THE THAW

Soviet Society and Culture during the 1950s and 1960s

The period from Stalin's death in 1953 to the end of the 1960s marked a crucial epoch in Soviet history. Though not overtly revolutionary, this era produced significant shifts in policies, ideas, language, artistic practices, daily behaviours, and material life. It was also during this time that social, cultural, and intellectual processes in the USSR began to parallel those in the West (and particularly in Europe) as never before.

This volume examines in fascinating detail the various facets of Soviet life during the 1950s and 1960s, a period termed the 'Thaw.' Featuring innovative research by historical, literary, and film scholars from across the world, this book helps to answer fundamental questions about the nature and ultimate fortune of the Soviet order – both in its internal dynamics and in its long-term and global perspectives.

DENIS KOZLOV is an assistant professor in the Department of History and the Department of Russian Studies at Dalhousie University.

ELEONORY GILBURD is an assistant professor in the Department of History and the Department of Russian and Slavic Studies at New York University.

The Thaw

Soviet Society and Culture during the 1950s and 1960s

EDITED BY DENIS KOZLOV AND
ELEONORY GILBURD

UNIVERSITY OF TORONTO PRESS
Toronto Buffalo London

Toronto Buffalo London
www.utppublishing.com

Reprinted in paperback 2014

ISBN 978-1-4426-4460-1
ISBN 978-1-4426-2864-9

Library and Archives Canada Cataloguing in Publication

The thaw : Soviet society and culture during the 1950s and 1960s / edited by Denis Kozlov and Eleonory Gilburd.

Includes bibliographical references and index.
ISBN 978-1-4426-4460-1 (bound). — ISBN 978-1-4426-2864-9 (pbk.)

1. Soviet Union – Social life and customs – 1917–1970. 2. Soviet Union – Intellectual life – 1917–1970. 3. Popular culture – Soviet Union – History – 20th century. 4. Soviet Union – History – 1953–1985. I. Kozlov, D.A. (Denis Anatol'evich), editor II. Gilburd, Eleonory, editor

DK276.T53 2013 947.085 C2012-906368-1

University of Toronto Press acknowledges the financial assistance to its publishing program of the Canada Council for the Arts and the Ontario Arts Council, an agency of the Government of Ontario.

Canada Council for the Arts Conseil des Arts du Canada

University of Toronto Press acknowledges the financial support of the Government of Canada through the Canada Book Fund for its publishing activities.

Contents

Illustrations, Figures, and Tables

Illustrations

Figures

Tables

Archival Abbreviations

APRK	Arkhiv Prezidenta Respubliki Kazakhstan (Archive of the President of the Republic of Kazakhstan)
DAMVSU	Derzhavnyi Arkhiv Ministerstva Vnutrishnikh Sprav Ukrainy (State Archive of the Ministry of the Interior of Ukraine)
EKLA	Eesti kultuurilooline Arhiiv (Estonian Cultural History Archives)
ERAF	Eesti Riigiarhiivi Filiaali (Estonian State Archives, Branch)
GARF	Gosudarstvenyi Arkhiv Rossisskoi Federatsii (State Archive of the Russian Federation)
GURK NARK 1	Gosudarstvennoe uchrezhdenie Respubliki, Komi Natsional'nyi Arkhiv Respubliki Komi, Fondokhranilishche no. 1 (State Institution of the Komi Republic, National Archive of the Komi Republic, Repository 1)
GURK NARK 2	Gosudarstvennoe uchrezhdenie Respubliki, Komi Natsional'nyy Arkhiv Respubliki Komi, Fondokhranilishche no. 2 (State Institution of the Komi Republic, National Archive of the Komi Republic, Repository 2)
LYA	Lietuvos ypatingasis archyvas (Lithuanian Special Archive)
NARB	Natsyianal'ny arkhiu Respubliki Belarus' (National Archive of Belarus)
OPDAO	Otdelenie partiinoi dokumentatsii Akmolinskoi oblasti (archive of the former regional committee of the Communist Party in Akmola, Kazakhstan)
RGAE	Rossiiskii gosudarstvennyi arkhiv ekonomiki (Russian State Archive of the Economy)

RGAKFD	Rossiiskii gosudartvennyi arkhiv kinofotodokumentov (Russian State Archive of Documentary Films and Photographs)
RGALI	Rossiiskii gosudarstvennyi arkhiv literatury i iskusstva (Russian State Archive of Literature and Art)
RGANI	Rossiiskii gosudarstvennyi arkhiv noveishei istorii (Russian State Archive of Contemporary History)
RGASPI	Rossiiskii gosudarstvennyi arkhiv sotsial'no-politicheskoi istorii (Russian State Archive of Socio-Political History)
RGASPI-M	Rossiiskii gosudarstvennyi arkhiv sotsial'no-politicheskoi istorii, Dokumenty molodezhnykh organizatsii (Russian State Archive of Socio-Political History, reading room for documents of youth organizations)
TsAE i ADM	Tsentral'nyi arkhiv elektronnykh i audiovizual'nykh dokumentov Moskvy (Central Archive of Electronic and Audiovisual Documents of Moscow)
TsAGM	Tsentral'nyi arkhiv goroda Moskvy (Central Archive of Moscow)
TsAOPIM	Tsentral'nyi arkhiv obshchestvenno-politicheskoi istorii Moskvy (Central Archive of Socio-Political History of Moscow)
TsDAHOU	Tsentral'nyi Derzhavnyi Arkhiv Hromads'kykh Ob'iednan Ukraïny (Central State Archive of Public Organizations of Ukraine)
TsGA SPb	Tsentral'nyi gosudarstvennyi arkhiv Sankt-Peterburga (Central State Archive of Saint Petersburg)
VMKM OF	Vorkutinskii Mezhraionnyi Kraevedcheskii Muzei, osnovnoi fond (Vorkuta Interdistrict Regional Studies Museum, main fund)
ch.	*chast'*, part
d.	*delo,* file
f.	*fond,* record group
l.	*list,* page
op.	*opis'*, inventory

Acknowledgments

This book grew out of the productive discussions at the international and interdisciplinary conference, 'The Thaw: Soviet Society and Culture during the 1950s and 1960s,' which took place at the University of California, Berkeley, 12–15 May 2005, and brought together participants from Russia, the United States, Canada, Britain, France, and Germany.[1] We want to express our gratitude to everyone who helped our project to materialize. Funding came from the National Endowment for the Humanities; the Sheila Fitzpatrick/Mellon Foundation; the Centre for European, Russian, and Eurasian Studies at the Munk Centre for Global Affairs at the University of Toronto; the Faculty of Arts and Social Sciences at Dalhousie University; and the University of California, Berkeley, where we thank the Social Sciences Division of the College of Letters and Sciences, the Arts and Humanities Division of the College of Letters and Sciences, the Institute for Slavic, East European, and Eurasian Studies, the Institute of International Studies, the Institute of European Studies, the Department of Slavic Languages and Literatures, the Department of History, the Graduate Division, the Doreen B. Townsend Center for the Humanities, and the Abigail Reynolds Hodgen Fund at the Social Sciences Division.

Behind institutions are, of course, people. Our colleagues welcomed this project from the very start, and it was only with their generous help that it became possible. Our thanks go to Yuri Slezkine, Lynne Viola, Thomas Lahusen, and Sheila Fitzpatrick for their vital contributions to the various phases of this work – from organizing and taking part in the conference, to reading numerous (lengthy!) drafts, to offering invaluable advice about publication. Without their help, on more occasions than we can count, this book would not have seen the light of day. At

Berkeley, we also thank George Breslauer, Victoria Bonnell, Martin Jay, David Frick, Mary Ann Mason, Olga Matich, Candace Slater, Matthew Tiews, Steven Weber, as well as the late Gerald Feldman and Reginald Zelnik. At the University of Toronto, we thank Peter Solomon for his advice and support of this work at its earliest stages. Edward Walker, Barbara Voytek, and the staff of the Institute for Slavic, East European, and Eurasian Studies at UC Berkeley helped in many ways with both the conference and the book. At the University of Toronto Press, we are grateful to our editor, Richard Ratzlaff, who took enthusiastic interest in the volume while it was still in manuscript form and, throughout our numerous conversations and email exchanges, helped us immensely in structuring and shaping the book on its way to print. We also thank the anonymous reviewers who read the manuscript and offered many helpful suggestions that made it better. The inevitable errors and omissions are, of course, our own. We can only hope that, with all the valuable advice we received, there will not be too many of them in the book.

NOTE

1 The conference had a workshop format, with participants reading each other's papers in advance. The presenters and discussants were Alan Barenberg, Steven A. Barnes, Stephen Bittner, Victoria Bonnell, George W. Breslauer, Per Brodersen, Katerina Clark, Susan Costanzo, Miriam Dobson, Marc Elie, Sheila Fitzpatrick, Gregory Freidin, Eleonory Gilburd, Anne Gorsuch, Steven E. Harris, Polly Jones, Denis Kozlov, Brian LaPierre, Ann Livschiz, Karl Loewenstein, Olga Matich, Eric Naiman, Benjamin Nathans, Nordica Nettleton, Irina Paperno, Michaela Pohl, Alexander Prokhorov, Susan E. Reid, Kristin Roth-Ey, Galina Rylkova, Shawn Salmon, Peter Schmelz, Yuri Slezkine, Kathleen E. Smith, Christine Varga-Harris, Lynne Viola, Amir Weiner, and Larissa Zakharova.

THE THAW

Soviet Society and Culture during the 1950s and 1960s

Introduction

DENIS KOZLOV

This book examines major problems of the Thaw – the epoch in Soviet history that spans the post-Stalin 1950s and most of the 1960s. We interpret these years as a paradigmatically defining moment for the entire period from Stalin's death until – and largely also beyond – the collapse of the Soviet Union. Not overtly revolutionary, the Thaw nonetheless produced crucial shifts in policies, ideas, artistic practices, daily behaviours, and material life. The immense diversification of culture and language undermined the outward semblance of stability, uniformity, and coherence that had existed under Stalin. Distant historical legacies gained increasing cultural prominence. As never before, the social, cultural, and intellectual processes in the USSR began to parallel those in the West, particularly in Western Europe.

Exploring the Thaw thus helps to answer fundamental questions about the nature and ultimate fortunes of the Soviet order in its internal dynamics, as well as its long-term and global perspectives. Accordingly, in this volume our goal is twofold. Firstly, we want to tell the story of the Thaw in some of its key aspects, examining in detail (and with inevitable selectivity) various facets of Soviet life during the 1950s and 1960s. Secondly, where possible, we seek to place that story within broader Russian and international contexts, analysing the Thaw as part of larger historical frameworks – or at least to suggest a few potential paths for such contextualization.

One such path is to discuss Soviet phenomena as integrated in a modern Russian cultural tradition that crossed the 1917 divide and dated back to the imperial era, if not to more distant times. Another path, parallel and closely related, is to consider the Soviet Union as one of the twentieth-century European societies that went through similar, if not identical, historical experiences and faced similar, often common problems. This approach is particularly relevant to the post–Second World War decades, when, as it is becoming increasingly clear, cultures and societies east and west of the Iron Curtain interacted in the realms of ideas, artistic trends, demographic and social change, material life, and consumption. Marked by a major increase in the circulation of information and cultural products, these decades regularly brought the two parts of the divided continent into meaningful contact with each other.

Historians have started a detailed systematic exploration of the Soviet 1950s and 1960s fairly recently. Nonetheless – or probably because of this – research on this period is becoming increasingly popular among both established and young scholars. It is not a great exaggeration to say that, at least in the field of Soviet studies in the West, these decades have lately moved from the margins to the centre of scholarly attention. What makes this growing body of research unique is that, possibly for the first time in the history of the field, conceptualization develops hand in hand with the incorporation of remarkably vast and fresh empirical evidence available from the Russian archives. However, the other side of the excitement of novelty and the numerous opportunities for discovery is that scholars who work on the Thaw are only beginning to relate to each other's arguments. A major goal of the present volume is to promote such scholarly dialogue and reflection on how this new research may affect a broader interpretation of modern Russian history.

During the Thaw, Soviet people made historic choices that still resonate in the current politics, culture, and media of many European and Asian societies, in open and private conversations, in individual memories and family histories. The chapters in the volume combine new archival research with interpretations in an effort to discuss some of these choices and their outcomes. With some exceptions, we have deliberately eschewed the 'top-down,' leadership-heavy approach that focuses on the personalities of political leaders or evolution of high authority. While important, such aspects in the history of the Thaw have by now received fairly extensive scholarly attention.[1] Taking this scholarship as a valuable point of departure, our volume focuses on issues of society and culture, on the large-scale and long-term tectonic shifts in cultural authority, social agency, and consciousness that the Thaw set in motion.

These objectives have determined the structure of the book. It opens with a chapter by the editors that introduces the reader to this historical period and discusses interpretations of the term *Thaw* as well as alternative designations for the Soviet 1950s and 1960s. We emphasize the broader significance of this epoch in the Soviet, long-term Russian, and European contexts, particularly highlighting the legacies of twentieth-century mass violence, the increasing role of international contacts and cross-cultural transfers, issues of material culture and consumption, problems of language, and generational identities.

The main body of the volume comprises two parts: 'Looking Back' and 'Looking Forward.' This is not a neat subdivision, because evaluating the past and envisaging the future during the Thaw were unthinkable without one another. Experiences of state repression and contemporary literary or artistic debates, Gulag legacies and government-initiated economic reforms, memories of 'anti-cosmopolitan' struggles and the country's opening to the outside world informed and contextualized each other throughout these years. Nonetheless, the subdivision may alert the reader to the complexities and inner tensions of the Thaw culture, where yesterday and tomorrow kept in a constant dialogue.

A discussion of a somewhat more distant 'yesterday' is a good starting point for situating the Thaw in modern Russian history. Part One opens with the chapter by Katerina Clark, who raises the issue of the Thaw's historical uniqueness. Clark begins by considering the 'Thaw' metaphor as characteristic of Russia's historical and cultural evolution – thaw as a recurrent natural phenomenon that has a seasonal and cyclical rhythm. Questioning the perception of Stalin's death in 1953 as 'an absolute BC/AD dividing line,' she argues that many of the shifts in Soviet culture with which the Thaw is commonly credited might have had earlier predecessors. Clark draws unexpected parallels – not between the late Stalin years and the Thaw (such parallels would be obvious and not very surprising), but instead between the culture of the early Thaw (1953–7) and the late 1930s, the peak of terror. She argues that, as early as 1937–40, a group of young writers and poets put in circulation some of the terms that would be central in the literary discourse of the 1950s – genuine (*podlinnyi*), sincerity (*iskrennost'*), or the lyric (*lirika*). The participants in the polemics of the late 1930s, such as Konstantin Simonov and Olga Berggol'ts, were among those authors who would subsequently coin the vocabulary of the early Thaw. When put in this context, the story of the Thaw becomes part of longer-term cycles of ideas and generational continuities – little-analysed yet crucial features of the Soviet intellectual landscape that Clark reveals.

Despite the continuities, Clark notes one fundamental difference between the late 1930s and the Thaw. Whereas the literary debates of the

1930s took place at the height of terror, in the 1950s mass repression came to an end, producing a political environment vastly different from that of twenty years earlier. Following Clark's piece are several chapters devoted to this central theme of the Thaw – ending the terror. First of all, they focus on the dismantling of the Gulag. In his work, Marc Elie describes how the Gulag shrank to a fraction of its Stalin-era size and ceased to be the backbone of Soviet economy.[2] This was a long and complicated process. The main tension accumulated between three conceptual approaches to the penal system – something Elie terms a 'conservative' approach, embodied by many senior officers in the Ministry of the Interior (MVD) who favoured the old Stalin-time system; a 'functionalist' approach, personified by Beria who, before his 1953 downfall, had been preoccupied with the Gulag's economic efficiency; and finally what we may term a futuristic approach, which insisted on mitigating the brutality of the old penal regime and on the genuine re-education of prisoners. The main proponents of this last approach were the short-term Minister of the Interior Nikolai Dudorov and his patron, Khrushchev himself. From Elie's account it follows that their noble initiatives of transforming the camps into smaller colonies for re-educating prisoners with more humane treatment, little isolation from local society, and moderate economic exploitation proved too advanced for the majority of the MVD personnel. A pragmatic approach based on the conservative notions of state expediency prevailed over considerations of humaneness. Similarly, many amnesties of the Khrushchev years were dictated by pragmatic rather than humanitarian reasons – budgetary constraints and camp overpopulation. In the early 1960s, the penal system went through a conservative shift, embodied in the 1961 statute of places of detention, which hardened the regime and reversed some of the earlier reformist achievements.

It remains to be seen whether the economic rationale of the Gulag bosses in the 1950s and 1960s completely excluded any other pro-reform considerations on their part, or whether the language and logic of pragmatism (as opposed to futuristic humanism) were the only ones the reformists could successfully employ to ensure changes. Be that as it may, while showing the lukewarm attitude of many senior police officials to the Khrushchev-inspired humanitarian impulses, Elie demonstrates that the conservatives did not quite end up winning. Neither the concept nor the practice of the Soviet penal system ever actually returned to the Stalin-era model. Separation of inmates in different regimes of detention, the enhanced role of courts, and the obligation to detain convicts in regions where they were sentenced were important – if incomplete – gains that remained in place in the 1960s. Most importantly, pragmatic reasoning, even if not necessarily accompanied by a conceptual desire to 'end the terror,' ultimately did contribute to the unmaking of the Gulag. The economically minded administrators gradually moved away from using the cheap yet inefficient convict labour in many industrial projects, except for the most labour-intensive and hazardous. As Elie concludes, during the Thaw the Gulag was not only reduced to a small part of its original population but also, from a major presence in the economy, evolved into 'a supply company of mobile workforce capable of filling gaps and clearing backlogs.' What came to replace the empire of slave labour was a rather conventional network of corrective institutions with marginal economic significance.

What happened to those three-quarters of the prisoners who had left the camps and now had to find their ways back into society? In his chapter, Alan Barenberg investigates life after Gulag in Vorkuta, a city above the Arctic Circle in the northeastern extreme of European Russia. During the 1950s, when Vorkutlag, the local camp branch of the Gulag, was gradually dismantled, Vorkuta made the transition from penal colony to what Barenberg describes as an industrial 'company town' – a story quite comparable to Elie's. Tens of thousands of men and women released from prison sentences and terms of exile sought to build careers, families, and lives outside the 'zone.' Although many returned home or struck out anew in places as far as the Virgin Lands in Kazakhstan, others chose to remain in Vorkuta for the rest of their lives, or eventually to return there, despite the harsh environment, painful memories, and physical vestiges of brutality. Exploring the social reintegration of the former prisoners, Barenberg shows all the mistrust and discrimination these people often faced in their new life.[3] Nonetheless, an important aspect of his work is that he also treats reintegration as a real possibility and analyses factors that aided it. Thus, the scarcity of labour urged employers to overlook the camp backgrounds of their (often highly qualified) new hires. More importantly, the personal networks that the ex-prisoners had built in the camps persisted in their new lives. Outside the barbed wire, these people reconstituted and relied on those networks, using them to find housing and jobs, to restore old and form new families.

If we extrapolate these findings to the larger question of how successful the reintegration of the former prisoners ultimately proved to be, then Barenberg's work suggests that the answer is in the nuances. The term *reintegration* embraces a complex, multifaceted phenomenon. On the one hand, the fact of an ex-prisoner staying in his geographic area of incarceration or even returning there after a failed attempt to rebuild life at a former home does not exactly project the image of successful reintegration. On the other hand, Barenberg shows that quite a few of the former prisoners did manage to build meaningful lives for themselves, if in Vorkuta. His work thus proposes a plausible middle ground between the two polarized perspectives on the prisoners' return from the Gulag – the intelligentsia narrative of a welcome back[4] and the later scholarly argument that the Soviet population generally clung to the stereotype of 'enemies of the people,' largely rejecting the returnees.[5] The reality, as Barenberg shows, was somewhere in between. Meticulously reconstructing the ex-prisoners' life stories, he reveals the constraints these people faced, but also the choices they made, the ideas they developed and voiced, as well as the important successes they achieved.

Reintegration was an intellectual as much as a socio-cultural process, inseparable from how society – which now included both the Gulag returnees and all others whom they faced upon return from the camps – conceptualized the experiences of the recent catastrophic political violence. The people of the Thaw thought and acted with constant references to historical realities that had had a formative impact on their lives and now had to be re-evaluated.[6] As often in modern Russia, historical interpretation was centred on literature, the prime mover of intellectual evolution and public self-expression in this country of readers. In his chapter Denis Kozlov analyses the pivotal moment of this evolution of consciousness – the early 1960s, when, for a few years following the 22nd Party Congress (1961), the polemics about the Stalin-era executions and camps became relatively legitimate, overflowing into print. On the basis of archival readers' letters, Kozlov discusses the impact of the two literary publications that for decades defined the parameters of conceptualizing the Stalin terror. One was Ilya Ehrenburg's memoir *People, Years, Life,* while the other was Aleksandr Solzhenitsyn's *One Day in the Life of Ivan Denisovich.* For the first time vividly describing the human experiences of arrests and imprisonment of Stalin's time, these texts provoked a crisis in the readers' established world view. People began to see their country's twentieth-century history through the prism of terror, drawing the lineage of the Soviet order not so much from the revolution but from the state violence that had followed it – not from 1917 but from 1937.

Literature of the Thaw did much to discredit the established venues and language of mass persuasion. Many time-honoured literary and journalistic devices were compromised by association with the time when they had originated – the Stalin time, which was now inescapably tied to the image of terror. Also, the media's language and ethos proved unfit for explaining or even describing the tragic past. Asking themselves why they had kept silent during the 1930s as thousands of people were disappearing, many letter-writers of the 1960s concluded that fear had not been the only reason for silence. They also noted the absence, either then or now, of words and categories for describing and evaluating this massive destruction of lives. By proposing the centrality of individual human existence, and by greatly diversifying the literary language, the writings by Ehrenburg and Solzhenitsyn became landmarks in the emergence of new ethical and verbal standards of formulating experience. Quite a few readers engaged in this historical, linguistic, and moral quest with remarkable willingness to share a degree of responsibility for the recent tragedy.

Ultimately, the principle of a critical reassessment of the Soviet past, which the party leadership under Khrushchev espoused, and which made publications such as Ehrenburg's and Solzhenitsyn's possible, threatened nothing less than the regime's historical legitimacy. This was clear to many observers, certainly not all of whom accepted the critical paradigm. In her chapter, Polly Jones examines the conservative intellectual opposition to the Thaw, a phenomenon that has received little scholarly attention.[7] What was the relationship between the conservatives' personalities, political ideas, and literary-aesthetic visions? How did they imagine resisting the intellectual turmoil that endangered the regime's foundations? Jones focuses on a group of writers such as Vsevolod Kochetov, Anatolii Sofronov, Nikolai Gribachev, and Vadim Kozhevnikov, who rallied around several major literary periodicals – the journals *Oktiabr'* (edited by Kochetov), *Ogonek* (Sofronov), *Znamia* (Kozhevnikov), and the newspaper *Literaturnaia Rossiia.* Often labelled by their opponents as 'Stalinists,' these writers (together with several leading politicians in the Central Committee) were indeed cautious about the dismantling of the Stalin cult and admitting the crimes and blunders of the past. However, Jones complicates the picture by examining not so much the relationship between the literary conservatives and their political patrons as, rather, the infighting within the literary environment itself. Party authorities, she suggests, played a secondary and often balancing role in the struggle between the conservatives and their opponents in the journals

Novyi mir and *Iunost'* (whom she terms 'liberal'). Rather, pride of place in the rivalry belonged to personal factors. The tactics and methods of the two literary camps had much in common: both parties eagerly employed connections, patronage politics, ties of mutual responsibility, and a variety of ad hominem arguments.

In this sense, the literary politics of the Thaw might not differ significantly from those of the Stalin years. However, Jones also shows that both camps took shape in the characteristic Thaw atmosphere of conceptual uncertainty, including uncertainty over the meanings of the key concept of 'Stalinism.' Ultimately, the notion of Stalinism itself, as well as the broader aesthetic and political platforms it denoted, evolved in the context of these personal literary hostilities. It remains to be seen whether the frictions between the two literary camps were indeed 'not based on deeper understanding of the ideological stakes of the debate,' as Jones argues. It might well be that the polemic also did involve more serious historical and philosophical reflection. Nonetheless, Jones's work deepens our own understanding of the literary environment of the 1950s and 1960s. The world of the 'villains' of the Thaw, just as that of its 'heroes,' was far from linear.

The Stalin past was in a constant dialogue with the daily realities of the Thaw, as well as with how contemporaries envisioned and built the future. Part Two of the volume opens with a chapter that amply demonstrates this connection. Under Khrushchev, in a visible rupture with the Stalin years, the Soviet regime openly premised the validity of socialism not only on the departure from mass violence but also upon the immediate satisfaction of the people's material needs. The economic reforms of the Thaw were also ideological ventures, intended at once to improve the citizens' living standards and to reinvigorate the socialist ideal. In her chapter, Michaela Pohl explores one of the most important such ventures – the Virgin Lands campaign. Launched in 1954 to cultivate the vast territories in Kazakhstan and Siberia and thus remedy the agricultural crisis, this initiative was propagated as a specifically socialist endeavour of voluntary, enthusiastic labour: thousands of young people were mobilized for the task. However, the Virgin Lands were not exactly virgin. Pohl shows that they were populated by present and former Gulag inmates, Chechen, Ingush, and German exiles, as well as indigenous Kazakhs. Whether staying in Kazakhstan or (recently) homeward bound, these people interacted with each other, often in a tense and hostile way. It was in this explosive milieu that the new settlers landed, with hundreds of violent episodes and ethnic clashes rocking the north of Kazakhstan.

Like the story of Vorkuta told by Barenberg, Pohl's story of the Virgin Lands depicts the transition of a former Gulag terrain to life without terror. In either case, there was much chaos and violence, but in Kazakhstan, furthermore, a new ambitious economic initiative was unfolding at the same time in the same place. And yet in both cases the transition inspired hope among contemporaries, while chaos eventually yielded to some order. Among other aspects, the value of Pohl's work is that she questions the widespread interpretation of any Soviet project as a failure. Ultimately, Pohl argues, the Virgin Lands cultivation proved a success, both for the government and for the many people it involved. The massive investment benefited the national and regional economy while bringing tangible advantages to the settlers. The Virgin Lands 'passport' offered geographical and status mobility to numerous young collective farmers, and the cultivated lands eventually yielded not only larger harvests but also higher living standards than anything the settlers had enjoyed in Russian or Ukrainian villages. The ethnic groups that clashed with each other eventually found ways of coexistence. The town formerly known as 'White Grave' was renamed Tselinograd and became a model city, acquiring new apartment buildings, roads, clubs, theatres, schools, and newspapers. Not incidentally, perhaps, it was this new city that, under the name of Astana, would decades later become the capital of Kazakhstan. Pohl's work adds a significant and previously unwritten chapter to the history of the Thaw, exploring the relationship between ideology, mobilization, and human agency in an important Soviet periphery, as well as the ultimate implications of Khrushchev's reforms.

These implications, and the crucial role of the periphery in the Thaw, become even clearer in Amir Weiner's chapter, which focuses on Ukraine and the Baltic states – the areas where the Soviet rule was least established and nationalist resistance to the regime was the strongest. Weiner explores the fate of thousands of Ukrainian and Baltic nationalists and former guerrilla fighters who were released from the camps during the Thaw and bound for their homes. With this mass exodus, two empires met in the western borderlands of the Soviet Union – the disintegrating empire of the Gulag and the post–Second World War empire of newly Sovietized Eastern Europe. The encounter proved all the more turbulent since the western regions acutely felt the impact of the 1956 uprisings in Hungary and Poland.

What was it that prompted the Khrushchev leadership to make the paradoxical, seemingly self-destructive step of granting amnesty to those who had fought against Soviet power only a few years earlier and made no secret of their continued hostility to the regime? Drawing on evidence from the Ukrainian, Russian, Belarusan, Estonian, and Lithuanian archives, Weiner observes the remarkable degree of the regime's flexibility, resolve, and confidence in its own stability, as well as in the success of its efforts to relinquish mass violence and become a less repressive polity based on citizens' voluntary political participation. What boosted the confidence was that a great share of the population in the western borderlands was now committed to the Soviet order, seeing it as permanent and stable. In this environment, strange and unfamiliar to them, the Gulag returnees were not necessarily welcome, especially since the wounds of the war and bitter ethnic strife were still fresh, and the ex-prisoners' homecoming was complicated by memories of who they had been in wartime. As Weiner shows, in response to these shifts, the very nature of opposition to the Soviet regime in the western borderlands began to change. From an overt, violent anti-Soviet stance of the late Stalin years, the oppositionists moved to political dissidence, working within the system and, importantly, embracing the legal culture that the authorities now promoted.[8]

Weiner's work, whose arguments find many parallels in the chapters by Barenberg and Pohl, makes it evident that the Thaw was neither an exclusively Russian phenomenon nor a prerogative of the capitals. Regional variables and experiences, particularly those of non-Russian ethnicities, were essential in the key processes of the epoch. His work elucidates the origins and dimensions of the Soviet human rights movement, rooted in the Thaw-era transition from mass repression to extensive participatory politics and the growing importance of legality. Most significantly, Weiner highlights the interconnectedness of the intellectual and political processes of the 1950s and 1960s in the Soviet Union and Eastern Europe – or more broadly, Europe. The mutual influence and the exchange of information were widespread and constant. In western Ukraine and the Baltics, thousands of people listened to Western radio broadcasts, while repatriates or their relatives moved across the recently established Soviet borders. Weiner thus shows a much more important and versatile presence of the West in the Thaw than was known before.

In fact, Western presence in Soviet society and culture at the time was ubiquitous. These were the years of the country's extraordinary opening to the outside world, especially to Western cultural imports. How foreignness became a regular presence in this culture is the subject of Eleonory

Gilburd's chapter, which examines the revival of Soviet internationalism through the prism of cultural exchange with Western countries. Gilburd presents cultural relations with the West as a case of 'governmental internationalism.' In the mid to late 1950s, she argues, the government initiated an unprecedented campaign for popular diplomacy. The idea flared briefly and died down by the early 1960s, but the impulse behind it remained, sustaining the continued Soviet participation in international cultural traffic for years to come. That impulse was the notion of a shared language called 'culture.' From the mid-1950s and early 1960s, a group of Soviet philosophers and experts in international cultural affairs began to postulate a set of 'universal values' – fundamental behavioural norms, science, anti-militarism, and a 'world culture.' The class approach to social life and ethics was not abandoned, and socialism and capitalism were still seen as incompatible. However, certain creations of 'capitalist culture' were recognized as having a universal value. This new language of 'common humanity' helped to justify the new ties with the West.

Internationalism was the Soviet Union's 'back door to power,' another way of achieving political supremacy, creating an international audience, and gaining recognition in the West. The USSR was a latecomer to the circulation of cultural and consumer goods in post-war Europe – the process usually termed 'Americanization.' American goods and symbols, movies and music had made it to many places first, so that by the mid-1950s the Soviets had a lot of winning over to do. The projects of confirming Soviet political ascendancy and gaining cultural supremacy coalesced in the Sixth International Youth Festival in Moscow during the summer of 1957. This was an event of unparalleled scale, investment, excitement, and impact on the lives of its participants, as well as on the cityscape itself. The festival launched cultural institutions, artistic styles, careers, and biographies. Gilburd explores how the festival became conceivable, how it was fashioned at home and abroad despite the recent Hungarian Revolution, and how it was experienced and remembered. The legitimacy of foreign presence in Moscow squares and on street corners – the stamp of government approval and sponsorship that the event bore – was as central to the festival experience as the presence of foreigners themselves. From now on, foreign cultural imports became integral to the official public face of the USSR, at home and abroad. As Gilburd argues, the festival facilitated the transformation of the Soviet Union, from an alleged beacon for communist, socialist, and other 'progressive' causes into a big European city, a centre of international 'mega-events'

– film festivals, exhibitions, or Olympics – on a par with major Western capitals. Experienced by vast audiences of readers, viewers, listeners, and consumers, the opening to the West became crucial in the evolution of the Soviet order, up to and beyond its collapse.

The new imports and ideas, of course, landed in an environment of long-developed notions and cultural perceptions. The country's opening to the world, and the Thaw-era projects of satisfying the Soviet public in its daily demands, were inseparable from endeavours of shaping and regulating those demands, of differentiating between the healthy and the harmful, the beautiful and the ugly. One place where such endeavours were especially conspicuous, but also ran into endemic crises, was fashion. In her chapter, Larissa Zakharova takes up the Soviet clothing industry in the 1950s and 1960s as a case study of reforms that were meant to overcome the shortages, poor quality, and aesthetic deficiencies of consumer goods. In what is also a study of the place of aesthetics in Soviet daily life, Zakharova argues that the economic reforms were accompanied by the policing and suppression of numerous illegal and semi-legal private entrepreneurs who filled the gaps between the inefficient industry and the consumer. Policing extended to fashion itself: the suppression of the private sector paralleled an intensified regulation of stylistic practices. Tracing what it meant to be 'tasteful,' 'fashionable,' and 'beautiful,' Zakharova shows how a set of prescribed fashions was aggressively forced upon consumers through state tailoring enterprises, fashion magazines, manuals on cutting and sewing, and the like.

These strategies of regulation and indoctrination – which, we may surmise, originated not only in the vicissitudes of Soviet economy but also in the time-honoured intelligentsia's ideals of culture and 'culturedness'[9] – suffered from the same chronic ills and shortages as the entire system. There was, for example, a shortage of textiles and sewing machines. More importantly, perhaps against the will of its authors, the official orientation toward promoting fashion encouraged a variety of semi-independent activities in clothing production and a fashion-oriented consumption culture. Ironically, domestic clothing production followed the same illicit paths that the authorities were trying to eliminate. Moreover, tailors and consumers gleaned fashionable models not so much from Soviet magazines as from the newly accessible Western films and clothing items, as well as from foreigners and those few who travelled to the West. Zakharova's work thus is an exploration of the mutually constitutive relationships among Soviet economic structures, government policies, consumption strategies, and aesthetic ideals.

While Soviet consumers were borrowing the fashionable looks of Western film stars, European moviegoers and festival juries were watching Soviet films. The Soviet Union became a regular presence at international film festivals, up to earning the Palme d'Or at the 1958 Cannes festival. Soviet films, perceived as archaic in the late Stalin years, became understandable to Western audiences, while Western critics could now describe them in familiar terms, situating them within national and transnational trends. In her chapter, Oksana Bulgakowa examines how in the 1950s and 1960s Soviet film rejoined the global cinematic culture. From the familiar models of liberalization and 'de-Stalinization,' she shifts the reader's attention to a radical alteration in perception paradigms, a visual and aesthetic revolution for millions of spectators in Europe, America, Asia, and the Soviet Union. For the first time, Soviet studio directors, cultural officials, and film-makers alike perceived their efforts as part of global stylistic and technological phenomena. The changes in cinematic technology – Cinemascope, wide screen, colour film, or television – arrived in the USSR at about the same time as elsewhere. Soviet films were also inscribed within transnational stylistic aspirations to rescue physical reality from linguistic conventions. As Bulgakowa suggests, in its search for image beyond interpretation, for accident and ambiguity, in its rejection of professional actors, artificial lighting, and voice training, Thaw cinema shared aesthetic projects and approaches with Italian neorealism, French cinéma vérité, the Free Cinema movement in Britain, Brazilian *cinema novo*, and Direct Cinema in North America. Young film directors such as Andrei Tarkovskii and Andrei Konchalovskii saw their work as adaptations of Bergman, Kurosawa, or Buñuel to Soviet reality. The relationship was not unidirectional but rather mutual and diachronic, as some French and Italian directors also acknowledged having been influenced by the early Soviet filmmakers of the 1920s. The films of all these schools had another thing in common: thanks to simplified filming techniques, they were relatively low-budget productions. Whereas under Stalin, Soviet studios had produced a handful of expensive films per year, from the mid-1950s the film industry expanded dramatically, requiring significantly more people and tighter budgets per film.

All this expansion, innovation, and the emergence of a new generation of film-makers who promoted and benefited from the changes led to the integration of Soviet film in the international visual culture. Offering a panorama of shifts in cinema across national borders, Bulgakowa integrates the aesthetic, technical, financial, political, and generational aspects of Soviet film, analysing it in its broad context.

All the chapters thus demonstrate the formative impact that the Thaw had on many aspects of Soviet, and often post-Soviet, societies and cultures. Its repercussions are still heard, as it occupies a special place – or, rather, a variety of special places – in the memory and mythology of the past century. In her afterword to the volume, Sheila Fitzpatrick reflects on some of the themes raised by the contributors. Examining the memories and significance of the Thaw as an event and a myth, she discusses the possible meanings of the Thaw, and of the 'Sixties' with which it is often associated, in the Soviet, post-Soviet, American, and (East) European contexts. Fitzpatrick's essay suggests new possibilities for the study of the Thaw in a broad historical and cross-cultural perspective. On our part, we hope that the volume, as a whole and in its constituent parts, does justice to this epoch, whose importance is becoming increasingly evident.

NOTES

1 See, e.g., Oleg Leibovich, *Reforma i modernizatsiia v 1953–1964 gg.* (Perm', 1993); Vladimir Naumov, 'Repression and Rehabilitation,' in *Nikita Khrushchev*, ed. William Taubman, Sergei Khrushchev, and Abbott Gleason (New Haven, 2000), 85–112; Aleksandr Pyzhikov, *Khrushchevskaia ottepel', 1953–1964* (Moscow, 2002); Pyzhikov, *Opyt modernizatsii sovetskogo obshchestva v 1953–1964 godakh: Obshchestvenno-politicheskii aspekt* (Moscow, 1998); Anatolii Strelianyi, 'Khrushchev and the Countryside,' in Taubman, Khrushchev, and Gleason, *Nikita Khrushchev*, 113–37; William Taubman, *Khrushchev: The Man and His Era* (New York, 2003); William J. Tompson, 'Industrial Management and Economic Reform under Khrushchev,' in Taubman, Khrushchev, and Gleason, *Nikita Khrushchev*, 138–59; Tompson, *Khrushchev: A Political Life* (New York, 1995); Mariia Zezina, 'Shokovaia terapiia: ot 1953-go k 1956 godu,' *Otechestvennaia istoriia* 2 (1995): 121–35; Zezina, *Sovetskaia khudozhestvennai intelligentsia i vlast' v 1950-e – 60-e gody* (Moscow, 1999); Elena Zubkova, 'The Rivalry with Malenkov,' in Taubman, Khrushchev, and Gleason, *Nikita Khrushchev*, 67–84; Melanie Ilic and Jeremy Smith, eds., *Khrushchev in the Kremlin: Policy and Government in the Soviet Union, 1953–1964* (New York, 2011).

2 On the Gulag's role in Soviet economy under Stalin, see Steven A. Barnes, *Death and Redemption: The Gulag and the Shaping of Soviet Society* (Princeton, 2011); James R. Harris, *The Great Urals: Regionalism and the Evolution of the Soviet System* (Ithaca, 1999), 105–22; Galina Ivanova, *Gulag v sisteme totalitarnogo gosudarstva* (Moscow, 1997), esp. 69–126, 188–90; Oleg Khlevniuk, *The History of the Gulag: From Collectivization to the Great Terror* (New Haven, 2004), e.g., 332–8.

3 For another detailed exploration of this issue, see Miriam Dobson, *Khrushchev's Cold Summer: Gulag Returnees, Crime, and the Fate of Reform after Stalin* (Ithaca, 2009).
4 E.g., Evgeniia Ginzburg, *Krutoi marshrut: Khronika vremen kul'ta lichnosti* (Moscow, 1990).
5 E.g., Nanci Adler, *The Gulag Survivor: Beyond the Soviet System* (New Brunswick, NJ, 2002), 88–9, 110–11, 136–7, 139–46, 156–62, 178–9.
6 On this, see also Irina Paperno, *Stories of the Soviet Experience: Memoirs, Diaries, and Dreams* (Ithaca, 2009).
7 In the Russian-language literature, the only major work exploring the anti-Thaw intellectual tendencies is Nikolai Mitrokhin, *Russkaia partiia: Dvizhenie russkikh natsionalistov v SSSR, 1953–1985* (Moscow, 2003) – a valuable unconventional study, which, however, does not exhaust the subject. In the English-language literature, notable is the study by Yitzhak Brudny, which focuses on Russian nationalism while paying less attention to other agendas of anti-Thaw thinkers. Brudny, *Reinventing Russia: Russian Nationalism and the Soviet State, 1953–1991* (Cambridge, MA, 1998).
8 In her history of dissidence in the USSR, Ludmilla Alekseeva makes a point that in Ukraine the human rights movement was much stronger and better organized than in Russia. Alekseeva, *Istoriia inakomysliia v SSSR: Noveishii period* (Moscow, 1984), 7–44, 396–413.
9 On 'culturedness,' see Vera Dunham, *In Stalin's Time: Middleclass Values in Soviet Fiction* (Cambridge, MA, 1976; republished Duke, 1990), 22; Sheila Fitzpatrick, 'Becoming Cultured: Socialist Realism and the Representation of Privilege and Taste,' in her *The Cultural Front: Power and Culture in Revolutionary Russia* (Ithaca, 1992): 216–37.

1 The Thaw as an Event in Russian History

DENIS KOZLOV AND ELEONORY GILBURD

The epoch that was born when Joseph Stalin died in March 1953 was a time of great expectations. Contemporaries described these years as a moment of awakening. With metaphors of air, freshness, and light, writers and film-makers created an image of dawn. And the fiery publicist Ilya Ehrenburg (1891–1967) gave his otherwise inconspicuous novella the title that has demarcated the Soviet 1950s and 1960s. Ehrenburg titled his book *The Thaw.*

Metaphor

Ehrenburg's title belonged to, but also worked against, some of the most stable and meaningful associations in Russian poetry and lyrical imagination. For many poets, thaw was not a favourite time. Pushkin decried it for 'stench and filth': a spring thaw made him sick with melancholy and boredom. By contrast, 'severe winter' brought energy and freshness, planting colour on the cheeks of maidens and exciting passions.[1] Nineteenth-century poets lauded winter's purity, describing it as a young beauty, enchantress, and dream. For them, winter often was an allegory of Russia itself.[2]

The severity of Russian winter has also traditionally provided a less benign association, with the stern and repressive power of the state. In Ivan Lazhechnikov's (1792–1869) famous historical novel *The House of Ice* (1835), the phantasmagoric ice palace epitomizes the rule of Empress Anna Ioannovna (1730–40) and her favourite, Ernst Johann von Biron. The palace is inspired by an ugly sculpture, a man frozen to death as a punishment for truth-telling, and embodies Anna's much-hated reign of police repression, fear, denunciation, and torture (as represented by her successor Elizabeth and recorded in history).[3] In his depiction of a political winter, Lazhechnikov also may have referred to his own times, the reign of Nicholas I – at least this was how the censors read his novel.[4] But ice palaces inevitably melt, and in the novel a 'thaw' (*ottepel'*) succeeds the 'cruel frosts,' destroying the House of Ice shortly before Anna's death. The new sovereign, Elizabeth, 'throws off the people's chains,' 'heals their wounds,' 'tears off a black seal' from their hearts and mouths, promotes science, and founds Moscow University. The people bless the new empress and soon forget about the 'bloody *Bironovshchina*.'[5]

Lazhechnikov's contemporary Fedor Tiutchev (1803–73) certainly did have Nicholaevan Russia in mind when he represented the autocracy as 'iron winter' (*zima zheleznaia*) and a 'heap of ice' (*gromada l'dov*).[6] Upon Nicholas's death, Tiutchev transferred the meteorological term *thaw* onto the Russian political and emotional environment. The educated society received the new metaphor as wonderfully refreshing, a mot juste, because in the spring of 1855 the changes Tiutchev felt were indeed atmospheric, intangible. Nobody was yet sure of specific policies that Alexander II would adopt, but Tiutchev did capture a certain anticipatory mood 'of things getting easier with regard ... to spirit.'[7] He was a poet of spring. Tiutchev's thaw was not all mud and melancholy, but a vigorous, audible herald of spring: a 'fair child' (*prekrasnoe ditia*) or a youth, it 'ran,' 'rang,' and 'laughed.' Winter could be resilient, but spring was inexorable and irresistible:[8]

No matter what severe trials
Upon you life may ever bring –
What can resist the first encounter
And breath of the arriving spring![9]

Many decades later, it was this verse of Tiutchev's that the young Ilya Ehrenburg, then an exile in Europe, liked to recall in his days of hardship. Ehrenburg felt an affinity for Tiutchev. He often cited or mentioned the poet and even wrote a poem about Tiutchev's last love, while living through the last years of his own.[10] In 1953, deliberately or not, Ehrenburg reinvented Tiutchev's forgotten metaphor of thaw, for a different audience but at a similar historical juncture. The metaphor embodied familiar images – motion, awakened feelings, and above all, anticipation.

The Thaw's action takes place mostly in the winter, in an atmosphere anguished and expectant. The main protagonists are desperate for reasons they know not: they are lonely, bored, and almost nauseous from malaise and cold. Ehrenburg offers dozens of synonyms for this cosmic winter. Snowflakes flutter like scared birds, birds freeze amid flight and fall dead on the ground, and breath turns into ice. Winter suffering is both physical and linguistic: one of the characters is blinded by a snowstorm, while another feels as if he lost words in the snow.[11] The only language the characters know is frozen bureaucratese. They speak in hollow words and of things for which they do not care, keep silent when conscience orders them to speak, act in theatrical performances that contain 'not a single living word' (*ni odnogo zhivogo slova*), sit in awkward silences, arrest each other's confessions, and suffer throughout.[12]

A blizzard puts an end to the languished immobility of winter, and a spring thaw sets the frozen town in motion. Icicles drip, surfaces shine, birds chirp, women wash windows, children scamper, and an inveterate cynic follows suit, rushing to break floating chunks of ice. Thawing nature suggests an emotional, linguistic, and implicitly also political emancipation: the sounds of spring encourage simple, natural words, lifting the fear of human communication.[13] In his memoirs, Ehrenburg pointed to how important speech was 'after the long months of silence, after the cold that was kin to loneliness, after the trial of winter.'[14] For him, the thaw was a new freedom in behaviours and relationships, a kinetic and verbal spontaneity. The thaw heralded a lyrical, intimate disposition – after all, the novella told of late love as the last chance for deliverance from an emotional winter. With the thaw metaphor, Ehrenburg wished to depict, and perhaps also create, a psychological climate (*dushevnyi klimat*).[15]

What outraged his critics, Khrushchev above all, was this very metaphor. To them, thaw suggested nothing but slush and mud, sickly confusion and instability – a reading that reflected the word's longstanding connotations of disarray, slackening, and enfeeblement.[16] In a few decades, after the collapse of the Soviet Union, disenchanted Russians would mock the Thaw in similar terms – as 'short-lived and unreliable,' 'snotty' in the sense of pathetically naive, ridiculous, and altogether embarrassing.[17] As late as 2008, following the Russian presidential succession, the deputy head of the president's administration Vladislav Surkov dismissed hopes for a liberalization by declaring, 'There will be no thaw or any other political slush [*sliakot'*]' – a remark that provoked an outrage among the intelligentsia.[18] Some remembered that the identification of a political thaw with 'slush' itself dated back to the 1950s and 1960s, when the ideologically militant press used this derisive label to smear the alleged home-grown 'agents of bourgeois ideology.' 'State power is remarkably rude and disrespectful,' exploded in September 2008 the popular radio host Matvei Ganapol'skii, born in 1953. 'They know perfectly well what the word "thaw" means in Russia.... And yet they utter such words, and they do so deliberately ... they have invoked "slush." Well, history will determine who is slush in Russia.... You know, people gave their lives for that thaw.... One cannot use such words: this is an insult to the living and to people's memory.'[19]

Historians usually avoid such value judgments, but even they sometimes use the thaw metaphor in a similar sense of 'slush,' underscoring confusion and instability.[20] This is precisely the interpretation against which Ehrenburg objected. In his memoirs, he dismissed it with a dictionary definition: 'Thaw – warm weather in the midst of winter or at the arrival of spring, causing snow and ice to melt.'[21] The title of his novella, he argued, heralded above all this arrival of spring, 'the spring that *had to come*.'[22] In 1958, Ehrenburg returned to the metaphor and remade his novella into a poem about waiting for spring.[23] Again there were cruel winters, whose 'March frosts' brought despair, and whose 'dry blizzards' blinded. Incarceration was verbally tangible: '*grown into* such cold,' '*in* solid, icy bitterness,' Ehrenburg's 'we' 'waited and waited until the bulky ice began to budge.' Three years later, in 1961, Grigorii Chukhrai made the metaphor visible in his film *Clear Skies*, which depicted the ordeal of an ex-POW suspected of treason and expelled from the party. In the final shot, symbolizing the triumph of justice and absolution from the Stalin past, the entire expanse of the screen fills with a huge block of ice beginning to drift.[24] In so turning word back into image, Chukhrai materialized and reinforced the already stable metaphor.

What was it in the thaw metaphor that assured it such stability in art and literature? In common expressions, weather is a fickle thing beyond human agency. Weather metaphors suggest instability and unpredictability.[25] However, the cyclicality and recurrence of meteorological phenomena also impart to such metaphors a sense of outwitting nature by anticipation and prognosis.[26] Furthermore, seasonal changes affect everyone. Grounded in fundamental sensory experiences – warmth, natural sounds, and levity (thanks to lightweight clothing) – the thaw metaphor made sense of complex politics and ambivalent emotions by making them immediate and physiological.[27]

Organic and mechanistic metaphors had long vied with each other in Soviet rhetorical efforts in relating the individual to the community. In the late 1920s and early 1930s, 'the root metaphor' for Soviet society was the machine.[28] The metaphor ascribed to people 'a flaming motor instead of a heart' and, to use Stalin's dictum, transformed humans into 'cogs' with little individual value other than as parts of the grand mechanism.[29] Products of fascination with technology and rationality, mechanistic metaphors connote uniformity, rigidity, and standardization.[30] Organic metaphors, on the other hand, specifically those for weather, allow for contingency and flexibility. In the symbolic ordering of Soviet society, machine metaphors yielded to organic ones, to the garden and the family, as early as the mid-1930s. Nature became the setting where the Soviet man stood trial, conquered space, the elements, and his own limitations, emerging victorious and 'tempered' by fires and snowstorms.[31] During the 1950s, such scenarios were played out anew in Thaw culture, but with a fundamental difference. If previously natural disasters were the hero's chief antagonists, in Ehrenburg's novella the snowstorm was the champion of justice: it destroyed the workers' shabby dwellings, thus toppling the evil bureaucrat who had refused to invest in new housing. The coming spring embodied not only environmental but also emotional and social harmony. Later, in the 1960s, the conquest of nature became an increasingly ambivalent image, as the Soviet man began to fail the test of the elements. In the literature and film of the 1960s, man returned to nature as its fraction, not its subjugator, to learn from it rather than to battle it – and when he did try to battle, fires and snowstorms often effortlessly wiped him off the face of the earth.[32] By the 1970s, most visibly in village prose, nature as a symbol of eternal normality had become an object of veneration, while struggle against nature was now represented as useless, harmful, and altogether immoral.[33]

Ehrenburg's 1953 thaw metaphor may have been an early herald of these new sensibilities, a desire for a harmonious, non-conflicted relationship between nature and society.[34] Emerging in direct opposition to the conceptualization of society as a machine, the metaphor focused not on mechanism but on nature in a transitional stage and thereby suggested a world in the making, a cultural system open to chance and change.

As it sought to impose coherence upon polyvalent societal developments, the thaw metaphor inevitably concealed a great deal. But metaphors are meant to conceal, highlighting what their inventors and users see as essential while suppressing other aspects of reality.[35] Scholars have taken the thaw metaphor to task for what it obscures and have identified the mentalities and practices (such as continuing surveillance, anxieties about returning camp prisoners, and the persistent imagery of enemies and social strife), which do not accord well with the metaphor's optimistic interpretation.[36] In this approach, the metaphor is taken to reflect historical reality, whether accurately or poorly. Yet what if we consider the thaw metaphor not as reflective but as constitutive of historical phenomena?[37] The metaphor became operative precisely because it singled out what the contemporaries saw as consequential about the Thaw, what they hoped for and desired. Even the post-Soviet disappointment with the Thaw was itself a product of the metaphor's promising, positive implications, of its capacity to be a formative 'self-fulfilling prophecy' that structured reality.[38]

No metaphor is perfectly consistent with all its possible connotations, let alone capable of accounting for all aspects of politics and society. *Thaw* is not an entirely coherent metaphor. It is, for example, not as cheerful as it seems: to push it to its ultimate logic (as contemporaries understood only too well), the metaphor foretold as much of another winter as of arriving spring in the unbreakable cycle of seasons. In linking weather and politics, it presented climate as destiny.

And yet the thaw metaphor is heuristically useful. It created an environment of anticipation. It was inclusive, accessible, and broadly comprehensible. It reconstituted the relationship between social and natural orders. It admitted chance and alternative into a deterministic ideology. It highlighted the issue of language, with which Soviet writers, journalists, artists, and ordinary citizens would grapple henceforth. It heralded lyricism and emotionality. In all these ways, the thaw metaphor shaped social, political, and cultural realities.

Ilya Ehrenburg defended his interpretation of the word *thaw* with a contemporary dictionary definition, but he also shaped the way subsequent dictionaries came to define the word. In Tiutchev's time, thaw as metaphor was a witticism of limited circulation. In Ehrenburg's time, the dictionary listed only the meteorological definition. After Ehrenburg, *thaw* became a conventional metaphor, a stable concept habituated in the common language and established in the cultural tradition. Today's dictionaries list two meanings for *thaw*: one meteorological, the other metaphoric and political.[39]

Histories of the Thaw

Until the early twenty-first century, the Thaw was underprivileged in historical writing. It was as if historians presumed the Soviet order to have taken final shape by the late 1930s, perhaps by the end of the Second World War at the latest, viewing the subsequent decades as a postscript. Even today, textbook chapters on the 1950s and 1960s remain relatively cursory, compared to the better-rounded examinations of the 1920s and 1930s.[40] Yet writing about the Thaw has a rich history.

Some of the earliest students of the Thaw were its memoirists, and its first story was the intelligentsia's tale of nostalgic remembrance, reinforced ex post facto by the negative perception of the subsequent Brezhnev years that made the Thaw look all the brighter.[41] Memoirists often wrote themselves into the intelligentsia's conventional saga of martyrdom for liberty, portraying their noble standoff against various incarnations of 'power.' Members of 'the Thaw generation,' to use Ludmilla Alexeyeva's term, many of them had matured in the 1950s and 1960s and later became proponents of Gorbachev's reforms, seeing the perestroika as a logical continuation of the Thaw's unfinished business.[42] It was not accidental that the voices of human rights activists, countercultural figures, escapists, and professed nonconformists became prominent in writings about the Thaw from the late 1980s to the mid-1990s, or that the voices of conservative loyalists and *étatistes* were muted at that point.[43] Perestroika claimed the Thaw heritage, and the first historical scholarship on the 'lessons of the Twentieth Congress' appeared in the party press of the final Soviet years.[44]

Yet, for the most part, historical research on the Thaw in Russia emerged in a different epoch – following the collapse of the Soviet Union. Both before and after the collapse, historians also tended to see the Thaw as an unfinished business resumed twenty years later. Some remained fairly optimistic. Thus, drawing parallels between the Khrushchev and Gorbachev years, Elena Zubkova looked back from the historical moment when, seemingly, the unresolved issues of the Thaw (a word she did not use) could at last find appropriate resolution. Noting the wavering leadership and 'the lack of a culture of reformism' among the population, Zubkova still welcomed the intellectual shifts of the 1950s and early 1960s, especially the rise of independent political opinions, a process whose origins she traced to the hopes, expectations, and a new sense of self-worth among the victors in the Second World War.[45]

Generally, though, the Soviet Union's collapse led to a sceptical shift in evaluations of the Thaw. From the mid-1990s, Russian authors began to emphasize its legacy of unsuccessful top-down reforms, poorly thought out and ill performed.[46] Parallels between the Khrushchev and Gorbachev years grew bleaker, to the point that some historians associated both of these periods with the political crisis of the early 1900s. In all these cases, they implied, the system's capacity for change from within proved limited, with inconsistent reforms leading to political catastrophe.[47] Like the earlier intelligentsia's representations, this one painted the Thaw and the perestroika with the same brush, only in darker colours: the emphasis now was not so much on the progress of democracy as on the collapse of statehood. For radical conservatives, whose previously muted voices now became prominent, this suggested a correlation between the two processes. The sceptical shift was not universally shared, and appreciative interpretations persisted after 1991, occasionally coming even from the critically minded.[48] On a broader political stage, admiration for the Thaw became part of the time-honoured intelligentsia narrative of struggle for liberty, which revived following Putin's rise to power. After 2000 the Thaw enjoyed a limited comeback in what could be termed oppositional social commentary based on the traditional intelligentsia values.[49] Yet the sceptical view of the epoch retained strong positions as well.[50]

Recent Western scholarship at times displays a similar scepticism toward the Thaw, although rooted in another political/intellectual tradition – the paradigm of 'continuity and change' between the Stalin years and their aftermath. Western studies of the Thaw began during the Thaw itself, at the time when the Stalin era constituted most of Soviet history. Kremlinologists monitored new developments in the USSR with an eye to the regime's political stability, often considering the reforms in instrumental terms, as a factor in power struggles.[51] Many of the earlier scholars did eventually come to believe that the impulse for change was substantial and persistent, potentially leading to outcomes the Soviet leaders could not foresee.[52] At the same time, the scepticism survived, and revived several decades later, when the Thaw became a subject of historical writing. A common emphasis now was on continuity, not so much in high politics as in culture. Scholars of the late 1990s and early 2000s stressed the post-1953 persistence of a political culture formed during the early Soviet years, especially under Stalin. Historians underscored the incompleteness of the Khrushchev reforms, the continuing recourse to repressive methods of social discipline, mobilization, and control, the still widespread secrecy and mistrust, the persistent reverence for Stalin, the lasting tendency to blame society's misfortunes on scapegoats, and the tight limits on cultural openness and discussion.[53] This description, of course, does not fully portray the recent literature, as many authors do emphasize the watershed role that Stalin's death played in Soviet society, the new pluralism of opinions and the media after 1953, the intense exchange of ideas, greater personal security, and higher living standards.[54] Still, a widespread emphasis in the tonality of some recent writings has been on the frailty and/or limitations of the Thaw enterprise.

There seems to have emerged a chorus of sceptics about the Thaw, all the more peculiar since the chorus is international and includes Russian and Western historians who would disagree on many issues except this one. Yet, valid as some of the observations about the Thaw-Stalin continuities are, one issue is that an emphasis on such continuities tends to perpetuate the view of the post-1953 decades as a postscript to the Stalin years, casting doubt on the need to study the entire second half (in fact, more than half) of Soviet history. Does a postscript really have to be read? Another, more important issue is that a focus on the continuity-change paradigm within the narrow Soviet framework may obscure the broader chronological and transnational contexts of modern Russia, such as the legacies of the imperial epoch and the numerous parallels and ties between the Soviet Union and its counterparts on the international stage.

One problem with the Thaw-Stalin continuity thesis is that it has a limited explanatory potential. How surprising is it, after all, that two adjacent and relatively brief periods, together spanning the duration of a short human life, had much in common? Yes, it was still the same country, culture, and century. Except for the very youngest, most of those who were active in 1962 had been active in 1952 as well. Many, furthermore, had also lived through 1942 and 1932. Naturally, people inherited values, beliefs, interests, affections, and forms of self-expression from their recent past. And of course, the leaders, opinion-makers, high culture–bearers, and their audiences operated within a set of historically conditioned assumptions about themselves and the outside world. It is true that some of the changes commonly associated with the Khrushchev years – the housing reform, the new party program, the emphasis on 'collective leadership' and 'intra-party democracy' – were proposed, discussed, and sometimes initiated during the late Stalin period.[55] There had been amnesties and releases from the Gulag before 1953, and a Western-oriented youth subculture had emerged as early as the immediate post-war years.[56] The literary stirrings, such as the publication of Viktor Nekrasov's *Stalingrad* (1946) and Valentin Ovechkin's *District Routine* (1952), both of which inspired a constellation of Thaw writers, dated back to the late Stalin years as well. It is equally true that many of the (socialist) realist tastes, heroes, and devices persisted long after Stalin.[57]

The Thaw certainly did originate in the late Stalin years – most importantly perhaps, in the Soviet experience of the Second World War. Victory in the war brought about a new sense of self-worth in people who had fought and seen that the country's fate depended on them.

After 1945 many, especially the intelligentsia, hoped that repressive policies would be relaxed, burdens on the collectivized peasantry would be alleviated, the militarized economy would be modified toward the people's everyday needs, intellectual life would be liberalized, and in general the government would show some degree of appreciation for the citizens' contribution to victory. Frustrated in the late 1940s and early 1950s, these aspirations nonetheless survived, and the pressing desire for change prepared ground for the actual changes later.[58] Just as importantly, many among the country's leadership under Stalin, and likely Stalin himself, did realize how dangerously ineffective the economic and political system was and did envision its improvement.

However, for every precedent of historical phenomena originating in the Stalin era there is a counter-example of unprecedented shifts that started in the 1950s and 1960s. Among those are the mass exculpation of political prisoners, the open reassessment of society's fundamental principles, the immense diversification of language and the overall cultural landscape, as well as the government-sponsored opening to the West. The scope and dynamism of transformation also made these years distinctive. Compared to the late Stalin years, changes were drastically accelerated, to the effect that the country emerging out of the Thaw was quite different from the one that had entered it.[59] Many people differed greatly in 1966 from what they had been in 1946 – in the ways they dressed, walked, and talked, in the books they read, conversations they held, letters they wrote, radio and (completely new) TV broadcasts they listened to and watched, music, songs, and dances they enjoyed, art exhibits they visited, homes they inhabited, and accoutrements they had inside those homes. Movies, which themselves altered perceptions and behaviours, registered the changes best. Soviet films of the 1950s and 1960s encompassed new dress, gestures, and bearings, all pointing to a 'liberation of body language.'[60] Motility was a key element in Thaw cinema – and indeed, motility and spontaneity were important elements of the thaw metaphor itself.

To explain these developments, and to speak meaningfully about continuity and change during the Thaw, it is insufficient to measure these years against the Stalin epoch. What is necessary is to place the Thaw in a broader interpretive context, Russian and international, considering these years from a long-term diachronic and synchronic historical perspective while also highlighting their distinct significance. In what follows, we offer several possible ways for such contextualization. This chapter emphasizes the distant origins of many Thaw phenomena in modern Russian culture, imperial as well as Soviet. We also stress parallels between the similar, although not identical, processes that took place simultaneously in the Soviet Union and several other European societies. One of our arguments is that during the 1950s and 1960s the USSR increasingly became an integral part of the larger world where governments and people dealt with very similar issues – a country among many others.

The Thaw as an Event

One traditional way of reaching beyond Stalin to longer historical processes is to view the Thaw through the prism of reform, as a link in the long chain of reforms that runs through modern Russian history.[61] Much as the specifics and circumstances varied, the goals of reforms had often been similar: modernizing the military, stimulating the economy, streamlining the administration, education, and justice, and thus 'catching up' with the ever-advancing and so-unreachable West. Reforms were regularly initiated from above, often in response to crises, proceeded unevenly, amidst much bureaucratic strife, and inspired forceful debates in the educated society.[62] All these similarities amounted to what Alfred Rieber designated as a 'reforming tradition' in Russian history.[63] Indeed, in the imperial age, reforms, or 'counter-reforms,' marked almost every major reign, as a new monarch initially publicized a break with the efforts of the immediate predecessor, performing a 'symbolic rupture,' to use Richard Wortman's expression. At the same time, (counter-) reformers often cast mnemonic glances to distant ancestors. Many invoked the image of the archetypal reformer, Peter I, and legitimated their work as return to a sacred tradition – whether Petrine modernization, pre-Petrine patriarchality, or Catherinian enlightenment.[64] These alternations have prompted scholars to propose that Russian history unfolds in a 'regime of inversions' – swings and returns between repression and reprieve, xenophobia and open-mindedness, traditionalism and experimentation, and so forth.[65]

It is beyond the scope of this chapter to explain the origins of this long-lasting reform cycle, although one possible (and inevitably vague) explanation might be the chronic crisis of political legitimacy in modern Russia that added to the vicissitudes of the country's modernization. For our purposes, it is important to note that the cycle apparently revived in the Soviet years. Against the imperial background, Khrushchev's denunciation of his predecessor and the appeal to a distant and pure source of origin (uncorrupted Leninism) appears to have belonged in the political tradition. So did the ever-present standard of the West, which inspired many Thaw undertakings. So did the curbing of repression, the release of prisoners incarcerated under the previous regime, the liberalization of the press, and the educated society's delight at the start of the new reign. All these had earlier precedents – say, in Elizabeth's attack on Anna, 'the beautiful beginning of Alexander's days,' or the release of the surviving Decembrists from Siberian exile in 1856, on the eve of the Great Reforms and exactly 100 years before the Twentieth Party Congress.

When placed in this broader perspective, the inconsistency of Khrushchev's reforms and the inertia of the populace unprepared for revelations and amnesties – these are the main arguments with which scholars question the Thaw project[66] – are neither distinctive nor surprising. Most reforms in Russia had been executed without sufficient planning or prognoses and were foisted upon an unready population.[67] Yet this does not necessarily detract from the reforms' ultimate significance.

The reform model is not unproblematic, one problem being that each set of reforms evolved in unique historical circumstances.[68] The experience of earlier reforms mattered as well: what some historians view as 'counter-reforms,' others interpret as a regular adjustment, evaluation, and trial of previously introduced methods of governance.[69] Perhaps the main problem is that interpreting reforms as cyclical predetermines continuity as failure. If viewed as part of a never-ending cycle, any 'reforms' (including those of the Thaw) are doomed to 'fail,' just as the previous and subsequent ones did – otherwise the cycle would break and the model would have to be discarded.

A different way of connecting the Thaw to long-term historical developments is to look for continuities not so much in government action as in cultural practices and imagery. Given the multiplicity of historical legacies, it indeed makes sense to speak not of continuity but of *continuities* in the plural.[70] The people of the 1950s and 1960s carried a baggage of traditions and conventions dating back decades and sometimes centuries. Thus, the literary polemics of the time could be traced simultaneously to several epochs. Lyrics had been a theme of literary conversations already in the 1930s, the division between archaists and innovators dated back to the 1920s, the Silver Age, or perhaps even to the age of Pushkin, while the strong societal impact of literature had characterized Russian culture at least since the 1790s. Contemporaries in the 1960s compared *Novyi mir* to *Sovremennik* and *Otechestvennye zapiski*, the thick journals of the other 'thaw,' a century earlier.[71]

This plurality of continuities explains why we prefer the designation *Thaw* to another common label for these years – *de-Stalinization,* a term of Western origin born in the mid-1950s and still widely used in the literature half a century later. The term is somewhat limiting. It prompts the reader to view the Soviet system as a single-handed creation and epitome of Stalin's will, thus unwittingly following the 'cult of personality' reasoning that Khrushchev advanced in 1956. Such terminology reduces the controversies of the 1950s and 1960s to a clash between a 'Stalinist' and a 'Khrushchevian' vision of socialism, threatening to bypass the larger social and cultural implications of those controversies. *De-Stalinization* obscures the possibility that the Soviet order, as well as attempts to reform or conserve it, had origins extending beyond Stalin's or Khrushchev's personalities, and that the personalities themselves were products of broader national, and perhaps even transnational, contexts. After all, nobody today would call the post–Second World War overcoming of the Nazi legacies in Germany 'de-Hitlerization.'

Rather than ousting the term *de-Stalinization* altogether, we propose to narrow its application to phenomena directly related to Stalin's figure and imagery. *De-Stalinization* may apply, for example, to the dismantling of the Stalin cult in the media or the arts. But *de-Stalinization* is less useful in analysing shifts of language, growing pluralism of self-expression, diversification of artistic and literary life, relations with the West, and even coping with the legacy of mass violence – phenomena whose origins and nature transcended Stalin's persona.

Continuities notwithstanding, the Thaw also had unique significance, and what helps to see it is the paradigm of event. In modern culture there is a widespread understanding of events as created by subjective perspectives, notably those of the media – just about any occasion can be turned into an 'event,' if spun properly. Yet this may not be the only useful interpretation of the concept. While agreeing that events are products of cultural construction and interpretation,[72] in what follows we also view them as having a formative and experiential quality, a lasting impact that is also helpful in historical analysis.

During the 1950s and 1960s, precisely when Soviet studies focused on 'continuity and change,' this same issue was actively debated by the *Annales* school in France. Much of the debate revolved around Fernand Braudel's 1958 concept of the *longue durée* that urged historians to privilege lengthy time spans and processes over brief periods, short-term changes, and a 'history of events.'[73] One of Braudel's critics, Michel Vovelle, doubted the utility of this approach. Rather than writing events and short-term changes out of existence, he argued, it was necessary to find 'a new dialectic of the shorter and longer time-frame in history.' The mentalities of eighteenth-century French peasants could be defined by centuries-old inertia, but the French Revolution did affect their lives, as it created lasting ruptures and divided traditional communities into conflicting political parties. Not only a revolution but also a smaller occurrence within it could be meaningful for subsequent decades and even centuries.[74] Insisting on the significance of the event, the 'shorter time frame,' or the rupture of continuity – all these terms, as he tacitly acknowledged, were largely synonymous with 'change' – Vovelle suggested such venues for exploring the power of events as 'historical traumatism' (an event studied together with its legacy) and 'constitutive event' (an event giving rise to a new process, practice, or tradition).[75]

It is within this framework of a constitutive event that we consider the Thaw. We focus on the specific phenomena of the 1950s and 1960s that prompted new trends of thought, patterns of behaviour, material life, and language – including some of the terms in which the Thaw would be subsequently interpreted. We also highlight the widespread perception of the epoch by its contemporaries as a time of imminent historic change, or at least of expectations for such change – the perception that would last for decades.

The sense of living in historic times had long characterized Soviet consciousness, but in the 1950s and 1960s the sense became particularly acute. In twentieth-century Russia, the point about the significance of events – or, to use Vovelle's terminology, 'shorter time frames' and 'ruptures' – pertains not only to the upheavals of the first half of the century but also to many occurrences within a decade after Stalin's death in 1953 (another indisputable historic event). In fact, the Thaw was a time particularly rich in events. The year 1956 alone witnessed Khrushchev's 'Secret Speech' at the Twentieth Party Congress, uprisings in Poland, the Hungarian Revolution, the release of exiled nationalities, the publication and triumphant reception of Vladimir Dudintsev's novel *Not by Bread Alone,* the Picasso exhibition, and Yves Montand's visit to Moscow – so many events that historians now devote separate studies to this year alone.[76] In 1957 followed the Moscow Youth Festival and the launch of Sputnik. These and other occasions – such as Gagarin's spaceflight in 1961, the Twenty-Second Party Congress in the same year, and the 1962 publication of Aleksandr Solzhenitsyn's *One Day in the Life of Ivan Denisovich* – were not momentary happenings causing short-term reactions conditioned by, and sinking back into, the mire of a certain 'Stalinist mentality.' On the contrary, these developments had a transformative impact, catalysing long-term historical processes.

But the density with which events arrived may be explained not only by their ultimate impact. What also created the sense, and the lasting memory, of these occasions as 'events' was the widespread *expectation* of an event. One historian has noted the 'domestic climate of exhilarating optimism' among the Soviet population on the verge of the 1960s. The optimism reflected improvements in material life, but also many people's genuine confidence and pride in their society's ethical and cultural values, political ideas, and prospects for the future that, many believed, would now be uninhibited, with rapid positive change just around the corner. Despite the later disillusionments, this optimism has left its trace in history and is still visible – in memories of the Thaw but also in the temperament, world outlook, and speech of those who grew up during those years.[77] It was this hopeful optimism that drove exuberant young people to turn streets, squares, university clubs, and exhibition halls into places of spontaneous (indeed) poetry readings, demonstrations, celebrations, and debates.[78] The common anticipation of events, the zeitgeist that attributed at once public and personal significance to contemporary occasions, made the time *eventful*. Taken together and called 'the Thaw,' all these events may also be considered a larger event in its own right.

The Thaw and the Past

Central to the Thaw and its historic impact was the drastic reduction of political violence in Soviet society. In February 1956 Nikita Khrushchev delivered his famous 'Secret Speech' at the Twentieth Party Congress in Moscow, in which he slammed the dead Stalin for having created his own 'cult of personality,' unleashing terror against millions of innocent people, and committing grave blunders in state leadership. The denunciation of Stalin produced an earth-shattering impact, both within the Soviet Union and throughout the world. In Eastern Europe – Poland, and especially Hungary – it led to major political crises and armed struggles, raising apprehensions about the stability of the socialist order. Five years later, though, at the Twenty-Second Party Congress in 1961, Khrushchev resumed his attack on Stalin and the terror. This time he dealt the final blow to the commemoration of Stalin's name and image: in 1961, places named after the deceased leader were renamed, his monuments were destroyed, and his mummified body was taken out of the Lenin Mausoleum and reburied in a simpler grave by the Kremlin wall. For a brief but influential period in the early to mid-1960s, relatively direct and detailed descriptions of the recent state violence were allowed into print – Solzhenitsyn's 1962 *One Day* being the most famous example. Literary publications proved particularly influential, transforming the ways in which thousands of people interpreted history. Sparked by such writers as Ehrenburg and Solzhenitsyn, conversations about arrests, executions, and prison camps unsettled the established linguistic universe and historical rationale, urging readers to seek different intellectual foundations. The intensity of societal reactions to this literary polemic was such that the regime deemed it dangerous and gradually shut it down by the late 1960s. When it resumed in the 1980s, the polemic proceeded largely in the literature-centred forms cast by the Thaw – only this time the terror debate indeed proved politically explosive.

Ending the terror also had an immediate and tangible human effect that preceded Khrushchev's speeches at party congresses, transcended the dismantling of the Stalin cult, and mattered even for those who hardly read literature.[79] Between 1953 and 1956, more than 3.3 million inmates were released from camps, colonies, and prisons. Despite the simultaneous convictions, the Gulag population shrank to a third of its earlier size in these years, from 2,467,893 to 810,755, never again to reach the Stalin-era heights. The number and proportion of political prisoners declined yet more drastically, from 539,718 to only 9,596 and from 22 per cent to a mere 1.6 per cent in 1953–60 – never to return to the Stalin-time levels, either.[80] With the releases, accompanied by uprisings on the 'inside' and crime waves on the 'outside,' came the major downsizing and reshaping of the Gulag, from a prison labour empire to a much smaller and less ambitious penal institution. By the mid-1960s the camps had shifted from the centre to the margins of Soviet economy.[81] Besides the camp prisoners, entire nations (Balkars, Chechens, Ingush, Kalmyks, and Karachaevans) deported during the Second World War as 'unreliable' now returned to their original areas of residence. Other deported nations – Crimean Tatars, Finns, Germans, Koreans, and Meskhetian Turks – began a decades-long struggle for the right to return home. Together with the released 'kulaks,' 'Vlasovites,' Ukrainian nationalists, and several other groups, the total number of deportees ('special settlers') dropped from 2,753,356 to just about 153,400 people in 1953–8.[82]

Several million former prisoners and exiles began their difficult reintegration in society. Their paths were diverse and success varied, as they often faced suspicion, surveillance, and discrimination.[83] Outside the barbed wire, many former prisoners continued to rely on personal networks they had built in the camps, now using those networks to find housing and jobs, to restore old and form new families. With that aim, some opted to stay in the areas of their former incarceration or even returned there later.[84] For others, who sought to build a new life on the 'mainland,' homecoming was complicated by memories of who they had been before the arrest or exile, as well as by the new environment, often strange and unfamiliar.

Reintegration was not simply a matter of society's accepting or rejecting the returnees on the basis of preconceived opinions about who they were ('criminals,' 'enemies of the people,' etc.). The meanings of all the components in the equation – *society, returnees, acceptance,* and *rejection* – varied, depending on specific circumstances. It mattered who was returning, from where, and where to. Returning from the Kolyma region was not the same as returning from Kazakhstan, where the dismantling of camps and special settlements overlapped with a new ambitious agricultural mobilization, so that Russian and Ukrainian workers arrived in the 'Virgin Lands' just as thousands of Chechen and Ingush deportees flooded the train stations trying to leave.[85] Returning to Moscow or Leningrad was different from returning to a Russian province, and still different from returning to western Ukraine or the Baltics. In the recently Sovietized western borderlands, thus, the ex-prisoners found themselves in an environment permeated with fresh memories of war, the Holocaust, a succession of repressive regimes, and multi-sided ethnic violence. Consequently, many things mattered in reintegration. It mattered whether the return happened before, during, or after the 1956 events in Hungary and Poland. It mattered whether, and at what point, the local authorities received the directives to integrate the ex-prisoners or to obstruct their return, and how they reacted to those directives. It mattered *who* the returnee had been – what his ethnicity was, whether he had been politically active in the past, and especially whether he had fought in the Second World War. It mattered on whose side and *how* he had fought. It also mattered whom he would face upon his return – while some might welcome him back as a hero, others who had fought against him and whose families he had killed were not likely to forgive and forget.[86]

Rejection and acceptance of the former Gulag prisoners were thus not constants but variables dictated by many overlapping factors: location, timing, political conjuncture, dispositions and memories of the local population, and the returnees themselves. There were mechanisms that made reintegration possible, and, despite the obstacles, many returnees were able to make choices as well as celebrate modest yet vital successes. The variables suggest that in the ex-prisoners' reintegration, as elsewhere, the Thaw had many faces. It was not one project but a number of different multi-directional 'projects' – Russian and non-Russian, central and regional, intelligentsia- and government-driven, with many subgroups and agendas in between.

The countryside was another place where, as in the borderlands and areas of imprisonment and exile, state violence had been particularly methodical. The Thaw brought considerable relief to the peasantry. By cutting agricultural taxes, writing off peasant debts, investing in agriculture, and easing restrictions on migration from collective farms, the government improved the situation in the village. Although later Khrushchev's 1958–9 euphoric struggle against private land plots and household livestock undermined much of this improvement, the mid-1950s marked major steps toward ending the new serfdom to which the peasantry had been subjected since collectivization. The easing of repressive policies would continue, with collective farmers beginning to receive salaries in 1966 and permanent passports after 1974–6.[87] Perhaps as important as the material improvements was the fact that Russian educated society was now more willing to listen to peasant voices than in the 1930s and 1940s, if not directly then at least through those members of the intelligentsia who began to speak on the peasants' behalf. Part of the broader re-evaluation of the past during the late Soviet decades, 'village prose' and agricultural journalism gradually reassessed the legacy of collectivization. The new attention to the countryside began to undermine the dismissive, exploitative attitude to the peasantry that had been central to the Stalin epoch.[88]

In October 1961, the Third Party Program redefined the Soviet Union as an 'all-people's state' (*obschenarodnoe gosudarstvo*), thus discarding the regime's original self-definition, 'dictatorship of the proletariat,' which the party had formulated in its first program (1903), confirmed in the second program (1919), and maintained since.[89] The Third Party Program is usually regarded sceptically, as the ultimate embodiment of Khrushchev's hopeless utopianism, and more broadly, the utopianism of the 'Soviet project.'[90] Meanwhile, 1961 was the only time in Soviet history when the country officially changed its raison d'être. Endorsed later in the 1977 Constitution, the elimination of the term *dictatorship* from the strategic party and state documents meant the rejection of mass violence as a fundamental tenet of the Soviet political doctrine.

Coping with the legacy of the recent violence – remembering and chronicling it, striving to explain it and to prevent its resumption – became a major characteristic of the country's political, intellectual, and artistic life. Ending the terror was a process that directly touched individual biographies, as millions of people faced disturbing questions about their past and the social order that had consumed their lives.[91]

Soviet society was not the only one that scrutinized the recent past. During the 1950s and 1960s, discussions about mass political violence in the USSR in some ways paralleled those in the West. After the Second World War, European societies nearly simultaneously arrived at very similar questions: How to exit the recent violence and what to do with its institutions and machinery? How to reorganize politics and rebuild trust in justice? How, and whether, to discuss repression and its legacy? What to do with the old imagery, language, and ideas, and what could emerge in their stead? Finally, how to avoid the return of this past? On the one hand, the discussion of these issues took paths in France, Germany, or Italy that were different from those in the Soviet Union. In the West, the intense polemic about the recent mass violence came as a consequence of the collapse of the polities that had created or abetted this violence. Except in Spain and Portugal, the post-war governments and media largely distanced themselves from the regimes that had produced concentration camps and mass extermination. In the USSR, on the contrary, the political order that had brought collectivization, the terror of 1936–8, and the Gulag not only survived 1945 (1953, 1956), but also proclaimed itself ever more stable and successful. Accordingly, in the Soviet Union a reverse order of political developments took place: unlike in Italy, Germany, or France, the collapse of the regime followed, rather than preceded, a long period of historical reflection and polemics. The reinterpretation of the past in the USSR emerged within the original, if modified, political structure, only gradually reaching an explosive stage and itself contributing to the structure's collapse. More than elsewhere, then, remembrance of state violence in the Soviet Union had to work against the state's efforts at maintaining historical legitimacy. The persistence of the established political order made identifying the nature of the recent violence, its victims and perpetrators, as well as strategies of memorialization and prosecution, considerably more difficult in the Soviet case than nearly anywhere in Western Europe.[92]

On the other hand, underneath the seemingly obvious differences there were commonalities between the processes of remembrance east and west of the Cold War divide. The 1950s and especially 1960s were the time when both in the West and in the USSR the critical issues of twentieth-century past entered the focus of public attention.[93] In both cases the trajectories of remembrance, commemoration, and retribution were neither linear nor straightforward.[94] Certainly not everyone who had lived under the authoritarian regimes disapproved of them, and along with remembering there were strong tendencies not to remember, encouraged by politicians who favoured putting the past behind.[95] In the Soviet Union, as in the West, it took multi-decade efforts of intellectuals and dedicated political activists to set collective historical reflection in motion.

We are used to thinking about Russia as a literature-centred civilization and therefore accept that in Soviet society literature played a crucial role in launching the polemics on the Stalin terror. However, writers played an important role in drawing attention to the past in post-war Western societies as well. In West Germany, the first surge of widespread concern with the Holocaust and the question of German guilt came in 1955, after *The Diary of Anne Frank* was published in paperback – by 1960, the best-selling paperback in West German history. It was a writer, Annie Romein-Verschoor, who together with her husband made the publication of the document possible. As a result, concentration camp memorials and museums (particularly the former camp of Bergen-Belsen, where Anne Frank had died), recently almost devoid of visitors, now saw thousands of teenagers coming on excursions to honour the victims' memory.[96] In 1959, Günter Grass published *The Tin Drum*, one of the most vivid German literary representations of the Nazi past.[97] In the early 1960s, the years when Solzhenitsyn's *One Day* and Ehrenburg's memoir were published in the USSR, two major trials drew public attention in Germany to the Nazi crimes – the 1961 trial of Adolf Eichmann in Jerusalem and the 1963–5 trial of Auschwitz camp guards in Frankfurt am Main.[98] No less significant than the trials themselves and their media coverage were the literary responses. In 1963, a few months after the Eichmann trial, Rolf Hochhuth produced his famous play *The Deputy*, focusing on the Vatican's inaction despite awareness of the Holocaust.[99] In 1964, Hannah Arendt's *Eichmann in Jerusalem* introduced the broad reading public in Germany to the 'banality' of Nazi evil.[100] Next year, Peter Weiss responded to the Auschwitz trial with his famous play *The Investigation*, presenting the Nazi criminals not as an aberration but as legitimate offspring of Western society. Along with Hochhut's *The Deputy*, Weiss's play became one of the most widely discussed literary texts in West Germany.[101] Thus promoted by writers, from the 1960s on the German *Vergangenheitsbewältigung* debate and similar controversies in other countries only grew in intensity.[102] As recently suggested, intellectuals played an ever more important role in post–Second World War societies throughout and beyond Europe, voicing and widely broadcasting alternative political ideas as well as mobilizing the consciousness of their increasingly well-educated, informed audiences.[103]

These were also years when both Soviets and West Europeans sought to place their time in a long-term historical perspective. After the attack on Stalin had threatened to de-legitimate most if not all of Soviet history, many people increasingly looked for new historical foundations that could give meaning to their own and the country's existence. Not incidentally, the theme of 'tradition and innovation' (*traditsii i novatorstvo*) re-emerged during the Thaw, becoming a constant presence in Soviet cultural polemics for the next three decades. Absorbing the best minds since the first revolutionary years, the 'tradition/innovation' controversy was itself a tradition in Soviet and pre-revolutionary Russian culture.[104] With the rupture of historical legitimacy in 1953–6, the controversy took a new turn: unlike in the earlier discussions (say, in the 1920s), the polemical emphasis during the 1950s and 1960s was not so much on innovation as on tradition. It was not only the professed conservatives – defenders of realism, figurative art, and the 'classical legacy' – who advocated the various renditions and incarnations of the past. Their rivals, the proponents of artistic and literary innovation, also promoted a return to the past – to the turn-of-the-century's artistic and literary experimentation, to the legacy of modernism and avant-garde.[105] During and after the Thaw, many intellectuals made conscious efforts to bring back hundreds of names of early-twentieth-century artists, writers, poets, and composers, earlier struck (often physically) from the cultural memory. Ehrenburg's memoir was but one, although the most influential of such resuscitation projects. Like the new 'traditionalists,' the new 'innovators' of the 1950s and 1960s sought to ground themselves in a legacy, even as the specific legacies in question were very different. To a great extent, the polemic about 'tradition and innovation' was a controversy among various traditions and groups of tradition-seekers. The longevity of the polemic throughout the 1970s and 1980s shows how significant this search for origins and historical legitimacy was.[106]

For many, the search became a retreat into the past. The pursuit of an evanescent ideal knocked down consecutive historical beacons, which, upon closer scrutiny, proved not so radiant. One could move back to the New Economic Policy (NEP) of the 1920s, to Lenin, to the romantics of the first revolutionary years, and then to the pre-revolutionary times – with the numerous and often contradictory objects of nostalgia and idealization that Imperial Russia could offer. The objects ranged from the grandeur of the emperors' courts and the prowess of their regiments led by noble officers, to the same nobles' learned pursuits, dignity, and impeccable manners in glittering ballrooms, to the harmonious pastoral landscapes, the aesthetic appeal of old architecture, and unhurried lifestyles, to the uprightness of the *zemstvo* doctors and teachers or the noble camaraderie, self-sacrificing courage, and perfect French of the Decembrists. Imperial splendour was not the end of the retreat, for other continuity-seekers would look into pre-Petrine Russia – the centuries of Orthodoxy and peasant patriarchality, the esoteric beauty of icons by Andrei Rublev and Theophanes the Greek, the austere magnificence of pre-Mongol cathedrals, and the invulnerable eight-hundred-year-old passages from *The Tale of Bygone Years*. Building bridges to the distant past became one of the most visible and important themes for decades after 1953, as historical polemics transformed and diversified late Soviet culture.[107]

The quest had parallels in post-war Western Europe, notably West Germany, where, just as in the Soviet Union, the quest for alternative historical continuities and grounds for legitimacy originated in the discrediting of the recent past. In what Jeffrey Herf has called 'multiple restorations,' West German intellectuals and statesmen of the late 1940s and early 1950s looked for the country's ties to distant history. Konrad Adenauer, Theodor Heuss, and Kurt Schumacher sought to rebuild society's confidence, bringing back the ideas of Weimar, the Second Reich, or perhaps even the 1848 Frankfurt Parliament. Centrist conservatism and Christian democracy, social democracy and liberalism came back into the political play.[108]

East and west of the Iron Curtain, the 1950s and 1960s witnessed a resurgence of the language of legality, democracy, and human rights, which many saw as guarantees against a return of the recent past. The centrality of law in preventing the re-emergence of Nazism achieved remarkable prominence in post-war West Germany, showing, for instance, in the supreme importance given to the courts, particularly the Constitutional Court. The primary objective of this approach was to ensure maximum stability and survival of democracy amidst the widespread anxiety that 'Bonn would become Weimar.' The 1949 constitution included the principle of 'super-legality,' a provision that the highest institutions of power could not, under any circumstances, abrogate the fundamental principles of liberal democracy. Super-legality was intended to prevent a replay of the 'democratic suicide' that the Reichstag had committed in 1933 precisely by abrogating those principles and thus paving the legal path for the Nazi dictatorship. The same anxiety over 'Bonn turning into Weimar' drove the debates among post-war West German political thinkers about 'militant democracy,' which, unlike Weimar, would be capable of defending itself in the face of an authoritarian threat.[109]

Legal doctrines in West Germany and France also evolved in response to the trials of wartime collaborators and perpetrators. In 1960, 1965, 1969, and 1979 the Bundestag held four major debates to extend the statute of limitations for murder, crucial for the prosecution of the Nazi genocide, crimes against humanity, and war crimes. Each of those *Verjährungsdebatten* extended the term of prosecution for such crimes, until in 1979 the statute of limitations was abolished altogether. In France as well, law assumed major public importance in dispensing post-war justice. The 1953 Bordeaux trial and amnesty of the perpetrators of the 1944 massacre at Oradour-sur-Glane triggered a controversy not only among intellectuals but also between the country's two regions – Limousin, where the massacre had taken place, and Alsace, from where some of the perpetrators hailed. Thousands of people took to the streets, and extensive polemics on the amnesty law broke out during the 1950s. In 1964, reacting to West German parliamentary debates, the French National Assembly suspended the statute of limitations for crimes against humanity. In 1966, *Eichmann in Jerusalem* came out in French, causing yet another storm of debate on the perpetrators' legal accountability.[110]

In the Soviet Union, similarly, extensive legal polemics of the 1950s and 1960s originated in a widespread perception that distortions of legality were at the root of mass violence, in this case the repression during the Stalin years.[111] Although the doctrine of the presumption of innocence would not enter Soviet law expressly until 1989, during the Thaw it was no longer rejected as a bourgeois leftover, unlike often in the early Soviet years. Discussions on the presumption of innocence had started in the legal profession already during the late Stalin period and intensified afterwards. Experts, as well as their Western observers, split into those who believed that Soviet law implicitly contained the presumption of innocence and others who argued that it did not and/or should not. By the 1970s, advocates of the presumption of innocence had slowly gained the upper hand, their victory secured by a 1978 ruling of the USSR Supreme Court.[112]

As early as the 1960s, Soviet law underwent important changes. In 1960, the new Code of Criminal Procedure of the Russian Federation replaced the 1923 one. The new code rejected the use of confession as decisive proof of guilt, thus refuting Andrei Vyshinskii's arguments of the 1930s to early 1950s about establishing guilt in political 'conspiracy' cases.[113] In the 1960s and 1970s, a number of legal theorists launched a fairly successful attack on Vyshinskii's ideas.[114] The new 1961 Criminal Code of the Russian Federation, which replaced the 1926 one, prevented, at least on paper, the repression of individuals who had committed no formal crime, as well as members of their families. The code also ruled out extrajudicial repression, such as the *troikas, dvoikas,* and the Special Conference of the Stalin years, by stating that criminal punishment be meted out only by courts.[115] These and other shifts undermined some of the foundations of Stalin-time criminal justice. Significantly, during the Gorbachev years Soviet legal theorists returned to their Thaw debates.[116]

Law became important not only to legal professionals but also to a broad non-specialist educated audience. The Soviet human rights movement grew largely out of the widespread concern for preventing, by means of legality, the return of mass repression. In 1965–6, many people wrote letters of protest against the trial of the writers Andrei Siniavskii and Iulii Daniel', comparing it to the show trials of the 1930s and insisting that proper legal procedure, such as openness of trial and presumption of innocence, be observed. They also expressly defended the norms of a democratic society, where open disagreement with an official ideological line was perfectly possible.[117] Thus, during the same years, legality and democracy became crucial concepts for intellectuals, political leaders, and human rights activists both in the West and in the Soviet Union.

On the Soviet side, perhaps the most prominent human rights activist of the time was Andrei Sakharov (1924–1990). Notably, his political philosophy evolved in the 1960s under the impact of the contemporary polemics about the recent historical tragedies. Sakharov's first major treatise, *Progress, Coexistence, and Intellectual Freedom* (1968), abounded in references to Solzhenitsyn, as well as to the history of Nazi Germany.[118] Not incidentally perhaps, in this work Sakharov discussed the Soviet Union and the West in the same breath, as parts of one world – not only with regard to the past but also in reference to the present and future. He wrote at the time when Soviet and Western cultures began sharing important agendas. Reflection on the recent pan-European experience of political violence was one of them.

Taken broadly, in both of the Cold War camps the massive involvement of intellectuals in politics, the quest for alternative historical legitimacy, and the widespread emphasis on law were parts of the increasingly common engagement with the legacy of the twentieth-century turbulent past. The parallels between the East and the West are, of course, not perfect, given the vast differences in political and intellectual cultures and the many distinctions one could draw between the nature of political violence in each particular case. And yet the parallels are worth emphasizing. If anything, they suggest that Europeans of the 1950s and 1960s responded to the common questions about the past with similar, if not identical, answers that ultimately transcended the Cold War divide.

Material Life

The physical and psychological homecoming of Gulag and exile survivors was only one out of many voyages of the Thaw. Images of departure and arrival became prominent in the press, literature, and the arts during the 1950s and 1960s. The country was on the move.

Rural poverty, memories of collectivization, and unpredictable government policies urged millions of peasants to use the new migration opportunities and leave collective farms for the cities. By the end of the 1950s, for the first time in its history, Russia had become a predominantly urban country. In the Russian Federation, the urban population exceeded 50 per cent in 1958, in the USSR overall in 1962.[119] This exodus from the countryside paralleled contemporary demographic trends in some other regions of Europe with large rural populations. Italy, particularly in 1958–63, experienced the 'great migration' from the villages to the cities and from the South to Rome and the North.[120] In France of the late 1950s and 1960s, intellectuals lamented the disappearance of 'authentic' rural culture as rural youths moved to the cities and populated monotonous new apartment complexes.[121]

Within the cities, millions of Soviet people moved from decrepit communal dwellings to standardized individual apartments, poorly built yet supplied with running hot and cold water, sewerage, and central heating, and thus offering a solution to the desperate shortage of urban housing. Between 1955 and 1970, 35,688,000 separate apartments were built in the Soviet Union, accommodating more than half of the country's population.[122] The new apartments raised the question of privacy as an experience for millions and a conundrum for the ideologues.[123] The apartments also redefined the citizens' daily expectations of socialism in personal, consumerist, and welfare terms.[124] Ironically, the success of housing construction proved disturbing for the regime, stimulating new material demands that the economy could not meet.[125] Soon enough, the standardized apartment complexes made of prefabricated parts became the object of criticism and ingenious humour.[126]

The new apartment blocks also connected, visually and experientially, Soviet to other European cityscapes. Soviet 'micro-districts' of the 1950s looked much like the *grands ensembles* in France, social housing in West Germany, 'satellite cities' in East Germany, high-rise complexes in Britain, and public construction projects in Italy.[127] While the housing shortage in Russia dated back to the rapid industrialization and urbanization in the early decades of the century, the colossal destruction of the Second World War put Russians and West Europeans in similar housing situations.[128] Forced by the war into shacks, barracks, and dugouts, millions of people all over Europe lived in overcrowded shared lodgings with terrible sanitation facilities. France lost about a fifth of its housing stock. In the late 1940s, approximately half of the French population did not have running water, and only 3 per cent enjoyed running hot water, while public fountains continued to supply water for many working-class households well into the mid-1950s. Contemporary photographs showed families of five or six crammed into one room, not unlike in Soviet communal apartments. Young French couples dreamed of a place of their own.[129] A third of German housing was destroyed during the war; and even after the living conditions improved, getting 'a room of one's own' was 'a memorable event' for a child.[130] In Italy, even before the war, hundreds of thousands of people were packed in attics and cellars. Wartime bombings left hundreds of thousands more homeless. In the early 1950s, Italian housing was still overcrowded and lacked basic amenities. Skyrocketing rural-urban migration made the housing crisis yet worse.[131]

Facing the same imperative to build quickly, post-war European governments adopted the same solution: standardized mass construction. In Italy, construction expanded so rapidly that the decade of 1953–63 has been called 'the great building boom.'[132] Just as in Moscow or Leningrad, the high-rise districts in Rome or Milan were located on city outskirts and poorly integrated in the urban infrastructure.[133] West German government-subsidized apartment complexes were built speedily, without much care for beauty but with a megalomaniac notion of progress, prompting residents and architects alike to consider the box-like structures 'inhuman, isolating, frightening, unecological, and unhealthy,' a West German 'mass housing catastrophe.'[134] Similarly dull 'dormitory suburbs' sprawled around urban centres in East Germany. Prefabricated panels provided poor insulation from cold, heat, and sound, while the apartment layout was awkward and the rooms small. By the late 1960s and

1970s, the new construction came to be criticized East and West for supposedly neglecting aesthetics, sophistication, and all but basic comforts.

Back in the 1950s, however, these dwellings did not mean crudeness only, and they did not create just nationwide landscapes of unrelieved monotony. Initially, the new apartment blocks meant new principles of housing – modern and democratic. Constructivism, rationalism, and functionalism were back in vogue. And the new apartments did improve countless lives. In France, starting in 1953, government initiative spurred no less than 'a revolution in housing.' 'For millions of French families unable to afford a home of their own, the new apartment buildings represented a veritable leap into modernity. They extended to the bulk of the population advantages previously enjoyed only by the wealthy.'[135] The dreams of young French couples were shared by other European couples, just as their governments' efforts reflected transnational developments in housing.[136]

The Soviet Union was part of this picture. Unprecedented in the domestic context, Khrushchev's mass housing campaign belonged with contemporary trends in urban planning, construction technology, welfare, and aesthetic vision. Similar forms of material life emerged in the 1950s all over Europe, connecting both parts of the divided continent.[137]

Providing each family with a separate apartment was but one, although the principal, symbol of the Soviet regime's new materialism. The Thaw manifested the leadership's effort to stake the domestic and international legitimacy of the Soviet order upon the immediate, not distant, material prosperity of ordinary citizens. Next to the U.S.-sponsored 'economic miracle' and booming consumption in Western Europe, the advantages of socialism as a world system were to be demonstrated through better living. Khrushchev portrayed communism as a land of milk and honey – and indeed, milk and meat, if not honey, figured prominently in his assurances at home and in his bravado abroad.[138]

The economic reforms emphasized greater investment in the production and accessibility of consumer goods. With the newly available commodities, such as home appliances, came expert counsel on how to use them – advice manuals that put homemaking on a 'rational' basis.[139] Scholars view the proliferation of normative literature in these years as an indication that the new apartments did not bring much privacy.[140] That may have been so, but the 'intrusion of experts' into the home dispelled privacy in Western Europe as well. In France, home economics classes had been de rigueur as far back as under Vichy, popularizing the 'scientific' organization of time and space at home. In the 1950s the same ideas were widely disseminated through women's magazines. Studies on French housing and consumption often begin with a caveat that the home was neither apolitical nor entirely private. The same was true for Germany, East and West, where consumption and homemaking were explicitly politicized: West Germany in particular relied on economic prosperity and welfare in the wake of the national catastrophe and postwar privation. Consumption became a defining 'vector of the nation,' and the market a 'guarantor of political freedoms.'[141]

Soviet leaders, too, welded together consumption and citizenship in search of legitimacy. Khrushchev, at least until the price hike of 1962, claimed welfare provisions as his forte, announcing a break with the past precisely in the production and supply of consumer goods, food, housing, and services. Moreover, in the Cold War context rivals sought to legitimize themselves by claiming economic superiority. The comparisons were so frequent that shortages and poor-quality goods under socialism convinced Soviet consumers of an intrinsic value to things Western.[142] Enormous crowds visited the exhibits of Finnish design, American appliances and graphics, British plastics, Parisian haute couture, Austrian footwear, and much more. There was a certain pleasure in looking at this remote yet tangible world: displays made consumer fancies material and therefore real.[143] Western labels, by virtue of their lettering and design, became prized possessions in socialist societies, linking the drab here-and-now to the fantastic.[144]

The lure of Western consumerism offered a dual challenge to Soviet ideologues, economic planners, and designers – to invent its distinctly socialist equivalent as well as to 'catch up and overtake.'[145] Fashion best exemplifies the attempts to distinguish Soviet consumer culture – as culture indeed – from its profligate capitalist counterpart.[146] The very concept of fashion was thorny: it implied changeability, while Soviet goods were supposed to be durable. The idea of durability also went hand-in-glove with chronic economic shortages: things, from cupboards to socks, would get fixed, mended, or stored, but rarely thrown out.[147] The malfunctioning economy intertwined with established cultural practices and perceptions, so that designers would often fall back on familiar arguments for promoting 'cultured' consumption and educating 'good taste.' Meanwhile, the shortages in clothing were eagerly filled by the legal and not-so-legal retailers and entrepreneurs well-attuned to consumer demand.

And yet, despite all this persistent economic and cultural rigidity, it was during the Thaw that daily practices and choices became greatly diversified. Soviet consumers now drew on multiple strategies and new sources of inspiration. Illustrated magazines, shows at the houses of fashion, Western films, and foreign tourism fired imaginations. The result was a heterogeneous consumer environment and the Westernization of the Soviet material world. [148]

The Thaw and the West

The impact of Western material culture was part of a much larger phenomenon of the 1950s and 1960s – the unprecedented opening of the Soviet Union to the outside world, especially to the West.[149]

In Europe and the United States, these decades were remarkable for the extraordinary scope of cultural exchange that effectively spurred a 'cultural revolution.'[150] The post-war presence of American GIs, businesses, and products in Europe, although important, does not entirely account for this effervescence. Another reason was the new communication and travel technologies: the European mid-1950s were the dawn of family automobiles and television, democratized leisure, tourism, and record migrations.[151] The technological changes of the 1950s – Cinemascope, wide screen, colour film, and television – radically altered perception, amounting to a visual revolution for millions of spectators worldwide. In the 1960s, British rock/pop – drawing on jazz, blues, and rock 'n' roll – burst onto the American scene, while the miniskirt and Sassoon hairstyles overtook Paris, that citadel of fashion. Italian cinema offered the world some of the most iconic (and beautiful) faces and some of the most stylistically influential films.[152]

The Soviet Union did not remain isolated from the transnational cultural flows of the time. On the contrary, it became an integral participant in exhibitions, film festivals, and book fairs. The changes in cinematic technologies were global and arrived in the USSR at about the same time as elsewhere. Thaw cinema also partook of the transnational visual style: Soviet films became part of the international cinematic aspirations to rescue physical reality from linguistic conventions. Italian neo-realism, indeed all Italian film, had a profound impact on Soviet cinema, which, too, began to depict ordinary apartment-dwellers and crowds rushing through rain-drenched streets. In its search for accidental events and ambiguous moments, in the rejection of artificial lighting, elaborate sets, and voice training, Thaw cinema shared the faith in the redeeming power of the documentary with contemporary Western cinematic trends. Western films introduced to the Soviet screen new dances,

American teenage heroes of the James Dean variety, risqué femininity à la Brigitte Bardot, and the bittersweet clumsiness of Giulietta Masina. Archaic in the late Stalin time, Soviet films at last became understandable to Western audiences and critics, who could now discuss them in familiar terms. The transformation of the Soviet film industry and the emergence of a new generation of filmmakers met the aesthetic revolution in the West.[153]

Another example of the Soviet Union's partaking of the international visual culture was the famed 1959 American National Exhibition in Moscow. The Sokol'niki Park welcomed, at once grudgingly and hungrily, a cornucopia of objects and images, hundreds of consumer items, dozens of paintings and photographs, refreshments, glossy magazines, books, home and garden appliances, information charts, and dazzling colours. All these were not created for Moscow alone but amalgamated from different displays in different countries. The golden geodesic dome, a much remembered sight, arrived from Delhi. The 'typical American family home,' which brought so much political commotion as the site of the Khrushchev-Nixon 'kitchen debate,' had been a success at the Brussels World Fair the year before. And Edward Steichen's photography exhibit 'The Family of Man' had been displayed at the Museum of Modern Art in New York in 1955 and had travelled around the world since then. The exhibit was also heir to the turn-of-the-century photographic collection, 'Archives of the Planet,' created by Albert Kahn in Paris.[154] Among the numerous meanings of the 1959 exhibition – consumption, modern art, welfare, American myth and reality – was this one: millions of Soviet visitors now saw the same images as viewers in Delhi, Brussels, Paris, and New York.[155]

Western presence during the Thaw was not limited to the capitals. People eagerly listened to Western radio broadcasts not only in Moscow but also (perhaps more so) in western Ukraine and the Baltics. Finnish students visited not only Leningrad but also Tartu, while at least some Estonian students were able to go to Helsinki. Hundreds of thousands of repatriates moved across the western Soviet border, heavily policed as it was, in both directions, carrying experiences to share and stories to tell. Some even managed to cross the border from Hungary to call on their relatives in Soviet Transcarpathia. In the western Soviet regions, older people's interwar memories of free contact with the West, such as opportunities to travel abroad and study in British or Swedish colleges, were part of the emotional environment, too. The Thaw-era visits from the West to the USSR were not figurative but very tangible and real.[156]

The words *Cold War* often bring to mind a bipolar world divided by the Iron Curtain: on the one side, the impenetrable socialist bloc, on the other side, the European economic revival moulding American-style consumer societies. Indeed, post-war European elites felt beleaguered by American mass culture, media, consumer objects, and tastes.[157] For their part, Soviet cultural diplomats played up European fears of American cultural invasion, moralizing about violent Westerns, profligate stars, corrupting dances, coarse manners, dumb comics, and great books shredded into Cliffs Notes.[158] The importance of American presence in Europe for the Soviet understanding of cultural exchange cannot be overstated: in part, the exchange agreements were the Soviet response to the American exercise of 'soft power.'[159] In the cultural Cold War, the Soviet Union stood little chance from the start, the argument goes, because it was much poorer. America's wealth bears the weight of most arguments about the success of U.S. cultural imports in Europe. Historians have vividly described just how well-fed and well-stocked with goods – the proverbial hosiery, cigarettes, and chocolate – American GIs in Europe were.[160] If America won the political Cold War, it is because it had first, and early on, won 'the cool war': the Soviet Union was not as rich, fun, and colourful. The America of European fantasies and envy was nylon and neon.[161]

The America of Soviet fantasies and envy was nylon and neon, too. But importantly, not only America: nylon and neon was also the *Europe* of Soviet fantasies. Most accounts reduce post-war cross-cultural traffic to 'Americanization,' in which Western Europe, let alone the USSR, rarely exported songs, films, books, or paintings. Meanwhile, Soviet exposure to the West during the Thaw was part of intra-European cultural traffic. Italian films, French chanson and painting, as well as English drama, mixed with Hollywood, jazz, abstract expressionism, and American novels on Soviet screens, radio sets, bookshelves, and exhibition displays. The Soviet Union also circulated books and journals in Europe and beyond, sent art exhibitions, performing troupes, and delegations, and participated in international film festivals.[162] Ineffective abroad, Soviet cultural export was consequential at home: the exchanges were reciprocal, and Soviet ballet tours and movie sales brought Western cultural imports to the USSR. It was this nexus of mutually constitutive export and import that reintroduced the country to European, cross-Atlantic, and indeed global cultural networks.

Historiographically speaking, the Soviet Union of the Thaw may rescue Europe from the vortex of 'Americanization.' The multiplicity of sides and agents of exchange complicates the bilateral view of cultural traffic and the bipolar vision of the world that has dominated scholarly literature. Viktor Krasil'shchikov's 'glass curtain' and György Péteri's 'nylon curtain' metaphors refer to the attraction of Western goods for socialist consumers.[163] But these metaphors also imply a transparency and permeability in the Cold War divide.[164] There were multiple points of intersection and diffusion, spatial and temporal, relationships not only between the countries of origin and destination but also among cultural imports in circulation, synchronically as well as diachronically.[165] Thus, classical ballet, perhaps the best-known Soviet cultural export, had inherited the imperial tradition of dance, which in turn owed much to eighteenth- and nineteenth-century French choreographers.[166] The films and paintings of Russian revolutionary avant-garde had been an integral part of European modernism. Forbidden and forgotten in the Soviet Union later, they returned during the Thaw as European creations. And, while young Soviet directors of the 1950s and 1960s emulated Italian neo-realists, the latter claimed to have learned their craft from early Soviet filmmakers, just as their French counterparts admiringly looked to Dziga Vertov. The cultural flow from Europe to the USSR occasionally retraced back the earlier flow from the USSR to Europe, while many products of exchange had a rich history that transcended the 1917 divide.

The presence of imports from multiple countries in the Soviet cultural space made for a pluralistic aesthetic experience. The imports became a ground for demarcating difference in Soviet society.[167] Sometimes they were appropriated to stage a rebellion, or were condemned as such. More often, they denoted material, cultural, or intellectual privilege. They were a threat when embraced by youngsters evading 'socially useful labour' and obsessing with fashion and jazz, yet they were a reward when carefully picked workers and activists went on closely supervised trips abroad.[168] But whether it meant trips or personal contacts, objets d'art or home gadgets and clothing, translated books or music records, foreignness was a claim to distinction.[169] Foreignness was a prominent way of staying different from the supposedly uniform collectivity. However, in the process of cross-cultural transfer, foreignness, and thus difference, became habitual and everyday.

Languages of the Thaw

Perhaps nowhere else did the new proliferation and normalization of difference manifest itself more clearly than in language. The Thaw provoked a crisis and eventual disintegration of the established literary and propagandistic word. As recently suggested, the language became ossified, to a large extent because after March 1953 there was no longer a single undisputed linguistic authority, while the innumerable repetitions of the same verbal formulae drained them of meaning.[170] Another reason that Soviet propagandistic language lost dynamism and credence was its inability to describe, let alone explain, the central phenomenon in the country's recent history, the mass violence that now attracted increasingly critical attention. Journalistic, literary, and academic efforts to write the terror into a positive historical narrative or pass it over in silence backfired, as the audiences rejected both strategies. To discuss the human costs of the Soviet past, writers, journalists, and their readers had to find different words.

The language issues of the Thaw were not only about the erosion of propaganda. At the heart of the search for new words was the question of reflecting the emotional and experiential universe that the press and literature of socialist realism had failed to depict. Returning, like Solzhenitsyn, to cultural roots, linguistic origins, and distant legacies was one answer to this question, but there were other answers as well – revolutionary romantics, lyrical poetry, irony, youth slang, and Western borrowings.[171] Each of the arts insisted on the specificity of its own language. In the visual arts, critics debated altogether dispensing with narrative.[172] The Thaw cinematic canon rejected the 'theatricality,' verbosity, 'varnishing of reality,' and static composition of the late 1940s films. As the camera arrived in the street, the dormitory, or a modest apartment, the documentary approach supplanted the hyperbole of the late 1930s and 1940s. Escaping from grand rhetoric, the 'new objectivity' pursued the random flow of life, relishing the concreteness and tangibility of everyday detail.[173]

The language polemics that would eventually result in the recognition of linguistic multiplicity began with monologues, and the first one was about the lyric. Katerina Clark suggests that the issue of the lyric had political undertones, as it hinted at the primacy of the 'I' over collectivity. Reprising the polemics of the late 1930s in her spring 1953 article 'Conversation about the Lyric,' Ol'ga Berggol'ts insisted that, to be persuasive, poetry should speak in passionate words, convey genuine emotions, and create a lyrical hero with whom the reader could identify.[174] In December 1953, Vladimir Pomerantsev's article 'On Sincerity in Literature' raised similar issues, making the case for confessional prose and rejecting clichéd language, plots, and characters.[175] Komsomol propagandists lamented the devaluation of 'exalted words.' Literary critics denounced empty rhetoric and stilted characters. Literary characters, for their part, rejected 'verbal fetishes' or vowed to 'purify grand words,' while writers sought to reanimate prose. Everyone's most persistent question was, how to return power and authority to words?

Why was there a perception that words needed to regain power, and why did this need become so urgent? As the writer Kornei Chukovskii (1887–1969), a consistently active language polemicist, observed, the issue was not only lexicon and syntax per se. It was primarily ethics – the values that words denoted. Here were 'philistinism' (*poshlost'*), fear, callousness, insincerity, and deceit (*strakh, fal'sh', litsemerie, obman*).[176] The use of worn-out words that had lost meaning supposedly revealed the flawed ethical standards of the speaker/writer. This also implied a political tension. The Thaw-era arguments about language often associated the overlapping linguistic and ethical flaws with government bureaucracy. Much of the polemic revolved around purging 'bureaucratese' (*kantseliarit*) – the office-and-newspaper lingo full of predictable clichéd phraseology now seen as a mark of ethical inadequacy.[177]

Some of this was not particularly new. Very similar attacks on bureaucratese had marked the 1920s and 1930s. Chukovskii in fact (just as Mayakovskii, Zoshchenko, Ilf and Petrov, and many others), had long argued about the evils of *kantseliarit*, thus maintaining a decades-old tradition of linguistic criticism of officialdom, to which the polemicists of the 1950s and 1960s eagerly returned.[178] However, the linguistic/literary debates of the Thaw were replete with ethical, intellectual, and political urgency – not unprecedented perhaps, but arguably more acute than before. The assault on the legitimacy of the Stalin epoch, at the time nearly synonymous with Soviet history, undermined the legitimacy of both the language and the moral values this epoch had produced.[179] The terror theme was at the core of practically all major disputes among the Thaw-era literary parties. Indeed, it was precisely in these literary disputes that the parties themselves took shape, and the distinctly negative idea of 'Stalinism' evolved, acquiring connotations of arbitrary political violence and profound ethical corruption.[180]

What could replace the historically compromised language was 'the living word' (*zhivoe slovo*), again an echo from the 1920s.[181] The idea reached specifically beyond the sanitized lexicon of the Soviet dictionaries from the 1930s and 1940s, which, as Dmitrii Ushakov's 1934–40 classic did, had sought to set the linguistic norm by purging Russian from both archaisms and colloquialisms. Now both were in vogue again. Much like during the NEP, the spoken word invaded literature of the Thaw, disturbing not just bureaucratese but also the cornerstone of (socialist) realism – 'cultured' speech.[182] The question was, whose living word would it be? Neo-archaists like Solzhenitsyn, emerging village prose authors, and renascent Russian nationalists reinstated and imitated peasant speech, criminal jargon, proverbs, and forgotten Slavonicisms from Vladimir Dal's 1863–6 *Dictionary of the Living Great Russian Language.*[183] Their opponents had little patience for the presumably popular (*narodnaia*) speech, maintaining classical literary norms and wondering 'why take such tender care to protect a thief's spelling mistakes.'[184] In 1953–4 the press held discussions on 'the culture of speech,' with many similar polemics to follow in the next three decades. Debates about a single standard of verbal expression during and after the Thaw revealed a quest for stability in a cultural environment commonly perceived as unsettled and flawed. Yet, as the debates unfolded, the standard looked ever less attainable.

The norm also came under attack from the other side of the literary spectrum: youth poetry and prose. In the search for the living word, youthful inarticulateness temporarily came to bear a mark of authenticity. In 1954, a group of Moscow Komsomols proposed to replace monotonous reading from 'crib sheets' with improvised spontaneous talk, not entirely smooth yet passionate, incoherent perhaps but spoken 'in one's own words,' 'simply,' 'from the heart.'[185] On the screen as well, during the late 1950s and early 1960s muffled and faltering voices supplanted the perfect diction of the late 1930s and 1940s. Thaw film, in its pursuit of 'art without artifice,' prized incoherence over refined speech.[186] Similarly, the youngster speaking in his own garbled slang became an emblematic protagonist of youth prose, published during the 1960s in perfectly official editions such as *Iunost.* Until then, slang had not been a legitimate subject of discussion: like the *stiliagi* jargon, it could only be ridiculed and censured.[187] But in the 1960s, educators and Komsomol propagandists increasingly accepted, if not slang itself, then at least the fact of linguistic fragmentation, recognizing that young people spoke differently.[188] Youth jargon and conversational speech flooded mainstream literature, eliciting protest from purists yet gradually habituating the audience to the new words. In everyday life, slang had been furtive and ephemeral; print publicized and authorized it. Just as with the previously forbidden themes and names, official publication sanctioned linguistic novelty.

The same ideas of authentic spontaneity were behind the mass poetry readings. This was a time when young people read poems in streets and squares, and when poets such as Andrei Voznesenskii, Evgenii Evtushenko, Bella Akhmadulina, and Bulat Okudzhava gathered hundreds or even thousands of listeners. Indeed, poets – these especially – became iconic figures of the Thaw. Underscoring the significance of oral expression, the public readings extended poetry beyond written texts to behaviours, relationships, and social spaces. Poetry as acting out, a happening – an *event* – drew such enormous crowds that the poetic revival of the Thaw has been retrospectively criticized for debasing poetry to a variety show (*estrada*).[189] Today it is strange to picture hundreds of people collectively listening to something as intimate as love poetry, and yet the sight was common at the time. It was the poets who appeared to possess the new words, sounds, postures, and intonations suitable for verbalizing emotions and experiences, and it was this appearance that drew listeners together.[190] Poetry heralded new sensibilities, proposing a new language and setting new codes of behaviour.

From the 1950s and 1960s, the quest for a different language took myriad forms, broadening the horizons of literature, journalism, art, theatre, and film, as well as undermining the semblance of linguistic coherence that had existed before. As a result, the Thaw and its aftermath greatly diversified the Russian linguistic landscape, ultimately dispensing with illusions of uniformity. Increasingly many people, whether archaists, innovators, or their eager audiences, began to recognize that language was 'a living, developing organism.'[191] From now on, the idea of a norm would be on the decline, yielding to a much more variegated, controversial, and dynamic panorama of language.

Postscript: *Shestidesiatniki*

In Russian culture, the people of the Thaw have been associated with the 1960s more readily than with the 1950s. The term is *shestidesiatniki* – literally, 'the people of the Sixties.'[192] During the post-Soviet years this term became divisive, as it was increasingly unclear who could or could not legitimately claim the name and why. But in the year 1960, when the term was coined by the literary critic Stanislav Rassadin, it was integrated into the vocabulary of the time quickly and matter-of-factly.

Just as the Thaw itself, the word *shestidesiatniki* had literary origins. It first appeared as the title of Rassadin's seemingly unremarkable review of contemporary youth fiction (actually of the late 1950s) in the literary journal *Iunost*.[193] The decade was still ahead, and the term was by necessity suggestive rather than descriptive. It announced the arrival of a new kind of literary hero and, characteristically for Russian culture that never radically separated literature from reality, a new kind of people as well. Accepted by contemporaries as a self-identification, the term *shestidesiatniki* became formative: it created what it purported to analyse.

The term was also retrospective. Rassadin did not identify his source of inspiration, but the name *shestidesiatniki* originated in the nineteenth century. It was borrowed from, and referred directly to, the 1860s, thus modelling a generation on the image of the radical intelligentsia of the Great Reforms era – who were also known as *shestidesiatniki.* Immortalized by Chernyshevskii, their image was that of men who scorned comfort, ignored appearances, rejected old certainties, ridiculed manners and high-society gloss, behaved 'naturally,' trusted in science, desired freedom, polemicized in journals, and assumed a self-delegated moral mission easily translatable into political action. The nineteenth-century parallels surfaced in some of the earliest uses of the term a hundred years later. 'The bearded men of the Sixties,' his contemporaries who had passed 'the Virgin Lands test,' reminded a 1962 poet of the earlier men of the Sixties: 'That one, in glasses, looks like Dobroliubov, and this one resembles Maklai.'[194] Glasses were common among both the old and the new *shestidesiatniki,* as both were primarily intelligentsia self-names. Beards were a regular presence, too. Mentioned in the poem, the Russian ethnographer Nikolai Miklukho-Maklai (1846–88) was famous for his studies of Oceania and New Guinea, where he spent many years living among the aboriginal people. Portraits of Maklai usually depicted him sporting abundant hair and a rich, full beard, which, along with his aura of a voyager, may have accounted for the poetic association. Interestingly, the image of a twentieth-century *shestidesiatnik* has been much more visibly associated with male than with female characters. The issue of female emancipation, prominent in the 1860s, became muted a century later and, unlike many other motifs of their ancestors, was not picked up by the new *shestidesiatniki.* One always hears about a *shestidesiatnik,* but practically never about a *shestidesiatnitsa.*

Describing 'this century's men of the Sixties,' the 1962 poet reproduced a gamut of contemporary romantic clichés. The men were returning home from the Virgin Lands, all grown up, preferring the intimate guitar to thunderous trumpets, avoiding 'loud phrases,' donning beards and sailor jerseys, and maintaining an ironic stance to disguise inner tenderness and ingenuity.[195] In his 1960 review Rassadin, too, recited several key lines of the Thaw. He cautioned against the inflation of words, insisted that young men needed to be sceptical, and hailed passion as opposed to bureaucratic indifference.[196] This, then, was the image of *shestidesiatniki* in the early 1960s – young men, always urban, at once lyrical and ironic, altruistic and critical, who cherished lofty ideals but shunned lofty rhetoric, who wished (often in a company of friends) to test words against experiences and try everything first-hand with scientific scepticism, and who somehow retained childlike artlessness, despite the scepticism and the beards. A throng of such characters populated Soviet literature, journalism, film, theatre, and songs in the 1960s. Their creators were commonly considered *shestidesiatniki* as well.

Shestidesitaniki, of course, was a self-description of the intelligentsia, or, more precisely, one of several intellectual currents within the intelligentsia. The most vocal inspiration, supporter (and sometimes opponent) of change, its most influential interpreter in modern Russia, the intelligentsia played a crucial role in the Thaw. The self-styled descendants of Maklai and Dobroliubov once again claimed the role of the nation's conscience. But this was an intelligentsia very different from its customary nineteenth-century images. Rather than a tight circle of savants, conspiracy of revolutionaries, artistic elite, or populist movement, the intelligentsia of the 1950s and 1960s was a sizeable and fast-growing cohort of educated professionals inseparable in origin and lifestyle from the rest of the people.[197] Ultimately, it was this demographic prominence of the intelligentsia that made the effects of the Thaw lasting.

Three decades later many of the qualities associated with the *shestidesiatniki*'s image – civic-mindedness and naive masculinity, idealism and idealization of science, lyricism and romanticism – seemed passé, ridiculous, or, worse yet, harmful. Critics attacked them for moralistic authoritarianism, utopianism, collectivism, trust in enlightenment and in a truth-telling mission of literature and art – in other words, for being not so much the children of the Twentieth Congress as Stalin's heirs. From the critics' standpoint, perfected since the 1970s, art had an autonomous value and no mission apart from its own existence.[198] In response, Rassadin, who lived to see the new times, defended the image of the *shestidesiatniki*. In his view, the moral relativism and social disengagement of the 1970s and 1980s made art irrelevant. After all, he considered himself a man of the Sixties, too – except that in his late Soviet reflections the 'men of the Sixties' were not so much a community of people as a spirit of the times.[199]

The times he remembered were breezy, just as they were portrayed in Mikhail Kozakov's 1982 film *The Pokrov Gates*, an instant classic and a nostalgic tribute to the Thaw. For Rassadin, the film, in which even older characters were taken by youthful passions, captured the lightheartedness of simpletons and oddballs, perfectly conveying the zeitgeist. He described these cinematic characters-cum-people as appealing yet pathetic, eliciting 'serious pity' but also admiration precisely for the qualities their critics attacked: for conflating art and ethics, for demanding that art speak the truth. These were the *shestidesiatniki* in the updated definition. Interestingly, although the film's action takes place in 1956–7, during the months preceding the Moscow Festival, Rassadin continued to refer to the 1960s to designate the spirit of the time the film captured.[200]

Attempts to define the *shestidesiatniki* proliferated in the post-Soviet years, displaying both the nostalgic and the sceptical attitudes. In 2007, two related symposia in Moscow positioned the conversation as a generational dialogue between those speaking on behalf of the 1960s and others presenting a view from the 1970s and 1980s.[201] One participant claimed that the university students of the 1970s had viewed *shestidesiatniki* as liars or fools who advanced ridiculous slogans, such as 'Back to Lenin.' They also were allegedly too direct and explicit to the taste of the 1970s that valued subtext and 'indirect statements' (*nepriamye vyskazyvaniia*).[202] Others, speaking on behalf of the *shestidesiatniki*, countered that their civic-mindedness was not so ridiculous or primitive. The literary critic Marietta Chudakova, who had started writing during the Thaw, phrased this idea in a generational language that again took the reader back to the 1860s, although a century later at issue was not so much a conflict between, as connectedness of, generations. Collectivism and idealism, Chudakova admitted, indeed had been common among the *shestidesiatniki*: they did seek to act together and did aspire to a certain ideal, which stood not so far from the socialist ideals of their fathers. But many of the fathers had perished for those ideals. For the sons, Chudakova insisted, restoring the purity of the fathers' ideals was an act of retribution against their (implied but largely unidentified) hangmen.[203]

If accurate, her observations suggest an interesting generational dynamic of the Thaw, which potentially makes the Soviet 'men of the 1960s' different from their West European counterparts. A common argument is that in West Germany and France of the 1960s and early 1970s generational conflict propelled the resurgence of interest in the past. Young people who had not seen the war began asking poignant questions about what their parents had done then, and to a large extent, it was this questioning that inspired the mass reassessment of the recent catastrophe.[204] In the Soviet case, such generational conflicts might have mattered less, as the *shestidesiatniki*, at least initially, professed many of the same political beliefs as their fathers had – or, for that matter, the hangmen, even though Chudakova did not acknowledge this.[205] Indeed, as early as the 1960s many among the 'fathers' as well as the 'sons' came to admit a measure of responsibility for the past.[206]

Not everyone, though, would agree that overt political engagement, for which they are praised or blamed, depending on the critic's affiliation, was a salient feature of the *shestidesiatniki.* Rassadin, for one thing, presented them as a diverse assemblage of urbanites who shared a common language but were not necessarily dissidents.[207] Another participant of the 2007 symposia, the trend-setting Thaw writer Vasilii Aksenov, defined the *shestidesiatniki* as intersecting Bohemian groupings united not so much by political dissidence as by 'stylistic *fronde.*' They were not a movement but a milieu, embodied in individuals, personal relationships, friendships, love affairs, break-ups, reunions, literary and artistic feedbacks, and jealousies. The interlocking intimate circles created an environment based less on politics than on ethics and aesthetics.[208]

Politics, however, returned through the back door. Their presumed abstinence from political action in favour of sociability, reading, movie-going, romantic travel, poetry recitals, and singing accompanied by guitar became the ground for attacks on the *shestidesiatniki* by some of the more militant dissidents. In 1999 Valeriia Novodvorskaia (born in 1950) charged them with betrayal of the dissidents who had died in labour colonies and psychiatric wards. She sarcastically upturned the Thaw romantics: their bonfires supplied conveniently dim lighting so that the *shestidesiatniki* might not have to look each other in the eye, singing to the guitar covered up their silence on matters of principle, and carrying a backpack was easier than carrying the 'burden of the country's problems.' In Novodvorskaia's rendition, the *shestidesiatniki* were cowards, opportunists, idlers, and whiners – not Dobroliubovs but Oblomovs.[209]

Novodvorskaia's diatribe sounded amazingly similar to the post-Soviet attacks on the *shestidesiatniki* from the opposite political camp – the militant statists and Russian nationalists. One of them, the writer Stanislav Kuniaev (born in 1932), who had also matured during the 1960s, hardly considered himself a *shestidesiatnik.* In his description, too, they were Oblomovs – lazy no-gooders who could only socialize in the kitchens, drink, flip through Western journals, and cultivate their worthless personal emotions. For Kuniaev, just as for Novodvorskaia, the archetypal *shestidesiatniki* contributed nothing positive to society. Only, his understanding of a positive societal contribution was different: while for Novodvorskaia it lay in political dissent and uncompromised opposition to the regime, for Kuniaev it meant working together with the regime, for the benefit of the Russian state – or the Soviet state: he made no difference between the two.[210] After 1991, Kuniaev's attitude found many sympathizers. Following the collapse of the Soviet Union, the ridicule often turned into hatred: the *shestidesiatniki* were held accountable for the country's ruin.

What strikes the eye in these retrospective attempts to define the *shestidesiatniki* is the prominence of art and especially literature. Among the principal polemicists are the literary critics Chudakova and Rassadin (who, we remember, coined the term in reference to fiction) and writers of all shades in the political spectrum, from Aksenov to Kuniaev. Even those unaffiliated with the literary world resort to literary images: witness Novodvorskaia on 'Oblomovschina,' as well as the title of her tirade, 'Shestidesiatniki and Emptiness,' borrowed from a novel – Viktor Pelevin's *Chapaev and Emptiness.*[211] In fact, her entire article was conceived as an 'epitaph' to the *shestidesiatniki's* emblem – the thick literary journal.

The constant literary allusions are not incidental, and perhaps they testify better than anything else to the futility of efforts to neatly identify the *shestidesiatniki* in actual society and history. Born in literature and developed in art, the term *shestidesiatniki* refers first of all to a host of literary and artistic images. Trying to find its exact flesh-and-blood equivalents means conflating art and reality. The 2007 symposia, as well as many other efforts to coin a definition, were identity performances – quite literally, as people got up to identify themselves or others as *shestidesiatniki,* citing books, films, poets and the experiences of reading, viewing, and listening as the criteria for self-identification. Gatherings and publications on the *shestidesiatniki* are roll-calls, listing name after name and drawing camps on the way toward a viable definition.[212] But perhaps a viable definition cannot be reached, and the debate cannot go beyond the performances and the roll-calls.

This does not mean that there was no correspondence between image and reality. The books, articles, films, poems, and songs of the 1950s and 1960s that created the image of a *shestidesiatnik* were enthusiastically received by thousands of people. Readers, listeners, and viewers identified with these images, perceiving them as reflections of reality and as role models, shaping their own behaviour, speech, style, and attitudes according to literature and art. The *shestidesiatniki* were not only real people but also – and primarily – a host of ethical attributes, an emotional condition, and an imaginative language created by a characteristically close relationship between art, literature, and society in modern Russia. As characters and as people, they approached all manner of social and political problems, employing the lens of ethics, vowing to live 'not by bread alone' and 'not by lies.'[213] The ethical perspective inspired new behaviours and languages, investing new meanings into old words. On that basis, those who identified with the name *shestidesiatniki* tried to make their own image into historical reality. And indeed, they are now remembered as reality – a distinct group and a cultural milestone.

The fact that debates about *shestidesiatniki* are still going on today indicates that the agendas of the Thaw are not yet exhausted. Indeed, it is hardly possible – or necessary – to produce a single definitive termination date for the Thaw. The legacies of twentieth-century mass violence, which came in the focus of society's attention in the 1950s and 1960s, would remain a defining cultural and political factor for the next several decades, to a large extent until the present. So did the country's opening to the outside world and the new presence of Western imports, which continued to shape lives and minds long after arriving on the Soviet stage. As never before, social and cultural processes in the Soviet Union began to parallel those in the West. The erosion of the old and the search for new words, the new artistic means of self-expression, and the general diversification of the cultural and linguistic landscape persisted well beyond the end of the Soviet Union itself. The Thaw determined much of late Soviet and post-Soviet culture, profoundly transforming the country's urban and rural terrain, people's behaviours and lives.

The epoch began in 1953, but when did it end? Sceptics terminate it as early as 1957, when, in the wake of the 1956 civic commotion at home and the political crises in Hungary and Poland, the authorities backed down on reforms, fearing massive unrest and systemic disintegration.[214] Others suggest that it was Khrushchev's removal from power in October 1964 that spelled the end of the Thaw.[215] Still others point to the invasion of Czechoslovakia in 1968 and the tightening of ideological control thereafter. A definitive answer as to when the Thaw ended does not seem in sight. And perhaps identifying such a distinct and clear 'end' may not be the historian's most important objective. Instead, to use Michel Vovelle's formulation, it makes sense to regard the Thaw as a constitutive event – one that gave rise to new processes, practices, and traditions. In many ways, the agendas and legacies of the Thaw still matter today.

NOTES

1 A.S. Pushkin, 'Osen',' in *Polnoe sobranie sochinenii* (Moscow, 1954), 2:148–50; see also M.N. Epshtein, *Priroda, mir, tainik vselennoi ... Sistema peizazhnykh obrazov v russkoi poezii* (Moscow, 1990), 158, 173–5.
2 Epshtein, *Priroda, mir, tainik vselennoi*, 170–3, 177–81.
3 Ivan Lazhechnikov, *Ledianoi dom* (Moscow, 1958); N. Petrunina, 'Roman "Ledianoi dom" i ego avtor,' in Lazhechnikov, *Ledianoi dom* (Minsk, 1985).
4 Dan Ungurianu, '*Ledianoi dom* Lazhechnikova i peterburgskii kanon (K voprosu o genezise peterburgskogo teksta),' *Russian Literature* 51 (2002): 471–81, here 477.
5 Lazhechnikov, *Ledianoi dom*, 357–60.
6 I.O. Shaitanov, *Fedor Ivanovich Tiutchev: poeticheskoe otkrytie prirody* (Moscow, 1998), 45, 91; F.I. Tiutchev, '14-oe dekabria 1825,' in *Polnoe sobranie stikhotvorenii* (Moscow, 1994), 1:133.
7 Vera Aksakova, *Dnevnik Very Sergeevny Aksakovoi 1854–1855* (Saint Petersburg, 1913), 102.
8 F.I. Tiutchev, 'Vesennie vody,' 'Zima nedarom zlitsia,' 'Eshche zemli pechalen vid,' 'Vesenniaia groza,' and 'I v bozh'em mire to zh byvaet,' in *Polnoe sobranie*, 1:168, 230, 235, 154, 2:174 respectively; on Tiutchev's spring: Shaitanov, *Fedor Ivanovich Tiutchev*, 38–41.
9 F.I. Tiutchev, 'Vesna,' in *Polnoe sobranie*, 1:258 (trans. D. Kozlov).
10 Ilya Ehrenburg, *Dai oglianut'sia ... Pis'ma 1908–1930* (Moscow, 2004), 142, 151; Ehrenburg, 'Posledniaia liubov',' in *Sobranie sochinenii* (Moscow, 1990), 1:201.
11 Ilya Ehrenburg, 'Ottepel',' in *Sobranie sochinenii* (Moscow, 1965), 6:10–12, 16–17, 31–7, 54, 64, 68–9, 76.
12 Ibid., 9, 15–16, 31, 34, 53–4, 68, 88–9.
13 Ilya Ehrenburg, 'Ottepel',' 121–8.
14 Ilya Ehrenburg, 'Liudi, gody, zhizn,' in *Sobranie sochinenii* (1990), 8:389–90.
15 Ibid., 8:394–5.
16 Nikita Khrushchev, 'Vysokaia ideinost' i khudozhestvennoe masterstvo – velikaia sila sovetskoi literatury i iskusstva' (speech of 8 March 1963), in Khrushchev, *Vysokoe prizvanie literatury i iskusstva* (Moscow, 1963), 224.
17 Aleksandr Gorodnitskii, *I vblizi, i vdali* (Moscow, 1991), 293, 299; Iurii Nagibin, *T'ma v kontse tunnelia: povest'* (Moscow, 1994), 107.
18 Natal'ia Kostenko, Maria Tsvetkova, and Anastasia Kornia, 'Ottepeli ne budet,' *Vedomosti*, 11 September 2008.
19 Matvei Ganapol'skii, interview with Leonid Radzikhovskii, *Ekho Moskvy*

radio station, 12 September 2008. http://echo.msk.ru/programs/personalno/539990-echo/.

20 Stephen Bittner, *The Many Lives of Khrushchev's Thaw: Experience and Memory in Moscow's Arbat* (Ithaca, 2008), 3, 4, 13; Nancy Condee, 'Cultural Codes of the Thaw,' in *Nikita Khrushchev*, ed. William Taubman, Sergei Khrushchev, and Abbott Gleason (New Haven, 2000), 169; Juliane Fürst, 'The Arrival of Spring? Changes and Continuities in Soviet Youth Culture and Policy between Stalin and Khrushchev,' in *The Dilemmas of De-Stalinization: Negotiating Cultural and Social Change in the Khrushchev Era*, ed. Polly Jones (London, 2006), 135–53.

21 Ilya Ehrenburg referred to *Tolkovyi slovar' russkogo iazyka*, ed. B.M. Volin and D.N. Ushakov, 4 vols. (Moscow, 1934–40), 2:998.

22 'Toi vesny, chto *dolzhna* byla priiti.' Ehrenburg, *Sobranie sochinenii* (1990), 8:390, emphasis added.

23 Ilya Ehrenburg, 'Da razve mogut deti iuga,' in *Sobranie sochinenii* (1990), 1:189.

24 Grigorii Chukhrai, *Moe kino* (Moscow, 2002), 136–47.

25 Mary Favret, 'War in the Air,' *Modern Language Quarterly* 65, no. 4 (December 2004): 531–59.

26 Ibid., 534–7, 546.

27 On the importance of physicality and bodily knowledge for the understanding and use of metaphors, see George Lakoff and Mark Johnson, *Metaphors We Live By* (Chicago, 1980), 56–60, 112, 117–21, 146, 175–82; also Favret, 'War in the Air.'

28 Katerina Clark, *The Soviet Novel: History as Ritual* (Chicago, 1985), 94–6; Rolf Hellebust, *Flesh to Metal: Soviet Literature and the Alchemy of Revolution* (Ithaca, 2003), 17–19, 124–6.

29 'Priem v Kremle v chest' uchastnikov parada Pobedy,' *Pravda*, 27 June 1945; see also Hellebust, *Flesh to Metal*, 19, 22, 29, 59, 77–80, 86–9, 113–14, 124–6.

30 Daniel Rigney, *The Metaphorical Society: An Invitation to Social Theory* (Lanham, MD, 2001), 41–3, 48–58.

31 Clark, *Soviet Novel*, 98–135, 164–6.

32 Ibid., 225–30; Epshtein, *Priroda, mir, tainik vselennoi*, 266–8; Evgenii Margolit, 'Peizazh s geroem,' in *Kinematograf ottepeli* (Moscow, 1996), 106–9; Yuri Slezkine, *Arctic Mirrors: Russia and the Small Peoples of the North* (Ithaca, 1994), 358–64.

33 E.g., Epshtein, *Priroda, mir, tainik vselennoi*, 31, 119–24, 142–3, 271–2; Kathleen Parthé, *Russian Village Prose: The Radiant Past* (Princeton, 1992), 7–8, 72–80; Valentin Rasputin, *Farewell to Matyora* (New York, 1979).

34 Margolit, 'Peizazh s geroem,' 104–5.

35 Lakoff and Johnson, *Metaphors We Live By*, 81–3, 139–41, 147–52.
36 Fürst, 'Arrival of Spring?'; Oleg Kharkhordin, *The Collective and the Individual in Russia: A Study in Practices* (Berkeley, 1999), 279–302.
37 Lakoff and Johnson, *Metaphors We Live By*, chap. 23.
38 Ibid., 156.
39 *Tolkovyi slovar' russkogo iazyka*, ed. S.I. Ozhegov and N. Iu. Shvedova (Moscow, 1992); compare Ozhegov, *Slovar' russkogo iazyka*, ed. N. Iu. Shvedova (Moscow, 1984), 425; *Slovar' russkikh politicheskikh metafor*, ed. A.N. Baranov and Iu. N. Karaulov (Moscow, 1994), xiii, 169.
40 E.g., Michael Kort, *The Soviet Colossus: History and Aftermath* (Armonk, 2006); Robert Service, *A History of Modern Russia from Nicholas II to Vladimir Putin* (Cambridge, MA, 2005).
41 Bittner, *Many Lives*, 6–7.
42 Ludmilla Alexeyeva, *The Thaw Generation: Coming of Age in the Post-Stalin Era* (Pittsburgh, 1990); Robert English, *Russia and the Idea of the West: Gorbachev, Intellectuals, and the End of the Cold War* (New York, 2000).
43 Maria Zezina has noted the lack of memoirs from 'the conservative-preservationist camp,' in Zezina, *Sovetskaia khudozhestvennaia intelligentsia i vlast' v 1950e-60e gody* (Moscow, 1999), 43. For memoirs, see also Anatolii Naiman, *Rasskazy o Anne Akhmatovoi* (Moscow, 1989); Naiman, *Slavnyi konets besslavnykh pokolenii* (Moscow, 1998); Liudmila Polikovskaia, *My predchuvstvie ... predtecha ... : Ploshchad' Maiakovskogo, 1958–1965* (Moscow, 1997); Evgenii Rein, *Mne skuchno bez Dovlatova: novye stseny iz zhizni moskovskoi bogemy* (Saint Petersburg, 1997); Viktor Slavkin, *Pamiatnik neizvestnomu stiliage* (Moscow, 1996); Mikhail Veller, 'Deti pobeditelei. Konets shestidesiatykh. Rekviem rovesnikam' [1988], in Veller, *Randevu so znamenitost'iu* (Tallinn, 1990), 6–29.
44 See the discussions in *Voprosy istorii KPSS* 4 (1988): 57–88; 8 (1988): 52–65; 9 (1988): 35–49; 1 (1989): 36–49; 4 (1989): 62–71; (1990): 19–21; *XX s"ezd KPSS i ego istoricheskie real'nosti*, ed. V.V. Zhuravlev (Moscow, 1991), 4, 414.
45 Elena Zubkova, *Obshchestvo i reformy, 1945–1964* (Moscow, 1993), 150, 182–8.
46 Iurii Aksiutin, 'Popular Responses to Khrushchev,' in Taubman, Khrushchev, and Gleason, *Nikita Khrushchev*, 177–208; Aksiutin, *Khrushchevskaia 'ottepel'' i obshchestvennye nastroeniia v SSSR v 1953–1964 gg.* (Moscow, 2004); Liubov' Sidorova, *Ottepel' v istoricheskoi nauke: sovetskaia istoriografiia pervogo poslestalinskogo desiatiletiia* (Moscow, 1997), 95–101, 197, 218–19; Zezina, *Sovetskaia.*
47 Aleksandr Pyzhikov, *Khrushchevskaia 'ottepel''* (Moscow, 2002), 54–6, 69, 316–17, 323; Lada Silina, *Nastroeniia sovetskogo studenchestva, 1945–1964*

(Moscow, 2004), 112, 117–18, 121, 128–9, 145–55, 158–9, 168; Zezina, *Sovetskaia,* 381–6.

48 Aksiutin, *Khrushchevskaia,* 483; Nikolai Barsukov, 'The Rise to Power,' in Taubman, Khrushchev, and Gleason, *Nikita Khrushchev,* 44–66.

49 In 2009–10 *Echo of Moscow* hosted a series of broadcasts on Khrushchev, titled 'Our Dear Nikita Sergeevich' and thus sympathetically echoing the title of a laudatory 1964 film documentary produced for Khrushchev's seventieth birthday. http://www.echo.msk.ru/programs/hrushev/.

50 E.g., the forum on Khrushchev at http://savok.name/forum/topic_740/1.

51 E.g., Charles Kenney, 'The Twentieth Party Congress: A Study in Collective Moderation,' *American Political Science Review* 50, no. 3 (September 1956): 764–86; Wolfgang Leonhard, 'Return to Stalinism in the USSR,' *International Affairs* 33, no. 3 (July 1957): 280–8; Harold Swayze, *Political Control over Literature in the USSR, 1946–1959* (Cambridge, MA, 1962), esp. 259–66; Robert Tucker, 'The Politics of Soviet De-Stalinization,' *World Politics* 9, no. 4 (July 1957): 550–78.

52 George W. Breslauer, *Khrushchev and Brezhnev as Leaders: Building Authority in Soviet Politics* (London, 1982), 270, 281, 284, 289; Breslauer, 'Khrushchev Reconsidered,' in *The Soviet Union since Stalin,* ed. Stephen F. Cohen, Alexander Rabinowitch, and Robert Sharlet (Bloomington, 1980), 50–70; Stephen F. Cohen, 'The Friends and Foes of Change: Reformism and Conservatism in the Soviet Union,' in Cohen, Rabinowitch, and Sharlet, *Soviet Union since Stalin,* 11–31; Cohen, 'The Stalin Question since Stalin,' in Cohen, *Rethinking the Soviet Experience: Politics and History since 1917* (New York, 1985), 93–127, here 125–6; Priscilla Johnson, 'The Politics of Soviet Culture, 1962–1964,' in *Khrushchev and the Arts,* ed. Johnson and Leopold Labedz (Cambridge, MA, 1965), 1–89, esp. 84–9; Carl Linden, *Khrushchev and the Soviet Leadership, 1957–1964* (Baltimore, 1967), 220–1.

53 E.g., Nanci Adler, *The Gulag Survivor: Beyond the Soviet System* (New Brunswick, NJ, 2002), esp. 77–105, 175–8, 191–8, 263–7; Miriam Dobson, 'Contesting the Paradigms of De-Stalinization: Readers' Responses to *One Day in the Life of Ivan Denisovich,*' *Slavic Review* 64, no. 3 (2005): 580–600; Dobson, *Khrushchev's Cold Summer: Gulag Returnees, Crime, and the Fate of Reform after Stalin* (Ithaca, 2009); Dobson, 'POWs and Purge Victims: Attitudes towards Party Rehabilitation, 1956–57,' *Slavonic and East European Review* 86, no. 2 (April 2008): 328–45; Dobson, '"Show the Bandit-Enemies No Mercy!" Amnesty, Criminality and Public Response in 1953,' in *Dilemmas,* 21–40; Fürst, 'The Arrival of Spring?'; Cynthia Hooper, 'What Can and Cannot Be Said: Between the Stalinist Past and New Soviet Future,' *Slavonic and East European Review* 86, no. 2 (April 2008): 306–27; Polly Jones, 'From Stalinism

to Post-Stalinism: De-Mythologising Stalin, 1953–56,' in *Redefining Stalinism,* ed. Harold Shukman (London, 2002), 127–48; also her '"I've Held, and I Still Hold, Stalin in the Highest Esteem": Discourses and Strategies of Resistance to De-Stalinisation in the USSR, 1953–62,' in *The Leader Cult in Communist Dictatorships: Stalin and the Eastern Bloc,* ed. Balázs Apor, Jan Behrends, Polly Jones, and E.A. Rees (Houndmills, UK, 2004), 227–45; Brian LaPierre, 'Making Hooliganism on a Mass Scale: The Campaign against Petty Hooliganism in the Soviet Union, 1956–1964,' *Cahiers du Monde russe* 47, nos. 1–2 (January–June 2006): 349–75; Kharkhordin, *The Collective and the Individual,* 279–302; Susanne Schattenberg, 'Democracy or Despotism? How the Secret Speech Was Translated into Everyday Life,' in *Dilemmas,* 64–79, esp. 76.

54 E.g., Steven A. Barnes, *Death and Redemption: The Gulag and the Shaping of Soviet Society* (Princeton, 2011), 202–4; Bittner, *Many Lives*; Laurent Coumel, 'L'appareil du parti et la réforme scolaire de 1958: Un cas d'opposition à Hruščev,' *Cahiers du Monde russe* 47, nos. 1–2 (January–June 2006): 173–94; Steven E. Harris, 'Moving to the Separate Apartment: Building, Distributing, Furnishing, and Living in Urban Housing in Soviet Russia, 1950s–1960s' (PhD diss., University of Chicago, 2003); Susan E. Reid, 'In the Name of the People: The Manège Affair Revisited,' *Kritika: Explorations in Russian and Eurasian History* (hereafter *Kritika*) 6, no. 4 (Fall 2005): 673–716; Thomas C. Wolfe, *Governing Soviet Journalism: The Press and the Socialist Person after Stalin* (Bloomington, 2005); Wolfe, *Russia's Sputnik Generation: Soviet Baby Boomers Talk about Their Lives,* ed. Donald Raleigh (Bloomington, 2006), esp. 1–23. For a valid argument about a possible combination of an 'optimistic' and an 'authoritarian' interpretation of the Thaw, see Anne E. Gorsuch, *All This Is Your World: Soviet Tourism at Home and Abroad after Stalin* (New York, 2011), 3.

55 Yoram Gorlizki, 'Party Revivalism and the Death of Stalin,' *Slavic Review* 54, no. 1 (1995): 1–22; Gorlizki and Oleg Khlevniuk, *Cold Peace: Stalin and the Soviet Ruling Circle, 1945–1953* (Oxford, 2004), 166; Steven Harris, 'Moving,' 46, 48, 49, 51, 59; Aleksandr Pyzhikov, 'Poisk putei obshchestvennoi modernizatsii (1945–1964),' in *Rossiia v XX veke: Reformy i revoliutsii,* ed. G.N. Sevost'ianov, 2 vols. (Moscow, 2002), 2:245–63.

56 Golfo Alexopoulos, 'Amnesty 1945: The Revolving Door of Stalin's Gulag,' *Slavic Review* 64, no. 2 (2005): 274–306; Mark Edele, 'Strange Young Men in Stalin's Moscow: The Birth and Life of the Stiliagi, 1945–1953,' *Jahrbücher für Geschichte Osteuropas* 50, no. 1 (2002): 37–61; Juliane Fürst, 'The Importance of Being Stylish: Youth, Culture and Identity in Late Stalinism,' in *Late Stalinist Russia: Society between Reconstruction and Reinvention,* ed. Fürst (London,

2006), 209–30; Fürst, *Stalin's Last Generation: Soviet Post-War Youth and the Emergence of Mature Socialism* (Oxford, 2010), 5, 20, 23, 323.

57 Clark, *Soviet Novel*; Aleksandr Prokhorov, *Unasledovannyi diskurs: Paradigmy stalinskoi kul'tury v literature i kinematografe 'ottepeli'* (Saint Petersburg, 2007).

58 Zubkova, *Obshchestvo i reformy*.

59 On the acceleration, see Barnes, *Death and Redemption*, 202–4.

60 Oksana Bulgakowa, 'Cine-Weathers: Soviet Thaw Cinema in the International Context,' in this volume.

61 Donald Filtzer, *The Khrushchev Era: De-Stalinisation and the Limits of Reform in the USSR, 1953–1964* (Basingstoke, 1993); Oleg Leibovich, *Reforma i modernizatsiia v 1953–1964 gg.* (Perm', 1993); Pyzhikov, *Khrushchevskaia*; Zezina, *Sovetskaia*; Zubkova, *Obshchestvo i reformy*.

62 I.L. Andreev, 'Etapy i tendentsii formirovaniia sistemy upravleniia tsentralizovannogo gosudarstva v XV–XVII vv.,' in *Administrativnye reformy v Rossii: istoriia i sovremennost'* (Moscow, 2006), 40–6, 50; Ben Eklof, John Bushnell, and Larissa Zakharova, eds., *Russia's Great Reforms, 1855–1881* (Bloomington, 1994); Daniel Field, *The End of Serfdom: Nobility and Bureaucracy in Russia, 1855–1861* (Cambridge, MA, 1976); A.B. Kamenskii, 'Administrativnoe upravlenie v Rossii XVIII v.,' in *Administrativnye reformy v Rossii*, 62–5, 67; Kamenskii, *Ot Petra I do Pavla I. Reformy v Rossii XVIII veka: opyt tselostnogo analiza* (Moscow, 2001), esp. 54–7, 89–90; Kamenskii, 'Preobrazovaniia administrativnoi sfery pervoi chetverti XIX v.: zamysly i real'nost',' in *Administrativnye reformy v Rossii*, 116–38; I.A. Khristoforov, '"Kamen" pretknoveniia': problema administrativnykh reform poslednei chetverti XIX – nachala XX vv.,' in *Administrativnye reformy v Rossii*, 221–2; V.A. Krasil'shchikov, *Vdogonku za proshedshim vekom: razvitie Rossii v XX veke s tochki zreniia mirovykh modernizatsii* (Moscow, 1998); Bruce W. Lincoln, *In the Vanguard of Reform: Russia's Enlightened Bureaucrats, 1825–1861* (DeKalb, 1982), 162–211; Alfred J. Rieber, 'The Reforming Tradition in Russian and Soviet History: A Commentary,' in *Reform in Modern Russian History: Progress or Cycle?* ed. Theodore Taranovski (New York, 1995), 237–43; Blair A. Ruble, 'Reform and Revolution: Commentary,' in Taranovski, 407–11, here 408.

63 Rieber, 'Reforming Tradition.'

64 Andreev, 'Etapy,' 34; Kamenskii, 'Administrativnoe,' 91; Richard Wortman, *Scenarios of Power: Myth and Ceremony in Russian Monarchy* (Princeton, 2000), 2:23–4, 204–5, 235–70; abridged version (Princeton, 2006), 189–91, 304, 314.

65 Kamenskii, *Ot Petra*, 10–11, 39; Khristoforov, '"Kamen,"' 220; Leibovich, *Reforma*, 16–18; Ruble, 'Reform and Revolution'; Iu. A. Poliakov, 'Oktiabr' 1917 goda v kontekste rossiiskoi istorii,' in *Rossiia v XX veke*, 1:9–19, here

14–15; Theodore Taranovski, 'The Problem of Reform in Russian and Soviet History,' in Taranovski, *Reform*, 20; Wortman, *Scenarios of Power*. On the cyclicality of Soviet reforms, see N.A. Khrenov, ed., *Perekhodnye protsessy v russkoi khudozhestvennoi kul'ture: novoe i noveishee vremia* (Moscow, 2003), 6–7; Robert Service, 'Reforma v Sovetskom Soiuze: strukturirovannaia povest',' in *Rossiia v XX veke*, 1:70–80; Vladimir Papernyi, *Kul'tura Dva* (Ann Arbor, 1985).

66 Aksiutin, *Khrushchevskaia*; Aksiutin, 'Obshchestvennye nastroeniia v SSSR (1953–1982),' and S.S. Zgorzhel'skaia, 'Obshchestvennoe soznanie 1950–1960-kh godov: faktor tormozheniia,' in *Rossiia v XX veke*, 2:339–50 and 367–70, respectively; Dobson, *Khrushchev's Cold Summer*.

67 Andreev, 'Etapy,' 30–1, 33; Evgenii Anisimov, *The Reforms of Peter the Great: Progress through Coercion in Russia* (Armonk, 1993); V.V. Shelokhaev, 'Rossiiskie reformy kak teoretiko-metodologicheskaia problema,' and A.S. Seniavskii, 'Problemy modernizatsii Rossii v XX veke: dialektika reformizma i revoliutsionnosti,' in *Rossiia v XX veke*, 1:46–54 and 55–69, respectively. Of course, some reformers, notably Catherine II, emphasized gradual rather than speedy transformation.

68 Rieber, 'Reforming Tradition.'

69 Kamenskii, *Ot Petra*, 57, 184–213, 219–52, 520–4.

70 Alexander Dallin, 'The Uses and Abuses of Russian History,' in *Soviet Society and Culture: Essays in Honor of Vera S. Dunham*, ed. Terry Thompson and Richard Sheldon (Boulder, 1988), 181–94, esp. 187.

71 E.g., Vladimir Lakshin, *Novyi mir vo vremena Khrushcheva: Dnevnik i poputnoe (1953–1964)* (Moscow, 1991), 134, 189 (diary entries, 13 June 1963 and 29 January 1964).

72 Marshall Sahlins, *Islands of History* (Chicago, 1987), vii, xiii.

73 Fernand Braudel, 'History and the Social Sciences: The *Longue Durée*,' in Braudel, *On History* (Chicago, 1982), 25–54, esp. 27–8; Olivia Harris, 'Braudel: Historical Time and the Horror of Discontinuity,' *History Workshop Journal* 57 (2004): 161–74.

74 Mona Ozouf, *Festivals and the French Revolution* (Cambridge, MA, 1988); Brian Singer, 'Violence in the French Revolution: Forms of Ingestion / Forms of Expulsion,' in *The French Revolution and the Birth of Modernity*, ed. Ferenc Feher (Berkeley, 1990), 150–73; Michel Vovelle, 'The *Longue Durée*,' in Vovelle, *Ideologies and Mentalities* (Chicago, 1990), 126–53, esp. 141, 145–50.

75 Colin Jones, 'Michel Vovelle and the French Revolution,' *French History* 19, no. 2 (June 2005): 168–76, esp. 175; Michel Vovelle, 'The Event in the History of Mentalities,' in Vovelle, *Ideologies*, 228–231; Vovelle, 'History of

Mentalities, History of Resistances, or the Prisons of the *Longue Durée*,' in Vovelle, *Ideologies*, 154–76, esp. 175.

76 Carole Fink, Frank Hadler, and Thomasz Schramm, eds., *1956: European and Global Perspectives* (Leipzig, 2006); Lev Lur'e and Irina Maliarova, *1956 god: seredina veka* (Saint Petersburg, 2007). Kathleen Smith is working on a book-length project on the year 1956.

77 Raleigh, *Russia's Sputnik Generation*, esp. 7, 16.

78 Fürst, 'Arrival,' 139–42; Eleonory Gilburd, 'Picasso in Thaw Culture,' *Cahiers du monde russe* 47, no. 1–2 (January–June 2006): 65–108, here 89–93; Susan E. Reid, 'The Exhibition Art of Socialist Countries, Moscow 1958–9, and the Contemporary Style of Painting,' in *Style and Socialism: Modernity and Material Culture in Post-War Eastern Europe*, ed. Reid and David Crowley (Oxford, 2000), 101–32, here 116–24; Kathleen E. Smith, 'A New Generation of Political Prisoners: "Anti-Soviet" Students, 1956–1957,' *Soviet and Post-Soviet Review* 32, nos. 2–3 (2005): 191–208; Petr Vail' and Aleksandr Genis, *60-e: mir sovetskogo cheloveka* (Moscow, 1996), 70, 142–3, 148; Benjamin Tromly, 'Re-imagining the Soviet Intelligentsia: Student Politics and University Life, 1948–1964' (PhD diss., Harvard University, 2007), 206–8, 214–21, 224–40, 250–7, 296–302.

79 For the concept of 'ending the terror,' see Bronislaw Baczko, *Ending the Terror: The French Revolution after Robespierre* (Cambridge, 1994). On these issues in the Soviet context, see Aksiutin, 'Popular Responses'; Dobson, *Khrushchev's Cold Summer*; Polly Jones, 'From Stalinism'; see also her 'I've Held'; and her 'Memories of Terror or Terrorizing Memories? Terror, Trauma, and Survival in Soviet Culture of the Thaw,' *Slavonic and East European Review* 86, no. 2 (2008): 346–71.

80 Marc Elie, 'Khrushchev's Gulag: The Soviet Penitentiary System after Stalin's Death, 1953–1964,' in this volume; Elie, 'Les politiques à l'égard des libérés du Goulag: Amnistiés et réhabilités dans la région de Novosibirsk, 1953–1960,' *Cahiers du monde russe* 47, no. 1–2 (January–June 2006): 327–48. For slightly different figures – 2,624,861 inmates in 1953 and 940,880 in 1956, see Galina Ivanova, *Labor Camp Socialism: The Gulag in the Soviet Totalitarian System* (Armonk, 2000), 187, table 5.

81 Elie, 'Khrushchev's Gulag.' On the Gulag's role in Soviet economy, see Barnes, *Death and Redemption*; Steven A. Barnes, '"In a Manner Befitting Soviet Citizens": An Uprising in the Post-Stalin Gulag,' *Slavic Review* 64, no. 4 (Winter 2005): 823–50; James R. Harris, *The Great Urals: Regionalism and the Evolution of the Soviet System* (Ithaca, 1999), 105–22; Ivanova, *Labor Camp Socialism*, 69–126, 188–90; Oleg Khlevniuk, *The History of the Gulag: From Collectivization to the Great Terror* (New Haven, 2004), 332–8.

82 Pavel Polian, *Against Their Will: The History and Geography of Forced Migrations in the USSR* (Budapest, 2004), 185–6, 194–223, 361–6; Viktor Zemskov, 'K voprosu o repatriatsii sovetskikh grazhdan, 1944–1951,' *Istoriia SSSR* 4 (1990): 26–41; Zemskov, 'Repatriatsiia sovetskikh grazhdan i ikh dal'neishaia sud'ba, 1944–1956,' *Sotsiologicheskie issledovaniia* 5 (1995): 3–13.

83 Adler, *Gulag Survivor*, 88–9, 110–11, 136–7, 139–46, 156–62, 178–9; Dobson, *Khrushchev's Cold Summer.*

84 Alan Barenberg, 'From Prisoners to Citizens: Ex-Prisoners in Vorkuta during the Thaw,' in this volume.

85 Michaela Pohl, 'From White Grave to Tselinograd to Astana: The Virgin Lands Opening, Khrushchev's Forgotten First Reform,' in this volume.

86 For a detaled analysis of these issues, see Amir Weiner, 'The Empires Pay a Visit: Gulag Returnees, East European Rebellions, and Soviet Frontier Politics,' in this volume.

87 M.A. Beznin and T.M. Dimoni, 'Zavershenie raskrest'ianivaniia Rossii (vtoraia polovina XX veka),' in *Rossiia v XX veke*, 1:632–44, esp. 634–5; Liubov' Denisova, *Ischezaiushchaia derevnia Rossii: Nechernozem'e v 1960-e – 1980-e gody* (Moscow, 1996), 18, 48, 152; Leibovich, *Reforma i modernizatsiia*, 138–40, 145, 151; Mervyn Matthews, *The Passport Society: Controlling Movement in Russia and the USSR* (Boulder, 1993), 33–5; Rudolf Pikhoia, *Sovetskii Soiuz: Istoriia vlasti, 1945–1991* (Moscow, 1998), 169; Ilya Zelenin, *Agrarnaia politika N.S. Khrushcheva i sel'skoe khoziaistvo* (Moscow, 2001) 80–4, 136–50, 232.

88 E.g., Parthé, *Russian Village Prose*, 29–31, 50–1, 66–7.

89 *Programma Kommunisticheskoi partii Sovetskogo Soiuza: priniata XXII s'ezdom KPSS* (Moscow, 1961), 100–1 (section III, preamble); compare *Programma i ustav VKP(b)* (Moscow, 1937), esp. preamble; Pyzhikov, *Khrushchevskaia*, 31–2, 115–51. Pyzhikov mentions that the Central Committee prepared a first draft of the new program as early as 1947. However, the 1947 draft was shelved. It also retained a heavy emphasis on 'dictatorship of the people' and the future eminent role of the police, rather than on an all-people's state.

90 E.g. Prokhorov, *Unasledovannyi*, 16; Vail' and Genis, *60-e*, 12–18.

91 Adler, *Gulag Survivor*, 205–38; Orlando Figes, *The Whisperers: Private Life in Stalin's Russia* (New York, 2007), 535–656; Denis Kozlov, 'The Readers of Novyi mir, 1945–1970: Twentieth-Century Experience and Soviet Historical Consciousness (PhD diss., University of Toronto, 2005); Catherine Merridale, *Night of Stone: Death and Memory in Twentieth-Century Russia* (London, 2002).

92 Among the vast literature on these issues in Western Europe, see, e.g., Sarah

Farmer, *Martyred Village: Commemorating the 1944 Massacre at Oradour-sur-Glane* (Berkeley, 1999); Farmer, 'Postwar Justice in France: Bordeaux 1953,' in *The Politics of Retribution in Europe: World War II and Its Aftermath*, ed. István Deák, Jan T. Gross, and Tony Judt (Princeton, 2000), 194–211; Konrad Jarausch, 'Critical Memory and Civil Society: The Impact of the 1960s on German Debates about the Past,' in *Coping with the Past: West German Debates on Nazism and Generational Conflict, 1955–1975*, ed. Philipp Gassert and Alan E. Steinweis (New York, 2006): 11–30, esp. 20–2; Tony Judt, 'The Past Is Another Country: Myth and Memory in Postwar Europe,' in Deák, Gross, and Judt, *Politics of Retribution*, 293–323, esp. 300–3; Judt, *Postwar: A History of Europe since 1945* (New York, 2005), 41–62, 416–17; Harold Marcuse, *Legacies of Dachau: The Uses and Abuses of a Concentration Camp, 1933–2001* (Cambridge, UK, 2001), 201, 212–13, 249–61; Henry Rousso, *The Vichy Syndrome: History and Memory in France since 1944* (Cambridge, MA, 1991), 98–101; Detlef Siegfried, 'Don't Look Back in Anger: Youth, Pop Culture, and the Nazi Past,' in Gassert and Steinweis, *Coping with the Past*, 144–60; Rebecca Wittmann, *Beyond Justice: The Auschwitz Trial* (Cambridge, MA, 2005), e.g., 262–6. On the Soviet Union, see, e.g., Kathleen E. Smith, *Remembering Stalin's Victims: Popular Memory and the End of the USSR* (Ithaca, 1996), esp. 1–2, 154, 166–73; Boris Sokolov, *Beriia: Sud'ba vsesil'nogo narkoma* (Moscow, 2003), 318, 369, 374–7.

93 Judt, *Postwar*, 300–1, 416–18, 810; Marcuse, *Dachau*, 199–220; Rousso, *Vichy Syndrome*, 99; Wittmann, *Beyond Justice*, 13, 246–7.

94 On the West, see Luisa Passerini, *Fascism in Popular Memory: The Cultural Experiences of the Turin Working Class* (Cambridge, UK, 1987); Rousso, *Vichy Syndrome*; Jeffrey Herf, *Divided Memory: The Nazi Past in the Two Germanys* (Cambridge, MA, 1997), 6–7, 274–5; Jarausch, 'Critical Memory,' 19. For the memories recorded in the 1990s–2000s, see Eric A. Johnson and Karl-Heinz Reuband, *What We Knew: Terror, Mass Murder and Everyday Life in Nazi Germany: An Oral History* (Cambridge, MA, 2005), esp. xvi, xxii, 387–98; Judt, *Postwar*, 416–418; Judt, 'The Past Is Another Country,' 305; Marcuse, *Legacies of Dachau*, 200–6; Samuel Moyn, *A Holocaust Controversy: The Treblinka Affair in Postwar France* (Waltham, 2005), 9, 89–90; Rousso, *Vichy Syndrome*, 98–100; Wittmann, *Beyond Justice*, 262–3.

95 Herf, *Divided Memory*, 6–7, 274–5.

96 The first German-language translation of Anne Frank's diary came out in 1950, but the 1955 one was a mass edition that quickly conquered German reading audiences. In five years the book sustained eighteen printings with over 700,000 copies. Marcuse, *Legacies of Dachau*, 200–1. On literature and memory in West Germany, see also Jarausch, 'Critical Memory,' 20.

97 Günter Grass, *Die Blechtrommel* (Neuwied, [1959]).

98 Judt, *Postwar*, 416–17; Devin Pendas, *The Frankfurt Auchwitz Trial, 1963–1965: Genocide, History, and the Limits of the Law* (Cambridge, UK, 2006); Wittmann, *Beyond Justice*, 188–9.

99 Rolf Hochhuth, *Der Stellvertreter* [Reinbek bei Hamburg, 1963]; Marcuse, *Legacies of Dachau*, 213.

100 Hannah Arendt, *Eichmann in Jerusalem: ein Bericht von der Banalität des Bösen* (Munich, 1964); Wittmann, *Beyond Justice*, 14, 188, 246–7.

101 Peter Weiss, *Die Ermittlung* [Velber bei Hannover, 1965]; Wittmann, *Beyond Justice*, 247, 269–71.

102 Claudia Koonz, 'Between Memory and Oblivion: Concentration Camps in German Memory,' in *Commemorations: The Politics of National Identity*, ed. John Gillis (Princeton, 1994), 258–80, esp. 259, 261, 265, 268.

103 Jeremi Suri, *Power and Protest: Global Revolution and the Rise of Détente* (Cambridge, MA, 2003), 88–94.

104 E.g., Leopol'd Averbakh, 'O kul'turnoi preemstvennosti i proletarskoi kul'ture,' *Krasnaia nov'* 6 (1929): 166–84; Aleksandr Bogdanov, 'O khudozhestvennom nasledii,' *Proletarskaia kul'tura* 2 (1918); Katerina Clark, *Petersburg: Crucible of Cultural Revolution* (Cambridge, MA, 1995); V. Kerzhentsev, 'Mezhdunarodnaia revoliutsiia i proletarskaia kul'tura,' *Proletarskaia kul'tura* 6 (1919): 1; G. Lelevich, 'Otkazyvaemsia li my ot nasledstva?' *Na postu* 2 (1923); Anatolii Lunacharskii, 'Pushkin i Nekrasov,' *Izvestiia*, 4 December 1921; Lunacharskii, 'Vchera, segodnia i zavtra russkoi poezii,' *Pechat' i revoliutsiia* 7 (1922); V. Pertsov, 'Kul't predkov i literaturnaia sovremennost',' *Novyi lef* 1 (1928); Viktor Shklovskii, 'Novootkrytyi Pushkin,' *Novyi lef* 11 (1928); Iurii Tynianov, *Arkhaisty i novatory* (Leningrad, 1929); P.S. Vykhodtsev, 'V bor'be za razvitie natsional'nykh traditsii,' in *Russkaia sovetskaia poeziia: traditsii i novatorstvo 1917–1945*, ed. V.V. Timofeeva (Leningrad, 1972), 6–61.

105 E.g., P.S. Vykhodtsev, 'Problema traditsii i novatorstva na sovremennom etape,' in *Russkaia sovetskaia poeziia: traditsii i novatorstvo 1946–1975* (Leningrad, 1978), 3–20.

106 See also Susan E. Reid, 'Modernizing Socialist Realism in the Khrushchev Thaw: The Struggle for a "Contemporary Style" in Soviet Art,' in *Dilemmas*, 209–30, here 210.

107 Bittner, *Many Lives*; Katerina Clark, 'Changing Historical Paradigms in Soviet Culture,' in *Late Soviet Culture: From Perestroika to Novostroika*, ed. Thomas Lahusen and Gene Kuperman (Durham, NC, 1993): 289–306; Denis Kozlov, 'The Historical Turn in Late Soviet Culture, 1953–1991,' *Kritika* 2 no. 3 (2001): 577–600.

108 Herf, *Divided Memory*, 11, 212, 236–7, 243–6.

109 Jan-Werner Müller, *A Dangerous Mind: Carl Schmitt in Post-War European Thought* (New Haven, CT, 2003), 63–8.

110 Farmer, *Martyred Village*, 135–70; Herf, *Divided Memory*, 334–42; Moyn, *Holocaust Controversy*, 142–9; Rousso, *Vichy Syndrome*, 96–7; Wittmann, *Beyond Justice*, 48–53.

111 Denis Kozlov, '"I Have Not Read, but I Will Say": Soviet Literary Audiences and Changing Ideas of Social Membership, 1958–1966,' *Kritika* 7, no. 3 (2006): 557–97. On the late Soviet ideas of rights, see Benjamin Nathans, 'The Dictatorship of Reason: Aleksandr Vol'pin and the Idea of Rights under "Developed Socialism,"' *Slavic Review* 66, no. 4 (2007): 630–63; Nathans, 'Soviet Rights-Talk in the Post-Stalin Era,' in *Human Rights in the Twentieth Century*, ed. Stefan-Ludwig Hoffmann (Cambridge, UK, 2011), 166–90; see also Nathans's forthcoming work on the late Soviet human rights movement and legal culture. Unfortunately, our efforts to include a contribution by Nathans in this volume were unsuccessful. For other aspects of Thaw-era legality, see, e.g., Sheila Fitzpatrick, 'Social Parasites: How Tramps, Idle Youth and Busy Entrepreneurs Impeded the Soviet March to Communism,' *Cahiers du Monde russe* 47, nos. 1–2 (January–June 2006): 377–408.

112 Harold J. Berman, 'The Presumption of Innocence: Another Reply,' *American Journal of Comparative Law* 28, no. 4 (1980): 615–23; L.V. Boitsova, 'Tolkovanie somnenii v pol'zu podsudimogo v sudebnom poriadke,' *Pravovedenie* 3 (1989): 94–9; Vladimir Kudriavtsev and Aleksei Trusov, *Politicheskaia iustitsiia v SSSR* (Saint Petersburg, 2002), 263–4, 351; 'Postanovlenie Plenuma Verkhovnogo Suda SSSR ot 16 iiunia 1978 g. no. 5 "O praktike primeneniia sudami zakonov, obespechivaiushchikh obviniaemomu pravo na zashchitu,"' *Biulleten' Verkhovnogo Suda SSSR* 4 (1978), 9; Mikhail Strogovich, *Uchenie o material'noi istine v ugolovnom protsesse* (Moscow, 1947), 227–59.

113 'The Code of Criminal Procedure of the RSFSR,' articles 74, 77, in *Soviet Criminal Law and Procedures: The RSFSR Codes*, ed. Harold J. Berman (Cambridge, MA, 1966), 280–1; Kudriavtsev and Trusov, *Politicheskaia iustitsiia v SSSR*, 247–59, 340–1; Andrei Vyshinskii, *Teoriia sudebnykh dokazatel'stv v sovetskom prave* (Moscow, 1941), 180–1.

114 'Do kontsa likvidirovat' vrednye posledstviia kul'ta lichnosti v sovetskoi iurisprudentsii,' *Sovetskoe gosudarstvo i pravo*, 4 (1962): 3–16; D. Karev, 'Likvidirovat' posledstviia kul'ta lichnosti v sovetskoi pravovoi nauke,' *Sotsialisticheskaia zakonnost'* 2 (1962): 54–62; *Problemy sudebnoi etiki*, ed. Mikhail Strogovich (Moscow, 1974), 124–6, 146; Peter H. Solomon, *Soviet Crimi-*

nal Justice under Stalin (Cambridge, UK, 1996), 360–4; N.V. Zhogin, 'Ob izvrashcheniiakh Vyshinskogo v teorii sovetskogo prava i praktike,' *Sovetskoe gosudarstvo i pravo* 3 (1965): 22–31.

115 'Criminal Code of the RSFSR,' article 3, in *Soviet Criminal Law*, 145.

116 Peter H. Solomon, 'Judicial Reform under Gorbachev and Russian History,' *The Impact of Perestroika on Soviet Law*, ed. Albert J. Schmidt (Dordrecht, 1990), 18.

117 Kozlov, '"I Have Not Read."'

118 Andrei Sakharov, *Razmyshleniia o progresse, mirnom sosushchestvovanii i intellektual'noi svobode: s prilozheniem vseobshchei deklaratsii prav cheloveka* (Frankfurt/Main, 1968), 19–27, 30–1, 34, 50.

119 Liubov' Denisova, 'Rossiiskaia nechernozemnaia derevnia 1960–1980-kh godov,' in *Rossiia v XX veke*, 618–31; Efim Pivovar, 'Sovetskoe obshchestvo v 1960–1980-e gody. K voprosu o sotsial'nykh i politicheskikh posledstviiakh modernizatsii,' in *Rossiia v XX veke*, 2:372; *Naselenie Rossii v XX veke: Istoricheskie ocherki*, ed. Iurii Poliakov and Valentina Zhiromskaya, 2 vols. (Moscow, 2001), 2:361; R. Popov, 'Kolichestvennye kharakteristiki urbanizatsii v regionakh Evropeiskoi Rossii za 100 let,' in *Gorod i derevnia v Evropeiskoi Rossii: sto let peremen*, ed. T. Nefedova, P. Polian, and A. Treivish (Moscow, 2001), 155; Ilya Zelenin, 'Sovetskaia agrarnaia politika v 1950 – nachale 1980-kh godov,' in *Rossiia v XX veke*, 1:605–17, esp. 605.

120 Percy Allum, 'Italian Society Transformed,' in *Italy since 1945*, ed. Patrick McCarthy (Oxford, 2000), 14–16; Paul Ginsborg, *A History of Contemporary Italy: Society and Politics, 1943–1988* (London, 1990), 211, 217–25.

121 Susan E. Weiner, 'The *Consommatrice* of the 1950s in Elsa Triolet's *Roses à crédit*,' *French Cultural Studies*, 6 (1995): 123–44, here 125–7, 133, 136–7.

122 In 1955–70, 131.8 million individuals moved into the newly constructed housing. The total USSR population was 208.8 million by 1 January 1959. The years 1956–1960 marked the peak of housing construction. Steven Harris, 'Moving,' 1; Poliakov and Zhiromskaya, *Naselenie Rossii*, 2:353.

123 Steven Harris, 'Moving,' 11, 61, 381–8, 393, 401–14; Christine Varga-Harris, 'Constructing the Soviet Hearth: Home, Citizenship and Socialism, 1956–1964' (PhD diss., University of Illinois at Urbana—Champaign, 2005), 6, 14, 132–86; Susan E. Reid, 'The Meaning of Home: 'The Only Bit of the World You Can Have to Yourself',' in *Borders of Socialism: Private Spheres of Soviet Russia*, ed. Lewis H. Siegelbaum (New York, 2006), 145–70.

124 Steven Harris, 'Moving,' 7, 11, 467, 536–45, 549; Krasil'shchikov, *Vdogonku za proshedshim vekom.*

125 Steven Harris, 'Moving,' 549; Blair A. Ruble, 'From *Khrushcheby* to *Korobki*,' in *Russian Housing in the Modern Age: Design and Social History*, ed. William

Craft Brumfield and Ruble (Cambridge, 1993), 238–43, 251, 256–7, 260–1.

126 Ruble, 'From *Khrushcheby*'; *Ironiia sud'by, ili s legkim parom*, dir. El'dar Riazanov (Mosfil'm, 1975).

127 Photographs in *Housing in Europe*, ed. Martin Wynn (London, 1984), 21, 57, 63, 88, 137–8.

128 Steven Harris, 'Moving,' 34–5, 42–9; Ruble, 'From *Khrushcheby*,' 235.

129 *A History of Private Life: Riddles of Identity in Modern Times*, ed. Antoine Prost and Gerard Vincent (Cambridge, MA, 1991), 52, 55–7, 62–3, 66; Susan Weiner, '*Consommatrice*,' 124; Anne Power, *Hovels to High Rise: State Housing in Europe since 1850* (London, 1993), chap. 3; Wynn, *Housing*, 11–12.

130 Greg Castillo, 'Domesticating the Cold War: Household Consumption as Propaganda in Marshall Plan Germany,' *Journal of Contemporary History* 40, no. 2 (2005): 261–88, here 269; Clara Oberle, 'City in Transit: Ruins, Railways, and the Search for Order in Postwar Berlin (1945–1948)' (PhD diss., Princeton University, 2006); Hanna Schissler, 'Writing about 1950s West Germany,' in *The Miracle Years: A Cultural History of West Germany, 1949–1968*, ed. Schissler (Princeton, 2001), 7–8; Wynn, *Housing*, 55.

131 Allum, 'Italian Society Transformed,' 14; Ginsborg, *History of Contemporary Italy*, 19, 36–7, 187–8; Wynn, *Housing*, 247–8, 252; Paolo Scrivano, 'Signs of Americanization in Italian Domestic Life: Italy's Postwar Conversion to Consumerism,' *Journal of Contemporary History* 40, no. 2 (2005): 317–40, here 318–20.

132 Ginsborg, *History of Contemporary Italy*, 246–7; Wynn, *Housing*, 255, 263–4.

133 Allum, 'Italian Society Transformed,' 15; John Foot, 'Mapping Diversity in Milan: Historical Approaches to Urban Immigration,' FEEM Working Paper No. 110.06 (August 2006), http://papers.ssrn.com/sol3/papers.cfm?abstract_id=927745.

134 Wynn, *Housing*, 56–7, 62–4 (quotation at 63).

135 Prost and Vincent, *A History of Private Life*, 56–7.

136 Wynn, *Housing*, 13–14, 20–4, 29, 222–5, 241.

137 Paul Betts and David Crowley, 'Introduction,' *Journal of Contemporary History* 40, no. 2 (2005): 213–36, here 228–30. See also Steven Harris, *Two Lessons in Modernism: What the Architectural Review and America's Mass Media Taught Soviet Architects about the West* (Trondheim, 2010), and most recently his *Communism on Tomorrow Street: Mass Housing and Everyday Life after Stalin* (Washington, DC, 2012); *Mark B. Smith, Property of Communists: The Urban Housing Program from Stalin to Khrushchev* (DeKalb, 2010). Similar government-subsidized mass housing projects were undertaken in the 1950s in North America, particularly Canada. John Bacher, *Keeping to the Market-*

place: The Evolution of Canadian Housing Policy (Montreal, 1993). We thank Shirley Tillotson for this reference.

138 For details, see Susan E. Reid, 'Cold War in the Kitchen: Gender and the De-Stalinization of Consumer Taste in the Soviet Union under Khrushchev,' *Slavic Review* 61, no. 2 (2002): 212–52. See also Nikita Khrushchev, *Bor'ba za uvelichenie proizvodstva miasa – vsenarodnaia zadacha* (Moscow, 1957); Khrushchev, *Povyshenie blagosostoianiia naroda i zadachi dal'neishego uvelicheniia proizvodstva sel'skokhoziaistvennykh produktov* (Moscow, 1961) 22–37.

139 Catriona Kelly, *Refining Russia: Advice Literature, Polite Culture, and Gender from Catherine to Yeltsin* (Oxford, 2001), 312–53, esp. 317–20; Susan E. Reid, 'The Khrushchev Kitchen: Domesticating the Scientific-Technological Revolution,' *Journal of Contemporary History* 40, no. 2 (2005): 289–316.

140 Betts and Crowley, 'Introduction,' 227; N.B. Lebina and A.N. Chistikov, *Obyvatel' i reformy: kartiny povsednevnoi zhizni gorozhan* (Saint Petersburg, 2003), 184; Reid, 'Khrushchev Kitchen,' 298–301; Varga-Harris, 'Constructing the Soviet Hearth,' chap. 3. For a revised perspective, see Susan E. Reid, 'Khrushchev Modern: Agency and Modernization in the Soviet Home,' *Cahiers du monde russe* 47, nos. 1–2 (January–June 2006): 227–68, here 262–5.

141 Betts and Crowley, 'Introduction'; Erica Carter, *How German Is She? Postwar West German Reconstruction and the Consuming Woman* (Ann Arbor, 1997), 5–6, 22–43, 78–80, quotations in 81; David F. Crew, 'Consuming Germany in the Cold War: Consumption and National Identity in East and West Germany, 1949–1989, An Introduction,' in *Consuming Germany in the Cold War*, ed. Crew (Oxford, 2003), 7; Claire Duchen, 'Occupation Housewife: The Domestic Ideal in 1950s France,' *French Cultural Studies* 2, no. 1 (1991): 1–11; Matthew Hilton and Martin Daunton, 'Material Politics: An Introduction,' in *The Politics of Consumption: Material Culture and Citizenship in Europe and America*, ed. Daunton and Hilton (Oxford, 2001), esp. 10–13, 21; Mary Nolan, 'Consuming America, Producing Gender,' *The American Century in Europe*, ed. R. Laurence Moore and Maurizio Vaudagna (Ithaca, 2003), 243–61, here 246–7; Katherine Pence, '"A World in Miniature": The Leipzig Trade Fairs in the 1950s and East German Consumer Citizenship,' in Crew, *Consuming Germany*, 21–50, esp. 27–32; André Steiner, 'Dissolution of the "Dictatorship over Needs"? Consumer Behavior and Economic Reform in East Germany in the 1960s,' in Strasser, *Getting and Spending*, 167–85, here 170; Judd Stitziel, 'On the Seam between Socialism and Capitalism: East German Fashion Shows,' in Crew, *Consuming Germany*, 51–85, here 53; Susan Strasser, Charles McGovern, and Matthias Judt, 'Introduction,' in

Getting and Spending: European and American Consumer Societies in the Twentieth Century, ed. Strasser, McGovern, and Judt (Cambridge, UK, 1998), 4; Jonathan Wiesen, 'Miracles for Sale: Consumer Displays and Advertising in Postwar West Germany,' in Crew, *Consuming Germany*, 151–78, here 154; Michael Woldt, 'Changes in Consumption as Social Practice in West Germany during the 1950s,' in Strasser, *Getting and Spending*, 301–16, here 315.

142 Castillo, 'Domesticating the Cold War,' 284–6; Crew, 'Consuming Germany,' 3–4; Ina Merkel, 'Consumer Culture in the GDR, or How the Struggle for Antimodernity Was Lost on the Battleground of Consumer Culture,' in Strasser, *Getting and Spending*, 281–99. For a broad and comparative consideration of socialist consumption, see David Crowley and Susan E. Reid, 'Introduction: Pleasures in Socialism?' in *Pleasures in Socialism: Leisure and Luxury in the Eastern Bloc*, ed. Crowley and Reid (Evanston, 2010), 3–51.

143 Also Pence, '"A World"'; Stitziel, 'On the Seam,' 76.

144 Crew, 'Consuming Germany,' 6; Wiesen, 154–8, 162, 168–9; Merkel, 'Consumer Culture,' 284–5; Alexei Yurchak, *Everything Was Forever, Until It Was No More: The Last Soviet Generation* (Princeton, 2006), 194–5.

145 Crowley and Reid, 'Introduction'; György Péteri, 'Introduction: The Oblique Coordinate Systems of Modern Identity,' in *Imagining the West in Eastern Europe and the Soviet Union*, ed. György Péteri (Pittsburgh, 2010), 1–12; Reid, 'Khrushchev Modern.'

146 Djurdja Bartlett, *FashionEast: The Spectre That Haunted Socialism* (Cambridge, MA, 2010).

147 Ekaterina Gerasimova and Sof'ia Chuikina, 'Obshchestvo remonta,' *Neprikosnovennyi zapas* 2 (2004): 70–7; Kelly, *Refining Russia*, 318; Merkel, 'Consumer Culture,' 288–90; Eli Rubin, 'The Order of Substitutes: Plastic Consumer Goods in the *Volkswirtschaft* and Everyday Domestic Life in the GDR,' in Crew, *Consuming Germany*, 87–121, here 112–13; Stitziel, 'On the Seam,' 54, 56–7.

148 On these issues, see Larissa Zakharova, 'Soviet Fashion in the 1950s–1960s: Regimentation, Western Influences, and Consumption Strategies,' in this volume. On professional expertise, taste wars, and negotiations, see also Reid, 'Khrushchev Modern.'

149 Eleonory Gilburd, '"To See Paris and Die": Western Culture in the Soviet Union, 1950s and 1960s' (PhD diss., University of California—Berkeley, 2010); Anne E. Gorsuch, *All This Is Your World*, 5; see also her 'From Iron Curtain to Silver Screen: Imagining the West in the Khrushchev Era,' in Péteri, *Imagining the West*, 153–71; Sergei I. Zhuk, *Rock and Roll in the Rocket City: The West, Identity, and Ideology in Soviet Dniepropetrovsk, 1960–1985*

(Baltimore, 2010); Vladislav Zubok, *Zhivago's Children: The Last Russian Intelligentsia* (Cambridge, MA, 2009), esp. chap. 3. On openings elsewhere, see Sudha Rajagopalan, *Leave Disco Dancer Alone! Indian Cinema and Soviet Movie-Going after Stalin* (New Delhi, 2008).

150 Arthur Marwick, *The Sixties: Cultural Revolution in Britain, France, Italy, and the United States, c. 1958–c. 1974* (Oxford, 1998), esp. 18, 36, 319, 329, 406.

151 Michael Geyer, 'The Subject(s) of Europe,' in *Conflicted Memories: Europeanizing Contemporary Histories*, ed. Konrad Jarausch and Thomas Lindenberger (New York, 2007), 254–80; Krasil'shchikov, *Vdogonku za proshedshim vekom*, 124–5, 140; Thomas Mergel, 'Europe as Leisure Time Communication: Tourism and Transnational Interaction since 1945,' in *Conflicted Memories*, 133–53; Arnold Sywottek, 'From Starvation to Excess? Trends in the Consumer Society from the 1940s to the 1970s,' in Schissler, *Miracle Years*, 346–7, 349.

152 Marwick, *Sixties*, 35–6, 66–71, 78–9, 107–9, 165, 173–7, 183–91, 406–11, 417–21, 455–61, 464–9.

153 Bulgakowa, 'Cine-Weathers.'

154 Jay Winter, *Dreams of Peace and Freedom: Utopian Moments in the Twentieth Century* (New Haven, CT, 2006), 11–47, Steichen comparisons at 26, 36.

155 Walter Hixson, *Parting the Curtain: Propaganda, Culture, and the Cold War, 1945–1961* (New York, 1997), chap. 7; Marilyn Kushner, 'Exhibiting Art at the American National Exhibition in Moscow, 1959: Domestic Politics and Cultural Diplomacy,' *Journal of Cold War Studies* 4, no. 1 (2002): 6–26; Rosa Magnusdottir, 'Keeping Up Appearances: How the Soviet State Failed to Control Popular Attitudes toward the United States of America, 1945–1959' (PhD diss., University of North Carolina, Chapel Hill, 2006), esp. 220–2; Karal Marling, *As Seen on TV: The Visual Culture of Everyday Life in the 1950s* (Cambridge, MA, 1994), 243–52, 271–83; Reid, 'Cold War'; Susan E. Reid, 'Who Will Beat Whom? Soviet Popular Reception of the American National Exhibition in Moscow, 1959,' *Kritika* 9, no. 4 (Fall 2008): 855–904; specifically on the transformative presence of Western cultural phenomena in Soviet media, see Kristin Roth-Ey, *Moscow Prime Time: How the Soviet Union Built the Media Empire That Lost the Cultural Cold War* (Ithaca, 2011).

156 Weiner, 'Empires Pay a Visit.'

157 Mike-Frank Epitropoulos and Victor Roudometof, 'Introduction: America and Europe, Fragile Objects of Discourse,' in *American Culture in Europe: Interdisciplinary Perspectives*, ed. Epitropoulos and Roudometof (Westport, CT, 1998), 2–3; Richard Kuisel, *Seducing the French: The Dilemma of Americanization* (Berkeley, 1993), 30–6, 40–7, 52–69, 100–2, 108–21; Richard Pells, *Not Like Us: How Europeans Have Loved, Hated, and Transformed American*

Culture since World War II (New York, 1997), 51–2, 67–9, 163–82, 191–203, 236–9; Uta Poiger, *Jazz, Rock, and Rebels: Cold War Politics and American Culture in a Divided Germany* (Berkeley, 2000); Reinhold Wagnleitner, *Coca-Colonization and the Cold War: The Cultural Mission of the United States in Austria after the Second World War* (Chapel Hill, NC, 1994).

158 On the struggle over 'culture' and 'barbarity,' see Greg Castillo, 'East as True West: Redeeming Bourgeois Culture, from Socialist Realism to *Ostalgie*,' in Péteri, *Imagining the West*, 87–104; Gilburd, 'Picasso in Thaw Culture.'

159 Gilburd, '"To See Paris and Die,"' chap. 1.

160 Schissler, 'Writing about 1950s West Germany,' in Schissler, *Miracle Years*, 10; Wagnleitner, *Coca-Colonization*, ix, 44, 68–9; Reinhold Wagnleitner, 'The Empire of the Fun, or Talkin' Soviet Union Blues: The Sound of Freedom and U.S. Cultural Hegemony in Europe,' *Diplomatic History* 23, no. 3 (Summer 1999): 499–524.

161 Pells, *Not Like Us*, 40–1, 158–9, 163–8, 196; Wagnleitner, 'Empire.'

162 David Caute, *The Dancer Defects: The Struggle for Cultural Supremacy during the Cold War* (Oxford, 2003); Pells, *Not Like Us*, 84–5.

163 Krasil'shchikov, *Vdogonku za proshedshim vekom*; György Péteri, 'Nylon Curtain: Transnational and Transsystemic Tendencies in the Cultural Life of State-Socialist Russia and East-Central Europe,' *Slavonica* 10, no. 2 (2004): 113–23.

164 On permeability, see also the editorial article 'Passing through the Iron Curtain,' *Kritika* 9, no. 4 (2008): 703–9; Gorsuch, 'From Iron Curtain.'

165 Michael Werner and Bénédicte Zimmermann, 'Beyond Comparison: *Histoire croisée* and the Challenge of Reflexivity,' *History and Theory* 45 (February 2006): 30–50; for a musical example, see Peter J. Schmelz, *Such Freedom, If Only Musical: Unofficial Soviet Music during the Thaw* (Oxford, 2009), ch. 2,

166 Tim Scholl, *From Petipa to Balanchine: Classical Revival and the Modernization of Ballet* (London, 1994).

167 Gorsuch, 'From Iron Curtain.'

168 Edele, 'Strange Young Men'; Fürst, *Stalin's Last Generation*, chap. 6; Anne Gorsuch, 'Time Travelers: Soviet Tourists to Eastern Europe,' in *Turizm: The Russian and East European Tourist Under Capitalism and Socialism*, ed. Gorsuch and Diane Koenker (Ithaca, 2006), 205–26.

169 On the centrality of the encounter with Western imports for late Soviet culture and identity, see Zhuk, *Rock and Roll*; Yurchak, *Everything Was Forever*, chap. 5.

170 Yurchak, *Everything Was Forever*, 36–76.

171 On irony, see Prokhorov, *Unasledovannyi*.

172 Reid, 'Modernizing.'
173 Bulgakowa, 'Cine-Weathers.'
174 Katerina Clark, '"Wait for Me and I Shall Return": The Early Thaw as a Reprise of Late Thirties Culture,' in this volume.
175 Vladimir Pomerantsev, 'Ob iskrennosti v literature,' *Novyi mir* 12 (1953): 218–45.
176 Kornei Chukovskii, *Za zhivoe, obraznoe slovo* (Moscow, 1967); Chukovskii, *Zhivoi kak zhizn'* (Moscow, 1962).
177 Vit. Bianki, 'Mysli vslukh,' *Zvezda* 7 (July 1955): 136, 138, here 138; Aleksandr Morozov, 'Zametki o iazyke,' *Zvezda* 11 (November 1954): 143–6, here 143; Pavel Nilin, 'Opasnost' ne tam…' *Novyi mir* 4 (1958): 276–7; S. Radin, 'Iazyk i slovar'. Pis'mo v redaktsiiu,' *Zvezda* 1 (January 1959): 217–19.
178 Kornei Chukovskii, *Ot dvukh do piati* (Leningrad, 1939, first published 1933); Irina Lukianova, *Kornei Chukovskii* (Moscow, 2006), 589, 617–19, 621.
179 On the production of this language, see Michael S. Gorham, *Speaking in Soviet Tongues: Language Culture and the Politics of Voice in Revolutionary Russia* (DeKalb, 2003); Matthew E. Lenoe, *Closer to the Masses: Stalinist Culture, Social Revolution, and Soviet Newspapers* (Cambridge, MA, 2004).
180 Polly Jones, 'The Personal and the Political: Opposition to the "Thaw" and the Politics of Literary Identity in the 1950s and 1960s,' in this volume.
181 Gorham, *Speaking in Soviet Tongues,* 7–15, 39–42, 59–70.
182 Clark, *Petersburg,* 224–41, 284–8; M. Golubkov, *Utrachennye al'ternativy: formirovanie monicheskoi kontseptsii sovetskoi literatury, 20–30-e gody* (Moscow, 1992), 56–64; Gorham, *Speaking in Soviet Tongues,* 134–6; N. Primochkina, *Pisatel' i vlast': M. Gor'kii v literaturnom dvizhenii 20-kh godov* (Moscow, 1996), 138–45.
183 Aleksei Iugov, *Sud'by rodnogo slova* (Moscow, 1962); Iugov, 'Tak chto zhe nam delat'?' *Literatura i zhizn',* 30 March 1962; Morozov, 'Zametki,' 144–6.
184 'Berech' russkii iazyk,' *Literaturnaia gazeta,* 3 March 1959; V. Kostomarov, *Kul'tura rechi i stil'* (Moscow, 1960); S. Tsalanchuk, 'Prav li A. Iugov?' and L. Barlas, 'Spornaia pozitsiia,' *Literaturnaia gazeta,* 28 April 1959.
185 I. Dukhovnyi, 'Ne govorit' gotovymi formulami,' *Komsomol'skaia pravda,* 31 October 1954; E. Dunaev, L. Tsakunov, V. Shvedko, and L. Shibina, 'Krasnorechie po shpargalkam: Pis'mo v redaktsiiu,' *Komsomol'skaia pravda,* 17 August 1954; P. Konoplev, 'Sila dushevnogo slova: bez bumazhek,' A. Lukin, 'Sila dushevnogo slova: Shpargalka vredna,' *Komsomol'skaia pravda,* 18 November 1954; Ia. Levin, 'Govorit' po sushchestvu: Oshibesh'sia – popraviat' and V. Morozenko, 'Govorit' po sushchestvu: O liubiteliakh bumag,' *Komsomol'skaia pravda,* 21 November 1954.

186 Bulgakowa, 'Cine-Weathers.'
187 N. Aleksandrova and L. Pochivalov, 'Otstupnik – tak on i nazyvaetsia,' *Komsomol'skaia pravda*, 9 July 1958.
188 E.G. Borisova-Lukashanets, 'O leksike sovremennogo molodezhnogo zhargona (Angloiazychnye zaimstvovaniia v studencheskom slenge 60–70-x godov),' in *Literaturnaia norma v leksike i frazeologii*, ed. Lev I. Skvortsov and Boris S. Shvartskopf (Moscow, 1983), 104–20; N.A. Leonova, 'O proiznoshenii sovremennoi molodezhi,' *Uchenye zapiski Kurskogo gosudarstvennogo pedagogicheskogo instituta* 25, no. 2 (1966): 106–13; L.I. Skvortsov, 'Literaturnyi iazyk, prostorechie i zhargony v ikh vzaimodeistvii,' in Skvortsov, *Literaturnaia norma i prostorechie* (Moscow, 1977); Skvortsov, 'Ob otsenkakh iazyka molodezhi,' *Voprosy kul'tury rechi* 5 (Moscow, 1964), 45–70.
189 Vladislav Kulakov, *Poeziia kak fakt* (Moscow, 1999), 42–59; Stanislav Rassadin, 'Vremia stikhov i vremia poetov,' *Arion* 4 (1996): 18–29; on poetry, see also Tromly, 'Re-Imagining the Soviet Intelligentsia,' 432–43, 474–6.
190 Katharine Hodgson, '"Russia is Reading Us Once More": The Rehabilitation of Poetry, 1953–64,' in *Dilemmas*, 231–49.
191 This discussion is based on E.A. Bakhmutova, *Kul'tura rechi. Orfoepoiia. Leksicheskie normy. Uchebnoe posobie* (Kazan', 1960), 5; Chukovskii, *Zhivoi*, 3–12, 22–4; Kostomarov, *Kul'tura rechi i stil'*, 42, 10; S.I. Ozhegov, ed., *Pravil'nost' russkoi rechi. Slovar'-spravochnik* (Moscow, 1965), 4–5.
192 For a contrary emphasis on the 1950s, see Vladimir Ufliand, 'Piatidesiatnyi shestidesiatnik,' *Literaturnoe obozrenie* 5 (1997): 72–8; Andrei Zorin, 'Sekta piatidesiatnikov,' in his *Gde sidit fazan: Ocherki poslednikh let* (Moscow, 2003), 13–25.
193 Stanislav Rassadin, 'Shestidesiatniki: Knigi o molodom sovremennike,' *Iunost'* 12 (December 1960): 58–62.
194 Iakov Khelemskii, 'Borodatye shestidesiatniki,' *Iunost'* 7 (1962): 37.
195 Ibid.
196 Stanislav Rassadin, 'Borodatye shestidesiatniki'; Rassadin, 'Teatr "Sovremennik" ishchet p'esu,' *Iunost'* 8 (1962): 68–75.
197 Sakharov, *Razmyshleniia*, 5. According to the official statistics, 28.8 million people in the USSR were 'engaged in intellectual labour' in 1968, compared to 2.6 million in 1926 and 20.5 million in 1959. In 1939 there were 8 persons with higher education per 1,000 people over ten years old in the USSR. In 1959 the ratio was 23:1,000, and by 1970 it went up to 42:1,000. In 1967 the country boasted of 6.4 million people with higher education, compared to 1.2 million in 1939 and 3.8 million in 1959; by January 1970 their number reached 8.3 million. In addition, there were over 4.5 million college students by 1969–70, compared to just 812,000 in 1940–1 and 2.4 million in 1960–1. *Narodnoe khoziaistvo SSSR v 1967 g.: statisticheskii*

ezhegodnik (Moscow, 1968), 34, 35, 788; *Narodnoe khoziaistvo SSSR v 1970 g.* (Moscow, 1971), 23, 637.

198 Aleksandr Timofeevskii, 'Poslednie romantiki,' *Iskusstvo kino* 5 (1989): 59–66. For 'the children of the 20th Congress,' see Evgenii Evtushenko, *Talant est' chudo nesluchainoe* (Moscow, 1980), 310. For 'Stalin's heirs,' see Evtushenko, 'Nasledniki Stalina,' *Pravda*, 21 October 1962. See also Schmelz, *Such Freedom*, 17–18.

199 Stanislav Rassadin, 'Prostaki, ili Vospominaniia u televizora,' *Iskusstvo kino* 1 (1990): 14–31, here 18; Sergei Korotkov, 'Shlagbaum dlia romantikov shestidesiatnikov ubila perestroika,' *Stolichnye novosti*, 14–19 April 2004, http://cn.com.ua/N305/society/generation/generation.html, accessed 1 December 2008; and Korotkov, 'Shestidesiatniki,' *Literaturnaia gazeta*, 7–13 August 2002.

200 Rassadin, 'Prostaki,' 14–17.

201 *Shestidesiatniki*, ed. M. Barbakadze (Moscow, 2007).

202 Ibid., 32–3; see also Svetlana Boym, *Common Places: Mythologies of Everyday Life in Russia* (Cambridge, MA, 1994); Yurchak, *Everything Was Forever*, 102–25.

203 Marietta Chudakova, 'Tri kachestva ne daiutsia v odnom nabore – um, partiinost' i poriadochnost''; and Chudakova, 'Ubezhdennost' u menia ot ottsa,' *Shestidesiatniki*, 22–31, esp. 24, 67–70.

204 Jarausch, 'Critical Memory,' 20–2; Judt, *Postwar*, 416–17; Marcuse, *Legacies of Dachau*, 201, 212–13; Rousso, *Vichy Syndrome*, 98–101; Wittmann, *Beyond Justice*, 262–6.

205 On the political beliefs of the late Soviet intelligentsia, see Zubok, *Zhivago's Children.*

206 Denis Kozlov, 'Remembering and Explaining the Terror during the Thaw: Soviet Readers of Ehrenburg and Solzhenitsyn in the 1960s,' in this volume.

207 Stanislav Rassadin, 'A potom zhloby poedaiut sami sebia,' *Novaia gazeta*, 2 October 2002.

208 Barbakadze, *Shestidesiatniki*, 55 (quotation), 57; Korotkov, 'Shlagbaum dlia romantikov. Shestidesiatnikov ubila perestroika'; for an application of the milieu concept in another scenario, see Tromly, 'Re-Imagining the Soviet Intelligentsia,' 102–8, 135, 141–9.

209 Valeriia Novodvorskaia, 'Shestidesiatniki i pustota,' *Novaia Iunost* 1 (1999). http://magazines.russ.ru/nov_yun/1999/1/novodvor.html.

210 Stanislav Kuniaev, 'Dobro – sila dukhovnaia,' interview with Sergei Kaznacheev, *Trud*, 27 November 2002; Kuniaev, *Poeziia. Sud'ba. Rossiia*, 3 vols. (Moscow, 2001) 1:78–80.

211 Viktor Pelevin, *Chapaev i pustota* (Moscow, 1996).
212 E.g., *Shestidesiatniki*; E.A. Semenova and O.A. Salynskii, eds., *Miry Bulata Okudzhavy: Materialy Tret'ei mezhdunarodnoi nauchnoi konferentsii, 18–20 marta 2005 g., Peredelkino* (Moscow, 2007), 104–18.
213 The famous titles of, respectively, Vladimir Dudintsev's 1956 novel and Aleksandr Solzhenitsyn's 1974 article.
214 E.g., Karl Loewenstein, 'The Thaw: Writers and the Public Sphere in the Soviet Union, 1951–1957' (PhD diss., Duke University, 1999), 422–36.
215 E.g., Filtzer, *Khrushchev Era*; Leibovich, *Reforma i modernizatsiia*; Pyzhikov, *Khrushchevskaia.*

PART ONE

Looking Back

2 'Wait for Me and I Shall Return': The Early Thaw as a Reprise of Late Thirties Culture?

KATERINA CLARK

What is a thaw? Most commentators on the post-Stalin thaws have seen them as periods of 'liberalization,' by analogy with what happens when ice is thawed and what was frigid and rigid becomes more fluid. Another way of looking at a thaw, and particularly a Russian thaw, would be to see it as a moment when the snow, accumulated over a long winter, finally melts, revealing what lies beneath, what was always there, if invisible, but dormant and drab under the impact of the cold and lack of light, and which can now come into its own, turn green, sprout new shoots, and blossom. A third interpretation, and one foregrounded in the title of Vera Panova's 'thaw' novel of 1953–4, would be to see a thaw as one of the 'seasons of the year' (*Vremena goda*), or in other words as a recurrent, as one phase in a repeated cycle. All three possible interpretations have merit as tropes for the cultural changes that took place during the first decade after Stalin's death.

Here I want to focus on the early phases of the post-Stalin thaw, the years 1953–7, which are conventionally seen as having experienced two thaws, one of 1953–4, the other of 1956. I want to discuss them in terms of that hopelessly timeworn debate about Soviet culture, about whether this or that development represents 'continuity or change' – or for that matter whether it marks a 'great retreat.'[1] I will be focusing on the aspect of recurrence, as I suggest with my title's somewhat facetious invocation of that beloved poem from the Second World War by Konstantin Simonov – 'Wait for Me, and I Shall Return' (1941). Moreover, in the poem Simonov also invokes nature's cyclicity as his 'I' urges his beloved to wait steadfastly through the successive harsh seasons to come. As it were, our spring will return again.

Unfortunately, in looking at cultural evolution such analogies with the world of nature can take us only so far. When in nature spring comes, a familiar scenario is replayed in more or less the same sequence as in previous years and with the same events: by the Russian sense of things, starting with snowdrops (*podsnezhniki*), to be followed by new leaves, after which comes the lilac blossom. Cultural evolution is more complex, less 'natural' or pre-programmed, less automatic. A particular phase with its particular characteristic values, discourse and practices never recurs, so to speak, intact. A closer analogy might be the dynamic discussed in several theories of memory, including that of Bergson, whereby at any given moment when a memory occurs it does not do so in isolation but interacts in the mind with other material, including current impressions, which are of course themselves shaped by memory. Moreover, over time a particular memory may be conflated with another, or elements in its narrative may be lost or accrue to other memories; or a memory can undergo what Freud called displacement or may be in some other way distorted. In consequence, particular memory elements weave in and out of our consciousness over time. A given experience, once committed to memory, is rarely replayed in the mind intact, but when it is replayed it is reinflected by both intervening experiences and the other material present in the mental stream at the time it recurs. An obvious problem with this comparison with Bergson is that it suggests that the thaw was all in the mind, whereas in fact it had to be the product of political developments. But of course naming these developments and their aftermath a 'thaw' is to categorize our perceptions of what has transpired.

Our sense of the post-Stalin thaws has undergone an evolution. At the time, the changes that came with the initial thaws were heralded by Western commentators as virtually a revolution in Soviet values and cultural practices. As George Gibian put it in his book *Interval of Freedom*, 'Between the years 1954 and 1957 opinions were expressed by Soviet writers which during Stalin's rule certainly would have been repressed by the writers themselves – or by those in charge of controlling Soviet cultural life.'[2] Yet, as some scholars have since established, including myself, several of the attitudes that at the time appeared so radical and defining for these thaws were in fact expressed in works published earlier in the infamous Zhdanov period, although admittedly they were then expressed in more muted form and were not blazoned forth as they were to be during the post-Stalin thaws.[3] In some instances, authors of works deemed bombshells of the thaws had, during the Zhdanov years, published works that made much the same points.[4] One also has to ask how politically radical were the works of thaw years. So often those authors who most vociferously called for 'Truth! Truth!' and denounced the false 'truths' of the Stalin era, and especially if they drew a radical contrast between 'two truths,' were actually not as interested in intellectual freedom or any such 'liberalization,' much as Western commentators were anxious to impute such motives to them, as in paying obeisance to the new regime by publicly distancing themselves from the old ('The king is dead, long live the king!').[5]

Stalin's death in 1953 did not mark an absolute BC/AD dividing line. Many of the shifts charted as post-1953 can be seen to have begun in the immediately preceding years, facilitated by such things as the relative recovery from the war and the renewed concern for human welfare reflected, for example, in speeches made at the Nineteenth Party Congress in 1952, and even Stalin's essay on linguistics (his attack there on the linguist Marr's 'Arakcheev-like regime' was in some senses picked up by Vladimir Dudintsev in his thaw novel *Not by Bread Alone* (*Ne khlebom edinym*) of 1956, where he also used that expression). In positing a blurred divide between the Stalin and immediately post-Stalin periods, a case in point would be Leonid Leonov's novel *The Russian Forest*, which came out in December 1953 and can be read as a critique of Stalinist repression: Leonov's stress on Russia's abundant forests as a national treasure ('green gold') can be taken to stand for the Russian people, so that when in the novel he decries the wilful cutting down of the forests, one can take this to be a trope for the great human cost of the purges, which is at the same time a loss to the nation (one could take as a cue for this interpretation a passage where Leonov invokes in connection with this criminal waste of the national treasure that famous maxim used in Stalin's time to justify instances when innocents were purged – 'When you cut down a forest, the chips will fly' [*Les rubiat – shchepki letiat*]).[6] In this sense, the novel could be read as anticipating Khrushchev's 'Secret Speech' of February 1956, yet it could *at the same time* be seen as an elaborate celebration of Stalin's recent program for aforestation.[7] Indeed, given that the novel was written between January and September of 1953, in other words, largely before post-Stalin liberalization was much in evidence, one can see it as straddling both eras.

Even if, then, the initial thaws can be seen as less times of *radical* change than as providing a difference of degree, an intensification of ongoing changes, still in a highly conventionalized culture, such as one found in the Soviet Union, the slightest degree of modification can be all-important. After all, the Stalin era's little red book, *The Short Course* (*Kratkii kurs istorii VKP[b]*) of 1938, foregrounds as an analogy for the structure of revolution the moment when progressive increases in degrees of heat or cold become critical, and suddenly water is turned to steam or ice in a qualitative change. There is also the question of the degree of prominence that a particular view enjoyed on the political or cultural horizon. Attitudes may be present at a given moment but *at that time* marginal or muted, not typical. If they became typical of a subsequent time, should that be considered as showing continuity or change? It could be argued, for example, that what might be called the Ovechkin/Tendriakov/Troepol'skii line in the post-Stalin thaws that questioned rigid enforcement of the principle of *edinonachalie* (one-man management) and putting production considerations above those of human welfare – a line that was so prominent in the initial thaws – bespeaks the relative continuity between late- and post-Stalin culture.[8]

Here, however, I want to focus not on such continuity but on ways in which the early thaws could be seen as a 'return' to attitudes and patterns to be found in that most unlikely of precedent times: the late 1930s, those years of 'high Stalinism.' Here I shall be treating not discussions about management and politics but another element in the thaws.

Simonov's 'Wait for Me, and I Shall Return' is not only about return, but primarily a love poem written in the circumstances of war. In it the poem's 'I' implores his addressee to 'wait intensely' (*ochen' zhdi*), to wait beyond the point where everyone else has given up on his returning, leaving a 'just you and me.' The theme of heroic defence of the motherland, and all that, is nowhere in sight in the text; there is no indication that the poem's 'I' is a fearless and determined fighter (though perhaps that is implicit, given that Simonov was associated with the military). This foregrounding of private, intimate emotions can be seen as symptomatic of the ideological concessions made by the regime in the interests of national unification in a time of war, but the poem is underpinned by values that anticipate defining aspects of the initial post-Stalin thaws.

On 16 April 1953, just six weeks after Stalin died, Ol'ga Berggol'ts published in *Literaturnaia gazeta* a programmatic article 'A Conversation about the Lyric' (*Razgovor o lirike*). The ideas Berggol'ts set out in this article, which have been picked up by Western commentators as signs of 'thaw,' were reiterated in various ways in a series of articles published over the next year or so and appearing largely in *Literaturnaia gazeta* or *Novyi mir*. I will focus on just the one article by Berggol'ts here.[9]

Berggol'ts argues in this article that Soviet literature is in crying need of true lyric poetry. In her experience, at poetry readings the audience keeps demanding it. There are, she allows, so-called lyrics published, but they are not *true* lyrics at all and are scorned by the readership because the Soviet public and its authors have developed, become more sophisticated, and now need a more sophisticated literature ('the inner life of Soviet man and consequently of the Soviet poet' has 'grown so much, broadened and been enriched').[10]

Lyric poetry Berggol'ts defines at the outset as 'self-expression,' and central to self-expression in her account is expression of one's own inner emotions and intimate feelings – love in particular. What she and others who took similar positions at this time objected to was the overly schematic accounts of love relations presented in socialist realist texts where the love plot – the private lives of protagonists – became subordinated to the account of the hero's public life. Consequently, any love object that might tempt a positive hero to adultery *could only be* both politically dangerous and of the wrong sociological category. Moreover, the positive hero, as a *positive* hero, must have a sudden insight into her true nature and be able to resist her in the nick of time. But in standard Stalinist novels, even the less risqué theme of young love leading to marriage was presented in ludicrously politicized love plots, which critics of these initial post-Stalin thaws delighted in parodying. As Berggol'ts puts it in this article, in Soviet poetry we find 'the replacement of true [*podlinnykh*] feelings and passions with erzats surrogates,' such that, for example, rather than show the sorrows of love unrequited, an all-too-typical lyric will show how 'the rejected lover has overfulfilled the plan for hay gathering.'[11]

Berggol'ts is in effect calling for a different attitude to private life in Soviet literature as a whole. She argues that representation of love should not only be more realistic, but should also be more autonomous within a text, 'in a society that is building communism where love has been liberated from "the corrupting power of money," where it has acquired the possibility of being "more grandiose than Onegin's love."' This campaign of Berggol'ts and others for 'the lyric' was soon followed by a shift in the treatment of love in literature and film which increasingly liberated themselves from the stricture that positive heroes could not indulge in adultery and also to a significant but of course limited degree from overly puritanical and politicized love plots.[12]

But Berggol'ts's concern was not just plot conventions. Her interest in this article is not so much the formal characteristics of a genre, genre purity, as a nexus of desired attributes in poetry, and by implication in literature and culture in general. Her article recurrently uses three terms that were to become emblematic of the early thaws: besides 'the lyric' (*lirika*), 'sincerity' (*iskrennost'*), and 'genuine' or 'true' (*podlinnyi*). Berggol'ts in her opening paragraph states, 'The hero [of the lyric] is the poet himself, the individual person who is speaking of himself and from himself, from his own "I."' If he really does, he is being 'sincere,' and his lyric poem is then 'genuine.' The term used here for individual person is *lichnost'*, a word that also means 'personality.' She insists that it is the lyric poetry that most fully and *sincerely* [emphasis mine] expresses his cherished and multi-faceted [*mnogogrannye* – complex] feelings.'[13]

Individualized self-expression was of course a problematical proposal, but Berggol'ts covers herself from potential attacks on her article in various ways that were standard among those writers campaigning for a 'true lyric': allegedly, self-expression would not mean pure and self-indulgent subjectivity, for a 'true' poet 'expresses and formulates masterfully the basic, the best and the dominant emotions of his age.' Lyric poetry is 'profoundly individual,' she insists, 'yet at the same time typical for the great majority of people.' In other words, the sort of reinvigorated lyric she sought would be no exercise in dissidence, in solipsism or self-indulgent wallowing in one's own emotions. Somehow, given that (this argument typically ran) the author of today is a product of socialist society, the private emotions expressed would inevitably coincide with the official line; as it were, they would be only more individually, more personally depicted. Casuistry or conviction? Who can say? Also, typically again, Berggol'ts buttresses her argument with endorsing citations from authority figures (a Belinsky article on Lermontov, a recent statement by Malenkov) and even argues that her version of the 'lyric' has greater utility: allegedly, sincere poems have 'great pedagogical power' because with a good lyric the reader 'appropriates this "I" as his own "I," his personal one,' while crude, declamatory, or direct treatment of themes is not very effective in influencing the reader.[14]

To some extent, Berggol'ts's position could be seen as a development out of a new line in literature to be seen already in the early 1950s. Even before Stalin died, in 1952, critics were attacking contemporary Soviet literature on the grounds that it was overly 'varnished' (*lakirovka*) and also suffered from tepid plots because of the doctrine of conflictlessness (*beskonfliktnost'*).[15] The doctrine of 'conflictlessness' held that Soviet society had progressed so far towards communism that now literature, instead of conflicts between positive and negative characters, should have conflicts between positive and less-than-entirely-positive characters. But clearly Berggol'ts's article is more than an extension of this new line, and indeed the campaign that went under the sign of 'the lyric' and 'sincerity' was largely attacked by the literary establishment, who reiterated the late Stalin doctrine that *beskonfliktnost'* had to go but suggested that the new slogans such as 'sincerity' threatened to undermine party-mindedness (*partiinost'*).[16]

The demand that writers overcome what Berggol'ts called a 'fear of sincerity' was a more cautious and tentative version of the demand for '*pravda*' of 1956.[17] In that year Ia. Strochkov published an article in *Voprosy istorii* (for which heads rolled) that could be considered taking the campaign for 'the lyric' to one of its logical conclusions. In the article Strochkov suggests that Lenin in his article of 1905, which is the locus classicus for the doctrine of mandatory *partiinost'* in literature, never meant that principle to apply at all times but only in the extraordinary conditions of a revolutionary situation, such as in 1905, the year Lenin wrote this.[18] Much of the discussion of '*pravda*' in literary works of 1956 was in fact about artistic truth.[19]

In 1956 several writers suggested that citizens are not only entitled, but actually have a duty to their conscience, to exercise what Daniil Granin called in the title of his short story of that year, 'One's Own Opinion.' However, though the demand for 'sincerity' might seem vaguer than the demand for 'truth,' and perhaps even a trifle naive or sentimental, in some respects Berggol'ts's program for bringing back a genuine 'lyric' was more radical than was advocated in 1956. For a start, it was less tied to Soviet literature's function of extolling official policies.

Berggol'ts in this article implicitly, and to a large degree explicitly, proposes reorienting Soviet literature. Rather than feature putatively 'typical' characters who are depicted purely in external characteristics and in terms of their sociological categories (such as 'Party member since ...' or 'former kulak [wealthy farmer]'), literary works should, she maintains, show the inner life of the characters and individualize them, changes that would potentially undermine the entire tradition of socialist realism and even bedrock values of Soviet ideology. In recent lyric poems, she complains, the hero is defined by the sorts of data one might find in an 'average personnel file' (social origins, education, party record, war experience, employment record). Thus, typically, 'bulldozer or excavator drivers are described, and gardeners, and sometimes they are described well, even with mastery, but they are described in terms of *external features* [emphasis mine], and in poetry there is not the main thing, the lyrical hero, his individual attitude to events.' In the poetry of today, 'the main thing is missing, man himself.' The hero should be given 'his own biography' and not just the 'average personnel file data.' And, she adds, '*be-*

skonfliktnost" has been condemned by the party but '*beskonfliktnost'* and *bezlichnost'* [facelessness, having no individuality] are sisters.'[20]

What *bezlichnost'* really means here is a totally conventionalized, non-individualized representation of characters. In Stalinist socialist realist novels, a 'character' is, as it were, not a person in his or her own right, but a mask made up of standardized, codified markers that establish the character's socio-political identity and triangulate his position on the road to full Marxist-Leninist consciousness, but have only token or glancing reference to his personality.[21] It is not just the fact that there were – and this is something Fedor Abramov went to town about in his 1954 article 'Kolkhoz Villagers in Post-war Prose' – all those execrable kolkhoz idylls published in the Zhdanov era, idylls where reality was totally 'varnished.'[22] Berggol'ts, who in her article also deplores what she calls the 'idyllic-odic intonation' of so much recent literature is not, unlike Abramov, asking primarily for more realistic depiction of reality. She is proposing what effectively amounts to recentring literature to focus characterization not on the exterior mask but on the inner man and his emotions.

It could be argued that thaw writers such as Berggol'ts were not really demanding that those wishy-washy and ultimately unverifiable qualities of 'sincerity' and 'the genuine' become criteria for evaluating lyric poetry. As has recently been discussed in the West, the romantics also called for 'sincerity' or 'spontaneity' in poetry, but 'these now old-fashioned terms point to a set of stylistic conventions developed by the romantics to give the illusion of 'spontaneous overflow' to their verse.[23] If lyric poets specialized in sincere outpourings, then the result is in danger of becoming schoolboy mush. After all, T.S. Eliot argues in his well-known article 'Tradition and the Individual Talent' that a process of depersonalization is critical in the creation of good poetry, describing such poetry as 'a continual self-sacrifice, a continual extinction of personality,' and adding, 'the more perfect the artist, the more completely separate in him will be the man who suffers and the mind which creates.'[24] Lydia Ginzburg, in her major study of the pre-revolutionary lyric *O lirike*, published in 1964, argues for a more restrained version of a similar position, contending that good lyric poetry requires 'the interaction of tradition, of the heritage of the past with an affirmation of the new.' She rejects completely the notion – which she says was proposed 'at one time' and here one cannot help speculating that she has in mind precisely the insistence on 'sincerity' among those who campaigned in the previous decade for the 'true lyric' – that the lyric poem should present 'the unmediated expression of the feelings of a particular, single individual [*lichnosti*]. Such unmediated expression would not only be uninteresting (if it was really about the one person), but also impossible inasmuch as art is the experience of the one in which the many must find and understand themselves.' In poetry, moreover, human feelings are presented in 'poetic discourse,' and this, of course, means they are mediated.[25]

Berggol'ts's advocacy of 'the lyric' as a panacea for the stiltedness of socialist realism should not be seen as a post-Stalin development. She and Margarita Aliger, another poet, made much the same points as appear in 'Conversation about the Lyric' in their speeches to a meeting of Moscow poets in January 1953, the same month as the Doctor's Plot was 'uncovered'![26] Were they, then, *podsnezhniki* (snowdrops), harbingers of a spring to come? Certainly, this near simultaneity of what appear to have been radically different events bespeaks the complexity of cultural evolution. What we see in the campaign for 'the lyric' is a debate conducted within the literary establishment on both sides of the March 1953 divide. Berggol'ts was no marginal figure at the start of the 1953–4 thaws, having been elected in 1952 as head of the poetry section of the Leningrad Branch of the Writers Union (Panova, the author of the early thaw classic *Seasons of the Year*, was made head of its prose section at the same time).[27] Berggol'ts joined the Party in 1940, Aliger (who was close to Aleksandr Fadeev, the general secretary of the Writers Union), in 1942. Indeed, many of the prominent thaw writers, such as Granin and Valentin Ovechkin, were party members. At the same time, the points made in what have been classified as 'thaw' works met stolid opposition from authority figures in literature who reaffirmed that *beskonfliktnost'* was no longer acceptable and even spoke of the desirability of 'multifaceted' characters in literature, but attacked the demand for 'sincerity' by advocates of 'the lyric.'[28] Berggol'ts and Aliger had been attacked for what they said in January 1953, too. Moreover, even after Stalin died, during the initial thaw, it was not at all clear what direction the political platform would take, and it is reported that many of those attacked were extremely apprehensive about what might be the consequences of their stands,[29] though this did not prevent Berggol'ts and Aliger from reiterating their positions at the Second Writers' Congress of 1954.[30]

The strong opposition of most who were authoritative in literature to the campaign for 'the lyric' of the 1950s was arguably because that campaign was not just about the lyric, or at any rate not in its potential implications. Though the points Berggol'ts made in 1953 were ostensibly to apply to just one sub-genre of poetry, regardless of what she intended or did not intend, they were in effect directed at restoring the 'I' to its due status, along with the lyric element in life (love, the emotions) and in literary representation. Potentially, the campaign threatened 'the collective' as an absolute, inviolate value and also the principle that Soviet citizens assume an extra-personal identity. Nadezhda Mandelshtam in her memoirs pronounced as a defining – and to her appalling – aspect of Stalinist culture the elimination of the pronoun *I* in any meaningful sense. Now, it would seem, writers were campaigning to have it restored. A fundamental of Stalinist culture would be eliminated.

Not so fast. The campaign for the 'lyric' should not be seen as a phenomenon of the 1950s. The very arguments made, and the characteristic discourse used by Berggol'ts and company in 1953–4, were widely to be found in literary debates and practices in those infamous years of the late 1930s, 1937–40.[31]

A good example would be the article 'Notes on Poetry' published in *Literaturnaia gazeta* of 28 December 1939 by Konstantin Simonov, then a young poet and literary critic. Simonov's first subheading in this article, one that others used in allied articles as a catchphrase, was 'On the Right to the Lyric.' Simonov asserts here, somewhat as Berggol'ts would do in 1953, that 'an honest lyrical book is always convincing.' Such a book, he continues, 'tells [*povestvuet*] about a person, but not about a typical person who with a firm, sometimes overly firm, stride progresses through novels and epic poems.' Rather, 'a hero of a true [*pravdivyi*] lyrical book is an author operating with his own poetic self-perception [*samovospriiatii*].' 'The author does not try to make him a composite person [*sobiratel'naia*].' If he did, the work would become a 'poetic falsehood [*fal'sh'*].' It is only in time, looking back, that we see in what appears to be an individualized lyric persona the typical traits of his time. But, Simonov observes, in contemporary literature all too often if two lovers meet in a work, the boy has to be a 'tank driver' and the girl a 'parachute jumper.' And if they meet somewhere in Moscow, before them they must see glowing the 'red letters of the metro [sign].' Simonov also attacks the demand for overt political content and sociological data in poetry: 'Following that logic, Pushkin in [his famous love poem] *'Ia pomniu chudnoe mgnovenie'* would have to list the number of serfs owned by [its addressee] A.P. Kern.' 'Some think the task of literature ... is now just to respond to the events of the day in straight, unmediated agitation,' he continues, but this is only a 'masked justification for the paltriness [*melkovodnosti*][32] of one's talents, which are not capable of seeing at a deeper level, beneath the hundreds of daily tasks, the overall movement of the epoch.' Though literature will not cease to address burning issues of the day, there should be no 'lowering to the lowest common denominator' (*nivelirovka*). Rather, 'as we approach Communism in literature there will develop a multifacetedness [*mnogogrannost'*], a breadth of horizons.'

Effectively, as in the Berggol'ts article of 1953, behind the front of discussing the lyric, we have here a demand to dismantle the conventions of socialist realism ('the typical,' the 'composite' character, 'unmediated agitation,' the focus on current issues, and couples treated not as individuals but as such poster categories as the 'tank driver' and the 'female parachute jumper'). Simonov's call for 'multifacetedness' could be read as a demand for greater pluralism and sophistication, for a less simplistic interpretation of the doctrine of mandatory *partiinost'*.

Simonov's article was outspoken and controversial but was far from the first or last such article advocating a return to the 'true' lyric. In fact the case was made at the First Writers Congress in 1934 by Nikolai Bukharin. In 1937–8, Bukharin was arrested and tried in the most public of the show trials and was not rehabilitated until perestroika. And yet, in those infamous years of the late 1930s, 1937–40, a campaign for the 'lyric' that used many arguments similar to his, became prominent in Soviet criticism and poetic practice.[33] It evolved progressively, especially after the Writers Union plenum of February 1937, where the 'lyric' was discussed. The campaign could also be seen as a development out of the cult of Vladimir Maiakovskii who, as soon as Stalin pronounced in 1935 that 'Maiakovskii was and remains the best and most talented poet of our Soviet epoch. Indifference to his memory is a crime,'[34] had been rescued from the problematic status his reputation had enjoyed since 1930 when he committed suicide. One result of Stalin's pronouncement was a recommendation that Soviet literature pay greater attention to poetry,[35] made both at the Writers Union plenum of 1935 and at a meeting of the Writers Union Presidium that October.[36] The percentage of poetry increased in both the literary journals and the publishing house lists.[37]

This shift prepared the way for the new attention to 'the lyric' that emerged later. Many of the key issues in the late 1930s campaign for 'the lyric' crystallized in the debate about 'political poetry' of early 1937. One of the most controversial and central articles in this debate, one that argues against simplistic poetry that translates the political platform directly into verse, was 'On Political Poetry' published in the May number for 1937 of the journal *Literaturnyi kritik* by its editor Elena Usievich. Here we see several of the arguments and the same code terms as in the campaign for the lyric of the 1950s. 'Paradoxical as it might sound,' Usievich insists, 'in Maiakovskii's cries about love unrequited there was more social content than in many lamentations on political themes written by the minor epigones of populist poetry.' Directly political poems are often 'prosaic and impersonal [*bezlichnost'*]' and often comprise no more than 'hastily rhymed slogans.' A worker of today is too sophisticated for this, she contends: he 'himself insists on his right to experience the most varied human feelings, including love.' 'Man is not a machine set up exclusively to "produce steel" and to express lyrically his love for the factory work bench, "My darling work bench, I don't want to go home."' Such verse is not 'genuine.' Poets need to be 'sincere.'[38]

In a later article of 1939, while discussing the lyric poet Stepan Schipachev,[39] Usievich observes,

> Some literati might call Shchipachev's poems 'apolitical.' But they show a complete misunderstanding about what the political in poetry, in art, means. It is in no way obligatory that in order to express a socialist sense of the world a poem has to begin or end with a hail to socialism or has to consist of a long list of parallels on the theme of 'us and them,' or 'it used to be, and now.' Very often a so-called political lyric is unpoetic and expresses nothing other than political slogans that have been assimilated very superficially. In Shchipachev's poetry the words *socialism* and *communism* rarely appear. And yet they are reflected in his poetry, but reflected precisely in a poetic way.'

The thing about Shchipachev is that he 'apprehends reality in a poetic way rather than attempts to put into poetry a perception which is utterly prosaic ... consequently several of his lyric poems that express completely personal feelings are particularly fine.'[40]

A long debate on the lyric and the political in literature ensued over the remaining years of the 1930s, generating dozens of articles like those of Simonov and Usievch.[41] What is important here is that the key terms of the discourse from 1937–40 – 'genuine [*podlinnyi*],' 'sincerity [*iskrennost'*],'[42] 'the lyric [*lirika*]' – were in effect picked up again in the early years of the fifties' thaws. In both instances the terms were invoked in the cause of dismantling the facile standard narrative of the production novel, the backbone of Soviet cultural production, in which the love plot was always subordinated to the twin overarching plots that chronicled the hero's fulfilment of the plan and political development.[43]

In the late 1930s several novels appeared that present the agonies and complexities of love in a more realistic vein, giving them a greater role in their heroes' lives, not just as subplots that are essentially subordinate to the plot about production.[44] To some extent this shift was reflected in film, too, most strikingly in Konstantin Iudin's *Four Hearts* (*Serdtsa chetyrekh*, 1941), where the focus is on love. Incidentally, one of the film's female leads was allegedly the real-life addressee of Simonov's 'Wait for Me.' In many respects *Four Hearts* represents a Soviet appropriation of the 'Ninotchka' plot, with the heroine a humourless mathematician who regards her younger sister's focus on clothes and love life as reprehensively frivolous and immature – until she herself is smitten by an army officer, even as her sister also finds her true love. In this film there is no monumental Moscow with its politically resonant landmarks such as the Kremlin and the Bolshoi, but rather a Moscow full of sites of assignation: phone booths, Gorky Park, and the dacha. At the end, the two couples who have been at a dacha go to a local station to buy tickets to Moscow. By the conventions of socialist realism, this journey to Moscow would be a fitting resolution of the love plot, the moment when the hero, brimming with self-realization, naturally impends towards the nation's 'centre.'[45] But the two couples change their minds, let the train leave, and return to the dacha. Admittedly, this film was banned when it was released on the very eve of the Nazi invasion, but largely because the principal male character was an army officer, and his distraction in love was deemed inappropriate for a military man, though the ban was also because the film was deemed too 'frivolous [*legkomyslennyi*].'[46]

As in the thaws of the 1950s, then, efforts to reinstate a 'genuine lyric' in culture recurrently met authoritative opposition, but also had a powerful lobby. For example, undeterred by attacks of early 1937, in late 1937 and early 1938 a series of meetings of poets were held in Moscow to try to foster more lyric poetry.[47] Somewhat as, in the thaws of the 1950s, particular literary periodicals advocated what was cryptically referred to as 'the lyric' (*Novyi mir, Literaturnaia gazeta*) and were attacked by writers publishing in others (*Oktiabr', Pravda*), in the late 1930s both lobbies had institutional affiliations.[48] The campaign for the lyric was centred in the journal *Literaturnyi kritik*, edited by Usievich, in *Literaturnaia gazeta*, and in the Moscow Institute for Philosophy, Literature and History (IFLI). Mikhail Lifshits, a Marxist literary theoretician and advocate of the lyric, was prominent in all three.[49]

It was not only an older generation of critics like Lifshits and Usievich who were proselytizers for a 'genuine' lyric. A conspicuous feature of this campaign in the late 1930s was the extent to which it was taken up by a new generation of writers, who were primarily poets rather than prose writers and included Simonov and Aliger.[50] In the mid- to late 1930s many of these new young poets had studied in either IFLI or the Literary Institute (Simonov had been at the Literary Institute from 1935 to 1938 and in IFLI from 1938 to 1939, while Aliger had studied at the Literary Institute from 1934 to 1937). Similarly, later, in the 1950s, a new generation emerged into literature under the banner of 'sincerity' and a more personal literature; the list includes the poets Evgenii Evtushenko[51] and Andrei Voznesenskii, and authors of 'youth prose,' such as Vasilii Aksenov.[52] As if to confirm these similarities, there was some continuity between those advocating the 'lyric' in the late 1930s and those advocating it in 1953 (e.g., Aliger and Lifshits). The list of those who participated in both campaigns could not include Berggol'ts, even though she had already been publishing in the 1930s, however, because she was excluded from the Writers Union during the purges of 1937.[53]

This mention of the purges throws into focus a problem alluded to earlier. In seeking to identify the campaign for the 'lyric' in the 1950s as a 'reprise' of a marked trend of the late 1930s – though one can establish much continuity in the arguments[54] and in the highly codified vocabulary used, and even to some extent in the participants – can one really identify the two campaigns, given that they took place in radically different circumstances? The campaign for the lyric of the 1930s developed in its initial stages more or less in tandem with the purges. The Writers Union plenum on poetry (the 'Pushkin plenum') of February 1937 finished the day before Bukharin was arrested (on 27 February 1937), and at its last session the poet Aleksandr Bezymenskii (himself a target of Bukharin's criticisms) attacked the speeches made by Bukharin and Radek at the First Congress of the Writers Union in 1934.[55] The day after Bukharin's arrest, an unsigned article appeared in *Pravda*, 'On Political Poetry,' which reported that *Pravda* had recently convened a meeting on this very topic at which speakers had discussed the dangerous recent tendency to advocate the Bukharinite position on poetry and claim that it need not be directly political.[56] At the party plenum, which came shortly after the writers' plenum, Stalin made two speeches (3 and 5 March) that provided the official narrative rationalizing the purges.[57] In other words, as in the 1950s, indeed probably more so, the stakes were high and the risks for those advocating a less crudely politicized poetry were palpable.

The campaign for 'the lyric' in the 1930s was inflected by the mentality of the purges and could even be seen as linked to them. In other words, the relative continuity of vocabulary between the campaign for 'the lyric' in the 1930s and the one of the 1950s should not blind us to differences.

During the campaign of the late 1930s both sides of the debate about 'the lyric' used purge accusations as weapons against their opponents. Usievich's 1937 article 'On Political Poetry' is quite distasteful in that again and again she buttresses her position by denouncing, in stock purge formulations, some writer or group recently purged and attributing to them, often questionably, the position she is arguing against. Similarly, once the leaders of the militant proletarian literary organization RAPP, which had been so powerful in the 1920s, were purged as Trotskyites in 1937, several campaigners for 'the lyric' jumped on the bandwagon and (unfairly) attributed 'schematicism, varnishing reality' to that organization, alleging that the theoreticians of their Litfront did not want 'human character' depicted but rather 'a schema of a human being as a bearer of a social tendency,' when in reality it had campaigned for representing the 'living man' and showing his inner conflicts.[58] This camp's detractors, in turn, suggested (not without a point) that the argument advanced by Usievich and others for less crudely politicized poetry, made in terms of the Soviet public having become more sophisticated and therefore needing a different kind of literature (an argument Berggol'ts was also to make in 1953), was very like the points made by Bukharin in his address to the First Congress of the Writers Union in 1934.[59]

One should not write such machinations off as *only* casuistry. The campaign of the late 1930s for 'the lyric' could be seen as an integral part of a terror campaign, with its rhetoric about tearing off 'masks' and its insistence that citizens not be deceived by appearances and even by apparently impeccable sociological and work profiles and instead look deep within their fellow citizens to reveal the 'true' self within. The campaign for 'the lyric' coincided with a turn to more inward-looking literary genres such as the diary; indeed one of the major controversies of 1939 was around poems by Vera Inber about her travels in Georgia, presented as a 'lyrical diary.'[60] Even the public heroes of the day, such as the polar explorer Papanin, were generating diaries. Though the diaries of these public figures were not particularly intimate or revelatory, the accompanying rhetoric was like that used by advocates of 'the lyric.'[61] Consider also Stanislavskii's *An Actor Prepares* (*Rabota aktera nad soboi*, 1938), which not only takes the diary form but also advocates an approach to acting whereby the actor in performing a role delves deep into *himself* and draws on his personal memories and emotions; he is actually to be preoccupied with his own emotional experiences while he acts out those of another. This technique is represented by Stanislavskii as the only way of creating on stage a *genuine* (*podlinnyi*), convincing character.

Other stark differences between the two contexts for the campaigns for 'the lyric' would include the fact that the one from the 1930s was conducted at a time when the cult of personality was coming into full gear, whereas in the initial post-Stalin years that cult was somewhat dismantled.

As we know, the late 1930s were marked by a cult of nineteenth-century Russian writers, and especially of Pushkin and Lermontov, whose anniversaries were celebrated in 1937 and 1939, respectively.[62] But these canonical writers were also appropriated in the service of the campaign for 'the lyric,' and hence accounts of them were very specifically inflected. Lermontov, for example, was characterized as a poet who was very involved in the 'personal' and 'feverishly sought his own expression for his feelings and thoughts' so that he began to 'look intensely [*pristal'no*] within himself.'[63]

The cults of Pushkin and Lermontov in the late 1930s have also been taken by Western historiography as signs of a retrograde Russian chauvinism.[64] By contrast, the initial post-Stalin thaws were fairly internationalist and were marked by the Moscow Youth Festival of 1957 and the revival of *Inostrannaia literatura*.

But the late 1930s were not only a chauvinist time. An important factor then, which also had bearing on the campaign for 'the lyric,' was the Spanish Civil War of 1936–9, which, linked as it was with the Soviet involvement in the international anti-fascist movement, gave much of its cultural life an internationalist colouring. In 1937 a major anti-fascist literary conference was held in Madrid and Valencia as shells were bursting all around, and at that venue Byron was advanced as the poet of the hour, or more specifically the Byron who had (by the accounts of him advanced there and in the Soviet press) perished fighting for freedom and independence for Greece. In Soviet Russia, Byron quickly became *the* exemplum of the lyric poet,[65] and the campaign for a less politicized poetry began to be identified with 'the lyric.'

This appropriation of Byron draws attention to another defining factor in the campaign for 'the lyric' of the 1930s, one that might set it apart from the campaign of the 1950s: the extent to which it was conducted in expectation of, and during, war. Indeed, the campaign intensified as the danger of war increased; it is no accident that 1939 was a high point in it.

The firebrand lyrical poets of IFLI were part of a new wave of patriotism among the young and romantic who took up the cause of the Spanish Civil War. When the Russo-Finnish War began, many signed up as volunteers, and several of them were killed in individual tragedies that were often represented as following the example of Byron. Simonov was one of these enthusiasts who took the Spanish Civil War and its martyred commander of an International Brigade, the Hungarian Communist writer Mate Zalka, there called General Lukacs, as his icon (Simonov wrote several poems extolling Zalka).[66] Simonov did not, for health reasons, participate in the war in Finland but did see battle in an earlier intense military engagement of the summer of 1939 in the East with the Japanese at Khalkhin-Gol.[67]

Although war was relatively absent as a context for the thaws of the 1950s – in fact, if anything this was a time of eased international tensions – the ethos of that earlier generation of firebrands inspired by the Spanish Civil War was central to the sense of identity of its emerging young generation. This is reflected, for example, in the cult of Ehrenburg and Hemingway, two bards of love and war who had spent time in Spain and written about it. Spain became the gold standard for many, who were also particularly taken by those Soviet authors who had sung of Spain in the late 1930s, such as Simonov and Pavel Kogan.[68]

Many young writers who emerged in the 1950s sought to revive the pathos and the passion they saw as defining this particular strand of the culture of the late 1930s. It offered them a possibility for a Soviet tradition alternative to the Stalinist 'excesses,' which were discredited in Khrushchev's 'secret' speech to the Twentieth Party Congress of February 1956 and elsewhere (after all, many of the heroes of Spain had been purged while the new generation of the late 1930s, who were inspired by their example, often made the ultimate sacrifice). They, along with Ol'ga Berggol'ts in 'Conversation about the Lyric,' decried the 'composure' (*ravnovesie*) that they saw as endemic to the culture of their time. Many writers of the initial thaws, as they sought to revive 'Spain,' sent their heroes to remote parts – the Virgin Lands, the taiga, Siberia, the Far North. And Anatolii Gladilin titled his youth prose novella of 1957 *Brigantine Raises Its Sails* – an allusion to the refrain of a poem by Pavel Kogan.

Youth prose, we will note, emerged during a period of relative reaction following the thaw of 1956 (due in part to the Hungarian uprising). Another marked theme in the culture of the second half of the 1950s – war fiction and films – can also be related to a trend among the young firebrands of the late 1930s. The war fiction and films that began appearing around 1957 were written as conscious re-evaluations of the standard heroic war fiction of late Stalinism. In particular – and this was hailed as a 'humanism' – they questioned the human cost of war and posed the

Dostoevskian question as to whether gaining an 'inch of ground' (*piad' zemli*), to cite the title of a novel by Grigorii Baklanov of 1959, could justify the extensive loss of life.[69] In the late 1930s a number of writers, and Simonov in particular, had argued for a more realistic depiction of war that would eschew the standard heroism and triumphalism and the simplistic poetry where the enemy is routed in just a few days, in favour of a more truthful (*pravdivyi*) account that shows the huge human cost and the difficulties.[70]

The demands for greater realism, for an end to purely external, superficial representation of characters, and to positive heroes who stride through the workplace with seven-league boots, have in fact, and not surprisingly, been recurrent in Soviet literature ever since the early harbingers of what was later codified as socialist realism first began to appear.[71] However, the specific terms of the two debates we have been following here – 'the lyric,' 'sincerity,' 'the true' or 'genuine' – were features only two times, in 1937–40, and in 1953–4.

'Wait for Me, and I Shall Return,' asked Simonov, but in what form will he return? Will the 'I' be unchanged by the dramatic circumstances he will have gone through in the interim? In the recurrent debate on 'the lyric,' this question applies, ironically, especially to Simonov himself who, by the time that debate resurfaced in 1953, had become an establishment figure and even replaced Aleksandr Tvardovskii (in 1954) as editor of *Novyi mir*. When in the initial thaw years Simonov entered the debates on 'the lyric,' he essentially followed the official line and advocated a literature that was 'multi-faceted' (*mnogogrannost'*), but not 'sincerity.' Someone had not waited intensely enough (*ochen' zhdi*). Recurrence can be a wily thing.

NOTES

1 The reference here is to Nicholas S. Timasheff, *The Great Retreat: The Growth and Decline of Communism in Russia* (New York, 1946).

2 George Gibian, *Interval of Freedom: Soviet Literature during the Thaw, 1954–57* (Minneapolis, 1960), 3.

3 See e.g., V. Grossman, 'Za pravoe delo,' *Novyi mir* 7 (1952): 3–131; 8 (1952): 74–227; 9 (1952): 5–122; 10 (1952): 128–209, esp. 7:178 and 8:157, 225; V. Kochetov, 'Zhurbiny,' *Zvezda* 1 (January 1952), esp. 57, and 2 (February 1952), esp. 18; V. Ovechkin, 'Lavuliruiushchie' (first published 1952), in his *Gosti v Stukachakh: Rasskazy i ocherki* (Moscow, 1978), 209–13; and

even his 'S frontovym privetom,' *Oktiabr'* 5–6 (1945) (Kochetov, Ovechkin, and Panferov were party members, and the first two are generally labelled conservatives); F. Panferov, 'Volga-matushka reka,' *Znamia* 8 (August 1953), and 9 (September 1953), which must have been substantially written before Stalin's death; V. Panova, 'Kruzhilikha,' *Znamia* 11 (November 1947), esp. 72. It is also to be noted that A. Nove argues in 'Some Notes on the 1953 Budget and the Peasants,' *Soviet Studies* 5, no. 3 (January 1954): 228–9, that the policies announced to the September 1953 plenum were essentially formulated before Stalin died. As if to confirm this point, several works published in early 1953 (passed for publication before Stalin died) suggest some of the policies outlined there, e.g., V. Tendriakov, 'Sredi lesov,' *Nash sovremennik* 2 (1953); and G. Troepol'skii, 'Iz zapisok agronoma,' *Novyi mir* 3 (1953): 78–112; 8 (1953): 52–99. See also Katerina Clark, 'Public Values in Post-Stalin Fiction' (MA thesis, Australian National University, 1966), esp. 22–43, 355–6.

4 E.g., D. Granin, 'Variant vtoroi,' *Zvezda* 1 (1949); and Granin, 'Sobstvennoe mnenie,' *Novyi mir* 8 (1956); V. Kaverin, parts 2 and 3 of the trilogy *Otkrytaia kniga.* Part 1 appeared in 1949, but the last two thirds of part 2, 'Dr Vlasenkova,' published in *Novyi mir* 2, 3, and 4 (1952), show a shift towards attitudes expressed more blatantly in part 3, 'Poiski i nadezhdy,' published in *Literaturnaia Moskva* 2 (1956).

5 A. Chakovskii, 'God zhizni,' *Oktiabr'* 8 and 9 (1956).

6 See such statements as 'And so once more the bearded forest bows to the ground and submits to arbitrary felling by agents of foreign dominions' (*Znamia* 10 [1953]: 80). Leonov also emphasizes the value of each human life (ibid., 94) and invokes disparagingly the maxim about the chips flying (*Znamia* 11 [1953]: 49, 99). D. Granin also uses this maxim negatively in 'Iskateli,' *Zvezda* 8 (1954): 50.

7 One of the most publicized measures in the late Stalin period was the law of 24 October 1948, which proposed the planting of fifteen million acres of new forest land, a law that was meant to redress the effects of severe erosion in the Russian countryside. That Leonov was genuinely concerned about forests was also evident later, when, under Brezhnev, he emerged again as a passionate environmentalist especially concerned with preserving Russia's forests.

8 I refer here to a series of sketches and novellas published by the writer Valentin Ovechkin between 1952 and 1954 (generally the same sketch was published both in *Pravda* and in *Literaturnaia gazeta*), culminating in 'Trudnaia vesna' of 1956: *Novyi mir* 3 (1956): 30–78; 5 (1956): 37–68; and 9 (1956): 121–78. These sketches effectively proposed major changes in the manage-

ment of agriculture that the party promulgated at around the same time. Similar views were presented in works by Gavril Troepol'skii and Vladimir Tendriakov.

9 The list includes Ilya Ehrenburg, 'O rabote pisatelia,' *Znamia* 10 (October 1953): 160–83; V. Pomerantsev, 'Ob iskrennosti v literature,' *Novyi mir* 12 (December 1953): 218–45; F. Abramov, 'Liudi kolkhoznoi derevni v poslevoennoi proze (Literaturnye zametki),' *Novyi mir* 1 (January 1954): 210–31; Mikhail Lifshits, 'Dnevnik Marietty Shaginian,' *Novyi mir* 2 (February 1954): 206–31; Mark Shcheglov, '"Russkii les" Leonida Leonova,' *Novyi mir* 5 (May 1954): 220–41; Ol'ga Berggol'ts, 'Protiv likvidatsii liriki,' *Literaturnaia gazeta,* 28 October 1954.

10 Ol'ga Berggol'ts, 'Razgovor o lirike,' *Literaturnaia gazeta,* 16 April 1953.

11 Ibid.

12 Film examples include Marlen Khutsiev and Feliks Mironer's *Vesna na Zarechnoi ulitse* (1956); El'dar Riazanov's *Karnaval'naia noch'* (1956); and Mikhail Kalatozov's *Letiat zhuravli* (1957). In literature one should note not only the love plot of Dudintsev's *Ne khlebom edinym,* with its motivated adultery, but more particularly the progressive development of the love plot in Viktor Nekrasov's works of this time: compare 'V rodnom gorode,' *Novyi mir* 10 (1954): 3–68; and 11 (1954): 97–178, to his 'Kira Georgievna,' *Novyi mir* 6 (1961): 70–126.

13 Berggol'ts, 'Razgovor o lirike.'

14 Ibid.

15 E.g., 'Preodolet' otstavanie v dramaturgii,' *Literaturnaia gazeta,* 16 March 1952.

16 See the collection of articles *Razgovor pered s"ezdom. Sbornik statei opublikovannykh pered vtorym vsesoiuznym s"ezdom pisatelei* (Moscow, 1954). Most of these articles were originally published in *Pravda* between 1953 and 1954.

17 As if to confirm this, Berggol'ts even decries the cult of personality, though she ostensibly associates that with bourgeois society, and in an article of 1956, 'Napisat' by takuiu knigu!' *Literaturnaia gazeta,* 21 April 1956, in which she praises Lenin, she calls for more '*pravda.*'

18 Ia. M. Strochkov, 'O stat'e V. Lenina 'Partiinaia organizatsiia i partiinaia literatura',' *Voprosy istorii* 4 (1956): 29–37.

19 See Ilya Ehrenburg, 'Ottepel',' part 2, *Znamia* 4 (1956), 41–6, 57–8, 68, 77–8.

20 Berggol'ts, 'Razgovor o lirike.'

21 Katerina Clark, 'Socialist Realism *with* Shores: The Conventions for the Positive Hero,' in *Socialist Realism without Shores,* ed. Evgeny Dobrenko and Thomas Lahusen (Durham, 1997), 27–50.

22 Abramov, 'Liudi kolkhoznoi derevni v poslevoennoi proze.'

23 Jerome J. McGann, *Romantic Ideology: A Critical Investigation* (Chicago, 1983), 63.

24 T.S. Eliot, 'Tradition and the Individual Talent,' *The Sacred Wood: Essays on Poetry and Criticism* (New York, 1998), 27–33, here 30, 31.

25 L. Ginzburg, *O lirike* (Moscow, 1964), 5.

26 [TASS], 'Arest gruppy vrachei-vreditelei,' *Literaturnaia gazeta*, 14 January 1953; 'K itogam poeticheskogo goda. V sektsii poezii Soiuza sovetskikh pisatelei,' *Literaturnaia gazeta*, 10 January 1953, reports that at a recent meeting 'Ol'ga Berggol'ts reproached contemporary lyricists with "fear of themselves" [*samoboiazni*], with a fear of expressing all the complexity, the unrepeatable particularity of the lyric persona.' Also note, 'The young poet E. Evtushenko' attacked N. Gribachev for the very 'fear of the self' Berggol'ts discussed. M. Aliger spoke in the same vein.

27 'V tvorcheskikh sektsiiakh,' *Literaturnaia gazeta*, 19 January 1952.

28 E.g., A. Surkov, 'Pod znamenem sotsialisticheskogo realizma,' *Pravda*, 25 May 1954, in which Surkov attacks Berggol'ts, Pomerantsev, Abramov, Lifshits, and Shcheglov, but also 'the antipatriotic activities of the cosmopolitans' – perhaps one of the reasons why Leonid Zorin, whose play *Guests* was also attacked in the article, was particularly nervous (see next note); V. Ermilov, 'Za sotsialisticheskii realizm,' *Pravda*, 3 June 1954 (who also brings up the negative example of Zoshchenko, as attacked in the Zhdanovist 'O zhurnalakh "Zvezda" i "Leningrad". Iz postanovleniia TsK VKP [b] ot 14 avgusta 1946 g.,' *Novyi mir* 1 [1946]: 1–3; and 'Doklad t. Zhdanova o zhurnalakh "Zvezda" i "Leningrad,"' *Novyi mir* 1 [1946]: 4–19; as well as the example of Pasternak: 'Let his poem ... be completely sincere. That does not prevent him from being false in his content').

29 Conversation of 30 April 2005 with Andrei Zorin, son of the dramatist Leonid Zorin. Leonid Zorin published in *Teatr* 2 (1954) his play *Guests* [*Gosti*], which depicted three generations of a Soviet family, with the middle generation represented by a corrupt and authoritarian high-ranking official. The play was produced in Leningrad, but when it opened at the Ermolova Theatre in Moscow, it was closed after one performance, and a sharp attack appeared in *Pravda*. The play was invariably listed thereafter when excesses of recent literature were cited. Zorin himself was so terrified by this turn of events that he developed acute tuberculosis and was considered to be dying (though in actuality he is still alive today).

30 See O. Berggol'ts, 'Protiv likvidatsii liriki'; 'Rech' M. Aliger,' and 'Vtoroi vsesoiuznyi s"ezd pisatelei. Vystupleniia uchastnikov s"ezda,' *Literaturnaia gazeta*, 23 December 1954; 'Rech' O. Berggol'ts,' *Literaturnaia gazeta*, 24 December 1954.

31 One also finds in the late 1930s attacks on '*beskonfliktnost'*.' See, for example,

'Obraz sovetskogo cheloveka v sovremennoi proze. Iz doklada P. Pavlenko i F. Levina na otkrytom sobranii partiinoi organizatsii Soiuza sovetskikh pisatelei 31 ianvaria,' *Literaturnaia gazeta*, 5 February 1941.

32 One is reminded here of Melkovodsk – the name of the backward town in provincial Russia that is the setting for G. Aleksandrov's film *Volga-Volga* of 1938.

33 See also note 31.

34 *Literaturnaia gazeta*, 12 December 1935.

35 E.g., B. Runin, 'Lirik-tribun,' *Literaturnoe obozrenie* 3 (1939): 3–7.

36 'Stenogramma zasedaniia Presidiuma SSP SSSR 15/X 1935 goda,' Rossiiskii gosudarstvennyi arkhiv literatury i iskusstva (RGALI), 631/15/17/14, 48; this reweighting in poetry's favour was intensified in 1938, when the State Literary Publishing House decided to increase significantly both the number of titles in poetry and their print runs (Vladimir Grib, 'Obsuzhdenie plana Goslitizdata na 1939 god,' *Literaturnaia gazeta*, 20 October 1938.

37 Initially, the return to poetry was also to some extent occasioned by the policy of promoting 'folk epics,' which extolled the achievements of the Soviet Union and the feats of its hero-leaders Lenin and Stalin. One could even speculate that the campaign for 'the lyric' was to some extent a reaction against the doggerel pseudo-folk poetry published in 1936–7.

38 E. Usievich, 'K sporam o politicheskoi poezii,' *Literaturnyi kritik* 5 (1937): 70, 87, 90, 89, 90 and 102, respectively.

39 A potential difference between the two campaigns might be the fact that O. Berggol'ts in 'Razgovor o lirike' (1953) finds Shchipachev too 'rational' and insufficiently 'lyrical,' while Usievich in 1939 extols him as an example of the lyric poet. E. Usievich, 'Lirika,' *Literaturnaia gazeta*, 30 June 1939.

40 E. Usievich, 'Lirika,' *Literaturnaia gazeta*, 30 June 1939.

41 E. Usievich, 'V zashchitu politicheskoi poezii,' *Literaturnyi kritik* 5 (1937); and the response: Dzhek Al'tauzen, 'V zashchitu politicheskoi poezii,' *Literaturnaia gazeta*, 1 November 1937. In no. 63 there is a whole page of criticism in which, among other things, Usievich is accused of peddling the Bukharin line (she is also attacked in 'O politicheskoi poezii,' *Pravda*, 28 February 1937; E. Usievich, 'Lirika,' *Literaturnaia gazeta*, 30 June 1939: 'a socialist attitude to life without "*vykriki*"'; E. Usievich [review of] 'Molodaia Moskva. Sbornik stikhov,' *Literaturnoe obozrenie* 10 (1937): 9.

42 E.g., A. Evgen'ev, 'Proshchanie s liubimym. O chetyrekh sonetakh S. Kirsanova,' *Literaturnaia gazeta*, 1938, no. 57.

43 E.g., M. Gus, 'A gde zhe liubov'?,' *Literaturnaia gazeta*, 13 October 1940: 'Love relations in literature are too tied to politics. Engels believed that true socialism will come from true marriage and choice in love.'

44 E.g., R. Fraerman, *Dikaia sobaka dingo* (Moscow, 1939), about first love between adolescents, a love complicated by divorce and step-siblings, or V. Kaverin'a *Dva kapitana* (1938–44). Kaverin also wrote about the need to restore the love plot to its due place in Soviet literature so that readers would have '*pravdivye knigi.*' V. Kaverin, 'Nenapisannye knigi,' *Literaturnaia gazeta* 1939, no. 45.

45 See S. Gerasimov's film *Semero smelykh* of 1936, where the hero and heroine opt to stay at the research station (i.e., opt for duty in the most testing conditions rather than return to a comfortable life).

46 See documents nos. 64, 65, 66 in *Vlast' i khudozhestvennaia intelligentsia. Dokumenty TsK RKP (b) – VKP (b) – VChK – OGPU – NKVD o kul'turnoi politike 1917–1953 gg.*, comp. Andrei Artizov and Oleg Naumov (Moscow, 1999), 470–3.

47 See, e.g., 'Satira i lirika,' *Literaturnaia gazeta* 1938, no. 12.

48 One could speculate, for example, that the fact that the campaign was at its height in 1939, when Simonov wrote his article, had something to do with the demise in that year of Vladimir Stavsky as head of the Writers' Union.

49 Grigorii Pomerants, 'Zapiski gadkogo utenka,' *Znamia* 7 (1993): 143. A complication in discussing the campaign for the lyric in the 1930s is the fact that Lifshits was Lukacs's closest Soviet associate, and in his writings of this time Lukacs had identified the epic as the quintessential genre of socialist realism – a position Bakhtin was effectively attacking in his essay 'Epos i roman.' Mikhail Bakhtin. 'Epos i roman: O metodologii issledovaniia romana,' *Voprosy literatury i estetiki* (Moscow, 1975): 447–83.

50 Margarita Aliger, 'Vo ves' golos,' *Literaturnaia gazeta* 1940, no. 31.

51 The theme of 'sincerity' and the cause of truly representing the self were also taken up by the new generation of poets, especially by Evtushenko, whose 'Stantsiia Zima' is presented as a leaf out of the poet's own autobiography, a personal response to the 'revelations' of 1956 (though in producing this work he could also be seen as a court poet celebrating the change of ruler).

52 Incidentally, both Simonov's poetry and youth prose were distinguished by breaking with the heavy formal language of conventional Soviet literature and using conversational speech (in the case of Vasilii Aksenov, slang).

53 'Averbakhovskie prispeshniki v Leningrade,' *Literaturnaia gazeta*, 20 May 1937.

54 For example, Vissarion Belinsky's comments on Lermontov were frequently cited during both campaigns as supporting evidence.

55 'Plenum pravleniia Soiuza pisatelei,' *Literaturnaia gazeta*, 27 February 1937.

Bukharin's expulsion from the party was announced in *Literaturnaia gazeta* on 10 March.

56 'O politicheskoi poezii,' *Pravda,* 28 February 1937.

57 The publication of these speeches in *Pravda* was delayed, appearing on 29 March and 1 April respectively.

58 'Vykorchevat' bez ostatka,' *Literaturnaia gazeta,* 18 May 1937.

59 'Doklad N. I. Bukharina o poezii, poetike i zadachakh poeticheskogo tvorchestva v SSSR,' *Pervyi s"ezd pisatelei. Stenograficheskii otchet* (Moscow, 1934), 479–503.

60 E.g., A. Fadeev, 'O poeme Very Inber,' *Literaturnaia gazeta,* 5 December 1938; 'Poemy Very Inber i ee kritiki,' *Literaturnoe obozrenie* 3 (1939): 59–62.

61 *Sovetskoe iskusstvo* 47, 12 April 1938.

62 Actually, some resisted imposing great writers from the past as models for contemporary literature. For example, Aleksandr Fadeev, at a meeting of Moscow writers in April 1939, insisted that poets should not be made to imitate Pushkin and Maiakovskii. 'Obshchemoskovskoe sobranie pisatelei. Doklad tov. A Fadeeva ob itogakh XVIII s"ezda VKP(b),' *Literaturnaia gazeta* 1939, no. 22.

63 P. Antokol'skii, 'Lermontov,' *Literaturnaia gazeta* 1938, no. 56.

64 David Brandenberger, *National Bolshevism: Stalinist Mass Culture and the Formation of Modern Russian National Identity, 1931–1956* (Cambridge, MA, 2002), 2.

65 Mikhail Zabludovskii, 'Poemy Bairona,' in Dzhordzh Bairon [George Byron], *Poemy,* trans. Georgii Shengeli (Moscow, 1940), 1:5–26.

66 L.I. Lazarev, *Konstantin Simonov. Zhizn' i tvorchestvo* (Moscow, 1990), 17.

67 I. Vishnevskaia, *Konstantin Simonov. Ocherk tvorchestva* (Moscow, 1966), 7.

68 See, e.g., Simonov's poem 'General' about Lukacs.

69 Grigorii Baklanov, 'Piad' zemli,' *Novyi mir* 5 (1959): 3–45; and 6 (1959): 62–111. Other examples include Iu. Bondarev, 'Batal'ony prosiat ognia,' *Molodaia gvardiia* 5 and 6 (1956); M. Sholokhov, 'Sud'ba cheloveka,' *Pravda,* 31 December 1956 and 1 January 1957; and V. Starikov, 'Shchedroe serdtse,' *Moskva* 6 (1957). Note also Simonov's own 'Panteleev,' *Moskva* 11 (1957), esp. 114.

70 Lazarev, *Konstantin Simonov,* 34. This position was also shared by other poets, such as Aleksei Surkov and Aleksandr Tvardovskii, who served in the Russo-Finnish Campaign of the winter of 1939–40.

71 See, e.g., A. Voronskii, 'Literaturnye zametki,' *Prozhektor* 5 (1925): 25. Note also the debate on the theatre of 1929 in 'S potolkom ili bez potolka?' and the RAPP theory of the 'living hero' of 1929–30 which was opposed to 'revolutionary romanticism.'

3 Khrushchev's Gulag: The Soviet Penitentiary System after Stalin's Death, 1953–1964

MARC ELIE

The camps aren't our ideal.

– Georgii Malenkov, at the Central Committee Presidium Session, 8 February 1954[1]

With the understatement in the epigraph of this article, the head of the Soviet government summed up the dissatisfaction of the post-Stalin party elite with the GULag (*Glavnoe upravlenie lagerei*, Main Camp Administration).[2] In the post-war years, if the need for profound reforms in the detention system was obvious for most of the higher party functionaries, they were unable to take any substantial step until Stalin's death. In 1953–4, the Soviet camp system experienced a major crisis, as it went through an unprecedented series of prisoners' strikes and uprisings. Stalin's heirs were worried about the hideous penitentiary machine and inefficient economic colossus the dictator left to them. Despite their discontent with the Stalinist model of the camp as giant unit of confinement and production located in a remote place and committed to supplying a workforce to great industrial projects, in February 1954 the Soviet leaders could not agree on an 'ideal' penal system to replace the old one.

Given the importance of the Gulag in Stalin's government and the menace it represented for the social order after his death, its future was a central issue in his heirs' reform agenda. As with other pending structural reforms of the Thaw, though, the reconfiguration of the Gulag was a matter of disagreement and debate among officials of central agencies. Depending on how they envisioned the post-Stalin societal system as a whole, they expressed contradicting views on how the Gulag should be reshaped. Should the detention system remain a lighter version of Stalin's Gulag, or should it be based on new organizational and disciplinary principles? Answering this question implied defining the size of the penitentiary network, its place in the economy and state budget, and the role of the re-education of prisoners in their economic exploitation. Along with discussions of principles, bureaucratic conflicts and personal rivalries among leaders played an important part in the rambling developments of the Gulag reform. Lavrentii Beria, Georgii Malenkov, and Nikita Khrushchev successively attempted to implement their projects for reforming the Gulag.

Relatively little attention has been given to the evolution of the Gulag after Stalin's death.[3] The opinion is widespread that, with the crisis of 1953–4 and the liberation of most political prisoners, the Gulag was quickly dismantled.[4] Mitigating this perspective, I argue that in the ebb and flow of the Thaw, the penitentiary system appears as transitional and highly versatile, as it evolved from Stalin's camp model into a mechanism of limited political and penal repression. The Gulag, though suppressed as an all-Union agency in 1960, went through constant reorganizations until the mid-1960s and maintained throughout some fundamental organizational features it had had under Stalin.

Saving the Gulag, 1953–1956

Immediately after Stalin's death in March 1953, Lavrentii Beria, appointed minister of a reunited Ministry of Internal Affairs (MVD) including the State Security (MGB), launched a broad reform to rationalize the repressive system around three priorities:[5] dividing up the police, imprisonment, and economic functions formerly merged in a single agency, the MVD, among different ministries; cutting most of the MVD construction program; and radically reducing the incarcerated population. It is important to note that this purely organizational reform was not directed against the massive use of forced labour in the Soviet economy.[6] On the contrary, Beria and his party colleagues saw this reform as necessary for maintaining the camp system. However, the reform deepened the crisis it was deemed to cure and was therefore partially reversed after Beria's arrest in the summer of 1953.

By the end of Stalin's reign, the MVD had grown into one of the biggest economic agencies in the USSR. It supervised sixteen economic Main Directorates (*Glavnye upravlenia*, GU): Some of them covered the economic structures of entire regions (like Eniseistroi in Krasnoiarsk Territory or Dal'stroi in the Northeast), others encompassed entire industrial sectors (like the Main Directorates for the Mica and Asbestos Industries), others still were created for the sake of a unique grand enterprise (like the construction of the Volga–Baltic Sea canal). Each directorate had its own network of camps extracting forced labour.[7] In addition to its own economic sites, the GULag as an MVD Main Directorate controlled the regional and republican administrations of the camps and colonies (such as the camp administrations of the Sverdlovsk region, of Byelorussia). Subordinated to one of the directorates, the camp (*ispravitel'no-trudovoi lager', ITL*) was the key unit of workforce detention and management. The camp included up to several tens of thousands of inmates and was subdivided into camp sections, officially up to 3,000 prisoners each. By Stalin's death the MVD detained 2,624,537 convicts.[8]

Beria's first steps were to dismantle the economic empire of the Gulag, with the goal to free the MVD from its industrial and economic activities. The MVD was to become a pure police agency without production tasks. A few weeks after the death of his master, Beria obtained an almost 50 per cent reduction of the MVD 105-billion ruble construction program by scrapping the most gigantic and unworkable canal, road, and railroad construction projects of the late Stalin era operated by the MVD. The so-called great construction projects of socialism, such as the Turkmenistan canal and the railroad track Chum–Salekhard–Igarka, had dubious economic prospects and were a waste of human and material resources, Beria argued.[9] Earlier still, he obtained the transfer of all economic directorates and their subordinate industrial and construction enterprises from the MVD to the corresponding economic ministries.[10] This separation of economic and penal functions had important consequences for the camp administration. Camp commanders lost control over the economic enterprises that had belonged to the MVD. Their competence was now limited to watching over prisoners and farming them out to construction and production projects, while the economic ministries appointed their own personnel to manage the enterprises they received.

Separating the camp hierarchy and the industrial management put an end to the principle of *edinonachalie* (one-man management). However, some large industrial complexes were ultimately excluded from the reform.[11] In the logging industry, the reform was carried out with difficulty. The MVD Main Directorate of Timber Industry Camps (GULLP) with all its branches was transferred to the civilian Ministry of Forest and Paper

Industry and renamed *Glavspetsles*. To get prison labourers, the logging enterprises henceforth had to contract with the regional camp administration. However, MVD camp bosses and the ministry's high-ranking officials were pressed hard to work with each other. Both parties claimed *edinonachalie* for themselves. The minister of timber and paper industry, Georgii Orlov, maintained in May 1953 that in the new configuration the camp administration was preoccupied only by the issue of discipline, while the management cared only about plan fulfilment, and each authority ignored the concerns of the other. Meant to rationalize the workforce management, the reform led to a sharp decrease in productivity and failure to fulfil the timber plan in 1953.[12]

As Beria wanted the MVD to lose not only its economic power but also most of its penal responsibilities, he transferred the GULag from the MVD to the Ministry of Justice.[13] Furthermore, several hundred camps formerly administered by the MVD economic directorates were shifted to the GULag. The MVD retained only the most severe camp network of the GULag's detention system, the 'special camps' (*osobye lageria*) and 'special prisons,' designed to confine 221,435 'especially dangerous' political, war, and common criminals in the hardest possible conditions.[14] For its part, the Ministry of Justice was in charge of carrying out the sentences of the majority of prisoners. After the redistribution of its economic and penal functions, Beria could now focus the MVD on what he considered its core objective: the protection of state security.[15]

On 27 March 1953, the Presidium of the Supreme Soviet adopted an amnesty edict, following Beria's recommendations to remove all prisoners serving short sentences (less than five years) and all prisoners condemned for small economic and office crimes.[16] The prisoners unfit for labour, who were a financial burden to the camps (too young, too old, pregnant or with young children, disabled, ill), were to recover their freedom, too, except for those condemned for counter-revolutionary and the most dangerous common crimes.[17] Under the March amnesty, 1,201,738 prisoners left the camps and colonies.[18] In October, there remained 1,055,950 prisoners in the camps and colonies of the Ministry of Justice.[19] The mass release of prisoners brought about a drastic reduction in the 'Gulag Archipelago': 40 per cent of 3,274 camp units were closed in 1953, implying an equivalent 40 per cent cutback in GULag personnel.[20]

The massive release had a detrimental effect on the prisoners who were left behind. In the summer of 1953, the situation became incontrollable in the camps where hardened prisoners, dangerous recidivists, and resolute nationalists, among others, were still detained.[21] In some places,

Inmate population, USSR, 1940–70: Camps, colonies, and prisons of the NKVD-MVD-MGB (1940–60); camps and colonies of the MVD (without prisons) (1962–70).

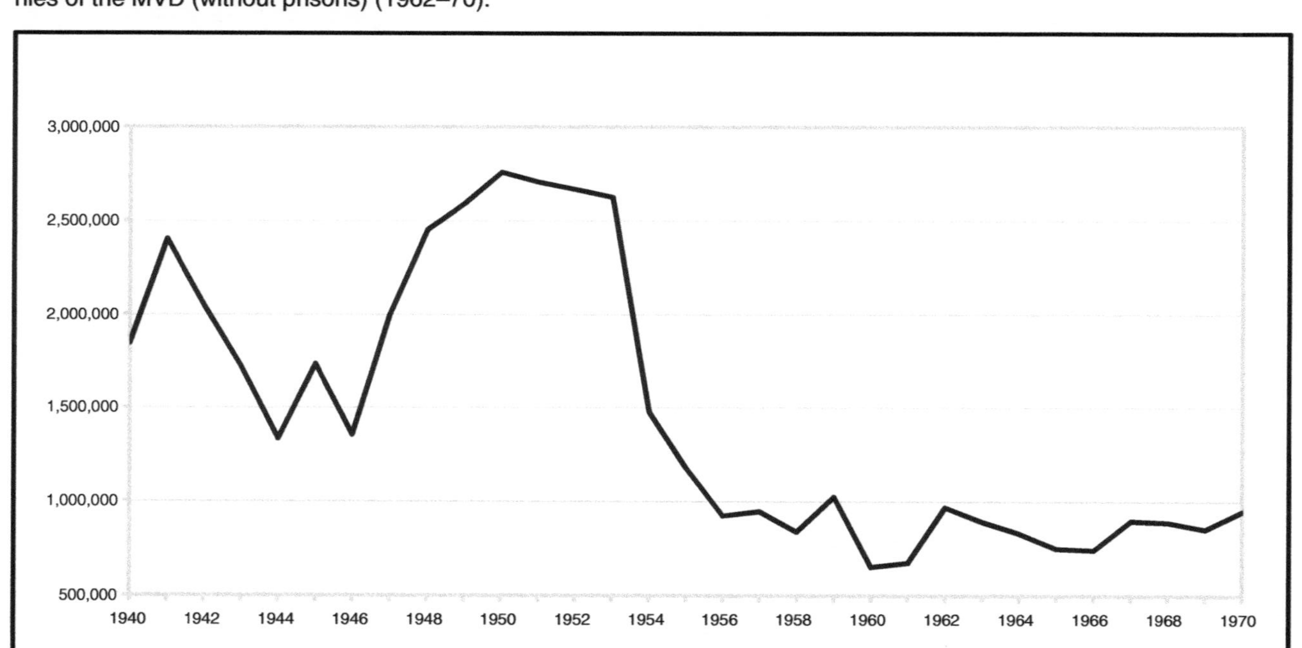

Sources: Viktor Zemskov, 'Deportatsii naseleniia. Spetsposelentsy i ssyl'nye. Zakliuchennye,' in *Naselenie Rossii v XX veke: Istoricheskie ocherki*, ed. V.B. Zhiromskaia (Moscow, 2001), 2:183; GARF R-7523/95a/109/99–101 (1961); R-7523/95a/110/29 (1962); R-9492/6/290/3 (1963–70).

the camp bosses, disoriented by the turmoil of changes, had lost the control over the situation. There was mass disorder in the special camps – in Gorlag in May to July, Noril'sk and Viatlag in July, Rechlag during July and August, and Pechorlag in November 1953. In Steplag from May to June 1954 the prisoners staged a forty-day rebellion, demanding an improvement of living and working conditions as well as a review of their cases. The revolt was quelled in a bloodbath.[22]

The reorganization of the Gulag that Beria sought to implement partly failed. The amnesty did not break the penal machine; on the contrary, the panic created by mass rumours of crimes committed by the amnestied led the party leadership to take harsh law-and-order measures in the fall of 1953, increasing the monthly influx of new Gulag convicts.[23] Moreover, the difficulties in the camps convinced the leaders that the Ministry of Justice was unable to manage the confusion within the GULag.[24] By the beginning of 1954, the directorate was transferred back to the MVD.[25] At the same moment, the MVD lost the secret services, which were now entrusted to a new separate agency, the KGB (Committee for State Security).[26] Thus, the pre-March 1953 organizational scheme of the repressive agencies was re-established. Sergei Kruglov, who had been in charge of the MVD during the whole post-war period and became its head again after Beria's arrest, applied himself to fulfilling Malenkov's reform endeavour of maintaining the ministry's economic power and ensuring its financial viability. Beria's model of contractual relations between camps and enterprises lost ground: the proportion of prisoners farmed out fell from 67.6 per cent in October 1953 to 43.3 per cent in July 1954.[27] Kruglov consolidated the ministry's economic potential by recreating some economic main directorates and re-establishing the principle of *edinonachalie* within them. The timber industry was reintegrated in the MVD with fifteen timber camp directions. At the beginning of 1956, 237,909 convict workers, one-third of all inmates, were felling trees for the GULLP.[28]

Moreover, the political leadership still entrusted the MVD with the in-house carrying out of strategic economic projects. It transferred back to the MVD two industrial main directorates (*glavnye upravleniia*, or *glavki*) from the recently created Ministry of Medium Machine-Building, the Main Directorates for Special Construction (*Glavspetsstroi*) and for Industrial Construction (*Glavpromstroi*), fulfilling secret construction assignments for the Soviet nuclear project. These *glavki* took control over some twenty camps delivering roughly 126,500 convict labourers. The MVD even played a vanguard – if fairly short-lived – role in the newly launched campaign for Virgin Lands' conquest.[29] In July 1954, Kruglov proposed to Khrushchev the idea of developing the farming camp of Karaganda and building ten new grain state farms in the Karaganda region.[30] The Central Committee (CC) and the Council of Ministers entrusted the forced-labour system with a still broader program: it was to build thirty-one grain state farms, 129 grain storage facilities, and a harvester plant in Pavlodar. In March 1955, Kruglov went on a three-week journey to Kazakhstan to supervise the operations.[31] These construction works employed 17,085 prisoners in the summer of 1955, and Kruglov anticipated providing some 14,000 more.[32] Moreover, the party leadership needed specialists to tame nature in Kazakhstan. In the spring of 1954, Khrushchev ordered Kruglov to free 8,000 convicted agriculture specialists from the camps and colonies. These tractor drivers, repair mechanics, agronomists, and veterinarians were assigned to the Virgin Lands for compulsory work.[33]

As second priority, the political leadership established or re-established release mechanisms to free prisoners regularly. This was a long-sought progress for Kruglov, who, in an attempt to step up labour productivity, had for years petitioned Stalin to release detainees incapable of working and to create real incentives for prison labour.[34] In July 1954, Kruglov obtained the reintroduction of early conditional release for good behaviour, suppressed in 1939.[35] Moreover, the 1954 Statute of the Corrective Labour Camps and Colonies brought the system of work credits into general use: for one workday, a detainee could get up to a three-day sentence reduction if employed in common works, and up to a two-day sentence reduction if employed in subsidiary works, depending on his or her performance.[36] The economic agencies encouraged such measures because they were strongly interested in offering incentives to the prisoners working on their sites.[37] These early release mechanisms hastened mass exits from the camps, as did specific mass amnesties meant to free the Gulag finances of those prisoners who where a 'burden.' In the summer of 1955, the Gulag detained 122,148 invalids, 16,345 persons aged sixty or more, and 8,556 pregnant women or mothers with newborns (16 per cent of all prisoners) whom it couldn't farm out to enterprises and who cost him 650 million rubles yearly.[38] An amnesty released 77,333 of them on 3 September 1955.[39]

From Camps to Colonies? 1956–1960

By the beginning of 1956 the Gulag had slimmed down to a third of its 1953 level with 781,630 inmates.[40] Even though the majority of the unworkable industrial projects had been cancelled under Beria, the MVD under Premier Malenkov and Minister Kruglov stabilized as an important economic agency. However, Khrushchev, who was becoming *primus inter pares* at the CC Presidium, advocated a different reform vision. To him the problem with Stalin's Gulag was not primarily in the ministerial organization or in the technocratic viewpoint on how to raise the profitability of forced labour. The problem was ideological and social. Khrushchev advocated a regionalized system of small penitentiary units (called colonies) focused upon prisoner reform, with less separation from the familiar environment, with skilled work, and with regime relaxation as a reward for good behaviour. Khrushchev idealized the penitentiary system of the 1920s, what he called 'Dzerzhinsky's system,' and opposed it to the model of huge camp complexes at the core of the Soviet penitentiary and economic organization under Beria and Kruglov. The emphasis on re-education implied the end not only of the MVD's own great projects, but of the contract system as well. Under the colony system, the prisoners could no longer be farmed out to enterprises to do the job free workers refused to do – hard physical and unqualified labour in dangerous working conditions on remote industrial sites. The colonies had to create their own production facilities.[41] Symbolically enough, the GULag (Main Directorate of the Camps) was renamed Main Directorate of Corrective Labour Colonies (GUITK) at the end of 1956, to signify the end of the camp era.[42]

The first secretary set up a new reform agenda for the MVD, implying the participation of central and regional party organizations. At the end of 1955, Kruglov was dismissed. The party leadership accused him of concealing the real state of affairs in the MVD and managing the Gulag without much party interference. In particular, he was charged with organizing mass amnesties to save on Gulag budget without regard for their social consequences: since 1953 the political elite had been concerned with disorders during liberation operations and high recidivism rates among ex-convicts.[43] To break with the past, Khrushchev appointed his man at the top of the MVD, a devoted party official without Chekist ties – Nikolai Dudorov (1906–77).[44] Khrushchev expected Dudorov, a specialist in construction known as an effective organizer, to build a new network of penitentiary institutions replacing the camps. The aim was to create a downsized penitential system that would not constantly menace public order with upheavals and massive violence. Dudorov's appointment heralded an intensification of the party's role in the Gulag reform. This change hit Premier Malenkov, who had protected Kruglov and promoted the MVD's role as industrial operator.[45] Indeed, Dudorov's first step was to remove the production directorates from the MVD's purview.[46]

Two months after his appointment, on 5 April 1956, Dudorov presented the CC with an ambitious reform project for the Gulag to 'renew the approach to re-educating prisoners.' The minister drew up a disastrous picture of the state of affairs in the places of detention. Revealingly, he named the social organization of professional criminals in the camps – and not economic or managerial issues – as the greatest ill. To him the challenge was to get rid of the unofficial network of power created by the 'recidivists and other hardened criminals' who 'exert a corrupt influence on' the other prisoners, 'commit pillage, murder, and other grave crimes,' and 'live the life of parasites at the expense of the work of honest prisoners.' For Dudorov this category of prisoners represented a real danger to the penal system: criminals grouped in rival gangs and were so well organized that the camp administration had no effective means to fight against them. In his memo, Dudorov said no single word on the 'counter-revolutionaries,' until then the greatest political and social foe in the camps and elsewhere.[47] Most of the politicals had been already liberated by the time Dudorov became minister: only 92,000 of them remained by April 1956, some 10 per cent of the overall prison population (against 460,000 representing 22 per cent of all prisoners at the beginning of 1953).[48] Since 1955 the professional criminals had replaced the politicals as enemy number one for the Gulag bosses in Moscow.[49]

The camp system in Dudorov's presentation was the breeding ground for these perverted social phenomena. In giant camps, the physical separation of different categories of prisoners' activities after work, and organization of vocational training were next to impossible: Criminals made use of this confused situation to impose their rule on the other prisoners.

The minister suggested 'a revision of the current forms and methods of the corrective labour institutions' activities.' Demanding a stricter separation of prisoner categories from each other, he claimed that professional criminals could not be re-educated, because in their 'consciousness [*soznanie*] anti-social views had set up.'[50] As their mindsets were deeply affected by 'parasite' principles, none of the means usually employed by the camp administration would bring them into line. Dudorov suggested shutting these prisoners away in two special corrective labour prisons beyond the polar circle to resume the construction of the unfinished railroad track Salekhard–Igarka that Beria had cancelled in 1953. This unusual concept of a 'corrective labour prison,' almost an oxymoron in Soviet penal theory, was meant to combine the hardness and isolation of prison detention with the possibility of employing the prisoners as a labour force in the most exhausting outdoor jobs.[51] Although contradicting the principles of Khrushchev's re-education policy, the conviction that the professional criminals were 'incorrigible' had been widespread among the Gulag headship since at least 1954. After the suppression of the special camps in 1954, it was admitted that gang members could not be returned to normal camps and had to be locked up in prison. In the camps, they 'could not be reformed' and exerted a corrupting influence on the other inmates. Already by May 1954, 11,560 'incorrigible prisoners' had been transferred to prisons.[52]

To perfect the separation of different categories of prisoners, Dudorov suggested increasing the number of common prisons for severe offenders. The rest of the convicts, sentenced for minor offenses, were to be held in corrective labour colonies. The camps had to be fully liquidated as a detention form. Furthermore, the practice of mass displacing of convicts (*massovye etapirovaniia*) from one corner of the Soviet Union to another was to cease. In order to make their social reintegration easier, prisoners were to serve their sentences with a minimum of isolation from the rest of society – in the regions where they had been condemned.

In the labour colonies, as the projected new core of the Gulag system, re-education by labour was to become the main goal of detention. Within the system of great camp complexes and the managerial contract model, able-bodied inmates were overwhelmingly employed as 'gross workforce' (*valovaia rabochaia sila*) at hard physical labour in timbering, mining, and construction.[53] The use of prison labour in the economy was the pride and joy of Kruglov, but it was fairly incompatible with the now proclaimed goal of re-education.[54] In Dudorov's view labour should serve the prisoners' re-education rather than economic priorities. Therefore, hard physical and unqualified labour would be banned from the colonies, which instead were to be involved in consumer goods industries and other local industrial and agricultural enterprises. During their detention, prisoners would acquire useful training to increase their ability to find a job upon release.

Dudorov's proposal was the product of a compromise between three

Proportion of Political Prisoners in the GULag, 1951–60

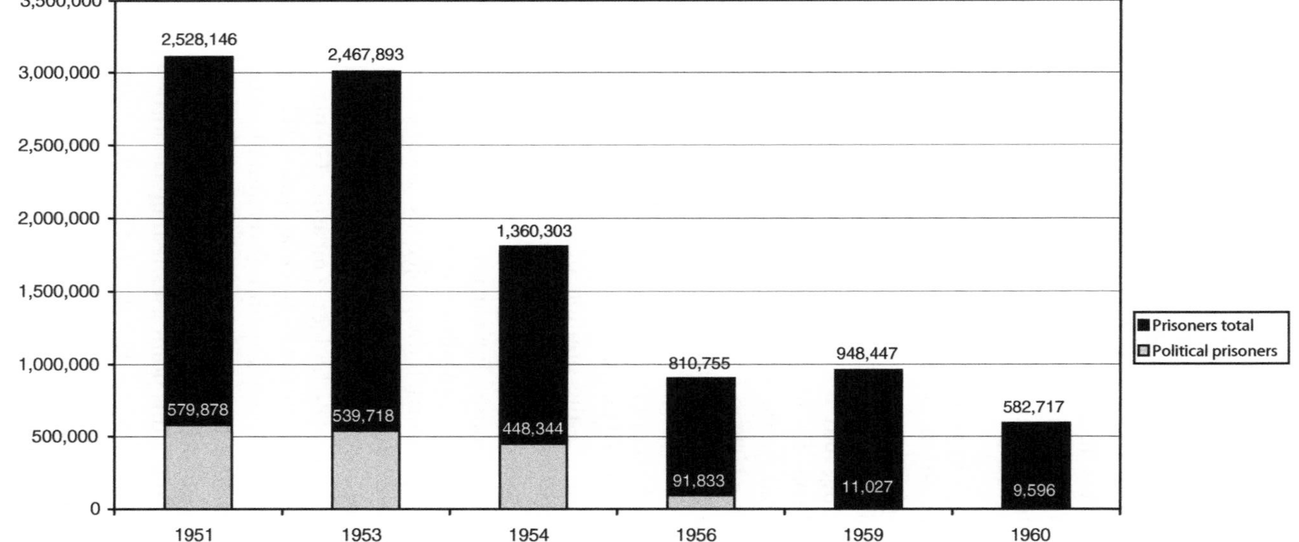

Sources: (1951 and 1959), Viktor Zemskov, 'GULAG (istoriko-sotsiologicheskii aspekt),' *Sotsiologicheskie issledovaniia* 6 (1991): 10–27, and 7:3–16; (1953) GARF R-9414/1/507/69–73; (1 April 1954), GARF R-9401/2/450/463–79; (1 April 1956); and (1960), Kokurin and Petrov, GULAG, 401–2 and 443.

tendencies: Khrushchev's ideas of smaller colonies, the Stalinist penitentiary model of extensive industrial development, and criminological ideas among the MVD leadership. The proposal to see the 'Death Road' project resurrected may have come from the nostalgia among Gulag high functionaries for the spectacular construction enterprises of the Stalin era. As for the effort to isolate the gang members from the rest of the prisoners, it was borrowed from new criminological thoughts in the Gulag administration on the existence of dangerous criminal structures in the camps and the inability of the penitentiary system to re-educate gang members.[55]

The commission in charge of examining Dudorov's project turned it down. The chairman of the KGB, Ivan Serov, opposed every single suggestion: the suppression of the camps, the creation of regional colonies, the softening of the regime in the process of re-education, the turn to vocational training, and the extension of the prison network without forced labour. From his ideological standpoint, he actually supported the traditional Stalinist model of huge camps located in remote regions and employing convicts in low-skilled, hard physical labour.[56] But, contrarily to what is generally assumed, Serov's radical criticism was not the strongest argument against the reform project.[57] The majority of the commission members did not share Serov's viewpoint on the necessity of remote camps and hard labour.

More important was the opinion of the central planning agencies. Gosplan (the USSR Council of Ministers State Committee for Advanced Planning) and Gosekonomkomissiia (the USSR Council of Ministers State Economic Committee for Current Planning) came down against Dudorov's proposal to accomplish the construction of the railroad Salekhard–Igarka. They dismissed the project as unworkable, refusing to give Dudorov the seventy million rubles he needed to build the two special prisons. The most controversial point was the request of the MVD to include the Gulag in the state budget, a measure Gosplan and the Ministry of Finance insistently opposed.[58] Since at least 1947, the MVD had unsuccessfully petitioned the party and government to finance the Gulag entirely from the state budget. Although the 1954 statute of camps and colonies foresaw including the Gulag in the state budget, the Ministry of Finance had cancelled this point. At the time Dudorov wrote his memo, the camps and colonies (except for the strong regime sections) were 87 per cent self-financed, the rest of the money coming from budget allocation. For Dudorov the inclusion of the Gulag in the state budget was the key to reorienting the Gulag's attention toward its penal duties.

Without complete state funding, the Gulag was urged to finance itself, concentrating its entire activities on fulfilling the economic plans and securing the financial viability of the camps and colonies. That implied utterly exploiting the workforce of the inmates, to the detriment of their re-education.[59]

The political leadership returned to the reform of the Gulag in October 1956. In the wake of the 20th Party Congress, the reformist wing in the party led by Khrushchev received support from the regional party leaders, after hundreds of them worked for weeks in the camps as heads of liberation commissions in 1956.[60] The decree reforming the MVD, which the CC and the Council of Ministers finally issued on 25 October 1956, was a compromise between the views Dudorov expressed in his memorandum and the needs of the central planning agencies.[61] The decree met Dudorov's demand to reorganize the penal system around colonies, endowed with their own production facilities. There prisoners were to be employed according to their qualification or receive appropriate training. Re-education was made a priority in the decree, although in general terms only. The decree confined itself to declarative statements that the prisoners sentenced for petty crimes should be separated from the ones sentenced for dangerous crimes, and that leaders and active members of criminal groups should be locked up in prisons or held in strong regime colony subdivisions. More alarmingly still, the decree was passed in a money-saving mode: the political leadership did not allot any funds for reorganizing camps into colonies.

The reorganization of the Gulag into smaller penitentiary units failed for a number of reasons. The main one lay in the correlation between the permanence of the giant camp model and the fluctuation in the numbers of the Gulag population. A simple scheme was at work after Stalin's death: even a short-term increase in the detained population created financial and disciplinary difficulties for the Gulag, as this meant increasing the number of non-working prisoners who had to be maintained. The prisoner surplus motivated the MVD to keep the camp model alive and to postpone the creation of colonies: for the Gulag administrators, camps were a flexible system, able to adapt to greatly varying convict numbers, as camp sections could accommodate huge number of prisoners, and prisoner surplus in one camp could always be shifted to another. In the colonies, on the contrary, accommodation regulations were less adjustable: ceilings for prisoner numbers were limited and convicts were to serve their sentences in their home regions. New colonies lacked work assignments: the creation of in-house production facilities in every colony necessitated serious investments. For the Gulag, adapting to the jolts of the government criminal policy was problematic.

To understand this mechanism, one has to become accustomed to the idea that, although an abysmal reduction in prisoner figures is the general trend, there were indeed months and years during the Thaw when the Gulag population was increasing: thus, it increased by 10 per cent in 1956 in the wake of a law-and-order campaign against petty criminality, notwithstanding massive release operations and the 'Secret Speech.'[62] The Gulag retained its 'revolving door' that historians of Stalinism have aptly described: vast numbers of prisoners entered the camps, and vast numbers left them every year.[63] The fluctuations in the numbers of prisoners exerted a tremendous influence on how reformable the Gulag was. Overpopulation and unemployment meant severe losses for the Gulag economy and danger for the camp discipline. Confronted with such problems, the Gulag leadership petitioned the political authorities to enact mass amnesties and to offer 'work fronts' by transferring labour-intensive enterprises (such as construction and timbering) into the Gulag or by widening the contract system. The economic need to obtain 'work fronts' in mass hard labour contradicted the proclaimed refocusing on re-education, hampering the transformation of the penitentiary system.

The MVD was caught in an overpopulation crisis beginning in the spring of 1957, when Dudorov claimed that 70,000 prisoners were unemployed. He proposed that the party and government create 'a set of colonies on great construction sites in remote regions of the country,' which actually amounted to creating new camps. The transfer back to the MVD of a greater GULLP, of Glavspetsstroi, Dalstroj, and the enterprises of the Vorkuta region was equally recommended to put prisoners to work, a year only after the same Dudorov had managed to 'free' the MVD of its economic directorates.[64] By the summer, the government had enacted some of his proposals. In blatant contradiction to the decree of 25 October 1956, the MVD obtained the right to open new *camps* for construction and timbering in November 1958, which would house 60,000 to 70,000 prisoners for up to five years. The MVD took over three large construction projects to be linked to these new camps (a mineral processing plant, Plant 530, and a cellulose plant). The old economic directorates were not recreated to supervise the camps and the enterprises. Instead, the MVD had to work together with the newly established Soviets of the National Economy (*sovnarkhozy*) in the regions where the industrial sites were situated – Sverdlovsk *oblast'* and the autonomous republic of Buriat-Mongolia. Remarkably, the system of forced labour inherited from the Stalin years was made compatible with Khrushchev's reorganization of the command economy on a regional basis.[65]

The second reason for the reform failure lay, paradoxically, in the efforts of industrial managers to limit the use of forced labour in economic sectors and regions traditionally relying on convict workforce. Whenever they could, industry managers and party bosses had been moving to free labour since 1955, accentuating the unemployment crisis in the Gulag.[66] Furthermore, managers still employing prisoners refused those convicted for serious crimes. 'The Forest, Coal and Non-Ferrous Metal Ministries refuse categorically to employ in their enterprises criminals and bandits among the prisoners,' claimed Dudorov at the end of 1956.[67] Indeed, the Vorkutugol' industrial complex asked in April 1956 to transfer from Vorkutlag all hardened criminals to other camps.[68] In August, the Inta Region and Intaugol' mine complex asked the MVD to send the workforce they keenly needed to fulfil the plan requirements, but insisted on obtaining only light or regular regime prisoners.[69] To Dudorov, this request was impossible to meet, because the majority of convict newcomers had to be detained on strong regime. The relative weight of prisoners condemned for serious offences rose continuously from 1956, representing a fifth of all detainees in 1958 and a third in 1960.[70] The reduction in the demand for forced labour and the ever-higher requirements of the managers, far from encouraging the change of paradigm Khrushchev imposed in 1956, put a considerable financial burden on the MVD and motivated it to open new camps and new large-scale projects.[71]

The third reason the colony project did not succeed was that, in traditionally non-camp regions, republican and regional leaders deliberately impeded colony founding. While the old system allowed them to relegate local convicts to camps outside of the region, the colony system implied that the delinquents would serve their sentence in the region where they had lived prior to conviction.[72] To avoid keeping their criminals at home, regional leaders built only 43 out of the 276 colonies they were obliged to build in 1957.[73] In traditional penitentiary regions, like Perm, Irkutsk, and Kemerovo, *obkom* secretaries refused to receive the new prisoner influx from the republics and regions that had not built enough colonies to accommodate their own convicts.[74] The MVD was thus put in a strained situation, as it was ever more difficult to house new prisoners. To release the financial burden of unemployment and overpopulation, the ministry had to resort regularly to mass amnesties, in November 1957 (196,713 liberations) and 1959–60 (471,858 liberations).[75]

Liberation from detention and conviction to deprivation of freedom, USSR, 1950–66

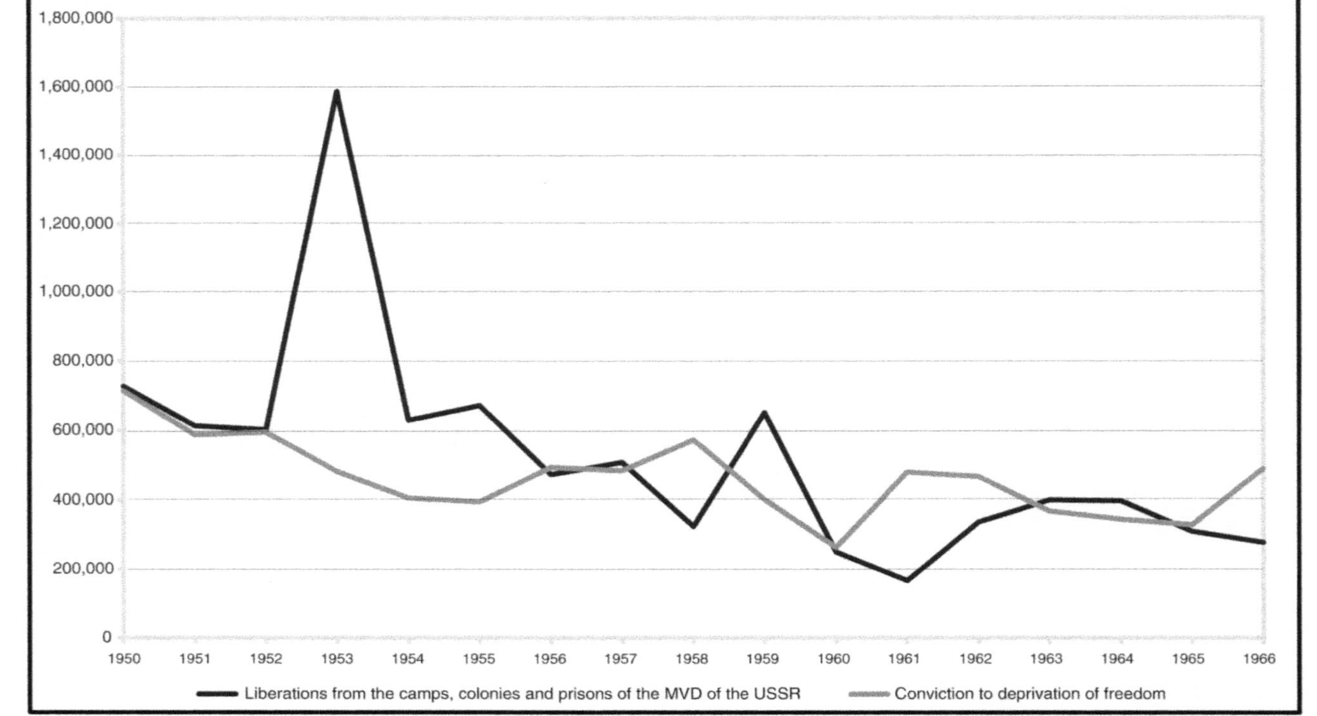

Liberation curve: *Istoriia stalinskogo Gulaga. Konets 1920-kh – pervaia polovina 1950-kh godov*; I.V. Bezborodov, ed., *Naselenie Gulaga: chislennost' i usloviia soderzhaniia* (Moscow, 2004), 4:134–6 (1950–53); GARF R-9414/1/1426/5 (1954–8); GARF R-9492/6/133/82 (1959–66).

Conviction curve: GARF R-9492/2/112/111 (1950–54); GARF R-9492/6/290/3 (1955–66). This is the lowest evaluation of conviction rates, as it does not include convictions by military tribunals or special courts (camp tribunals until 1954 and tribunals of the line until 1956), or by extrajudicial bodies (Special Conference until 1953).

Fourth, the government insufficiently subsidized the reorganization of the camp archipelago into a network of colonies. At the beginning of 1957, the MVD was denied the necessary financial resources to acquire buildings and facilities for the colonies.[76] From the end of 1957, a rule authorized the MVD to finance the renovation of old and the creation of new colonies by appropriating 60 per cent of income from the prisoners' work until 1960.[77] This rule, though insufficient to cope with the colony construction program, encouraged the contracting out of prisoners, contradicting the spirit of the 1956 reform. In 1959, twenty-eight huge camps were still in place, detaining 45 per cent of all inmates.[78] This was progress compared to 1956, when 71.4 per cent of all inmates were detained in camps.[79] However, at the end of the decade, two-thirds of all prisoners were contracted out to do hard physical work, mainly for the timber and mining industries, and for the construction sites of nuclear projects belonging to the Ministry of Medium Machine-Building.[80] This meant that many colonies were colonies in name only, and functioned in reality like camps, ruthlessly exploiting prisoners.

The Conservative Shift, 1960–1964

At the beginning of 1960, Soviet penitential institutions held only 582,717 prisoners, the smallest number since 1935.[81] The 1960 dissolution of the All-Union MVD remains a highly symbolic event in the political history of the Thaw. The Ministries of the Interior of the republican level inherited the police and penitentiary functions of the former MVD of the USSR.[82] The decision seems to have been taken quickly and in great secret, as even the minister himself was caught unprepared.[83] It could be interpreted as a climax in the period of legal reforms: at last, the leviathan's terrifying centralized imprisonment structure inherited from the Stalinist past was destroyed. The Ministries of Internal Affairs of the Soviet Republics took over its remains. (The absence of the MVD at the all-Union level did not last long, however. In 1966 it was revived under the name of the USSR Ministry of the Protection of Public Order [Ministerstvo okhrany obshchestvennogo poriadka, MOOP SSSR], and in 1968 it recovered its previous name.)[84] However, the dismantling of the USSR MVD, this apogee of reform and decentralization, coincides, quite unexpectedly, with the end of the wave of penal reforms that started in 1956. The eviction in January 1960 of the reformist Dudorov gave way to the conservative wing within Russian MVD officialdom.[85]

In the early summer of 1960, data on the ongoing last massive liberation of the decade poured into the CC. The party leadership of the Russian federation was indignant: 12.7 per cent of the most dangerous crimes registered in the first semester of 1960 had been committed by individuals liberated under the amnesty of the summer of 1959.[86] Recidivism occurred in a context of a sharp increase in registered serious crimes, after eighteen months of strong diminution. The political leadership attributed the crime wave to the liberated prisoners, and so to a laxity of repression. Reports on the state of mind of the Soviet population were a second influence on Soviet decision-making. Supporters of a more rigid detention system were able to prove that fifteen hundred letters to the editor argued against the 'privileged life' inmates allegedly led in detention, which a painstaking special report issued in the Russian daily *Sovetskaia Rossiia* fiercely denounced in August 1960. According to the reporters, as a result of recent reforms, the detainees, even those condemned for dangerous crimes, were so well treated in places of detention that they tried to commit new crimes upon release in order to be sentenced again. In detention, they enjoyed high living standards free of charge, which not every free citizen could afford: plentiful food, high-quality medical care, entertainment (music, sports, games, and movies), and easy work with high wages.[87] The newspaper article provoked a debate within the CC over the definition and interpretation of the party line in penitential matters. The reformists remained attached to the softening of detention conditions implemented since 1956, thinking it to be the official line supported by Khrushchev. Their conservative opponents leaned on the anti-parasite campaign of the summer of 1960 – which was Khrushchev's venture as well – with the slogan 'Who doesn't work doesn't eat,' demanding a change in penal matters.[88] The combination of rough statistical data and indignant citizens' letters allowed the conservative wing to convince Khrushchev to impose a U-turn on punitive institutions.[89] In 1961, the first secretary partially recanted the policy of social participation and penal humanness he had advocated since 1956. The militia, the courts, and the procuracy were enjoined to display harshness toward every kind of social deviance.[90] On 1 September 1961, the Bureau of the CC for the RSFSR passed a new statute of places of detention for the RSFSR, which was a real step back in penitentiary matters.[91] In 1958 the enactment of its predecessor, the Statute of Corrective Labour Colonies and Prisons of the MVD of the USSR, had been a victory for the reformist camp. It had proclaimed that 'prisoners enjoy all civilian rights, apart from the rights they lost by the court's sentence and also from the rights they cannot exercise by virtue of their deprivation of freedom.' This meant, for instance, that prisoners were subjected to the same labour rules as free workers, especially to the same workday length. It had bound the penitentiary administration to 'a humane, fair attitude to the prisoners,' forbidding measures 'whose aim is to occasion physical pain or violation of human dignity.'[92] In the new statute, these references to humaneness disappeared, replacing the three kinds of regime – light, common, and severe – with a system of four colony types, each with its own regime – common, reinforced, severe, and special. Therefore, it hardened the whole scale of regimes by removing the lightest one and adding an especially tough one. Detainees in special colonies could not receive food parcels, had a right to receive no more than one letter a month and a visit every six months. Common colonies saw a drastic reduction of the rights granted to prisoners regarding correspondence, use of money, visits, etc., compared to the old common regime. Prisons were subjected to a similar hardening of regime. Every convict had to pay for and to wear a uniform.[93]

At the same time, the 1961 statute reinforced some reformist tendencies of the past years: strict separation among detainees in different kinds of detention regime, institution of the court as the only office capable of deciding upon and changing the regime type for a given prisoner (in the 1958 statute, this was still the domain of the administration of penal institutions), organization of labour on intra-colony production facilities, and obligation to detain the convicts in the region where they had been sentenced. In this sense, the 1961 statute was a counter-reform but not a return to the Stalinist system. However, there was much political hypocrisy in the introduction of these novelties, because, as we will see, many of them were obviously unenforceable, given the repressive drive of 1961, of which the new statute was a product.

The hardening of criminal and penal policy in 1961 brought new difficulties and adverse reactions. As a direct consequence of the repudiation of the lenient criminal policy of the second half of the 1950s, the number of prisoners rose. The Russian minister of internal affairs, Nikolai Stakhanov, signalled that 'the number of prisoners had decreased sharply [in 1959–60 as a result of the amnesty] and the RSFSR MVD had been forced to liquidate 184 ... colonies with 106,900 places ... But in the time from August 1, 1960 to April 1, 1961 the number of prisoners has grown by almost 60,000 persons.'[94] In the summer of 1961, he complained that the corrective labour system had an excess of 24,000 prisoners.[95] As in 1955, 1957, and 1959, this new augmentation was a financial burden for the MVD. If the MVD were to respect the legislation, which prescribed a colony for each of the four regime types in every region, it would have had to create seventy new colonies in the second half of 1961, their total cost being 100 million rubles.[96] The MVD could not afford these costs, given that its request to budget the camps and colonies had been dismissed anew in the summer of 1961.[97]

The rise in penal population, together with the legal obligation to increase the number of colonies, drove the RSFSR leadership to introduce a new, cheaper colony type, the corrective labour colony-settlement (*ispravitel'no-trudovaia koloniia-poselenie*) for criminals who behaved well and had already served a significant part of their sentence. Some 20,000 inmates belonged to this category.[98] In practice, the detention conditions in such establishments were similar to the abolished light-regime colonies: the inmates could wear civilian clothes, meet relatives, receive mail and parcels, and use money with little restriction. They were paid regular salaries, and their working day was of the same length as that of free workers. They had the right to move freely during the day in the territory of the colony and to invite their families to live with them.[99] For the MVD, this colony type had the financial advantage of saving on the numbers of guard troops.[100]

The convict reform through labour that strongly developed in 1956–60 was revoked in the course of the subsequent repressive shift. The MVD and party leadership henceforth fully accepted the primarily economic purpose of convict labour, as was obvious in the efforts to raise the manufacturing significance of the camps and colonies in Russia. A 1963 party memorandum on the economic activities of penal institutions in Russia hailed the results: 'The production volume in the camps and colonies increases from year to year. Whereas in 1956 gross output amounted to 164 million rubles, in 1962 it reached 359 million rubles and 462 millions in 1963.'[101]

But this economic boom (an increase of 182 per cent in seven years) was still deemed insufficient. The cost of production in camps and colonies was too high and labour productivity too low, as their production was still run on a managerial and economic model 'created some thirty years ago,' notwithstanding the 'big changes that occurred in the national economy' since. The memo proposed to modernize the use of convict labour in order to increase the colonies' output.[102] In 1961, the party and state leadership had obliged corrective labour colonies to produce 'more sophisticated and modern goods.' The *sovnarkhozy* had to give them the old 'equipment of subordinate organizations freed by the introduction of new technologies.' In the textile industry, for instance, colonies had to concentrate on low-quality items, leaving high-quality production to civilian factories.[103] In 1963, penal institutions manufactured equipment for the textile and food industry, electrical items, spare parts for tractors and cars, etc. The colonies were even producing goods for export.[104] The political leadership tried to foster economic rationalization by improving the integration of penal manufacturing in the national economy. In 1963, this meant better coordination with the *sovnarkhozy* planning. According to the memo, colonies produced too many different things, thus lowering profitability, as some goods found no realization in trade. The memo recommended specialization as a means to fit the penal institutions in the regional economic process, so the manufacturing industries of the colony system were reconfigured in 1961–3 to make them more profitable, their role in the national economy now defined as supplying goods with low added value.[105]

The practice of contracting out labour from the penal premises on key construction projects continued. In 1961, the MVD organized new colonies to rent out 33,500 prisoners to *sovnarkhoz* construction projects. To cite only the biggest contracts, the ministry appointed 8,000 inmates to the construction of the Plesetskii aluminium factory, up to 3,000 to the construction of the Emtsovskii cement factory (Archangelsk *sovnarkhoz*), 1,500 to the construction of the Beloretskii mines (Altai *sovnarkhoz*), and the same number to the construction of a silk-weaving industrial complex and a heat-electric generating station (Orenburg *sovnarkhoz*). The plan foresaw contracting out inmates not only to construction sites, but also to stone quarries, brickworks, and automobile and machine-building industry, all around Russia.[106]

Convict labour still performed important functions in the 1960s. In construction and other spheres, the labour of free citizens could be too expensive to employ or virtually unavailable, because of extremely bad working or living conditions. In these cases, the economic organizations continued using convict labour. To give an example, immediately after the enactment of the 1961 statute, the Ministry of Medium Machine-Building lobbied the CC to keep the reinforced regime at the Pavlovskaia Colony (former Pavlovskoe Camp Subsection), located in Elektrostal' next to Moscow. The colony was supposed to switch to common regime under the new statute. This change would have endangered the production of Factory No. 12, which produced propellants for nuclear-power stations and nuclear icebreakers, and to which the colony labour force was contracted out.[107] If the new regulation were put into practice, all qualified 650 convict workers, condemned to long sentences and having worked there already for three years, would have to be removed and replaced by inexperienced new prisoners, who were sentenced for short periods only, thereby creating high turnover in this crucial and secret industry. Interestingly, the minister did not envisage the possibility of using free labour in place of convict labour in these hazardous assignments.[108]

The gold-mining industry was the second sphere of economic activity where convict labour was deemed irreplaceable in the first half of the 1960s.[109] Yet another striking example of the key role of convict labour in some priority sectors comes from the history of the woodcutting industry. By 1960, four timber camps had been shut down in the Russian Federation, but eleven remained. They detained almost 200,000 prisoners, logging twenty to twenty-two million cubic metres of timber yearly.[110] At this point, the Russian government ordered the *sovnarkhozy* to organize the accommodation of the first 35,000 free workers to gradually replace the convicts at timber assignments. However, the fulfilment of this instruction had been delayed, and one year later, in the summer of 1961 only 7,000 free workers had arrived in woodcutting units, which comprised only 20 per cent of the government prescription. Thus, some 134,000 convict workers from the camps were still needed to fulfil the timber plan, the MVD claimed. The rise in overall detained population following the penitentiary counter-reform of 1961 came as an additional reason not to close the camps. The economic priority (fulfilling the timber plan) and the political priority (sentencing more people to custodial penalty) prevented their dissolution. The Russian MVD petitioned the CC Russian Federation Bureau in the summer of 1961 to maintain the camps. The minister asked as well for the right to transfer prisoners from one camp to another and from one colony type to another, in direct violation of the 1961 statute of penal institutions.[111] The bureau acceded to this demands and gave penal labour with logging enterprises top priority in the RSFSR economic plan.[112]

More significantly still, at the same time, during that same summer of 1961, the Russian Council of Ministers and MVD asked the party leadership to allow them to send 10,000 more convicts to the timber camps of the Komi Republic, Krasnoiarsk territory, Perm, and Sverdlovsk regions. The Russian *sovnarkhozy* had missed the goal of the first quarter plan by 1.5 million cubic metres of timber and needed support to realize it.[113] The Russian Bureau instructed the petitioners to catch up with the general woodcutting plan by resorting to forced labour in the old GULag fashion. This practice continued in 1963–4: 24,000 detainees were transferred from all corners of the RSFSR to the timber camps.[114] At the end of 1963, the total number of camps in the RSFSR did not fall, as planned, but instead rose to fifteen, as opposed to twelve in 1961.[115]

Despite the intention to abandon the forced labour system, the party leadership clearly was not ready to renounce the use of convict labour if this meant endangering the economic achievements it deemed vital.[116] The enforcement of regulations for the organization of penal institutions could still be sacrificed to economic priorities. While the conversion of the penitentiary economy to free labour was quick in many sectors and regions, in a few the model of forced labour economy created in the 1930s proved difficult to discard, because the replacement of convicts by free workers was in fact complicated and extremely costly.[117] It implied new ways of organizing economic activities. During the years of slavery, nobody had to take care of organizing proper working conditions, housing, schooling, transport, and health care – in a word, of making life possible for workers and their families in remote and unwelcoming regions. These facts make it necessary to carefully approach the claim that convict labour was universally recognized as inefficient by the party leadership after 1953 and that it quickly lost all economic meaning.[118]

At the end of Khrushchev's era, the political leadership sought new ways of mobilizing inmates to provide labour for construction sites. In 1964, a CC decree refined the system of convict labour,[119] prescribing the systematic liberation of small offenders from the colonies with their compulsory transfer to construction sites in the chemical, oil-refining, and petrochemical industries, as well as the chemical and oil-refining engineering industries, and some others (hence inmates' use of the term *chemistry* (*khimiia*) for this type of early conditional release). These former inmates were subject to common labour regulations, with the notable exception that work was compulsory until the end of their sentence. Moreover, they had to register with the local police every three months, and the possibility of being retransferred to the colony hung over them.[120] This law secured a permanent source of labour for economic sectors and regions needing it the most, and it unblocked a detention system confronted with an increasing penal population that could hardly be accommodated in penal institutions under the 1961 regulations. In the first year of its application, 49,274 inmates were granted transfer to the construction sector – 12.4 per cent of all freed prisoners. In 1965, 29,938 prisoners were also sent to construction sites, and as many were sent there in the following year.[121] There is evidence that economic managers were satisfied with this new system. Second-offense criminality and alcoholism were rare occurrences among the liberated detainees,[122] so this system of semi-forced labour was amplified in the following years, to the detriment of other forms of early release:[123] from 1968 to 1973, 820,659 people were sent to finish their sentence working in economic enterprises – an average of almost 137,000 a year, representing 27 per cent of all prisoners over this period.[124]

The overview of the Gulag under Khrushchev is one of economic marginalization, shrinking inmate population, and drastic limitation of penal repression for political crimes. The Gulag underwent a transformation from an economic empire of its own into a supply company of a mobile workforce capable of filling gaps and clearing backlogs. It was no longer the centre of the Soviet economy but rather on its fringes. As its population experienced a fourfold decrease, with political prisoners becoming a statistically limited convict category, the Gulag evolved from a gigantic and omnipresent repressive machine into an agency of narrowly limited purposes, designed to inhibit public disorder and political opposition.

In the overall context of Soviet history, Khrushchev's Gulag emerges as a transitional and hybrid system, typical for the transformations of the Thaw. It was transitional as it evolved from a penal-economic model of giant camps into a more regular imprisonment system with Soviet features, based on graduated isolation from society according to court decisions as well as on prisoner reform, understood as social integration through work experience and vocational training. Given the consensus that Stalin's Gulag was unviable, but also in a context of political tensions and uncertainty, several projects of reforming the Gulag were tested during these years. There was a functionalist trend, expressed by Beria, who understood the Gulag crisis as a managerial and institutional problem, to be solved by separating the managerial and penitentiary functions previously merged in the MVD. Malenkov, Kruglov, and Serov were proponents of a conservative trend, common in the MVD leadership, and envisioned a powerful MVD endowed with broad economic prerogatives as industrial operator and workforce supplier. They diagnosed a crisis of labour productivity and cost control in the Gulag, and they intended to resolve it by introducing work incentives and mass releases from the camps. Lastly, Khrushchev and Dudorov understood the main problem of the Gulag as the prevalence of economic priorities over re-educational goals. This imbalance could be overcome only by breaking up the Stalinist institution of a camp and reorganizing the penal system around smaller, regional units.

The Gulag of the Thaw was a hybrid construct. The inertia of the Stalinist model was so strong that giant camps in remote regions remained an important part of the system, at least until 1964. Notwithstanding official insistence on prisoner reform and regionalized colonies, the penal institutions remained profit oriented, even those that had set up their own work facilities for re-education. Convict labour remained the only way to finance the penal system. Moreover, the economic and political leadership was reluctant to abandon the mobilization capacities of the camp forced-labour system.[125] The camp paradigm was still haunting the detention system.

NOTES

This paper benefited from exchanges with Klaus Gestwa, Alan Barenberg, Simon Ertz, Brian LaPierre, and Oleg Khlevniuk. I am grateful to Eleonory Gilburd and Denis Kozlov for their help in reshaping it.

1 *Prezidium TsK KPSS. 1954–1964. Chernovye protokol'nye zapiski zasedanii. Stenogrammy. Postanovleniia*, ed. Andrei Fursenko (Moscow, 2003), 1:22.
2 Hereafter, two versions of spelling are adopted: *GULag* stands for the particular institution, while *Gulag* applies to the entire system of forced labour (Ed.).
3 Ann Applebaum, *Gulag: A History* (New York, 2003): 476–563; Alan Barenberg, 'From Prison Camp to Mining Town: The Gulag and Its Legacy in Vorkuta, 1938–65' (PhD diss., University of Chicago, 2007); Steven Barnes, *Death and Redemption: The Gulag and the Shaping of Soviet Society* (Princeton, 2011): 201–53; Jeffrey S. Hardy, 'Khrushchev's Gulag: The Evolution of Punishment in the Post-Stalin Soviet Union, 1953–1964' (PhD diss., Princeton University, 2011).
4 Andrei Sokolov, 'Forced Labor in Soviet Industry: The End of the 1930s to the Mid-1950s: An Overview,' in *The Economics of Forced Labor: The Soviet Gulag*, ed. Paul R. Gregory and Valery Lazarev (Stanford, 2003), 23–42, here 41.
5 Beria had been People's Commissar of Internal Affairs from 1938 to 1945.
6 The accessible documentation shows no evidence of Beria condemning the use of prison labour for national economic ventures. The famous quotation Boris Starkov attributes, with no archival reference, to Beria ('Beria proposed to "liquidate the existing system of forced labour given its economic inefficiency and lack of prospects"') is dubious. Starkov, 'Sto dnei "Lubian-

skogo Marshala,"' *Istochnik. Dokumenty russkoi istorii,* 4 (1993): 82–90, here 89.

7 *Sistema ispravitel'no-trudovykh lagerei v SSSR, 1923–1960: spravochnik,* ed. M.B. Smirnov (Moscow, 1998), 100–27.

8 Alexander Kokurin and Nikita Petrov, eds., *GULAG: Glavnoe upravlenie lagerei. 1917–1960* (Moscow, 2000), 169; Viktor Zemskov, 'Deportatsii naseleniia. Spetsposelentsy i ssyl'nye. Zakliuchennye,' in *Naselenie Rossii v XX veke: Istoricheskie ocherki,* ed. V.B. Zhiromskaia, 3 vols. (Moscow, 2001), 2:183.

9 Marta Craveri and Oleg Khlevniuk, 'Krizis ekonomiki MVD (konets 1940-kh–1950-e gody)', *Cahiers du monde russe* 36, nos. 1–2 (1995): 179–90, here 181; and Kokurin and Petrov, *GULAG,* 786–9.

10 Oleg Khlevniuk, 'The Economy of the OGPU, NKVD, and MVD of the USSR, 1930–1953: The Scale, Structure, and Trends of Development,' in Gregory and Valery Lazarev, *Economics of Forced Labor,* 43–66, here 54.

11 While Dal'stroi – the giant construction trust of the Far North-East – and Noril'sk trust, both extracting non-ferrous metals like gold and tin, were handed out to the Ministry of Metal Industry, they retained the principle of undivided management: the chief of Dal'stroi industrial complex remained the chief of the regional camp administration. Gosudarstvennyi arkhiv Rossiiskoi Federatsii (State Archive of the Russian Federation, hereafter GARF) R-9492/5/196/78. Moreover, the camp networks Karlag in Kazakhstan and Siblag in Kemerovo region did not switch to the contractual system. *Istoriia stalinskogo Gulaga. Konets 1920-kh – pervaia polovina 1950-kh godov.* Vol. 3, *Ekonomika Gulaga,* ed. Oleg Khlevniuk (Moscow, 2004), 356.

12 Immediately after the transfer of the timber enterprises from the MVD to his ministry, Orlov petitioned the Council of Ministers for appointing the economic manager *edinonachal'nik* over the camps and the enterprises. GARF R-9492/5/198/193–201. At the same time, the headship of the North-Ural Camps was lobbying to recover the *edinonachalie* over the wood enterprises by transferring *Glavspetsles* to the Ministry of Justice, next to the Gulag. It complained about the 'additional expenditures' and 'rise in personnel' brought about by the creation of two 'parallel apparatuses' – one in the Ministry of Justice and the other in the Ministry of Timber Industry. GARF R-9492/5/196/21–3. The end of *edinonachalie* was contested as well by the party leaders of the Kuibyshev region, who claimed that the hierarchical separation of the Kuibyshev hydroelectric project and the Kuneevskii camp caused a drop in labour productivity. GARF R-9492/5/196/62–3. Similarly, the managers of Vorkuta's mine were dissatisfied with the end of *edinonachalie.* Alan Barenberg, 'Prisoners without Borders: Zazonniki and the Transformation of Vorkuta after Stalin,' *Jahrbücher für Geschichte Osteuropas* 57, no. 4 (2009): 513–34, here 520.

13 This included the entire central and regional penal administration, all colonies and prisons, labour colonies for minor offenders, the Inspection of Corrective Labour, and all their subordinate enterprises and organizations. Kokurin and Petrov, *GULAG*, 792.

14 Ibid., 788, 791–3; A. Yakovlev, V. Naumov, and Iu. Sigachev, eds., *Lavrentii Beriia. 1953. Stenogramma iiul'skogo plenuma TsK KPSS i drugie dokument* (Moscow, 1999), 19. It seems that in Beria's plan the special settlers would stay in the domain of the MVD.

15 See the project of 'Statute for the MVD of the USSR' he submitted on 16 July 1953, in Alexander Kokurin and Nikita Petrov, *Lubianka: organy VChK-OGPU-NKVD-NKGB-MGB-MVD-KGB. 1917–1991. Spravochnik* (Moscow, 2003), 681–4.

16 'Edict of the Presidium of the Supreme Soviet of the USSR "On the Amnesty,"' *Pravda* and *Izvestia*, 28 March 1953.

17 Yakovlev, Naumov, and Sigachev, *Lavrentii Beriia*, 19–21.

18 On the March Amnesty and subsequent mass release operations of the Thaw, see Marc Elie, 'Les politiques à l'égard des libérés du Goulag: amnistiés et réhabilités dans la région de Novossibirsk, 1953–1960,' *Cahiers du monde russe* 47, nos. 1–2 (2006): 327–48; and Marc Elie, 'Unmögliche Rehabilitation: Die Revisionskommissionen 1956 und die Unsicherheiten des Tauwetters,' *Osteuropa* 57, no. 6 (2007): 369–86.

19 GARF R-9414/1a/1331/186–7.

20 *Istoriia stalinskogo Gulaga. Konets 1920-kh – pervaia polovina 1950-kh godov.* Vol. 2, *Karatel'naia sistema: struktura i kadry*, ed. Nikita Petrov (Moscow, 2004), 452–3.

21 Few of the prisoners of the MVD special camps could benefit from the amnesty. In December 1953, 205,573 were left. A.N. Artizov, Iu. V. Sigachev, I.N. Shevchuk, and V. Khlopov, eds., *Reabilitatsiia: kak eto bylo. Dokumenty Prezidiuma (Politiuro) TsK KPSS i drugie materialy. V 3-kh tomakh* (Moscow, 2000), 1:83.

22 *Istoriia stalinskogo Gulaga. Konets 1920-kh – pervaia polovina 1950-kh godov.* Vol. 6, *Vostaniia, bunty i zabastovki*, ed. Vladimir Kozlov (Moscow, 2004), 309–648. On the Rechlag uprising, see Barenberg, 'From Prison Camp to Mining Town,' 227–60. On Steplag, see Marta Craveri, 'Krizis GULaga. Kengirskoe vosstanie 1954 goda v dokumentakh MVD,' *Cahiers du monde russe* 36, no. 3 (1995): 319–44; and Steven Barnes, '"In a Manner Befitting Soviet Citizens": An Uprising in the Post-Stalin Gulag,' *Slavic Review* 64, no. 4 (2005): 823–50. Large-scale unrest remained common in 1955, as the mutiny of some six hundred prisoners of the 20th, 28th, and 17th camp sections of Noril'lag on 23–4 and 27–8 June and the three-day strike of up to nine hundred miners detained in the 5th and 15th camp sections of Vorkutlag on 18–20 July show. GARF R-9401/2/465/342, 259–64.

23 Miriam Dobson, *Khrushchev's Cold Summer: Gulag Returnees, Crime, and the Fate of Reform after Stalin* (Ithaca, 2009), 21–49; Marc Elie, 'Slukh o banditskom razgule v 1953–1954 gg.,' in *Slukhi v istorii Rossii XIX–XX vekov. Neformal'naia kommunikatsiia i krutye povoroty rossiiskoi istorii*, ed. Igor' Narskii (Cheliabinsk, 2011), 146–67.

24 Kokurin and Petrov, *GULAG*, 372–3. The Ministry of Justice and the Gulag were furthermore in a state of permanent conflict. See, for instance, GARF R-9414/1ch1/151/1–13 and 95–105. In particular, the Gulag administration held the Ministry of Justice responsible for the deterioration of life conditions of the prison camp staff. Petrov, *Karatel'naia sistema*, 455–62.

25 The special camps were now included in the Gulag. See Kokurin and Petrov, *GULAG*, 386–90. Two months later, as a consequence of mass disorders, they merged progressively with the regular camps. Khlevniuk, *Ekonomika Gulaga*, 365.

26 Fursenko, *Prezidium*, 879.

27 Compare to the mere 11 per cent at the beginning of 1953. Khlevniuk, *Ekonomika Gulaga*, 356; and Kokurin and Petrov, *GULAG*, 667.

28 Smirnov, *Sistema*, 59, 112.

29 Ibid., 59, 113–7. On the Virgin Lands campaign, see Michaela Pohl's article in the present volume.

30 GARF R-9401/2/451/45–53.

31 GARF R-9401/2/463/410a.

32 GARF R-9401/2/465/109–18. Atbasarskii Camp was specially created to build these state farms and silos. Karlag was involved, too. Smirnov, *Sistema*, 259–60, 285.

33 GARF R-9401/2/450/233–4. The construction of the Kuibyshev power station can serve as another example of the Gulag participation in prestigious projects. In 1957, as the construction works of the power station entered their final stage, 21,484 inmates from Kunevskii ITL were involved. GARF R-9401/2/491/180–1. At the beginning of 1956, 34,594 inmates worked on hydroelectric projects. Kokurin and Petrov, *GULAG*, 169.

34 Khlevniuk, *Ekonomika Gulaga*, 292–5 and 361; see the plans that had been circulating since 1949 among higher MVD officials, as described by Aleksei Tikhonov, 'The End of the Gulag,' in Gregory and Lazarev, *Economics of Forced Labor*, 67–74.

35 N.S. Zaharov and V.P. Malkov, *Sbornik dokumentov po istorii ugolovnogo zakonodatel'stva SSSR i RSFSR 1953–1991 v 2-kh tomakh* (Kazan: 1992), 1:23.

36 Kokurin and Petrov, *GULAG*, 156. Prisoners held on the strong detention regime were not eligible for this system.

37 See, for instance, how the Ministry of Coal industry and the MVD attempted to stimulate further work productivity in the Vorkutlag and Minlag mines in December 1955. GARF R-9492/2/111/88–94.

38 GARF R-9401/2/465/370–4.

39 GARF R-9401/2/500/316–23.

40 Between the reincorporation of the Gulag within the MVD in early 1954 and the beginning of 1956, the number of camps diminished somewhat, but far less than the convict population: from 53 (with 1521 camp sections) to 47 (with 1398 camp sections) camp complexes and from 700 to 524 regional camps and colonies. GARF R-9401/2/478/264–9.

41 Fursenko, *Prezidium*, 22. A report of 1920 gives an idea of 'Dzerzhinky's system': Petrov, *Karatelnaia sistema*, 557–8.

42 Kokurin and Petrov, *GULAG*, 186.

43 Kruglov had dared to contest the opinion of the deputy head of the CC Department of Administrative services, Valentin Zolotukhin, on the scope of one of the 1955 amnesties. Furthermore, he had reportedly concealed unpleasant statistical data on the state of criminality in the USSR. See Fursenko, *Prezidium*, 77; and GARF R-9401/2/467/253–60.

44 On Dudorov, see *Tsentral'nyi komitet KPSS, VKP(b), RSDRP(b): Istoriko-biograficheskii spravochnik*, ed. Iurii Goriachev (Moscow, 2005), 198.

45 It was Malenkov who suggested reintegrating the *glavki* in the MVD in February 1954. Fursenko, *Prezidium*, 23. As Kruglov lost his position in the MVD, Malenkov appointed him deputy minister for the construction of electric power stations. Later, he insisted in vain on keeping Kruglov at this post. The latter was ultimately downgraded and sent away to Bratsk. *Molotov, Malenkov, Kaganovich. 1957: Stenogramma iun'skogo plenuma CK KPSS i drugie dokumenty*, ed. N. Kovaleva, A. Korotkov, S. Mel'chin, Iu. Sigachev, and A. Stepanov (Moscow, 1998), 245.

46 Dudorov used Beria's wording to justify the removal of the *glavki*: to 'free the MVD from industrial and economic functions unrelated to its purpose (*nesvoistvennye emu*).' Among them the Main Directorate for timber industry (GULLP) and the Directorate of the Construction Site no. 304 were handed out respectively to the Ministry of Timber Industry and the Ministry of Medium Machine-Building. Dudorov also obtained the exclusion of the Gulag from participation in the Virgin Lands campaign (the construction of the Pavlodar Harvester Plan and of state farms and silos). Kokurin and Petrov, *GULAG*, 794.

47 Ibid., 164–8.

48 Ibid., 402, 435, 437.

49 Marc Elie, 'Banditen und Juristen im Tauwetter. GULag-Reform, kriminelle

Gegenkultur und kriminologische Expertise,' *Jahrbücher für Geschichte Osteuropas* 56, no. 4 (2009): 492–512.
50 Kokurin and Petrov, *GULAG*, 166.
51 Ibid., 165, 166, 174.
52 Artizov et al., *Reabilitatsiia*, 1:151.
53 Kokurin and Petrov, *GULAG*, 169.
54 Ibid., 667.
55 Elie, 'Banditen und Juristen.'
56 Craveri and Khlevniuk, 'Krizis ekonomiki,' 188–9; Rossiiskii gosudarstvennyi arkhiv noveishei istorii (Russian State Archive of Contemporary History, hereafter RGANI) 89/18/36/1–4. Procurator General Rudenko, also a member of the commission, supported some of the views aired in Dudorov's text, such as the statement on colonies instead of camps, but was against the creation of special prisons and the broader use of imprisonment sentences. See GARF R-8131/32/4577/284–5.
57 See, e.g., Petrov, *Karatel'naia sistema*, 2:50–1.
58 RGANI 89/16/1/86–8.
59 Kokurin and Petrov, *GULAG*, 394–5.
60 Elie, 'Unmögliche Rehabilitation.'
61 Kokurin and Petrov, *GULAG*, 187–92.
62 Brian LaPierre, 'Making Hooliganism on a Mass Scale: The Campaign against Petty Hooliganism in the Soviet Union, 1956–1964,' *Cahiers du monde russe* 1–2 (2006): 1–28.
63 Golfo Alexopoulos, 'Amnesty 1945: The Revolving Door of Stalin's Gulag,' *Slavic Review* 64, no. 2 (2005): 274–306.
64 GARF 9401/2/490/262–3, 492/108–10; and Khlevniuk, *Ekonomika Gulaga*, 362–3 and 571–2.
65 Khlevniuk, *Ekonomika Gulaga*, 363–4; and Kokurin and Petrov, *GULAG*, 207. On the *sovnarkhoz* reform, see Natalya Kibita, 'Moscow–Kiev Relations and the *Sovnarkhoz* Reform,' in *Khrushchev in the Kremlin: Policy and Government in the Soviet Union, 1956–64*, ed. Jeremy Smith and Melanie Ilic (London, 2008): 94–111; and Valery Vasiliev, 'Failings of the *Sovknarkhoz* reform: The Ukrainian Experience,' in ibid., 112–32.
66 Thus, the management of one of the most prestigious hydroelectric projects of the Thaw, the Bratsk hydroelectric power plant construction, energetically dismissed the Gulag administrators' offers to employ convict labour. Prisoners were employed there only for auxiliary construction works. Klaus Gestwa, *Die Stalinschen Großbauten des Kommunismus. Sowjetische Technik- und Umweltgeschichte, 1948–1967* (Munich, 2010), 438.
67 GARF R-9401/2/482/196–7.

68 GARF R-9401/2/480/67–8.
69 Intaugol' needed 1,650–1,700 prisoners for the mines and 2,100 for construction. GARF R-9401/2/481/229–30 and 252–3.
70 Khlevniuk, *Ekonomika Gulaga*, 366–7; Kokurin and Petrov, *GULAG*, 443.
71 GARF R-9401/490/262–3.
72 In his 1959 report, Dudorov cited Belorussia as an example of reluctance to construct colonies: the republic had built only two new colonies and was unable to accommodate all its convicts who had to be transported to camps outside Belorussia. Kokurin and Petrov, *GULAG*, 208.
73 Khlevniuk, *Ekonomika Gulaga*, 367–8.
74 GARF R-9401/2/492/195–6; R-9401/2/506/22–3 and 209–10.
75 GARF R-9414/1/1427/1, and GARF R-7523/95/3/169.
76 GARF R-9401/2/490/262–3.
77 Khlevniuk, *Ekonomika Gulaga*, 368.
78 Kokurin and Petrov, *GULAG*, 207.
79 Zemskov, 'Deportatsii,' 183.
80 Kokurin and Petrov, *GULAG*, 211, 220.
81 Ibid., 443.
82 Kokurin and Petrov, *Lubianka*, 698–702.
83 Vladimir Nekrasov, *Trinadtsat' 'zheleznykh' narkomov. Istoriia NKVD – MVD ot A.I. Rykova do N.A. Shchelokova, 1917–1982* (Moscow, 1995), 320.
84 Vladimir I. Ivkin, *Gosudarstvennaia vlast' SSSR. Vysshchie organy vlasti i upravleniia i ikh rukovoditeli. 1923–1991 gg. Istoriko-bibliograficheskii spravochnik* (Moscow, 1999), 180.
85 The MVD officials have kept an unhappy memory of the Dudorovian era until today. See the negative evaluation of Dudorov by Vladimir Nekrasov, who served in the MVD for forty-five years: 'It was, of course, hard for a constructor by profession and work experience to run such a ministry as the MVD.' Dudorov himself claimed on several occasions to have been the victim of 'attacks and reprisals' by conservative party leaders after his dismissal. See Nekrasov, *Trinadtsat'*, 321–2.
86 RGANI 13/1/764/127–32.
87 *Sovetskaia Rossiia* 27 August 1960 (report), and 19 September 1960 (review of readers' letters).
88 RGANI 13/1/788/32–75. On the anti-parasite legislation, see Sheila Fitzpatrick, 'Social Parasites: How Tramps, Idle Youth, and Busy Entrepreneurs Impeded the Soviet March to Communism,' *Cahiers du monde russe* 47, nos. 1–2 (2006): 377–408.
89 Witnesses have noticed this turn: Valerii F. Abramkin and Valentina F. Chesnokova, *Tiuremnyi mir glazami politzakliuchennykh, 1940–1980gg* (Moscow,

1993), 12–6; Anatolii Marchenko, *Moi pokazaniia,* chapter 'Vladimirka' (June 2006). http://www.memo.ru/history/diss/books/MAP4EHKO/index.htm; Alexander Solzhenitsyn, *Arkhipelag GULAG, 1918–1956: Opyt khudozhestvennogo issledovaniia* (Moscow, 1990) 3:171–85.

90 'I think that the Presidium was afraid to display courage, it played liberal (*sliberal'nichal*) [in 1959–60]. Yes, I publicly took the position that it is cruel (*zhestoko*) [to execute people]. But now, is it really cruelty? ... No, the people are awaiting this, they demand executions,' Khrushchev said at a Central Committee session in June 1961. Fursenko, *Prezidium,* 525–8. On the repressive drive and its causes, see Dobson, *Khrushchev's Cold Summer,* 156–85. On the new role given to the militia in the fight against social disorder, see Yoram Gorlizki, 'Policing Post-Stalin society: The *Militsiia* and Public Order under Khrushchev,' *Cahiers du monde russe* 44, nos. 2–3 (2003): 465–80.

91 'Minutes of the Bureau session no. 134, item 1g, 1 September 1961, "On the Measures to Carry Out the Decree of the CC of the CPSU," and the Council of Ministers of the USSR of 3 April 1961, no. 331–143, "On Measures to Ameliorate the Work of Corrective Labour Establishments of the MVD of Socialist Republics,"' RGANI 13/1/295. The CC had adopted an outline statute in April 1961 that served as a model for all republican statutes. RGANI 13/1/872/44–73.

92 Kokurin and Petrov, *GULAG,* 195–207.

93 RGANI 13/2/894/87–104.

94 RGANI 13/1/768/25–55.

95 RGANI 13/1/891/9.

96 RGANI 13/1/891/10–2.

97 It was not included in the 1961 Statute. RGANI 13/1/872/45–73.

98 *Organy i voiska MVD Rossii. Kratkii istoricheskii ocherk* (Moscow, 1996), 386.

99 RGANI 13/2/174/38–40.

100 RGANI 13/2/567/164.

101 In new rubles (after the 1961 monetary reform). RGANI 13/2/618/27–31. For the entire USSR. the plan assigned the Gulag 380 million of gross output in 1954 and 544.3 million in 1958 (in new rubles). Comparisons in time were complicated though, as the GULag farmed out most of its prisoners in the second half of the 1950s (62.7% in 1958): their work yielded considerable amounts of money (437 million expressed in new rubles) that were not included in the gross output figures. Kokurin and Petrov, *GULAG,* 217, 220, 378.

102 RGANI 13/2/618/26–31, here 27–8.

103 RGANI 13/2/894/79–81.

104 RGANI 13/2/618/27.
105 RGANI 13/2/618/28–31.
106 RGANI 13/2/894/83–5.
107 Since the mid-1940s, Elektrostal' had become an important centre for nuclear projects and had a big uranium plant. In 1945, Factory No. 12 began processing uranium for the first Soviet atom bomb. Paul Josephson, *Red Atom: Russia's Nuclear Power Program from Stalin to Today* (Pittsburgh, 2005), 284.
108 RGANI 13/2/372/163–8.
109 RGANI 5/30/373/90–2.
110 RGANI 13/2/891/9–12. Compare with 152,400 prisoners working in forest industry, logging 21.1 million cubic metres in the entire USSR in 1958. Compare as well with the total number of workers employed in forestry – 227,000 – and with the total amount of logging – 317 million cubic metres in the RSFSR by 1961 (including self-supply in agriculture). *Narodnoe khoziaistvo SSSR v 1961 godu. Statisticheskii ezhegodnik* (Moscow, 1962), 235 and 570.
111 RGANI 13/1/891/7–21.
112 RGANI 13/2/894/81.
113 RGANI 13/2/894/133–5.
114 According to the 1961 statute, the camps did not have the right to let dangerous prisoners move freely out of the camp territory. However, the advances in mechanization increased the need for convict specialists (drivers of tractors, trucks, and engines) who would be free to move. Therefore, the MVD of RSFSR felt compelled to import from other places of detention prisoners condemned to short sentences for petty crimes who could be permitted to move around without convoy. GARF A-385/26/251/1.
115 RGANI 13/2/618/26–31 and 13/2/891/10–12. There were 583 colonies in the RSFSR; 390 of them had their own production facilities. The rest had to contract out prisoners to enterprises.
116 Avraham Shefrin reports several high-risk work assignments in decisive industry fields where prisoners were used in the 1960s and 1970s. Shefrin, *The First Guidebook to Prisons and Concentration Camps of the Soviet Union* (Toronto, 1982), 31–5 and 345–52.
117 See Alan Barenberg's article in this volume on *Vorkuta* as an example of a successful conversion.
118 Galina Ivanova, *Labour Camp Socialism: The Gulag in the Soviet Totalitarian System* (Armonk, NY, 2000), 124.
119 *Organy i voiska*, 387.
120 GARF R-7523/83/1184/198–200.

121 GARF R-9492/6/122/62–3.

122 GARF R-7523/83/1184/112–16.

123 Whereas 70% of all liberated convicts in 1963 were given an early conditional release, only a third received it in 1966. GARF R-9492/6/122/62–3.

124 GARF R-9492/6/210/51–6.

125 In 1974 General Secretary Leonid Brezhnev reflected on the need to mobilize the workforce to build the immense railroad construction project of the Baikal-Amur Mainline (BAM). He proposed naturally to his Politburo colleagues to recourse – along with volunteers and soldiers – to the 'special contingent of comrade Shchelokov,' then minister of the interior, that is, to prisoners, who were easy to mobilize and seemingly cheap. *Vestnik Arkhiva Prezidenta. Spetsial'noe izdanie: General'nyi sekretar' L.I. Brezhnev 1964–1982* (Moscow, 2006), 169.

4 From Prisoners to Citizens? Ex-Prisoners in Vorkuta during the Thaw

ALAN BARENBERG

Then there's another thing – people do live in the camps, you know, and they come out of the camps as people. And they don't live or come out too badly at that. They have real friends, they read good books, study things.

– Yury Dombrovsky, *The Faculty of Useless Knowledge*[1]

Vorkuta – my alma mater.

– Mikhail Baital'skii, *Notebooks for the Grandchildren*[2]

On 25 December 1954 a young engineer named Leonid Pavlovich Markizov moved to Vorkuta. This was not Markizov's first time in the city – he had been a prisoner there from 1951 to 1954. Granted parole in October 1954, he was given a choice of where in the Soviet Union he wished to settle, and he chose Chkalovskaia *oblast'* in the Virgin Lands of Kazakhstan, where his wife and family had moved earlier that year. Markizov was reunited with his family on a state farm but found conditions there so appalling that he did not even stay long enough to find work. 'In a word,' writes Markizov, 'we saw the situation for what it was and decided to go to Vorkuta, where there was work.'[3] Less than two months after he had been released from Vorkuta, he returned to the place where he had spent three long years behind barbed wire. In Vorkuta he was hired as a department head in a mine construction bureau, a position that put him in an elite category of engineers. His family joined him the following March. The Markizovs lived in Vorkuta until 1972, when they moved to Syktyvkar, because Leonid Pavlovich finished a graduate degree and found a better job in the capital of Komi ASSR.[4]

At first glance, Vorkuta hardly seems a desirable place to settle down and raise a family in 1954. Geography and climate alone made it an extraordinarily difficult place to live. Located above the Arctic Circle, just to the west of the Ural Mountains in European Russia, temperatures in the city dip as low as –55°C during winters that typically last nine to ten months. In Vorkuta, the built environment was just as harsh as the natural one; the area was dominated by two prison camps, Vorkutlag and Rechlag, which formed a complex that was among the most notorious and deadly in the Soviet Gulag.[5] By 1954, to be sure, this camp complex was shrinking. But this process was still far from complete, and by the time that Markizov moved back to the city there were still some 60,000 prisoners in addition to the 84,000 non-prisoners living in the area.[6] Having been imprisoned there for three years, Markizov would have been well aware of both the harsh environment and the presence of an enormous prison camp complex. Why did he choose to come back?

This chapter is an attempt to understand why Markizov, and thousands of other former prisoners like him, chose to stay in Vorkuta. Of the nearly 106,000 prisoners who were released from the Vorkuta camps from 1953 to 1958, perhaps 25,000 opted to remain in the city for some time after they were released.[7] In answering this question, this chapter adopts a novel approach to the study of the place of former Gulag prisoners in Soviet society during the Thaw. Rather than following the historiographical convention of focusing on those prisoners who attempted to return to where they had lived before arrest and imprisonment,[8] I instead examine the experiences of those who decided to settle in or near their former places of incarceration. Using archival records, oral history, and memoirs, this chapter traces the path of prisoners who chose to live in Vorkuta after their terms in the Gulag ended. As I will show, examining those prisoners who stayed adds an important dimension to the study of the Gulag's legacy and allows us to draw important conclusions about Soviet society during the Thaw.

This chapter points out, first of all, that a significant proportion of former Gulag prisoners settled near their former places of incarceration. It argues that in order to more fully understand the experiences of ex-prisoners during the Thaw, historians need to shift their focus from Moscow to the vast industrial hinterland that made up the Gulag empire. By focusing study of ex-prisoners on a place rather than on a particular group of people, be it members of the Moscow intelligentsia, Ukrainian nationalists, or common criminals released during the 1953 amnesty, this chapter integrates the experiences of a broad range of former prisoners who came from many geographic regions in Russia, belonged to

Leonid Markizov, a former prisoner. Syktyvkar, April 2003. Photograph by the author. Used with permission.

different social classes, and had different national backgrounds.[9] A location-based study brings new issues into focus, such as intergroup conflict among ex-prisoners, and helps to integrate a variety of experiences into the narrative. Studying former prisoners in Vorkuta has other benefits as well. By choosing a city in the Soviet periphery, I am able to explore how central state policies were implemented regionally and locally. Finally, and most importantly, this chapter integrates the study of informal practices and social networks into the study of former prisoners. Just as in every other aspect of life in the Soviet Union in the 1950s and 1960s, it is impossible to understand the way that the political, economic, and social system operated without taking into account the many informal practices that operated alongside formal state policy.[10]

This chapter follows the experiences of ex-prisoners as they attempted to build new lives for themselves after release from the Vorkuta camp complex. While exploring the prejudices and discrimination that former prisoners faced after release, it argues that it was indeed possible for many former prisoners to successfully rejoin Soviet society. While other historians, most notably Nanci Adler, have pointed out that it was exceptionally difficult for former prisoners to readjust to life in Moscow and Leningrad, I will demonstrate that many former prisoners were successfully reintegrated in or near their former places of incarceration. Former prisoners in Vorkuta faced a difficult reception from non-prisoners, party and state authorities, and even other groups of former prisoners. They also had to contend with formal discrimination that limited their occupational mobility, particularly for those former prisoners who were engineers or specialists.[11] In this regard, Vorkuta was much like any other Soviet city. Yet official, state-sponsored discrimination against former prisoners was mitigated to a large degree in Vorkuta and other former Gulag locations. Social networks that prisoners acquired while on the 'inside' eased the transition to life on the 'outside,' especially in securing scarce resources like desirable jobs and housing. Just as important was the fact that the departure of many thousands of prisoners from camp industries ensured a significant shortage of skilled workers, putting former prisoners in a strong bargaining position vis-à-vis their employers. Local bosses and managers devised informal practices to minimize or sidestep state campaigns discriminating against former prisoners in the workplace. The case of Vorkuta suggests that, for a variety of reasons, former prison camp cities became magnets for ex-prisoners and served as locations for the successful reintegration of tens if not hundreds of thousands of former prisoners into Soviet society during the 1950s and 1960s.

The Reception of Prisoners

For many of the more than 100,000 prisoners released from the Vorkuta camp complex during the Thaw, release was followed by euphoria.[12] Aleksandr Solomonovich Klein's poem 'Miracle' (*Chudo*), written after his release from Vorkutlag in 1955, conveys the emotions that he felt as he first left the camp. The poem opens with incredulity and celebration:

I walk – and do not believe:
alone,
without guards?
And there is joy,
and tenderness,
and shyness in me,
And everything surprises,
and it seems strange,
That I do not have to
wear a number
on my back.[13]

Klein associates child-like delight and curiosity with his newfound freedom. It is as if he were now the inhabitant of an entirely new world, a world free of guard towers and camp dogs. As a result of this 'miracle' of release, he can explore this new world without fear of violence. Yet the poem ends on an ambiguous note. In the final stanza Klein writes, 'But my hands / out of habit / I hold behind my back.'[14] The disbelief that accompanied euphoria at the beginning of the poem has re-emerged as uneasiness, symbolized by the author's habitual holding of his hands behind his back, as a prisoner would. Like other ex-prisoners, Klein faced an uncertain future outside of the 'zone.' After years of imprisonment, he had to contend with the difficult and often contradictory process of starting a civilian life in Soviet society.

Former prisoners faced misunderstanding, prejudice, and sometimes open hostility from the society that they were attempting to rejoin. Even in a city like Vorkuta, where much of the population consisted of former prisoners and exiles, mass releases of prisoners were greeted by some of the non-prisoner population with a mixture of fear and trepidation. What would happen when thousands of prisoners were set free in the city? Would neighbourhoods be safe when convicted murderers and thieves wandered the streets? Would those former prisoners who had

Vorkutinskaia mine, Vorkuta. This mine was formerly known as mine no. 40 (and is referred to in the text). The shot also overlooks Rudnik, the abandoned old city. Photograph by the author, May 2003. Used with permission.

been convicted of serious political crimes, such as anti-Soviet agitation or terrorism, spread sedition and anti-Soviet views among the general population? Would they be able to readjust to Soviet society? Would they even want to?

This picture was complicated by the fact that Gulag prisoners did not necessarily identify with each other as belonging to the same group. To be sure, having been a *zek* was an important identity marker for former prisoners, and it could play an important role in post-Gulag social interactions.[15] But on the other hand, former prisoners often identified first and foremost with a certain subgroup of the camp population. For many, the key identity factor was belonging to a particular nationality, especially for those prisoners who had belonged to underground self-help organizations in the camps that had been organized on the basis of national identity.[16] Others identified with criminal castes, such as the *vory-v-zakone*.[17] Many prisoners felt that there was a stark division between those who had been convicted of political offences and others who had been convicted of other types of crime – this is the famous distinction between 'politicals' and 'criminals' that is so often found in Gulag memoirs. By that same token, other non-prisoners did not necessarily perceive released prisoners as a homogenous mass. Particularly in a place like Vorkuta, where so much of the population consisted of former prisoners or camp officials, it was likely that the general population would see former prisoners as continuing to belong to the same identity groups that they had in the Gulag. The result was that the perception and reception of former prisoners was far more complex and nuanced than would appear at first glance.

Perhaps no group of prisoners inspired more anxiety among the general population than those freed by the so-called Beria amnesty of 27 March 1953.[18] This amnesty, which resulted in the release of over a million prisoners over the course of a few short months, set off a crime wave across the Soviet Union that was serious enough to warrant significant attention from the country's top leadership.[19] As Miriam Dobson has pointed out, these releases generated local panic and indignation, despite the best efforts of the central leadership to discount the threat that the newly released prisoners posed to society at large.[20] Vorkuta was no exception in this regard, and the rapid release of some 7,000 prisoners from the Vorkuta camp complex led both to violence and to increased fears on the part of the local population.[21] Poor organization of the amnesty, particularly in the case of the first groups of released prisoners, led to large numbers of former prisoners wandering around the city of

Vorkuta buying alcohol, drinking, and then brawling in public. Several prisoners were hospitalized during the confusion and violence, which included serious assault and rape. The violence continued on trains departing the city, where even the most basic security measures were not followed, including the separation of men from women.[22] As was the case elsewhere, most of the violence perpetrated by the departing prisoners was directed against other former prisoners;[23] nevertheless, such incidents contributed to locals' perception that former prisoners were dangerous and did little to inspire confidence that the authorities could control them as they were being set free.

Tensions between the local population and newly released prisoners were exacerbated by violence between camp guards and amnestied prisoners. On one hand, many former prisoners had scores to settle now that they were free; on the other, camp guards were reluctant to give up the arbitrary authority that they had so recently wielded over the prisoners. Under such circumstances, violent confrontations were frequent. On 17 May 1953 a recently released prisoner who was leaving a store with a loaf of bread was accosted by drunken, off-duty camp guards and beaten with a belt. After being beaten, the ex-prisoner returned with nearly forty former prisoners who lived in a nearby converted camp barracks, hoping to dispense payback. Faced with a large crowd of angry ex-prisoners, the guards summoned some sixty of their comrades to what soon became an all-out brawl. Belts, bricks, knives, and picks were among the weapons used, although miraculously there appear to have been no serious injuries among the ten wounded participants.[24]

The blame for the incident landed squarely on the guards and camp officials who had instigated the violence without provocation.[25] This was not surprising, as it was not unusual for camp guards, usually in a state of intoxication, to victimize erstwhile peaceful city residents, as had been happening for a number of years.[26] But even if they did not bear the official blame for the violence, former prisoners, especially those who were perceived to have come from the ranks of the Gulag's 'criminals,' remained subject to suspicion and fear, if not outright hostility. The outbreak of violent confrontations between former prisoners and others only heightened tensions and increased mutual suspicions.

Public fears about the potential criminality of ex-prisoners were confirmed by newspaper reports on crime and punishment in the city. Throughout the 1950s Vorkuta's local newspaper *Zapoliar'e* published brief descriptions of court proceedings under the heading 'From the Courtroom.'[27] Many of the articles publicized cases of former prisoners being convicted of new crimes, usually petty theft, apartment burglary, or hooliganism. For instance, an article on 21 October 1956 described how one recently released prisoner was sentenced to twenty-five years' imprisonment for a series of twelve thefts from May to July 1956.[28] Such fears that former prisoners represented a risk to public safety were not completely unfounded; one report to the City Party Committee (Gorkom) in September 1960 pointed out that 31 per cent of all crimes in the first half of that year were committed by ex-prisoners.[29]

Some former prisoners were themselves fearful of the danger that other ex-prisoners posed. In particular, former prisoners who identified themselves as 'politicals' or 'counter-revolutionaries' were often afraid of being victims of violent crimes at the hands of former 'criminal' prisoners. Former 'political' Oleg Borovskii recalled that in 1956 there was widespread fear of being robbed and beaten by members of the criminal world who had recently been released from the Gulag, especially during the twenty-four-hour darkness of the polar night. As he wrote, 'We ... strong men left [work in] the city [for an outlying settlement] in small groups ... some of us even [armed] with knives.'[30] Thus, it was not simply a matter of non-prisoner suspicions of ex-prisoners, but also of mutual suspicions between different groups of released prisoners.

Hostility and suspicion were not directed only at 'criminals,' however. Local and regional state and party officials, particularly those representing the state political police (KGB), voiced fears at party meetings that some former counter-revolutionaries represented an active danger to Soviet society. The potential threat posed by former prisoners came into particular focus after the Hungarian uprising, which had broken out on 23 October 1956 and been crushed by Soviet tanks and troops less than two weeks later.[31] In its wake, on 19 December 1956 a letter drafted by the Central Committee was sent to all party organizations in the Soviet Union at the republican, regional, local, and district levels, calling for these organizations to strengthen their vigilance and actively fight against recent manifestations of 'active operations of anti-Soviet and enemy elements' that were taking place as the result of recent unrest in Hungary. Among the potential sources of threat identified in the letter, recently released prisoners were singled out. Although the letter acknowledged that the majority of prisoners were making honest and successful efforts to readjust to civilian life, it pointed out that there were a few 'former Trotskyites, right opportunists, and bourgeois nationalists' who were continuing their anti-Soviet activities. Using strong language, the letter urged that 'party organizations and Soviet organs must take the most decisive measures to intercept [them] and act as we always have against people who are enemies of our system.'[32]

The language of the letter was echoed directly in a speech that the first secretary of the Vorkuta Gorkom, V.A. Shikhov, delivered a month later at a city party conference. As he stated, 'Among them [former prisoners], especially former Trotskyites and bourgeois nationalists, there are people who are evilly disposed against Soviet power, who gather around themselves anti-Soviet elements, who attempt to resume their hostile and anti-Soviet activities.' In order to thwart these people, the party was to take a two-pronged approach: first, it had to educate 'the population and former prisoners' in order to inoculate them against pernicious influences; second, it had to keep a watchful eye and act swiftly to thwart truly anti-Soviet elements.[33] Although there were no truly drastic measures taken against former prisoners, the Central Committee's letter and general anxieties about the Hungarian events did lead to increased scrutiny of the activities of some former prisoners, and certainly to an increase of KGB surveillance.

This KGB surveillance was focused on three types of potential opposition among former prisoners: political, nationalist, and religious. The first category, that of political opposition, was the most amorphous of the three. Politically suspicious activities included criticism of Soviet foreign policy, particularly in Hungary.[34] It also included allegations of distributing anti-Soviet material, as in the case of a former prisoner who gave his notebook containing 'anti-Soviet poetry' to a young woman who came to the city as a volunteer.[35] Listening to foreign radio broadcasts, such as the BBC, was also a particular focus of the KGB.[36] That said, such garden-variety anti-Soviet activities were not given nearly as much attention as nationalist and religious opposition.

Suspicion of former prisoners for participating in dangerous political speech and action extended not only to ex-prisoners, but to their families as well. While Stalin was still alive, romantic associations or sexual relations with former prisoners usually resulted in serious consequences for party and Komsomol members. For example, in January 1952 the local Komsomol took up the case of a young woman who 'attempted to marry a former prisoner convicted under Article 58-10.' She was not kicked out of the Komsomol, but she was formally reprimanded, and the Komsomol Gorkom asked her employer to demote her.[37] Such practices continued well into the Thaw, suggesting significant continuity in the treatment of non-prisoners who associated with former prisoners. In 1958, for instance, several party members who had married former prisoners (all women) were singled out for harsh words at various meetings of the Gorkom. It does not appear that any of them were expelled from the party for their relationships with former prisoners, but the negative attention sent a clear message that the loyalties of those party members who married former prisoners were highly suspect.[38] As was the case in the western borderland regions of the Soviet Union,[39] suspicious activity by former nationalists was a particular area of interest for the KGB in Vorkuta. By the early 1950s the majority of the prisoner population in the Vorkuta camp system was not Russian, so non-Russians made up a majority of the prisoners released in the 1950s.[40] Local KGB officials noted a wide range of potentially subversive nationalist activity in Vorkuta and its environs throughout the Thaw. In 1956, a group of almost two hundred former prisoners from Latvia gathered in a cemetery in Inta (Vorkuta's near southern neighbour) for the unveiling of a monument commemorating Latvians who had died in the camps. According to Kurashov, the head of the local KGB, at this gathering 'anti-Soviet speeches' were delivered and 'bourgeois' Latvia's national anthem was sung to the accompaniment of a brass orchestra.[41] Thus, a gathering intended to honour dead comrades became, in the eyes of the KGB at least, a politicized event with dangerous nationalist overtones.

Networks connecting prisoners of common nationality within the camps were frequently reconstructed outside the camps, making them an easy target for those with suspicions that unrepentant nationalist rebels were on the loose in the city. The fact that many convicted nationalists were forced to return to Vorkuta in the late 1950s after unsuccessful attempts to return to their homes in the western borderlands only added to the atmosphere of suspicion and unease.[42] For local KGB representatives, the re-deportations of former prisoners reinforced prejudices and suspicions about non-Russian former prisoners, particularly those from the western Ukraine. For the prisoners deported, being sent back to Vorkuta was a painful reminder of how the Soviet Union's system of identity politics ascribed labels and stigmas that were remarkably persistent. This could only have strengthened social networks of co-nationals in the post-Stalin decade.

What made allegedly nationalist activity so dangerous in the eyes of party and KGB officials was the potential danger of anti-Soviet, nationalist contagion being spread from former prisoners to the many young recruits who came to the city to work in the 1950s and 1960s. Take, for instance, a birthday celebration that took place in an apartment in 1958. At this gathering, former prisoners from Lithuania 'sang nationalist songs,

songs from bourgeois Lithuania.'[43] What worried party officials most was that this celebration was for a newly arrived demobilized soldier, not for a former prisoner. Thus the significance was far greater, because it suggested the possibility that an impressionable youth was being corrupted by incorrigible nationalists who had rightfully served time for fighting Soviet power in the Baltics. In light of the directives received from the Central Committee, this birthday party represented a dangerous attempt to indoctrinate a loyal Soviet citizen.

The final area of potential opposition that was the focus of the KGB in Vorkuta during the Thaw was a result of Khrushchev's revival of anti-religious propaganda and his sustained campaign against religious belief in the Soviet Union.[44] In Vorkuta, religious 'sectarians' became a frequent target for KGB surveillance in connection with this campaign. In 1957 the city's KGB representative reported that religious groups of all kinds, including Jehovah's Witnesses, Baptists, and Mennonites, were active in Vorkuta. Not surprisingly, former prisoners and their families figured prominently in reports on their alleged activities. Jehovah's Witnesses were singled out in particular. As one report stated, 'Jehovah's Witnesses gather illegally in many parts of the city in order to carry out religious services, recruit new members to their sect, distribute religious literature among citizens and believers, and maintain ties with co-religionists in other regions of the Soviet Union, and with missionaries from capitalist countries.'[45] Religious groups often met in the apartments of former prisoners, many of whom had already served sentences in the 1940s and early 1950s for their heterodox religious beliefs. Men like Korol' Prokop'evich Nishchii, an ex-convict who now worked as a blacksmith in Mine No. 30, led regular weekly gatherings that included as many as twenty-six participants. But the most threatening activity of the Jehovah's Witnesses was the outspoken refusal of many to participate in elections.[46]

As in most cases of potentially dangerous 'anti-Soviet' activity, the local KGB and party organization pursued a policy of arresting ringleaders and aggressive measures to stop the spread of religious propaganda. Prophylactic measures included the publication of material in the local newspaper meant to attack and debunk the sectarians. For instance, a major feature appeared in the local newspaper in March 1959 telling the story of Krivchuk, a former prisoner who had become a Jehovah's Witness while serving time in a camp for Ukrainian nationalist activity. Drafted into the army soon after his release in 1955, he had been arrested a second time, this time for recruiting Jehovah's Witnesses from among his fellow soldiers.[47] Now living in Vorkuta, 'having finally broken with the Jehovah's Witnesses, he began to work.... He is cheerful, outgoing and grateful to his comrades at work, who have accepted him into their working family.' The lesson here was that inner peace was not to be found in religion, but through labour in a collective.[48] Despite repression and propaganda, the presence of 'sectarians' persisted, especially Jehovah's Witnesses; in 1961 one leader named Kazak, who worked in Mine No. 9, was arrested in connection with the confiscation of large amounts of religious literature found in his home.[49] Surveillance of ex-prisoners suspected of illegal religious activities persisted throughout the Thaw and into the late 1960s.

In fact, KGB surveillance of former prisoners continued long after the end of the Thaw. In 1967, former prisoner Pavel Negretov was formally questioned by the KGB in connection with his wife's planned trip to visit family in West Germany. The questioning began when he was met at a bus stop by an unknown man who later identified himself as a KGB agent and called him in for questioning. Although the conversation was ostensibly about his wife's trip, it quickly became clear to Negretov that he was being harassed for his activities during the Second World War. During the war, he had joined the National-Workers' Union of the New Generation (a proto-fascist organization that originated among Russian émigrés in the West), and that had earned him a fifteen-year sentence in the Gulag. Now, some twenty years later, the Vorkuta KGB asked Negretov to write a letter denouncing the group, which had been reincarnated as the National Workers' Union, an anti-Communist organization. Negretov flatly refused.[50]

Continued KGB surveillance of Negretov and other former prisoners was a constant reminder of the outsider status that was ascribed to certain groups of former prisoners. Those suspected of potentially anti-Soviet political, nationalist, and religious activities faced suspicion, surveillance, harassment, and even arrest, long after they had been released. For Negretov, the ultimate expression of the alienation and frustration that he felt was the publication of two of his works abroad: the first, published in English translation in Britain in 1977, was a journal article on the origins of Vorkuta and its camp system; the second, published in Russian in the United States in 1985, was a version of his memoirs.[51] Even in the 1975, Negretov was denied a job as archivist for one of Vorkuta's coal mines on the basis of his suspect past.[52] For many prisoners, the stigma of having been 'counter-revolutionary' prisoner was all but impossible to erase.

Employment Discrimination

Many former prisoners in Vorkuta also faced a significant formal obstacle to their successful reintegration into Soviet society: discrimination in the workplace. Ex-prisoners were a frequent target of state policies aimed at excluding them from important positions in a variety of fields. Engineering and technical workers, the so-called ITR in Soviet parlance, were subject to formal discrimination during the Thaw.[53] These managers, engineers, and technicians were the experts on which the proper and efficient operation of the mines depended. Because of their importance, local, regional, and central party bodies were concerned with their qualifications and political reliability. As a result, the cadres department of the Vorkutaugol' (Vorkuta Coal) kombinat (KVU hereafter) collected data on specialists that it did not collect on ordinary workers. These data were used throughout the 1950s and 1960s to practise discrimination against specialists who were former prisoners and exiles. This discrimination may have been to some degree systematic, but it followed no simple formula. There was no blanket policy against hiring ex-prisoners for ITR positions. Nor was it random; rather, it ebbed and flowed in accordance with party oversight, which was done, like so many other things in the Soviet Union, 'campaign-style.'[54]

Formal discrimination against ex-prisoners was discussed in party meetings under the rubric of the 'selection, allocation, and preparation of cadres' (*podbor, rasstanovka i vospitanie kadrov*). Campaigns to purge the ranks of specialists of ex-prisoners were carried out in 1950–1,[55] 1954–5, 1959, and 1966, usually initiated as a result of discussions at the level of central and regional party bodies. The purge of 1959 provides a good example because it is well documented. The campaign in Vorkuta began at a Gorkom plenum on 21 March 1959. Launched in a speech by the second secretary Vorob'ev, it took place in accordance with decisions made at the Twenty-First Party Congress. The logic behind the purge was explained in the following manner: 'Comrades! The Communist Party teaches that in order to make the most objective measure of a worker one must first know his political and professional qualities.... Many of our managers, while making promotions to important posts, forget these Leninist instructions and are guided by only one of these qualities, either choosing on the basis of professional qualities, forgetting about political qualities, or the other way around.' In other words, specialists needed a combination of know-how *and* political reliability in order to be suitable candidates for important posts.[56]

As evidence for this, Vorob'ev pointed out that of 2,405 ITR positions in KVU, 712 were filled by people 'formerly convicted of serious crimes against the motherland.' By contrast, there were only 163 Communist Party and 456 Komsomol members in ITR positions.[57] In terms of 'professional qualities,' the ITR workers of KVU were wanting as well: over half were *praktiki*, people with no formal training.[58] As Vorob'ev continued his speech, it became increasingly clear that lack of requisite political and professional qualities often coexisted. As an example, Vorob'ev pointed out that none of the section heads in Mine No. 26 had any formal mining training, and at the same time, all had been convicted of serious crimes.[59] This blurring of categories between politically unreliable and technically unqualified was a consistent feature of campaigns against former prisoners. Its logic was probably self-evident to contemporaries. Most ex-prisoner specialists had not come to coal mining after graduating from mining institutes or technical schools, but rather had been brought to the city as prisoners. Consequently many lacked formal training.

Vorob'ev proceeded to provide concrete examples of appointment 'mistakes' throughout a range of mines. One personnel decision that he found particularly disturbing took place at Mine No. 9/10 in 1957. In that case, Efimov, a Communist Party member who had worked as a section head from 1950 to 1957, was demoted for mismanaging work in his section. He became a deputy to Artym, an ex-prisoner (allegedly a West Ukrainian nationalist) with no formal training. According to Vorob'ev, making a Communist the deputy of an unqualified ex-prisoner was a blatant violation of party policy.[60]

The resolution of the Gorkom plenum called for several measures to be taken in order to rectify the situation. First and foremost, in the first half of 1959, relevant authorities were to fill decisive positions in all organizations with people who were known to be both 'technically literate and faithful to our party.' Particular attention was to be paid to promoting young specialists who were not yet employed in ITR jobs despite having formal training. All party organizations were to participate in the ritual of criticism and self-criticism regarding the management of cadres. Secretaries of party organizations in Vorkuta were to discuss the Gorkom resolution in closed party meetings. The management of KVU, as well as individual enterprises (like Mine Nos. 26 and 9/10) were singled out as those that needed to change their hiring practices most of all.[61]

How successful was this campaign against ex-prisoners? The 1959 purge, from the point of view of local party leadership, was partially successful, although it seemed to fall short of expectations. Directors of individual enterprises continued to be singled out and criticized for their poor implementation of the new policy. In June 1959, the director of Mine No. 26 was called in front of the Gorkom and disciplined for not implementing the new policy properly.[62] Even in 1961, two years after the original plenum discussion, the Gorkom was having trouble enforcing it. On 28 March 1961 the head of Construction Department 19, Meleshko, was given a formal reprimand by the Gorkom for ignoring the resolution. In addition to not firing ex-prisoners under his employ, he had even gone so far as to hire newly released prisoners after the resolution had been passed.[63] According to a status update from the Gorkom bureau on 20 May 1961, two years after the plenum resolution, 312 ITR positions in KVU were filled by ex-prisoners, as opposed to 712 before the campaign began. While this was a significant reduction in the number of ex-prisoners in ITR jobs, Gorkom officials were unsatisfied, and various managers were warned and disciplined.[64]

Thanks to reasonably systematic recordkeeping within KVU on the number of ex-prisoners working as specialists, it is possible to discern overall trends in discrimination from 1955 to 1966, as depicted in table 4.1. These data suggest a general downward trend in the employment of ex-prisoners as specialists, although increases in the employment of ex-prisoners in 1961 and 1966 underscore the episodic nature of discrimination. Whereas in 1955 nearly half of KVU's ITR workers were ex-prisoners, by 1966 the proportion was about 14 per cent. This confirms what other evidence suggests: as the prison camps in Vorkuta shrank, fewer and fewer ex-prisoners held responsible posts in the city. This was partly due to the fact that as time passed, more and more qualified ex-prisoners left the city or retired. It could also, to some degree, reflect informal practices used to keep ex-prisoners 'off the books' (see below). But formal discrimination was the dominant factor.

Data in this table also suggest the existence of a glass ceiling for ex-prisoners. A selection of ITR jobs at various levels in the hierarchy (in descending order of importance) shows how far former prisoners could advance in the KVU hierarchy and how this changed over time. No former prisoner held the job of mine director during this eleven-year period, although in 1954 two of ten mine directors had been ex-prisoners.[65] A few former prisoners managed to occupy the second most important job in a mine (head engineer), but this ceased after 1960. Former prisoners did work in slightly less important positions, like head mechanic (or assistant head mechanic) in greater numbers and further into the 1960s. But by

Table 4.1 Former prisoners occupying ITR positions in KVU, 1955–66

Occupation (descending by importance)		Date (dd.mm.yy)							
		15.07.55	01.01.59	01.01.60	01.12.60	01.12.61	01.12.62	01.12.64	01.01.66
Mine director	*n*	–	–	–	–	–	–	–	–
	%	–	–	–	–	–	–	–	–
Head mine engineer	*n*	2	2	1	–	–	–	–	–
	%	12.50	9.52	6.25	–	–	–	–	–
Deputy head mine engineer	*n*	3	1	1	–	–	–	–	2
	%	18.75	5.26	6.25	–	–	–	–	3.85
Head mine mechanic	*n*	5	8	3	1	–	–	–	1
	%	26.32	38.10	18.75	5.56	–	–	–	5.88
Deputy head mine mechanic	*n*	–	13	2	3	1	1	–	11
	%	–	50.00	6.45	13.04	7.69	5.56	–	18.33
Mine geologist	*n*	–	7	2	–	1	1	–	–
	%	–	77.78	28.57	–	12.50	11.11	–	–
Mine economist	*n*	–	1	–	7	–	–	–	–
	%	–	5.88	–	53.85	–	–	–	–
Section head (extraction and tunnelling)	*n*	41[a]	42	11	10	11	2	9	8
	%	34.75	36.21	12.36	10.87	11.58	2.13	10.00	7.34
Mining master	*n*	–	240	71	60	64	42	29	58
	%	–	33.29	11.97	10.20	11.59	7.61	6.65	11.39
ITR overall	*n*	1034[b]	712	312	247	397	271	342	474
	%	46.95	29.60	13.09	10.56	14.23	10.21	11.88	14.07

[a]Includes 16 prisoners

[b]Includes 261 prisoners

Source: 15.07.55: GURK NARK 1 R-1675/1/1778/15; 01.01.59: GURK NARK 1 R-1675/1/1709/147–9; 01.01.60: GURK NARK 1 R-1675/1/1710/35–6; 01.12.60: GURK NARK 1 R-1675/1/1711/29–30; 01.12.61: GURK NARK 1 R-1675/1/1712/32–4; 01.12.62: GURK NARK 1 R-1675/1/1713/21–3; 01.12.64: GURK NARK 1 R-1675/1/1714/61–2; 01.01.66: GURK NARK 1 R-1675/1/1716/39–40.

1964, the only ITR positions at a mine that were realistically within the reach of former prisoners were decidedly less prominent, such as section head or mining master. Whereas in 1954 a former prisoner had been the director of one of KVU's two 'trusts' (in other words, he managed half of Vorkuta's mines),[66] by 1966 few prisoners were entrusted with management of even a mine section.

Despite the general decline in the use of ex-prisoners in ITR positions and the glass ceiling outlined above, it is important to underline the limited success of discrimination in keeping former prisoners out of important posts. Even on 1 January 1966, 56 of 277 ITR positions in Mine No. 1 were filled by former prisoners (about 20 per cent), many of them formerly convicted of counter-revolutionary crimes.[67] Overall, official discrimination kept former prisoners out of the highest ITR positions, but not less important jobs. Why was it that campaigns to remove political unreliables from positions of responsibility met with limited and uneven success? One part of the answer is undoubtedly the ambiguous language of the resolutions passed by the Gorkom. It was never explicitly stated against whom the campaign was directed, nor was anyone expressly forbidden to hire or employ former prisoners. This ambiguity could only have been underscored by the fact that the Gorkom, in September 1959, was criticizing KVU for not hiring enough newly released prisoners in accordance with a Supreme Soviet decree from earlier in the year.[68] That said, the examples discussed in Gorkom meetings should have made the target of the campaign fairly obvious.

In fact, the limited success of the formal policy of discrimination exposes widespread informal practices that undermined it. In some cases, former prisoners were simply too valuable to fire or demote. Although many lacked formal training, they were often more experienced than the young, formally trained specialists who were sent to Vorkuta. In an atmosphere of a general labour shortage and high labour turnover rates, it seemed foolish to fire long-term residents and dependable specialists in favour of new arrivals who might not stay in Vorkuta for long. The livelihood of virtually every person working in a mine, from the director to those working at the coal face, depended on meeting production quotas, and the work of ex-prisoner specialists was essential in meeting these targets. It was one thing for Gorkom officials to institute a policy of formal discrimination, but these same officials also demanded that mines meet output plans. In the end, it was individual enterprise managers who conducted hiring, and they had to balance conformity with party campaigns and plan fulfilment. For their part, KVU top brass never seemed wholly committed to implementing discrimination policy. In the midst of the 1959 campaign, even the head of the cadres department of KVU, K. Plastinina, herself a long-time city resident, admitted that ex-prisoners were still employed in ITR positions and that they were also still being hired to fill vacancies. Those former prisoners who 'recommended themselves positively by their work' often remained unpurged.[69]

Mine directors and those in charge of personnel deployed various techniques to minimize the potentially negative effects of purges on their enterprises. One strategy was to name an ex-prisoner specialist to a relatively low post, but appoint him the 'acting' (*ispol'niaiushchii obiazannosti*) occupant of a higher post. This was one way to make it appear as though an enterprise employed few ex-prisoners as specialists. Another strategy was to comply with party orders to demote a specialist, but then promote her later. Mikhail T., a young specialist who came to Vorkuta in 1962 from Novocherkassk, described how this worked in the case of an ex-prisoner who had once been a high-ranking civilian official in the German occupation administration of Kharkov. This ex-prisoner was an unacceptable candidate for an important post in a mine because he was considered politically unreliable. Yet he was an extraordinarily competent manager and so worked as the deputy mine director in charge of supplies in Mine No. 27.[70] As Mikhail T. explained,

> The order came to remove him [from his post]. He is removed from that position, and he begins to work as a master in the lumber depot. Time passes, and the mine begins to choke without lumber [for tunnel supports] ... the lumber depot works in three shifts, and there is still not enough lumber for the mine ... So he [the ex-prisoner], whether it is allowed or not, is reappointed deputy mine director in charge of supplies. Time passes, and lumber appears in the mine. More time passes, and he suggests that the lumber depot only work in two shifts. They work in two shifts, and there is still lumber for the mine. More time passes, and two shifts are no longer needed, one will suffice. The lumber depot works in one shift and there is sufficient lumber in the mine. The party organs once again order that he must be removed – 'How can there be a deputy mine director with that kind of biography [*anketa*]?' They remove him ... the lumber depot begins to work in two shifts, then in three, and there isn't enough lumber in the mine.[71]

Using a cycle of demotion and promotion of former prisoners, managers navigated the dual pitfalls of punishment for not following party directives and penalties for falling short of plan targets.

Why Vorkuta?

The previous two sections have explored some of the handicaps that ex-prisoners faced on the 'outside' in Vorkuta. As I have pointed out, some aspects of life in Vorkuta made these obstacles potentially less important for the experiences of ex-prisoners in the city than they might have been elsewhere. Yet the story of why so many former prisoners remained in Vorkuta is not simply a negative one, that things were not quite as difficult for ex-prisoners there as they were elsewhere. The city of Vorkuta also offered positive inducements for ex-prisoners to settle there over the short or long term.

One advantage was that Vorkuta, like other cities in the Gulag empire, was familiar to most ex-prisoners – not simply the environment, but also the people. When Valentin Frid was released from a camp in Inta (a city near Vorkuta) on 8 January 1954, he was relieved to learn that he would be allowed to live in that city rather than being sent elsewhere. He writes, 'It was very lucky [to be released in Inta and not exiled elsewhere]. Here everything was familiar, here there were friends, here there were greater opportunities to find tolerable work.'[72] The advantages of being released in a place where one had friends and acquaintances became immediately apparent to Frid in his first days on the 'outside.' With no place to live, he stayed temporarily in the house of another ex-prisoner, a convicted thief named Vasia Nikulin, whom he had met in the camp.[73] Living there was a harrowing experience because of Nikulin's proclivity for drinking binges (not to mention a vicious dog), but in January it was essential to have a warm place to stay, and without the kindness of this acquaintance Frid might have been left without a roof over his head.

Nanci Adler, in her groundbreaking book on Gulag survivors, rightfully points out that 'the deforming effects of the camps continued to wreak havoc on the ex-prisoners, along with their social networks.'[74] But, as the story above shows, prisoners' experiences in the camps led to the creation of new social networks that could facilitate adjustments to life on the 'outside.'[75] These social networks were especially valuable in cities like Vorkuta that were dominated by prison camps. Here ex-prisoners were everywhere, if not a majority then a sizeable minority of the population. They were more likely to be in positions of power than elsewhere, so were able to help their camp acquaintances obtain scarce resources like housing. Even if two people had not been imprisoned together, sharing the experience of imprisonment in the Gulag could be enough to strengthen otherwise weak social bonds.

The case of Galina S. shows both the power and the limits of ex-prisoner social networks. Unable to return permanently to Moscow because of limitations in her passport, recently widowed, and with a newborn baby, she lived in a fellow ex-prisoner's apartment for some time after she was released. Her first job was as a guard in a store. Her boss was a fellow ex-prisoner who hired her out of sympathy for her struggles as a single mother. The job required her to work one twenty-four-hour shift and then gave her three days off at a stretch – an arrangement that allowed her to take care of her baby. But assistance from other ex-prisoners was not adequate for her to obtain permanent housing or a stable financial situation. For that, she got married, to a man who had been recruited to come to Vorkuta to run a new cafeteria, and who had been introduced to her by the woman in whose apartment she was staying. Her husband had a good job and had been offered housing when he was recruited. After their nuptials, the young family moved into a 'family dormitory,' essentially a large communal apartment, but one in which she, her husband, and her baby shared their own room. About five years later, in 1962, they moved into two rooms in a communal apartment that they shared with one other family. In 1971 they moved into a two-room separate apartment across the street. Recalling the marriage decades later, she maintained that the main reason for getting married was her husband's access to housing. As a single mother with a small child, she had little other choice.[76] In this case, contacts among ex-prisoners helped her find temporary work and housing, but were inadequate when it came to obtaining long-term housing and financial stability.

The case of Pavel Negretov is similarly instructive. Released in November 1955, he had no real place to live for a year and a half. He split his nights between the apartment of his childhood friend Vitalii (an ex-prisoner), the laboratory where he worked, and the apartments of colleagues while they were on vacation (many of whom were also ex-prisoners). He wrote, 'In this manner I spent the entire summer of 1956 living in the apartment of Olga Pavlovna Bazhovaia, my boss, who was away on two years' worth of vacation.' It was not until he and his wife Ursula married in May 1957 that he obtained permanent housing and they moved into a dormitory room with Ursula's sister.[77] By 1962 the couple had moved into a two-room apartment in a former camp barracks. In January 1967 they moved into a separate apartment in a new five-story reinforced concrete apartment block.[78]

Many ex-prisoners found jobs through the networks they had built inside the 'zone.' If a prisoner left Vorkuta for a new city, he would likely have to rely on strangers to hire him. Even when returning to a place of former residence, there was no guarantee that previous ties would still be extant or useful in finding a job. But in Vorkuta, former prisoners often relied on friends and acquaintances they had acquired while in the camps. An anonymous letter sent to the Ministry of Coal from a worker in Mine No. 25 in 1954 contended that an ex-prisoner named Niurin, who worked as the head accountant in the mine, was directly responsible for the mine hiring a number of his ex-prisoner friends. The letter specifically alleged that Niurin had conspired with Bak, a good friend of his from Vorkutlag, under the following conditions: Niurin hired Bak for a lucrative position and paid him a travel allowance of almost six thousand rubles. The allegedly conspiratorial behaviour took place when the two met in Moscow after release. Obviously, this anonymous letter was meant to denounce Niurin and Bak. But it merely confirmed what was a widespread, and perfectly legal, practice: former prisoners often hired their friends.[79]

In Vorkuta some former prisoners held positions where they were responsible for hiring others. Even though employer and potential employee might not be personally acquainted, they did share a common experience in the camps, and this could be a deciding factor in the hiring process. Gadzhiev, a machine operator from Mine No. 40, complained that some ex-prisoners had exclusive say in the hiring process and were using it to hire ex-prisoners. As he stated at a session of the Gorkom plenum in 1959, 'There are still former prisoners who command Komsomol members and Communists. In my opinion it is necessary to make it so that they cannot personally decide on hiring or firing workers, because otherwise they will hire "their own" as they are freed from the camps.'[80] Hiring 'their own' is exactly what a Komsomol representative alleged was happening at the Vorkuta machine-repair factory in 1956: in that factory, 'most of the shop managers and masters are former convicts, and because of this they are interested in hiring only qualified workers from among prisoners, and avoid [hiring] youths.'[81]

As the use of the expression 'qualified worker' in the last example suggests, it was not simply a matter of ex-prisoners preferring to hire other ex-prisoners. Managers of mines and enterprises who had never been prisoners were often desperate to retain the former convicts who were being released from Vorkutlag or from exile in huge numbers. The alternative sources of labour were prisoners provided by Vorkutlag, who were becoming increasingly unruly and unproductive, or new recruits from outside the city, who were often unskilled and unlikely to stay in the city for long once they realized how difficult life there could be. In order to retain released prisoners, mine directors made requests in 1955 to 1956 to be allowed to offer 'northern bonuses,' significant wage incentives to which only outside recruits were normally entitled, to former prisoners who remained.[82] These requests made their way to the USSR Council of Ministers via both the Ministry of Coal Industry and the Komi Obkom, resulting in a Council of Ministers circular on 7 May 1956 that allowed mine directors to sign contracts with released prisoners and exiles.[83] Now able to offer 'northern bonuses' to ex-prisoners, mines and enterprises in Vorkuta were far better able to retain the services of prisoners being released from Vorkutlag.[84]

For some, at least in hindsight, the transition from prisoner to 'free' worker was relatively seamless. This was apparently the case for Stepan Mikhailovich Semegen, a prisoner who worked in Mine No. 27 beginning in 1953. When interviewed for a book of recollections about this mine published in 2002, he described his personal transition in very simple terms, stating, 'In 1957–1958 the substitution of prisoners for free workers gradually began, and as of April 1958 I also began to work as a free worker. But my production status was not affected by this: I had been a tunnelling brigade leader, and remained one.'[85] This may be a dramatic oversimplification of the transition from prisoner to comrade, but it does show that from the standpoint of work, it did not necessarily make an enormous difference. Many former prisoners continued working in the same mines, had the same jobs, and even led the same work brigades. In fact, continuity among brigade leaders and foremen was quite high; even as late as 1964, almost one-fifth of the brigade leaders and foremen working in Mine No. 1 were former prisoners, most of whom had been released from 1955 to 1957.[86]

Unfortunately, systematic data on the number of former prisoners hired by KVU have not been preserved in the company records. Still, it is possible to get an impressionistic view of the quantitative scale of this phenomenon. According to company records, of 13,268 prisoners released in 1954, 2,823 remained in Vorkuta. All but 312 of them were still gainfully employed as of 1 January 1955.[87] In 1958, 3,161 people were hired directly by KVU after release from Vorkutlag.[88] Such calculations do not include the many who returned to the city after trying their luck elsewhere. Still, it is clear that over the course of the 1950s many thousands of ex-prisoners chose to remain in Vorkuta. Even in 1960, when Vorkutlag had already been largely dismantled, 652 ex-prisoners were hired directly after release by KVU.[89] The eagerness of managers to hire experienced former prisoners and the presence of potentially useful social networks in the city were important factors that prisoners weighed when choosing where to settle after release. These factors combined to make Vorkuta and other former Gulag communities magnets that attracted a large proportion of the Soviet Union's millions of ex-prisoners during the Thaw.

In 1957 Iurii P. left his native Ukraine for Vorkuta. Like many others who settled there, he was recently released from the Gulag. But his story was different: although he spent almost six years in Soviet prisons and camps, he came nowhere near Vorkutlag. After being released from a camp in Kuibyshev in 1956, he returned to his home town in western Ukraine. He found work in a sugar factory but found life at home difficult because of the KGB. They asked him to inform on a local man who had emigrated from the United States, and when he refused, the KGB began to harass him. In 1957, a school friend of his, an ex-prisoner then living in Vorkuta, was visiting on summer vacation and presented Iurii P. with a solution: 'He said, you know what, come to Vorkuta – there, everyone is like you and me. And no one is going to keep you under surveillance.'[90] Iurii P. came to Vorkuta, and his wife and daughter soon followed. From 1957 to 1959, he worked in Mine No. 2, and from 1959 until his retirement in 1983, in Mine No. 40 (now known as *Vorkutinskaia*). Whereas his home village in Ukraine had rejected him, Vorkuta accepted him as a citizen.

This man's story, like those of many other ex-prisoners, resonates with an officially endorsed parable that cast Vorkuta as a place where ex-prisoners could be successfully reintegrated into Soviet society. Perhaps the best example of this story is a version that was told in the pages of the local newspaper on 7 December 1960, entitled 'The Road to Big Life.' Stretching across three of the paper's four pages, this article relates the life of Victor Babkin, an ex-prisoner living in Vorkuta. Arrested for theft as a teenager in Moscow *oblast'* and sentenced to fifteen years' imprisonment in the late 1940s, he was freed early by a commission. After his release, he began his new life as a coal miner in the following fashion: 'At the mine he was simply hired. No one asked about the past, in his brigade he was considered an equal and respected for his diligence.' By 1959, Viktor had been elected leader of a brigade, joined the Komsomol, and was nominated as a candidate member of the Communist Party. His brigade had been given a great honour, the title of Brigade of Communist Labour. This is how he reflected on his new life: 'Viktor thought for a long time about his comrades, real friends, with whom he had resolved

A monument to Gulag victims in Vorkuta. It overlooks Rudnik, the abandoned old city. Photograph by the author, May 2003. Used with permission.

to live by the principle "one for all and all for one." What broad horizons this life had opened up before him – a big life, rushing into the future.'[91]

As I have argued, beginning life on the 'outside' for most ex-prisoners in Vorkuta was more difficult than suggested by the narratives of Iurii P. or Viktor Babkin. Former prisoners faced serious obstacles in establishing new lives outside the 'zone' in Vorkuta: prejudice, surveillance, and discrimination in the workplace. These were obstacles that former prisoners had to contend with all over the Soviet Union. Yet there is much that rings true even in the parable of Babkin, because as Vorkuta underwent its transition from prison camp complex to 'company town,' there were opportunities for ex-prisoners that were unlikely to have existed where they had originally come from. Given the social, economic, and political upheaval taking place around them, enterprise managers actively sought ex-prisoners as the anchors who could ensure that production targets were met. Former prisoners were hired for many jobs without any questions asked about their backgrounds. This was an important factor in the individual decisions of ex-prisoners who chose to remain in the city. Another of no less importance was the familiarity of the city and its inhabitants. During their time in the 'zone,' prisoners made important personal connections that proved to be useful on the 'outside.'

For former prisoners in Vorkuta, there would always be reminders of the camps. Many lived in, worked at, or saw the physical vestiges of Vorkutlag and Rechlag regularly (some of these vestiges remain in the city even in the twenty-first century). An interaction with a former camp official, even a decade after release, might bring back unhappy memories of imprisonment, as happened to Galina S. when her husband invited a former camp chief to their home to share a bottle of vodka.[92] Suspicion over past behaviour might mean being turned down for a promotion that one deserved, as happened to Pavel Negretov in 1975 (see above). As Nanci Adler concluded in her study of Gulag survivors from among the urban intelligentsia, 'The consequences of their experience as prisoners and the further consequences of their status as ex-prisoners hindered all efforts toward readjustment and reassimilation.'[93] But in Vorkuta, hindrances hardly rendered readjustment or reassimilation impossible. Many former prisoners grew proud of their city and their own contributions to its construction. In personal narratives related by ex-prisoners like Leonid Markizov and Iurii P., this pride is what frames the story of their post-Gulag lives in Vorkuta, not the obstacles they faced as ex-prisoners. Such framing suggests that it was indeed possible for former prisoners to be reintegrated into Soviet society, at least in former Gulag cities like Vorkuta.

NOTES

Funding for the research and writing of this article was provided by the Council on Library and Information Resources Mellon Fellowship for Dissertation Research in Original Sources in the Humanities, the University of Chicago, and the Eurasia Program of the Social Science Research Council with funds provided by the State Department under the Program for Research and Training on Eastern Europe and the Independent States of the Former Soviet Union (Title VIII). The author wishes to thank Judy Cole, Marc Elie, Sheila Fitzpatrick, Michael Geyer, Eleonory Gilburd, Denis Kozlov, Abigail Swingen, and Lynne Viola for their helpful comments and criticism.

1 Yury Osipovich Dombrovsky, *The Faculty of Useless Knowledge*, trans. Alan Myers (London, 1996), 285.
2 M. Baital'skii, *Notebooks for the Grandchildren: Recollections of a Trotskyist Who Survived the Stalin Terror* (Atlantic Highlands, NJ, 1995), 401.
3 Leonid Pavlovich Markizov, *Do i posle 1945* (Syktyvkar, 2003), 155.
4 Ibid., 145–55.
5 Vorkutlag, or *Vorkutinskii lager'*, was first established as a separate camp on 10 May 1938. GARF f. R-9401, op. 1a, d. 22, ll. 67–7ob. Rechlag, or *Rechnoi lager'*, was established on 27 August 1948. A.B. Roginskii, M.B. Smirnov, and N.G. Okhotin, *Sistema ispravitel'no-trudovykh lagerei v SSSR, 1923–1960: spravochnik* (Moscow, 1998), 291–92.
6 GARF R-9414/1 ch. 2/511; Gosudarstvennoe uchrezhdenie Respubliki Komi Natsional'nyi Arkhiv Respubliki Komi (GURK NARK) 1 R-1941/1/83/6.
7 Archival records provide surprisingly scanty evidence on the exact number of former prisoners who settled in Vorkuta. However, a mine director, speaking at a Gorkom plenum in April 1959, estimated that 20–30 per cent of the city's workforce consisted of former prisoners. GURK NARK 2 2216/14/56/27.
8 For studies that follow this approach, see Nanci Adler, *The Gulag Survivor: Beyond the Soviet System* (New Brunswick, NJ, 2002); Orlando Figes, *The Whisperers: Private Life in Stalin's Russia* (New York, 2007); Amir Weiner, 'The Empires Pay a Visit: Gulag Returnees, East European Rebellions, and Soviet Frontier Politics,' in this volume.
9 For approaches that study particular social groups, see, e.g., Adler, *Gulag Survivor*; Stephen F. Cohen, *The Victims Return* (Exeter, NH, 2010); Miriam Dobson, '"Show the Bandit-Enemies No Mercy!": Amnesty, Criminality, and Public Response in 1953,' in *The Dilemmas of De-Stalinization: Negotiating Cultural and Social Change in the Khrushchev Era*, ed. Polly Jones, 21–40 (London,

2006); Weiner, 'Empires Pay a Visit.' Of particular note is the approach of Miriam Dobson in her groundbreaking monograph on the Khrushchev era, where she examines the cases of former prisoners who were subsequently re-arrested. As she demonstrates, reintegration was hindered by deep suspicion and hostility to returnees, and by the alternative world views that many former Gulag prisoners had acquired. Dobson, *Khrushchev's Cold Summer: Gulag Returnees, Crime, and the Fate of Reform after Stalin* (Ithaca, NY, 2009), chap. 4.

10 Only two studies have systematically attempted to explore the importance of informal social networks and informal practices in the lives of former prisoners: Marc Elie, 'Les politiques à l'égard des libérés du Goulag,' *Cahiers du monde russe* 47, nos. 1–2 (2006): 327–48; and Figes, *Whisperers.*

11 On discrimination against former prisoners, see Marc Elie, 'Les anciens détenus du Goulag: libérations massives, réinsertion et réhabilitation dans l'URSS poststalinienne, 1953–1964' (PhD diss., l'École des hautes études en sciences sociales, 2007), chap. 8.

12 One of the most moving descriptions of this feeling was written by Evgeniia Ginzburg. Evgeniia Semenovna Ginzburg, *Within the Whirlwind* (New York, 1981), 173.

13 Aleksandr Klein, *Moi nomer '2P-904': avtobiograficheskie stikhi i poema* (Syktyvkar, 1992), 60.

14 Ibid.

15 Of the many stories explaining the remarkable power of the shared prisoner experience, perhaps the most interesting is Jacques Rossi's 'Twenty Years Later' [Dvadtsat' let spustia]. The story describes a chance encounter in Warsaw in the 1970s, where Rossi was targeted on the street as the dupe in a money-changing scheme. However, when Rossi and his would-be assailant recognized each other as former Gulag inmates, the encounter turned friendly. As he wrote, 'What an amazing event! Two foreigners meet on the streets of a strange city in a strange country; after recognizing each other, they name "their" Moscow prison, after which one abandons the idea of cheating the other.' Jacques Rossi, 'Dvadtsat' let spustia,' *Volia* 8–9 (2002): 143.

16 For a classic view of nationalist self-help organizations in Vorkuta, see Joseph Scholmer, *Vorkuta* (New York, 1955), chap. 6. On the role of nationalist organizations in the postwar Gulag, see Steven A. Barnes, '"In a Manner Befitting Soviet Citizens": An Uprising in the Post-Stalin Gulag,' *Slavic Review* 64, no. 4 (2005): 823–50.

17 On the *vory-v-zakone,* see Federico Varese, 'The Society of the vory-v-zakone, 1930s–1950s,' *Cahiers du monde russe* 39, no. 4 (1998): 515–38.

18 The best summary of the terms of this amnesty remains Nicolas Werth, 'L'amnistie du 27 mars 1953. La première grande sortie du Goulag,' *Communisme* 42–44 (1995): 211–24.

19 On the increase in crime that followed the amnesty and the discussion of measures to curb violence, see GARF R-7523/85/34/1–31. For secondary studies of this crime wave, see Dobson, *Khrushchev's Cold Summer*, 37–49; Elie, 'Les politiques à l'égard,' 334–7; V.A. Kozlov, *Massovye besporiadki v SSSR pri Khrushcheve i Brezhneve (1953 – nachalo 1980-kh gg.)* (Moscow, 2010), 83–9.

20 The Soviet public's reception of the amnesty and the amnestied has been explored by Dobson, *Khrushchev's Cold Summer*, 37–49.

21 One report, produced no earlier than 1 August 1956, stated that 7,123 prisoners were released from Vorkutlag and Rechlag under the amnesty in 1953. GARF R-9414/1 ch. 2/519/2. It should be noted that while this was a significant release of prisoners, only approximately 10 per cent of the prisoners in Vorkutlag and Rechlag were released, well below the average for Gulag camps and colonies.

22 GARF R-8131/32/3032/62, 176–7. This problem was noted throughout the Gulag. See Iurii Nikolaevich Afanas'ev and V.P. Kozlov, eds., *Istoriia stalinskogo Gulaga: konets 1920-kh-pervaia polovina 1950-kh godov*, 7 vols. (Moscow, 2004), 2:430–1. Although actions were soon taken to limit the violence associated with the amnesty, such as banning the sale of alcohol when prisoners were being released and increasing security, disorganization surrounding mass prisoner releases persisted. In the last few months of 1955, when some six thousand convicted Nazi collaborators were amnestied, Vorkuta's railroad station became an encampment for scores of prisoners waiting to be issued railroad tickets. GURK NARK 2 2216/6/63/65.

23 Elie, 'Les anciens détenus du Goulag,' 38.

24 Two versions of events, the first from the point of view of camp officials and the second from the militia, can be found in GURK NARK 2 2216/6/63/37–41; GURK NARK 2 2216/6/62/10–11. On the disciplining of those responsible, see GURK NARK 2 2216/6/54/158.

25 Violent conflicts between soldiers and other parts of the location population (e.g., ex-prisoners, students) broke out periodically over the course of the 1950s. For a discussion of similar conflicts elsewhere in the Soviet periphery, see Kozlov, *Massovye besporiadki.*

26 One such incident, when off-duty camp guards beat students and other city residents, took place on 22 June 1952. GURK NARK 2 2216/1/7/107–11.

27 These features began to appear on 26 July 1953. Miriam Dobson discusses

these news items within the broader context of the Khrushchev period. Dobson, *Khrushchev's Cold Summer*, 44–8.

28 *Zapoliar'e*, 21 October 1956.

29 GURK NARK 2 2216/14/108a/154.

30 Muzeino-Vystavochnyi Tsentr (VMVTs) OF/3094/1–2/336.

31 For a brief account of the political background to the uprising, see William Taubman, *Khrushchev: The Man and His Era* (New York, 2003), 294–9. According to Taubman, some twenty thousand Hungarians were killed during the course of events.

32 A. Artizov, Iu. Sigachev, I. Shevchuk, and V. Khlopov, eds., *Reabilitatsiia: Kak eto bylo*, 3 vols. (Moscow: 'Demokratiia,' 2000–2004), 2:208–14. Quotation from 2:213.

33 GURK NARK 2 2216/7/92/43.

34 GURK NARK 2 2216/6/27/51–5.

35 GURK NARK 2 2216/14/17a/53.

36 One such incident is described in GURK NARK 2 2216/6/27/45–6.

37 GURK NARK 2 1791/1/27/24–25.

38 GURK NARK 2 2216/14/19a/49; GURK NARK 2 2216/14/19, l. 94; GURK NARK 2 2216/14/17a/56.

39 Weiner, 'Empires Pay a Visit,' 336–47.

40 As of 1 January 1953, only 31 per cent of the population of the Vorkuta camp complex was categorized as Russian. GARF R-9414/1 ch. 2/492.

41 GURK NARK 2 2216/92/106.

42 Many officials in the western borderlands did not want convicted nationalists to return home and took measures to ensure that they remained in (or were returned to) Vorkutlag and other camps in Russia and Kazakhstan. For example, representatives of the Ukrainian KGB wrote to their central counterparts in 1956 asking that specific prisoners who were 'active participants in the OUN underground, had committed terrorist acts and other heinous crimes' be returned to camps to serve out their full sentences because their return to the Western Ukraine was 'premature and unjustified.' GARF R-8131/32/4851/22. One such ex-prisoner was Mikhail Vasil'evich Drabat, who had allegedly led an armed band of Ukrainian nationalists who were captured in 1947. Drabat was freed by the commission in Vorkuta on 15 August 1956. The Ukrainian KGB wrote to their central counterparts and requested that this decision be overturned on 10 November 1956. The central KGB assented and forwarded the case to the Presidium of the Supreme Soviet on 23 November. On 3 January 1957, the Presidium overturned the commission's decision in response to the severity of Drabat's crime. GARF

R-8131/32/4851/43, 117, 132. On the expulsion of returnees from the western borderlands, see Weiner, 'Empires Pay a Visit.'

43 GURK NARK 2 2216/14/17a/53.

44 On the anti-religious campaign, see Irina Paert, 'Demistifying the Heavens: Women, Religion and Khrushchev's Anti-Religious Campaign, 1954–64,' in *Women in the Khrushchev Era*, ed. Melanie Ilic, Susan E. Reid, and Lynne Attwood, 203–21 (New York, 2004); Elena Zhidkova, 'The Antireligious Campaign in Kuibyshev Oblast during the Thaw,' *Russian Studies in History* 50, no. 1 (2011): 3–18.

45 GURK NARK 2 2216/6/27/48.

46 Ibid., 48–51.

47 'Krivchuk Obviniaet,' *Zapoliar'e*, 21 March 1959.

48 Ibid., *Zapoliar'e*, 22 March 1959.

49 GURK NARK 2 2216/15/13/20.

50 Pavel Negretov, *Vse dorogi vedut na Vorkutu* (Benson, VT, 1985), 142–5.

51 Pavel Negretov, 'How Vorkuta Began,' *Soviet Studies* 29, no. 4 (1977): 565–75; Negretov, *Vse dorogi vedut na Vorkutu*. These were published with the assistance of dissident historian Roy Medvedev.

52 Negretov, *Vse dorogi vedut na Vorkutu*, 17–18.

53 Other groups suffered discrimination as well. On discrimination against teachers, for instance, see GURK NARK 2 2216/14/61/120–4.

54 Although the Gorkom did specifiy in reference to the 1959 resolution (see below) that work with cadres was not to have a 'campaign character' (*kampaneiskii kharakter*), this is the way it operated in practice. GURK NARK 2 2216/15/18a/71.

55 Over the course of 1950, 140 people were purged from ITR positions in KVU for lack of political reliability; most were ex-prisoners and exiles. GURK NARK 2 1/4/979/25–7.

56 GURK NARK 2 2216/14/54/59.

57 Ibid.

58 Ibid., l. 60.

59 Ibid., l. 61.

60 Ibid., ll. 62–3, 101.

61 Ibid., ll. 122–6.

62 GURK NARK 2 2216/14/65/4–6.

63 GURK NARK 2 2216/15/17/107–8.

64 GURK NARK 2 2216/15/18a/68–71.

65 GURK NARK 1 R-1675/1/1746/95.

66 GURK NARK 1 R-1675/1/1745/183.

67 GURK NARK 1 R-1688/1/274/16–19.

68 GURK NARK 2 2216/14/68/97–8.

69 GURK NARK 1 R-1675/1/1711/13–14. It is hardly surprising that Plastinina pursued formal discrimination with less zeal than was expected. In 1956, when she had been the director of mining administration no. 2 (a collection of small mines), she was accused of refusing to hire Komsomol specialists in lieu of ex-prisoners, going so far as to 'speak to them rudely and send them packing.' GURK NARK 2 2216/7/57/51.

70 This was hardly the only example of a high-placed German collaborator holding an important position in KVU. A man named Korabilo, who had once been the *burgomistr* of Dnepropetrovsk, was fired as head mechanic of mine no. 7, only to be hired as the deputy head mechanic of mine no. 30. GURK NARK 2 2216/14/54/64.

71 Mikhail T., interview by author, digital recording, Syktyvkar, Russia, 31 October 2004. All interviews were conducted under the auspices of the University of Chicago Social and Behavioral Sciences Institutional Research Board Protocol 103-1008. The names of the interview subjects have been changed for their protection.

72 V. Frid, *58 1/2: zapiski lagernogo pridurka* (Moscow, 1996), 363.

73 Ibid., 368–70.

74 Adler, *Gulag Survivor,* 109.

75 Orlando Figes has recently pointed out the importance of such networks for former prisoners. As he writes, 'People who had been in the camps together tended to be more supportive of each other than relatives and friends at home. In a society where former prisoners were frequently the victims of prejudice and malice, they forged special bonds of trust and mutual reliance.' Figes, *Whisperers,* 566.

76 Galina S., interview by author, digital recording, Vorkuta, Russia, 14 May 2003.

77 Negretov, *Vse dorogi vedut na Vorkutu,* 37–9.

78 Ibid., 140–1.

79 GURK NARK 1 R-1675/1/1707/91. Similar allegations were made that former prisoners hired only other former prisoners of their nationality. GURK NARK 2 2216/14/17a/52.

80 GURK NARK 2 2216/14/54/110.

81 GURK NARK 2 70/3/6/28.

82 A response to one such request from mine no. 40, dated 26 October 1955, can be found in RGAE 8225/27/490/104.

83 For correspondence lobbying on behalf of KVU and the mine directors,

see RGAE 8225/27/506/184–8; RGAE 8225/27/509/37–9. The circular is referred to in RGAE 8225/27/504/14.

84 The importance of these bonuses is illustrated by the case of Leonid Markizov (see introduction). As a non-citizen, he avoided exile when he was paroled in 1954. Thus, when he returned to Vorkuta in 1954, he was able to sign a contract and enjoy 'northern bonuses' within six months of being hired. By 1957, he was receiving a 50 per cent bonus on his wages. When he received his official rehabilitation in September of that year, his time in Rechlag began to be included in the calculation of his total tenure in the north. Thus, he began to receive a 100 per cent bonus, a doubling of his wages, an increase that certainly made a difference in his family's budget. Markizov, *Do I posle 1945*, 155.

85 Al'bert Efimovich Bernshtein, *Na rubezhe vekov* (Syktyvkar, 2002), 115–17.

86 GURK NARK 1 R-1688/1/273/226–7.

87 GURK NARK 1 R-1941/1/128/11.

88 GURK NARK 1 R-1675/1/2281/21.

89 Ibid., ll. 14–15.

90 Iurii P., interview by author, digital recording, Vorkuta, Russia, 1 June 2003.

91 'Doroga v bol'shuiu zhizn',' *Zapoliar'e*, 7 December 1960.

92 Galina S., interview by author, digital recording, Vorkuta, Russia, 14 May 2003.

93 Adler, *Gulag Survivor*, 42, 109. Adler does not rule out the possibility that some prisoners might have been able to readjust and reassimilate completely, but none of the returnees she studied were able to. Dobson, on the other hand, concludes that, 'Of the millions who came back from the camps, many no doubt *did* return home and find work, but stories of successful reintegration leave little trace in the archives.' Dobson, *Khrushchev's Cold Summer*, 112.

5 Remembering and Explaining the Terror during the Thaw: Soviet Readers of Ehrenburg and Solzhenitsyn in the 1960s

DENIS KOZLOV

For Soviet readers during the Thaw, two publications were especially significant in opening the discussion of twentieth-century mass political violence and of the forms it had taken in the Soviet Union under Stalin. Both texts appeared in the journal *Novyi mir,* then edited by Aleksandr Tvardovskii. One, of course, was Aleksandr Solzhenitsyn's *One Day in the Life of Ivan Denisovich,* which came out in November 1962. But the readers began debating what later came to be known as 'the Stalin terror' at least a full year before Solzhenitsyn. They did so in response to Ilya Ehrenburg's memoir *People, Years, Life,* which *Novyi mir* published in 1960–3 and 1965.[1]

The books by Solzhenitsyn and Ehrenburg were not the first or only publications of the Thaw that brought up the terror, and reactions to them were not the earliest instances when readers wrote letters mentioning the arrests, executions, and prison camps of the Stalin decades. With varying degrees of subtlety, such references surfaced in many literary publications and discussions of the Thaw. Ehrenburg's own eponymous 1954 book was an early example.[2] The overt and detailed conversation, however, reached print only in 1961, following or shortly preceding the Twenty-Second Party Congress with its renewed attack on Stalin's legacy.[3] It was the books by Ehrenburg and Solzhenitsyn that touched the audience's nerve and provoked a polemic specifically about the nature of the recent violence.

Letter writers of the 1960s rarely used the word *terror* to describe the tragedy of the Stalin years. More often than not, they left this phenomenon without any name, and in the early twenty-first century that name is still missing from the Russian language. Despite the collapse of the Soviet Union and its ideology, despite decades of discussion about the mass arrests, imprisonments, and executions, the language still lacks a definitive overarching term to describe what happened. The terms currently in use – *the terror, Stalin Terror, Great Terror, Great Purges,* or *(mass) repression* – are calques from Western languages. Some of these words, such as *repression,* became operational early in the history of Soviet bureaucratese, while others took many years after Stalin to make their way into broad circulation.[4] Thus, it was a Western author, Robert Conquest, who coined the term *the Great Terror* in the late 1960s, in a parallel with revolutionary France. Only two decades later, during the explosive historical debates of the Gorbachev perestroika, the term became common in the Soviet and then post-Soviet cultural and linguistic space.[5] Yet, while established among the highbrow intelligentsia, *terror* is not in much use among the Russians otherwise. When they invoke the tragedy of the Stalin years, people most often use a different word, referring to this phenomenon exactly as they, their parents, or grandparents did back in the 1960s. They call it by the date when the arrests and executions reached their peak – 'the year thirty-seven.' Hardly anyone needs an explanation for what the year means.

In this chapter, I also use the word *terror* – in awareness of the terminological problem, but for the lack of a better word. The existing language gap in reference to one of the central phenomena in Russia's modern history indicates better than anything else that the accounting for the unprecedented extermination of human lives in this country is far from over.[6] At the same time, more than half a century of reflection and polemics on this theme has had major implications for society and culture. Perhaps to an even greater extent than in many other European countries, the legacy of twentieth-century mass violence has become central to historical and political consciousness in Russia, defining the relationship between the state and the individual.

The conversation that brought about this fundamental self-perception originated in the Thaw, and as often the case in modern Russia, it first unfolded in literature. The two writers who gave shape to it in the early 1960s were Ehrenburg and Solzhenitsyn.

The Art of Remembrance and Its Critics

A biographer of Ehrenburg has aptly called his 1,400-page memoir 'nothing less than an attempt to restore the country's cultural history.'[7] One of Ehrenburg's many accomplishments was to return, and often introduce, to public circulation scores of historical events and hundreds of names of writers, artists, and statesmen who had been rhetorically, and often surgically, removed from Russian cultural memory. Above all, he described the arrests of 1937–8, mentioning, for the first time in a quarter of a century, the names of many people imprisoned and killed. Indeed, one integrating theme of the memoir was life in the times of terror – human survival under a constant, decades-long threat of physical extermination.

Right away from the 1960s, *People, Years, Life* became just as famous for what Ehrenburg said as for what he did not. The point of highest controversy was his laconically understated description of the arrests and disappearances. Except for once in the chapters published in 1960–3, his references to the terror were brief, elusive, and achingly incomplete for an information-hungry reader – a maze of elaborately disguised words and half-sentences. Heart-rending as it was, his description of Vsevolod Meyerhold's or Isaac Babel's arrest and death took only one brief paragraph.[8] A short section described Soviet writers vilifying 'enemies of the people' at a literary congress in Paris in July 1937,[9] and another one, equally brief, showed Ehrenburg calling Moscow by telephone from Spain in the spring of that year and asking about the strange disappearance of his fellow journalist, Mirova – only to be told by his daughter Irina that the weather in Moscow was remarkably good.[10]

Censorship was one reason for omission and circumvention. Thus, Ehrenburg had to take out the chapter about his youth friends Grigorii Sokol'nikov and Nikolai Bukharin, both of whom had perished in the terror. He left himself the small satisfaction of coding his messages, so that an undisclosed 'Nikolai Ivanovich' appeared in the text, making happy those few readers who understood.[11] Self-censorship and the author's discretion also played a role. Intentionally selective in what he remembered, Ehrenburg defended his right of choice. Several times in the memoir he turned to the theme of keeping silent as an integral part of his remembrance effort. Silence and selectivity, he argued, were dictated not only by political considerations but also by his personal preferences and ethical concerns. He declared his wish to write only about the people he liked. Also, the years he remembered were fairly recent, and he had to be careful not to hurt those who were still alive.[12]

There were also issues in the past he preferred not to disclose. In a half-sentence Ehrenburg mentioned a certain letter that he had refused to sign in 1952 (1953?). He did not explain what the letter was about, noting that the time had not yet come to tell.[13] Some scholars argue that this was the orchestrated collective petition on behalf of the Jewish intelligentsia urging the government to deport the Jews to Siberia, in order to 'protect' them from the 'people's wrath' during the Doctors' Plot.[14] Others deny that the deportation project ever existed, while pointing out that Ehrenburg did sign a (never-published) collective letter to *Pravda* in January 1953, which expressed the Jewish people's loyalty to the Soviet cause but also demanded punishment for the arrested doctors. Separately, though, Ehrenburg wrote another letter, this time to Stalin, discouraging as inexpedient the massive attention in the press to the Jews or any other ethnically defined community.[15] However the actual events had developed, remembering them required extreme caution. Had Ehrenburg even wanted to tell the whole story, he would not have been able to publish it, and the only choice was to allude to it in this disturbingly vague fashion.

Overall, the description of the terror in *People, Years, Life* ended up at best laconic. Only once in the chapters published in 1960–3 did Ehrenburg talk about the reprisals at considerable length – in the seven pages describing his six-month stay in Moscow from December 1937 through May 1938, between trips to Republican Spain. These seven pages remain, even today, an interesting account of the Moscow intelligentsia's life during the peak of terror – with a posting in the elevator forbidding residents to flush books down the toilet, with name slots on doors at the *Izvestiia* editorial office staying perpetually empty as the result of revolving-door appointments, and with the journalist Mikhail Kol'tsov, who would himself soon perish, taking the author to the bathroom to tell him a fresh joke: 'They took Teruel. – And what about his wife?' – a palimpsest of fear shining through the politically acceptable conversation about the Spanish Civil War.[16]

Camouflaged as it was, Ehrenburg's account of the terror produced much of the readers' fascination with his book. At the time, extracting information about the terror from contemporary Soviet publications was an exercise in comparative Aesopianism, and the only alternative to his hazy descriptions was to read the dried-up, filtered, and processed formulas of newspaper editorials. Between those options, most readers definitely preferred Ehrenburg, since he at least began telling the human story of the terror, something the media almost completely bypassed. For the audience ready to grasp every fresh word about this nearly forbidden subject and used to reading between the lines, Ehrenburg's understated references meant much.[17] Readers noticed them immediately and began responding – long before *One Day in the Life of Ivan Denisovich*. Out of 336 letters to Ehrenburg in *Novyi mir*'s archive, 147 came before the publication of Solzhenitsyn's novella, and of those a quarter (36 letters) referred to the terror. 'We have taken all your hints,' wrote in October 1961 the young physicist Leonid Rinenglaz from Sukhumi, for whom Ehrenburg's obituary to his murdered friends became an elusive yet preciously rare personal account of 'the terrible days of the year 37.'[18] Compared to anyone else at the moment, the memoirist was hiding less and telling more of what the readers desired to know.[19]

Yet they wanted to know still more – and not only for informational purposes. Some people were upset by Ehrenburg's fragmentary reminiscences and justly suspected a censor's hand.[20] Criticizing him for excessive caution, they described him as writing 'with half-strokes and half-hints,'[21] or, as another letter writer put it, 'with hands tied up.'[22] Few letter writers pressed serious ethical charges against him on those grounds, and yet the very possibility of such charges revealed the centrality of ethics to the crisis of Soviet consciousness in the 1960s. Before it could proceed to generalizations about history, politics, or culture, a reassessment of the terror and its legacy meant a re-evaluation of individual biographies and life choices. The tragedy was recent, and any interpreter of the past was to begin with the issue of his or her own accountability.

This ethical dimension became crucial to the polemic around Ehrenburg's memoir and its depiction of the terror. At the centre of this polemic, which unfolded both in print and in readers' letters, stood the question of silence.

Why Did You Keep Silent? The Question and Its Formulations

The question was born long before the publication of *People, Years, Life.* As early as 1956, it had resounded at numerous conferences and meetings that followed Khrushchev's revelations about Stalin at the Twentieth Party Congress. Men of letters were among the first to raise the issue. Thus, on 29–30 March 1956, at a party meeting in the editorial board of the newspaper *Izvestiia,* several journalists admitted their guilt of having kept silent in times of repression. One of them, Grigorii Ryklin (1894–1975, editor-in-chief of the satirical journal *Krokodil* in 1938–48), argued, 'Many of us began hesitating in 1937. We saw that something was going wrong. We were appalled, and yet we kept silent.' Another newspaper veteran, Konstantin Sevrikov (1907–1985), agreed: 'We, Communists, saw a lot, and sensed even more that something was going wrong with the reprisals and arrests of many party members. We also felt that Stalin was being deified, and yet we kept silent, we were afraid of speaking up.' A 'comrade Syrtsov' added, 'We the newspapermen did a lot for the creation of the cult of personality, singing praises and varnishing reality.... We sang many praises and often passed over major flaws in silence.' Other *Izvestiia* journalists at the meeting, however, strongly objected to such statements, and a passionate debate broke out. Again and again, agitated people spoke up, trying to explain their silence during the extermination of their colleagues, friends, and relatives.[23]

The question of silence under terror was one of the more disturbing questions of the Thaw, because it posed the problem of personal responsibility, the issue of whether compliance equalled complicity, whether it was possible to maintain human dignity in times of fear and to act politically rather than being a blind prisoner of the circumstances. This was an ethical question, because answering it involved intense moral self-assessment, in which the answerer had to judge himself or herself on the scale of good and evil, while at the same time revisiting these fundamental notions. It was also a historical and political question, because defining individual responsibility could not proceed without evaluating the sociopolitical order on the same ethical scale.

Who asked the question of silence during the Thaw? To whom was the question addressed, and exactly how was it formulated? Was it limited to a bifurcation between 'fathers' and 'sons,' with young people demanding answers from their fathers and grandfathers as to why *they*, the older ones, had kept silent? In other words, was the issue of silence – and thus of origins, responsibilities, and effects of the terror – a generational issue? Answering this may also allow for a comparison between historical consciousness of the 1960s in the Soviet and other European societies, especially in West Germany and France where, as many studies suggest, generational tensions played a crucial role in drawing society's attention to the recent (Nazi or Vichy) past.[24]

In the Soviet Union, it seems, the picture was different. The question of silence did exist and was indeed addressed to eyewitnesses of the recent state violence. However, the formulation 'Why did *you* keep silent?' was rarely in use.[25] On the one hand, the agency in raising the question did not necessarily belong to young people blaming their fathers: often the fathers themselves would eagerly speak up. At the 1956 meeting of the *Izvestiia* editorial board, there was no 'you' in the question of silence: for the journalists, many of whom had lived through the late 1930s, the question was rather, 'Why did *we* keep silent?' On the other hand, although young people did actively discuss the terror, they usually refrained from inter-generational interrogations, but rather assumed their own belonging to, if not exactly accountability for, the terror environment.[26] The same *we* was overwhelmingly present in the letters of the 1960s, from readers old and young alike.

The distinction between *you* and *we* is crucial. The use of the first-person pronoun suggests that the letter writers, largely regardless of age, perceived their lives as integrally connected to the Stalin past, with even the youngest viewing themselves as its eyewitnesses and products. There certainly was a note of historical passivity in such statements, a self-perception of being acted upon, rather than acting, in history. Yet the sense of belonging to the system of values formed during the Stalin years potentially prepared the letter writers for acknowledging a measure of their own responsibility for the past. Rather than trying to lay guilt on someone else's shoulders, many of them sought explanations by critically re-examining their own lives. In this respect, Soviet readers of the 1960s displayed a remarkably high degree of intellectual maturity in addressing one of the most formidable questions of their time.

Why Did We Keep Silent? Readers and the Media Campaign against Ehrenburg

If most letter writers did not stop admiring Ehrenburg's memoir for its understatements, and if charges of calculated duplicity, servility, and 'lack of heroism' were relatively few, those charges nonetheless became central to the media campaign against him. On 30 January 1963 *Izvestiia* published an article by the well-known literary critic Vladimir Ermilov (1904–65) titled 'The Need to Argue: Reading I. Ehrenburg's Memoir *People, Years, Life*.'[27] The article came out shortly after the publication of *One Day in the Life of Ivan Denisovich*, and many people responded to the Ermilov-Ehrenburg controversy under the fresh impression of reading and discussing Solzhenitsyn. Other crucial developments took place that winter as well. Following Khrushchev's notorious visit to the Manège (1 December 1962), Central Committee Secretary Leonid Il'ichev delivered his speeches attempting to reimpose ideological orthodoxy in literature and the arts – one at the meeting between party leaders and 'the creative intelligentsia' on 17 December,[28] the other at the session of the CC Ideological Committee on 26 December 1962, in the presence of 140 young writers and artists.[29] On 7–8 March 1963, at the second meeting between party leaders and the intelligentsia, Khrushchev and Il'ichev also delivered speeches, with Khrushchev specifically attacking Ehrenburg's alleged doctrine of silence.[30] According to Aleksei Adzhubei, then *Izvestiia*'s editor-in-chief, it was none other than Leonid Brezhnev who commissioned Ermilov's article.[31] Against this background, and with the polemics on Ehrenburg and Solzhenitsyn going simultaneously, the winter of 1962–3 became the peak of the Thaw-era literary-historical polemics about the terror.[32]

The brunt of Ermilov's criticism was directed against Ehrenburg's alleged credo of informed silence. Quoting several passages from the memoir where Ehrenburg described silence as a survival skill, 'the need to live with my teeth clenched,' which he had learned from reality, Ermilov denied that this fairly portrayed the moods of the 1930s. 'Living with your teeth clenched' meant understanding that things were going wrong and yet continuing to accept the status quo. For Ermilov, this separated Ehrenburg from the majority of Soviet people, because, while Ehrenburg had realized back in 1937–8 that the terror was wrongful and criminal, most people had not. Ermilov also proposed that, while the majority had supported the purges, there was also open protest against them during the 1930s. He was remarkably unspecific, mentioning neither names nor concrete instances of protest, and instead speaking of 'a certain action,' 'this or that individual,' 'an individual fact,' or 'a particular phenomenon.'[33]

Ermilov did not need to be specific, because the subject of his article was not the terror but, rather, Ehrenburg's political persona. Protest or no protest, Ermilov's main theme was loyalty to the cause, which in his article seamlessly translated into loyalty to the leadership. His argument favoured belief above rationality, and selflessness above self-interest: in all situations, a transparent, predictable devotee was preferable to a tongue-in-cheek sceptic. Within the media ethos of heroic selfless devotion to the cause, the lack of protest against evil looked better as a product of earnest delusion than informed calculation. 'We kept silent because we did not know the purges were wrong' was safer than 'We kept silent because we knew and yet minded our best interests.' Calculated non-resistance to the terror meant hidden opposition to the regime, and Ermilov portrayed Ehrenburg exactly as such a calculating sceptic, whose silence was redolent of disloyalty.

'The Need to Argue' was one of the more sophisticated propaganda pieces of its time, not only because Ermilov praised Solzhenitsyn (he did), condemned the terror, and on his own initiative took up the complex issue of people's reactions to the purges of 1937–8 – and not even because he played (as he did) with the title of another, Stalin-time article, 'Comrade Ehrenburg Simplifies,' which back in 1945 had temporarily made Ehrenburg a political outcast by accusing him of indiscriminate Germanophobia.[34] Ermilov's originality was that he used the relatively unexplored set of socio-ethical issues involved in the terror to justify and reassert the same regime that had produced the terror. Skilfully, he disguised his redemption of the regime behind the redemption of ordinary citizens, covering this political agenda with an ostensibly proper ethical argument.

And yet the argument did not work. As soon as Ehrenburg reacted to the article, Ermilov attacked again, declaring that Ehrenburg's informed silence and calculated behaviour during the terror had contradicted Leo Tolstoy's principle, 'I cannot keep silent.'[35] It was at this point that massive reaction to the debate came from readers. With more than a third of letters about *People, Years, Life* in *Novyi mir*'s archive (117 out of 336) dated February and March 1963, these months marked the peak of public response to Ehrenburg's memoir.

Very few letter writers agreed with Ermilov,[36] while most challenged him on precisely the ethical grounds he chose for the polemic. First of all, they argued, Ermilov was a poor candidate for wearing a Tolstoyan garb and appealing to the Russian tradition of a writer's protest against social ills. Under Stalin, he himself had acted very differently from Tolstoy's 'I cannot keep silent.' Two students found a 1949 issue of *Literaturnaia gazeta* that featured Ermilov's article, 'The Great Friend of Soviet Literature,' praising Stalin on his seventieth birthday.[37] 'The title conveys all the content of this well-rounded narrative,' they caustically remarked.[38] Ermilov qualified poorly for pressing ethical charges against those who had kept silent, because much worse charges could be pressed against him. People often referred to his servility, far worse than Ehrenburg's, and the frequent 'Comrade Ermilov' and 'dear Comrade Ermilov' in their letters were thickly sarcastic, framing the debate in passable officialese but also reminding that Ermilov had mastered that language like no one else. They also pointed to the logical inconsistencies in his article. As one letter writer succinctly put it, Ermilov presented the situation as if, during the purges, 'ordinary people' had not known of the evil and yet somehow struggled against it.[39]

The basis on which the letter writers challenged Ermilov's rendition of the past was their personal experience. Two-thirds of the letters that indicated at least the approximate ages of their authors, thirty out of forty-four, came from those who well remembered the terror. Time came for them to speak up.

Why We Kept Silent: Fear, Belief, Accountability

Without exception, every one of those who remembered 1937–8 disagreed with Ermilov about open protest during the purges. Open protest had been impossible, they argued, because any such attempt would have been suicidal. A great admirer of Ehrenburg, Boris Pavlovich Vishnevskii from Orenburg region had been 'already a man of mature age' during the 1930s.[40] Rejecting Ermilov's journalistic moralization, he did not view silence as offensive to him and his contemporaries: it was only normal to keep silent not to risk one's life and the lives of many people around.[41] Many of his age agreed, and so did some younger letter writers.[42] In a collective letter, five of them argued that not only was this silence beyond reproach, but it might also be a sign of courage – say, when someone refused to renounce a family member.[43] It was also worth remembering, they continued, that today's party leaders (no names mentioned, but Khrushchev obviously implied) had also witnessed the purges and kept silent. Using a characteristic legitimization device, the letter writers defeated Ermilov's thesis about the culpability of informed silence with a sure-fire appeal to the flawlessness of the current leadership. No Ermilov could object if Khrushchev himself had known but did not dare speak. '"I cannot keep silent!" is a beautiful concept,' they concluded. 'The only problem is that it hardly applies to the issue and the epoch under consideration.' After-the-fact moral judgments and newspaper heroism had nothing to do with the real choices of people for whom silence had been the only way to stay alive.[44]

Fear was a powerful and often sufficient explanation for why few people had openly protested. But the letter writers did not attribute their silence to fear alone. Many of them produced extensive deliberations about their own and others' behaviour back in 1937. In such analyses, fear tortuously overlapped with belief. Iurii Aleksandrovich Fridman, a sixty-three-year-old 'rehabilitated communist' who had spent fifteen years in the prison camps and was outraged by Ermilov's cavalier moralizing, reformulated the question of silence in a way he saw as more ethically acceptable and historically accurate. It was understandable, he wrote, that an average individual did not dare protest. But how was it possible that Old Bolsheviks, the guard of the Revolution, the veteran fighters who had risked their lives for it and went to tsarist prisons or even to the gallows – how was it possible that they did not struggle? The answer, to Fridman, would be the key to the silence of 1937.[45]

His explanation was that, although they did not necessarily have warm feelings for Stalin, the Old Bolsheviks viewed protest against him as discrediting the Soviet cause by unleashing internal factional struggles and disputation. That was inadmissible. 'To speak against Stalin and the system of arbitrariness was tantamount to speaking against the party and Soviet power, and no true Communist would do that. "I'd better die," they reasoned, "but let the party and Soviet power be well and prosper, because sooner or later everything will become clear, and mistakes will be corrected."'[46]

The silence of the veteran communists came not necessarily from fear or blind admiration for the leader. At the root of the silence was a characteristic understanding of loyalty to the cause: a concern for the unity of the ranks, an apprehension that open criticism of government policies would undermine that unity and endanger the cause itself. Regardless of whether such unity had ever existed, many people in the 1930s considered it a blessing – especially in view of the inevitable battle against Nazi Germany.[47]

The tragedy of silence in 1937 was that numerous people who realized the injustice or repression refrained from disagreeing with it openly – not even because they feared for their own lives, but because they feared the very idea of disagreement. Preoccupation with maintaining an appearance of unity, Fridman argued, was what distinguished the Soviet mind from its tsarist intellectual forebears. When Leo Tolstoy protested against the Stolypin executions of peasants in 1908, he proclaimed, 'I cannot keep silent!' in Russia of the tsars, where the democratic intelligentsia took a split between state and society for granted. Presuming it an issue of honour to oppose the monarchical authority, it was in these traditionally confrontational terms that many educated Russian readers received Tolstoy's call for above-party clemency and forgiveness.[48] But in the Soviet Union of the 1930s, where an opposition between state and society was declared impossible, and where indeed many presumed those two concepts to mean one and the same, the Tolstoyan stance was not only physically deadly – it just did not make sense.[49]

Here was something that distinguished the minds of the 1960s from those of the 1930s. Now, in 1963, Fridman did not fear disagreement any more, and in fact he disagreed as intensely as possible. What previously did not make sense, even if for a select circle of dedicated believers, received a meaning again. The traditional state-society fractures, which had marked Russian political culture before the Revolution and remained latent in the early Soviet years, resurfaced during the Thaw.[50] The idea of difference, the principle of remonstrance against authority as a moral duty of an educated person, became an ethical norm again. Concern for the unity of the ranks, on the other hand, was becoming visibly less significant. In the winter of 1962–3, the readers' massive protest against journalistic attempts to employ the theme of terror for the regime's self-congratulatory reaffirmation showed that, even for those who had once built the Soviet order, identification with socialism no longer meant automatic acceptance of any government policy or message. Silence was to be no more.

The way in which the terror eyewitnesses rejected the ostensibly convenient journalistic theory of open protest to the purges was remarkable. One might imagine that some of those who had lived through 1937 would be tempted to embellish their own past behaviour by grabbing onto Ermilov's idea and arguing that they had in fact protested. Yet practically none of the letter writers assumed this heroic posture. Instead, they sought an explanation of what had made the arrests, the executions, and the silence that accompanied them possible. Finding out what hopefully would be the truth was more valuable to them than achieving peace of mind by a quick fix of historical myth-making.

It was hardly possible, though, to do without myth-making altogether. This became a stumbling block, particularly when a discussion of the terror approached the issue of personal responsibility – the other side of the question of belief. The letters suggest that in the 1960s the discussion of historical accountability for the terror had reached only an embryonic, if important, stage – the one at which memories of fear and belief mostly served the purposes of self-absolution, rather than repentance. This refers in particular to the older letter writers who had had the most intense exposure to repression. Some of them tried radically dissociating from the past, although their language suggested that they shared more tenets of the militant mentality than they were ready to admit.[51] But the most common motif for them, which sometimes broke out even in the best-argued and cogent letters, was self-justification. Boris Vishnevskii wrote, 'We, rank-and-file, ordinary Soviet people have nothing to blush for. Let those blush, if they are alive and capable of feeling shame, let those be responsible before history who created Stalin's cult of personality, who glorified Stalin in all their public statements, who reported "personally" to Stalin and elected honorary presidia invariably headed by Stalin ... Let them blush, and let shame fall upon their heads, rather than the heads of those who became victims of Stalin's cult of personality against their will.'[52]

It was the emotionality of such statements that revealed their authors' unease – and perhaps also lack of confidence in what they so passionately proclaimed. What revealed this, too, was the frequent 'we' that they used instead of the lonely, disconcerting 'I.' The 'we' came not only and not principally from the habitual Soviet fashion of public speaking on behalf of a collective. It was also safer to feel part of a group, a cohort, to be not alone when facing the ocean of blood spilled for reasons increasingly unclear.

But then, inevitably, came the time when one had to face it alone, and at this point people became far more reflective and less confident. Even the authors of the most upbeat statements about their innocence did not seem to find their own words very uplifting. Despite proclaiming that his cohort had nothing to blush for, Vishnevskii did blush. 'This was a strange and difficult time,' he wrote. 'You remember it – and deep inside you feel something unpleasant, so much trash has accumulated there ... At my advanced age, I finally should not lie. The time comes when I need to tell the truth.'[53]

The striving toward self-absolution was an initial promising step, not a definitive conclusion in the increasingly introspective remembrance of the terror. Self-absolution was not yet repentance, but it surely was one step above a 'zero' stage of (non-) remembering – denial. None of those who wrote to Ehrenburg, and indeed none of the thousands of people who wrote to *Novyi mir* throughout the 1950s and 1960s, ever denied that massive political violence had taken place and was a tragedy of universal scale.[54] It was the recognition of this universal impact of the terror that kept the letter writers thinking. Self-absolution, also, was not too far from repentance. Indeed, theology, whether Orthodox, Catholic, or Lutheran, views absolution and repentance as inseparable – provided, of course, that the repentant does not absolve himself or herself but seeks the higher ethical authority for that sake.

An additional problem was that many letter writers did not know a higher ethical authority. The time when they wrote witnessed the collapse of such authorities, especially those considered stable only a few years before. During the Thaw, thousands of people were looking for different ethical criteria and systems of values – new, old, sometimes ancient – for assessing their past and present. Adding to the cultural tradition, this was yet another reason why writers became such moral authorities for their contemporaries. The quest was to take years, even decades. What was reassuring was the visible restlessness and discomfort with which people remembered their behaviour of 1937, the fact that on their own initiative they spent long hours writing dozens of pages about how the terror had affected their lives. Better than anything else, this showed that, for them, reflection on responsibility for the recent past was far from over. It was only beginning.

'I Am Afraid This Past May Come Back'

The terror had a powerful grip on present-day existence. Again and again, the letter writers suggested that the disappearances and executions, together with years of enforced silence about them, had irreparably damaged society's moral fibre.[55] The growing awareness of lives destroyed for no apparent reason and long prohibited from mentioning, undermined the readers' confidence in the country's path and in their own integrity. A world replete with ethical disorientation, a sense of lost markers between the very basic ethical categories framing human existence, opened in a letter by the thirty-nine-year old V. Grigor'eva. 'Your book,' she wrote to Ehrenburg in early 1961, 'is good because the white is called white in it and the black is called black. Many people have long stopped understanding what is white and what is black.' Ehrenburg in fact did not differentiate between white and black as clearly as she proposed – he much preferred shades to polar colourations of human action. And yet this was what Grigor'eva carried from the book: a clearer identification of basic ethical values that, she believed, society had forsaken.[56] A. Vorob'ev, a history teacher in his early thirties, had been five or six years old in 1937–8. He remembered how his elder sister would come home from school and tell him that Marshal Bliukher was an enemy of the people and that she had to blot him out of the textbook – 'a man whom everyone had mentioned with respect just the day before. It is only now that one realizes how the souls were mutilated, not only of adults but of schoolchildren as well.'[57]

For many readers, the ethical crisis originating in the past suggested that this past was not safely gone. With minds distorted by decades of living in the repressive environment, the purges could return at any moment.[58] 'Today things have become quite lively, but, time and again, there comes a harsh administrative bellowing suggestive of the recent past! And quite frankly, I am afraid this past may come back,' wrote the thirty-four-year-old Iurii Boglovskii from Leningrad. 'There is yet so much trash within people.'[59]

Perhaps the one who most vividly expressed the idea of permanent ethical damage that the past had inflicted by dragging everyone in, either as a victim or a hangman but with no bystanders, was Eva Vil'gel'movna Miuntser, the sixty-year-old widow of a Polish communist arrested and murdered in 1937.[60] Back then, she had a ten-year-old son and was pregnant. After her husband had been arrested, everyone around without exception – neighbours, friends, her son's schoolteacher – turned away from her and the child. In April 1938 she was at the hospital, in labour that lasted for fourteen hours. Reluctant to deal with an 'enemy's' wife, none of the medical personnel came up to her, and only a nurse whose husband had also been arrested finally called for a doctor when the patient lost consciousness. In the end, the baby suffocated and died. 'Why, among everything I have been through, does this haunt me the most? It seems to me that the birth of a child brings forth something bright, human, and compassionate, even in the worst kind of people. And here is some fascist savagery. This is incomprehensible, and it is frightening that something like that could exist within people. But shall we only say, "could"? Several generations have been trained in the "Stalinist" spirit – the spirit of suspicion and mistrust of the individual. And all these "trainees" now occupy leading administrative positions, especially in the provinces.'[61]

What emerged from accounts such as Miuntser's was the idea of the terror as a long-term moral catastrophe, a chasm that remained directly underneath present-day existence. Together with several other letter writers of her age, she did not hesitate to bring charges against her people – charges of complicity in murder. This was why Eva Vil'gel'movna made the analogy between 1937 and fascism – an analogy that did not escape Ehrenburg, either. This was also why she subscribed to Ehrenburg's words, which he made the leitmotif, overtly publishable but incisively unnerving, of his writing about the terror and its legacy: 'It was not the idea that received a blow. It was the people.'[62] Ehrenburg, in fact, had phrased that slightly differently. He wrote, 'fatal blow.'[63]

Solzhenitsyn: The Readership Divided

While Ehrenburg's memoir introduced many important themes to the readers' discussion of mass political violence and its effects, this discussion reached its peak when, parallel with the continuing publication of *People, Years, Life*, *Novyi mir* published Aleksandr Solzhenitsyn's *One Day in the Life of Ivan Denisovich*.[64] *One Day* is the best-remembered work of literature that appeared in Tvardovskii's *Novyi mir*, and it is widely considered the most famous literary product of the Thaw. Indeed, the journal's archive, thus far yielding 532 letters about *One Day* from more than 579 readers dated 1962–9, confirms that the novella was important for the readers. If the numbers of available responses at least partly reflect the societal impact of literary works, Solzhenitsyn's book was one of the most influential publications in *Novyi mir*'s history from the late 1940s through the late 1960s, bested perhaps only by Vladimir Dudintsev's 1956 *Not by Bread Alone* (720 letters from over 820 letter writers).[65] Solzhenitsyn did not initiate the literary polemic on terror, but with his appearance the polemic, and the readers' reactions to it, received an important direction.

A longtime champion of Solzhenitsyn's novella, who must be credited with its publication (particularly for obtaining Khrushchev's personal sanction to publish), Tvardovskii correctly anticipated a surge of readers' responses.[66] He also predicted that they would vary. On the eve of the publication, in the atmosphere of growing suspense and fast accumulating rumours in Moscow's literary circles about the forthcoming sensation, he wrote to Solzhenitsyn, 'There will be good press, there will be enormous mail, and I am sure this mail will be *diverse*.'[67] When *One Day* came out and the responses began flooding in, the jubilant Tvardovskii wrote again, 'The torrent of letters in my name and in yours keeps coming to the editorial board, and the responses, take courage, are diverse – and this is how it should be. But the bad ones, of course, comprise only a small part, and as a rule they are anonymous, which sufficiently characterizes their authors.... In a word, all is going well, dear A.[leksandr] I.[saevich], and hopefully will go the same way in the future.'[68]

I will return to the anonymity of responses, but let us first examine their variety. Reactions to *One Day* indeed varied, more so than responses to Ehrenburg's memoir or, in fact, any major publication in *Novyi mir* from the late 1940s through the late 1960s. From the total of 532 letters, the vast majority of 422 (79.3 per cent, 478 letter writers) overall approved the novella. Still, another 100 letters (18.8 per cent, 109 letter writers) evaluated it largely negatively, while 10 more letters were rather neutral or unspecific. Be it an editorial preference for keeping positive letters, the readers' inclination to send mostly approvals, or, perchance, the actual distribution of opinions, in *Novyi mir*'s archive one-fifth was a high proportion of negative reactions to a publication.

Readers' responses, of course, cannot be divided unequivocally into negative and positive, as many combined elements of both attitudes. In addition, different attitudes did not manifest incompatible world views. Most responses, be they positive or negative, were written in a similar language that reflected a fairly coherent, although dynamic, order of political and historical reasoning. This order of reasoning is the main subject of my analysis.

Words, Ages, Truth

It is useful to begin with some general characteristics of the letter writers. Apparently, none of such categories as gender, ethnicity, place of residence, and party or komsomol membership made responses to *One Day* special or determined the readers' attitudes to the novella. Age, on the other hand, was a distinct characteristic of Solzhenitsyn's correspondents. Middle-aged and older readers were always prominent in *Novyi mir*'s audience, but in response to *One Day* the journal received more responses from older people and fewer from the younger than at any other time in the previous two decades.[69] But even age did not necessarily determine whether the readers accepted or rejected Solzhenitsyn's text. Although the younger seem to have particularly welcomed *One Day* (forty out of forty-two among them did so), most of the middle-aged and pension-aged letter writers also reacted to it positively (ninety-nine to twenty-two, and twenty-eight to ten in these two groups, respectively).[70] As in Ehrenburg's case, the disagreements about *One Day* did not split neatly along the lines of age, cutting not between but within age groups, and often within the same reader, who could accept some of Solzhenitsyn's agendas but reject others.

Age mattered, though, in how the readers evaluated Solzhenitsyn's language. The prose was indeed unusual, since *One Day* was the first published Russian literary text in decades where the author used swear words. They appeared in print nearly openly, with only one letter changed, *f* instead of *kh*, masking an obscenity like a fig leaf.[71] *Fuiaslitse, fuimetsia, smefuëchki*, etc. – by the standards of today's Russian fiction, these euphemisms look timid, but in 1962–3 they brought the readers' intense criticism. Language became one of the most frequent targets of the readers' attack on Solzhenitsyn: no fewer than 73 letters out of 532 contained critical comments about it. For 31 out of these 73 letters, I know the letter writers' age, and 24 out of those 31 came from people aged fifty-five and above.[72]

In addition to his thinly disguised obscenities, they also attacked Solzhenitsyn for the many neologisms or, rather, neo-archaisms that he used in *One Day* and that later became his trademark. In order to verbalize human senses in an environment of brutal repression, especially the senses of uneducated people outside the customary intelligentsia circle, Solzhenitsyn introduced words imitating 'simple,' popular speech. At least from the mid-1960s on, neo-archaic linguistic experimentation became part of his deliberate effort at enriching the presumably impoverished, Sovietized Russian literary language.[73] Some of these words he invented, others he borrowed from Vladimir Dal's nineteenth-century dictionary,[74] in an attempt to replenish Russian prose 'by a judicious use ... of such words which, although they do not exist in the modern spoken language ... are used so clearly by the author that they may meet with the approval of speakers, attract the speakers, and in this way return to the language.'[75]

Solzhenitsyn was not the only author in the early 1960s who experimented with language and introduced jargon to literature, and not the only one against whom readers revolted for that reason. Another writer, very different from him in form and spirit, was Vasilii Aksenov, whose short story 'Halfway to the Moon,' replete with 'youthful' slang, appeared in *Novyi mir* in the same year 1962, bringing similarly furious reactions.[76] Occasionally the letter writers criticized Aksenov's and Solzhenitsyn's linguistic innovations in the same breath.[77] But vigilance against innovation, jargon, and presumably impending subversion of the Russian language had long preceded the literary debates on either Solzhenitsyn or Aksenov. At least as early as 1953, linguistic conservatism had shown itself in the numerous press discussions about the 'proper' ways of writing and speaking, 'proper' stresses, spellings, or forms of polite address. During Tvardovskii's first editorship (1950–4), *Novyi mir* had participated in these discussions, in 1953 publishing, for instance, Fedor Gladkov's linguistically conservative article 'On the Culture of Speech,' to which the readers reacted approvingly. One reader then even suggested forming 'an authoritative all-Union organ for the protection of the purity of our mother tongue.'[78]

These Thaw-era discussions were part of the general crisis of the spoken and printed word, the widespread perception of the abnormality of the contemporary language, of a search for new ways of verbal and artistic expression. The ethical and the linguistic crises of the post–Second World War decades were two sides of the same coin, indicating that Russian culture had entered a time of profound transformation. Resistance to linguistic innovation and the desire for a single standard of verbal expression revealed the readers' quest for stability in the cultural environment that they increasingly perceived as unsettled and flawed. Classical

Russian literature readily offered itself as one anchor of stability, especially since it had long been legitimized by the socialist realist doctrine, itself deeply classicist.[79] Now that socialist realism had come into a crisis, many people eagerly distanced from its didactic straightforwardness by resorting to the presumably more refined, ethically and emotionally complex, as well as legitimate poetry and prose of the past century. And so in their letters they duly appealed to the literary norms set by Pushkin, Gogol', and Tolstoy.[80] At the core of their revulsion against Solzhenitsyn's language was this search for stability expressed in a linguistic norm, an anxious cultural preservationism premised on the notion of a classical static language, once carved in stone and never changing.

It is not incidental that so many of the language critics were of advanced age. People who had for decades learned to measure literature (and often life) by the classical literary standard could not easily part with this ideal. Solzhenitsyn violated the linguistic norm to which these readers were accustomed. But the origins of their linguistic conservatism were far more distant than the Soviet epoch. Thus, one letter criticizing Solzhenitsyn's use of swear words came from an old Russian émigré who resided far away from the shores of socialist realism – in Florida, USA.[81] Another émigré, Vera Carpovich, who compiled a glossary of Solzhenitsyn's language, noted in 1976, 'Many Western readers, including native Russians, find his books "difficult"; some are actually discouraged from reading them.'[82] It might be that such attitudes, coming from people who had not set foot on Soviet soil for a long time, if ever, were distant repercussions of the fin-de-siècle cultural debates and upheavals. The continuum of crisis that Russia entered at the turn of the twentieth century may have had a linguistic dimension that, just as its other dimensions, had a long life, extending for decades and ultimately resurfacing in the polemics of the Thaw.[83]

The readers' frequent rejection of Solzhenitsyn's language did not necessarily mean a rejection of his other agendas, first of all his representation of the camps and the prisoners, nor did they mean rejection of the actual camp returnees. In fact, many of those who attacked his language had been camp prisoners themselves, and probably a few more chose not to declare such backgrounds.[84] Just as in responses to Ehrenburg's memoir, regardless of age practically all the letter writers saw the terror as a formidable problem with which they personally were obligated to deal, as was society at large. Although resenting the author's prose, most of them still welcomed his book, recognizing its political and historical significance.[85]

Why – and this question applies to all readers' letters to *Novyi mir* – would somebody write several dozen pages of a response that would go essentially nowhere, into the void, bringing the letter writer no recognition, no credit? There was practically no chance for publication: only a few people (just 5 out of more than 579) expressly desired to see their letters published.[86] Many more knew and predicted that this would never happen. Instead, they often wrote that their letters were not for publication, but only for the reader's information. Who was their intended reader? Who were the letter writers? What did they write, and what for?

The letters blended together eyewitness accounts, statements of political opinion, and efforts to explain the terror historically, strengthened by the desire to leave a lasting record of this phenomenon. Many were intended to share experiences with a sympathetic, informed listener, and it was in this capacity that the letter writers envisioned Solzhenitsyn or Tvardovskii – their most frequent addressees. The presence of a listener, as the theory of testimony argues (based predominantly on studies of the Holocaust), is crucial for the testimonial process.[87] Solzhenitsyn was presumably a particularly good listener, because he himself had gone through the camps. This was the therapeutic writing that Tvardovskii, about this time, recommended to his correspondents who had been to the Gulag, arguing that the very process of putting memories on paper would help them come to terms with their experiences. He could not publish their reminiscences, but he nonetheless urged people to write, promising that their writings would not be lost: he would store them in *Novyi mir*'s archive, for the future use of writers and historians. So he did, and the letter writers' degree of trust in him, as well as in writers such as Ehrenburg and Solzhenitsyn, was impressive.[88]

At the same time, the readers' letters were not only testimonies of individual traumatic experiences. Many were also political statements and attempts at historical interpretation. Those who wrote about their Gulag experiences viewed themselves as political subjects, citizens eager not only to tell their life stories but also to interpret them in a larger historical context, to rationalize the causes and implications of the terror.[89] Many letter writers continued to identify with the (still existing) political order that had generated the prison camps and the mass extermination of human lives. This might be an important difference between the accounts of the Holocaust and the Soviet prison camps. Many of the Soviet eyewitnesses did not, could not, and did not wish to distance themselves from the regime that had brought the camps into being. On the contrary, they associated with this regime and often wrote in a desperate, tragic attempt to salvage its history, inseparably tied to their lives.

Former camp prisoners wrote 159 of the 532 letters to Solzhenitsyn available in *Novyi mir*'s archive. A further 15 letters came from ex–camp guards or those who had once worked in the camps as freely hired personnel (*vol'nonaemnye*). Thus, no fewer than one-third of responses to *One Day* came from people who knew the Gulag from the inside. Considering that these were only self-identified former prisoners (guards, free hires), and that a few others might not disclose their camp backgrounds, the share of ex-inmates or camp personnel may have been larger – not to mention relatives and acquaintances of the repressed, who would make this share grow progressively.

One Day was a book about them, and repeatedly the letter writers would stress that everything Solzhenitsyn wrote was pure truth. Vsevolod Golitsyn, a fifty-five-year-old engineer who had spent ten years in the camps and was then sentenced to Siberian exile for life, even specified the year in which the action of *One Day* took place, 1951.[90] Several other readers recognized not only the time but also the location, stating that *One Day* described the Ekibastuz special camp in Kazakhstan (where Solzhenitsyn indeed had spent part of his term) and claimed to have met Solzhenitsyn in the camp.[91] Some identified the prototypes for the various characters in the novella.[92] Interestingly, while these letter writers placed the action of the novella in Kazakhstan, others made different geographical attributions. 'Dear Editors,' wrote a navy officer O.A. Bliuman,

> In 1950–51, I lived in the area where the action of this novella takes place. My father worked in the settlement of Ust-Omchug in the Kolyma region. I studied at a night school and worked at the CRMW (Central Repair Mechanical Workshop), in the technical design bureau, if you could apply that name to a small wooden hut with an iron stove and four tables inside. There were five of us: four prisoners and one free hire, myself.... We were friends. I learned a lot from them about life in the camps, and [Solzhenitsyn's] novella strikes me precisely with its deep truthfulness.... It would be interesting to learn about the fate of my comrades at work, although that is hardly possible.[93]

That was indeed hardly possible: Solzhenitsyn had never been either to Ust-Omchug or to the Kolyma region. *Novyi mir*'s deputy editor Aleksei Kondratovich had to disappoint Bliuman, writing that Solzhenitsyn had served his term in a different area and therefore could not know anything about Bliuman's former camp mates.[94]

One may certainly interpret Bliuman's response as a culmination of socialist realism, the satisfaction of readers' demands for life-likeness, verisimilitude, and 'total realism' that had originally stood at the source of the new creative method.[95] But it also makes sense to shed condescension and listen to Kondratovich, who explained Bliuman's misrecognition by the fact that Solzhenitsyn did manage to capture some universal Gulag reality, which, Kondratovich supposed, had been very similar for Kolyma and elsewhere.[96] Solzhenitsyn himself emphasized authenticity as one of his strongest creative sides, and Bliuman's letter testified to the success of the writer's project.[97]

Curiously, the Far Eastern prison camp settlement of Ust-Omchug, in 1949–56 the home of the Ten'kinsky correctional labour camp (Ten'lag), left its record in literary history more than once. Back at the time when Bliuman was working at the 'Central Repair Mechanical Workshop,' no fewer than 180 readers from Ust-Omchug sent a telegram to the writer Vasilii Azhaev, praising his novel *Far from Moscow*, 'a highly ideological and patriotic book that brings up Soviet readers in the spirit of communism.'[98] It might be that Bliuman, together with his father and the four prisoners of the workshop, were among those 180 signatories. We do not know if another letter writer, Ivan Sergeevich Korolev from Tadzhikistan, had ever been to Ust-Omchug, but he did spend thirteen years (1937–50) in the camps. And he also read Azhaev's book, which now he had a chance to compare to *One Day*:

> I have read the novel *Far from Moscow* by the author Azhuev [*sic*], who took it from construction site no. 115 Sofiisk [illegible] Komsomol'sk, where there was a dense network of prison camps and arbitrariness exclusively 70–80% article 58 and the rest was the criminal [*blatnoi*] world, and following the bosses' directions they exterminated beat honest Soviet people, but the author V. Azhuev placed there improbable [*nepravdopodobnykh*] heroes, I think [two words illegible]. Solzhenitsyn's novella that you published is truthful, and it opened Soviet people's eyes, because such a cult of personality and the victims of its arbitrariness are innumerable. I have spent more than 4,000 such days. I am an eyewitness of how thousands of honest Soviet people perished.[99]

Transfigured into a picture of model socialist labour, Azhaev's own camp experiences were buried too deeply in *Far from Moscow* for this reader to recognize them.[100] But now, in 1962, the two worlds, Azhaev's socialist realist 'montage of life'[101] and the world of prisoners who populated the actual construction sites of the Far East, came face to face with each other. Thanks to *One Day,* the prison camp underworld of Azhaev's images rose to the surface: the second layer of text in his literary palimpsest exposed itself to the readers' eyes. Perhaps there were not two but three worlds clashing here: Azhaev's 'montage of life'; Solzhenitsyn's *One Day* (which was, after all, a literary text and thus also a 'montage'), and finally, the camp reality. Or, still more precisely, the palimpsest had not three but four layers, as the readers' memory was also, in a sense, a 'montage,' a construct put on paper after the fact and phrased in the politically acceptable language of public self-expression? The layers were probably innumerable: there were as many memories and representations of the terror as there were memoirists and writers.

The clash of these worlds did not produce an immediate revolution of the mind. The reader Korolev continued to speak the language of the 'Big Other'[102] ('victims of arbitrariness,' 'opened Soviet people's eyes') and praised social truthfulness above all else in literature. In his literary preferences he remained loyal to the standards of realism, and in his self-expression he stayed within the limits of the acceptable. But the limits themselves had become far broader than those he knew a decade earlier, when reading Azhaev. *Far from Moscow* probably had never persuaded him, but now, having read Solzhenitsyn in a legitimate publication, Korolev could openly explain why that was so. Realism remained in place, but now it had new, previously forbidden themes at its disposal. Legitimacy of publication, something on which Tvardovskii had always insisted, was crucial for the impact of Solzhenitsyn's prose. The importance of his text appearing in print openly and officially – with the highest sanction, as many knew at the time – was that his readers received a *public* opportunity to talk about the part of their lives they previously could share only with the chosen few.

They also now had new words for such a conversation. Boris Stepanovich Khokhlov, a pensioner who had spent ten years in the camps, wrote to Solzhenitsyn,

> A few days ago, I read your novella, *One Day in the Life of Ivan Denisovich.*
>
> I read it THREE TIMES, in order to re-live, again and again (in my heart, my soul, my thoughts, and somehow even in my body, physically) the TRUTH – I repeat, the TRUTH of my past, from 1936 to 1946....
>
> And you know what? I re-lived again everything I had been through in 1936–46 and even later, up to the rehabilitation.
>
> Time has taken the edge off a few things and sharpened others. And still, impressed by your truthful novella, I lived through everything again.

> Everything, everything, and everything, WHAT and HOW you describe in your novella – everything, everything is authentic, everything is truthful to the utmost and is also rendered in a simple, human way.[103]

Accustomed to academic scepticism toward the notion of truth, a scholar is tempted to brand such statements as manifestations of realism, socialist or otherwise, and to hurry on, looking for some 'thesis' of what the reader argued, for a certain 'substantive' point that could provide grist for analysing his or her political opinions, cultural viewpoints, and the like. Yet perhaps it makes sense to slow down. Excited commentaries about Solzhenitsyn's truth were legion among the readers' responses to *One Day*.[104] Some resented his jargon, but many more conveyed a clear sense of liberation by truth, a delight in both 'what' and 'how' Solzhenitsyn described. It was not by chance that Khokhlov wrote all three words in capital letters – TRUTH, WHAT, and HOW. In this and many other readers' responses, all three categories were inseparable from one another. The truth that so many readers found in Solzhenitsyn's novella was both in the authentic detail of the prison camps he brought to light and in the language he found to portray this reality. Not accidentally, some of those who admired Solzhenitsyn's truth also explicitly praised his language – and not despite, but specifically thanks to, the swear words and neologisms he employed.[105] It was both 'what' and 'how' that mattered for these letter writers – 'what,' because a wealth of genuine detail about the camps was now unearthed, and 'how,' because a language, a terminology for making these details known had finally entered the public domain. The novella's impact was both in its detail and its language, fused together and indivisible.

Combined, these three factors – the authenticity of depicting human existence in the camps, the fact that this depiction was published legitimately, and the new language that the writer adopted – produced the effect of *One Day in the Life of Ivan Denisovich*: Solzhenitsyn coined the terms, ideas, and categories in which a discussion of the terror could, and to a large extent would, proceed.

The Terror: A People's History

To share their memories of repression, to speak out without any self-interest or possibility of gain, was a common, remarkably altruistic explanation the letter writers gave as the goal of their letter writing. But they also had a practical reason. The readers wrote for the information of the author whose judgment and mastery they trusted – and who, they believed, could and ought to use their letters when creating an unwritten chapter in the country's history, a chapter about the terror. 'Please bear in mind that my letter is *by no means intended for publication.* This is just my need to express my opinion and feelings,' wrote Daniil Il'ich Markelov from Kerch', a fifty-four-year-old veteran of the Second World War. His biography was remarkable. A POW, Markelov escaped from German captivity to Switzerland, organized a guerrilla detachment in France to fight against the Germans, returned home after the war and was first greeted as a hero, with the newspaper *Izvestiia* even publishing an article about his wartime courage. Then he was arrested and spent the next ten years in the Gulag.[106] 'This is truth, without any extra additives,' Markelov wrote in his twelve-page letter, 'truth expressed in magnificent artistic forms and vivid images. At last!'[107] Still, he argued, for all its accuracy *One Day* did not tell the whole story of the terror. A former prisoner of war, he admired not only Solzhenitsyn's *One Day* but also Mikhail Sholokhov's *The Fate of a Man* (1956), one of the first stories in Soviet literature to create a positive image of a former Soviet POW (named Sokolov), returning home.[108] What Markelov wanted was that some writer put together the messages of Solzhenitsyn's and Sholokhov's texts, add similar stories, and explain, at last, what they were about:

> This is what I want.
> While I am still alive, I would like to read and learn about this:
> Sokolov + Shukhov + X = …
> What does it equal? This is what I would like to know.
> Who and how will solve this difficult equation?
> And it has to be solved. Life demands this and will demand ever more pressingly.[109]

The aim of solving this equation with at least two unknowns was to answer why, in this country, innocent people had been proclaimed enemies, for what sake innumerable lives had been destroyed and mutilated. Remarkably, in this and many other readers' eyes, coming up with such a comprehensive explanation was the task not of a historian but of a writer, the most trusted intellectual figure there could be.

On the other side of the camp spectrum, Vadim Viktorovich Kasatskii, a doctor who had worked in the Kolyma camps as a free hire and must have compared himself to the doctors portrayed in *One Day*, also praised Solzhenitsyn's novella. Kasatskii noted its 'absolute photographic accuracy. Accuracy – but not more. Isn't that too little? Isn't it time to move toward generalizations? Let us presume that political generalizations have been made, but artistic generalizations are also necessary, to bring up in people an aversion toward what happened, bring that up by emotional means, by imagery.'[110]

Generalizations would be possible only on the basis of a more detailed and comprehensive description. Many readers who had experienced the terror firsthand suggested exactly what aspects of it Solzhenitsyn had missed and would need to cover in the future. I. Lilenkov, a former prisoner, proposed such themes as society's attitudes to the repressed, the fate of their wives who stayed behind, exile, and the experiences of rehabilitation.[111] Zhanna Blinova, a war veteran who had spent eleven years in the camps (1945–56), insisted that Solzhenitsyn had failed to tell about the prisoners' intellectual and spiritual life – the numerous conversations, the reciting of poetry, the writing of letters home – all that had indeed taken place and was indispensable to them.[112] S. Prokofieva, an old Bolshevik with seventeen years of Gulag behind her, would agree with Blinova, as she reproached Solzhenitsyn for his sarcastic scepticism of the intelligentsia with its egghead conversations about literature and film amidst the horror of the camps. No, argued Prokofieva, such conversations had been vital, as they saved the prisoner's mind and therefore body. She enclosed her poetry written in the camps.[113] Nikolai Vilenchik, a party member since 1931 who had spent sixteen years in the camps, added that Solzhenitsyn disregarded the intense political reflection, which had constantly taken place among the prisoners. And Mikhail Poliakov, a former technician at the Simferopol telephone station who had been in the camps for eighteen years, 1941–59, argued that *One Day* depicted too mild and beautified a picture of the camps.[114] Some, although not many, former prisoners even rejected *One Day* altogether because it was still a far cry from the full measure of atrocities they had seen.[115]

These responses were intended not only to share the burden of the readers' untold experiences. Filling the gaps in Solzhenitsyn's story, they were written to help develop that story into an all-encompassing interpretive history of the terror. The driving force behind these letters, and the reason they were so long and detailed, was personal and public at once: it was their authors' desire to see a history of their epoch written. Readers' responses to *One Day* were part of an immense, dispersed, and yet somehow coherent collective effort at creating a polyphonic history of the terror, a common text that was to be a meaningful interpretation of these readers' times and lives. Boris Khokhlov, the reader who praised both the form and the content of Solzhenitsyn's text, nonetheless saw *One Day* as only the first step in creating such a comprehensive history – of which, he argued, Solzhenitsyn was capable:

> You were courageous enough to step forward with a novella that sheds light only on one day of an innocent prisoner in the late [19]40s and early 50s. But who will dare – precisely, dare – tell, just as publicly [*tak zhe vsenarodno*], the truth about those innocent people who perished at the time of the Ezhov-Beria arbitrariness, or about the people who, although they survived, had suffered through all the horrors of the NKVD torture chambers of [19]36–46, be that a cellar, a prison, a Stolypin railway car, or a camp for prisoners who were at the time called 'enemies of the people'! And it is necessary to tell about all that, it is necessary, as N.S. Khrushchev said, 'while we are alive, to tell the truth about that to the party and to the people.'
>
> If we do not do it, then our children or grandchildren will do it – but they will do it, all the same!
>
> And it seems to me that this is your direct duty, your sacred obligation as a writer who has created, with amazing talent, with human truthfulness, and with Bolshevik honesty, a novella about one day of an innocent prisoner. I would like to know whether you are making plans for such a work.[116]

Solzhenitsyn did write such a work – it was *The Gulag Archipelago*. Written in 1958–68 and based on at least 227 oral and written testimonies he managed to collect, *The Gulag Archipelago* came as close as possible to what Khokhlov and other letter writers envisioned as a polyphonic, collectively authored, monumental history of the terror told through the stories of human lives.[117] In part, this immense project grew out of readers' responses to *One Day*. Solzhenitsyn could not reply to all the letters, but he did read and use them, occasionally tracking down and interviewing his correspondents.[118] A special chapter in *The Gulag Archipelago* contained excerpts from readers' letters about *One Day*. As the chapter did not seem to fit the main text, Solzhenitsyn circulated it via samizdat, and soon, even before the *Archipelago* itself, the chapter was published in the West as part of a documentary collection.[119] It contained excerpts from sixty-three readers' letters about *One Day*, accompanied by Solzhenitsyn's (rather moralistic) comments. Twenty-one out of these sixty-three letters have survived in the original – among them letters by Golitsyn, Markelov, Lilenkov, Vilenchik, and a few others cited here.[120]

Although a step toward a history of the terror, *One Day*, like all good literature, steered clear of providing ready answers. Solzhenitsyn left the job of explaining and generalizing to his readers. And so they tried hard to explain, frustrated and bewildered at the lack of answers. For the time being, Markelov's equation remained unsolved.

The Many Lives of Terror

One of the many powerful messages of *One Day* was that Solzhenitsyn treated all prisoners alike, making no distinction between the guilty and the innocent, right or wrong, be they political prisoners or common felons, Red Army veterans or Vlasovites, Banderovites or even, possibly, actual spies. In his picture of the camps, the notions of friend and foe meant little, as the ongoing struggle for survival could drive human beings together just as well as it could pit them against each other at any given moment, swapping the roles of enemy and friend several times a day. The magnitude of suffering and humiliation in the camps made every prisoner a victim, a tormented human being fighting to preserve his life, and this dwarfed all paper definitions, categorizations, and accusations into trifling insignificance. This was a strong statement, very much unlike what the readers were accustomed to seeing in print, and many rebelled against it. Quite a few argued that somewhere, be it at the helm of power or right there in the camps, there had been real enemies and real criminals, not just innocently imprisoned victims, and that treating every prisoner as innocent was simply not right.

What should we make of these voices? Shall we conclude that in the 1960s, despite a slight modification of rhetoric, the fundamental militant creeds often attributed to the Stalin era – the existence of enemies, the need to purify society, to cast out and exterminate infidels – stood effectively undamaged? The implications of this conclusion would be that the Thaw had not changed the fundamental aspects of a Soviet person's Weltanschauung, that the minds had remained the same as they had been in Stalin's time. Such pronouncements would be premature. Despite the frequent occurrence of 'enemy' images, readers' letters to Solzhenitsyn do not reveal an established and motionless world view of his readers. Rather, they reveal just the contrary.

I have located the variously formulated images of 'enemies' in at least 59 out of 532, that is, approximately 11 per cent of letters about *One Day in the Life of Ivan Denisovich.* Although not overwhelming, this is a substantial number, and it is not to be disregarded. Yet it is also necessary to look at who these people were. Again, just as with language, the letters point to age as an important factor in their authors' tendency to seek and find 'enemies.' Out of the 59 letters referring to 'enemies,' 24 indicate the exact or approximate age of the letter writers, and 19 out of those 24 came from people who described themselves as either pensioners or aged fifty-five and above.[121] In other words, just as with the critics of Solzhenitsyn's language, most letter writers who argued that the camps had contained at least some 'real' enemies were of fairly advanced age. Remarkably, no fewer than fifteen of these letter writers had themselves been imprisoned in the Gulag. The camps did not impair their inclination to divide humankind into the pure and impure.[122]

In their young years these people had gone through the revolution, the Civil War, and the decades when the military mentality inherited from those upheavals reigned supreme, surfacing in collectivization, industrialization, and ultimately the terror of 1937–8.[123] A few of them were Old Bolsheviks who had retained their world view even in the camps, seeing the guards and many fellow prisoners as real enemies, while at the same time regarding themselves as the torchbearers of a pure, untarnished idea. Formed by their experiences, in letters to Solzhenitsyn they continued to stand by their past.[124]

It was experience, rather than simply age, that determined the readers' reactions to Solzhenitsyn's agenda. Not everyone who attacked Solzhenitsyn and advocated the 'enemy' interpretation of the camps was of an advanced age. But whenever the letter writers described their lives, it was evident that they had gone through such experiences that by their nature would foster a vision of the world as divided between good and evil.

One such experience was the Second World War. A significant difference between *One Day* and Ehrenburg's *People, Years, Life* (at least as of the winter of 1962–3, when only the first parts of Ehrenburg's memoir had been published) was that these texts described different chronological stages of repression and different categories of victims. While Ehrenburg depicted the atmosphere of arrests in Moscow of 1937–8, Solzhenitsyn portrayed the camps of the early 1950s, the post-war years. This distinction was important to the readers in the 1960s. While they nearly unanimously saw the victims of the 1930s, the classical 'stream of 1937,' as innocent, the letter writers were far more ambivalent about admitting the innocence of those who ended up in the camps after the war.[125] Among the prisoners in *One Day* are former Ukrainian, Estonian, and Latvian 'nationalists,' and even Ivan Denisovich himself is shown, indirectly but transparently, as a former soldier in the Second Shock Army of General Vlasov.[126] None of these details escaped the readers' attention. If we look at what kinds of 'enemies' the letter writers identified in *One Day*, it becomes clear that the legacy of the Great Patriotic War was crucial in those identifications. Many correspondents of Solzhenitsyn were war veterans or, in any case, had lived through the war. Some had gone through it all – the fighting, the German captivity, and then the Soviet camps. It was hard for them to agree with Solzhenitsyn, who treated all prisoners alike. Someone identified as a militant Ukrainian nationalist ('Banderovite') or a former German occupation police officer (*Polizei*) was an enemy to the veterans, because they had faced those as real enemies during the war, in battle and in captivity.

Even Soviet prisoners of war subsequently transferred from German to Soviet camps were not necessarily innocent in the readers' eyes. An aging veteran and former prisoner of war, S. Zhuravlev was not sure that Ivan Denisovich was above suspicion. '*There were different prisoners of war*: martyrs and fighters, self-seekers [*shkurniki*] and traitors,' he wrote. 'I myself was a prisoner of war. I know the sufferings of our people and the beastly triumph of the *Polizei* and traitors of the Motherland who tormented us not less and often even more than the most bestial Fascists did, because they were serving their masters. And so, I do not see that *Ivan Denisovich feels himself* like a *Soviet* man.'[127] 'The author,' wrote the war veteran A. Stoliarov, 'did not take the trouble to distinguish between real criminals, who fed the Banderovites,[128] and honest people; [in the text] they all look the same. This is not true either. Barbed wire does not make brothers of people who treat their Motherland so differently.'[129] 'I do not feel pity for the dark individuals of the Patriotic War,' snapped a female reader, E.A. Ignatovich, who had faced the camp prisoners while working as a foreman on transport in Karaganda in 1954. In his chapter on the readers of *One Day*, Solzhenitsyn somewhat rashly cited her among the '"practical workers" [of the regime] and the well-intentioned.' Yet Ignatovich had also suffered from repression: her father had been killed in 1937.[130] 'Vlasovites,' 'Banderovites,' and 'traitors' figured prominently in the letter by Lev Arkad'evich Meerson, sixty-seven, who had spent six years in the camps in 1949–55 and now wrote about these prisoners with little sympathy.[131]

These responses did not come simply from a paranoid witch-hunting impulse or an abstract Manichean search for the social good and evil, the pure and the impure, which the war had perpetuated. The Second World War drew not only imaginary but also very real front lines across the territory of the Soviet Union, and for millions of Soviet people. The fighting forces of their wartime adversaries were not imaginary but very real enemies. After the unparalleled bloodshed and atrocities of this war, it was explicable that those who had witnessed it continued viewing their yesterday's opponents on the same wartime terms.

The war had had yet another effect. In letters to Solzhenitsyn, people often spoke unaffectedly and even condescendingly about the suffering he described. Such letters did not necessarily come from former camp inmates. They could also be written by war veterans and actually by anyone who had seen wartime or post-war life, in the army or in the rear, and had never seen the camps. 'I have never been imprisoned,' wrote P.S. Petrov from Moscow, 'but when I served in the army, I saw all this and much more. We used to cut bread with a saw because it was frozen, and for a few months we ate nothing but wheat for both the first and second course. People got dystrophy – and mind you, we were getting ready for the front.'[132] A veteran of the Second World War from Groznyi, A. Tambovtsev, claimed that life had not been much easier outside the camps after the war, and that had the camps had decent living conditions, everyone would have flocked there.[133] In 1943, a Red Army unit where Viktor Sorokin served was stationed in an abandoned prison camp: 'And so, we the soldiers lived in the very same barracks and dugouts where the "zeks" had lived before us. Bunk beds and single-pane windows covered with ice, mattresses (we, by the way, did not have them at all for awhile) – this was very much like what Solzhenitsyn describes. So, what do you suggest, should we have built solid structures for prisoners in 1946–50? How, then, would prisoners have been different from us, from a nation that had been through a severe disaster and was living in pits and dugouts, on the ashes of our homes?'[134]

Daily life during and immediately after the Second World War was such that Solzhenitsyn's text easily paled in comparison to reality, in and outside the camps. Many readers had been through trials even worse than those of Ivan Denisovich. Their wartime and post-war experiences habituated these people to privations, violence, and death, bringing up a hardened insensitivity to human suffering.[135]

The impact of the Second World War overlapped with the experiences of the camps, through which many letter writers had gone on either side of the barbed wire. In an outburst of chilling mockery, the forty-one-year-old Vasilii Sergeevich Zagorodskii from Kotlas, a war veteran who, according to his letter, had served at the front as a private throughout the war, wrote,

> How can we not feel pity over this poor, poor prisoner, that is, a Banderovite and a Vlasovite, subjected to such inhuman treatment by the Chekist hangmen! But what about the fact that during the war this very Banderovite

> and Vlasovite, like a cruel beast, committed horrible atrocities against little children and old women in the villages of Belorussia, Ukraine, and the Baltics, and, together with German soldiers, 'organized' the ditch graves of Katynshchina, where thousands and thousands of people, innocently shot and dug half-alive by you, Banderovite, are asleep and will never wake up? Well, that's a thing of the past![136]

The grim irony of Zagorodskii's letter was that Katyn, a place near Smolensk, was a site of mass executions of Polish army officers not by Banderovites, Vlasovites, or German troops, but by the NKVD in 1940, the fact that the Soviet government at the time denied, ascribing the execution to the Germans.[137]

Vasilii Sergeevich Zagorodskii may or may not have known the Katyn story, but he was not only a war veteran. In 1950, he wrote, the local party organs had 'directed' him to serve in the prison camps, doing 'educational work among the prisoners, including the category of political prisoners.' He served in the camps from 1950 to 1957, then spent a couple of years working in local administration, and then 'the party again directed' him to carry out 'political education work among the prisoners,' which he did from 1959 on.[138]

Zagorodskii's letter was a twenty-page handwritten attack on Solzhenitsyn, accusing the writer of badly and intentionally misrepresenting the camp guards. 'We,' wrote Zagorodskii on behalf of the guards, 'never allowed anything of the kind that Solzhenitsyn describes, to happen.'[139] Nobody ever beat the prisoners, he repeated again and again[140] – as did other ex-MVD officers, such as Aleksei Mikhailovich Egorov from Cherepovets, who claimed that a guard beating a prisoner would have gone straight to jail.[141] Many of the prisoners were guilty, too, Zagorodskii insisted – take those Banderovites and Vlasovites. And even if some of them were not guilty, he wrote, how were the guards supposed to distinguish between the guilty and the innocent? For the guards, every prisoner was in the camp for a reason.[142]

There were quite a few such letters in Solzhenitsyn's mail, coming from those who had been on the other side of the camp spectrum or somewhere in the middle. No fewer than ten of the fifty-nine letters advancing the 'enemy' argument and attacking the writer on these grounds came from the former guards, career NKVD/MVD officers, and free hire camp personnel.[143] Some of the former free hires accepted Solzhenitsyn's viewpoint,[144] but most of them, and all the officers and guards, rejected it.

We should not, of course, necessarily believe what they wrote about the camps, such as the statements that prisoners were never beaten. What exposes those statements is, for example, Zagorodskii's claim that, although they never beat the prisoners, the guards did have 'a moral right' to do so – as the prisoners were, again, nothing better than Banderovites, Vlasovites, *Polizei*, German-appointed village elders, or common criminals.[145] What we should do is try to understand why at all those camp guards wrote long autobiographical letters attacking Solzhenitsyn – the letters that would most likely get no response whatsoever, ending up with a laconic editorial verdict, 'To the archive.'

Zagorodskii continued his letter: 'During all these years, I was twice awarded the medal For Distinguished Service in the Organs of the MVD, received a Letter of Commendation numerous times, and have had a number of honourable citations.'[146] After *One Day in the Life of Ivan Denisovich*, the letter of commendation was a useless piece of paper, and the medal for distinguished service in the organs of the MVD, just as the word *honourable*, looked like a bad joke. And so they protested, poorly prepared to argue but furious over what they had read. It was certainly a reaction premised on the criteria of realism, a guild response to the writer's negative portrayal of their trade. But it was also something else. *One Day* gnawed at the very foundation, the core of these people's lives, exposing it and suggesting that the core was, and had always been, black and hollow. This was impossible to acknowledge, and this was why they wrote.

Again, the fact that the novella was published openly and legitimately cannot be overestimated. Its publication in the country's principal literary journal suggested to the readers that Solzhenitsyn's interpretation of the camps was now the official interpretation, automatically relegating the ex-guards and police officers to the unfortunate camp of social pariahs. The roles were being reversed, and the former guardians of the existing order found themselves in a position of its implicit rhetorical enemies. In their letters against Solzhenitsyn, these people not only desperately defended their own past and self-esteem but also struggled to maintain their membership and social status.

Apparently, *One Day*'s idea that what they had done in the camps was cruel came as big news to some MVD officers. Thus, Aleksei Grigor'evich Panchuk, a party member since 1940 and veteran of the Second World War, who had been an MVD officer for sixteen years and retired in 1962, wrote,

> Well, what did you expect? Perhaps you thought, Solzhenitsyn, that a prison camp is a health resort or something of the kind? Having committed a heav-

> iest crime against the state, you would like to stay warm, to be well fed and decently clothed, not to work, and to serve your term in that fashion? There are no such camps in the Soviet state, and they cannot exist....
>
> Solzhenitsyn's Shukhov sleeps for seven to eight hours, has felt boots, wadded pants, a padded jacket and a pea jacket, an ear-flap hat, and mittens. He goes to work in the temperature of 27 degrees and complains that it is cold. Solzhenitsyn had better visit a construction site today and see how construction workers function in the same or even worse cold, and what they wear. A man who works is not afraid of cold, while a sloth will freeze even in a sheepskin coat. Shukhov gets three hot meals a day, for breakfast he gets even three courses, and 900 grams of bread....
>
> It is unclear what facts of cruelty, arbitrariness, and what violations of socialist legality Tvardovskii sees in this novella. That prisoners were kept in intense custody, that they had to work, that they were clothed to the season and fed according to the norms, that they were required to observe the regimen, and that malicious violators were locked up? These are legitimate limitations to certain rights of a Soviet citizen who has committed a crime against the Soviet state.[147]

Declarations like this were not very frequent in Solzhenitsyn's mail,[148] and yet the justification of reprisals, the failure to recognize cruelty spoke volumes about the time and the culture. Such statements had to do not simply with the readers' overall insensitivity to suffering as a result of war and privations, not just with their background of service in the Gulag, and not only with their desire to justify the past and validate their social membership and status. The letter writers' confidence that such opinions could and should be expressed was *uninhibited.* Justification of repression came from an underdeveloped state of public discussion about the terror.

During the Thaw, it was becoming ever harder to defend the mass violence openly by quoting clichés from textbooks and newspaper editorials, because the clichés, the textbooks, and the editorials were being increasingly discredited. Yet such defence remained possible – more so than, say, during the late 1980s and early 1990s, when the terror again came in the spotlight of public attention and a much more resolute verdict upon it was pronounced. In the early 1960s, however, not only were the ideologues of the regime unwilling to push the analysis of the terror any further than it had at the Twenty-Second Party Congress, but even the ethical condemnation of the prison camps and executions had not yet reached a finality and decisiveness that it achieved two decades later. Up until 1961, the debate had been relegated largely to the innumerable kitchen conversations and left the public forums of political conversation with a big void on the issue.[149] Even though the situation changed after the Twenty-Second Congress, by 1962–3 too little had yet been published about the terror in the Soviet press, too timid a discussion had been openly held. It was this void in the media, the absence of a narrative of the terror, the lack of detailed information and comprehensive rejection of mass reprisals that allowed defenders of concentration camps to go public when, after the publication of Solzhenitsyn's *One Day*, Ehrenburg's memoir, and several other texts the discussion finally began. As of 1962–3, the forging of common ethical attitudes to the terror was only beginning. In the late 1980s and 1990s, people like Panchuk would more likely refrain from an open defence of the camps, but in 1963 they still thought it acceptable. Over time, arguments in favour of mass violence would be progressively compromised, and much credit for that goes to Ehrenburg and Solzhenitsyn, whose writings coined the terms for the discussion and formulated the main principle of approach to the problem – the supreme value of an individual human life.

Although few of the letter writers advanced 'enemy' arguments when either criticizing or praising Solzhenitsyn's picture of the camps, the enemy theme was present in many letters. The retention of this idea had specific reasons in each individual case, grounded in the letter writers' life experiences. Many of them were older people who had imbibed, from their young years, the socially divisive and militant ethos of the early years of the Soviet order. They had also gone through the Second World War, carrying from it an acute sense of real threats to the survival of their country, an apprehension that did not easily go away. In addition, a substantial number of the letter writers who mentioned 'enemies' had been directly involved in the functioning of the Gulag. Their attack on Solzhenitsyn was a defence of their own past, an attempt to justify their lives before others and perhaps also before themselves. But it was also a desperate effort to maintain a public face in society, a status that, with the publication of *One Day*, they were destined to lose.

The terror had many faces, and behind each face there was a person and a life.

The Power of *One Day*

Something new was in the air after *One Day* came out. In his letter of 25 December 1962, as we remember, Tvardovskii informed Solzhenitsyn that most of the negative responses to the novella were anonymous.[150]

In the archive, such responses are mostly signed, so technically speaking Tvardovskii could be wrong. But a few negative letters were indeed anonymous – either not signed at all or signed contractedly and illegibly and missing a return address.[151] Few as they were, they are not to be ignored. Even stronger than the former NKVD/MVD officers, these letter writers must have felt that with the publication of *One Day* the tide had been reversed, the prisoners' view of the terror became the new official line, and the opposite views, previously mainstream, now became alien and seditious. Although these readers expressed orthodox and callous opinions with no trace of dissent whatsoever, they opted to be on the safe side and remain incognito. Perhaps their intuition did not fail them. What started as the Thaw indeed portended a change of intellectual climate.

Negative or furious as they were, the letters nonetheless betrayed the major impact that *One Day* had on Solzhenitsyn's critics. Even if they wanted to, the readers could not ignore the strength of his prose. Pavel Kol'tsov, a veteran of three wars (Civil, Soviet-Finnish, and the Great Patriotic) and a camp prisoner for seven years (1949–56), spent several pages arguing that Solzhenitsyn did not show all the complexity of the terror, that he had missed important distinctions between categories of prisoners, and that his language, too, was inappropriate. Yet Kol'tsov felt compelled to add, 'I cannot but sense the power of this work.' Tvardovskii (it was to him that Kol'tsov wrote) underlined these words.[152]

The inability to withstand Solzhenitsyn's prose was disturbing. At times the letter writer would lose his nerve, and the argument slid into a frustrated, hysterical outcry of protest. 'The author simply does not know Soviet people, they are not like that at all, they are not cannibals,' exploded A. Stoliarov, a party worker and war veteran.[153] 'Who is this book going to bring up, what does the author want to express in this book, when he so much vilifies the Soviet countryside and thousands of Soviet people, the workers of the MVD and MGB, who are not like that, they are better, more humane, they are Soviet people, not self-seekers and bribe-takers, not hunters after a slice of lard, he vilifies not just the cult of personality but everything,' almost shrieked in his letter Mikhail Sykchin, a collective farm party organizer from Novosibirsk region.[154]

It was the details that killed, the minute record of human existence in the camp. Yuliia Pilipchuk from L'vov agued that, despite the numerous general words the press had used before to describe the terror, the readers were 'caught unawares' and shocked by the precise description of what the camps were about. 'Soviet [literary] criticism,' she wrote, 'had employed more than enough of the words *lawlessness*, *arbitrariness*, *flagrant, the cult,* and *despotism,* but after reading the novella, many highly educated and highly positioned people looked as if they were publicly exposed as having participated in anti-Soviet activities.'[155] Readers wrote about the 'horrible truth' of *One Day.* Some of them even felt that discussing the terror in the way Solzhenitsyn proposed could be dangerous, if not lethal for the regime. The fifty-nine-year-old Andrei Fedin, who had spent six years in the camps (1936–42) and five years in exile, admired *One Day* but suggested taking the book out of circulation, because Solzhenitsyn's truth was too dangerous for the minds of 'our sons and grandsons.'[156] Aleksei Kondratovich, deputy editor of *Novyi mir,* felt it necessary to respond to Fedin, insisting that 'such formidable truth as the truth about the year 1937' could not be concealed from the people, and that open and full discussion of the terror was the best guarantee against its return.[157]

'Oh no, I do not want this novella!' exclaimed Liudmila Sosnina, a middle-aged woman whose father had been expelled from the party in the 1930s. Her brother and sister had been sent to the camps, and after her brother had spent eight years there and was apparently sentenced to exile, Sosnina received permission to join him. She spent the next fifteen years in the North, working in the camps as a free hire. Never imprisoned, she technically stayed on the other side of the barbed wire, but if her story was accurate, she had obviously suffered from the repression. Still, in her remarkably long letter – forty handwritten pages – she protested against *One Day.*[158]

Why did she write these forty pages, replete with grammar mistakes, exclamation points, and question marks? 'It was hard for Solzhenitsyn to write this novella, but it was even harder for me to read it,' she answered.[159] Sosnina admired her father, a Bolshevik self-made man and an altruistic enthusiast of industrialization who had struggled, in the 1930s, to manage a large industrial plant and teach himself engineering in the process. The main part of her letter was actually not about the camps or exile – it was about her father and family in the 1930s. Solzhenitsyn invaded and threatened the world of her childhood that she portrayed as the time of family unity and happiness. Her letter was a defence of that time. She defended the spirit of selfless devotion to the cause, which had reigned in their family, and in which her father had raised her. And yes, he did believe in the existence of wreckers and enemies – foreign specialists, old tsarist engineers, and the like – and these images also constituted part of her fond remembrances. The purges had destroyed her family, but the notions that stood behind the purges made their way into an idyll that Sosnina created out of the 1930s. Perhaps that helped her survive her fifteen years in the Far North.[160]

At the same time, her letter was more than just a piece of nostalgic writing. Sosnina wanted to explain what had actually happened in the 1930s, how the ideals of her childhood could match the grim reality of the terror. 'The cult of personality deeply and powerfully touches me personally, and it makes me think endlessly,' she wrote. How was the industry created – was it the enthusiasm? Or 'perhaps, it was the iron will of the cult that built the country's industry, or helped to build it?' Why did her father, the enthusiast, get expelled from the party, why were her brother and sister arrested? 'I am not looking for consolation at all. I bear neither grudge nor malice. It's only thoughts, endless thoughts. This is some gigantic nonsense!'[161]

In part, Solzhenitsyn provoked many readers' protest because, by showing the survival-oriented, primeval underside of human nature that left no room for political convictions, high sentiments, or noble pursuits of the mind, he violated the conventions of socialist realism. But he also did much more than that. The readers' protest against *One Day* stemmed from biography and history. Solzhenitsyn threatened to erase these people's lives, in which many of them claimed to have seen or been the heroes, martyrs, intellectuals, and high-spirited enthusiasts he failed to portray. Not unlike Ehrenburg's opponent Vladimir Ermilov, Solzhenitsyn's critics, such as the reader Sosnina, initially wanted to write the terror into the mainstream Soviet history, to explain the violence while keeping their world view intact, to reassure themselves that, despite the camps, the country overall and they personally were, and had always been, on the right track. However, unlike Ermilov, Sosnina acknowledged the difficulties of such a papering-over project. After Solzhenitsyn, it was hardly possible to limit oneself to cosmetic revisions, otherwise maintaining the status quo. The power of *One Day* was that, no matter whether the readers agreed with its interpretation of the terror, the book, perhaps more than any other at the time, urged them to reconsider and question their past in its entirety.

This reconsideration was a prominent theme in the letter of a seventy-year-old agronomist D.A. Vakhrameev, a Civil War volunteer, a veteran, and a party member since 1918. Imprisoned in 1939 for 'praising Trotsky,' he spent the next seven years in the camps. His wife renounced him, and his daughter, who attempted to maintain ties with him, was driven to suicide. Inspired by Solzhenitsyn's *One Day*, which he described as 'a truthful work written in good language,' Vakhrameev's twenty-six-page handwritten letter was a detailed story of his imprisonment. Like many other readers, he did not intend his letter for publication but instead gave his life story away to another author, Solzhenitsyn, who might one day write a history of the terror. Also like many others, he insisted that creating such a history was the job not of historians but of writers: 'One must issue a call for all the participants of those events to send their memoirs and thoughts to the writers, so that the latter could rework this "raw material" into a literary form.... I am not going to join the literary circles, with my simple mug. But I would be happy if I got a note that someone used what I've written.'[162]

We cannot send him such a note, but we can interpret his letter, and all similar letters, as part in the creation of the history he so much wanted. Vakhrameev was one of the few letter writers who admitted their wilful contribution to the terror. After many days worse than the one of Ivan Denisovich, he came out of the camps with a sense of his own share of responsibility for the country's tragedy. Unlike many other former prisoners, he did not see himself as a victim and refused to dissociate himself from the hangmen. 'During the years of the personality cult, I conscientiously badgered "enemies of the people" at meetings. And in a private circle, I doubted (useless protest that no one can see).[163] I thought there was the party's will for everything ("God! I believe! God, help my disbelief!"). Therefore, I do not want to spit in my own face, and I consider myself just as guilty as Stalin was.'[164] After release from the camp, the Old Bolshevik and Civil War veteran Vakhrameev did not apply for reinstatement in the party. 'You and I are the two shores of one river,' he quoted a popular song when addressing Stalin's portrait, which was still hanging on his wall. 'One cannot throw a word out of a song. And I do not want to be reinstated in the party, because of my guilt.... As for the "father with moustache," I do not hold it against him. I treat him as one treats a natural disaster. The entire people together have created this nightmare.'[165]

Not many letter writers admitted their own responsibility as directly as Vakhrameev. A more common way of recognizing this responsibility was to confess having believed in the existence of 'enemies of the people' but to argue that one stopped believing after she or he or some family members and friends had been arrested. Still, even if in this indirect form, the letter writers gave bitter characteristics to contemporary society.[166] Many, like an economist Aleksei Filippov from Kazakhstan and a pensioner Mikhail Zabelkin from Vladimir-Volynskii, wrote about 'the epidemic of universal suspiciousness,' which had seized the country in Stalin's times, and to which they did not want to succumb again.[167] When he finally got hold of a library copy of *Novyi mir*, tattered and greased from readers' hands, the seventy-one-year-old S.A. Kolendovskii, who had spent fifteen years in the prison camps, noticed a pencilled question that someone had put in the margins: 'Why do camps and starvation constantly accompany socialism?'[168] Kolendovskii agreed: the camps, and the fact that they survived even after Stalin, were the country's shame. Why do we need them, he asked? For disinfection? By what political and social means? Should there be a new bloody revolution? Against whom now? Revolution has absolutely and forever become repulsive to everyone, he argued, because it has cruelly deceived all the 'Christian folk,' making them die not once of starvation and typhoid lice. Kolendovskii, too, suggested that writers apply themselves to creating a comprehensive history of the terror, 'in order for this all-national prison camp tragedy never to repeat with honest working people in Russia.'[169]

The desire to prevent the return of the terror, as well as the emerging sense of personal involvement and responsibility for it, inevitably drove one to think about the terror's origins. Ivan Alekseevich Pupyshev, a sixty-six-year-old retired village schoolteacher who had spent six years (1949–55) in the camps, admired *One Day* and responded to it with two letters, one in 1962, the other in 1964. In the second letter, he concluded that the origins of the violence lay in an 'exclusivity complex,' by which he meant someone's claim for undivided, undisputed possession of societal truth. Widespread in the revolutionary era, as well as in the 1920s and 1930s, this claim no longer looked convincing to him. Having read *One Day*, Ivan Alekseevich came back to his young years, to the revolutionary origins of the social order under which he had spent nearly all his life. Experience taught him to reject messianic ideas of monopolizing truth and claims of bringing light and happiness to humanity regardless of costs. Such claims, as he had ample opportunity to observe, brought people nothing but suffering.[170]

Such profound rethinking of the origins of the country's historic troubles was uncommon in *Novyi mir*'s mail. However, such letters were significant. Readers like Vakhrameev, Pupyshev, or Kolendovskii belonged to the generation that had brought the revolution to victory and for decades defended it against enemies, real and imaginary. This was the generation that commonly saw the revolution as an indispensable, vital development in Russian history and a blessing for their lives. Yet in the early 1960s the blessing looked far less obvious. The explosion of printed information and relatively open debate about the terror enabled and urged these people, perhaps even more so than their children and grandchildren, to look back and rethink the past. Many of them, perhaps most, kept defending it. Yet others came to judge this past and themselves soberly. They had seen it all and had nothing to fear anymore. For the most part, they did not regret what they had built. And yet at times they asked themselves whether the cost had not been too high.

Conclusion: Everyone's Living Past

Inspired to a great extent by Ilya Ehrenburg's memoir *People, Years, Life*, and Aleksandr Solzhenitsyn's *One Day in the Life of Ivan Denisovich*, the polemic about the nature and origins of mass violence in Soviet history stood at the centre of political and intellectual life during the Thaw. While revealing the power of conservative and residual tendencies in Soviet culture, the polemic at the same time suggested that those tendencies were on the decline, and that important new developments were taking place in the readers' minds. Looking at just a couple of years can mean holding the lens too closely to trace long-term intellectual change. On the other hand, holding the lens closely enables us to notice the moment when intellectual change begins to happen. The early 1960s were precisely one such moment. It was then that, with the legitimate publication of literary texts about the terror and the widespread, detailed, and relatively open discussion about it, the language and mentality shaped under Stalin received a heavy, and ultimately, to quote Ehrenburg, fatal blow.

A major problem of remembering and explaining the terror during the Thaw was that, unlike in many post–Second World War European societies where authoritarian regimes of mass extermination were crushed in 1944–5 and the new governments dissociated themselves from earlier policies, at least in general terms, the Soviet regime staked its legitimacy on continuity with the immediate past.[171] More than elsewhere, in Soviet reality remembrance of mass political violence had to work against the regime's strategic interests. Logically, after the initial revelations about the Stalin time, the Soviet media tried presenting it as an integral, overwhelmingly positive historical stage. Vladimir Ermilov's 1963 attack on Ehrenburg was one of the earliest attempts at this, an effort to write the terror into the established, non-controversial, and sanitized historical narrative, in which neither the system nor the people would bear responsibility for the recent human tragedy. The recent violence thus remained an unexplained momentary aberration, an accidental unfortunate sidetracking from the country's predominantly normal, progressive historical path.

The attempt failed spectacularly. It showed all the uncertainty and vulnerability of journalistic efforts to 'normalize' the terror, to write it neatly and in a politically acceptable language into mainstream Soviet history. Rather than easily lending itself to interpretations and uses, the violence proved inexplicable and unusable for any kind of didactic, propagandistic, or short-term political purposes. Instead, the terror itself turned out to have shaped, 'used,' and continued to 'use' those who tried to interpret it – or, unsuccessfully, cover it up. The terror proved a formidable tangle of problems, implicating everyone, impinging upon everyone's memories and current lives.

The readers' discussion of Ehrenburg's memoir showed that the existing language and ethos of the Soviet media were decidedly unfit for comprehending the twentieth-century experience of mass political violence. When it came to explaining the terror, the Thaw rapidly melted the ice of existing ideological constructs, ethical notions, and verbal formulas under the interpreters' feet. With time, the ice was becoming dangerously thin, and the option was either to risk drowning or look urgently for a new and firmer intellectual ground. Explaining the terror required a new system of values, while describing the terror required a new language. Both were manifestly absent.

This was the same issue over which Tvardovskii had agonized years before, and which he finally recognized as impregnable in the existing framework of political ideas, ethical models, and literary conventions. And this was why he was so jubilant in having found Solzhenitsyn – his greatest literary discovery of the Thaw. The power and significance of Ehrenburg's memoir and Solzhenitsyn's novella was that they not only urged the readers to rethink their past but also offered them the new ethical and linguistic terms for doing so. Whereas Ehrenburg for the first time emphasized the centrality of individual human experience to history, Solzhenitsyn brought the theme to its logical perfection as well as suggested new verbal approaches to it, the means to describe the previously indescribable historical reality.

The readers recognized that – some against their will. The anxious concern for the legitimacy and stability of the existing socio-political as well as cultural and linguistic order, the concern that we see in so many of the readers' letters, was rooted in a crisis of biography that numerous people began to face at the time. In their new roles of amateur historians, social psychologists, and political analysts, they were driven by the genuine desire to preserve the system, to salvage it in its predicament of dealing with the legacy of the terror. Thereby, many of them sought to justify their own lives. Experience played a crucial role in the readers' perceptions of repression and its literary depictions. People who had matured during the Revolution, the Civil War, and especially the Second World War often retained and defended the ethos of social militancy in which they had been raised, and frequently they continued to blame society's misfortunes on enemies and scapegoats. Persistent, at times desperate defence of their own past had a powerful impact on verbal representations of the terror in readers' letters.

And yet, under the impact of books they read – Solzhenitsyn's *One Day in the Life of Ivan Denisovich* and Ehrenburg's *People, Years, Life* in the first place – at least some people began reassessing the socio-ethical order that they, or their fathers, had brought to life. When putting their thoughts and memories on paper and sharing them with trusted authors and editors, the letter writers made an intense interpretive effort, coming to a sober, bitter reassessment of their past values and deeds – which, as they increasingly realized, had been an integral part of the recent tragedy. Some, if not too many, began to suspect that the roots of the terror were in their own minds.

Perhaps most importantly, in the early 1960s many readers began to realize that their society was, to a large extent, formed by the terror. Literature provoked the recognition that practically everyone had been privy to, indeed complicit in the mass violence of the recent past. On the one hand, this realization suggested that a society formed by the terror could not interpret the terror past at will. But on the other hand, here was the root and the first growth of departing from the terror – by being conscious of its impact, and by a resolution to gain distance from it.

NOTES

I am grateful to the participants of the conferences 'The Thaw: Soviet Society and Culture during the 1950s and 1960s' (University of California, Berkeley, 2005), 'The Pain of Words: Narratives of Suffering in Slavic Cultures' (Princeton University, 2008), and 'After the War, After Stalin' (University of Saint Petersburg, Russia, 2010), as well as the Stanford University Russian History Workshop (2007) for comments on several versions of this chapter. Part of this research appeared (in Russian) in *Noveishaia istoriia Rossii* 1 and 2 (2011). My special thanks to Eleonory Gilburd, Jochen Hellbeck, Yuri Slezkine, Lynne Viola, and Amir Weiner for their valuable suggestions about this work.

1 Ilya Ehrenburg, 'Liudi, gody, zhizn'' (hereafter LGZh), *Novyi mir* (hereafter

NM) 8–10 (1960); 1–2 (1961); 9–11 (1961); 4–6 (1962); 1–3 (1963); 1–4 (1965).

2 Ilya Ehrenburg, 'Ottepel',' *Znamia* 5 (1954): 14–87.

3 Among the publications that came out before the congress (October 1961) was Viktor Nekrasov's *Kira Georgievna* (*NM*, June 1961: 70–126). For an analysis, see Polly Jones, 'Memories of Terror or Terrorizing Memories? Terror, Trauma, and Survival in Soviet Culture of the Thaw,' *Slavonic and East European Review* 86, no. 2 (2008): 346–71, here 355–7. Nekrasov's novella, however, did not generate a large-scale polemic among readers comparable to discussions about Ehrenburg or Solzhenitsyn.

4 On the Soviet etymology of 'repression,' see David Fel'dman, *Terminologiia vlasti: Sovetskie politicheskie terminy v istoriko-kul'turnom kontekste* (Moscow, 2006), 118–261.

5 Robert Conquest, *The Great Terror: Stalin's Purge of the Thirties* (New York, 1968), in Russian as Robert Konkvest, *Bol'shoi terror* (Riga, 1991).

6 See also Cathy Frierson, 'An Open Call to Focus on Russia's Young Adults,' *Problems of Post-Communism* 54, no. 5 (2007): 3–18; Irina Paperno, *Stories of the Soviet Experience: Memoirs, Diaries, Dreams* (Ithaca, 2009).

7 Joshua Rubenstein, *Tangled Loyalties: The Life and Times of Ilya Ehrenburg* (New York, 1996), 339.

8 Ehrenburg, 'LGZh,' *NM* 9 (1961): 152; *NM* 4 (1962): 62.

9 Ehrenburg, 'LGZh,' *NM* 5 (1962): 143.

10 Ibid., 134.

11 See Boris Frezinskii's commentary in Ehrenburg, *Liudi, gody, zhizn'* (hereafter *LGZh*) (Moscow, 1990), 1:569; 3:233.

12 *LGZh* 1:48, 127, 250.

13 Ibid., 3:228.

14 Frezinskii's commentary in *LGZh* 3:396; Iakov Etinger, *Eto nevozmozhno zabyt'… : vospominaniia* (Moscow, 2001), 105–25; Benedikt Sarnov, *Sluchai Erenburga* (Moscow, 2004), 172–85, 234–77; Sarnov, 'U vremeni v plenu,' in *LGZh* 1:34–7.

15 Gennadii Kostyrchenko, 'Deportatsiia – mistifikatsiia (proshchanie s mifom stalinskoi epokhi),' *Otechestvennai istoriia* 1 (2003): 92–113, esp. 96.

16 'LGZh,' *NM* 5 (1962): 148–54. The town of Teruel changed hands several times in 1937–8 during the Spanish Civil War.

17 RGALI 1204/2/2617/39–41; RGALI 1204/2/2620/115; RGALI 1204/2/2626/89; RGALI 1204/2/2615/33ob; RGALI 1204/2/2625/80; RGALI 1702/8/632/1.

18 RGALI 1702/8/632/38.

19 RGALI 1702/8/735/130.

20 RGALI 1702/8/735/121 (registered 23 July 1962).
21 RGALI 1702/8/735/143 (Aleksandr Dunaev, Dushanbe, registered 10 August 1962).
22 RGALI 1702/10/250/13–14 (L. Ia., engineer, 23 April 1965). Also RGALI 1702/8/735/20–2 (Vsevolod Vibelius, actor, Irkutsk, 30 January 1962); RGALI 1702/8/735/113 (Skhodnev, steam boiler technician, Ivanovo region, 16 June 1962).
23 Tsentral'nyi arkhiv obshchestvenno-politicheskoi istorii Moskvy (TsAOPIM) 453/2/27/16–17, 19, 22, 27, 33–4.
24 Konrad Jarausch, 'Critical Memory and Civil Society: The Impact of the 1960s on German Debates about the Past,' in *Coping with the Past: West German Debates on Nazism and Generational Conflict, 1955–1975*, ed. Philipp Gassert and Alan Steinweis (New York, 2006), here 20–2; Tony Judt, *Postwar: A History of Europe since 1945* (New York, 2005), 416–17; Harold Marcuse, *Legacies of Dachau: The Uses and Abuses of a Concentration Camp, 1933–2001* (Cambridge, UK, 2001), 201, 212–13; Henry Rousso, *The Vichy Syndrome: History and Memory in France since 1944* (Cambridge, MA, 1991), 98–101; Rebecca Wittmann, *Beyond Justice: The Auschwitz Trial* (Cambridge, MA, 2005), 262–6.
25 A rare exception: RGALI 1702/10/82/1–3 (S.D. Serebrianyi, young age, Moscow, registered 1 March 1963).
26 RGALI 1702/8/632/37–8 (16 October 1961).
27 Vladimir Ermilov, 'Neobkhodimost' spora: chitaia memuary I. Erenburga "Liudi, gody, zhizn,"' *Izvestiia*, 30 January 1963.
28 Leonid Il'ichev, 'Tvorit' dlia naroda, vo imia kommunizma: Rech' sekretaria TsK KPSS na vstreche rukovoditelei partii i pravitel'stva s deiateliami literatury i iskusstva 17 dekabria 1962 goda,' *Pravda*, 22 December 1962.
29 For the stenogram of the session (24–6 December 1962), see *Ideologicheskie komissii TsK KPSS. 1958–1964: Dokumenty* (Moscow, 2000), 293–381. For Il'ichev's speech, see his 'Sily tvorcheskoi molodezhi – na sluzhbu velikim idealam,' *Sovetskaia kul'tura*, 10 January 1963.
30 Nikita Khrushchev, 'Vysokaia ideinost' i khudozhestvennoe masterstvo – velikaia sila sovetskoi literatury i iskusstva,' *Pravda*, 10 March 1963; Leonid Il'ichev, 'Ob otvetstvennosti khudozhnika pered narodom,' *Pravda*, 9 March 1963.
31 M. Levin, 'Ia veriu v propoved,' an interview with Aleksei Adzhubei, *Molodezh' Estonii*, 6 May 1988.
32 See Priscilla Johnson, 'The Politics of Soviet Culture, 1962–1964,' in *Khrushchev and the Arts*, ed. Priscilla Johnson and Leopold Labedz (Cambridge, MA, 1965), 1–89, esp. 84–9. On the Manège affair, see Susan E. Reid, 'In the

Name of the People: The Manège Affair Revisited,' *Kritika: Explorations in Russian and Eurasian History* 6, no. 4 (2005): 673–716.

33 Ermilov, 'Neobkhodimost' spora'; on silence, see also Ehrenburg, *LGZh* 1:250.

34 G. Aleksandrov, 'Tovarishch Erenburg uproshchaet,' *Pravda*, 14 April 1945.

35 Ilya Ehrenburg, 'Ne nado zamalchivat' sushchestvo spora,' *Izvestiia*, 6 February 1963; Ermilov, 'Otvet avtoru pis'ma,' *Izvestiia*, 6 February 1963.

36 E.g., RGALI 1702/10/82/1–3 (regestered 1 March 1963).

37 Vladimir Ermilov, 'Velikii drug sovetskoi literatury,' *Literaturnaia gazeta*, 21 December 1949.

38 RGALI 1702/10/82/73–4 (Emlin and Chervonyi, Sverdlovsk, 19 February 1963).

39 RGALI 1204/2/2646/158–9 (4 February 1963); also RGALI 1702/10/82/19; RGALI 1702/10/83/192 (Yulia Samarina, Cherepovets, [9 March 1963]).

40 RGALI 1702/10/83/211–22 (registered 5 March 1963). Vishnevskii did not indicate his profession or occupation, but the good prose of his long, typed letter suggests that he was well educated.

41 RGALI 1702/10/83/217–18.

42 RGALI 1204/2/2642/1–4 (Levshin, Moscow, 30 January 1963); RGALI 1204/2/2641/89ob-90 (Lilia Karpych, b. 1928, 19 February 1963), 110ob (Tatiana Bushinskaia, Tbilisi, 31 January 1963); RGALI 1702/10/83/92–92ob, 95–5ob.

43 RGALI 1702/10/82/41 (engineer Medova, economist N. Lysenko, agronomist G. Tolokonskii, college student E. Ramanovskaia, and personal pensioner B.G. Tolokonskaia, Leningrad, 25 February 1963).

44 Ibid. For similar legitimization devices, see RGALI 1204/2/2642/27–52ob, here 52–2ob (Irina Alekseeva, Mochishche-na-Obi, 11 February 1963).

45 RGALI 1702/10/82/19 (9 February 1963).

46 RGALI 1702/10/82/20.

47 Also RGALI 1204/2/2644/55–67, here 64–6 (Nikolai Tuchnin, associate professor, Kostroma pedagogical institute, 10 February 1963).

48 V.S. Spiridonov, '"Ne mogu molchat": Istoriia pisaniia i pechataniia,' ibid., 425–7; Leo Tolstoy, 'Ne mogu molchat',' in his *Polnoe sobranie sochinenii* (Moscow, 1928–58), 37 (1957): 83–96.

49 RGALI 1702/10/82/19–20. On these issues, see also Jochen Hellbeck, *Revolution on My Mind: Writing a Diary under Stalin* (Cambridge, MA, 2006), esp. 103–6.

50 See also Vladislav Zubok, *Zhivago's Children: The Last Russian Intelligentsia* (Cambridge, MA, 2009).

51 RGALI 1702/10/83/240–1 (Kolokolov, 61, Donetsk, registered 11 February 1963); RGALI 1702/10/83/92 (Briantseva, Novosibirsk, February 1963, registered 19 March 1963).
52 RGALI 1702/10/83/217–18.
53 RGALI 1702/10/83/214.
54 On denial, see Michael Shermer and Alex Grobman, *Denying History: Who Says the Holocaust Never Happened and Why Do They Say It?* (Berkeley, 2009), esp. 231–56.
55 RGALI 1204/2/2643/76ob (Neverov, 6 February 1963); RGALI 1702/10/83/191 (Samarina, Cherepovets, 9 March 1963); RGALI 1702/8/735/13–14 (Popov, journalist, Ukraine, 18 January 1962).
56 RGALI 1702/8/631/61 (Moscow); also RGALI 1204/2/2643/41–2ob (Valerii Buskis, 24, Kishinev 5 February 1963).
57 RGALI 1702/10/82/92 (Sarbala, Kemerovo region, February 1963).
58 RGALI 1204/2/2643/76ob; RGALI/1204/2/2634/53–4ob (Droznikas, Chita, 14 January 1962); RGALI 1702/10/83/185 (Mirkin, Omsk, 20 March 1963).
59 RGALI 1702/10/82/8; also RGALI 1702/10/82/104 (reg. 25 February 1963).
60 RGALI 1702/8/735/103 (5 June 1962).
61 RGALI 1702/8/735/104.
62 RGALI 1702/8/735/103.
63 *LGZh* 2:162 (*rokovoi udar*).
64 Aleksandr Solzhenitsyn, 'Odin den' Ivana Denisovicha,' *NM* 11 (1962): 8–74.
65 Denis Kozlov, 'Naming the Social Evil: The Readers of *Novyi mir* and Vladimir Dudintsev's *Not by Bread Alone*, 1956–1959 and Beyond,' in *The Dilemmas of De-Stalinization: A Social and Cultural History of Reform in the Khrushchev Era*, ed. Polly Jones, 80–98 (London, 2006).
66 On the writing and publication of *One Day*, see Liudmuila Saraskina's comprehensive *Aleksandr Solzhenitsyn* (Moscow, 2008), 287–322. On Tvardovskii's efforts to publish *One Day* (including his meeting with Khrushchev on 21 October 1962), see Aleksandr Tvardovskii, 'Rabochie tetradi 60-kh godov,' *Znamia* 7 (2000): 116 (diary entry for 3 July 1962), 118–19 (26 July 1962), 129 (16 September 1962), 130–1 (20–1 September 1962), 135–7 (19 and 21 October 1962); Vladimir Lakshin, *Golosa i litsa* (Moscow, 2004), 210–21; Lakshin, *Solzhenitsyn i koleso istorii* (Moscow, 2008), 192–214. Lakshin's memoir and diary generally match the story of *One Day*'s publication in Tvardovskii's diary.
67 RGALI 1702/9/80/70 (Tvardovskii to Solzhenitsyn, 8 November 1962), original emphasis.

68 RGALI 1702/9/81/73 (Tvardovskii to Solzhenitsyn, 25 December 1962).

69 'Younger' here refers to letter-writers of ages eligible for Komsomol membership (through twenty-eight). Most of them did not specify their age, instead identifying themselves as 'students.' 'Older' refers to individuals who had reached a legal retirement age by the time of writing. Established in the 1920s and confirmed by a comprehensive law on pensions in 1956, the standard pension age was fifty-five for women and sixty for men. Most of the older letter-writers did not specify their age, either, but identified themselves as 'pensioners.'

70 Here I count only letter-writers of identified age.

71 Solzhenitsyn, 'Odin den',' 9; Vladimir Voinovich, *Portret na fone mifa* (Moscow, 2002), 17, 29.

72 RGALI 1702/10/78/38–46ob (pensioner), 49–60 (Civil War veteran); RGALI 1702/10/2/16–17 (pensioner), 18–22 (age sixty-six), 81–1ob (pensioner); RGALI 1702/10/1/34–6 (age sixty-seven), 75 (pensioner), 115–17 (pensioner); RGALI 1702/10/3/60–1 (pensioner); RGALI 1702/10/75/69–70ob (age sixty-six), 88–91 (Grinberg, pensioner); RGALI 1702/10/76/69–70 (pensioner), 76–7ob (age sixty), 80–1 (pensioner), 82–3ob (pensioner), 86–93ob (party member since 1927), 94–6 (First World War veteran and party member since 1918), 97–8 (pensioner); RGALI 1702/10/79/55–70ob (pensioner), 76–7 (pensioner, as well as three other signatories); RGALI 1702/10/166/76–7ob (pensioner); RGALI 1702/10/173/87–7ob; RGALI 1702/10/74/7–8ob (pensioner), 78–9 (age sixty-seven). The remaining quarter of the letters looks as follows: one came from a fifty-two-year-old man: RGALI 1702/10/76/65; three letter-writers were in their forties: RGALI 1702/10/76/57–7ob (age forty to forty-two), 74–5ob (age forty-seven); RGALI 1702/10/79/82–3ob (age forty-four); while two were in their thirties: RGALI 1702/10/76/53–6 (approximately thirty-five); RGALI 1702/10/78/1–2 (thirty-five to forty). Only one letter-writer was in her twenties: RGALI 1702/10/1/70 (age twenty-five).

73 Vera V. Carpovich, *Solzhenitsyn's Peculiar Vocabulary: Russian-English Glossary* (New York, 1976), 3.

74 Ibid.; Georges Nivat, *Solzhenitsyn* (London, 1984), 175–91; Leonid Rzhevsky, *Solzhenitsyn: Creator and Heroic Deed* (n.p., 1978), 19–32.

75 Quoted in Carpovich, *Solzhenitsyn's Peculiar Vocabulary*, 3.

76 Vasilii Aksenov, 'Na polputi k Lune,' *Novyi mir* 7 (1962): 86–98; RGALI 1702/8/731/2–4, 11–12, 16, 20, 24–5, 32, 38–9, 41–2. Eight of the eleven letters available in the file attacked Aksenov's language.

77 RGALI 1702/10/76/100–10 (Oksamytnyi, literature teacher, Tiraspol', 14 January 1963).

78 RGALI 1702/6/85/61 (Alekseev, journalist, Leningrad, 1954); Fedor

Gladkov, 'O kul'ture rechi,' *NM* 6 (1953): 231–8; 'Tribuna chitatelia. O kul'ture rechi,' *NM* 4 (1954): 232; RGALI 1702/6/85/1–93.

79 Evgeny Dobrenko, *Formovka sovetskogo pisatelia: sotsial'nye i esteticheskie istoki sovetskoi literaturnoi kul'tury* (Saint Petersburg, 1999), 390–6; Maurice Friedberg, *Russian Classics in Soviet Jackets* (New York, 1962), esp. 156–66; Boris Grois, *The Total Art of Stalinism: Avant-garde, Aesthetic Dictatorship, and Beyond* (Princeton, 1992); Leonid Heller, 'A World of Prettiness: Socialist Realism and Its Aesthetic Categories,' in *Socialist Realism without Shores,* ed. Thomas Lahusen and Evgeny Dobrenko, 51–75 (Durham, 1997), esp. 54–9; Vladimir Papernyi, *Kul'tura Dva* (Moscow, 1996).

80 RGALI 1702/10/73/75, 76 (Sorokin, Moscow, 8 March 1963); RGALI 1702/10/78/1–2 (Negreus, thirty-five to forty, Leningrad, 11 March 1963), 38–46ob (Kuz'min, pensioner, Orel, 20 March 1963); RGALI 1702/10/76/53–6 (Lappo, approximately thirty-five, Severomorsk, registered 16 January 1963); RGALI 1702/10/2/81–1ob (Mel'nikov, pensioner, Moscow, 6 December 1962); RGALI 1702/10/2/16–17 (Naumova, pensioner, Kaluga, 30 December 1962), 63–3ob (anonymous, registered 22 December 1962); RGALI 1702/10/77/50 (Tarasov, Ivanovo, 4 February 1963).

81 RGALI 1702/10/76/122–3 (E.A. Tepper, 12 January 1963).

82 Carpovich, *Solzhenitsyn's Peculiar Vocabulary,* 5.

83 The term *continuum of crisis* comes from Peter Holquist, *Making War, Forging Revolution: Russia's Continuum of Crisis, 1914–1921* (Cambridge, MA, 2002).

84 RGALI 1702/10/1/13–13ob (anonymous, registered 4 December 1962), 34–6 (Leikand, sixty-seven, registered 7 December 1962), 75 (Petrovskii, pensioner, no date); RGALI 1702/10/2/18–22 (Golikov, sixty-six, 21 December 1962); RGALI 1702/10/75/69–70ob (Gorshunov, sixty-six, 8 January 1963), 88–91 (Grinberg, pensioner, registered 16 January 1963); RGALI 1702/10/77/52–69 (Konstantinov, 10 February 1963); RGALI 1702/10/76/69–70 (Chatskii, pensioner, registered 28 January 1963), 76–7ob (Artamonov, sixty, registered 15 January 1963), 82–3ob (Grigor'ev, pensioner, 20 January 1963), 94–6 (Leizin, 9 January 1963), 113–14ob (Shabalina, 18 January 1963), 115–17 (Rudinskaia, 14 January 1963); RGALI 1702/10/78/49–60 (Kol'tsov, 25 January 1963). Nearly half of Solzhenitsyn's older-aged critics had gone through the camps: Artamonov, Chatskii, Golikov, Gorshunov, Grigor'ev, Grinberg, Kol'tsov, Leikand, Leisin, and Petrovskii.

85 For a different interpretation of readers' responses, see Miriam Dobson, 'Contesting the Paradigms of De-Stalinization: Readers' Responses to "One Day in the Life of Ivan Denisovich," *Slavic Review* 64, no. 3 (Autumn 2005): 580–600; and Dobson, *Khrushchev's Cold Summer: Gulag Returnees, Crime,*

and the Fate of Reform after Stalin (Ithaca, NY, 2009), 215–28, esp. 219–23. Dobson's argument is that negative reactions to Solzhenitsyn's language revealed society's concern about the danger the Gulag returnees presumably posed to Soviet culture: 'If millions of prisoners released from the Gulag spoke and thought in the same way as Ivan Denisovich, the cultured behaviour that the party had fought so hard to inculcate was at risk' (*Khrushchev's Cold Summer*, 221). However, many of those who criticized Solzhenitsyn's language were themselves former Gulag prisoners. Others were old émigrés who lived abroad and had nothing to do with a Soviet fear of the returning inmates. So I doubt whether negative reactions to Solzhenitsyn's language had much to do with anxieties about the Gulag returnees. The origins of this linguistic aversion lay, rather, in the overall crisis of language and ethics, which Soviet culture experienced during the Thaw, but which also had distant roots in twentieth-century historic upheavals.

86 RGALI 1702/10/75/5–6 (Kuzanova, Baku, registered 30 January 1963); RGALI 1702/10/78/9–12 (Bazhanov, Kalinin, 5 March 1963); RGALI 1702/10/166/138–50 (Zinchenko, Kiev, 15 May 1964), 152–8 (Kolotusha, Mukachevo, 16 May 1964), 166–74 (Bashlakov, Grodno oblast', 10 July 1964).

87 Shoshana Felman and Dori Laub, *Testimony: Crises of Witnessing in Literature, Psychoanalysis, and History* (New York, 1992), 57–9, 68, 70–1.

88 Unlike Kerwin Klein, I am not convinced that arguments about therapeutic writing need to be dismissed as 'depressing,' and I accept them as a valid way of interpreting eyewitness accounts of mass violence. Kerwin Lee Klein, 'On the Emergence of *Memory* in Historical Discourse,' *Representations* 69 (Winter 2000): 136, 148n24.

89 On citizenship as a paradigm in letter-writing, see Sheila Fitzpatrick, 'Supplicants and Citizens: Public Letter-Writing in Soviet Russia in the 1930s,' *Slavic Review* 55, no. 1 (Spring 1996): 78–105. On the importance of interpretation of the twentieth-century past in Soviet documents of personal origin, see Hellbeck, *Revolution on My Mind*; Paperno, *Stories of the Soviet Experience.*

90 RGALI 1702/10/78/62 (Krasnoiarsk, registered 3 January 1963).

91 RGALI 1702/10/1/42 (Lipshits, 2 December 1962), 77 (Khmel'nitskii, 12 December 1962); RGALI 1702/10/75/19 (Tikhonov, registered 1 March 1963); RGALI 1702/10/76/44–6ob (Chubar', 15 January 1963).

92 RGALI 1702/10/76/44–6ob (Chubar', 15 January 1963).

93 RGALI 1702/10/75/66 (3 January 1963).

94 RGALI 1702/10/75/67 (11 April 1963).

95 Dobrenko, *Formovka*, 118, 125–6.

96 Kondratovich to Bliuman, 11 April 1963, RGALI 1702/10/75/67.
97 Nivat, *Solzhenitsyn*, 57–99; on *One Day* specifically, see 82–5.
98 Lahusen, *How Life Writes the Book: Real Socialism and Socialist Realism in Stalin's Russia* (Ithaca, NY, 1997), 173 (facsimile of the telegram).
99 RGALI 1702/10/74/75–5ob (Kuliab, Tadzhikistan, 30 December 1962). Original style and punctuation preserved, as closely as possible.
100 Lahusen, *How Life Writes the Book.*
101 Ibid., 46–7, 178.
102 Ibid., 163.
103 RGALI 1702/10/75/100 (Penza, registered 30 January 1963). Original emphasis.
104 E.g., RGALI 1702/10/2/18–22 (Golikov, 21 December 1962), 154–9ob (Markelov, 15 December 1962), 166–8 (Borisov, 14 December 1962); RGALI 1702/10/77/72–80 (Barbon, 22 February 1963); RGALI 1702/10/75/19 (Tikhonov, registered 1 March 1963), 22 (Rudkovskii, registered 23 February 1963), 32 (Radzinskaia, 6 March 1963), 66–6ob (Bliuman, 3 January 1963); RGALI 1702/10/1/42 (Lipshits, 2 December 1962), 50–1 (Pronman, 26 November 1962), 77 (Khmel'nitskii, registered 12 December 1962), 94 (Rakovskii, registered 12 December 1962), 103–4 (Stashevich, Vilnius, 12 December 1962), 126–7 (Dokuchaev, registered 22 December 1962); RGALI 1702/10/76/44–6ob (Chubar', 15 January 1963), 82–3ob (Grigor'ev, 20 January 1963); RGALI 1702/10/78/19 (Gress, 26 June 1963), 27 (Vasil'eva, 6 June 1963), 37 (Latyshev, 17 March 1963), 62–3 (Golitsyn, registered 3 January 1963); RGALI 1702/10/166/8–9 (Baranovskii, registered 13 February 1964), 32–6 (Fedin, 7 March 1964), 37–44 (Pupyshev, 12 March 1964); RGALI 1702/10/74/75–5ob (Korolev, 30 December 1962), 76–7ob (Tomashevskaia, 30 December 1962); RGALI 1702/10/75/94ob–94 (Solomakha, 29 December 1962); RGALI 1702/10/3/4–7 (Kolpakov, registered 22 December 1962), 10–14 (Zhevtun, registered 12 December 1962), 48–9 (Ignatenkov, registered 18 December 1962), 69–78ob (Einer-Biener, 20 December 1962); RGALI 1702/10/172/12–13 (Ivanov, n.d.); RGALI 1702/10/397/1–2ob (Lisiutin, 28 February 1967).
105 RGALI 1702/10/79/54 (Lisiutin, 27 March 1963); RGALI 1702/10/3/10–14 (Zhevtun, registered 12 December 1962), 48–9 (Ignatenkov, registered 18 December 1962); RGALI 1702/10/78/19 (Gress, 26 June 1963).
106 RGALI 1702/10/2/159ob (15 December 1962), original emphasis; 'Bezhavshie iz fashistskogo plena sovetskie ofitsery o svoem prebyvanii v Shveitsarii,' *Izvestiia*, 15 April 1945.
107 RGALI 1702/10/2/154.

108 Mikhail Sholokhov, 'Sud'ba cheloveka,' in Sholokhov, *Sobranie sochinenii v vos'mi tomakh* (Moscow, 1962), 8:22–54 (first published in *Pravda*, 31 December 1956 and 1 January 1957).
109 RGALI 1702/10/2/159–9ob.
110 RGALI 1702/10/74/14ob (Murmansk, 27 December 1962).
111 RGALI 1702/10/3/45–6 (Arzamas, registered 18 December 1962).
112 RGALI 1702/10/3/54–5ob (Gelendzhik, 10 December 1962).
113 RGALI 1702/10/1/98–8ob (registered 1 December 1962); RGALI 1702/9/82/127–8.
114 RGALI 1702/10/74/78–9ob (31 December 1962).
115 RGALI 1702/10/1/13–13ob (anonymous, former prisoner, registered 4 December 1962); RGALI 1702/10/77/1–4 (Kondratenko, old Bolshevik, spent 1937–56 in the camps; Krivoi Rog, 5 February 1963).
116 RGALI 1702/10/75/101.
117 Michael Scammell, *Solzhenitsyn: A Biography* (New York, 1984), 554, 559–60, 835. See also RGALI 1702/10/77/40–9ob (Ramm, pensioner, registered 2 February 1963); RGALI 1702/10/76/39–41ob (Kolendovskii, seventy-one, 20 January 1963); RGALI 1702/10/77/29–30ob (Kruglov, party member since 1917, 21 February 1963), 52–69 (Konstantinov, 10 February 1963); RGALI 1702/10/74/64–6ob (Luk'ianov, twenty-four, 30 December 1962), 49–53 (Galitskii, 16 January 1963); RGALI 1702/10/73/80–93ob (Vakhrameev, pensioner, 24 December 1962).
118 Scammell, *Solzhenitsyn*, 510–11, 542–3, 621–2.
119 Leopold Labedz, ed., *Solzhenitsyn: A Documentary Record* (1970; Harmondsworth, UK, 1972), 44–62. For the story of this chapter's publication, see Scammell, *Solzhenitsyn*, 621–2. On *The Gulag Archipelago* as a collective historical enterprise, see 560.
120 Labedz, ed., *Solzhenitsyn*, 44 (Markelov), 45 (Golitsyn), 48 (Lilenkov), 49 (Vilenchik, spelled as Vilenchuk). When quoting from the letters, Solzhenitsyn stayed true to the original texts and, at least for those I have, kept the original names.
121 RGALI 1702/10/1/115–17, 130–1; RGALI 1702/10/79/8–8ob, 76–7, 79ob–89ob; RGALI 1702/10/166/76–7ob; RGALI 1702/10/75/65; RGALI 1702/10/74/4–6ob, 35–9; RGALI 1702/10/1/99; RGALI 1702/10/73/36–7, 80–93ob; RGALI 1702/10/248/89–94; RGALI 1702/10/78/, 49–60, 62–3, 94–113, 132–5; RGALI 1702/10/3/69–78ob; RGALI 1702/10/74/15–22. Of the remaining five letters, four came from people in their forties; one letter writer was thirty-eight. RGALI 1702/10/2/6–15ob; RGALI 1702/10/76/74–5ob; RGALI 1702/10/78/33–4; RGALI 1702/10/79/9–19ob, 82–3ob.

122 RGALI 1702/10/1/99; RGALI 1702/10/73/36–7, 80–93; RGALI 1702/10/74/4–6ob, 15–22, 87–7ob; RGALI 1702/10/78/33–4, 49–60, 62–3, 94–113; RGALI 1702/10/3/69–78ob; RGALI 1702/10/76/44–6ob, 118–21ob, 132–42ob; RGALI 1702/10/79/9–19ob.

123 Sheila Fitzpatrick, 'The Legacy of the Civil War,' in *Party, State, and Society in the Russian Civil War: Explorations in Social History*, ed. Diane P. Koenker, William G. Rosenberg, and Ronald G. Suny, 385–98 (Bloomington, IN, 1989); Leopold H. Haimson, 'Civil War and the Problem of Social Identities in Early Twentieth-Century Russia,' 24–47; Moshe Lewin, 'The Civil War: Dynamics and Legacy,' 399–423.

124 E.g., RGALI 1702/10/74/4–6ob (Grachev, party member since 1918, prisoner 1936–56, Bugul'ma, registered 28 January 1963). My use of the notion of experience is different from the one employed by Joan Wallach Scott, who emphasizes its socially and, above all, linguistically constructed nature. See Scott, 'The Evidence of Experience,' *Critical Inquiry* 17 (1991): 773–97. I work on the assumption that the relationship between the past and the present in the conceptualization of experience is reciprocal and dialogical. Experiences may be constructed, but construction is not a purely rational and logical faculty that human beings possess. On the contrary, the terms of construction are themselves grounded in the past and influenced by the background of the one who formulates experience. The nature of experience is certainly discursive, but discourse itself is not emancipated from its historical context.

125 On the significance of the Second World War and the individual wartime records in defining postwar legitimacies, see Amir Weiner, *Making Sense of War: The Second World War and the Fate of the Bolshevik Revolution* (Princeton, 2001), esp. 314, 322–31, 378–80.

126 Aleksandr Solzhenitsyn, *Odin den' Ivana Denisovicha* (Moscow, 1963), 59.

127 RGALI 1702/10/79/79–9ob (Orenburg, 11 April 1963), original emphasis.

128 Stoliarov refers to a teenage character Gopchik in *One Day*, imprisoned for bringing food for 'Banderovite' guerrillas in the forest.

129 RGALI 1702/10/76/75 (Vinnitsa, registered 15 January 1963).

130 RGALI 1702/10/75/33 (Kimovsk, Tula oblast, registered 13 March 1963); Labedz, ed., *Solzhenitsyn*, 58.

131 RGALI 1702/10/78/104ob, 106, 110 (Gomel', 8 March 1963).

132 RGALI 1702/10/3/18 (Moscow, 8 December 1962).

133 RGALI 1702/10/166/198–9 (21 September 1964).

134 RGALI 1702/10/73/72–3 (Moscow, 8 March 1963).

135 Also RGALI 1702/10/75/49–51 (Sykchin, former schoolteacher, at the time a collective farm party organizer, Novosibirsk oblast, 9 February 1963); RGALI 1702/10/75/82–3ob (Astaf'ev, forty-four, mining technician, Irkutsk oblast, 25 March 1963); RGALI 1702/10/76/58–64 (L'vova, engineer-geologist, Irkutsk, 7 January 1963); RGALI 1702/10/78/84–4ob (anonymous Second World War veteran, 1965).

136 RGALI 1702/10/2/8ob–9 (Kotlas, 7 December 1962).

137 Stanislaw Swianiewicz, *In the Shadow of Katyn: Stalin's Terror* (Pender Island, BC, 2002).

138 RGALI 1702/10/2/14.

139 RGALI 1702/10/2/15.

140 RGALI 1702/10/2/13.

141 RGALI 1702/10/76/35 (Cherepovets, 7 January 1963).

142 RGALI 1702/10/2/12.

143 RGALI 1702/10/248/89–94; RGALI 1702/10/2/6–15ob; RGALI 1702/10/76/, 34–6, 58–64; RGALI 1702/10/79/20–25ob, 39–45, 71–4ob; RGALI 1702/10/166/109–29ob; RGALI 1702/10/75/33; RGALI 1702/10/78/14–14ob. The total number of letters from the former camp officers, guards, or free hires was larger, about fifteen, but the other letter-writers in this group did not explicitly advance the enemy thesis.

144 RGALI 1702/10/74/14ob; RGALI 1702/10/248/89–94 (Kasatskii, Govorko).

145 RGALI 1702/10/2/13.

146 RGALI 1702/10/2/14–14ob.

147 RGALI 1702/10/79/ll. 41, 44.

148 E.g., RGALI 1702/10/166/76–7ob (Krasikova, an old propagandist and party member for forty years, who also argued that a camp was 'not a health resort' – Moscow, registered 7 April 1964); RGALI 1702/10/78/14 (Nesterov, L'vov, 29 December 1962); RGALI 1702/10/79/73ob–74 (Samatskin, a war veteran and former MVD officer who had served in the camps – Karaganda, 23 March 1963). A few such letters (Panchuk's and Samatskin's among them) were initially intended not for *Novyi mir* but for *Pravda*, whose editors forwarded the letters to *Novyi mir*, possibly with an intent. RGALI 1702/10/79/39, 71.

149 RGALI 1702/10/1/38 (Golovin, 27, journalism student, Kurgan, registered 7 December 1962).

150 RGALI 1702/9/81/73.

151 RGALI 1702/10/1/112 (registered 22 December 1962); RGALI 1702/10/2/1 (registered 27 December 1962), 63–63ob (registered 22 December 1962); RGALI 1702/10/76/126–27 (20 February 1963).

152 RGALI 1702/10/78/59.
153 RGALI 1702/10/76/74ob (registered 15 January 1963).
154 RGALI 1702/10/75/51 (9 February 1963). Original punctuation preserved as closely as possible.
155 RGALI 1702/10/75/55 (1–5 April 1964).
156 RGALI 1702/10/166/32–6 (Rozhdestveno, Tatar ASSR, 7 March 1964).
157 RGALI 1702/10/166/29 (19 March 1964).
158 RGALI 1702/10/166/109–29ob (25 March 1964), here 110ob (quotation).
159 RGALI 1702/10/166/110.
160 RGALI 1702/10/166/111ob–117ob.
161 RGALI 1702/10/166/111–11ob, 117ob.
162 RGALI 1702/10/73/80–93ob, esp. 80, 81, 81ob, 93 (24 December 1962).
163 Vakrameev used a Russian idiom, *kukish v karmane,* of which this is an approximate translation.
164 RGALI 1702/10/73/83ob–84.
165 RGALI 1702/10/73/87ob.
166 RGALI 1702/10/2/18 (Golikov, sixty-six, prisoner 1938–46, Gor'kii, 21 December 1962); RGALI 1702/10/78/118 (Gor, pensioner, former camp prisoner, Vilnius, 23 February 1963).
167 RGALI 1702/10/2/82 (14 December 1962); RGALI 1702/10/2/39 (registered 22 December 1962).
168 RGALI 1702/10/76/39 (Kharkov, 20 January 1963).
169 RGALI 1702/10/76/39, 40–40ob, 41ob.
170 RGALI 1702/10/166/42ob, 43–3ob (12 March 1964). For his first letter, see RGALI 1702/10/2/114ob (registered 22 December 1962).
171 Literature on this topic abounds. For a brief discussion, see Introduction. For the German case, see, for example, Jeffrey Herf, *Divided Memory: The Nazi Past in the Two Germanys* (Cambridge, MA, 1997).

6 The Personal and the Political: Opposition to the Thaw and the Politics of Literary Identity in the 1950s and 1960s

POLLY JONES

Introduction

In early 1964, a now famous article appeared in *Novyi mir*, under the title 'Ivan Denisovich, His Friends and Foes.'[1] Critical attention to Solzhenitsyn's groundbreaking work had never waned since its publication in late 1962, but the controversy over Solzhenitsyn's subsequent works and the question of whether to award *Ivan Denisovich* the Lenin prize had put it squarely back in the centre of the literary agenda. Over the preceding few years, Vladimir Lakshin had risen to prominence as both a critic and editor at *Novyi mir*.[2] Intimately involved in the drama surrounding the publication and subsequent reception of Solzhenitsyn's work, he was in a good position to look back over the author's tumultuous critical fortunes.[3] In his article he contrasted the wholly positive reception of the work at the time of publication to the creeping tendency of some critics to find fault with it in the months and years that followed.

According to Lakshin, critical opposition to *Ivan Denisovich* did not take issue with the work's publication but it did carp at the work's portrayal of the world of the camps and of Ivan's attitude to his work, his fellow inmates, and his fate. He singled out some particularly egregious examples: articles appearing in *Oktiabr'*, *Literaturnaia Rossiia*, and *Don*, which had all accused both Solzhenitsyn and Ivan of narrowness, banality, and even indifference, in their understanding of the Gulag and incarceration. Citation from these articles was in each case followed by a meticulous and devastating critique. Solzhenitsyn's masterly literary skill and his deep moral commitment to the truth about the past were systematically opposed to the flawed logic, mendacity, and Stalinist mindset of his critics.

Lakshin's article exploded into the midst of an already tense situation, setting off another round of debate about de-Stalinization and attracting, in Lakshin's words, 'a hail of libellous comment, refutations and editorials.'[4] Solzhenitsyn's nomination for the Lenin prize had already seen tempers boil over in writers' meetings and readers' letters.[5] Lakshin's article, as the author later reflected, was 'correctly interpreted by both friend and foe' as a redrawing of the battle lines over the Thaw.[6] In defending both Solzhenitsyn and the Thaw that he epitomized, Lakshin felt sure that he had identified the Thaw's main opponents and their tactics. One reader wrote to *Novyi mir* to reassure him that he had: the journal indeed had 'non-friends and even implacable enemies from amongst the Stalinists.' Nonetheless, Lakshin should not worry, as the current era would be remembered for Solzhenitsyn and Tvardovskii, not for 'Kochetov, Chakovskii, and Sofronov with their ... anti-artistic works.'[7] As the letter writer noted, the forces ranged against the Thaw were politically motivated – they were 'Stalinists' – and they were also keen to conceal their aesthetic inferiority. Lakshin's article was the fullest exposé that these political and aesthetic explanations for opposition to the Thaw had received in the Soviet press.

The article hinted at the private accusations that had long circulated in the diaries, offices, and homes of not only the staff of *Novyi mir*, but of many other 'liberal' supporters of the Thaw. Opposition to the Thaw – which we define here as the aesthetic liberalization led by *Novyi mir* and *Iunost'* – was one of the big preoccupations and topics of conversation throughout the 1950s and 1960s. It had enormous subjective importance for the writers and editors in the vanguard of the Thaw.

However, although Khrushchev's own conservatism and that of some of his cultural officials has been analysed in the scholarship, there have been only scattered attempts to analyse the 'foes' who so troubled Lakshin and his colleagues.[8] The central insight into reform's 'friends and foes' inspired Stephen Cohen's eponymous dissection of the finely balanced forces of Soviet reformism and conservatism, but his analysis ranged beyond, and mostly outside, literature per se.[9] Western interest in Soviet liberalism and dissent has focused attention largely on literary 'freedoms' and struggles with the party authorities, overshadowing the internal constraints that bound the Soviet literary community and locked it into debate over the Thaw.[10] The paradigms developed to analyse literary liberalism – such as 'permitted dissent' and the Thaw-era emergence of a 'public sphere' – are more precise and more sophisticated than the terminology used to describe its opponents.[11] Conservative figures such as Vsevolod Kochetov and Anatoliii Sofronov have been termed 'Stalinists,' 'neo-Stalinists,' 'extreme pro-Stalinists,' 'Stalin's heirs,' the 'Stalinist old guard,' 'hardliners,' 'tough-liners,' 'dogmatists,' and the defenders of 'orthodoxy.'[12] These pithy formulations seem to attribute the 'conservative line' to both reactionary sentiment and the cynical desire of the 'old guard' to cling onto power, but do not probe this paradox further.[13] Indeed, until quite recently, this kind of scrutiny seemed both morally and intellectually dubious.[14] One reason for this, as I will argue, is that liberal writers themselves refused to take opposition to the Thaw seriously, on aesthetic, ideological, or moral grounds.

In what follows I analyse both the construction and deconstruction of opposition to the Thaw, tracing the arguments and counter-arguments put forth by both 'friends' and 'foes.' Opposition to the Thaw will be traced through the public and more private activities of the principal 'foes' identified in Lakshin's article – the journal *Oktiabr'* and its editor Vsevolod Kochetov, and the newspaper *Literaturnaia Rossiia* (and its previous incarnation, *Literatura i zhizn'*), along with its sponsoring institution, the RSFSR Union. What exactly did these institutions and individuals oppose in the Thaw, and how did they express their hostility to it in the years leading up to Lakshin's outburst? For conservatives, the concerns raised by the Thaw were aesthetic, ideological, moral, and personal. For their audiences too, the Thaw went beyond narrowly literary concerns. Recent scholarship on the popular reception of the Thaw has demonstrated that belief in *kul'turnost'* (culturedness), a deep-rooted aesthetic conservatism, and an affective attachment to Stalinism informed opposition to such Thaw landmarks as the Manezh exhibition and literary works by Dudintsev and Solzhenitsyn.[15] This diversity of concerns was not unique or unprecedented, if we take conservatism in its broader historical and international context.[16] My examination of conservative opposition to the Thaw and counter-attacks on it interrogates in turn the three dominant explanations of conservatism outlined above: the defence of aesthetic orthodoxy, the desire to retain power, and Stalinism.

In probing both the ideological and personal aspects of the struggle over the Thaw, it is important to acknowledge the nature and impact of the Soviet context. In ideological terms, since Soviet ideology was rooted in the progressive and the eschatological, ideas had to serve the progress toward the radiant future, and warring sides in any debate had to define themselves not only as more 'Soviet,' but specifically as more progressive, than their opponents. They also had to maintain a nominal sense of party unity and unanimity, especially regarding the broad contours of party policy. Personal factors had an impact too. Soviet literature had long operated through the accumulation of personal contacts and patronage networks.[17] These largely determined a writer's personal influence, wealth, and access to publication opportunities. Personal contacts were important, and therefore so was personal information, as the biographical politics of the terror and the anti-cosmopolitan campaigns demonstrated. The Khrushchev era disrupted Stalinist personal networks through institutional reform (including the creation of new union structures and new journals) while reigniting interest in the politics of biography through its revelations about the Stalinist past. These changes made 'personal' rivalries, enmities, and accusations even more important after 1953 than they had been before it. Mariia Zezina's analysis of the Writers' Union shows how quickly personal factors – especially conduct in the immediate past – came to the forefront of literary life after Stalin's death.[18] My analysis will demonstrate the persistence and significance of personal and moral criteria in shaping literary relations throughout the Khrushchev era.

The Khrushchev period can thus best be interpreted as a transitional phase, for all the wings of Soviet literature. Neither 'liberal' nor 'conservative' values were clearly differentiated or securely embedded in the fabric of Soviet cultural life. From the late 1960s onwards, as recent studies of Russian nationalism after Stalin have argued, a distinctive brand of neo-Stalinist conservatism started to emerge more clearly and more confidently.[19] However, the meanings of *Stalinism* were so uncertain in the 1950s and the first half of the 1960s that it is unhelpful to equate opposition to the Thaw with Stalinism without probing the latter term's meanings more fully. I argue below that it took the best part of a decade for both sides in the debate to understand the full aesthetic, ideological, and practical legacies of Stalinism and to reach a definition of the cult of personality. Despite or perhaps because of this lack of definition, however, both of these terms were frequently, sometimes indiscriminately, deployed in the struggle over the Thaw.

This struggle revolved around questions of literary form and content, and also broader cultural concerns, notably the entitlements and responsibilities of membership of the intelligentsia. The Khrushchev-era definition of *kul'turnost'* and *intelligentnost'* (intelligentsia behaviour) was rooted not only in literature but also in literary behaviour. Allegations of Stalinist behaviour, past and present, became especially important to constructing the 'liberal' counter-attack on opposition to the Thaw. Although the antagonism between liberals and conservatives in the late

Thaw was often unproductive and destructive, it also ultimately proved constructive by entrenching criteria – albeit increasingly polarized ones – not only for aesthetic judgment but also for 'cultured' behaviour in literature and life.

Constructing the Conservative Case against the Thaw

The Central Committee did more than any writer or literary institution to oppose the Thaw. For much of the Khrushchev era, the Soviet regime's default preference was for a conservative interpretation of Socialist realism and Soviet literature. In his diary in 1964 Lakshin bemoaned the fact that any sign of an official retreat from liberalization had an instantaneous and far deeper effect than any sign of party liberalism.[20] Such official 'retreats' were visible to editors and authors through prepublication bans – notably on the works of Pasternak, Grossman, and later Solzhenitsyn. More public evidence of party wariness of the Thaw were the frequent episodes of ex cathedra criticism of almost all of the published works that are now considered landmarks of the Thaw – from *Literaturnaia Moskva* in the mid-1950s and *Tarusskie stranitsy* in the early 1960s to the poetry of Evtushenko and Voznesenskii and the short stories of Solzhenitsyn and Iashin. Furthermore, all of Khrushchev's major public pronouncements on culture – although not all of his private decision-making – mounted a defence of literary tradition, *partiinost'* (party-mindedness), and 'life-affirming' literature.[21]

It is unsurprising, therefore, that in institution-building, the evolution of cultural policy in the 1950s and 1960s also favoured conservatism. The major new literary institution of the Thaw was actually established in order to control the Thaw's perceived potential for revisionism. The RSFSR Writers' Union, the sponsoring institution behind the conservative publications *Literatura i zhizn'* and later *Literaturnaia Rossiia*, was set up as a conservative counterweight to the Moscow Writers' Union in the aftermath of the first Thaw of 1954–6.[22] As we have already seen, the liberal wing of the Soviet intelligentsia was acutely conscious of, and hostile to, its attacks on the Thaw.

Vsevolod Kochetov, meanwhile, enjoys the special distinction of being the most frequently mentioned, and demonized, individual opponent of the Thaw. Again, Kochetov's power has been widely, and correctly, viewed as an intentional counterweight to the power of Tvardovskii and *Novyi mir*.[23] It was also explained, as I will show, with reference to the *Kochetovshchina*, an ultra-conservative approach to literature and literary bureaucracy that seemed firmly rooted in the literary establishment. At the beginning of the Khrushchev era, Kochetov was already rising to prominence, as an author (of *The Zhurbins*) and as a leading figure in the Leningrad branch of the Writers Union. However, the Khrushchev period saw Kochetov's career blossom in every branch of literary activity (though not always simultaneously). In the early post-Stalinist years, he became notorious as an opponent of the Thaw, through his leadership of the Leningrad Writers Union, and his editorship of *Literaturnaia gazeta.*[24] During the attacks on revisionism that followed Krushchev's 'Secret Speech,' Kochetov led *Literaturnaia gazeta* back to conservatism while dramatizing his impatience with the Thaw in his 1957 novel *The Ershov Brothers.* In the late Thaw, Kochetov spoke out against the Thaw, at the Twenty-Second Party Congress and in his novel *The Obkom Secretary* (both in 1961), and he also transformed *Oktiabr'* into the public face of literary conservatism from that year onwards.

The conservatism of the RSFSR Union and of Kochetov were not identical. However, they can usefully be examined in tandem, since each engaged with the Thaw on aesthetic, moral, ideological, and practical grounds. The Thaw provoked concerns arising out of general conservative aesthetic principles and from other more specific and personal factors. The conservative criticism of the Thaw concentrated above all on 'young' poetry and prose (especially the authors favoured by *Iunost'* and *Novyi mir*) and on the literary explorations of the Stalinist past epitomized by Tvardovskii's *Novyi mir* and the Moscow branch of the Writers Union. In attacking youth prose and poetry, the Thaw's opponents reproached the morality of both the works and their authors. Meanwhile, criticism of the cult of personality was rooted in normative aesthetic and psychological criteria. In turn, these moral concerns were articulated within a context of personal enmity and institutional rivalry and became all the sharper for it. Life and literature were intertwined in these assessments of cultural change and liberalization.

We will begin by examining conservative attempts to defend, but also to define, aesthetic orthodoxy. In some respects, as several scholars have argued, conservative writers' reservations about the Thaw were indistinguishable from party criticisms of it and appeared to be animated by the same set of literary ideals. However, there were important divergences of proportion and tone. Where party and literary opposition to the Thaw most closely coincided was in the criticism of the supposed absence of general socialist realist principles from many works appearing in the Thaw's flagship publications. In 1957, Khrushchev insisted that *Novyi mir,* the Moscow Writers' Union, and other renegade forces in Soviet literature had strayed because they had failed to maintain 'the close link to life.'[25] As one of the founding principles of the RSFSR Union, this theme went on to receive heavy coverage in *Literatura i zhizn'*.[26] For example, it granted pride of place to Kochetov's repeated admonitions to authors urging them to take their subjects and themes directly from life: as he put it in 1960, 'Contemporary material, new material is gathered in crumbs, in fragments – it's a hard, painstaking, but essential business.'[27] This trope of quasi-journalistic gathering of material directly from 'life itself' by plunging 'into the thick of society' was promoted by other like-minded authors too.[28] It also remained a central plank of RSFSR Union policy; in 1963, the union reflected proudly on the fact that the majority of its recent new members were authors 'closely linked to life of people,' who had backgrounds in agricultural and industrial labour and journalism.[29]

At the same time, it was not enough to document contemporary life (*sovremennost'*) indiscriminately and at random.[30] The 'real facts' that writers gathered had to be 'real achievements'; in other words, only heroic themes and characters from real life should be selected for narration.[31] The interpretation of contemporaneity as 'our historic today' meant that modern life should provide ample real-life heroes. Writers should strive for the 'creation of a bright, whole, memorable image of our heroic contemporary.'[32] The centrepiece of the strident defence of the 'positive hero' mounted by conservative publications was the normative notion that 'a person needs an ideal.'[33]

Literature, as this last statement suggests, also had to contain an ideological message. Kochetov was 'incapable,' as one of his contemporaries put it, 'of considering a work worthwhile if it was written beautifully, stylistically elegantly, with various formal innovations, if in his view it was ideologically immature or mistaken.'[34] His novels argued explicitly for *ideinost'* (ideological orthodoxy) as the central principle of Soviet art.[35] Likewise, *Literatura i zhizn'* within a year of its founding was already 'show[ing] signs of becoming a forum for the more doctrinaire defenders of ideological firmness'; in one typical article from 1960, for example, it claimed that the literary critic's number one priority was 'policing the ideological direction of literature, its ideological content.'[36]

According to the conservative critique of the Thaw, many Thaw works, while apparently about 'contemporary' life, actually lacked the principles of heroism and *ideinost'* that defined contemporaneity in party and literary conservative discourse. Conservative attacks on these defects as manifested in the 'young prose' by authors such as Vasilii Aksenov,

Vladimir Tendriakov, and Vladimir Voinovich were notably more sarcastic and aggressive than party criticism. Kochetov for one was horrified by the 'drawing from life and admiration of good-for-nothings' that he observed in these writers.[37] Such characters were not 'typical' of the Soviet masses.[38] They were isolated, solitary figures, and they were isolated examples of deviations from the Soviet norm.[39] They were consumed with 'everyday' (*budnichnyi*), trivial concerns rather than with contributing to the public good.[40] Some of these protagonists were actively sceptical and even nihilistic, abandoning Soviet ideals in favour of fruitless 'searching' and 'questing' for alternative ideals.[41] It was hardly surprising, then, that many had descended into immorality.[42]

Kochetov and the RSFSR Union did not stop there, however. They frequently extended their criticism of the immorality of Thaw literary heroes to the authors themselves, launching personal attacks on them. These writers were immoral because they disregarded the 'danger of a superficial, frivolous approach to life material' and seemed to 'consider themselves free from the burning themes of contemporary life.'[43] Popularizing such immoral role models was socially irresponsible and could be explained only by the authors' own lack of a moral compass. Such accusations were especially harsh in more private settings. A writer such as Evtushenko, his detractors claimed at one meeting of the RSFSR Union, was consumed by a 'petty' (*meshchanskii*) lust for fame, and his unseemly literary conduct was mirrored in his private life by a 'moral outlook' that was thoroughly 'debauched.' Speaker after speaker derided the *meshchanstvo* of Moscow writers who 'had lost the concept of the *ideinost'* of the Soviet writer,' becoming intoxicated by fame and by Western, bourgeois ideas.[44]

Kochetov meanwhile made no distinction between union meetings, the press, and the pages of his novels, using all of them as vehicles for his contempt for immoral writers. In the same year that he attacked the 'band of some teddy-boys writing something or other' (*kuchka nekikh chto-to pishushchikh pizhonov*) on the pages of *Literatura i zhizn'*, he also used his novel *The Obkom Secretary* to dramatize his impatience with wayward 'celebrity' authors.[45] The young poet Putushkov, modelled on Evtushenko, contrasts with Kochetov in every way – he is indolent (where Kochetov made himself ill through hard work), he dislikes drawing his material from life (and has to be sent by force to a local kolkhoz to do so), and he exploits the good graces of his local hosts and his local literary boss by using his time on the farm to craft a crude satirical attack on the regional leadership.[46]

The Obkom Secretary attacked young writers for immorality and sensationalism and simultaneously proposed a characteristically conservative solution. It pitched two approaches to literary management in unequal combat, opposing the weak and ineffective methods of *vospitanie* (education) initially used on Putushkov to the stricter approach favoured by the Kochetov-like writer Baksanov and the good *obkom* secretary, Denisov.[47] The saga of Putushkov comprehensively invalidated a patient, laissez-faire attitude to wayward writers. The novel as a whole proposed a 'freeze' on the Thaw through demonstrating the negative consequences of liberalism, echoing the extremely negative portrait of the 1956 Thaw in *The Ershov Brothers*.[48]

Kochetov's arguments against the liberalization of cultural controls and his polemic about the dangers of *vospitanie* and tolerance were echoed by the RSFSR Union. Its leadership argued that the Thaw was an assault on cultural, generational, and administrative hierarchies, and their desire for greater control reached a high point in the late Thaw. They called for supposedly dissolute authors such as Evtushenko to be punished rather than indulged, for the RSFSR Union to reassert control over the Moscow Union, and for the authority of older writers to be recognized rather than derided by colleagues.[49] The necessary restoration of administrative and generational hierarchy could be achieved only by curtailing the liberalism of the Thaw.

This 'administrative conservatism,' even more than the aesthetic conservatism that we began by examining, developed in the context of the personal and institutional rivalries of the period. The animus against *vospitanie* and the support for traditional hierarchies at least partly derived from personal experience of the Thaw as a time of administrative disruption and wounding attacks on personal integrity. Calls for the moral condemnation and administrative punishment of Moscow writers grew more shrill as institutional relations between the RSFSR and Moscow Unions worsened.[50] The 'Russianness' of the RSFSR Union in its first decade is inseparable from this context. The pro-Russian and pro-regional policies of the union in the Thaw were as much, if not more, about attacking metropolitan literary culture as they were about any principled stance on Russian identity or literary tradition.[51]

The liberal attacks on conservative positions, which reached a peak in 1962–3, were represented in appeals to the authorities and Soviet public as a form of 'persecution' and discrimination.[52] These appeals emphasized, rather than downplayed, the accusations of Stalinism at the heart of these attacks. In its heavy coverage of the 'problem of generations,'

Oktiabr' repeatedly informed its readers that real-life 'sons' were turning on 'fathers' for their past records.[53] The labels (*iarlyki*) being pinned on leading members of the RSFSR Union were likewise never far from the top of the union's agenda throughout the Khrushchev era. Its meetings, especially in the late Thaw, reveal an obsession with refuting the charges of 'varnishing reality' (that is, of being *lakirovshchiki*) and of being 'dumb slaves of the cult of personality' issuing from the Moscow Union and young writers.[54]

There was substance to these allegations of personal assault, as we shall see, but the emphasis on older writers' victimization was also highly strategic.[55] It painted them as victims of immorality and of ideological error (the conflation of conservatism with Stalinism). The supposed misidentification of conservative attitudes towards the cult of personality became increasingly important to these institutions' identities in the late Thaw. This made the cult of personality a frequent topic of debate, but it also imposed strategic limits on what could be said about it. Nevertheless, a distinctive attitude to the cult of personality and its role in the Thaw developed within the conservative press and literary organizations. In what ways, then, can this attitude be described as Stalinist?

Stalin himself was rarely invoked in arguments against the Thaw interpretation of the cult of personality. Public admiration of Stalin appears to have been virtually taboo during the Khrushchev era, hardly surprising in view of the party's attacks on him. Nevertheless, reluctance to accept the full extent of the attacks on Stalin did sometimes surface. In Kochetov's *The Ershov Brothers*, no character expresses outright hostility to Stalin, and there are several claims that de-Stalinization has gone too far in insulting him.[56] In *The Obkom Secretary*, the secretary Denisov expresses ambiguous feelings about de-Stalinization, finding it impossible to criticize Stalin directly.[57] On this count, at least, the contrast between Denisov and his supposedly Stalinist enemy Artamanov is not absolute. Kochetov was similarly reticent about publicly expressing his own views on Stalin.

Meanwhile, RSFSR Union meetings, not notable for their restraint in other regards, bypassed the Stalin question almost entirely, as did the conservative press. Instead, conservative opposition focused on the cult of personality in the broader sense of the exploration of traumatic aspects of the Stalin era. Discussions of the cult in this sense revealed a panoply of objections to this literary project, on aesthetic, moral, and personal grounds.

Kochetov's novels dramatized conservative attitudes to the cult most fully. In *The Ershov Brothers*, one of the main villains, Vorobeinyi, is a returnee whose record of collaboration with the Germans is proved beyond doubt by the end of the novel. On returning from the Gulag, he rises to power in the local factory, seemingly with the sole aim of stirring up trouble for honest party and factory workers. The immorality of these actions is matched by his irrational insistence that his Gulag experiences should be recounted in literature, 'laying it on thick.'[58] Vorobeinyi engages in both industrial and cultural sabotage. The cult of personality is as harmful to the Soviet project as 'wrecking,' and it is as morally repulsive as collaboration with the Nazis. Throughout, those who advocate concentrating on the cult also admire the Hungarian revolt, listen to foreign radio, sabotage Soviet industry, and represent the 'unhealthy' wing of Soviet literature, theatre, and art. All the 'good' characters, meanwhile, are notably impatient with the cult of personality. This extreme hostility towards the cult became more muted as party policy again turned back to de-Stalinization. However, even at the Twenty-Second Congress Kochetov openly expressed irritation and impatience with the 'memory politics' of the late Thaw and the apparent dominance of the literary agenda by cult victims – both literary and real.[59]

The literary press, and union politics, elaborated on both strands of Kochetov's arguments about the cult of personality. Above all, they warned against its potential to distort the overall 'optimistic,' 'life-affirming' agenda of Soviet literature. This argument was in line with party policy on limiting the 'hot topic' of the cult and its potential to spread pessimism, though conservatives frequently voiced these ideas in stronger terms than the party leadership. However, the conservative stance also echoed Kochetov's argument against victims' moral and cultural prerogatives. At first hesitantly and then increasingly boldly, it expressed a strong sense of suspicion of literary and real-life *zeks* and those who promoted them.

In the early period after the Twenty-Second Congress, though, the conservative press apparently embraced the cult of personality. *Oktiabr'* and *Literatura i zhizn'* (and later *Literaturnaia Rossiia*) carried many articles on the theme and published positive responses to several works about it.[60] However, even at the height of de-Stalinization, warnings were already sounding about Soviet literary priorities: 'denunciation' should never take precedence over 'assertion,' and literature must be 'life-affirming,' not pessimistic.[61] As the head of the RSFSR Union stated when summing up the Twenty-Second Congress, Soviet literature had never been, and would never be, concerned primarily with 'seeking out everything bad in life, gathering everything bad in a clump.'[62]

Two years, and two 'freezes,' later, the union was more forthright in criticizing 'those who tried to divert our literature on to side paths, who recommended that we should be inspired by the odours of burial pits, who saw our lives only from the dark side.'[63] This discursive emphasis on psychological aberration can perhaps best be seen in a controversy that befell *Literaturnaia Rossiia* immediately after its launch in 1963. In its second issue, the newspaper printed an extraordinary article by the critic Lidiia Fomenko, which unexpectedly claimed that the exploration of the 'tragic recent past' was Soviet literature's top priority.[64] The RSFSR Union responded with a prompt investigation that unleashed strong psychological arguments against the newspaper and the article's young author. The head of the investigation, Vadim Kozhevnikov, was adamant that the cult could not, and did not, dominate the mental horizon of Soviet citizens today: 'Surely now we don't only live for that?'[65] Another speaker accused Fomenko of making a 'psychological error [in] taking this theme to be the main thing.'[66] These charges directly influenced the newspaper's immediate reversion to a more hostile stance on the cult.[67]

Such arguments criticized liberal approaches to the cult in quantitative and qualitative terms. They expressed reservations about the overall proportion of works about the cult within Soviet literature, while probing the degree to which individual works qualified as 'Soviet' treatments of the theme. The latter aim was sometimes pursued through promoting alternative – and far more optimistic – 'cult narratives' in place of the works promoted by *Novyi mir*.[68] However, direct attacks on the narrative and moral choices of archetypal Thaw narratives of the cult also became increasingly frequent in the late Khrushchev era. As Lakshin had alleged, it was indeed the conservative press that pioneered the turn against the archetypal Thaw narrative of the cult. As Sofronov proudly recalled, 'At the very time when on the pages of our press there still swelled praises for Solzhenitsyn's opuses, it was precisely the journal *Oktiabr'* that was essentially the first to come out with criticism of Solzhenitsyn's writings.'[69] This criticism focused on Ivan Denisovich's moral and ideological failings: he had displayed no interest in Soviet principles, seemingly concerned only with brute survival.[70] The RSFSR Union also attacked Solzhenitsyn in similar terms.[71]

In fact, the distrust of Ivan as a literary character went deeper than the concern for optimism and ideological probity. Conservative criticisms also sometimes derived from personal distrust of victims themselves and resentment of their spectacular return to literary fame, as real-life authors and fictional heroes. Such sentiments were rare in the press of the 1960s but surfaced on occasion at union meetings. The discussions of the controversial *Literaturnaia Rossiia* article examined above, for example, touched on the personal and moral standing of cult victims. Anatolii Sofronov, one of the leading figures in the union, proposed the 'elementary truth' that Soviet society had endured because of its strength, a strength 'born not in the concentration camps [*sic*]' but rather 'in our society, in our party.' He located the 'fundamentals' of the Soviet experience in official literary culture, rather than in the peripheries of the Gulag and the perepeteia of rehabilitation policy.[72] Sofronov hinted that he distrusted the 'return of the repressed' – memories of Stalinism, and especially the Gulag – because he distrusted those who had been repressed under Stalin. Like Kochetov, he also used his own literary texts to dramatize his impatience with the memory politics of the Thaw.[73] In this, he found support amongst fellow union bosses: at a meeting in 1963, for example, his sardonic attacks on returnees were echoed by other speakers.[74]

More unexpectedly, though, victims themselves could also agree with these attacks on the Thaw. The writer Galina Serebriakova was perhaps the central character in the drama over the Fomenko article. As a rehabilitated former prisoner, she apparently stood to benefit from the article's insistent attention to Gulag narratives.[75] However, Serebriakova in fact considered the article an 'ideological lapse' and a 'major mistake,' claiming, 'I myself have spent many years in captivity but cannot agree with Comrade Fomenko.' She objected to the particular view of victims propounded by the article and by the Moscow Writers' Union: 'There they really love dead rehabilitated victims, but not live ones ... they don't think about the people who by some miracle escaped the grave.'[76] Serebriakova's negative perception of 'rival' victims meant that she found common ground with Sofronov in opposing the Thaw interpretation of the cult of personality. As someone who had undergone 'physical and mental torture,' she was henceforth granted the explicit prerogative to vet all articles on the cult before publication.[77]

The Stalinism of these conservative institutions was therefore complex. The conservative attitude to the literary treatment of the Stalinist past was mediated through, and legitimized by, the aesthetic doctrine of the party, which advocated a preponderance of 'optimism' in literature. It was also shaped by the official attacks on Stalin, which – unlike the calls to investigate the cult – were not fully retracted after 1961. This meant that Stalin himself was not a topic of debate in public or private. Soviet history, however, was up for debate, and a distinctively conservative, heroic view of the history of the Stalin era was more stridently articulated towards the end of the Khrushchev era. However, other personal factors also contributed to the complexity of attitudes towards the cult of personality. While Anatolii Sofronov's distrust of returnees and his desire to silence the cult altogether might be described as 'ultra-Stalinist' (and, as we shall see later, they came in response to a decade of allegations about his involvement in literary purges), figures such as Serebriakova – a conservative victim – defy easy categorization. However, as we will see, although positively inclined readers of conservatism responded to different facets of it, proponents of the Thaw insisted on a single, reductive interpretation of it.

Understanding Opposition to the Thaw: Conservatism and Its Audiences

In its struggle for legitimacy, the conservative press often emphasized that its favoured authors were not just ideologically correct, but also popular, acclaimed by the 'voice of the people' (*golos obshchestvennosti*).[78] Kochetov, it claimed, had a history of writing accessibly and efficiently about complex historical and social phenomena.[79] For that very reason, he also held tremendous popular appeal for the ordinary Soviet reader: 'People write, in hundreds of letters, that Kochetov's novels are true and lifelike.'[80] The newspaper concerned did not print these letters, but it did feature some reactions gathered from ordinary readers, who praised *The Obkom Secretary* for its closeness to life, the clarity of its style, and its provision of an ideal, sympathetic hero – Denisov – for emulation.[81]

Contrived as this 'model response' was, readers' actual responses, in letters and readers' conferences, suggest that some did genuinely enjoy Kochetov's novels for these reasons.[82] Readers who wrote in to *Literatura i zhizn'* about *The Obkom Secretary* endorsed Kochetov's decision to write about party leaders, and most found Denisov an inspiring hero whom they wanted to emulate.[83] Equally, the novel had succeeded in its main task of 'exposing the swindler … Artamanov.'[84] Kochetov's great virtue was the speed with which he translated contemporary problems – in this case the problem of leader cults – into fiction.[85] Sholokhov might have produced better-crafted works, but they appeared too late for readers hungry for guidance in interpreting the political and social change around them.[86] The obvious ideological message, and the prioritization of content over style were virtues for these readers.

If some readers thus responded positively to conservative aesthetic ideals, they also echoed, and even extended, the moral panic of the conservative press about the Thaw's values, or lack of them. This was particularly pronounced in reader response to *Literatura i zhizn*''s polemic against Vasilii Aksenov and his novella *A Ticket to the Stars*, a clear majority of which enthusiastically supported the newspaper.[87] In these letters, readers passionately deplored the immorality of Aksenov's (anti-) heroes and the pessimism and even 'nausea' generated by such 'trash and fungus,' 'deviants,' and '*stiliagi*' (teddy boys).[88] Moreover, they supported harsh measures against Aksenov himself, agreeing with the tone of the criticism and even urging it to go further, to counteract the positive reception the novel had received elsewhere, and to stem Aksenov's literary decline.[89] Their conviction about the impossibility of *perevospitanie* (re-education) for the novel's protagonists disposed them against the use of gentle methods of *vospitanie* on the author.

The popular enthusiasm for more repressive measures against 'liberals' also surfaced in the reception of both of Kochetov's Khrushchev-era novels. Not a single reader of *The Ershov Brothers* who wrote in to *Literatura i zhizn'* objected to Kochetov's decision to engage in what one called 'harsh condemnation of revisionism in all its manifestations.'[90] One relished the harsh treatment of the 'vulgar, careerist inner emigrant' Orleantsev and only wished that he had not been able to inflict so much suffering for so long on the good characters of the novel.[91] The same enthusiasm for an ultra-conservative cultural policy was voiced again in readers' letters of 1961, although such sentiments had by then become rarer in public settings. One letter writer in response to *The Obkom Secretary* was angered and perplexed that Putushkov, the dissolute poet, had enjoyed *any* success with his local audience.[92] He rejected Putushkov outright as a writer, pushing Kochetov to become even more intolerant in future literary representations of the Thaw.

There was therefore a receptive audience for the 'optimism,' heroism, and stringent morality of conservative literature. However, this popular support for some aspects of the conservative stance on the Thaw has often been overlooked. A key reason is that the liberal writers who have inspired much greater scholarly interest sought from the start to define post-Stalinist culture and the 'culture' of the intelligentsia in ways that excluded Kochetov and his ilk. These efforts focused on several aspects of their life and work: the low aesthetic quality of their works, their supposed lack of popularity with the Soviet reading public, and, above all, their infraction of the basic principles of proper conduct for the post-Stalinist intelligentsia.

In 1958, Aleksandr Tvardovskii noted the publication of *The Ershov Brothers* in his diary. At a time when *Novyi mir*, and Tvardovskii himself, were only just emerging from the literary doldrums, Kochetov's success was particularly galling. The novel was unliterary but still seemed to be enjoying an overwhelmingly positive official reception. Tvardovskii concluded bleakly that Soviet literature was now governed by criteria utterly at odds with his values: 'kind people' (*dobrye liudi*), whether literary heroes or real-life writers, seemed not to have a place in Soviet literature anymore.[93] This evaluation of Kochetov's work typified many other liberal writers' view of Kochetov and of other conservative writers. It combined confidence in literary taste with a lack of confidence in the political clout of these literary criteria. It also conflated literary and moral choices; good people would create good literature. It set liberal, cultured, literary taste in opposition to conservative aesthetic choices. It also counterposed the standards of *kul'turnost'* that should govern the private and public lives of Soviet writers to the personalities and actions of conservatives.

Tvardovskii's attempt to place Kochetov outside Soviet literature typified attempts to invalidate opposition to the Thaw on the grounds of literary quality. Kochetov was consistently the most criticized author on this count. Even at the subdued discussion of *The Ershov Brothers* at the Writers Union, there were myriad criticisms of the style of the novel, the poorly integrated storylines, the crude characterization, the inelegant language, and the 'rushed' feel to the work.[94] In the late Thaw, both the press and union discussions of Kochetov grew more bold, and reactions to *The Obkom Secretary* were often merciless in their dissection of the novel's stylistic flaws.[95] The most famous and longest of these aesthetic critiques appeared in *Novyi mir*. The critic Mariamov devoted several pages to Kochetov's total lack of literary finesse, his lack of attention to style, and the crude didacticism of the characterization and plot.[96]

Not all Mariamov's readers agreed with these aesthetic criticisms, but those who did developed them even further. One letter sent to *Novyi mir* rephrased Mariamov's critique, pointing to Kochetov's unsubtle staging of the conflict between 'the ultra-positive' Denisov and the 'negative' Artamanov, and deploring the obviousness of the message, clear to the reader 'from the first page.'[97] Some letters were franker still. 'The ground has been cut from beneath the *Kochetovshchina* – that particular brand of mediocrity,' crowed one letter from Leningrad, before detailing the many faults of Kochetov's primitive narrative. For others, Kochetov was entirely 'outside literature' (as Tvardovskii had also claimed) and 'anti-art.'[98] His works were 'grey, colourless,' and had no place in the Soviet canon.[99] One reader, a journalist from Novosibirsk, expressed indignation that Kochetov was on the Leningrad University syllabus and hoped that the *Novyi mir* article might change this, since it 'thoroughly and systematically expels Kochetov from the ranks of writers.'[100]

This celebration of exclusion indicates that, in constructing these arguments against Kochetov, these *Novyi mir* readers also constructed – or refined – their notions of the canon and their aesthetic criteria. One reader from Leningrad *oblast'* made explicit his politics of exclusion and inclusion: it was impossible to like both Gribachev and Kochetov, on the one hand, and Aksenov and Tendriakov on the other. He therefore rejected any article or review praising the first group of writers, since this was a priori proof that the author 'did not understand literature.'[101]

The literary communities thus constructed were unequal. Thaw authors and their readers were intellectually superior, since they 'understood' literature and could recognize authentic literary talent. Tvardovskii made sure that his colleagues were aware of the enormous qualitative gulf separating himself from Kochetov, despite comparable levels of their political influence; he found the idea that they might be thought of as 'comparable giants' hilarious.[102] His readers assured him that he was markedly superior to, and totally distinct from, the Kochetovs and Sofronovs of the literary world.[103] Tvardovskii saw *Novyi mir* in contrast to the 'inanity' of all the rest of Soviet literary culture.[104] While beleaguered and outnumbered, the Thaw was thought to be aesthetically and intellectually superior. It also seemed to have a genuinely receptive audience, unlike Kochetov (who was hardly read in the Soviet Union, and popular only in neo-Stalinist China) and *Literatura i zhizn'* (which had no readership to speak of).[105] Judged on all of these literary criteria, the Thaw embodied the true direction of literature and culture in the post-Stalin age.

This exclusionary rhetoric based on aesthetic criteria had its counterpart in the stringent behavioural and moral criteria that were invoked in the battle to protect the Thaw. According to this argument, conservatives were not just aesthetically unworthy, but should also forfeit their right to criticize the Thaw on moral grounds. The diaries and memoirs of the Thaw's proponents bubble over with invective against the conservative opposition, continuing a long tradition of using ego-documents to define inclusion in (and exclusion from) the intelligentsia.[106] To Evtushenko, the 'dogmatists' who opposed the Thaw were also 'bastards.'[107] For Chukovskii, the 'nonentities' attacking *Novyi mir* were also 'villains.'[108] According to Solzhenitsyn, the staff of *Oktiabr'* were 'scoundrels.'[109] For Tvardovskii too, the 'dark forces' in literature were both 'nonentities' and morally dissolute.[110] Accusations of immorality (*podlost', nizost', gnusnost'*) were legion in both diaries and private conversation.[111] The moral panic of the conservative press was thus countered by accusations of immorality that centred, as I will argue, primarily on Stalinist conduct in the past and present.

Kochetov, as the popularity of the term *Kochetovshchina* suggests, was 'investigated' most thoroughly on this count. However, equally harsh – and perhaps better-founded – personal allegations hounded certain of Kochetov's like-minded associates, particularly Anatolii Sofronov and the conservative writer and editor Nikolai Gribachev. The institutions that they represented – *Oktiabr'*, the RSFSR Union, and its press organs – also attracted criticisms for the tone of their criticism, for their dictatorial management style, and for the protection they offered to such conservative writers. All of these allegations constructed a derogatory counter-image of Stalinist literary culture.

Personal allegations surrounded Kochetov from the earliest days of the Thaw. As secretary of the Leningrad Union, he consistently attracted personal insults and accusations. His attacks on Vera Panova and Mikhail Zoshchenko in 1954 and 1955 resulted in a groundswell of hostility towards him for being dictatorial, aggressive, and clientelist.[112] Eventually this discontent found expression at the ballot box, and Kochetov was ousted from the leadership. During his editorship of *Literaturnaia gazeta*, he again faced waves of complaints of cronyism and of a cult of personality shielding him from his criticism, and these eventually led to his sacking.[113] In the antagonism expressed towards Kochetov, two personal factors were seen as central to his power: his natural desire for dictatorial control, and his personal ties to other writers in the conservative faction of the literary community.

The reception of Kochetov's Khrushchev-era novels deepened this fixation on the author's views and methods; the texts were seen as the direct counterpart of his political manoeuvring. In official and unofficial discussions of his novels, writers accused Kochetov of settling scores with his rivals through thinly veiled 'direct pamphlet sketches of famous Soviet writers.'[114] *The Ershov Brothers* apparently attacked the playwrights Shtein and Pogodin, the writers Ehrenburg and Dudintsev, and the Moscow Writers' Union, while *The Obkom Secretary* satirized Konstantin Simonov and Evgenii Evtushenko. Although sharply rebuked as parochial, these attempts to identify the real-life targets of Kochetov's ad hominem attacks continued to permeate writers' discussions with 'resentment and irritation.'[115]

More broadly, Kochetov stood accused of personal bias and self-interest in his depiction of the Thaw as a whole. Even the subdued discussion of *The Ershov Brothers* at the Writers Union took issue with the subjective biases of Kochetov's view of 1956 as a 'bad and murky time,' his 'irritable,' excessively negative picture of the state of Soviet culture, and his exaggeration of the scale of revisionism.[116] Here the references to Kochetov's irritability and 'highly strung' portrait of contemporary culture focused, if only temporarily, on the author's subjective, emotional perspective.[117] Many Moscow writers elaborated on these complaints in private, expressing horror at Kochetov's, 'scornful,' 'blackened,' 'poisonous' view of the Thaw and of the intelligentsia.[118] *The Ershov Brothers* was widely seen as a direct commentary on the current state of Soviet culture, informed by Kochetov's personal resentments and enmities. Kochetov's attention to the real-life characters of the Thaw was repaid by his opponents' equally merciless focus on Kochetov's character and opinions.

According to these accusations, Kochetov had a personal distaste for the Thaw, and he was using his novels to attack it in inappropriately personalized, aggressive terms. The same was later held to be true of his journal *Oktiabr'*. As *Oktiabr'* became more and more hostile towards the Thaw, its victims alleged that the journal had fallen under Kochetov's dictatorial control and that it was being used to pursue personal vendettas against Thaw authors and literary works.[119] The criticisms of the Thaw that appeared in *Oktiabr'* after Kochetov's takeover were frequently deplored at the Moscow Writers Union and in other liberal circles: *Oktiabr'*'s criticisms were a form of 'teeth-baring' and 'slander,' and they were linked directly to the new editor.[120] As we saw earlier, Kochetov had already become notorious for his own sarcastic criticism of the Thaw, and this past line in aggressive criticism coupled with his history of union and journal 'dictatorships' suggested that the journal's dogmatic 'line' against the Thaw was very much Kochetov's own.[121]

This model of understanding criticism of the Thaw as personally motivated and dictatorially executed can also be seen in reactions to *Literatura i zhizn'*. From its earliest days, the newspaper attracted criticism from both readers and writers for its 'frightening,' 'spiteful,' 'blasphemous' attacks on the Thaw.[122] One of the readers' letters sent in protest at its harsh treatment of Aksenov likened the criticism to 'a prison sentence' and advocated instead that 'this author should be saved for literature.'[123] The tone of these attacks provoked direct comparisons with Stalinist literary criticism, and part of the explanation lay in its 'Stalinist' management.[124] Though much less famous than Kochetov, the paper's editor Pozdniaev was attacked in similar terms for his suppression of dissent and his generally odious behaviour.[125]

According to these varied complaints, conservative opposition to the Thaw was guilty of *mauvais ton*. It discussed – or rather denounced – Thaw literature in an uncivilized way.[126] It failed to live up to the requisite standards of collegiality and humaneness and its motives were far from pure. However, there was more to these attacks than a sense of cultural and moral superiority. The aggression of conservative criticism and the dictatorial institutions that sponsored it called to mind not just the style of criticism of the Stalin era, but also the mechanisms of terror and exclusion that were the dark heart of Stalinist literary culture. Comparisons between opposition to the Thaw and Stalinist persecution were born of fear of a Stalinist revival, but also displayed a strategic awareness of the discursive and political explosiveness of references to terror.

In the late 1950s, fear was still dominant. The many writers who refused to criticize *The Ershov Brothers* in public 'feared unpleasantness and tried to save their nerves' by staying away from the Moscow discussion and staying out of Kochetov's sights.[127] The 'decorous' tone of the union meeting held to discuss the novel confirmed their fears of Kochetov's stranglehold on literary politics.[128] There were in fact some allusions even here to Kochetov's ability to scare his critics into silence.[129] Some ordinary readers also subsequently alluded to this apparent suppression of criticism.[130] Those who played truant from the meeting openly expected the criticisms that had been voiced to provoke punishment from Kochetov and his cronies: as one alleged, 'That group will now seek out any pretext to deal with [*raspravit'sia*] the critics of the novel.'[131] The fear of intra-literary reprisals was much greater than any fear of reprisals from the authorities, as evidenced in writers' willingness to convey to the authorities (but not to Kochetov himself) their feelings about Kochetov.[132]

The fear of Kochetov's methods of *rasprava* (reckoning) led most writers to stay under the radar until the Thaw had garnered more official support. Fresh from the Twenty-Second Congress, as we have seen, writers were more confident in attacking Kochetov and *The Obkom Secretary*, and his editorship of *Oktiabr'*. Though less and less fearful of speaking out, they still saw Kochetov as a frightening figure, who made editors 'tremble' and who seemed to have at his disposal a willing 'phalanx' and 'legion' of troops to lead the charge against the Thaw.[133]

Kochetov's fondness for *rasprava* was the main point of comparison with Stalin, but it was bolstered by rumours of his love for the leader. The liberal press critique of *The Obkom Secretary* had hinted at Kochetov's own opposition to de-Stalinization through lengthy critiques of Denisov's ambiguous attitude to Stalin.[134] At the Moscow Union, speakers openly accused Kochetov of 'defending the cult of personality'; all of his activities were driven by the 'political credo' of Stalinism and by a reluctance to see Stalinism criticized.[135] Many ordinary readers of the novel responding to Mariamov's critique also agreed. 'One sensed a kind of regret that the cult of Stalin has been exposed,' wrote one pensioner from Gor'kii, likening the novel's heroes and Kochetov himself to the *obkom* secretaries in his region who had criticized the 'Secret Speech' for bringing shame on Stalin.[136] Another called for the 'unmasking' in which Mariamov had engaged to go further; the whole novel was intended to reverse the message of the Twenty-Second Congress by stealth, and Kochetov must be 'exposed' as pro-Stalinist.[137] Throughout the Khrushchev era, then, Kochetov was held to be guilty of *rasprava* through his work as an editor, critic, union boss, and writer. Rumours about his fondness for Stalin then confirmed the view of Kochetov as a modern-day literary Stalin, nostalgic for the times and methods of *Zhdanovshchina*.[138]

Kochetov was not, however, the only writer to be accused of Stalinist-style repressive cultural politics. In the case of Kochetov's close associates, Sofronov and Gribachev, the Stalinism and deadliness of their methods were revealed to be literal rather than metaphorical. According to recurrent accusations during the period, they were the two principal henchmen in Stalin's anti-cosmopolitanism campaign.[139] Their records of *rasprava* and repression were the subject of frequent complaint, starting as early as 1953 and peaking in 1956 and 1961–2.[140] These complaints, as articulated at the Moscow Union, were deeply personal – the perpetrators were personally identified, and their accusers included rehabilitated victims of their campaign and others traumatized by the memory of late Stalinist anti-Semitism. The allegations focused on their rule of fear ('they terrified us') and the traumatic, divisive effects of their policies of *rasprava*; they had victimized individuals and damaged the entire literary community.[141] Gribachev and Sofronov's enduring anti-Semitism was central to these accusations, but so too was their love of power: they had done the party's bidding in order to further their careers.[142]

The Moscow Union was not the only place where these memories of Sofronov's and Gribachev's actions were aired. They remained a widespread preoccupation, as well as a source of frustration as it increasingly seemed that they would go unpunished. As one reader urged, in a 1963 letter written to *Novyi mir* to protest the power of literary conservatism, 'Let us remember how Sofronov, Shkernik and Gribachev dealt with [*raspravlialis'*] these people on the pages of amenable journals.'[143] The same desire for *rasprava* to be remembered and punished was expressed in an anonymous letter, sent to the Central Committee a few years prior to this letter, in protest against Sofronov's continued high office in the Writers Union. With his record of persecution (*izbienie, rasprava*), pursued with the sole aim of creating a 'vacuum' in Soviet literature, Sofronov should have been sacked long ago. Instead, the author claimed, he was compounding his sins by engaging in violent, intolerant literary criticism (*prorabotka, obvineniia, dubinka*). In every respect, Sofronov was personally and morally unsuitable for high office; he had a dissolute home life, while at work he showed a desire to 'deal with people [*raspravliat'sia*] left and right.'[144]

However, it was the film director Mikhail Romm who was responsible for the most direct and most controversial accusations of Stalinism levelled at Gribachev and Sofronov. In a long speech to the Moscow Institute of Art History at the end of 1962, he attacked 'the ideology of the Black Hundreds,' seeing it as responsible for both the anti-cosmopolitan *rasprava* carried out by Gribachev and Sofronov and the current wave of criticism of the Thaw in Kochetov's *Oktiabr'*.[145] Investigated by the Central Committee after all three writers wrote to complain, Romm reiterated his strong critique of Soviet anti-Semitism and claimed that 'the unpopularity of Gribachev and Sofronov in the Moscow writers organization is primarily down to their activity in the anti-cosmopolitan campaign.'[146] He did, however, apologize for 'involuntarily' including Kochetov in his accusations of involvement in the repressions and of anti-Semitism. It was simply, he explained, that he had 'long been used to seeing all three of them as occupying the same general literary position which is incorrect and moreover harmful to literature.'[147]

Romm's instinctive correlation of Gribachev, Sofronov, and Kochetov was the least of the authorities' worries; the long *samokritika* that he was forced to perform focused above all on his allegations of systemic anti-Semitism.[148] However, the 'error' he made in placing all three writers under the banner of the 'Black Hundreds' was far from unique.[149] One obvious reason to group the writers together was the patronage network that linked them from their days in Leningrad.[150] Kochetov clearly tolerated his friends' odious beliefs and may have actively sympathized with them. Either way, he was on the wrong side of the ideological and moral divide.

This slippage between the present and the past, and between anti-Semitism and other forms of 'persecution,' in these conceptualizations of conservative opposition reflected the high emotions of the Thaw, but also the conceptual broadness of the emergent idea of Stalinism and the cult of personality in the literary community. *Rasprava* and anti-Semitism were linked to all the forces of opposition, and so too was the notion of the cult of personality. As some enthusiastic supporters of *Novyi mir*'s attacks on Kochetov put it, Kochetov was the 'embodiment of everything backward, conservative and talentless that was generated by the cult of personality,' and he was 'the worst consequence of the cult of personality of Stalin.'[151] As these letters suggest, the counter-attacks mounted against opposition to the Thaw transformed the cult of personality into an umbrella term for Stalinism's legacies to literature – aesthetically weak works, a tradition of harsh criticism and persecution, impenetrable patronage networks, and belief in Stalinism and anti-Semitism. It was a hybrid, even hydra-headed, phenomenon that took time to emerge and was hard to grasp in its entirety.[152] However, the principal foes that Lakshin identified were amongst the most perfect embodiments of literary Stalinism, and their names offered a convenient short-hand for dismissing both the Stalin period and present-day opposition to the Thaw.

Conclusion

In 1963, Aleksandr Iashin confided his thoughts about the Thaw to his diary. Despite the problems that he and his works had suffered during the Thaw, Iashin was in an upbeat mood. He claimed that the 'revitalization advancing in literature was an irreversible process,' as was the 'course of democratization' started by the Twentieth Congress. However, he had to admit that 'not everyone implements this course with the same consistency, and some are simply ill-disposed towards it – that's the whole problem.'[153] At roughly the same time, Evgenii Evtushenko, another victim of attacks on the Thaw, assessed the situation in these terms: 'It goes without saying that the dogmatists used, still use, and will go on using every opportunity they can find to arrest the process of democratization in our society ... I know equally well that the dogmatists have reared a new crop of young people to replace them ... but they are easily outnumbered by our progressive-minded young people, and there is no doubt in my mind that dogmatism is doomed.'[154] Both writers – one young, one much older – expressed a surprising confidence in the Thaw. It would win out over its 'dogmatic' and 'ill-disposed' opponents because those opponents were in the minority and were not on the side of history; liberalization was moving forward, buoyed by the support of the majority.

The long view and quiet confidence adopted by Iashin and Evtushenko usually eluded the many writers caught up in the drama of the Thaw. As I have argued, the debate over the Thaw was highly emotional and often narrowly focused on particular statements, even particular phrases, specific episodes, and specific actions. Writers rarely seemed to lift their heads above the parapet to take in the panorama of the battlefield. Both sides saw themselves as victims, and neither felt that its position or power was secure. Nevertheless, the sense of destiny manifest in these two views of the Thaw was not untypical. Many proponents of the Thaw were convinced that right was on their side in the battle for the soul of Soviet literature. The personal and moral defects of their opponents were simply too great to allow them the ultimate victory. However, caught up in ongoing, unresolved conflicts over these defects, writers often felt much more pessimistic. Victory *within* the literary community was far from certain. Iashin and Evtushenko typify liberal attempts to place the Thaw and its impact within a wider historical and social context. Their hints about the broader successes of the Thaw raise the question of where and how we should measure the impact of the discursive politics of the Thaw that I have examined in this chapter.

Analyses of the Thaw have generally measured success by the degree to which conservative or liberal arguments convinced the Soviet authorities to move in their favour.[155] The influence of both sets of arguments on the authorities would require a separate study and more archival material than is currently available to researchers, but it is clear that the debate deliberately sought to involve the party authorities and sometimes succeeded in getting them to act in favour of one or other side. Khrushchev's defence of the beleaguered so-called *lakirovshchiki* (varnishers) in 1957 and again in 1963 is one example of the direct influence that conservative discourse could have on aesthetic policy. The moral arguments against conservatism, for their part, succeeded in ousting Kochetov from *Literaturnaia gazeta* (but not from *Oktiabr'*), and some minor post-holders from positions of power in the Writers Union, but the authorities remained deaf to calls to remove Gribachev and Sofronov from high office.[156] In general, official aesthetic policy, while it may seem to have been persuaded by writers' arguments at certain moments, sought above all to balance conservative and liberal approaches to literature.[157] In this respect, the 'official' impact of the discursive politics examined above was negligible. The debates that I have traced raged within a predetermined policy framework and, while isolated successes were possible, the victory of one or other side was impossible.

However, a different perspective may reveal deeper and longer-lasting effects of the debate over the Thaw. The failure to persuade the authorities of the validity of aesthetic and moral arguments against conservatism, for example, led their proponents to potentially revolutionary reflections on the nature of Soviet culture. The fact that there appeared to be an 'untouchable sect' of 'remnants of the cult' amongst writers – including Gribachev and Sofronov – reflected badly on the system that gave them personal and institutional protection.[158] While conservative writers had formidable resources at their disposal to influence the authorities – their 'collective responsibility' networks, and the 'dark forces' that clustered around them – they were not the sole culprits; the authorities seemed to be colluding in their desire to limit de-Stalinization.

However, again, focusing on attitudes towards the authorities overshadows the more interesting, far-reaching dynamics *within* the cultural community. One sure consequence of the quarrel over the Thaw was the deepening of hostility between the two sides in the debate. However, these deepened divisions were not based on deeper understanding of the ideological stakes of the debate over the future of Soviet literature. Moral and personal concerns dominated the literary debates of the Thaw, leading to caricatural depictions of each side (as 'Black Hundreds' and 'rebellious sons,' to take the two principal examples). However, these debates were not entirely unproductive, since they also led to reflections on the Stalinization and de-Stalinization of Soviet literary culture.

There was more similarity than difference in the ways that both sides negotiated the mechanisms and methods of Soviet literary culture.[159] As I have argued, both sides were guilty of personal attacks and of settling scores, although there were important differences of tone and approach. Both sides recognized the importance of the authorities' patronage and expended much energy on informal networking with Soviet leaders. Finally, *Novyi mir* and its 'friends' were bound by ties of mutual responsibility (*krugovaia poruka*) at least as strong as those that they observed and deplored between Gribachev, Sofronov, and Kochetov.[160] These were all necessary survival strategies, not only in the Khrushchev era, but in the longer history of Soviet literature. However, the revelations about terror and debates about morality imbued all of these aspects of Soviet literary culture with the taint of Stalinism and made them the object of contestation and controversy.

These silences about common ground were filled not only with noisy allegations of Stalinism in criticism and management, but also by emergent ideas about the broader social constituencies served by Soviet literature. Kornei Chukovsky, as one of the elders of the Soviet intelligentsia, frequently reflected on the subject in his diaries. He saw the publication of his own works and many of the banner works of the Thaw as 'the victory of the intelligentsia over the Kochetovs ... and other Black Hundreds types.'[161] Like other seasoned observers of the Thaw and its cyclical nature, he foresaw the Black Hundreds' revenge. However, he also professed substantial confidence in real, lasting change, claiming, 'You've got a large, new technical intelligentsia the government is dependent on, and this large new group has taken on the function of the humanistic intelligentsia and constitutes a kind of public opinion.'[162]

Thus, although pessimism about cultural policy might persist, the Thaw's legacy in social change was irreversible. Chukovsky echoed Iashin and Evtushenko in looking over the heads of their fellow writers and the Soviet authorities to the broader social constituencies served by the Thaw and supportive of it. For liberals, the very persistence of conservatism and the resulting attacks on the Thaw forced them to seek out signs of success outside the frustrating and unproductive battles over literature. These battles were going nowhere, because too many Soviet writers still seemed to have an appetite for outmoded ideas and practices; in other words, they were less *intelligentnyi* and *kul'turnyi* than the Soviet reading public. Within this community, Chukovsky was sure that 'Black Hundreds' ideas had no audience.[163]

The validation of the Thaw therefore increasingly came not from official approval or the sense of victory over literary rivals – both elusive and easily reversed – but from the teleological growth of an imagined community of readers. Lakshin's article about Solzhenitsyn, which we began by examining, left him feeling disappointed with the Soviet authorities, but he derived enormous comfort from the gestures of solidarity and letters of support that he received from the *Novyi mir* community.[164] Tvardovskii's second editorship of *Novyi mir*, as consumed as it was with struggles with the authorities and with his fellow writers, was clearly founded on this emergent idea of his intelligentsia audience.[165] At several crucial junctures of the Thaw, he and Lakshin used readers' letters to sustain it in the face of opposition from the authorities and literary rivals.[166]

The battle over the Thaw reflected and in turn produced new understandings of the operation of power and authority. In the post-Stalinist literary world, authority and power were mutable concepts, at times deriving directly from rank and position (as seemed to be the case with Kochetov, Sofronov, and Gribachev), and at times from moral authority, 'cultured' behaviour, literary talent, and the hope of an enthusiastic and reciprocal reader response. Suspended between multiple understandings of Stalinist literary culture and embattled post-Stalinist norms, the debate over the Thaw was as impassioned as it was impossible to resolve.

NOTES

1 Vladimir Lakshin, 'Ivan Denisovich, ego druz'ia i nedrugi,' *Novyi mir* 1 (1964): 223–45.
2 E.g., Lakshin, 'Doverie,' *Novyi mir* 11 (1962): 229–41.
3 Vladimir Lakshin, *Solzhenitsyn, Tvardovsky and Novy mir*, trans. and ed. M. Glenny (Cambridge, MA, 1980), esp. 148–51.
4 Lakshin, *Solzhenitsyn*, 5; Lakshin, *Novyi mir vo vremena Khrushcheva. Dnevnik i poputnoe* (Moscow, 1991), 192–203.
5 Examples of letters to *Kommunist*, RGASPI 599/1/447/23, 27; Lakshin, *Novyi mir*, 223; Aleksandr Solzhenitsyn, *The Oak and Calf: Sketches of Literary Life in the Soviet Union* (London, 1980), 70–2.
6 Lakshin, *Solzhenitsyn*, 5.
7 RGALI 1702/9/139/40.
8 E.g., Priscilla Johnson, *Khrushchev and the Arts: The Politics of Soviet Culture, 1962–64* (Cambridge, MA, 1965); Mariia Zezina, *Sovetskaia khudozhestvennaia intelligentsia i vlast' v 1950-e i 1960-e gody* (Moscow, 1999), esp. 278–93.
9 Stephen Cohen, 'The Friends and Foes of Change: Soviet Reformism and Conservatism,' in his *Rethinking the Soviet Experience: Politics and History since 1917* (Oxford, 1986).
10 On the importance of 'freedom' and 'opposition' to understanding of the period, see, for example, J. Augustyn, 'Vsevolod Kochetov: A Soviet Literary Conservative' (MA thesis, Brown University, 1971), 1; George Gibian, *Interval of Freedom: Soviet Literature during the Thaw, 1954–57* (Minneapolis, 1960); T. Scriven, 'The Literary Opposition,' *Problems of Communism* 1 (1958): 28–34.
11 Max Hayward and Edward Crowley, *Soviet Literature in the Sixties* (London, 1965), 92; Karl Loewenstein, 'Writers and the Public Sphere in the Soviet Union, 1951–57' (PhD diss., Duke University, 1999); Dina Spechler, *Permitted Dissent in the Soviet Union: Novy mir and the Soviet Regime* (New York, 1982).

12 Augustyn, 'Vsevolod Kochetov'; Yitzhak Brudny, *Reinventing Russia: Russian Nationalism and the Soviet State 1953–91* (Cambridge, MA, 1998), 54–6; Gibian, *Interval*, 16, 23; Hayward and Crowley, *Soviet Literature*, 198; Johnson, *Khrushchev and the Arts*, 7; Lakshin, *Solzhenitsyn*, 22, 169; Loewenstein, 'Writers and the Public Sphere,' 94; Harold Swayze, *Political Control of Literature in the USSR, 1946–59* (Oxford, 1962), 214.

13 Edith Frankel, *Novy mir: A Case Study in the Politics of Literature, 1952–58* (Cambridge, MA, 1981), 47; Johnson attributes conservatism and struggle against Thaw 'above all [to] the struggle by bureaucrats left over from the Stalin era to hang on to their power and positions' (Johnson, *Khrushchev and the Arts*, 4; see 42). Cohen argues for a more nuanced view of opposition to de-Stalinization, which accommodates pro-Stalin feeling but also more general 'conservative political attitudes' (Cohen, 'The Stalin Question since Stalin,' in Cohen, *Rethinking the Soviet Experience*).

14 Ronald Hingley, in *Problems of Communism* (September–October 1962): 44, typifies this disgust with conservatism. Richard Pipes polemicizes against ignoring 'proponents' of the 'status quo,' in Pipes, *Russian Conservatism and Its Critics* (New Haven, CT, 2005), xii–xiii.

15 Miriam Dobson, 'Contesting the Paradigms of De-Stalinization: Readers' Responses to *One Day in the Life of Ivan Denisovich*,' *Slavic Review* 64, no. 4 (2005): 580–600; Denis Kozlov, 'Naming the Social Evil: The Readers of Vladimir Dudintsev's *Not by Bread Alone*, 1956–59 and Beyond,' in *The Dilemmas of De-Stalinization*, ed. Polly Jones, 80–98 (London, 2006); Susan E. Reid, 'In the Name of the People: The Manège Affair Revisited,' *Kritika* 6, no. 4 (2005): 673–716.

16 Vladimir Bondarenko, *Plamennye reaktsionery: Tri lika russkogo patriotizma* (Moscow, 2003), 6–14; Kevin Gilmartin, *Writing against Revolution: Literary Conservatism in Britain, 1790–1832* (Cambridge, MA, 2007), 1–11; Pipes, *Russian Conservatism*, xii.

17 Sheila Fitzpatrick, 'Patrons and Clients,' in Fitzpatrick, *Tear Off the Masks! Identity and Imposture in Twentieth-Century Russia* (Princeton, 2005); Nikolai Mitrokhin, *Russkaia partiia. Dvizhenie russkikh natsionalistov v SSSR, 1953–1985* (Moscow, 2003), 142–7; Vera Tolz, 'Cultural Bosses as Patrons and Clients: The Functioning of the Soviet Creative Unions in the Postwar Period,' *Contemporary European History* 11, no. 1 (2002): 87–105.

18 Mariia Zezina, 'Crisis in the Union of Soviet Writers in the Early 1950s,' *Europe-Asia Studies* 46, no. 4 (1994): 649–61.

19 Brudny, *Reinventing Russia*, 28–59; Hosking, *Rulers and Victims: The Russians in the Soviet Union* (Cambridge, MA, 2006), 338–71; Mitrokhin, *Russkaia partiia*, 141–78; See Bondarenko, *Plamennye reaktsionery*.

20 Lakshin, *Novyi mir*, 252.

21 E.g., 'Za tesnuiu sviaz' literatury i iskusstva s zhizn'iu naroda,' *Kommunist* 12 (1957): 10–29; 'K novym uspekham literatury i iskusstva,' *Kommunist* 7 (1961): 3–16; Johnson, *Khrushchev on Culture* (London, 1964); *Literaturnaia gazeta* (hereafter *LG*), 12 March 1963.
22 Gibian, *Interval of Freedom*, 20–2; Hosking, *Rulers and Victims*, 350; Swayze, *Political Control*, 199–200.
23 E.g., *Apparat Tsk KPSS i kul'tura 1958–64. Dokumenty* (hereafter *Apparat TsK, 1958–64*) (Moscow, 2000), 474–85; Solzhenitsyn, *Oak and Calf*, 169; Zezina, *Sovetskaia*, 282.
24 E.g., his attacks on Vera Panova in 1954 (see Frankel, *Novy mir*, 53–4). On Kochetov and these two institutions, see Loewenstein, 'Writers and the Public Sphere,' 93–4, 298.
25 'Za tesnuiu sviaz'.'
26 'S narodom, s partiei,' *Literatura i zhizn'* (hereafter *LiZh*), 6 April 1958, 1; editorial discussions in RGALI 1572/1/1/1.
27 'Pisatel' i vremia,' *LiZh*, 18 March 1960, 1.
28 'Tipicheskoe – geroizm!,' *LiZh*, 25 March 1960, 3 (Vadim Kozhevnikov). Kochetov's literalist interpretation of the 'link to life' has been attributed in part to his journalistic background (Augustyn, *Vsevolod Kochetov*).
29 RGALI 2938/2/6/12.
30 Discussions of *sovremennost'* dominated the RSFSR Union agenda for much of the early period, e.g., 'Glavnaia tema,' *LiZh*, 4 June 1958, 1; 'Sovremennost' – dusha literatury,' *LiZh*, 18 June 1958, 2; 'Literatura i nasha sovremennost',' *LiZh*, 8 December 1958, 2–5.
31 'Istochnik pravdivosti- zhizn',' *LiZh*, 2 July 1958, 1; 'Chuvstvo okruzhaiushchego mira,' *LiZh*, 24 April 1960, 3.
32 ' Pisatel' i vremia,' *LiZh*, 18 March 1960, 1; RGALI 2938/1/130/2–3, 30.
33 'Cheloveku nuzhen ideal,' *LiZh*, 11 March 1960, 3; 'Chuvstvo okruzhaiushchego mira,' *LiZh*, 24 April 1960, 3; 'Besposhchadno borot'sia s revizionizmom,' *LiZh*, 28 December 1958, 2; 'Pafos sluzheniia narodu,' *LiZh*, 27 November 1961, 1–2; see V. Kochetov, 'Geroia vremeni vo ves' rost,' *Kommunist* 18 (1962): 83–91.
34 P. Strokov, 'Glavnyi redactor,' in *Vospominaniia o Vsevolode Kochetove* (Moscow, 1986), 106.
35 E.g., Vsevolod Kochetov, 'The Ershov Brothers,' *Soviet Literature* 1–3 (1959), chaps 13, 26, 27; Kochetov, *Sekretar' obkoma* (Moscow, 1975), 37, 402.
36 'Fal'shivyi bilet,' *LiZh*, 6 October 1961, 3; Swayze, *Political Control*, 215.
37 'Oktiabr' k s"ezdu partii,' *LiZh*, 17 September 1961, 1.
38 'Kompas- partiinost',' *LiZh*, 25 June 1961, 3.
39 'O novatorstve i smysle zhizni,' *LiZh*, 3 February 1960, 2.

40 'Mnimaia ob"ektivnost' i pravda epokhi,' *LiZh*, 19 March 1961, 3; attack on 'poeticization of the banal' in 'Zhit' i rabotat' dlia partii i naroda,' *LiZh*, 6 September 1959, 1; 'Kak budto o sovremennosti,' *Oktiabr'* 9 (1963): 189–95.
41 'Ob iskaniiakh i pravde zhizni,' *Oktiabr'* 8 (1962); 'Fal'shivyi bilet', *LiZh*, 6 October 1961, 3; 'Takaia li ona pravda?,' *LiZh*, 7 October 1959, 2; RGALI 2938/2/1/127–8. Critique reprised in *Vtoroi s"ezd soiuza pisatelei RSFSR. Stenograficheskii otchet* (Moscow, 1966), 60–71.
42 'Za novogo cheloveka!,' *Oktiabr'* 6 (1962): 194–212; 'Ustarelo li izobrazhenie "dialektiki dushi"?,' *LiZh*, 3 February 1961, 2; 'Ideinost' i masterstvo,' *LiZh*, 5 March 1961, 3; 'Pravda i sovremennost',' *LiZh*, 26 July 1961, 1; 'Fal'shivyi bilet,' *LiZh*, 6 October 1961, 3.
43 'Iskusstvo pravdy i krasoty,' *LiZh*, 24 November 1961, 1.
44 RGALI 2938/2/1/64–6, 139, 160, 40–2.
45 'O litse pisatelia,' *LiZh*, 3 April 1961, 4.
46 Kochetov, *Sekretar' obkoma*, 148, 207, 239, chap. 36; criticism of Putushkov's *meshchanstvo* in 'Tvortsy prekrasnogo,' *LiZh*, 22 November 1961, 1.
47 Kochetov, *Sekretar' obkoma*, chaps 14, 15, 32, 37, 43, 46.
48 Kochetov, 'Ershov Brothers,' part 2, chap. 16.
49 Generational concerns: RGALI 2938/2/1/43; concerns about lack of control over Moscow: RGALI 2938/2/45/69; 2938/2/6/12; 2938/2/1/6, 20, 79–80, 100, 157, 171, 178, 230.
50 'Novoe, kommunisticheskoe v literature,' *Oktiabr'* 4 (1963): 178–92; RGALI 2938/2/1/162.
51 Examples of discussion of the Russian, pre-revolutionary literary tradition (as supporting the union's stance on *ideinost'* and the positive hero): RGALI 2938/2/45/60–116; 'Sila russkogo realizma,' *LiZh*, 5 August 1959, 1–3; 'Internatsional'naia sushchnost' sovetskoi literatury,' *LiZh*, 21 February 1960, 2.
52 RGALI 2938/2/1/273. See debate about 'victimization' of Kochetov, Gribachev, and Sofronov by Moscow writers in *Ideologicheskie komissii TsK KPSS, 1958–64* (Moscow, 1998), 305, 351, 366.
53 'Otkuda mal'chik?,' *Oktiabr'* 10 (1962); *Oktiabr'* 11 (1962): 172–91. Untitled article.
54 RGALI 2938/2/7/3–4, 54, 59, 62; RGALI 2938/2/1/41–5; 'Niza? Na priviazi,' *LiZh*, 3 June 1960, 1–2; *Vtoroi s"ezd*, 70.
55 It also appears to have garnered some sympathy from readers: one survey of letters sent to the authorities after March 1963 found unanimous support for conservatives such as Gribachev, Kochetov, and Sofronov against the attacks and neglect of younger and Muscovite writers (RGANI 5/30/409/112–23).

56 E.g., Kochetov, 'Ershov Brothers,' part 2, chap. 2.
57 Kochetov, *Sekretar' obkoma*, 22, chap. 10.
58 Kochetov, 'Ershov Brothers,' 89.
59 *XXII s"ezd. Stenograficheskii otchet* (Moscow, 1962), 183.
60 E.g., 'Gde zhizn,' tam i poeziia,' *LiZh*, 15 December 1961, 3; 'Ia chelovek, Ia communist!,' *LiZh*, 4 March 1962, 1–3; 'Iunost' o iunosti,' *LiZh*, 27 April 1962, 2–3; 'Zhiv chelovek,' *LiZh*, 28 November 1962, 3.
61 'Pafos sluzheniia narodu,' *LiZh*, 27 November 1961, 1–2; 'Za polnuiu iasnost',' *LiZh*, 29 December 1961, 3; 'Za kommunisticheskuiu nov',' *Oktiabr'* 5 (1962); RGALI 2938/1/130/2.
62 'Za ideinuiu iasnost,' *LiZh*, 29 December 1961, 3.
63 RGALI 2938/2/7/3–4.
64 'Bol'shie ozhidaniia,' *Literaturnaia Rossiia* 2 (1963): 6–7.
65 RGALI 2938/2/3/38.
66 Ibid., l. 52.
67 E.g., *Literaturnaia Rossiia* 3 (1963): 6–7.
68 E.g., RGALI 2938/1/45/76, 150, 221; RGALI 2938/2/1/287–343.
69 A. Sofronov, 'Knigi ostaiutsia,' in *Vospominaniia o Vsevolode Kochetove*, 167.
70 'Tragediia odinochestva i "sploshnoi byt,"' *Oktiabr'* 4 (1963): 198–207; 'Nesgibaemye dukhom,' *Oktiabr'* 10 (1963): 210.
71 RGALI 2938/2/45/ 69, 219, 255, 273; *Literaturnaia Rossiia* 13 (1964): 11.
72 RGALI 2938/2/3/61.
73 A Sofronov, 'Beregite zhivykh synovei,' *Teatr* 2 (1963): 162–92. On Sofronov, see Polly Jones, 'Memories of Terror or Terrorizing Memories? Terror, Trauma and Survival in Soviet Culture of the Thaw,' *Slavonic and East European Review* 81, no. 2 (2008): 346–71.
74 RGALI 2938/2/1/51, 61–2.
75 See Jones, 'Memories of Terror.'
76 RGALI 2938/2/3/88–91.
77 Ibid., ll. 98, 106; RGALI 2938/2/4/71–2.
78 'Pafos sluzheniia narodu,' *LiZh*, 27 November 1961, 1–2.
79 'Brat'ia Ershovy vedut boi,' *LiZh*, 3 September 1958, 1–3; 'Takoi zhe zhivoi, smelyi,' *LiZh*, 28 December 1962, 2.
80 Ibid.
81 'Goriacho i talantlivo,' *LiZh*, 22 November 1961, 3.
82 Zezina, while dismissing the aesthetic worth of his works, concedes that readers did like them (Zezina, *Sovetskaia*, 281).
83 RGALI 1572/1/228/119–20, 150–1, 162–3; see letter to *Novyi mir* in a similar vein: RGALI 1702/8/738/8–11.
84 Ibid., l. 67.

85 Ibid., l. 70.
86 Ibid., ll. 20–1.
87 RGALI 1572/1/228/72–82, 94–101, 119–24.
88 Ibid., ll. 53–5, 152, 94, 72–5, 82, 83, 123.
89 Ibid., ll. 95–9.
90 RGALI 1572/1/95/33–8, 40–4, 69–73, 74–6.
91 Ibid., ll. 40–4; see also ll. 69–73.
92 RGALI 1572/1/228/150–1.
93 Aleksandr Tvardovskii, 'Iz rabochikh tetradei,' *Znamia* 8 (1989): 179.
94 RGALI 2464/1/355/12, 21, 30, 59.
95 E.g., Zezina, *Sovetskaia*, 281. Complaint that 'no-one entirely positive about Kochetov's new novel' in 'Pafos sluzheniia narodu,' *LiZh*, 27 November 1961, 1–2.
96 'Snariazhenie v pokhode,' *Novyi mir* 1 (1962): 219–39. See Lakshin, *Novyi mir*, 52.
97 RGALI 1702/8/738/55–6.
98 Ibid., l. 93.
99 Ibid., l. 40.
100 Ibid., l. 100.
101 Ibid., l. 53; see ibid., ll. 45–6.
102 Lakshin, *Novyi mir*, 57.
103 RGALI 1702/10/251/21; RGALI 1702/10/252/23–31.
104 Aleksandr Tvardovskii, 'Rabochie tetradi 60-kh godov,' *Znamia* 6 (2000), entry for 27 May 1961; Tvardovskii, *Znamia* 11 (2000), entry for 22 March 1964.
105 K. Chukovsky, *Diary: 1901–69* (New Haven, 2005), 478; Lakshin, *Novyi mir*, 119.
106 Barbara Walker, 'On Reading Soviet Memoirs: A History of the "Contemporaries" Genre,' *Russian Review* 59, no. 3 (2000): 327–52.
107 Evgenii Evtushenko, *A Precocious Autobiography* (Harmondsworth, UK, 1965), 97, 121.
108 Chukovsky, *Diary*, 462.
109 Solzhenitsyn, *Oak and Calf*, 122.
110 Aleksandr Tvardovskii, 'Rabochie tetradi 60-kh godov,' *Znamia* 11 (2000), entry for 3 April 1961; Lakshin, *Novyi mir*, 124, 132, 57.
111 Lakshin, *Novyi mir*, 26, 47, 124, 132; Aleksandr Tvardovskii, 'Rabochie tetradi,' *Znamia* 9 (2000), entry for 29 November 1963.
112 *Apparat TsK i kul'tura. 1953–1957. Dokumenty* (hereafter *Apparat TsK, 1953–1957*) (Moscow, 2001) 218–22, 228–48, 364–5, 269, 328, 331–5.
113 RGALI 8132/1/9/2; *Apparat TsK, 1958–64*, 137–50.

114 *Apparat TsK, 1958–64*, 102–5.
115 Ibid.; RGALI 2464/1/355/3, 56, 80.
116 Ibid., ll. 6–7, 9–11, 46, 49, 53–4.
117 Ibid., l. 9. See critical review in *Novyi mir* accusing Kochetov of 'irritation and nervousness' in assessing the Thaw. 'Zametki kritika,' *Novyi mir* 11 (1958), 234–6.
118 RGALI 2464/1/355/102–5, 114–17.
119 E.g., Lakshin, *Novyi mir*, 168.
120 RGALI 2938/2/45/320, 325; TsAOPIM 8132/1/41/119. See also film director Mikhail Romm's attack on *Oktiabr'* 'absolutely inadmissible tone of political denunciation' reminiscent of 'articles published 15 years ago,' in Johnson, *Krushchev and the Arts*, 99; and *Apparat TsK, 1958–64*, 560.
121 Vera Panova in 1954 had objected to Kochetov's 'rude, supercilious, absolutely RAPP-ist' tone (*Apparat TsK, 1953–57*, 221). Other allegations in TsAOPIM 8132/1/41/119–23; RGALI 2738/2/45/325.
122 RGALI 1572/1/228/99–101, 119–20, 124–7; RGALI 1572/1/1/21, 24, 40–4; Lakshin, *Novyi mir*, 91.
123 RGALI 1572/1/228/84–5.
124 RGALI 1572/1/228/91.
125 RGALI 2938/2/5 contains numerous complaints and requests to leave the editorial board from liberal writers claiming mistreatment by editor Pozdniaev; see RGALI 2938/2/4/114–21; TsAOPIM 8132/1/41/174.
126 The press frequently discussed the aggressive nature of Stalin-era criticism (e.g., *LG* 8 January 1963, 22 January 1963).
127 *Apparat TsK, 1958–64*, 117.
128 Ibid., 116.
129 RGALI 2464/1/355/28, 52, 65.
130 RGALI 1702/8/738/30–3, 45–6, 53, 85–7, 88–9.
131 *Apparat TsK, 1958–64*, 116.
132 See also Boris Polevoi's complaint to the Central Committee in December 1958 about *Literaturnaia gazeta* and its 'unethical' biases, particularly in favour of Kochetov's works. Ibid., 137–48.
133 Lakshin, *Novyi mir*, 53–4, 193; Aleksandr Tvardovskii, 'Rabochie tetradi 60-kh godov,' *Znamia* 9 (2000), entry for 28 November 1963; Lakshin, *Novyi mir*, 193; Chukovsky, *Diary*, 462, 478.
134 'Snariazhenie v pokhode.'
135 *Apparat TsK, 1958–64*, 489; TsAOPIM 8132/1/36/80–3, 109, 115; RGALI 1702/8/728/9–11.
136 RGALI 1702/8/738/30–3.
137 Ibid., ll. 85–7.

138 Ibid., l. 81.

139 Reference to the *Sofronovshchina*, e.g., TsAOPIM 8132/1/6/59. For plentiful evidence of Sofronov's and Gribachev's leading roles, see A. Borshchagovskii, *Zapiski balovnia sud'by* (Moscow, 1991), 78, 101, 106–7; G. Kostyrchenko, *Out of the Red Shadows: Anti-Semitism in Stalin's Russia* (Amherst, NY, 1995), 153–78; *Stalin i kosmopolitizm. Dokumenty agitpropa TsK KPSS, 1945–53* (Moscow, 2005).

140 *Apparat TsK, 1953–57*, 167–9, 174–7; Hosking, *Rulers and Victims*, 349; Zezina, 'Crisis'; Zezina, *Sovetskaia*, 147–5; Sensitivity, and sensationalism, of charges of anti-Semitism visible in e.g., Chukovsky, *Diary*, 394.

141 TsAOPIM 8132/1/6/59, 85; TsAOPIM 8132/1/7/122–3, 133. The resolution of this 1956 meeting named Gribachev and Sofronov as culprits and charged them with *rasprava*. Ibid., l. 168.

142 TsAOPIM 8132/1/6/63, 66, 110; TsAOPIM 8132/1/7/ 55, 67; see similarly mixed explanations in Borshchagovskii, *Zapiski*.

143 RGALI 1702/10/86/45.

144 *Apparat TsK, 1958–64*, 84–7.

145 Johnson, *Krushchev and the Arts*, 95–101.

146 *Apparat TsK, 1958–64*, 621–2 (party response to writers' letter); quotation from ibid., 555–6.

147 Ibid., 555–6.

148 Ibid., 621–3. On Khrushchev's policies on anti-Semitism, see Mitrokhin, *Russkaia partiia*, esp. 165–8.

149 Chukovsky, *Diary*, 409, 462, 477–8; Aleksandr Tvardovskii, 'Rabochie tetradi 60-kh godov,' *Znamia* 11 (2000), entry for 1 March 1964. This was a widespread liberal accusation (Hayward and Crowley, *Soviet Literature*, 188).

150 See the Gribachev and Sofronov chapters in *Vospominaniia o Vsevolode Kochetove*.

151 RGALI 1702/8/738/79, 85–7.

152 This point about the definitional complexity of Stalinism, especially late Stalinism, is raised in Hayward and Crowley, *Soviet Literature*, 187–9; and Kiril Tomoff, *Creative Union: The Professional Organization of Soviet Composers, 1939–1953* (Ithaca, NY, 2006), 152–89.

153 Aleksandr Iashin, *Sobranie sochinenii v trekh tomakh* (Moscow, 1986), 3:354.

154 Evtushenko, *Precocious Autobiography*, 122.

155 E.g., Spechler, *Permitted Dissent*.

156 Hayward and Crowley, *Soviet Literature*, 187, 196; Johnson, *Krushchev and the Arts*, 2, 7; *Problems of Communism* 1 (1963): 57–8.

157 E.g., *Apparat TsK, 1958–64*, 229, 474–91; 'Iskusstvo geroicheskoi epokhi,' *Kommunist* 10 (1964): 25–48.

158 TsAOPIM 8132/1/41/117.
159 Solzhenitsyn, *Oak and Calf*, 121–2.
160 Aleksandr Tvardovskii, 'Rabochie tetradi 60-kh godov,' *Znamia* 9 (2000), entry for 28 November 1963; Chukovsky, *Diary*, 462–3.
161 Chukovsky, *Diary*, 462.
162 Ibid., 480.
163 Ibid., 478.
164 Sense of betrayal by authorities in Lakshin, *Novyi mir*, 193; on intelligentsia solidarity and support, see ibid., 200–2, 209.
165 Denis Kozlov, 'The Readers of *Novyi mir*, 1945–70: Twentieth-Century Experience and Soviet Historical Consciousness' (PhD diss., University of Toronto, 2005).
166 Lakshin, *Novyi mir*, 209, 217.

PART TWO

Looking Forward

7 From White Grave to Tselinograd to Astana: The Virgin Lands Opening, Khrushchev's Forgotten First Reform

MICHAELA POHL

In 1954 new Soviet leader Nikita Khrushchev announced his first reform initiative, the Virgin Lands Program, a possible solution to the country's grain problems by cultivating unused and fallow land in Kazakhstan and Siberia. The region received massive investments, and the people who lived there (Kazakhs, Russians, deported Germans, deported people from the Caucasus, and former Gulag inmates) along with the volunteers sent by Khrushchev built a new political, economic, and cultural hub in northern Kazakhstan. They transformed Akmolinsk (1832–1961), an unknown railroad and Gulag outpost, into the capital of the Virgin Lands (it was called Tselinograd from 1961 to 1992). This makeover was one of the main successes of the Virgin Lands campaign. By the 1960s, the small steppe city whose name had been rumoured to mean 'white grave,' became a major centre of communications, transport, and light industry. After some initial conflicts, the mixed regional population found a consensus built on modest prosperity and a multicultural regional identity.[1] Many took advantage of the institutes of higher education that opened in the region. The Virgin Lands opening as a political and development process helped foster practical and independent thinking, bring forth skilled leaders, and investment in the institutions suitable for a capital city. More than any other factor, this laid the foundation for Tselinograd's transformation into President Nazarbaev's Astana, the national capital of post-communist independent Kazakhstan.

Khrushchev's first reform played a key role in the development of Kazakhstan, but it remains unrecognized and the least discussed of his many initiatives. It may be for this reason that many observers have been confused about President Nazarbaev's motives for moving the Kazakh capital. The connection between Tselinograd and Astana has been ob-

German youths in the Virgin Lands. Family archive, reproduced with permission.

An old Kazakh woman and her German neighbour in a former Virgin Lands sovkhoz. Photograph by the author. Used with permission.

scured in part by the fact that the city was called 'Akmola' for a few interim years (1992–8). Mainly we did not notice Tselinograd and all that it implied because during the Cold War years Western understanding of the Khrushchev period and its reforms was so limited to the study of Soviet leadership politics. The predominant view simply followed Brezhnev-era communist bosses in presenting the Virgin Lands as a failed 'hare-brained scheme.' In late 1997, when dozens of journalists went to Astana to cover Kazakhstan's new capital, many of them still relied on stereotypical views of the Virgin Lands as 'failed' and 'disastrous.'[2] They could hardly have concluded differently from Western Cold War literature, which dismissed the project as an 'attack on the agro-political front' in the Stalinist spirit, used by Khrushchev primarily as a 'forum for factional self-aggrandizement,'[3] or to 'bring himself into the limelight.'[4] Most Western authors continually repeated three stereotypes about the Virgin Lands: that those so-called volunteers were enlisted by 'semi-compulsory methods,'[5] that the project was a colonial policy that ran counter to the interests of the Kazakhs,[6] and that it failed to produce grain and led to disastrous dust storms.[7]

Yet the only Soviet-era monograph on the topic actually comes to a more balanced conclusion, as does the standard Western text on Kazakh history. Martin McCauley, who studied the sources available in the 1970s, argued that the project performed 'impressively' in grain production.[8] Martha Olcott, while drawing attention to Moscow's intense pressure on the Kazakh Communist Party and to the displacement of Kazakhs from allegedly 'empty' lands, did conclude that the project helped form a new Kazakh elite while integrating the Kazakh republic into the Soviet economy and the Kazakh party into the all-Union party organization.[9] Zhores Medvedev recognized the Virgin Lands program as 'a lasting success' among Khrushchev's many 'reorganization blunders.'[10] Western authors could not see the social implications, and only Roy and Zhores Medvedev noticed that it took place in regions with large populations of 'deported nations.'[11]

Astana was known as Tselinograd for decades, and its historical identity was determined by stereotypes about the Virgin Lands created under Brezhnev, during the 1970s. When I did field research there in the 1990s, public memory of the *tselina* (Virgin Lands) and what my respondents were able to articulate of it had been reduced to a few stock images of backward Kazakhs and heroic Russian settlers, making it difficult to critically examine what really happened. The official Virgin Lands legend totally obscured other aspects of the past and the complex nature of society in Kazakhstan when the settlers arrived. Only a few years before the *tselina* started, Kazakhstan had suffered a catastrophic famine caused by mass collectivization. Then the NKVD covered it with a web of labour camps to house millions of people deported under Stalin, especially Germans, Chechens, and Ingush.[12] Although officially the party sent the Virgin Lands settlers to 'empty' steppes, they actually encountered numerous victims of Stalin's terror. Their presence and the repressive legacy of the Stalin era in Kazakhstan meant that the *tselina* confronted Stalinism long before Khrushchev's 'secret speech.'

Khrushchev's First Reform

When Khrushchev became first secretary of the Communist Party in September 1953, he used his speech at the Central Committee's September Plenum to outline the approach that would shape the Soviet Union's agricultural policy for the next decade.[13] He introduced two major long-term policies: relieving the economic pressure on the peasantry, while improving political control over collective farms and machine tractor stations. Anticipating Gorbachev's glasnost by thirty years, Khrushchev also encouraged limited discussion of economic problems. Indeed, the Central Committee plenum was opened to dozens of guests, mostly agricultural specialists and managers.[14] Khrushchev's report on the condition of agriculture was highly critical of Stalin-era policies and their outcomes. He presented previously secret data about herd sizes and harvests that showed that the countryside had been ruined by collectivization and emptied of livestock.

The agricultural reforms announced at the September plenum were a major reversal of Stalin's anti-peasant policy, even if they left the institutional structures of collectivization intact. But if the state was to avoid the most oppressive forms of agricultural exploitation in the future, some other way had to be found to solve the chronic food crisis. The stenographic record of the plenum discussion shows that Khrushchev was not impressed with Zhumabai Shaiakhmetov, the party chief of Kazakhstan, because the Kazakh leader did not know much about the current livestock situation in his republic.[15] Khrushchev claimed that Shaiakhmetov withheld data about the amount of potentially arable land in Kazakhstan and that he 'kept arguing for a more modest goal.'[16] In his memoir, Khrushchev also stated that the plenum made a commitment to expand the area sown with grain by eight to ten million hectares. The published resolution does not mention any specific amount, only the goal to expand durum wheat production in southeast Russia, Kazakhstan, and Siberia.

Cultivating the Regional Party

Preparations for the new program started immediately. Khrushchev ordered Shaiakhmetov and the first secretaries of Kazakhstan's northern regions to present detailed plans to open new lands and develop agriculture in their region by 8 November 1953.[17] He asked for separate sets of plans so that the leadership in Alma-Ata would not water down the regional proposals. The republican leaders were to base their estimate on the regional proposals, not the other way round. A power struggle now ensued between the regions and Alma-Ata. According to the memoirs of Nikolai Zhurin, the party chief from Akmola *oblast'* (region) and one of Khrushchev's most enthusiastic supporters, leaders in Alma-Ata wanted the northern leaders to under-report the amount of arable land in their region – precisely what Khrushchev had hoped to avoid.[18]

The Kazakh Central Committee *biuro* (bureau) passed a number of agriculture-related resolutions after the September plenum, but none about opening new lands. Instead, local plenums and meetings held to disseminate plenum decisions focused primarily on the effort to create regional instructors' groups. In October and November the Alma-Ata leadership issued resolutions blaming, in the best Stalinist manner, the primary party organizations for discussing the September policies only 'formally' and 'shallowly.'[19]

In late November Shaiakhmetov presented a plan calling for a 2.5 million hectare increase in cultivated lands.[20] In the meantime, Khrushchev had invited a number of party leaders and agricultural specialists from north Kazakhstan to Moscow. The more enthusiastic participants offered proposals that were far in excess of what the republican leadership considered possible. Zhurin's proposal, for example, called for an increase of 2.84 million hectares in that region alone. The *oblast'* leadership estimated that in the period 1954–60 they would need about 71,000 workers, including 60,000 sent from other regions.[21] The Kazakh leaders dismissed the huge proposals as 'fantastic' and 'unrealizable' and argued that roads and grain elevators should be built before starting such a massive project.[22]

On 22 January 1954, Khrushchev proposed opening thirteen million hectares over the next two years.[23] He argued that the virgin lands of Siberia and Kazakhstan could yield 800–900 million poods[24] of grain. At this rate, investments of about six billion (old) rubles would be returned within a year. Opening the Virgin Lands would also allow the state to reduce its demands on central Russia and send aid to regions suffering from drought, without unduly depleting the state's grain reserves. Changing procurement practices would create material incentives to work harder, by allowing farmers to keep leftover grain for their own use.[25] Three days later, the Central Committee accepted his draft resolution and called a plenum devoted to the Virgin Lands question at the end of February.[26]

On 4 February 1954, Shaiakhmetov and his second-in-command were fired because they had 'underestimated the significance of the Virgin Lands opening.'[27] Former minister of culture Panteleimon Ponomarenko, a railroad engineer by training, became first secretary, while a young Leonid Brezhnev moved from first secretary in Moldova to second secretary in Kazakhstan. Their orders were to open 6.3 million hectares of new land and construct ninety-five new *sovkhozy* (state farms). Ponomarenko and Brezhnev oversaw the formation of a new state farms department and a department of procurements in the Kazakhstan Central Committee, along with new state farm departments in each Virgin Lands region. Full-time party secretaries were appointed to each of the new state farms, and the district committees were instructed to form inspectors' groups.[28] Ponomarenko flew to Akmolinsk on 10 February to announce the leadership changes to the city party organization.[29] An 'extraordinary' Seventh Congress of the Kazakh Communist Party was convened on 16–18 February to formalize the new policies.

Khrushchev's approach to the party organization in Kazakhstan was dual: he coerced or replaced the Alma-Ata–based party bosses, because they showed no interest in the resources of northern Kazakhstan. In the regions, he allowed a little bit of glasnost, and this in turn fired up real enthusiasm in those organizations, because the truth was that when administered efficiently the region could produce a very high yield. The agricultural labour camps and special farms established in the 1930s and 1940s and run by the NKVD-MVD in Akmola *oblast'* and in Karaganda had been quite successful. But in the rest of the region, the situation was grim. At the October 1953 plenum of the Akmolinsk party, Zhurin read a sensational paper in which he reported that the state of agriculture in his region was nothing short of catastrophic.[30] Collective farmers there received no cash at all well into the 1950s, only up to half a kilo of grain for each labour-day, which was less than one-quarter of the official average earnings reported in Kazakhstan at that time.[31] Shepherds in outlying pastures were never paid in money, and they were unfamiliar with basic goods like flour, sugar, tea, and matches.[32] Most agricultural work was done by hand, even though mechanization had been one of the goals of collectivization. In the spirit of Khrushchev's new agricultural glasnost, Zhurin presented statistics that showed that none of the major livestock herds had reached their pre-revolutionary size in 1953. The Kazakhs had been completely ruined by collectivization. Their horse herds, the mainstay of Kazakh households, remained at one-third of their pre-revolutionary size into the 1950s. Like Khrushchev, Zhurin did not mention the disappearance of people, but his listeners were stunned even by the livestock statistics revealed at the plenum. One participant stated, 'This is the first time that I am hearing a paper at the plenum in which some kind of analysis is given, and more fully, the kind with figures ... naming problems.'[33]

There was no pressing need to change the *oblast'* leadership in Akmolinsk in the spring of 1954. Zhurin and the other local leaders believed that great changes could be achieved with investments and machinery, and they were eager to see their backwater transformed. Major personnel turnovers came after the first Virgin Lands harvest, when performance had shown who was an efficient boss and who was not, and during the formation of the Virgin Lands *krai* (region) in the early 1960s.

New Arrivals and Old Residents

Khrushchev's main objective in the Virgin Lands was to grow wheat through 'technology plus people.' He would ship great numbers of workers, tractors, trucks, and harvesters to the 'empty' regions. Human labour was crucial to the undertaking, but workers were treated as an endlessly renewable resource. As a result, what started as a plan to resettle 100,000–200,000 people turned into a vast yearly labour mobilization when many workers quickly left as a result of the difficult conditions. Soon 100,000 new 'permanent' workers were needed *each* year, while up to half a million seasonal workers (about 300,000 Komsomols and students, and 100,000–200,000 soldiers) had to be mobilized for *each* harvest. The new workers were primarily from depressed areas of the western USSR and large cities: soldiers, young women, families, and prisoners.

Economic imperatives decided the ethnic composition of the workforce. Mechanized agriculture required a European workforce, so mainly Slavs were sent, despite loud proclamations that the 'whole country' was participating. Kazakh settlers displaced during the 1930s and wanting to return were ignored, because they were traditional livestock herders, and their skills were not needed on the *tselina*.[34]

The Virgin Lands region was hardly an empty swath of steppe. Khrushchev hoped to simultaneously expand the existing collective farms and special settlements. Nearly half of the 'new land' was opened in 'old' farms, bringing immediate economic relief to local villages. Yet this dimension is much less known, since local deportees like Germans, Chechens, or former prisoners never became part of the official Virgin Lands lore.

Hundreds of confrontations took place between arriving Virgin Landers and local people. The police and party records that I studied provide evidence of at least 135 separate violent crowd incidents in the Akmola region between 1954 and 1957.[35] The greatest number of group confrontations took place between *tselinniki* (Virgin Landers) and the Caucasian special settlers, the Chechens and Ingush, but dozens of *draki* (fistfights) and riots involved other national groups (Poles, Kazakhs, Germans), as well as soldiers, prisoners, Komsomols, construction workers, and even entire villages. Many of them were the kinds of cases that Vladimir Kozlov has termed 'Virgin Lands syndrome': the eruption of violence between locals and new arrivals because a 'flood of people torn from their customary social milieu poured into an unstable social environment characterized by weakened collective ties.'[36]

The police blamed the Virgin Landers for creating a hostile atmosphere and making locals afraid to go to local stores, cafeterias, dances, and movies. While deprivation and poor conditions may have increased the level of stress and competition for resources, confrontations actually increased when people had money to spend – especially on vodka. Most brawls involved single young men, but small-scale confrontations turned into riots or larger fights in district towns or Akmolinsk, where workers attending tractor courses lived in crowded dormitories or congregated at dances, parks, and clubs.

Most of the fights were about differing attitudes toward the Soviet regime, not ethnicity.[37] The *tselinniki* were unwilling to accept the deported or former prisoners and, as they had been taught, 'traitors' into their collective. Much of their daily anger was really directed against the authorities rather than their neighbours. The bosses used a heavy hand. Many of them got into drunken episodes that were more 'colourful' than those of the youth. They frequently came to blows with each other,[38] they beat Virgin Lands workers (one public prosecutor described the practice of physical punishment as 'widespread' in the local farms),[39] and they threatened the workers and locals with weapons. I recall my own surprise when I noticed in photos that the Virgin Lands directors wore revolvers on their belts. When I asked elderly Tselinograders about it, the men in particular were stunned that I had learned of this, and opened up about the fights. 'Why did your director carry a gun' turned out to be an excellent interview question, one that helped us talk with greater precision about the actual events of the past and set aside official language.

Not at Home: The Chechens and Ingush

The influx of the Virgin Landers coincided with a series of reforms of the exile system that started during the first Virgin Lands summer in 1954. At times, because of the fragmentary and hesitant way in which they were implemented, they led to great unrest among the special settlers, including periods of intense collective political and lobbying activities like letter-writing campaigns and demonstrations. Like the *tselina* itself, the timing of the reforms and the grass-roots political activities of the special settlers provide a distinct corrective to the notion of Khrushchev's 'secret speech' and the year 1956 as a great divide. On the contrary, one starts to see how necessary something like the speech became after years of unrest in the 'special' and Gulag regions. The number of complaint letters from exile was greatest in the two years immediately after Stalin's death, that is, in 1953 and 1954.[40] Such periods of heightened activity contributed to the outbreak of collective violence, as they caused the deportees to feel in turns greater hope and self-confidence – as well as frustration, when their efforts seemed blocked. It was clearly a period in which both they and the government were deeply engaged in redefining who belonged to the Soviet *kollektiv* (collective).

At the beginning of 1954, the special settler police counted 16,934 Chechens in the Akmola region, and 22,048 Ingush.[41] On 5 July 1954 the USSR Soviet of Ministers passed a decree that reduced the number of special settlers by a third at one stroke, by releasing all children and youth under sixteen and all students, regardless of their age, from their 'special' status. Along with these measures to reduce the numbers of special settlers came new regulations in July 1954 that eased the restrictions that the remaining deportees lived under. It became easier to travel and to change one's residence within the republic of exile. Fugitives' sentences were reduced from twenty to five years of hard labour, and the state essentially ceased to punish offenders. The numbers of actual convictions for fleeing from exile were reduced to nearly none, from over 8,000 in 1949 to 25 in 1954.[42] As soon as these new provisions were announced in December 1954, the Ingush and Chechens reacted. Many left rural areas for towns like Karaganda and Akmolinsk, in order to reunite with relatives or members of their *teip* (clan), and great streams of them began to leave the Virgin Lands areas altogether and to move to the south of Kazakhstan. Within two months, by February 1955, about 19,000 persons had left the northern regions.

The first really significant change in the political status of one of the deported national groups came with a decree of 13 December 1955, lifting the special regulations from the deported Germans. They received no compensation for their confiscated properties and did not receive the right to return to their former republics. The timing of this reform was linked to the visit of German chancellor Adenauer in Moscow in September 1955.[43] This change in the legal condition of the Germans caused great unrest and resentment among the remaining special settlers, especially the Muslims. Akmolinsk police reported that freeing the Germans had a 'negative effect' on the mood of the Chechen and Ingush.[44] To calm the remaining special settlers, in late 1955 instructions were issued to ease job restrictions and to improve access to education for the children of the remaining special settlers. These generated much paperwork and many reports, but little was actually done. An inspection group consisting of party and education ministry officials from Moscow and Almaty found that this resolution was routinely ignored in rural areas, including Akmola *oblast'*, and that the authorities continued to treat special settlers as 'second-class people,' while the Virgin Landers' relations with Caucasians frequently turned into 'open hostility.'[45]

On 16 July 1956, the Chechens and Ingush were finally freed from the provisions of the special regime. Their joy and the hope that they would be allowed to go home soon turned to dismay, as the authorities tried to force them to sign a release document stating that they waived all rights to their former property, and that they were aware that returning to their former home was forbidden.[46] In response, community and religious leaders organized a movement to prevent the signing of this paper.

A representative from the Kazakh Central Committee, who organized official meetings of Chechens and Ingush in the town of Makinsk to discuss the release, was surprised to find that he could find 'not one Chechen or Ingush' to speak in support of signing the release paper. Instead speakers denounced the procedure as undemocratic and the dissolution of their autonomous republic and confiscation of their property as illegal, and all demanded to be sent home.[47] Dozens of people began to travel to the Caucasus spontaneously, and altogether more than 7,000 Chechens and Ingush (of 17,032 adults remaining in this region) refused to sign in Akmola,[48] while in all of Kazakhstan over 35,000 people (of 200,000) refused to sign this release.[49]

The fall and winter of 1956–7 was an intense period. 1956 was the year of a record harvest in the Virgin Lands, and it was the year of Khrushchev' 'secret speech.' The harvest work brought tens of thousands of soldiers to the region, all the remaining special settlers were released from the *spetskomendatura* (special commandant's office), and in addition the labour camps were opened. Directly in the *oblast'* this affected about 8,000 women imprisoned in ALZhIR,[50] but the streams of former prisoners from the vast *KarLag* prison system were even greater. Akmolinsk and the district towns, especially Makinsk, became hotbeds of activity among the special settlers, as both Germans and Caucasians agitated to be allowed to go home. The Chechens and Ingush wrote a flood of letters and complaints, primarily to Khrushchev and the Central Committee, and to members of the Soviet government.[51]

The situation was becoming unmanageable and alarming. Chechen and Ingush men started showing up at the regional party committee building each day, asking for personal appointments with members of the local committee. Even in the countryside, collective farmers organized demonstrations and work stoppages in protest against their treatment, and demanding to be sent home. Many simply quit their jobs, sold their properties, and flocked to the train stations and towns of the region in great crowds. Periodically rumours spread about a 'special train' that would take all the Caucasians home. Most of the Chechens were waiting for the restoration of their republic, but dozens of groups began to travel to the Caucasus spontaneously. By October–November 1956, 80–100 tickets were sold to Caucasians in Akmolinsk *each day*, and they shipped hundreds of containers with their property, obviously not without some cooperation from local authorities.[52]

In December 1956, giving in to this massive pressure, the Central Committee passed a resolution that prepared the 'orderly' and 'gradual' repatriation of the Caucasians. Although this resolution was not published in the press, it was distributed immediately in the affected communities, to calm the volatile populations of north Kazakhstan. The Chechens and other small groups of people had autonomous *oblasts'* and republics restored to them in January 1957. Violent attacks on the Caucasians continued during this period, and they even became worse during the winter months of 1956–7.

The Chechen return home was not 'orderly.' In the Akmola region, train stations and railroad towns were swamped with streams of people for months. Republican and local authorities attempted to ease the pressure by announcing temporary stops on outmigration. This only brought more intense activity from the former deportees, including at least one 'large demonstration' in June 1957 by Chechens and Ingush in front of the regional party committee building, on the central square of Akmolinsk. In response, special representatives of the party leadership in Moscow, Alma-Ata, and Grozny (from the newly restored autonomous region) held a series of mass outdoor meetings in June 1957, in Akmolinsk, Makinsk, and Atbasar to discuss the situation.[53]

The German Virgin Landers

The Germans, who accommodated the larger goal of the Virgin Lands opening and who were praised often by the bosses, were not allowed to leave. On the contrary, the number of Germans grew: 71,442 Germans lived in the Akmolinsk region in 1954,[54] and by 1959 they made up 15.8 per cent of the *oblast'* population,[55] or about 100,000 of 633,000 inhabitants. Many of them initially did not see the *tselina* as 'home' and wanted to abandon it, either for their former places of settlement or for West Germany. On the surface of it, they used similar strategies as the Chechen and Ingush to accomplish their goal. Once they were taken off the special rolls, many individuals and families moved to larger towns within Kazakhstan to find employment, or they moved to reunite with relatives. At the height of the special settler reforms, roughly as many Germans moved about as did Caucasians. Like the latter, members of the German community wrote thousands of letters and complaints. Dozens of people from Akmolinsk travelled to Moscow personally, some with their own documents, while others went as couriers, with lists of names and letters from fellow villagers. Rumours spread that all Germans were supposed to be evacuated to West Germany. The authorities were very worried about the 'emigration mood,' as some among the Germans were quitting work and beginning to sell their houses and property.[56]

Unlike the Caucasians, however, the Germans did not refuse en masse to sign their release document, few of them took illegal actions of any kind (leaving the republic, participating in open demonstrations, getting involved in fights or crime), and they tended to bend to the russifying pressure of the surrounding environment, by attempting to 'blend in' and avoiding the use of the German language in public. Many of my informants told me that the use of German was 'illegal' (no such decree was ever issued) and that they were shamed into hiding their German identity by the use of the epithets *Fritzy* or *fashisty*. On the whole, the Germans were more committed to fitting into the Soviet collective and to not breaking the law, and this made it possible to keep them in the Virgin Lands. They were needed as the basic permanent workforce in the *tselina*, especially considering the substantial seasonal migration of Virgin Lands workers. Chechen, Ingush, and Kalmyks were considered 'half-wild' and 'more trouble than they were worth,' and thus they were allowed to go home.[57]

Worker Unrest

Workers in the Virgin Lands farms learned strategies to protest poor management, wages, and working and living conditions. These actions included 'individual' kinds of behaviour (absenteeism, quitting their jobs, slowing the pace of work), tactics like writing complaints and petitioning, and collective actions such as demonstrations, strikes, and violence.[58]

The behaviour of managers was a regular source of conflict. During 1954 and 1955, Komsomol officials reported that state farm bosses in the Akmola region were constantly drinking and rude towards the settlers, and they enjoyed acts of random and bureaucratic abuse, such as confiscating settlers' mail and passports and sending subordinates on frivolous errands. Several Komsomols perished in snowstorms, after being sent to find vodka.[59] 'Some of the managers do not treat the settler youth right,' wrote one complainant. 'They consider them loafers and drunkards, and they conduct their work with people on the basis of shouting, including the use of obscene language.'[60]

Central Committee advisors and plenipotentiaries from Moscow told the Akmola *oblast'* bosses that the Virgin Lands campaign required a new, dynamic approach to leadership. Instead, the *obkom* (regional party committee) managed 'through threats and warnings,' firing managers or denying them party membership when somebody needed to be punished. Local bosses called the process of having to appear at a session of the *obkom* bureau 'receiving a head washing,' 'going to the wall,' or 'getting one's mug polished.'[61] It is hardly surprising that the directors did not manage their subordinates any differently. Some workers resorted to violence.

By the summer of 1954, Akmola *oblast'* police officials reported at least twenty-five attacks directed at persons in authority, including state farm and MTS directors, accountants, and party and Komsomol secretaries.[62] Seven more attacks were noted in 1955, and another seven during 1956.[63] The attacks were carried out with knives, sticks, or bare fists, and in a few cases with firearms, but none fatal. The assailants were frequently intoxicated, and some had criminal records. Some demanded pay advances or releases from work. Others were responding to what they perceived as harassment or humiliation by workplace bosses. At the Kalachevskii state farm, for example, Director Klimentiev allegedly 'turned the entire collective against himself' and 'lost all authority.' The youth of the farm assured visiting inspectors from Moscow that they would drown Klimentiev in the Ishim River if he was not fired.[64]

However, after an initial wave of attacks in 1954, the directors were issued sidearms, and special security measures were taken for the harvest. The *oblast'* MVD forces were increased by forty-one additional officers, including seven posted at the *oblast'* grain elevators.[65] The attacks on farm bosses and party secretaries had ceased by July and August, possibly because of the harvest, and the initial wave of attacks did not recur in later years.

Virgin Lands workers wrote thousands of complaint letters to Soviet leaders and to newspapers. A few letters were anonymous, little more than denunciations, but most were signed by groups and work collectives. Between January and October 1955 the Akmola regional committee of the Komsomol received 600 letters and another 125 complaints transmitted in person, by phone, or by telegram.[66] The agriculture section of the All-Union Central Committee received about 100 letters from Kazakhstan each month – letters that were originally addressed to Khrushchev, Prime Minister Georgy Malenkov, Deputy Prime Minister Anastas Mikoian, Marshal Kliment Voroshilov, the Central Committee, and *Pravda*.[67]

The response to these complaints depended on where they landed. Overwhelmed by the flood of letters, the Akmolinsk Komsomol committee initially tried to ignore them, and piles of letters sat unanswered and unread.[68] The situation at the local party committee was similar, especially during the first months of the Virgin Lands project. During all of 1954, the Akmola *obkom* passed resolutions on only six written complaints. In two of the cases, people in authority (state farm directors, police officials) were fired, after investigations found severe cases of neglect and physical mistreatment.[69] Other letters led to citations and reprimands for 'neglectful-bureaucratic' and 'sloppy' attitudes toward the settlers. Some of the letters addressed to Khrushchev and the Central Committee were rerouted back to Akmola but monitored, including complaints about extreme neglect, heavy-handedness, and incompetence, rather than routine complaints about food shortages or housing difficulties. These letters had the greatest chance of getting serious attention, because the regional party committee was forced to take action and report back to Moscow. In October 1954 the head of the Akmola regional agriculture administration was reprimanded and several of his subordinates fired when an investigation showed that their office treated letters from workers and potential volunteers with 'criminal neglect.'[70]

Collective trips to party and Komsomol committees to confront people in authority in person were the most efficient means of complaint, but only for the very bravest. In one case an entire tractor brigade travelled from Aryktinskii state farm to Akmolinsk to complain about the poor organization of labour at their farm; their case was later discussed at the party plenum.[71] Two youths who worked in a construction unit at the Moskovskii state farm took the train all the way to Moscow and presented their complaint directly to the Komsomol Central Committee after written complaints – and pummelling the supervisor – had no effect. Their grievances included hunger, drunken bosses, corruption, pay problems, and refusals to work. Shelepin dispatched an investigator, who held meetings and arranged for food and medical supplies. Her efforts led to a number of firings and a complete revision of wages paid at the farm.[72]

Rural party officials lumped everything they did not like about the newcomers together, including the way they looked, their general brashness toward bosses, and their proclivity for collective protests. In particular, they did not like students from Moscow:

> Drinking and debauches, rampant vulgarities, and collective trips to the district party and Komsomol committees in search of the 'truth' take up the lion's share of the district authorities' time. We have barbershops in every state farm, but the majority of the volunteers from Moscow don't cut their hair or shave, they don't wash their hands and face. In one case [a teacher] came to a meeting in swimming trunks. Some of the youth, infected by foreign styles, call the management staff 'chief,' 'Sir,' 'boss,' 'local powers,' as if they had come to the district from a foreign country.... The volunteers from Stavropol', Brest, and Alma-Ata have achieved great successes in labour, but we have formed the worst opinion about half of the Muscovites.... That's supposed to be the working class? We don't understand where they found them.[73]

The workers in the Virgin Lands learned to go on strike. On 14 July 1955, for example, workers in the brick and lime workshops of the *Stalinstroi* construction organization organized a 'mass absence from work' because of food shortages. The following day, the strike spread to workers in the concrete workshops and housing construction units.[74] The authorities took seriously any incidents that threatened to cross the line between 'making demands' and 'striking,' and sent the KGB to investigate potentially political activities. A group of eighteen youth from Moldova began to avoid work soon after their arrival at a construction unit within *Akmolinskstroi.* When their requests for work in their specialty, higher pay, and normal living conditions were refused, they demanded the return of their passports and releases from work. The administration refused and put them to work as unskilled labourers. Four of the group then went on strike, covering their tent with painted caricatures of their bosses and slogans such as 'Don't touch us,' 'Hunger strike,' and 'Give us our passports.' KGB investigators characterized the writings as 'apolitical' and reported that they were working to 'turn around the unhealthy mood' among the remaining youth.[75]

By 1959 the enthusiasm of the workers had evaporated, and a number of youth planned to march to the *obkom* to protest living conditions at *Kazakhsel'mash* and the construction trusts. Their plan was described in an anonymous letter that spoke of 'strong discontent' among the young workers in Akmolinsk and denounced their plan as a 'conspiracy.' This case led the *obkom* to inspect living conditions in the dormitories in Akmolinsk, which revealed filth, hazing of newcomers, and more evidence of 'unhealthy moods' among the youth. Sergei Girich, a young metal worker at *Akmolinskstroi*, reportedly declared, 'The Russian *muzhik* can be oppressed, and oppressed, and he'll bear it – but finally he'll stand up, he'll rise up, and nothing can hold up against him.... The Russian bore it all until 1917, and then he destroyed the tsar, the landowners, and the capitalists. And who do the workers need to overthrow now?' Girich answered this question himself, naming the current head of the Soviet government.[76]

Such open and desperate threats against the regime were exceptional, and the large demonstration that some of the youth talked about apparently never materialized. However, small-scale collective actions to improve the situation at one farm or factory were common in northern Kazakhstan. Local collective farmers and townspeople were often swept up in the spreading conflict. Several major riots in Akmola *oblast'* broke out because the local men stood up to the Virgin Lands violence, whatever its cause, and took matters into their own hands. One such episode took place in the village of Krasnosel'skoe (Molotov district) in November 1956, after an exhausting – but record – harvest. As many as 10,000 soldiers from assorted army units were brought in to help with the harvest. Clashes between the soldiers and locals took several lives and injured scores of people.[77] After a few particularly brutal beatings and attacks on German and Ukrainian youth, the villagers rioted for three days, with the result that ten grain trucks were completely destroyed, and traffic to the local grain elevator was disrupted.[78]

These collective actions were almost entirely 'forgotten' locally when I talked to people in the 1990s. People in Kazakhstan saw a lot of wild behaviour over the years. They tended to uncritically lump together 'Muscovites' and 'hooligans,' and no one thought to celebrate their actions as a kind of resistance. Ultimately, the remote location of the state farms and the relatively small concentrations of workers prevented massive strikes and confrontations in the Virgin Lands that could threaten the regime, such as in East Germany or Hungary in the 1950s. The commissions sent to investigate complaints often did little more than 'fix' things for a few days. When they left, conditions returned to 'normal,' and things could get tricky for the complainers. All the same, the flood of complaints, and the many different tactics used to deliver them and make them count, forced the authorities to act at least in some cases and gradually built up higher-than-average expectations as well as a more disciplined workforce.

The Party Confronts the Problems

The Virgin Lands project also transformed the Kazakh Communist Party. Large sections in it came to be controlled more directly by Moscow in the interests of working more efficiently. When the campaign started, the Akmola party organization received instructions from both the All-Union Central Committee and the Kazakh Central Committee. The most important orders were transmitted verbally and personally, either over the telephone or during visits by Central Committee plenipotentiaries or instructors. Less important matters were relayed as written or telegraphed instructions. Resolutions passed at party plenums or at bureau sessions of the Central Committees in Moscow and Alma-Ata were accompanied by long lists detailing the concrete measures to be taken and who should carry them out. Often the operative instructions came well in advance of the formal resolutions, as with the entire Virgin Lands project. Personnel changes, for example, nearly always took effect weeks or months before the formal election of a new local party secretary.During the first Virgin Lands years, the Akmola region was divided into nine zones, each with its own permanent Central Committee plenipotentiary. But from the outset it was made clear that the local party was supposed to take the initiative to mobilize resources and resolve problems. If such initiatives were lacking, criticisms would appear in the press to spur the regional organization to greater efforts and to set an example for others. Just days after the February–March Plenum passed its Virgin Lands resolution, for instance, an article in the national newspaper *Pravda* criticized the regional party newspaper, *Akmolinskaia pravda*, for not preparing for the new policy in January and February 1954. The Akmola *obkom* was then forced to acknowledge this criticism as 'perfectly justified' and ordered the local newspaper to show greater discipline and to begin covering the Virgin Lands more systematically.[79] In May 1954 *Pravda* singled out the Akmola region in an article criticizing the slowness of the spring sowing campaign in the Virgin Lands regions. The very next day the local *obkom* passed a resolution promising to improve in this area.[80]

The *obkom* passed instructions and criticisms on to the regional and district organizations that were directly responsible for carrying out assigned tasks, such as the newly formed Akmolinsk and Atbasar state farm trusts, the regional agriculture, trade, and health organizations, the district party organizations, etc. Most of them were reactive, criticizing slowness and inactivity, pointing out tasks that had been not been carried out, like organizing tractor brigades, relocating machinery and trailers to sites, transporting fuel, and procuring consumer items.[81]

The *obkom* also issued warnings, reprimands, and reminders that those in authority bore 'full personal responsibility' for the work. Subordinate managers were regularly summoned to Akmolinsk to 'discuss' their shortcomings.[82] The Kazakh Central Committee apparently played a minor role, issuing very few resolutions relating to the Virgin Lands during the first years.[83]

The *obkom* tried to get the party district committees to work more efficiently and to focus on ploughing new lands. The district committees were supposed to send more communists to work in the farms and to provide active onsite leadership, but *raikom* (district party committee) instructors often interfered with economic decision-making and ended up taking over entirely for MTS directors and collective farm chairmen.[84] When the plan to plough 500,000 hectares in the farms of the Atbasar trust by 1 June 1954 was endangered, for example, the *obkom* stepped in with 'five-day assignments.'[85]

Input from Below

The *tselina* brought a noticeable democratization at party meetings and conferences, and especially during local party plenums. Before 1954, only party secretaries and members of the regional *nomenklatura* (key administrators) took part in plenum discussions. As soon as the Virgin Lands opening began, a great number of economic managers, members of the regional executive committee, the representatives of ministries, and even brigade leaders, tractor drivers, and other workers were invited to listen to the discussions and to present speeches. The general topics, speakers, and reports had to be cleared with the Central Committee in Alma-Ata prior to the event, but the subsequent debate and responses were not controlled entirely from above.[86] Meeting minutes reveal lively language, numerous interruptions, and arguments, and several investigations were launched after lower-ranking guest speakers complained about particularly grim problems at their farms.[87] The discussions that took place at the plenums of the *obkom* during the early Virgin Lands years (especially 1954–7) were so open and confrontational compared to the periods before and after that the stenogram records of these meetings were marked 'top secret.'

At the Fourth Akmola Party Plenum in November 1954 the party secretary of the Kievskii state farm, Kabaziev, accused the *obkom* of neglecting his farm; apparently an inspector came for a short visit but asked few questions, could not to answer any of the questions asked of him, and disappeared, never to be heard from again. Kabaziev also criticized the local *raikom*, whose secretary snapped, 'We don't hold seminars here' when Kabaziev asked what kind of activities to organize for the October holiday.[88] The secretaries of the state farm party cells were frequently criticized as undisciplined 'time-servers' who ended up in their posts 'by accident.'[89] The *obkom* practice of managing the directors through 'threats and warnings' came under fire at a party conference in December 1955. Citing the popular expressions describing what happened when directors were hauled before an *obkom* bureau session, Molotov district party secretary Serov complained, 'This is a form of leadership that has outlived its usefulness.... What is required are not head washings and threats, but businesslike demands from the party.... There should be fewer citations to the regional centre ... instead the members of the *obkom* bureau should go out to the sites. That would be significantly more useful.'[90] Similar criticisms of the new *obkom* and of the leaders of the agricultural administration in Akmolinsk came up at the June 1956 plenum: 'Some of [these leaders] relate to people from the districts callously, inattentively, without showing the proper respect. For some reason they think that only they are the guardians of the interests of the party, the people, and of the Soviet government, while their subordinates supposedly don't share these interests.'[91]

One of the most outspoken and revealing moments of criticism came at a party plenum in early 1957. P.A. Lysov, a former *obkom* secretary, alleged that the superior harvest of 1956 had made the current *oblast'* party leadership 'dizzy with success' and that the rudeness and haughtiness in the party's leadership methods stemmed from the management style of the new top secretaries, Borodin and Belov. He accused Borodin of ignoring others' advice and the principle of collegiality, instead ruling by giving orders and repressing criticism: 'Comrades! There used to be a time when unpopular and useless people were physically destroyed. That is not allowed now, they don't dare any longer. But you, comrades Borodin and Belov, you don't have the right to destroy people morally.... I'm not accusing [Borodin and Belov] of their own cult of personality, although there is an element of this cult [in their behaviour].... The main thing is that they forgot about collegiality, about the resolutions of the Twentieth Party Congress.'[92]

Lysov's remarks about 'destroying people morally' referred to his own dismissal as an *obkom* secretary. Apparently he had made himself a nuisance with constant criticism and was forced to take another job after being branded 'politically unreliable' and being 'advised to leave' through ominous questions about his health and hints that he should take a vacation.[93] Lysov's replacement, G.A. Mel'nik, decided not to punish Lysov for his speech, because 'hardly anyone would want to speak openly after that.' In a subsequent closed session, most of the party bosses dismissed Lysov's speech as a rant by a disgruntled former colleague, although some audience members were very receptive to his presentation.[94]

Cadre Turnover

Local party members had no influence on appointments to the top jobs in the region, which were made officially by the secretariat of the Kazakh party organization in Alma-Ata, in consultation with Moscow. After six years, Zhurin was formally removed in March 1956 (he actually left his post in late 1955). He survived in this enormously difficult job twice as long as the average tenure of regional party chiefs in the Soviet Union in the 1939–56 period.[95] A persistent rumour that Zhurin had 'compromised' himself somehow was put to rest at a party conference in 1958, when numerous written questions about this matter prompted an announcement that Zhurin had done nothing wrong but had been sent to another region because his leadership 'did not measure up to the demands that are now made of Kazakhstan.'[96] In the following years the region saw a rapid succession of party chiefs: Borodin (March 1956–March 1957), G.A. Mel'nik (March 1957–January 1958), and S.M. Novikov (January 1958 until the *krai* was formed in December 1960).[97]

Worker flight triggered the turnover. From 1954 to 1956, the *obkom* issued dozens of resolutions relating to the living conditions and conflicts at Virgin Lands farms, and it dealt with newspaper articles critical of the Akmola party organization and its treatment of the settlers.[98] The most striking thing about these resolutions is how repetitious they were, describing the same neglect of the settlers everywhere. Many of them mentioned the 'justified discontent' of the settlers. The huge lists of tasks in these resolutions, which ordered every organization in the region to improve every single aspect that needed fixing in the shortest possible time, were not realistic and were mainly for Moscow's consumption. The real work fell to Komsomol instructors and party officials who actually visited the sites and were expected to solve hundreds of operative or practical problems.

Brezhnev told a 1955 plenum in Akmolinsk that wherever he went in the region, he was surrounded and followed by crowds of desperate workers. The widespread 'loss of respect for superiors' that he had encountered undermined the program. Brezhnev urged the local party organization to change the way they treat the settlers:

> You give them bad water to drink, awful water, with clay sediments. Just that alone causes thousands of complaints and letters, which are all being sent to the CC of the party, and they're sent home, to relatives and friends. Some of them write straight out, 'It's all right, I'll live through it until fall, and then I'll leave this forced labour [*katorga*].' It's chilling to read these letters.... You have to realize that we have a new branch of the working class and a new *intelligentsiia* here, people that one needs to work with. You have to pay attention to them, to their living conditions.... Those are not simple questions, but very difficult ones, and you need to work [to resolve them].... Coming for short visits, taking down a few figures and collecting reports, delegating something – that's not work.[99]

Food shortages had ended largely by 1956, but attention to the settlers' problems did not get better between 1957 and 1959. Regional bosses became indifferent to the number of people streaming in and out of the region.[100] Housing and other construction quotas went unfulfilled year after year, and the turnover in construction labour was extremely high (80–100 per cent of the workforce annually was not unusual).[101] By the time the topic was raised at the Fifth Plenum in 1957, the catastrophically slow pace of housing construction was acknowledged as the main obstacle to keeping people on the *tselina.* The main speaker at the local plenum on housing was a Central Committee secretary from Alma-Ata, who blamed the construction bosses personally for waste, widespread theft, black market sales of construction materials, and other corrupt practices.[102] Year after year, their output was extremely low and shoddy, while administrative and overhead costs were huge. Conditions for construction workers were considerably worse than for other occupations.[103]

At this point, the party and the Komsomol started to study the problem of outmigration seriously. They focused entirely on the most important workers – the tractor drivers and mechanics needed for agricultural equipment called 'mechanizers' in Soviet parlance. By all accounts the situation was similar across northern Kazakhstan. Teams sent to study *oblast'* and state farm records in the late 1950s reported that 60–90 per cent of mechanizers were leaving each year, and only in 'rare cases' did about half the workforce stay.[104] In Kustanai, for instance, fewer than 5 per cent of the most important group of workers remained, after five years of constant mobilizations.[105] For the Virgin Lands regions as a whole, Komsomol inspectors reported that 253,000 of 378,000 mechanizers who came to northern Kazakhstan between 1954 and 1959 soon left.[106]

Akmolinsk had the highest turnover rates for directors and leading cadres (49 per cent compared with an average 40 per cent), and the fluidity of mechanizers was also greater than elsewhere.[107] By January 1958 outmigration in Akmola had reached nearly 100 per cent at both farms and construction units. Of 17,660 construction workers who came to the Akmola region in 1957, 17,000 left. Of 10,900–13,800 mechanizers brought in the same year, 12,000–12,300 left.[108] These people were hardly the 'useless weeds blown about by the wind' depicted in propaganda. The greatest irony of all the talk of 'deserters' and 'cowards' in the literature of the Virgin Lands cult is that the people who left most predictably each year were those who mattered the most: experienced mechanics, tractor drivers, and combine drivers. It was easy for them to take off: they earned the highest wages, they were tough and not easily bullied, and they could find work at any time in central Russia and Ukraine, where they were in high demand as well.

To stanch the outflow, in 1958 the *obkom* issued a resolution that threatened that 'even the smallest evidence of a neglectful attitude to the people living in the state farms will be considered a crime, and the guilty will be strictly punished.'[109] The *obkom* never really learned how to manage cadres or even the farm bosses. Zhurin ends his memoirs, published in 1982, with the misleading 'admission' that 'a few' directors did not measure up to the challenges and were fired. In fact, *dozens* of directors lost their jobs in the following years. At the November 1954 party plenum, Zhurin had been more honest: he spoke at length of leaders who were fired and who had lost all feeling of responsibility, systematically drank, and broke discipline.[110]

Ten state farm directors were fired in Akmola region in 1954, two of them for 'incompetence.'[111] In Zhurin's report to the Kazakh Central Committee at the end of 1955, the list was nearly twice as long. Nineteen state farm directors were fired from late 1954 to the end of 1955, twelve for incompetence and disruptions of work, two for 'moral dissolution,' and one for 'criminal neglect' of settlers. During the same period twenty-three district party secretaries and eighty-one farm technicians (assistant directors, agronomists, engineers, veterinarians, foremen, and accountants) were removed from their jobs, many for incompetence, insubordination or 'having compromised themselves.'[112] The 'fluidity' of the bosses continued to grow in the following years. In 1956 at least eleven directors were dismissed, and in 1957 thirteen were fired. In 1958, at least twenty-one directors were dismissed for incompetence (while fifty-three were replaced altogether), and ten were fired in 1959, not including people who were promoted, retired, or transferred for other reasons.[113]

The *obkom*'s Stalinist 'command' style of leadership had clearly outlived its usefulness. The party began to recognize the 'extremely negative' effect of seasonal migration on the productivity and infrastructure. In particular, they examined the 'barbaric' treatment of tractors and other equipment by workers who expected to use them for only a few months. One-fifth to one-quarter of the Virgin Lands machinery had to be written off each year, and all machines used in the program had a significantly shorter life expectancy than elsewhere. By 1959 only 94 of the 564 state farms in Kazakhstan even had repair shops (the rest repaired and housed the machines outside year round). Inexperienced and careless mechanizers did not carry out the most basic maintenance on tractors and combine harvesters, and accidents were frequent.[114]

The Virgin Lands *Krai*

At the end of the decade Khrushchev decided to impose discipline by creating a special Virgin Lands administrative region, the *Tselinnyi krai.* Soon after the Akmola party organization was reprimanded in November 1959, Khrushchev used the December 1959 Plenum of the Central Committee to severely criticize the Kazakh leadership for the state of agriculture in the republic. Khrushchev was especially upset that the 1959 harvest was not collected from more than 1.6 million hectares, that more than 18,000 tractors and 32,000 combine-harvesters did not participate in the harvest, and that Kazakhstan continued to rely on a yearly influx of students to manage the harvest.[115] Party chief Beliaev was replaced by Dinmukhamed Kunaev, previously chair of the Kazakh Council of Ministers.[116] In the spring of 1960 a special Bureau for Northern Regions and a new office of the Kazakhstan Ministry of Agriculture were set up in Akmolinsk to manage the Virgin Lands regions more directly.[117]

Similar to Khrushchev's decision to create industrial regional economic councils (*sovnarkhozy*) in 1957,[118] the *Tselinnyi krai* was meant to reduce the power of the Kazakh economic ministries, renew the regional party leadership, and weaken the influence of the Kazakhstan party organization in the northern regions. Thus, the most important functional result of the *krai* was the creation of a new *krai* party organization and of a *kraisovnarkhoz*.[119] The *krai* was officially created by Central Committee resolutions in Moscow and Alma-Ata on 16–17 December 1960 and comprised five regions or *oblasts*: Akmolinsk, Kustanai, Kokchetav, Pavlodar, and north Kazakhstan.[120]

Akmola *oblast'* ceased to exist as a separate administrative entity. Its districts were directly subordinated to the new *krai* administration, and the city of Akmolinsk became the *krai* capital, as well as the administrative seat of the new Virgin Lands economic region.[121] The entire regional leadership was now replaced, less than two years after receiving the prestigious Order of Lenin. On 20 March 1961, the Supreme Soviet of the Kazakh republic changed Akmolinsk's name to 'Tselinograd,' or 'Virgin Lands City.' The region was reconstituted on 24 April 1961 as Tselinograd region.[122]

The birth of the *krai* heralded a period of renewed investment, new volunteers from Russia, including many students and members of the intelligentsia, and – most importantly – a huge construction boom. Although workers' daily life did not change immediately, new vigorous attempts to improve their circumstances were made, especially by the newly formed *krai* Komsomol organization.[123] The *krai* years also marked the beginning of efforts to improve agricultural productivity, increase the use of technology, and assess the ecological damage associated with the Virgin Lands campaign. Wind erosion had been recognized as a potential danger in the early 1950s. In the summer of 1954, scientists had argued that deep ploughing was improper for soils in arid regions like Kazakhstan, but Khrushchev ignored the concerns.[124] The brilliant agronomist Alexander Baraev led a new, alternative scientific centre in Shortandy, not far from Akmolinsk, established in 1956 to design special ploughs and other machinery to cultivate the ground without turning over the top layer of soil.[125] The institute trained thousands of specialists, and many agronomists and farm managers came to Baraev for practical advice. Yet Khrushchev initially condemned his plan to use clean fallow to fight weeds, thinking it was a waste of land.[126]

In 1959 more than half of the four million hectares cultivated in Akmola were plagued by weeds and crop diseases, and the region had experienced its first dust storms.[127] By 1962 these storms occurred on up to twenty days per year in Akmola *oblast'* and even more frequently during drought years.[128] The Shortandy Institute sponsored several major conferences on the topic, and Baraev was vindicated. He was invited to speak about his methods and recommendations at a number of party conferences, plenums, and other gatherings between 1961 and 1963, and he published a book on soil erosion in 1963.[129]

While Khrushchev eventually admitted his mistake and took steps to correct the problem, he had wilfully ignored the advice of the Virgin Lands' most eminent scholar for years and contributed to widespread ecological damage. The experience of dust storms in the early 1960s 'permanently coloured perceptions of the region.'[130] The creation of the *krai*, the subsequent application of soil conservation techniques that led to a decline in wind erosion, and the improved grain production that followed went unnoticed in the West, and Khrushchev's Virgin Lands project was unjustly written off as a failure.

Khrushchev's colleagues in Moscow and the Kazakhstan party leadership were unhappy about the *krai* for yet another reason. Khrushchev had committed a serious blunder by supporting the attempt of first Virgin Lands *kraikom* secretary T. Sokolov to upgrade the *krai* to a sixteenth Union Soviet republic. The *krai* itself was already an affront to the Kazakh party organization based in Alma-Ata, because it formalized the republican leaders' complete lack of influence in the northern regions, but this went too far. It appears that Khrushchev was honestly astonished at the resistance to the idea of making it a republic, primarily from the first and second secretaries of the Kazakh party (Iusupov and Solomentsev): 'I don't quite understand why the republican organization isn't proud and happy that the *Tselinnyi krai* has been put on a special "red line."'[131]

In October 1965, a year after Khrushchev's ouster, Moscow dissolved the Virgin Lands *krai*. While economic and political control over the northern regions reverted to Alma-Ata, Khrushchev's successors continued to invest in the region, and they continued to receive grain and other agricultural products from it. In the Kazakh party literature of the 1970s and 1980s, the *krai* period was either ignored or criticized for 'voluntarism.' Martha Olcott argues that the optimism of the *krai* reorganization 'soon faded.'[132] Neither she nor Western Sovietologists like Martin McCauley see much good in the *krai* period, either for Kazakhstan or the national economy. The history of the *krai* remains one of the least known chapters in the Virgin Lands story. Even though it did not last long, it laid an important foundation for the future capital city by making Akmolinsk the capital of the entire Virgin Lands region, and by fostering a new kind of prosperity and regional identity.

Tselinograd

The former city of Akmolinsk experienced a tremendous transformation during the *krai* years. Khrushchev visited Akmolinsk in March 1961 and gave a speech to a gathering of agriculture leaders in which he compared the accomplishments in the Virgin Lands to those of the First Five-Year Plan, the victory in the Second World War, and space exploration. He proudly announced that the 'Russian word *tselina* has entered the consciousness of other nations just like [the expressions] *Five-Year Plan, kolkhoz, sputnik,* and *Lunik.*'[133] Khrushchev never spoke openly of the region's actual past as a part of the Gulag, although he did more than any other individual to rehabilitate it. Instead he praised the heroes who had transformed the 'untouched and uninhabited steppe.' He saw the *krai* as 'a region of the richest possibilities, a region with a great future' and promised that Akmolinsk would host institutes, schools, and industries. He expressed his dissatisfaction with the name 'Akmolinsk' to accompany his grandiose program.

> The city of Akmolinsk needs to be developed, not on the basis of the old city, but parallel to it.... Next to the old city you should choose a site, plan it out, and a new city should be constructed.... They told me that the name of Akmolinsk means 'white grave' in translation from the Kazakh language. This is hardly the fitting name for the workers of a city that is the capital of the Virgin Lands *krai.* (Applause.) Let the government and Central Committee of the Kazakh party think about it, maybe it would be useful to rename Akmolinsk, for instance, as 'Tselinograd.' (Stormy applause.) This name, it seems, would be appropriate for the present and future of your city. (Prolonged applause.)[134]

Tselinograd was completely transformed. Work on the first of three new high-rise housing districts began in 1963. In addition, the city received a number of new, monumental public buildings, including the Virgin Lands Palace (an enormous congress hall and recreational complex), a Palace of Youth, a House of Soviets, a new airport, and several sports complexes. Broad boulevards were lined with trees and city squares.[135] New housing appeared in the villages and state farms, while bridges and new roads were built across the region. Akmolinsk-Tselinograd grew into the largest centre of higher education in northern Kazakhstan. The new educational institutes and the new *krai* administrations provided work for many people released from the labour camps and for the special settler intelligentsia. New machine-building factories drew regional village youth to seek jobs in the city. Tselinograd had a booming economy and a flourishing public life. For a decade, it became an outpost of student culture, an important achievement. New television and radio stations, and the new *kraikom* Komsomol newspaper *Molodoi tselinnik* (Young Virgin Lander) brought enthusiastic young journalists and writers to the city. One could call *Molodoi tselinnik* a precursor of glasnost papers: it was critical, fresh, and read throughout the Soviet Union, not just in Kazakhstan. The newspaper's staff and the other youth of this second wave changed the image of the Virgin Lands briefly but profoundly. They were representatives of the national 'Thaw culture,' romantics who came to Kazakhstan to 'create culture.'[136] The lifestyle of local youths became more vibrant. Fights became less frequent, and 'going out' became more refined.[137] At night groups of nicely dressed young people filled the city, walking in groups.

> Because of my age I didn't make it into the beginning of the Virgin Lands, but I remember the flourishing that coincided with Khrushchev's thaw. In 1962 there were very few stores in Tselinograd, but a mass of dance squares.... Those who didn't go to the dances went for walks on the city squares. These walks were places of unannounced but inevitable [romantic] meetings, and it was rare day without concerts, with a loudspeaker in the worst case. It seemed that the whole city was made up of these sweet girls in braided hair and with rustling skirts like bells, and young men in white shirts with the sleeves pushed up to their elbows.[138]

My informants grew very animated when talking about the *krai*. Both men and women clearly loved Tselinograd, and they much preferred this part of the story to the hard memories of the 1950s. They spontaneously and fondly brought up entertainments and performances at the newly built Virgin Lands Palace, and the influential roles played by the new radio and television stations.

The *krai* period was crucial to the development of a separate Virgin Lands identity, as it brought a popular awareness that the region had undergone significant change. It is precisely in these years that local people built the first public monuments in honour of the *tselinniki* of 1954–5.[139] When the *krai* was dissolved in 1965, many of the journalists and the cadres of the *krai* administrations left, their organizations dissolved by order from above. The closure of the newspaper *Molodoi tselinnik* was experienced as a loss by many in Tselinograd. The city even experienced a wave of underground resistance to this 'closing of the Khrushchev reforms,' in the form of illegal youth circles (*kruzhki*). A few dozen *krai* enthusiasts, young writers and intellectuals, formed a club called *Vernost' tseliny* in the mid-sixties, which strove to uphold romantic and 'true' Virgin Lands ideals. I met some of them in the 1990s, now grey-haired and defensive of the *tselina* in the face of post-Soviet Kazakh criticism of the project.[140]

One special group who made Tselinograd their capital even as they grumbled about having to stay in the Soviet Union were the region's German deportees. The German special settlers had nowhere else to go, and they became the basic permanent workforce in the *tselina* and in associated industries. My German interviewees unanimously remembered the Virgin Lands and specifically their move from the village to Tselinograd as the time 'when things got better.' Staying in Kazakstan had many economic advantages, and the Germans were highly valued and respected as local organizers and administrators. By the 1970s and 1980s they had considerable influence in local party organizations. Tselinograd eventually became a major German cultural centre with a lively religious life, several official German churches, and even a German-language newspaper.[141] A very interesting attempt was made to create a separate German *oblast'* with Tselinograd as its capital – another project that pushed and prepared Tselinograders to think of their city as special (even if it was controversial and the project foundered against strong Kazakh opposition).

Residents who saw Akmolinsk grow into Tselinograd unanimously placed great emphasis on the economic transformation of the region and the city, but newcomers from other regions of the USSR in the 1960s were thrilled, as well, to find newly built housing and stores full of 'deficit' goods. 'Life was much easier here [in Tselinograd],' recalled one woman. 'It was easier to get an apartment and to get consumer goods than in Ukraine. In the stores here they had goods from East Germany, Poland, Czechoslovakia, they had shoes.'[142] Another recalled, 'Here they had shops, full of everything. They had good streets. Where we came from, everything had been destroyed by war.'[143] I collected numerous oral testimonies that showed how strongly people of all nationalities identified with these changes, but one of the most eloquent statements was published in an article entitled 'Virgin Lands Nostalgia,' in 1994: 'It seemed to us that we are living a new life, that the *tselina* represented a new planet, where people were nicer, better. According to Khrushchev's promise we had twenty years to go before communism – but here, in Tselinograd, it had already started.'[144]

Martin McCauley tracked official calculations of net income in the Virgin Lands and concluded that the Virgin Lands performed 'creditably' until 1960, as net income kept 'roughly in step' with investment. However, the additional investments undertaken during the *krai* years 'adversely affected the overall performance' of the project.[145] From our perspective there is nothing 'adverse' about the positive transformation of the lives of millions of people in the Virgin Lands regions. But they were far from Moscow, far from Alma-Ata, and far from debates in Western Sovietology, and so the successes of the Virgin Lands never became part of the Thaw story.

The Virgin Lands and Kazakhstan

During Kazakhstan's belated glasnost years in the 1990s, public debates of the *tselina* focused on the damage done to Kazakh culture as a result of the influx of Russians. Indeed, the percentage of Kazakhs in the republic fell significantly as a result of the Virgin Lands. Kazakh elementary schools were closed and replaced with Russian ones. Inconveniently located Kazakh villages were neglected in favour of the Virgin Lands settlements built close to major roads, and by the 1980s, many *auls* (Kazakh villages) in the north of Kazakhstan stood empty because families had moved in search of jobs and education.[146] Such criticisms, completely silenced during the Soviet period, were received with wounded hostility by the Virgin Lands elite in the period immediately after, and during the forty-year Virgin Lands anniversary. In my interviews, all of the Kazakh elders in Tselinograd and around it who witnessed the *tselina*, men and women, farm workers and professors, emphatically denied that the Virgin Lands project brought them harm. I participated in conversations in which younger Kazakh intellectuals openly accused them of being 'brainwashed' and tried to push them to speak of negative aspects of the Virgin Lands opening, but they resisted, saying they would not give in to 'fashionable' revaluations. Even those who recalled the fistfights and the exclusion of Communists from the party for openly participating in religious life placed more emphasis on the bitterness of the famine and the poverty of the post-war years, and angrily refused to 'malign' the project: 'I will not pull the *tselina* to pieces! Say what you want, the *tselina* gave us everything.'[147] Again and again, rural Kazakhs told me of the machines that were sent, of the roads, schools, and hospitals that were built, and of the way the shops filled with goods.

The Virgin Lands project amounted to a material rehabilitation that left the traumas of the Stalin era unaddressed in public discourse but did bring a flood of tractors and canned goods and winter jackets to the north of Kazakhstan. Kazakh culture became much less visible as a new multicultural society emerged there. Kazakh values like patience and hospitality, and the frequent choice of withdrawal over confrontation, made an enormously positive and largely unrecognized contribution to this new society. During the Brezhnev era, it was impossible to contradict the official Virgin Lands cult that presented Akmolinsk as 'primitive' before the Virgin Lands and as empty of culture, except for 'backward' religious practices. But the archives show that the same officials who made these proclamations paradoxically allowed religious revivals and the creation of small (and heavily monitored) churches among Germans, Poles, and Chechens right under their noses. Kazakh religiosity was condemned in public discourse, but increasing prosperity brought thousands more believers to the central mosque in Akmolinsk on major Muslim holidays like the end of Ramadan.[148] It is not revealing to reduce the Virgin Lands to an episode of demographic aggression, seeing the project's significance primarily in wreaking the 'crushing final disintegration of traditional Kazakh culture.'[149] The notion that the *tselina* was a disaster for the Kazakhs ignores the fact that the situation in the *tselina* was far more complicated than the simple 'Russian-Kazakh' confrontation that many imagine to have taken place. Why did the culture of the special settlers experience a modest revival in the Virgin Lands regions, even though they were on the receiving end of most of the violence of the first years, while that of the Kazakhs was supposedly 'crushed'? The Russian culture that came, the popular culture and daily *byt* (material conditions) of the *tselinniki* at the farm level, was rough but vibrant. It was a frontier culture of migrant agricultural and construction workers, and during the summer, students. It was neither monolithic nor oppressive, nor was it the mighty flow of Russian culture that the Virgin Lands cult would have us imagine. Hard work and the sharing of dangers, disappointments, and successes gradually engendered mutual respect. In interviews, people of all nationalities insisted that they did learn to value each other, even if that relationship had a stormy beginning and was somewhat different from the official 'friendship of nations.' From their point of view, Virgin Lands internationalism was not artificial. Virgin Lands society left previously unknown spaces to follow one's beliefs. It upheld a strong respect for other cultures, and people shared a high work ethic and valued education. It has served as one of the strongest foundations for a new post-communist Kazakhstani identity.

Conclusion

The *tselina* was one the most important sites of Khrushchev's reforms, but he never came out and openly talked about its Gulag past, nor the Kazakh famine. The closest he came to that was what seemed his impulsive dismissal of Akmolinsk as a 'white grave' and the renaming of the city as Tselinograd. These signals seem obvious now, but we should not blame Western Sovietologists for not 'getting' them. Even many people who came to Tselinograd in the 1970s and who lived there for two decades got a fuller picture of the region's past only during the glasnost era, as I learned from my interviews and the local press. The entire process was buried under hectic and grandiose proclamations about the grain campaign and later the Virgin Lands cult, a bureaucratized Soviet version of a Wild West epic. This obscured the very real rehabilitation through jobs and apartments of hundreds of thousands of deportees and former inmates of the Gulag, the creation of a cadre of successful and productive administrators and managers, and the growth of a disciplined and experienced regional workforce.

One of the greatest achievements of the Virgin Lands campaign was the transformation of Akmolinsk into Tselinograd, a city that boomed in the 1960s and 1970s and that was beloved by its many different inhabitants. This has become easier to see now, as a second momentous reform era has begun – the transformation of Tselinograd into Astana. Many varied processes have already contributed to the growth of something new in Kazakhstan's capital: Nazarbaev's will and direction, the enthusiasm that the project has unleashed among intellectuals (architects and designers foremost among them), the mass movement of Kazakhs from Almaty and other regions of Kazakhstan, the surprising level of international ties that the back-and-forth movement of Tselinograd's German *Aussiedler*[150] has caused, and a boom of church and mosque building that shows what a religious centre Tselinograd truly had been, beneath all the atheist propaganda. By making Astana the post-independence capital, President Nazarbaev has made the choice to claim the Virgin Lands heritage for everyone in Kazakhstan. Even if Khrushchev could not imagine an independent Kazakhstan, he made enormously successful investments in Kazakhstan's people and the country's future. It is time to rehabilitate Tselinograd and the Virgin Lands among Khrushchev's reforms and to recognize that his rehabilitation of this multi-ethnic Gulag region and the creation of such a vibrant city and regional economy were major achievements in their own right.

NOTES

1 I explore the ethnic aspects of the new Virgin Lands identity in greater detail in Michaela Pohl, 'The "Planet of One Hundred Languages": Ethnic Relations and Soviet Identity in the Virgin Lands,' in *Peopling the Russian Periphery: Borderland Colonization in Eurasian History*, ed. Nicholas Breyfogle, Abby Schrader, and Willard Sunderland (London, 2007), 238–61.

2 Richard Beeston, 'Kazakhs Protest as Capital Moves to Frozen North,' *Times*, 11 December 1997; Jeremy Bransten, 'Kazakhstan: Waiting for Nazarbaev in His New Capital,' *Radio Free Europe / Radio Liberty* feature, 14 October 1997, 1.

3 Sidney Ploss, *Conflict and Decision-Making in Soviet Russia: A Case Study of Agricultural Policy, 1953–1963* (Princeton, 1965), 71, 87.

4 Edward Crankshaw, *Khrushchev: A Career* (New York, 1966), 200. See also Carl Linden, *Khrushchev and the Soviet Leadership* (Baltimore, 1966), 29.

5 See, e.g., Crankshaw, *Khrushchev*, 201; Martin Gilbert, *Atlas of Russian History* (New York, 1985), 136; and, more recently, Gulnar Kendirbaeva, 'Migrations in Kazakhstan: Past and Present,' *Nationalities Papers* 25 (1997): 742; William Taubman, *Khrushchev: The Man and His Era* (New York, 2003), 263.

6 For a discussion of this issue, see V.I. Kulikov, 'Burzhuaznaia fal'sifikatsiia roli KPSS v osvoenii tselinnykh zemel',' *Voprosy Istorii KPSS* 5 (1964): 119–26.

7 This literature is discussed in Peter Craumer, 'Land Use and Agricultural Productivity in the Soviet Virgin Lands' (PhD diss., Columbia University, 1991).

8 Martin McCauley, *Khrushchev and the Development of Soviet Agriculture: The Virgin Land Programme 1953–64* (New York, 1976).

9 Martha Brill Olcott, *The Kazakhs*, 2nd ed. (Stanford, 1995), 224–40, 224.

10 Zhores A. Medvedev, *Soviet Agriculture* (New York, 1987), 175–6.

11 Roy A. Medvedev and Zhores A. Medvedev, *Khrushchev: The Years in Power* (New York, 1978), 122.

12 Nurtai Agubaev, 'Zdes' nashi korni, ili o tom kak Akmolinskaia oblast' stala mnogonatsional'noi,' *Info-Tses* (Akmola) 11 February 1994, 7; Michaela Pohl, '"It Cannot Be That Our Graves Will Be Here": The Survival of Chechen and Ingush Deportees in Kazakhstan, 1944–57,' *Journal of Genocide Research* 4, no. 3 (2002): 401–30.

13 RGANI 2/1/52/2–91; Nikita S. Khrushchev, 'O merakh dal'neishego razvitiia sel'skogo khoziaistva SSSR,' in his *Stroitel'stvo kommunizma v SSSR i razvitie sel'skogo khoziaistva* (Moscow, 1962) 1:7–84; William J. Tompson, *Khrushchev: A Political Life* (New York, 1995), 128–30; Medvedev and Medvedev, *Khrushchev*, 34–7; Medvedev, *Soviet Agriculture*, 163–7; Nikita S. Khrushchev, *Khrushchev Remembers: The Last Testament* (Boston, 1974), 119–22.

14 Medvedev, *Soviet Agriculture*, 163. The list of visitors included many regional party secretaries and representatives from a number of ministries. Almost all *oblast'* secretaries from Kazakhstan participated. RGANI 2/1/46/3–12.

15 RGANI 2/1/52/89–90.

16 Khrushchev, *Khrushchev Remembers*, 120–1.

17 RGANI 5/24/519/1.

18 Nikolai Zhurin, *Trudnye i schastlivye gody: Zapiski partiinogo rabotnika* (Moscow, 1982), 172.

19 Arkhiv Presidenta Respubliki Kazakhstan (APRK) 708/26/134/101–2; APRK 708/26/144/153; APRK 708/27/150.

20 *Kommunisticheskaia Partiia v bor'be za osvoenie tselinnykh zemel' v Kazakhstane*, ed. Z.A. Golikova, A.K. Kakimzhanov, and S.L. Koval'skii (Alma-Ata, 1969), 108.

21 RGANI 5/24/519/3–31, 161–225, 176.

22 Zhurin, *Trudnye i schastlivye gody*, 173.

23 RGANI 5/45/1/1–14. The published version contains minor editorial changes and one important omission; regarding the proposed use of prisoners to work in the Virgin Lands, see below. Nikita S. Khrushchev, 'Puti resheniia zernovoi problemy: Zapiska v Presidium TsK KPSS,' *Stroitel'stvo kommunizma*, 85–100.

24 A pood is the equivalent of 16.7 kilograms.

25 RGANI 5/45/1/10–12; Khrushchev, 'Puti resheniia,' 96–9.

26 RGANI 2/1/63/1–8.

27 Not two weeks later, at the party's 7th Congress, as most Soviet sources maintained (see also Kozybaev, *Istoriia Kazakhstana*, 340); APRK 708/27/28/2–11.

28 APRK 708/27/1600/26–7.

29 Zhurin, *Trudnye i schastlivye gody*, 174.

30 Otdelenie partiinoi dokumentatsii Akmolinskoi oblasti (OPDAO) 1/1/1577/16–17.
31 E.g., Bachmann, *Memories of Kazakhstan*, 60; anonymous interview, tape no. 27. The 'average' earnings reported in collective farms in 1952 were 1.8 kilos of bread and 1.04 rubles of cash, and even this was considered miserly by the reporting officials. RGANI 5/30/55/120–126.
32 OPDAO 1/1/1577/195–6.
33 OPDAO 1/1/1577/82.
34 Forty to fifty thousand Kazakh families lived in the Turkmen, Kirgiz, Tadzhik, Uzbek republics and in southern Siberia. During the 1950s they sent scouts to find out about resettlement, but nothing appears to have been done to help them. APRK 708/32/1476/1–3.
35 GARF, spetsfond 9479, dd. 903 and 847; OPDAO 1/1/1929–31, 2049–50, 2137–9, 2336, 2348, 2470–1, 2542, 2652, 2655, 2630, 2779, and 2852.
36 Vladimir A. Kozlov, *Mass Uprisings in the USSR: Protest and Rebellion in the Post-Stalin Years* (Armonk, NY, 2002), 25.
37 For more detail, see Mikaela Pol' [Michaela Pohl], '"Planeta Sta Iazykov." Etnicheskie otnosheniia i sovetskaia identichnost' na tseline,' *Vestnik Evrazii / Acta Evrasica* 1, no. 24 (2004): 5–33; Pohl, '"It Cannot Be."'
38 RGASPI-M 1/9/327/70–1; RGASPI-M 1/9/295/19–23.
39 OPDAO 1/1/1931/131–3.
40 GARF 9479/1/925/242.
41 GARF 9479/1/925/132.
42 Viktor Zemskov, 'Massovoe osvobozhdenie spetsposelentsev i ssyl'nykh (1954–1960 gg.),' *Sotsiologicheskie issledovaniia* 1 (1991): 5–26, 11.
43 Ibid., 15–16.
44 OPDAO 1/1/2336/1–4.
45 APRK 708/28/1339a/56–57.
46 Zemskov, 'Massovoe osvobozhdenie spetsposelentsev i ssyl'nykh,' 16.
47 OPDAO 1/1/2336/135; OPDAO 1/1/2336/134–5.
48 OPDAO 1/1/2336/128–131, 171.
49 Zemskov, 'Massovoe osvobozhdenie spetsposelentsev i ssyl'nykh,' 16.
50 Akmolinskii Lager Zhen Izmennikov Rodiny (Akmolinsk Camp for Wives of Traitors of the Motherland).
51 OPDAO 1/1/2470, 2360.
52 OPDAO 1/1/2336/128–31, 200.
53 OPDAO 1/1/2630/126–30.
54 GARF 9479/1/925/132.
55 OPDAO 1/1/2856/8.
56 OPDAO 1/1/2336/194–6.

57 Medvedev and Medvedev, *Khrushchev*, 122.

58 Donald Filtzer, *Soviet Workers and De-Stalinization: The Consolidation of the Modern System of Soviet Production Relations, 1953–64* (Cambridge, UK, 1992), 127–31.

59 RGASPI-M 1/9/327/61–74, 20 July 1955.

60 RGASPI-M 1/9/298/125.

61 OPDAO 1/1/2067/206.

62 OPDAO 1/1/2049/74–106.

63 My count, based on GARF, spetsfond 9479, dd. 903, 847; OPDAO 1/1, dd. 929–31, 2049–50, 2137–9, 2336, 2348, 2470–1, 2542, 2652, 2655, 2630, 2779, and 2852.

64 RGASPI-M 1/9/327/70.

65 RGASPI-M 1/9/339/5–16; OPDAO 1/1/1931/200.

66 RGASPI-M 1/6/915/63–7.

67 RGANI 5/45/3/127.

68 RGANI 5/45/3/64–6.

69 OPDAO 1/1/1878/13–14.

70 OPDAO 1/1/1876/25–7.

71 OPDAO 1/1/1852/172.

72 RGASPI-M 1/9/328/155–62; RGANI 5/45/96/45–7.

73 RGASPI-M 1/9/566/65.

74 RGASPI-M 1/9/327/68.

75 OPDAO 1/1/2336/150–1.

76 OPDAO 1/1/2852/113–1.

77 OPDAO 1/1/2471/224–5; OPDAO 1/1/2336/177; OPDAO 1/1/2470/181.

78 OPDAO 1/1/2336/215–18.

79 OPDAO 1/1/1857/31–3.

80 OPDAO 1/1/1861/7.

81 E.g., OPDAO 1/1/1859/25–9.

82 OPDAO 1/1/1875/4. About one hundred officials attended the discussion of this question at a session of the *obkom biuro*.

83 APRK 708/27–8; Zhurin, *Trudnye i schastlivye gody*, 218–22.

84 OPDAO 1/1/1861/34–40.

85 OPDAO 1/1/1861/48.

86 OPDAO 1/1/1915/51.

87 E.g., OPDAO 1/1/1882/41–4.

88 OPDAO 1/1/1852/152–4.

89 OPDAO 1/1/1852/202; OPDAO 1/1/2070/16–17; OPDAO 1/1/2286/77–8.

90 OPDAO 1/1/2067/206.

91 OPDAO 1/1/2286/68–71.
92 OPDAO 1/1/2487/179–81.
93 OPDAO 1/1/2487/176–9.
94 OPDAO 1/1/2487/228–34.
95 See Merle Fainsod, *How Russia Is Ruled* (Cambridge, MA, 1963), 226.
96 OPDAO 1/1/d. 2663.
97 OPDAO 1/1/2285/4; OPDAO 1/1/2487/228; OPDAO 1/1/2665/4–5.
98 OPDAO 1/1/2095/21; OPDAO 1/1/2292/5–6.
99 OPDAO 1/1/2070/119–20, 2–3 June 1955. See also Zhurin's misleading summary of Brezhnev's speech, in Zhurin, *Trudnye i schastlivye gody*, 221–2.
100 The 'weakening' of efforts was mentioned in many reports. See, e.g., OPDAO 1/1/2494/18–22; OPDAO 1/1/2673/40–6; OPDAO 1/1/2821/32–6.
101 OPDAO 1/1/2101/98–9; OPDAO 1/1/2297/22–6.
102 OPDAO 1/1/2487/6–9.
103 OPDAO 1/1/2487/9–12, 53.
104 APRK 708/32/1488/4.
105 RGASPI-M 1/9/470/1–11.
106 RGASPI-M 1/6/1113/10–19.
107 APRK 708/30/172/263–78.
108 OPDAO 1/1/2663/17–18, 45.
109 Ibid.
110 APRK 708/27/1619/7; OPDAO 1/1/1852/106, 115–16.
111 OPDAO 1/1/1957/159–63.
112 OPDAO 1/1/2135/43–74, 58–60.
113 OPDAO 1/1/2873/12–14, 77–83.
114 OPDAO 1/1/2873/89, and OPDAO 1/1/1113/10–19; see also Rossiiskii Gosudarstvenyi Arkhiv Sotsial'no-Polticheskoi Istorii (RGASPI-M) 1/9/392/2–5.
115 RGANI 2/1/445/85–6; see also Golikova et al., *Kommunisticheskaia Partiia*, 346–7; McCauley, *Krushchev*, 140–1.
116 Golikova et al., *Kommunisticheskaia Partiia*, 347; Olcott, *Kazakhs*, 227–8.
117 OPDAO 1/1/3031; McCauley, *Krushchev*, 141.
118 See Filtzer, *Soviet Workers*, 67–70.
119 The *sovnarkhozy*, formed in 1957 (North-Kazakhstan, Kustanai), were now dissolved, and the Akmola and Pavlodar regions were taken out of the Karaganda *sovnarkhoz* of which they had been part since 1957. Earlier reorganization had not affected them.
120 APRK 708/33/171/326. The Kazakh Central Committee had formally approved Khrushchev's suggestion on 11 November 1960, and a joint

resolution with the Soviet of Ministers requesting 'permission' to create the *krai* was passed a few days later. See APRK 708/33/171/233, 311–17. On 26 December 1960, the Presidium of the Supreme Soviet of Kazakhstan confirmed the changes in its decree on the formation of the *krai*.

121 APRK 708/33/171/326.

122 Andrei Dubitskii, *Proidemsia po ulitsam Tselinograda* (Tselinograd, 1990), 110; Guk et al., *Polveka v stroiu*, 80.

123 RGASPI-M 1/9/566/54–60; 'Iz doklada sekretaria TsK KPK, predstavitelia Biuro TsK KPK po Severnym oblastiam T.I. Sokolova na pervom respublikanskom slete molodykh tselinnikov v Kazakhstane, 29 November 1960,' in I.M. Volkov, *Velikii podvig partii i naroda – massovoe osvoenie tselinnykh i zalezhnykh zemel'. Sbornik dokumentov i materialov* (Moscow, 1979), 403–10.

124 Ilya E. Zelenin, 'Tselinnaia epopeia: Razrabotka, priniatie i osushchestvlenie pervoi khrushchevskoi "sverkhprogrammy,"' *Otechestvennaia istoriia* 4 (1998): 109–22, 115.

125 Alexander Baraev, A. Zaitseva, and E. Gossen, *Bor'ba s vetrovoi eroziei pochv* (Alma-Ata, 1963); fieldnotes, Shortandy, July 1994; Vladimir Gundarev and G. Roshchin, *Glavnyi agronom tseliny* (Alma-Ata, 1979).

126 Zelenin, *Agrarnaia politika N. S. Khrushcheva i sel'skoe khoziaistvo* (Moscow, 2001), 98–9.

127 RGASPI-M 1/9/470/87–90, 88.

128 Baraev, Zaitseva, and Gossen, *Bor'ba s vetrovoi eroziei pochv*, 3.

129 Golikova et al., *Kommunisticheskaia Partiia*, 349.

130 Craumer, 'Land Use.'

131 Cited in Aleksandr Pyzhikov, *Khrushchevskaia ottepel'* (Moscow, 2002), 172–3; Pyzhikov, *O nekotorykh aspektakh perestroiki partiino-sovetskikh organov po proizvodstvennomu printsipu (1962–1964)* (Moscow, 1998), 20.

132 Olcott, *Kazakhs*, 228.

133 OPDAO 3227/1/24/177.

134 OPDAO 3227/1/24/191–2. Bracketed notes about applause in original. See also B.G. Maevskii, *Rozhdennyi tselinoi* (Akmola, 1995), 11.

135 See Dubitskii, *Proidemsia po ulitsam Tselinograda*, 110; Guk et al., *Polveka v stroi*, 80–1; Maevskii, *Rozhdennyi tselinoi*.

136 Gul'nara Smagulova, 'Luchshaia v mire gazeta,' *Akmolinskaia Pravda*, 25 February 1994; interview with Vladimir Gundarev, 5 July 1996, Akmola, tape no. 20.

137 See also OPDAO 1/1/2794.

138 Efim Chirkov, 'Tselinnaia nostal'giia,' *Info-Tses* (Akmola) 25 February 1994, 7.

139 'Iz soobshcheniia gazety "Sel'skaia zhizn" ob ustanovlenii v sovkhoze

"Dvurechnyi" Akmolinskoi oblasti pamiatnika trudovoi slavy tselinnikam,' 8 December 1960, in Volkov, *Velikii podvig partii i naroda,* 410–11.

140 Interview at Akmola *oblast'* library, June 1994, tape nos. 1–2.

141 Berta Bachmann, *Memories of Kazakhstan: A Report on the Life Experiences of a German Woman in Russia* (Lincoln, NE, 1983); Joseph Schnurr, ed., *Die Kirchen und das religiose Leben der Russlanddeutschen* (Stuttgart, 1972), 265–8.

142 Anonymous interview, fieldnotes, 4 July 1996.

143 Anonymous interview, fieldnotes, 22 June 1996.

144 Chirkov, *Diary,* 2.

145 McCauley, *Krushchev,* 147.

146 N.E. Masanov et al., eds., *Istoriia Kazakstana: Narody i kul'tury* (Almaty, 2001), 341.

147 Anonymous interview, Kurgaldzhino, 7 July 1994, tape no. 94-XX.

148 OPDAO 1/1/1870/18–21.

149 Ingvar Svanberg, 'The Kazak Nation,' in *Contemporary Kazaks: Cultural and Social Perspectives,* ed. Ingvar Svanberg (New York, 1999), 3.

150 Individuals of German extraction who have moved back to Germany from Eastern and Southeastern Europe, where their families often had lived for centuries.

8 The Empires Pay a Visit: Gulag Returnees, East European Rebellions, and Soviet Frontier Politics

AMIR WEINER

In the wake of the 1956 Hungarian crisis, seven years passed before Soviet ideologues finally addressed in public the impact of one of its most sensitive and until then unspoken aspects. Writing on Soviet nationality policy in western Ukraine, Valentyn Malanchuk, the future secretary for ideology of the Ukrainian Central Committee, drew a link between Khrushchev's 'Secret Speech,' the Hungarian uprising, and the revival of anti-Soviet activity among Gulag returnees in the region. Beyond the now public vulnerability felt by the Soviets in response to the spillover of unrest into the Soviet interior – especially the western frontier – and its probable impact on the decision to invade Hungary, Malanchuk touched upon a critical dilemma facing the post-Stalinist order. In his account, the authorities were aware that not all of those released (mainly former nationalist and religious leaders) had renounced their anti-Soviet convictions; upon return to their homes, many resumed their hostile activities and efforts to recruit new supporters. For nationalist returnees, Malanchuk observed, the core issue was not the cult of personality but the Marxist-Leninist system itself: 'They questioned the basic principles of party activity in the western regions of the Soviet Union, especially the policy of industrialization and collectivization of agriculture, and the workers' struggle against the nationalists in the first postwar years.'[1]

Malanchuk had it right. The returning nationalists were not the dissidents who had begun to emerge at the time he was writing. Rather, they were the remnants of opposition forces in the Soviet Union who rejected co-optation and reform 'from within' while challenging the fundamentals of the system and seeking to replace it. The problem was not limited to the Ukrainian Republic, however. Throughout the preceding decade, party organizations and state security agencies across the western frontier – the territories between the Baltic and Black Seas that were initially annexed by the Soviets in 1939–40 – had bitterly complained about the premature release of former nationalist activists and guerrillas. Freeing these activists was a miscalculation that turned into a major debacle under the influence of the Polish and Hungarian unrest across the border.[2]

This essay explores the complex dynamic that fed Soviet anxieties over the border regions. This dynamic involved several interlocking aspects: the dismantling of the Gulag, including most notably the release of a significant number of convicted nationalist guerrillas and activists, who were allowed to return to their homes; the conflicting sentiments on the western frontier that led locals to embrace or reject the Gulag returnees on the basis of pre-Soviet memories, the experiences of the Second World War, and post-war Sovietization policies; the impact of the Polish and Hungarian upheavals, foreign radio broadcasts, and increased contacts with the outside world on the authorities and populations of the western republics; and finally, the attempt to counter these problems via the proliferation of communal surveillance and policing, the revival of class-based policies, and the intensified pursuit of ethno-national homogenization of the borderlands.

Indeed, the crisis sparked in 1956 raised several key questions for the post-Stalinist Soviet polity, especially on the western frontier: Why did a government as suspicious and seasoned as the Soviet regime consciously let a mass of sworn, unreformed enemies back into its midst? Was the era of social engineering over in the wake of the renunciation of mass terror and, if so, what came in its place? What were the boundaries of reform? What price was the regime willing to pay for the relative loss of control over information flow and communications? What accounted for the wide gap between a confident centre and its weary periphery, and what role did the latter play in shaping national policies? In 1956, all these issues came to the fore.

The Polish and Hungarian crises caught up with the Soviets at the very moment when cautious, gradual attempts to reform the Stalinist system grew bolder. It was there – and not just metaphorically – that the two Soviet empires met: the dismantled Gulag empire and the recently created socialist empire in Eastern Europe. The dismantling of the former was expected to revitalize the system. The creation of the latter was meant to guarantee its security. And both failed, at least temporarily. When Gulag returnees met the spillover from the rebellious People's Democracies of Poland and Hungary in 1956 on the Soviet western frontier, that already volatile region served as the last stand for an active anti-Soviet opposition and a testing ground for a regime committed to the continuation of its social engineering enterprise minus the hitherto primary tool of mass state violence. This would have been a delicate balancing act at any time. It became a critical turning point as Soviet citizens witnessed – most of them for the first time in their lives – the disintegration of an entrenched Communist regime across the border and a revived opposition with similar goals in their midst.

No one was in a better position than Nikita Khrushchev to capture the dilemmas and anxieties of the attempt to depart from the Stalinist legacy without sacrificing the fundamentals of the polity or bringing down the Soviet house. Reflecting on the Thaw era, the deposed Soviet leader admitted that the leadership was 'consciously in favor of the Thaw,' yet '[we] were scared – really scared. We were afraid the Thaw might unleash a flood which we would not be able to control and which would drown us. How could it drown us? It could have overflowed the banks of the Soviet riverbed and formed a tidal wave which would have washed away all the barriers and retaining walls of our society.'[3] It is remarkable that this did not stop Khrushchev from carrying on with reforms.

Indeed, the 1956–7 episode on the western frontier revealed a system torn between unrestrained optimism regarding its ability to pursue the revolutionary cause and an endemic sense of vulnerability; between an overly confident centre and a cautious periphery; between the unequivocal commitment to pursue the cleansing of unacculturated constituencies from society and the wish to break with the more brutal features of the recent past, such as mass deportations and executions; between the application of populist pressure on deviationists and the still formidable institutions of political policing; between belief that it accomplished the Sovietization of its ethno-national domain and the nightmarish vision of irredentist pressures among socialist countries. Above all, two decades after it declared itself free of antagonistic class divisions, class was a category to which it continued to return.

The latter paradox touched upon a key feature of the crisis in the western frontier and of Soviet socio-political life as a whole. Throughout this period and beyond, Soviet authorities persistently referred to all returnees as nationalists – a claim that often defied the recollections of these very people. One can hardly avoid the impression that in the western territories, where the authorities were still adjusting to the aftershocks of the civil war, collectivization and the spillover of upheaval from across the border, the term *nationalist* became a catchphrase for anyone perceived as a troublemaker. Aside from complicating the historian's task, such a gap between official claims and private perceptions was obviously detrimental to the advancement of the Soviet cause in this region. And yet, it could not and should not have concealed the ability of the regime to mould its constituency through the unilateral assignment of categories and their implementation via myriad institutions and practices. While many of the hundreds of thousands of those deported from the western frontiers may not have been nationalists or supporters of their cause, from that moment on their lives were structured as such. Whether as inmates of the Gulag camps and settlements – where they were grouped together, treated as an undifferentiated nationalist cohort and introduced to nationalist organizations, mythologies, and ideologies – or as amnestied inmates forced to cope with the obstacles of official documentation and social stigmas in practically every walk of life, these Soviet citizens had no option other than to lead their lives as members of this category. The outcome was typically Soviet. Either by design or by default or both, the regime managed to raise the stakes for everyone involved in its endeavour.

The Gulag Pays a Visit

The immediate aftermath of Stalin's death saw the emergence of the western frontier as a testing ground for the Soviet system's efforts and ability to reform itself. The post-Stalin era began with a surge of optimism and a sense that there was no returning to the turbulence that plagued the previous decade and a half. Nationalist guerrillas had been either exterminated or exiled, and occasional bursts of nationalist activity were easily contained. The countryside was collectivized, mass population movement was stabilized, including the exodus from the countryside to the cities, and the local party and state agencies were gradually being indigenized, easing the tensions that flared after Stalin's death.[4] And in the most visible display of confidence, a series of amnesty decrees allowed tens of thousands of former nationalist activists and their families – the largest, best organized, and most violent of anti-Soviet forces – to return from the Gulag to their native places of residence.[5]

In 1954–5 alone, some 48,000 inmates returned to their native Baltic republics, 17,000 to Belarus, and nearly 6,000 to Moldavia. The situation in the Ukrainian Republic was even more startling, given the presence of more than 20,000 convicted nationalists among those returning to the western provinces alone, as well as several hundred priests of the Greek Catholic Church – the core church of the nationalist camp. Unsurprisingly, the Ukrainian authorities were less than thrilled about the prospects of their sworn enemies' return en masse. Reports on the returnees were supplemented by detailed statistics of the recent bloody past that had cost the lives of more than 150,000 nationalists and 23,000 Soviet citizens, including 15,000 locals, in 1944–55. Furthermore, argued the local authorities, the bloody cycle had not abated since the 1955 amnesty. Clashes with remnants of the nationalist anti-Soviet guerrillas were still registered by the Baltic security forces in the spring of 1957, and some thirty-nine murders and attacks on Soviet officials were registered in western Ukraine in 1955–6, in addition to hundreds of threatening letters, confiscations of illegal weapons, and arrests of hundreds of returnees throughout the frontier.[6] For a regime that had just concluded the ruthless destruction of a mass guerrilla movement, the several hundred incidents associated with the returnees in 1955–6, most of which were classified as petty crimes, were little more than a trifle. This, however, was not the view in the localities.

The Belorussian authorities had already signalled their resistance to the return of nationalists, especially to their return to the western border regions, where most of the counter-revolutionary offences in the republic were registered after Stalin's death. Tolerance for political transgressions, especially those associated with wartime conduct, was not forthcoming, and the Presidium of the republic's Supreme Soviet terminated only a handful of such cases.[7] Not surprisingly, the Belorussian party objected to the wholesale return of former political inmates. As early as May 1955, the party secretary of the Hrodna region complained to Minsk that the anti-Soviet agitation and activities of some 1,356 returnees were causing major political and economic problems. In an ominous hint of things to come, the Belorussian officials focused mainly, though not only, on Polish nationals and Catholic activists who resumed their nationalist and religious activities upon returning from exile. Moreover, the local authorities did not shy away from criticizing the soft and formalistic approach of the Military District Procuracy officials, who were in charge of earlier releases and had often overruled the more cautious regional commissions.[8]

In Ukraine, the exasperated Committee for State Security (KGB) and the Administrative Department of the Central Committee did not hesitate to question the wisdom of the amnesty decree of 10 March 1956 by the Presidium of the Supreme Soviet of the Union of Soviet Socialist Republics, which allowed thousands of nationalist convicts to return to their homes in the western provinces. On 4 April 1956, the two organizations appealed to the party leader, Oleksii Kyrychenko, to immediately halt the return of some 80,000 people convicted for the worst violent crimes to the scenes of those crimes, where nationalist elements were still active. They offered a litany of objections such as the lack of housing (the property of deportees had already been divided among Soviet institutions, collective farms, and repatriated citizens from Poland), and the negative attitude of returnees who refused to work on the collective farms, incited others to join them, and threatened Soviet activists with revenge. Claiming to represent the consensus among Soviet and party activists in the localities, the agencies asked Kyrychenko to petition the Central Committee in Moscow for a ban on the return of released nationalists and their families and supporters to western Ukraine, as well as for a ban on the recovery of their property.[9]

And yet they kept coming. By 10 October 1956, the Ukrainian Ministry of Internal Affairs (MVD) registered over 45,000 former nationalists and affiliates who returned to the western provinces, including some 39,000 who had been convicted for counter-revolutionary crimes. The absolute majority (nearly 41,000 people) returned to the countryside, their traditional bastion. More than 16,000 were classified as members of the Organization of Ukrainian Nationalists (OUN) underground, 14,500 as members of guerrilla units, over 5,000 as family members and supporters, and some 5,000 as active collaborators with the Nazi occupiers. The MVD noted that the absolute majority integrated peacefully into workplaces, and some even excelled at work on the collective farms. Still, some 12,000 returnees were unemployed, creating a restless pool and a growing friction between the localities and the central authorities. The latter viewed the problem as basically economic, with full and proper employment of the returnees as the ultimate solution. While the Supreme Court and the Supreme Soviet of the Union of the Soviet Socialist Republics repeatedly reminded the state organs at all levels of their responsibility to find employment for returnees within two weeks of their petition for assistance, the reality in the localities was starkly different. Emboldened by the only partial rehabilitation of the inmates, the suspicious local police branches refused to exchange the returnees' passports, assign them proper housing, or admit qualified returnees to universities. The central authorities, however, were unmoved. Even when they reported on the increasing violence between amnestied nationalists and a population that allegedly objected to the return of these people to the villages, the Ukrainian MVD insisted that the issue was first and foremost employment and the proper dose of propaganda. The special commission that reviewed the dire state of the returnees in Lithuania went further and placed the blame squarely on the local authorities. Despite their awareness that the absolute majority of the returnees were released with no rights to recover confiscated property, many districts exacerbated the difficulty of their situation by arbitrarily curtailing their integration into the labour market and their lawful right to pursue the return of their property in court.[10]

The Calculus of Risk

Even by Soviet standards, allowing former nationalists to return home was nothing short of baffling. Barely four years after the authorities could finally claim a final victory over their most dogged enemy, they allowed him back in their midst, seemingly without great concern. Why did they do it? Was it in the hope of reconciliation now that the struggle was over? Did Moscow, Kiev, Vilnius, Riga, Tallinn, Minsk, and Chisinau entertain the thought that their most ardent opponents had had a change of heart? In its seventy-four years of existence the Soviet regime displayed many characteristics, but naivety was not one of them. Moreover, the authorities were aware that the camps and settlements were recruitment sites for the nationalist cause.[11]

The answer seems to lie in the nature of the release process, the reevaluation by Stalin's successors of the political worth of local cadres at their disposal, and their confidence in their ability to conquer the opposition without resorting to mass terror. Political deportees from the western borderlands were excluded from the initial release decrees in 1953–4. But as amnesty decrees kept pouring in, with each decree leading to another, these excluded categories were constantly being sliced into segments that were incorporated into other cohorts of political releases. As early as August 1953, the Central Committee decree on the special settlements abolished the decree of 26 November 1948, which imposed permanent exile on nationalities and guerrillas deported during and after the war, and it also released children under the age of sixteen in this cohort, regardless of class and political affiliation.[12] Many of the political deportees were released home under the 17 September 1955 amnesty of wartime collaborators, as were some 5,700 from the small Moldavian Republic alone.[13]

Gradually, the authorities began to broach the possible release of nationalists. A decree of 10 March 1956 by the Presidium of the All-Union Supreme Soviet released 'especially dangerous state criminals' who had been exiled upon completion of their term sentences on the basis of the now-abolished decree of 21 February 1948. The power to decide on the return of nationalists to the three Baltic republics was delegated to their governments based on individual applications.[14] On 15 May of that year, the regime finally addressed the group directly and ordered the release of the families of Ukrainian and Belorussian nationalists – an order that encompassed nearly 14,000 households. In Kiev and Minsk, the anxious and resentful authorities estimated that the decrees accounted for the return of 20,000 and 17,000 nationalists, respectively.[15]

At the same time, it appears that the authorities were making genuine efforts to run the amnesty process within the framework of the newly proclaimed socialist legality, however strained this term was by definition. One of their first steps was to move away from the imposition of undifferentiated categories and charges. Following the decision of 19 April 1956 to establish committees in the special settlements to review the convicts' cases, which was backed by the Estonian republic's Central Committee, the Estonian procurator pointed to the injustices resulting from the prevailing approach, especially the lumping together of members of nationalist organizations and participants in German wartime-created auxiliary forces, mainly *Omakaitse* (Self-Defence).[16] The latter, argued the Estonian official, should have been treated according to the amnesty of 17 September 1955, which was extended to wartime collaborators with no Soviet blood on their hands. Moreover, noted the official, since members of the review committees had no command of the Estonian language and the Estonian inmates barely spoke Russian, deliberations often resulted in unsubstantiated decisions and unnecessarily prolonged incarceration.[17]

Without disavowing the right of the party-state to use the law in the defence of the system, the authorities worked to reduce the numbers of political inmates to those 'with blood on their hands' – people who actually took Soviet lives during and after the war. One of those released in what he termed as the 'unforgettable spring of 1956' was Danylo Shumuk. A die-hard Communist-turned-nationalist who later broke with the nationalists in search of a more inclusive democratic path, Shumuk told the review commission that visited the special regime camp of his political journey from Communism to Ukrainian nationalism. His disillusionment with the Communist Party began with the 'liberation' of western Ukraine in 1939. He was disgusted by the 'formalistic, bureaucratic party-mindedness, soulless slogans and pompous speeches,' and by the forced collectivization; and his disenchantment was intensified, intriguingly, by his encounter as a Red Army soldier in 1941 with eastern Ukrainian peasants at the front who informed him about the famine of 1933 and the repressions of 1937. Still, it seemed that Shumuk's insistence that he had not taken part in battles or killed anyone, nor had he held a leading position in the nationalist movement, mattered more to the commission that annulled his conviction. 'Your court case is of no real account; I'm surprised that you received the death sentence or even twenty years of hard labour,' the head of the commission told Shumuk. Moreover, the commission let Shumuk turn the tables on the 'high-handed "feudal princes" and their *oprichniki*' who ran the camps by rebutting charges of his anti-Soviet activities there; they asked him to compose a detailed report on his time in the camps and send it to Moscow, and he did. Shumuk was released, although he was deprived of his citizenship rights.

The new emphasis on socialist legality was evident in the review of other cases, such as that of Fedosii Hloba, a former candidate for membership in the party and collective farm chairman, who under constant beating confessed to false charges and incriminated a multitude of other fellow Communists as members of the OUN-UPA (Ukrainian Insurgent Army). The review committee focused on the interrogation methods, threw out the conviction and twenty-five-year forced labour sentence, and, equally important, had Hloba sign each page of the new interrogation stenogram that concluded with a signed statement confirming the text was in accordance with his own words.[18] If Shumuk's and Hloba's cases are any indication, as they seem to be, then the release policy stemmed to a large degree from the desire to do away with the Gulag institution and the most blatant extrajudicial practices that accompanied it as soon as possible, or at least reduce it to a minimum. On average, recalled Shumuk, twenty out of every twenty-five inmates from each group reviewed were released, some had their sentences reduced by half, and a rare few sentences were left unchanged.[19]

Many inmates, however, did not wait for the regime to complete the gradual and convoluted dismantling of the Gulag but took the initiative into their own hands. By early November 1956, more than half of those deported from Moldavia between 1941 and 1951 (over 8,000 out of 15,865 families) had already been released from the special settlements. Many of those released, especially those who served at the front during the Great Patriotic War, not only returned to the republic's territory in defiance of the ban on doing so but also began bombarding the authorities with requests to retrieve their homes and official permission to reside in Moldavia. An effort by the MVD to compel the illegal returnees to sign an agreement to depart from the republic was met with hostility by the returnees and their families. The ministry concluded that the measure created a negative attitude toward Soviet power.[20] Earlier in April 1956, the All-Union minister of internal affairs explained to the party boss in Ukraine that, in accordance with the government decree of 21 October 1953, the nearly 24,000 nationalists released by the 10 March decree were allowed to return to their former place of residence, as long as it was not a passport regime location. In the very same note, the minister paved the way for a following decree on 15 May of that year that allowed family members of nationalists to leave the special settlements, since, he argued, it was unjust to keep them there for the crimes of others.[21]

The political arena offered another explanation for the regime's willingness to take such risks. With Stalin gone, Moscow's attitude toward the local cadres turned from suspicion to cultivation and respect. In the course of a series of regional party committee plenums in June 1953, party officials were inundated by bitter complaints by local Communists about the patronizing attitude of their counterparts who were arriving from the eastern regions. 'I do not and cannot trust you. You were not brought up the way we were,' was a typical retort levelled at veteran Communists and former partisan leaders.[22] It was not accidental that the indigenization drive coincided with an emphasis on vigilance in the continued struggle against Ukrainian bourgeois nationalists. With the renunciation of mass terror and the transition to communal policing, the cultivation and engagement of local cadres were deemed crucial. Moreover, the indigenous cadres had both ideological and personal stakes in the Soviet system. They began their climb up through the ranks during and immediately after the war in the course of the bitter struggle against nationalist separatists, who in turn viewed them as turncoats. Eradicating separatist nationalism was both an ideological creed and a ticket to the higher echelons of the system. It was, indeed, Mariia Kikh, Vasyl' Behma, Mykola Pidhornyi, Oleksii Kyrychenko, Antanas Sniečkus, Johannes Käbin, Arvīds Pelše, Kiril Mazurov and others like them throughout the western frontier who outlined an uncompromising stand against the nationalist movement that was often even harsher than the one articulated in Moscow.[23]

More concretely, Moscow and the republics' leaders appeared confident in their ability to remould their opponents, even when they abandoned the primary tool of mass physical terror in favour of sustained social and psychological coercion. The regime's self-assuredness was evident in the treatment of captured commanders. By now the security services sought nothing short of a change of heart. 'Both you and Orlan must realize your position,' Tymofii Strokach, the Internal Affairs chief in L'viv, told the wife of the captured nationalist leader Vasyl' Halasa (also known as Orlan) during an interrogation in July 1953 that would have been improbable only few months earlier. 'You will not leave [this prison] as the person who came here, your views and attitudes intact. Your only chance for survival is to be reborn, become different people. Of course, you would need to make amends to the government, exculpate your actions and the damage you have done. And this time we will not accept your words. You will have to do it with your deeds. You will have to help us liquidate the underground.'[24]

The rebirth, of course, was to be a Soviet one, which meant letting Halasa's wife out of the country but forcing her to leave behind her children and family who were still in exile for her activity, with the hope that this would be enough to turn her into an informant on émigré nationalist groups.[25] The efforts toward re-education and conversion of arch-enemies to informants included tours in the now Sovietized Ukrainian cities, as well as celebrations of 1 May and of the tercentennial of the signing of the Treaty of Pereiaslav, which brought left-bank Ukraine into the tsarist domain. Orlan's life was spared after he wrote a confession renouncing his nationalist past. His confession, along with those of other captured underground leaders, was published, and eventually he was pardoned and allowed to resume his education and professional career.

Moreover, the regime could count on several powerful sources of support for its cause. In a region where the wounds of the war were still open, stability and order had a strong appeal, especially since many among the exhausted population shared the authorities' revulsion for the uninhibited violence across the border and the fear of a chain reaction that might ignite the entire region. Recalling the Hungarian crisis more than a decade after its conclusion, Nikita Khrushchev was still incensed by the violence: 'Active party members and especially Chekists were being hunted down in the streets. Party committees and Chekist organizations were crushed. People were being murdered, strung from lampposts, and hanged by their feet.'[26] True to form, the Soviet leader was concerned largely with the blood of Communists and their allies ('there was always the risk that the counterrevolution might prevail temporarily, which would mean that much proletarian blood would be shed'[27]). Yet many in the western frontier, not just Communists, shared his anxieties.

In western Ukraine, the violence of the Hungarian rebellion seemed to deter even members of the younger generation, such as the group of students in Drohobych who commented, 'There will be disorder [in Hungary] until our "Russian Ivan" steps in, sticks it to them and tells them, "All right boys, it aches a little, now get down to work."' Others worried about the prospects of a spillover of the conflict in the Middle East leading to a third world war or interrupting their studies before they could graduate and enter a profession. Historical animosities, too, fed popular reactions such as the expressed satisfaction with Soviet power teaching the Hungarians a lesson for their crimes against Ukrainians in 1915 'when they hanged our people from telephone poles.' And there were those who had already developed a notion of the 'Soviet man's burden' and profound anger at the ungrateful Hungarians who 'murder and hang Communists while we send them bread.'[28]

Indeed, the return of released nationalists reopened the scars of the post–Second World War civil war and revealed a constituency split along the lines of this bitter strife. In their surveys of the countryside in October, the local police organs recognized a region that was sinking into a blood feud and a constituency paralysed by fear and animosities that effectively drained the landscape of Soviet power. In certain villages this blood feud formed the core of social life, the party-state, and KGB organs in the Stanyslaviv region claimed desperately. Peasants in the collective farms were reluctant to readmit the people who had terrorized them only a few years earlier and whom, in turn, they helped uncover and deport. In the villages of Pidhorode and Nova-Skvariva, children of deceased peasants attacked released UPA members, threatened to lynch them unless they departed immediately, and forced them to flee the villages. Widows complained bitterly against the injustice of having to watch the former killers of their husbands returning to normal life. 'You'll never hide from me. I'll kill you anyway. It's your wife's turn to become a widow,' one of them promised a former nationalist, after beating him in public. Elsewhere, relatives of peasants killed by nationalists in the course of the civil war employed the centuries-old weapon of social boycott, shunning amnestied returnees in public or introducing them to children as the murderers of their parents, effectively chasing the returnees out of the village, and in some cases, back to their place of exile.[29]

The returning nationalists faced a frontier different from the one they had left in the mid-1940s. Home was a foreign country, as many of them learned when confronted by locals' bewilderment or hostility. 'I find myself in an unrecognizable land. The native land that once nourished us with bread and salt now feeds us poisonous juices. The village is unrecognizable. People have changed. Where there was once love and friendship, there is now hatred and injustice, treachery at every step. They raise "Yanichars," with whom it's hard for me to communicate,' wrote one of the early returnees in the L'viv region to a former fellow inmate.[30]

The more intimate encounter was more painful. At home, Shumuk encountered an estranged wife and son as well as a new daughter, born out of wedlock when he was in the camps. His native village was equally alien. Few had actually recognized him upon arrival, and those who paid a visit confirmed his determination to leave the village. It was a Soviet village, a dispirited Shumuk realized. Exhausted by the mayhem of the war and the civil war that followed it and having gotten used to the omnipresence of Soviet power, the once fervently nationalist villagers were now fully engaged in the routine of everyday life on the collective farm. The number and quality of the buildings in the village had increased, as well as the number of educated people, but the old folk songs that embodied the cultural spirit of the village were no longer heard; they had been replaced by the wild shouting of drunks. The villagers, noted Shumuk, consumed more alcohol in a day than they had in a month before the war. Whatever politics was left in them had also become Soviet, Shumuk was soon to learn. His explanations to the curious villagers of the reasons for his disillusionment with Communism were conveyed to the KGB and would lead to his second imprisonment.[31]

Meanwhile in Tallinn, Jaan Kross, the now famed Estonian writer, was readjusting to civilian life after having spent eight years in the camps. In a pointed tale of a train ride from Tallinn to Tartu, Kross observes his surroundings through the eyes of a literary alter ego.[32] Burying himself literally and metaphorically in *Rahva Hääl*, reading Nikita Sergeevich's (Khrushchev) umpteenth speech on wheat production, he follows an encounter between the elderly wife of a headmaster who had recently returned from the camps, one of his former students, and other passengers who were also following the discussion. What he saw was a society where some were still trying to digest the avalanche of misfortune that had visited their lives over the last decade and a half, unafraid to ponder the issue out loud; others who did their best to avoid any public reference to the tormented past of occupation, denunciations, and deportations; and still others who could not care less. The woman, Ms Kaasik, expresses guarded optimism, but she still cannot comprehend why an innocent comment on the Soviet flag by her left-leaning husband, who opposed the authoritarian regime of Konstantin Päts (the interwar president), landed him in Soviet camps, or how his peers had no qualms about swearing allegiance to Päts and then to Stalin.

Most intriguing, however, was the linkage drawn between personal and national fates, a particularly poignant phenomenon in smaller nations. Ms Kaasik is still grieving over two of her four boys who fell in the war ('one on the right side, the other on the wrong side'), but she is even more troubled by her two sons who married non-Estonians, reside in Moscow and Brisbane, respectively, and are raising their children as Russians and Australians. 'Well, so what?' says Suursepp (the former student), 'as long as she's nice [referring to the Russian in-law] and the kids are too.' 'Yes, his wife is nice,' replies the woman. 'And so are the children. Nothing concrete to complain about. Love is something you don't inquire about. Only the thought crosses my mind: if there's too much of that kind of love, our nation will disappear off the face of the earth, won't it?' And so hope hinges on the only daughter who studies the Estonian language and will probably be admitted to the university, now that her father is back from the camps.

Yet the very characteristic that helped the headmaster, his wife, and their fellow countrymen to persevere is also a source of the trouble awaiting them. In the late 1950s, the stoic stubbornness that carried the family through both inside and outside the camps could only prolong the hardships. 'An Estonian is, of course, slow in matters of re-education,' reflected the woman. And with many seeking to put the troubled past behind them, it was the returnees, their families, and their adjustment that had turned into nothing more than the butt of crude jokes. When Kaasik tells of the tears she shed upon reuniting with her husband, one passenger winks and tells his companion, 'You 'eard 'er, Juss! Yon tears will come with all that merriment and the creaking bedsprings when the old man came home after six fallow years! But I wonder if old Pig's Ear or Droop-Ear Soekõrv [her employers] got the droops when dad returned, know what I mean? Hi-hi-hi.'

The regime's omnipotence took its toll on returnees who were still searching for popular support of the nationalist cause, especially when they contrasted the situation with that in Poland. 'The hope I nurtured and invested in the youth was in vain,' one of them told a KGB informant. 'The Bolsheviks succeeded in educating this youth so it can think only in Bolshevik terms. The overwhelming majority of elderly people are Bolsheviks.... They don't want to listen to anything and they say, especially after the events in Hungary, that Russia strangles everything that starts stirring up, and that's why we should seriously reorient ourselves in accordance with the Soviet way.'[33] True, there were those who did not hesitate to take to the street and call Ukrainians to arms and fight for their independence or to declare to a group of youngsters in a bus, 'The time has come for us to start the same process that is happening in Hungary. The end of Soviet dictatorship is approaching.' It is doubtful, however, that such incidents, often dismissed by the authorities as produced 'under the influence,' offered much comfort to veterans of the civil war and the Gulag who were desperately hoping for a chain reaction that would sweep the frontier. The mass youth movement across the border could also be a source of despair.[34]

Finally, as we shall see below, the authorities could always rely on the loyal and cohesive constituency of Red Army veterans in the western regions, who forged a blood bond with both the domestic order and the territorial claims of the Soviet polity. And when we recall the abovementioned view that the solution to the political problem was basically economic, the picture that emerged was one of a self-assured regime, confident in its ability to cope with any challenge.

Manageable Risk?

But was it enough to justify the risks taken? Were Stalin's successors getting dizzy with reforms? By all indications available to the authorities, the political attitudes of the returnees on the eve of their release spelled major problems. Few of them conveyed any sense of remorse or reconciliation the way many ethnic Russians and former party members did.[35] In January 1949 and April 1950, just three years before it launched mass amnesties, the regime converted the sentences of Baltic and Ukrainian nationalists into permanent exile and imposed twenty years of hard labour on those who tried to escape. Reactions recorded by the regime varied. Some inmates were fatalist or even recognized the right of the regime to keep some Ukrainians permanently in exile while claiming their own innocence.[36] Most, however, were not so accommodating, vehemently rejecting everything Soviet, or as they often viewed it, everything Russian. The initial despair was replaced with defiance. Some interpreted the decree as another sign of Soviet hatred of all Ukrainians, while others comforted themselves that this was a temporary setback that would soon be reversed 'because many youngsters join the [insurgent] army and God avenges treachery.' Still others vowed to escape, regardless of the consequence, since it is 'better to serve twenty years hard labour than to live forever in the forest [exile].'[37] News of the Korean War propelled hopes, or rather delusions that the Western Allies would invade the Soviet Union, bring down the regime, and set prisoners free. Estonian deportees who were urged to sign a condemnation of the 'imperialist aggression' refused to do so and expressed regret that the Americans had bombed only North Korea when they should have bombed the Soviet Union as well.[38]

Most relevant for the eventual conduct of the returnees when they reached their homes was their vehement resentment of the collective farm system, where most would soon be heading. For many inmates it was 'far better to stay in Karaganda and even summon our families here from Western Ukraine [since] collective farms are being established there at the moment.... Better live here and work in the factory.' Others were sure of the terror they inspired in the authorities, boasting, 'We are banned from returning to the homeland since Soviet power is afraid of a rebellion. Even if they [try to] hold us here permanently we won't be here for long. The young lads will arrive and set us free.'[39] This was no empty rhetoric. In Vorkuta, western Ukrainian and Baltic deportees were reputed to be the toughest and most violent political inmates. A German prisoner in Vorkuta, where Ukrainians comprised more than half of the inmate population, recalled their frequently being rounded up for killing informers and repeating over and over again, 'We want arms, that's all! We'll do the rest ourselves.'[40] Estonians impressed him with their uncompromising hostility to Soviet power, including their refusal to learn the 'state language,' Russian, even after six years in the camps, and their rough-and-tough reputation for killing camp guards who insulted them.[41] Baltic and Ukrainian nationalists, along with Red Army officers, spearheaded the wave of strikes and uprisings that swept through the Gulag camps in 1953–4.[42] Finally, camp life that often pitted nationalities against each other also brought them together unexpectedly. In one quasi-comic scene Joseph Scholmer found himself explaining to an astonished and delighted group of Estonians, Finns, Komis, and Hungarians that they all shared ancestry and languages.[43] Barely three years later, such scenes would look less unusual when events across the border transformed these ethnic-linguistic affinities into political realities.

Many of these individuals had already returned home when neighbouring Poland and Hungary exploded in 1956, putting to the test the regime's will, its belief in the system's reformability, and Moscow's actual familiarity with conditions in the periphery. In the non-Slavic republics, the KGB admitted it had difficulties penetrating the ranks of the Gulag returnees, largely because of the language barrier. In Lithuania the agency was particularly frustrated by its failure to infiltrate the Catholic Church, which it perceived as the spearhead of nationalist, anti-Russian sentiments. With the mass return of unreformed leaders and priests, the revived church, as well as other cohorts of returnees, appeared almost beyond reach. With barely 53 per cent of its agents having command of the indigenous language, infiltration of these cohorts was practically impossible.[44]

To make matters worse, the western frontier was already simmering in the wake of Khrushchev's not-so-secret speech in February of that year. Young Polish reformers made full use of the Polish-Ukrainian Friendship Month in October 1956 to spread the word among their Ukrainian counterparts. In a startling article in the official organ of the Ukrainian Ministry of Culture, the editor-in-chief of the Polish journal *Nowa kultura* related, 'Different people express different ideas.... We in Poland favour a variety of trends, a variety of artistic viewpoints. Our discussion has found an echo among the Czechs, Yugoslavs, and Hungarians. It would be a good thing if the Ukrainian artists had stated their opinions on this matter.'[45]

The Polish official was probably unaware that he was preaching to the choir. In meetings in March of that year, scores of writers and film-makers alarmed the authorities with their vociferous resentment of official actions: the slavish homage to the Russian people, the harsh attack on Volodymyr Sosiura for his famous 1944 poem 'Love the Ukraine,' the closure of Jewish journals and newspapers, and the glossing over of the famine of 1933 during the Twentieth Party Congress. They also raised the sensitive issue of Ukrainian artists repressed in 1937 and yet to be rehabilitated.[46] In a region flooded with tens of thousands of former inmates who perceived themselves as innocent victims, the very notion of rehabilitation was a time bomb.

Like the rest of their counterparts throughout the Soviet Union, the Communist Party organizations in the western republics conducted a series of meetings to discuss the resolutions of the Twentieth Party Congress and Khrushchev's speech on the 'cult of personality,' guaranteeing that the speech would become a household topic throughout the frontier. To a large degree, the reactions of local Communists were identical to those recorded elsewhere in the Soviet Union and Eastern Europe. Some congratulated the party for addressing the issue and engaging the population directly, in a clear break from past practices. Others wondered whether the cult should be viewed as a degenerate phenomenon and a repudiation of Marxism-Leninism, or why no one spoke about the violations of Leninist principles in the Nineteenth Congress (December 1952) when Stalin was still alive.[47] The Second World War figured highly in the reflections of ethnic Russian Communists, many of whom arrived in the frontier in the wake of the war. Condemnations of Stalin revolved upon his exaggerated role during the war, his strategic errors that cost the lives of many soldiers, unnerving questions regarding the validity of General Vlasov's anti-Soviet views in light of recent revelations, and comparison of the late Soviet leader with the his two arch-enemies Hitler and Churchill.[48] Party members in western Ukraine were more cautious than their Baltic and even their eastern Ukrainian counterparts, concerning themselves mainly with the fate of repressed veteran Communists. But even there, questions such as 'What is the situation with people who had not been rehabilitated?' and 'Will the deported nationalities return to their homelands?' were sharp reminders that these issues continued to unnerve party members.[49]

The authorities, however, were much more concerned by the evident loss of their monopoly over information, which led to a frenzy of rumours, especially in the villages – most alarmingly, regarding popular unrest in other non-Russian republics. Soviet anxieties over foreign broadcasts were evident: they constantly jammed those broadcasts and attempted to compete with the Western programs, especially in the non-Russian regions. The issue was of special concern in the territorially small Estonia, whose entire area was open to unhindered Western broadcasts, as the authorities found out well before the 1956 crises.[50] Alluding to the visible gap between the official silence over the 'Secret Speech' in the country and the constant references to it in the Western broadcasts, western Ukrainians wondered out loud why Khrushchev's speech was not published.[51] In Estonia, party members reported a series of rumours: the alleged dispatch of 15,000 agitators from Moscow to Georgia to answer questions on the cult of personality, broadcasts on an uprising that resulted in the seizure of government facilities, and the execution of 5,000 officers associated with the Tukhachevskii affair in 1937. And while Georgia was rocked by pro-Stalin demonstrations, monuments to the late leader were desecrated throughout Estonia. The authorities were further rattled by inquiries about the validity of Stalin's views on nationality policies and, even worse, regarding deportations from the republic: 'Was the resettlement of the kulaks necessary and will they be allowed to return?' came a question from Türi.[52] Six years earlier, the attempt by Nikolai Karotamm, first secretary of the Central Committee, to keep the de-kulakized peasants within the republic's borders had cost him his job and his party career. Peasants in the western Ukrainian region of Drohobych wondered what the principal and concrete mistakes were that Stalin had committed in guiding the rural economy.[53] In a region where collectivization was the worst calamity inflicted by the Soviet regime, few could be fooled by the seemingly innocent question. With deported kulaks and nationalist activists returning from exile, the wounds of that policy were reopened.

Things were already heating up when the Third Plenum of the Estonian Central Committee convened 23–25 October 1956, to discuss implementation of the Twentieth Congress resolutions on ideological work. Party members and agitators were criticized for neglecting the education of workers in the spirit of Soviet patriotism and internationalism, for struggling only half-heartedly against nationalist manifestations, and for catering to student delegations from capitalist Finland. The literary critic Laosson caused consternation when he condemned the 'national nihilism' among the cultural elite of Soviet Estonia, some of whom 'still confuse the sentiment and virtue of national pride with bourgeois nationalism, and attempt to forge the friendship of the peoples at the expense of and contempt for the past of the Estonian people, its merits and culture.' Other speakers criticized Estonian Communists arriving from other republics who were unfamiliar with the local conditions and population and were acting as a superior stratum. These speeches were roundly criticized, but they left an indelible mark on the proceedings.[54] By the time the Estonian plenum was concluded, the situation in Poland and Hungary was already at a crisis point.

Poland and Hungary Pay a Visit

The Twentieth Party Congress and the ensuing discussions inside and outside the party cells opened the wounds of the occupation and Sovietization policies in the western frontier and offered anti-Soviet activists a vast pool of memories and rhetoric upon which to draw. The amnesties and returns of political prisoners provided the required agency. However, there was a need for a cataclysm that would transform these dormant resentments into action. Such a spark arrived from across the border in November 1956. Early signs that locals in the western frontier were closely watching the turbulent events in Eastern Europe had already been spotted in the immediate aftermath of Khrushchev's speech. Inquiries about the legality of purges in the Eastern European satellites were tacit reminders of the view of Soviet power as an external force and the equation of the Estonian Republic with sovereign states. Significantly, such inquiries emerged from the party's rank and file. Against the backdrop of thousands of locals having been purged, deported, or executed, a request to clarify the validity of the cases against the Trotskyite-Bukharinite opposition and prominent Communists such as Traicho Kostov, Rudolf Slánský, and László Rajk was particularly troublesome. Questions thrown at top party leaders linked the party with domestic purges and external brutalities: 'Will Trotsky, Zinov'ev, and Kamenev be rehabilitated since they were ideologically harmless? Will Stalin be tried posthumously for the murder of many leaders and thousands of innocent workers? Many think that Stalin was also involved in the murder of Poles near Smolensk,' concluded a note in referring to the massacre of thousands of Polish officers in the Katyn forest.[55] When Poland and Hungary erupted a few months later, the importance of such inquiries became clear.

The echoes of the uprising in Hungary were soon heard in western Ukraine as well. On 3 November 1956, a day before the invasion of Hungary, the Ukrainian Central Committee sent Moscow a comprehensive report, *On Certain Statements regarding the Events in Poland and Hungary*. The report portrayed an agitated and fragmented republic. It opened with favourable reactions to the regime that condemned the upheaval in Poland and Hungary as the vile provocation of reactionary domestic elements joining forces with the agents of American-British imperialism. The statement of a worker from L'viv – who said, 'If the enemies of the People's Democracy of Poland try to repeat Poznan [the core site of unrest in Poland], they'll achieve nothing but death; to move against the people is like spitting against the wind' – was claimed to reflect the sentiments of the majority of the Ukrainian population. Others observed, 'If Father [*bat'ko*] Stalin were alive, he would have deported half [of the Hungarians] to Siberia and there would have been order in Hungary.' More potent, probably, were the voices of war veterans, whose anger at 'the fascist elements in Budapest and Poznan' had a distinct personal edge. 'As a surgeon and veteran of the Great Patriotic War, I could not avoid expressing my deep anger. Don't they understand, these petty, thuggish provocateurs, that they cannot destroy the erected building of the people's democracy and return to fascism?' roared one of them. Her voice was one of many. 'We liberated Hungary. Soviet people shed their blood there.... If this goes on, then a capitalist order will be established in Hungary,' declared another one in a meeting in L'viv.[56] What was won in blood was not up for negotiation.

At the same time, the Central Committee report revealed myriad vulnerabilities, if only unwittingly. First, the geography of opinions showed a sharp split between East and West. While the party paraded approving voices from both the eastern and western provinces, the condemnations of Soviet policies in the neighbouring countries, including disturbing comparisons with the policies of the tsarist regime, came solely from the western regions.[57]

Second, while people accused the government of distrust of its own population by concealing information on the course of events and thus helping the spread of provocative rumours, they seemed to be well informed. Many gathered information from Western radio broadcasts, the Hungarian news agency, Polish newspapers that continued to sell freely in western Ukraine during and after the crisis, and relatives and friends who were crossing and recrossing the border.[58] The contribution of the loss of the regime's monopoly over information to the rapid destabilization of the region was evident as national minorities began to draw their own interpretation of the upheaval across the border.[59] For western Ukrainian Poles it was mainly the living memory of statehood that fuelled their interest in the events in the external homeland. 'The Poles were always distinguished by their great desire for freedom and independence,' a senior instructor in one of L'viv's economic institutions told his colleagues. 'During their thirty years of independence they became accustomed to a different way of life.' Another one summed up the situation as the simple desire of Poland to bolt from under Russian control. Equally troublesome was the explicit expectation of a chain reaction that would shake the entire Soviet bloc and spill over to the western frontier. Poles in the region repeatedly invoked the name of Tito, the Yugoslav leader who, in their view, inspired the Polish and Hungarian governments to follow his path in relations with the Soviet Union. And, as the Soviets were fully aware, the living memory of lost sovereignty was even more problematic in the Baltic republics.

More dangerous, however, was the consternation among the nearly 50,000 strong Hungarian minority in the Transcarpathian region. As events were reaching their deadly climax in Hungary, the agitation in the region turned vehement and public. In late October, the streets of the regional centre of Uzhhorod were plastered with anti-Soviet and anti-Semitic leaflets, and locals insulted Soviet soldiers and non-Hungarians in public. 'You just wait. Soon you'll kneel down before me,' came one threat, echoing that of another worker, who promised a group of non-Hungarians that they would all 'go to church and kneel down in prayer when the Soviets leave the Transcarpathian region that will be reunited with Hungary.' Referred to as a revolution – a provocative term in the eyes of the Soviet authorities – the uprising was viewed by some as the long-awaited indigenization of power in their homeland. 'The Hungarian people got rid of the former Jewish prime minister and replaced him with one of their own, a Magyar,' gloated an employee at the municipal housing administration. And there was the young Kékesi who crossed the border to visit his parents in the village of Tiachev. 'Soon we'll have a new political course [in Hungary],' he declared.

> In two months there won't be collective farms any more. If they elect Imre Nagy, the first thing he will do is to abolish the collective farms.... The Russians will run away as the Germans did in 1944.... All of us immigrants have been at work, but here nobody does anything because you are afraid of getting twenty-five years [in prison] ... we'll continue to work for the return of Transcarpathia and other lands to Hungary. Greater Hungary will soon be restored to its 1914 borders.... If there is a third world war, we won't lose territory anymore, because America and West Germany are stronger than ever.[60]

Young Jewish activists, who viewed the developments in Poland as a revival of the very democratic socialism that the Soviets had abandoned, translated information into Russian and distributed it among the population. And amnestied Ukrainian nationalists fantasized about a chain reaction that would shake the frontier. 'After Poland come Hungary, Czechoslovakia and maybe Romania,' observed Mykola Ryvak. 'This will have a great impact on Ukraine, Belarus, and the Asian Soviet republics. There will be a brutal struggle here between the Russian element and the Ukrainians.'[61]

Hungarian rebels who were deported to the Soviet Union and imprisoned in western Ukraine described an excited atmosphere, buzzing with rumours, and a population that appeared sympathetic toward the Hungarian cause. Arriving at prisons in western Ukraine, where they replaced Polish inmates, the Hungarians encountered guards who showed them sympathy and friendliness, smuggled messages for them, and provided news on events in Hungary and student unrest in the Soviet Union.[62]

The countryside was equally agitated. Danylo Shumuk, who had just returned to his native village, recalled,

> In the Volhynian region, workers on the collective farms, especially the women, became so hostile to the authorities that the brigade leaders and heads of the collective farms were afraid to approach them. The collective farmers began warning officials, 'Soon the same will happen in Ukraine as

in Hungary. We'll drive you from our land too.' The uprising in Hungary and developments in Poland, together with the transportation of Soviet troops to the USSR's western borders, led many people to believe that a revolt inside the Soviet Union would also erupt and that the Soviet system would be toppled.[63]

Soviet activists were horrified by the return of people whom they thought they would never meet again. In 1949, Havryl Khrustiuk ignored the presence of nationalist forces in his village in Rivne and participated in the establishment of the collective farm. Now, however, he refrained from opposing them:

> That's how it is now. Work with your hands, but keep your mouth shut. Better to fasten your tongue behind your teeth, so it won't pop out even if it needs to. Why? ... Because you don't know from which side you'll get it. In the past I knew about some bandits, whom I could always avoid. But now try and guess which of the returnees is waiting for you in a dark corner. This is a very dangerous band of people and one must be careful of them. Will I move against them? It's enough that even without testifying I cannot step out of my home in the evenings.[64]

The increased anti-Soviet activity by the returnees brought the villages to a political and social standstill, with anxious activists avoiding enrolment in the Komsomol, attendance at village assemblies, and conferences in Moscow, and having their photographs taken for local exhibits. For the past three months, concluded the party, the collective farms had been practically surrendered to former nationalists.

Anxieties were exacerbated by the thorny issue of confiscated property, which Gulag returnees pursued relentlessly as soon as they resettled in their native places. In Moldavia, the authorities found out that the decree sanctioning the recovery of property only in cases where deportation was proven to be based on false charges had hardly deterred the former inmates. The rejected returnees bombarded the prosecutor office with demands for full rehabilitation, claiming they were deported on the basis of unsubstantiated denunciations.[65] Some worksites in Estonia took in only former Gulag inmates, prompting the authorities to quip that all that was needed was barbed wire around the base for it to fit the past of both the director and the employees.[66] In some western Ukrainian districts, the former inmates were welcomed as heroes and showered with honours and material support that allowed some to avoid work. True to form, returning nationalists refused to work on the collective farms, and most of them insisted on being employed, if at all, in the cities or industry. Moreover, nationalist groupings were often extensions of networks established in the camps. These enduring associations attracted non-active returnees by offering support and security by terrorizing villagers who had helped the authorities in the struggle against the nationalist forces or had testified against them in court.[67]

Baltic reactions to the crisis partially resembled those in the Slavic western republics, but they also differed in significant ways. First, expectations for a chain reaction that would sweep the region echoed those in western Ukraine and Belarus. The Lithuanian authorities noted the proliferation of pro-Polish and pro-Hungarian sentiments among individuals who hoped that the events in Hungary were 'the beginning of the end. Soon all the democratic countries will overthrow the hated system and break away from the Soviet Union. The unrest will then spread to the Baltics, which in the end will also be liberated from the Russians.' Agitated by foreign radio broadcasts and voluminous correspondence with Western countries, ordinary citizens, Gulag returnees, and Baltic Poles articulated expectations identical to those of their brethren in western Ukraine but embarked on a far more active course. Anticipating the abolition of collective farms in Poland and the restoration of the pre-1939 borders, many declined to work on the collective farms, sold their houses, and applied for exit to Poland, or waited for the opportunity to expel Lithuanians and Russians from districts that previously belonged to Poland.[68]

By late October the Estonian authorities grew increasingly alarmed by the impact of the upheaval in Poland and Hungary and the avalanche of Western broadcasts. On 27 October alone, a series of coordinated gatherings were held in Tallinn, during which dozens of former graduates of the Swedish and British colleges in interwar Tallinn and recently released anti-Soviet activists saluted the Polish and Hungarian uprisings, raised toasts to 'Free Hungary,' and sang 'Poland Has Not Perished Yet,' the Polish national anthem.

But it was Baltic students and youths who emerged as key actors in the unrest that swept the frontier, which helps explain the puzzle of why such an exhausted population was able to rally in such an active way. Initiating and leading the largest and best-organized anti-Soviet protests, students in Tallinn, Tartu, Vilnius, and Kaunas capitalized on an available organizational infrastructure, their closer contact with the outside world, their exposure to interwar political culture through the remaining older faculty, and the fact that, unlike the older generation in their respective republics and in contrast to their counterparts in the Slavic republics, they had passed through the crucible of the war relatively unscathed.[69] The authorities had already identified these features in the wake of Khrushchev's speech. Komsomol surveys of its ranks in Estonia and Lithuania in the spring of 1956 portrayed a cohort that was essentially isolated from Soviet life (some could not even name the first secretary of the Communist Party) and deeply anti-Russian. They were avid followers of foreign radio broadcasts, inspired by past sovereignty and the situation in the present-day West, and concerned with the fate of fellow nationals in other Soviet republics.[70] When Poland and Hungary erupted, these features assumed acute political meaning. Students from the Polytechnic Institute in Tallinn challenged a pillar of the totalitarian order when they invited their peers in other institutions to form an independent union, to which the latter responded enthusiastically. 'Life is getting very stormy.... There is a plan to form an All-Estonian Student Association. It's already moving ahead! The boys are full of enthusiasm. In general, the atmosphere is electric,' wrote one of them to a friend. In a gathering with several instructors present, students shouted, 'Long live Hungary!' and 'Long live Budapest!' and vowed to follow the Hungarian example, should similar circumstances arise. A student who attended the gathering described it in a letter to friend: 'You cannot imagine that we had a free discussion here. A year ago we didn't even dare to think about it. Some people want to liquidate the Komsomol and replace it with something new. Obviously the Hungarian events have had serious effects.' Moreover, the student was in awe after he met visiting students from Finland, with whom, he claimed, 'We have established regular interactions.' Others expressed their admiration for the Hungarian students who were the first to rebel, demanding that the Russian language and Marxism be excluded from the schools and inspiring the workers to join them.[71]

The mass eruptions in Lithuania overshadowed everything else. In well-prepared demonstrations, thousands of students from various institutions in Vilnius showed up at the old Rasos historical cemetery; the KGB estimated that some 30–40,000 people gathered at the Kaunas cemetery on the night of 2 November. The All Souls' Day tradition of lighting candles quickly turned into mass political demonstrations. Hungary was on the minds of the thousands who gathered there: 'Only God knows how many prayers were said that evening for fighting Hungary,' recalled one witness. After lighting candles and singing patriotic songs by the graves of fallen Lithuanian soldiers, the crowds in both cities marched to the city centres and clashed with the police, shouting 'Long live the Hungarian heroes!' 'Russians out of Lithuania!' and 'Long live independent Hungary, Poland, and Lithuania!'[72]

Nor was it lost on the authorities that in the hierarchy of animosities, ideology and politics took a backseat to ethnicity. Anti-Soviet leaflets or individuals shouting in the streets 'Down with the Russian government!' and 'Death to the Russian occupiers!' did not even bother with the Communist Party.[73] Alarmed ethnic Russians in Kaunas appealed directly to Moscow, citing their lack of confidence in the local party and KGB, which they accused of misleading Moscow and intentionally downplaying the political significance of the riots. Warning against the possible repetition of the murderous attacks on non-Lithuanians at the beginning of the German occupation, Russians lamented, 'This is the fate of the Great October in Kaunas, for which the Russian people fought and sacrificed millions of lives ... What's next?'[74]

The party's and KGB's analysis and measures in the wake of the crisis reflected the distinct features of the Baltic republics. A flabbergasted party cell at Tartu University admitted that it was out of touch with the political realities on campus, including the sharp rift between Estonian and Russian students, lacked the means to monitor the students, had no clue about the students' reactions to the unfolding crisis, and was rather ambivalent in its assessment of the 'capitalist threat.' While a loose admissions policy was blamed for the enrolment of 'bourgeois-nationalist elements and amnestied individuals,' no one offered an explanation for how these students were allowed to agitate uninterrupted. Similarly, the frequent encounters with Finnish students revealed a relaxed attitude that allowed the visiting Finns to discuss politics freely and to welcome Estonians visiting Helsinki with the pre-war Estonian flag, to which the Estonian representatives reacted with token disapproval.

The resolutions adopted were a balancing act, bereft of the trademark vehement rhetoric, and reflected the ambivalence of the local party activists. Calling for the strengthening of relations between Russian and Estonian students, the party cell vowed to 'react swiftly to occurrences of bourgeois nationalism and Great Russian chauvinism' and balanced the focused display of the evils and flaws of the capitalist system with 'objective Marxist assessment of the achievements of the capitalist countries in production technology.'[75] The Lithuanian KGB analysis of the unrest added an intriguing explanation for the proliferation of illegal organizations on campuses – the contacts between the young students and the old intelligentsia. The latter were especially active in raising money for political prisoners. Indeed, scores of leading writers and poets who returned from the Gulag between 1954 and 1956 were readmitted to the Writers Union and resumed publishing. Although the KGB did not provide a detailed list of members of the old intelligentsia who sought to incite the students, the purge of Vilnius academic institutions shortly thereafter for 'committing grave ideological errors; intensified nationalist tendencies, violation of Leninist principles in selection of cadres, and lack of attention to the multinational composition of the population of the republic' made clear that the group was marked by the authorities.[76]

Notably, the Lithuanian authorities tried to calm agitated Communists and Russian nationals by assuring them that the rioters were ordinary hooligans and that the entire episode was meaningless. The Estonian Central Committee did not report any arrests. It limited its response to political agitation and urged the primary party cells to lead the fight against nationalist and anti-Soviet sentiments, especially with the approaching anniversary of the October Revolution, and it hurriedly translated propaganda material into Estonian for use in the localities.

Yet the relatively moderate reactions of the Baltic authorities did little to counteract the venom of those inspired by the Hungarian violence and dreaming of life without Russians and Marxism-Leninism. Party agitators were bombarded with questions by a populace thirsty for information yet by no means bereft of opinions: 'The Soviet forces have intervened in the internal affairs of Poland and Hungary. Won't it lead to a war? Will there be collective farms in Hungary? Why does the Yugoslav radio station provide more detailed information on the situation in Hungary than our stations? What government was there in Hungary for twenty years if they had to form a new revolutionary workers'-peasants' government? Why do we use the slogan "Hands off Egypt!" but do not say this in reference to Hungary?' And on the eve of 7 November, leaflets calling for the exclusion of Russians from the student unions, the killing of traitors, and the expulsion of Russians from Estonia appeared in Tallinn and Tartu.[77]

The Hungarian uprising, noted party members, reignited anti-Communist sentiments and violence that paralysed the already isolated Communists, especially in the countryside. Kolkhoz meetings were regularly interrupted, and party members were routinely threatened by amnestied nationalists who held their own sessions to discuss possible action, should a situation similar to Hungary's develop.[78] Above all, they reached the chilling realization that some in the party were less than vigilant or even harboured sympathy for the uprising in Hungary. In the presence of a party district committee instructor who came to offer help in organizing political work in the collective, the secretary of the primary cell explained that he was drunk because he was 'celebrating Christmas. You are all blind. You don't know what has happened in Hungary and may soon happen in Yugoslavia and here.' Another Communist in the primary party cell of the Supreme Court of the republic decided to classify as simple hooliganism the act of citizens who tore apart and trampled on a portrait of Nikolai Bulganin (the chairman of the Council of Ministers) and shouted, 'Soon we'll have the same as what has taken place in Hungary.'[79]

Soviet anxieties were exacerbated by charges of Russification of culture made by delegations from the socialist satellites, and these were all the more explosive in the western border regions, as the first secretary of the Ukrainian Central Committee openly admitted in a detailed report to Moscow on 12 November 1956. In a balancing act that was to be expected from the head of the second Soviet republic, Kyrychenko voiced concerns over the problem of Russian speakers who were forced to cope with an insufficient number of Russian-language newspapers and too little instruction in Ukrainian in schools. At the same time, he vowed to guarantee the use of Ukrainian-language textbooks in schools. Most troubling was that the charges of Russification had receptive audiences – mainly returning nationalists, sectarian activists, and the Hungarian, Polish, and Jewish minorities, especially in the wake of the events in Poland, Hungary, and the Middle East.[80] Kyrychenko took comfort in the fact that nationalist demagoguery did not resonate with the population at large.[81] His own words and deeds, however, conveyed acute anxiety.

By then it was clear that the Twentieth Party Congress and the amnesties of political prisoners had shaken the world of party and non-party people alike, just as Khrushchev's rivals in the Kremlin had warned him at the time. But it was also evident that the Polish and Hungarian crises, especially the sight of a nearly toppled Communist regime and the flow of alternative information from both Western and socialist-bloc media, provided the spark that inspired anti-Soviet activists to act on deeply seated ethno-national and political-ideological resentments, offering hopes – or rather illusions – of realizing their agenda. Barely a decade earlier, similar actions and illusions had sunk the western frontier into a bloodbath, a fact that was always on the minds of the local authorities.

Gearing Up for Action

The growing anxiety over the conduct of former nationalists led the Ukrainian Central Committee to address Moscow in early September 1956 with specific recommendations it considered necessary in order to curtail the spreading chaos precipitated by their return. Fearing that the trickle was about to become a flood, and with demands to recover confiscated property already creating mayhem, the Ukrainian party requested an immediate halt to the further release of inmates to western Ukraine and the abolition of the rehabilitation commission under the auspices of the Presidium of the Supreme Soviet in Moscow. Citing numerous cases of premature release of defiant and unreformed nationalists ('Prison did not re-educate me. I am what I have always been and will continue to fight Soviet power for the rest of my life'; 'We will build an independent Ukraine in any case. We'll start with the extermination of Komsomolites. We learned the trade in the camps,' etc.), it demanded the establishment of a temporary commission in Ukraine that would review premature releases, declare L'viv and its surroundings a closed city, and impose a ban on the return of confiscated property to released nationalists.[82] Action followed: on 20 September 1956 the Council of Ministers placed L'viv under a special passport regime. A subsequent MVD order on 4 October authorized the ministry to expel violators of the restrictions, namely those who had not worked for three months or who refused registration. The ministry was authorized to intensify its surveillance among the returnees and to prosecute those who threatened Soviet personnel or who possessed arms. Two weeks later, the new passport regime had already claimed 345 violators marked for removal from the city.[83]

With mass terror no longer an option and the consequent reduction in the number of its employees, the KGB sought a coordinated response with the civilian authorities. Along with a sharp rebuke of the 'counterproductive and inadequate' cuts of its personnel in the western provinces and a demand to reactivate pro-Soviet political agitation among the returnees, the agency urged a more effective integration of the returnees in the labour force and called for an end to the practice of assigning pardoned nationalists with higher education to backward schools in remote rural districts. Nationalist groupings should be broken by separating those more susceptible to Communist agitation from the rest, recommended the KGB. This, however, was secondary to the assertion that the release of former nationalist guerrillas and activists to their former places of residence was premature. Stopping short of recommending the re-exile of the returnees, the KGB emphasized its unequivocal opposition to further releases of former nationalists into their jurisdictions.[84]

The pressure to get rid of nationalist returnees intensified in October, when the Ukrainian KGB appealed to the republic's Central Committee to obtain Moscow's permission to curtail, and in some cases to reverse, the resettlement of the former inmates in western Ukraine. In an urgent memorandum, the agency asked the central authorities to speed up the resolution of this matter by allowing it to exile from the republic those who violated restrictions within two months, imposing a special passport regime in all major western Ukrainian cities, and temporarily halting the removal of restrictions on family members of convicted nationalist activists. Party and state agencies were asked to register every nationalist who returned from exile and to place each promptly in useful jobs. Most important, however, the KGB asked Moscow to authorize the Ukrainian government to direct some 14,700 individuals to work in the southern and eastern provinces of the republic by the end of the year. The ministries of agriculture and state farms of these provinces were ordered to build proper housing for 1,400 families of former inmates scheduled to arrive there shortly. The agency also called for harsher sentences for the offenders and, together with the Prosecutor's Office, sought authorization to revoke the release of nationalist leaders and activists who were set free by various decrees of the Presidium of the Supreme Soviet before completing their terms or 'without sufficient grounds.'

Quite likely the most controversial recommendation was for the resurrection of articles in the Soviet Ukrainian Criminal Code that authorized the exile of socially dangerous people, which dated back to August 1938, the time of the Great Terror. Anticipating the uneasiness that such a recommendation might stir in 1956, the KGB chiefs went out of their way to emphasize the 'extraordinary and temporary' character of this measure, which they insisted was necessary in order to encourage frightened peasants to come forward and testify against the thugs who disrupted the work on the collective farms. Accordingly, the regional *ispolkoms* (executive committees) were authorized to mark for exile the returning nationalists who did not take part in 'socially useful labour.' At the same time, and in a marked departure from the earlier undifferentiated and unforgiving approach to the nationalist camp, the KGB called for publishing newspaper articles on individuals who after serving their sentences redeemed themselves through useful labour.[85]

The appeal did not fall on deaf ears, especially with violence steadily on the rise. On 9 November 1956, the Ukrainian authorities got their wish when the Presidium of the Supreme Soviet of the Republic issued a decree 'prohibiting former leaders and active members in the Ukrainian nationalist underground, who were tried and completed serving their sentences, to return to the western regions of Soviet Ukraine.' Violation of the decree was punishable by a five-year prison term.[86] By 1 January 1957, the KGB and the prosecutor's offices in the western Ukrainian regions reviewed and rejected 75,227 applications of inmates seeking to return to their former places of residence.[87] On 21 January 1957, the Lithuanian authorities followed suit and issued a similar decree that extended the ban to members of the former bourgeois government and parties and imposed five years' exile on those who violated the decree. On 12 October 1957 the Estonian and Latvian authorities adopted similar decrees that imposed one to three years' re-exile on violators of the decrees.[88]

On 19 December the Presidium of the Central Committee in Moscow finally weighed in with an extremely harsh and impatient letter addressed to all party organizations down to the level of primary cells: 'On Strengthening Political Work of the Party Organizations among the Masses and Preventing Attacks by Anti-Soviet, Hostile Elements.' Tying the recent events in Hungary to the impact of Western radio broadcasts, the Presidium lashed out first at the loss of vigilance among party cells that led to their failure to thwart the wave of negative reactions to Khrushchev's de-Stalinization speech and then at the behaviour of 'weaklings' in the creative intelligentsia, academia, and the media. The Presidium paid special attention to the returnees, some of whom were 'maliciously disposed against Soviet power, especially former Trotskyites, right-wing opportunists, and bourgeois nationalists [who surround themselves with] anti-Soviet elements and politically unstable individuals and try to resume their hostile anti-Soviet activities.' The Estonian student body was singled out for its nationalist demeanour, admiration for the counter-revolution in Hungary, proposals for liquidation of the Komsomol, and anti-Soviet agitation. 'We cannot have two opinions about how to struggle with hostile elements,' the stern warning went on. 'The dictatorship of the proletariat must be merciless with anti-Soviet elements. Communists ... must be vigilant in searching for hostile elements and, in accordance with the laws of Soviet power, must put an end to criminal actions in a timely manner.'[89] There were few, if any former 'Trotskyites and rightists' on the western frontier, where the focus turned almost exclusively to the returning nationalists.[90] In his native village in the Vohlyn region, Danylo Shumuk and his children were feeling the heat. His house was placed under surveillance, the collective farm manager pressured him to start working, and the KGB began paying evening visits. With the encouragement of one of his daughters the two signed up for resettlement in Dnipropetrovsk, and in mid-March 1957, under the cold and silent gaze of their neighbours, they left the village.[91]

The Belorussian Central Committee informed the Kremlin on 12 December 1956 that some 17,000 political prisoners had returned to the republic in the course of the last three years. The largest category was made up of 6,304 collaborators with the German occupiers, followed by 1,147 'bandits' and 704 alleged nationalists. The Belorussians were alarmed by the recent increase in violence by well-organized Polish and Belorussian nationalist returnees (veterans of the Union of Belorussian Patriots were singled out) and by the growing number of priests who defied the authorities. In line with their peers on the frontier, the Belorussians emphasized the public displeasure with the early releases of these criminals and with the permission given them to resettle in their former place of residence, and they pleaded with Moscow to review the expediency of these policies and to ban nationalists from returning to the border regions of the republic.[92]

Further north, in Estonia, party and state organizations were in a state of despair. Short-staffed and struggling to conceal the sympathies of many of its rank and file, the Estonian Communist Party seemed overwhelmed by the course of events. The loss of their monopoly on information was at the top of the agenda when the primary party organizations convened in mid-January to discuss the Presidium's letter. In some localities, such as the Antsla district, The Voice of America, broadcasting in Estonian and providing better reception than the Tallinn-based station was the major source for news. Equally disturbing was the sympathy amnestied returnees often found in the courts when they pursued the recovery of their property. The language barrier continued to block genuine inroads into the school-age cohort that, thirteen years after the return of Soviet power, was still more acquainted with Estonian 'bourgeois' literature than with the Russian-language Soviet literature.

The information on the schooling system confirmed an established pattern in the republic by which the authorities – at all levels – did their best not to wash dirty linen in public and to solve thorny problems without involving their superiors or external bodies. Facilities managers who kept Nazi paraphernalia and teachers who complained about the preferential treatment of (Russian) servicemen at the expense of the local population, who 'would be the ones called to fight in the event of war,' were not criticized or informed on to the party. Communists, too, were part of the problem, with some shielding former members of Kaitseliit (the banned Estonian Defence League), tuning in together to Voice of America broadcasts, observing in party meetings that the rural economy in bourgeois Estonia was more developed than the inadequate collective farm system, and denouncing Soviet propaganda as 'too imposing.' They went on to argue, 'We cannot thrust our ideology on everyone. Of course, every party member must recognize the statute of the Communist Party and subject himself to the majority, but what's going on within his soul is another matter, and here no one can impose anything.'[93]

Feeling the heat, the Estonian party primary cells and the Central Committee began pressuring Moscow to curtail the return of former nationalist activists to the localities. Peasants in the Voskhod collective farm were reportedly indignant about the return of confiscated property to a former merchant and active supporter of the Germans who was recently pardoned. The peasants were said to vow that they 'would never forgive someone who shot our people, beat us, served the fascists, and now lives among us.' The party cell reached the unanimous conclusion that such criminals, whose hands were soaked with the blood of honest Soviet people, should not be allowed to return to their former places of residence following the amnesty. [94] And with Gulag returnees comprising the majority of those who did not vote in the March 1957 elections ('When elections here are even half as democratic as they were in bourgeois Estonia, then I'll vote,' said those who remembered a different and more pluralistic era[95]), the road to the ban in the following October was paved.

In Moldavia, an equally frustrated KGB admitted that by August 1957 it had yet to assert control over the 20,000 returnees, especially in the thirty districts where it still had no institutional presence. Few of those amnestied had changed their anti-Soviet world view. They ignored any restrictions when they returned without permission to Moldavia, and once there they created havoc with their relentless struggle to recover their confiscated property. The Moldavian KGB, too, opted for a ban on the return of practically all political inmates and deportees. No returnees were allowed to resettle in the border districts.[96]

Needless to say, these measures paled in comparison to the bloody suppression of the three-day clashes in Hungary that resulted in tens of thousands of fatalities and injuries, hundreds of thousands of arrests, and hundreds of executions.[97] And yet the cleansing of the western frontier of alleged troublemakers was equally enduring and thorough.

Communal Cleansing

Beyond the concrete concerns for maintaining control during a turbulent time in a volatile region, the events of 1956–7 in the western frontier had far-reaching implications for the very nature and evolution of the Soviet enterprise. It was there, in the least expected place, that post-Stalinist totalitarianism exhibited a hitherto unthinkable confidence in its ability to engage its most resentful constituency in remoulding itself and displayed an impressive array of methods that filled the vacuum left by the renunciation of mass physical terror. The effort to draw the population into the implementation of state terror was not a novelty in itself. Part of the so-called revolutionary justice was carried out in public and with popular participation in the form of show trials, public deliberations, and signed denunciations. The late 1940s saw the introduction of myriad institutions that sought the expansion of popular engagement in state terror, such as housing and labour units (1948), courts of honour (1947–8), comrade courts (1951), collective farm assemblies charged with selection of deportees (1948), and the inclusion of thousands of locals in the actual deportation operations in the Baltic republics (1949). However, these were ad hoc institutions; the most extreme excesses were formulated by secret decrees and executed far from the public eye.

The attempts to expand popular participation in the anti-nationalist campaign on the western frontier before 1956 yielded mixed results. In between a series of mass-attended public trials in 1949 and 1951, the regime authorized collective farm assemblies in western Ukraine in May 1950 to deliberate over the fate of candidates for deportation from nationalist strongholds where collectivization appeared stalled. Peasants seemed to revel in the power they exercised over the fate of these individuals, reducing them to tearful recantations and vows to change, extending forgiveness to some and rejecting the pleas of most. Yet the authorities were forced to admit that the courts' poor command of Ukrainian and the prosecution's embarrassing performance only intensified the popular alienation. The collective farms' deliberations were conducted in villages cordoned off by police units, under rumours of an impending mass deportation, and with the participation of a carefully selected portion of the local population.[98]

Such dismal performances would not repeat themselves when the authorities resumed the campaign in the wake of the turmoil of 1956. With Nikita Khrushchev at the helm in Moscow, communal policing returned with a vengeance, this time as a permanent and ever-expanding feature of Soviet public life. On 2 January 1957 the Presidium of the Central Committee in Kiev concluded a detailed working paper on measures to cope with the problem of the nationalist returnees with a call to the Central Committee in Moscow to extend a decree from 2 June 1948, authorizing collective farm assemblies to exile 'anti-social and parasitic' elements beyond the republic's boundaries, to include the western Ukrainian regions – the very regions that were exempted from the decree when it was introduced eight years earlier.[99] There, the authorities were already busy cleansing the collective farms of nationalist presences.

The Red Partisan collective farm in the Demydiv district, Rivne region, was a case in point. Among its 369 households, the authorities counted thirty-seven former nationalist returnees, including seventeen who had served in UPA. Many of them had allegedly engaged in anti-Soviet activities from the arrival of the Soviets to as late as 1950, committing the most barbaric atrocities upon Soviet partisans and supporters. The collective farm became functional only with the actual liquidation of this partisan band. According to the farm's leadership, whose chairman was notably a former partisan and commander of the regional People's Commissariat of Internal Affairs (NKVD) destruction battalion, it was constantly improving until the return of the former nationalists, who shied away from work, resumed anti-Soviet agitation, and appeared to make inroads into segments of the local peasant population. Having spent years in camps, these nationalists seemed far from reformed. 'I did not "sit" ten years in prison only to work after that in a collective farm,' one of them told a group of peasants who asked him why he was not working.[100]

By December 1956, six nationalists had already been called to military service, removed to other places, or arrested upon returning to the village in violation of the 9 November decree. With the district branch of the KGB barely in sight, the collective farm leadership took matters into its own hands, isolating the returnees and depriving them of housing. The Central Committee instructor who studied the situation in the collective farm recommended a reversed family unification – sending those nationalist leaders and activists who still had families in exile back to the special settlements and directing the rest to industrial centres, exempting only those who were sick and those who had won the trust of Soviet people through their work and behaviour. He concluded with a call for a decree that would allow the collective farm assemblies or the executive committees of the rural soviets to decide on the exile of former nationalists who did not contribute to socially useful work and who hindered the development of Soviet social and state structure in the western provinces of Ukraine. The exile of these people should be carried out immediately after the assemblies made their decisions.[101] Nikita Khrushchev had already departed to Moscow some eight years earlier. His spirit and policies, however, were very much alive with his successors in the western frontier. Once again, under the auspices of their punitive organs, local communities and agencies were endowed with the task of policing and cleansing themselves.

It is not yet clear whether this initiative was a trial balloon for the all-Union campaign seeking public discussion of a draft law, On Intensification of the Fight against Antisocial, Parasitic Elements. The law authorized a general meeting of citizens – defined as a street committee or a commission of the public order of a housing unit in town and a village soviet in the countryside – to order the exile of 'able-bodied adults who lead an antisocial, parasitic life,' for a term of two to five years with compulsory labour. Hundreds of thousands of citizens were drawn into the public discussion of the law, including peasants who had been deported on similar charges in 1948 but now positioned themselves as its chief advocates. Peasants in the recently collectivized farms in western Ukraine displayed equal zeal in endorsing the law and sending their neighbours to work in industrial sites in the east.[102] However, the coincidence of the initiative with the intensification of the public onslaught on the *styliagi* (stylishly dressed youngsters), the enactment of the law by the Supreme Soviet of the Latvian Republic on the same day (12 October 1957) that it adopted the decree banning the return of former nationalist guerrillas and politicians to the republic, and the publicity accorded the procedure in the national and regional press suggest that it was part and parcel of the Khrushchevian enforcement of cohesion, conformity, and homogeneity through populist institutions and social norms.[103]

The village of Ustens'ke Pershe in the Rivne region offered a glimpse into this mode of operation. In March 1957, the authorities exhumed the bodies of sixteen local villagers who were murdered and dropped into wells by Ukrainian nationalists during the civil war of the late 1940s. While the initiative came from the local branch of the KGB, which also closely monitored the popular reactions, the entire population was drawn to the event, turning it into an unprecedented mass spectacle, as one witness wrote to his son. Nearly three thousand people from all the neighbouring villages, accompanied by dignitaries from Kiev and journalists, marched to the cemetery behind an orchestra, in a procession never seen before in the village. A sister of one of the murdered peasants brought people to tears when she described the murder she witnessed; she was followed by a writer who reminded the mourners that 'our Ukraine was invaded by Tatars, Turks, Poles, and Germans, but no one was worse than the Ukrainian nationalist bandits. Our fathers dug wells to drink water, but the cursed nationalists used them as mass graves. Our land rejects them.'

Emotions ran high when relatives of the victims identified five returnees as perpetrators and demanded their expulsion from the village. Efrosinia Kravchuk, whose parents were killed by nationalists, scolded Soviet power for its lenient treatment of bandits with blood on their hands. They should be cut to pieces, retorted the agitated peasant. Another peasant pointed to the five returnees as the ones who brutally murdered his parents, forbade him from giving them a proper burial, then robbed and flogged him. 'The return of Shevchuk [the leading perpetrator] to our village filled me with hatred and anger against the Soviet power that let him get away with such crimes unpunished,' exclaimed Boiko. 'I ask for permission to personally avenge the murder of my parents, the robbery of my property, and the beatings I suffered at the hands of Shevchuk. I want to see him and his likes punished and the returning nationalists removed from the region. They are politically untrustworthy and are capable of spilling blood at any moment.'[104]

In the lynch-mob atmosphere that engulfed the village, Boiko did not have to wait long. Fearing for their lives, the amnestied nationalists appealed to the kolkhoz chairman for permission to leave the region. One may wonder why the KGB went to so much trouble to remove a few individuals whom it could arrest and deport at will. This, however, was a small price to pay for a regime seeking not only to secure the stability of a volatile region but also to pre-empt its being singled out as the sole perpetrator in the cleansing campaign, and, even more ambitiously, to accelerate the folding of the local communities into the Soviet fabric.

The regional newspaper reminded readers about other atrocities the nationalists had committed in the region. It also warned against the enduring venom of the nationalists, who only recently tried to capitalize on the fascist uprising in Hungary and ganged up on the socialist fatherland with the help of the American imperialists and their radio broadcasts. The article opened with an ode to the serene, indescribable beauty of the village that had been violated by the vile actions of the butchers, and it concluded that a happier and brighter future depended on the removal of the eternally accursed perpetrators.[105] By then, the inflammatory rhetoric had already begun to yield results. Between 1 January and 10

April 1957, a total of 315 former nationalist guerrillas and activists were re-exiled from the Rivne region alone. The district branches of the KGB and the special regional commission reviewed the cases of some 112 former guerrillas and recommended their removal from the region; 108 of these were approved by the higher authorities. Forty-one people were resettled, another 83 departed through organized conscription for work in other regions, and 157 left the region voluntarily. Fourteen of those allowed to stay were recruited by the KGB as agents and informants.

Two years later, in March 1959, the region went through the same motions, this time with the public trial of five former nationalists, three of whom had already been deported and were still in exile in Magadan and Karaganda when they were arrested again.[106] The five were charged with heinous crimes against the population in 1943–4, ranging from murdering more than two hundred people, including fifty-five leading Soviet personnel, to terrorizing and robbing locals and killing Soviet Poles and Jews. A special operational group of party, state, and KGB employees organized maximum publicity of the trial in the republic's regional and district newspapers. The prosecutor's speech and sentencing were transmitted live throughout the district. The trial, meetings, and reactions of citizens were documented in a film and a photo album. Some 19,300 people in Chervonoarmiis'k and neighbouring districts participated in dozens of meetings that passed resolutions demanding death sentences for the accused. The party regional secretary noted with obvious satisfaction that thousands of citizens from neighbouring districts flocked to town during each day of the trial, the local paper was snatched off the shelves in the kiosks, and public readings were conducted at private homes and institutions.

The procedure in the local Palace of Culture was practically a lynch trial, with 500 attendants shouting down the relatives of the defendants who testified and throwing them out of the courtroom once they had concluded their testimonies. The carnival was concluded when the judge announced death sentences, which were greeted with unrestrained applause and chants: 'Death to the bandits!' In private letters to relatives outside the region, locals marvelled at the spectacle. 'Many foreign journalists and writers attended: Wanda Wasilewska, Pavlo Tychyna and many others, 150 people in all,' wrote Kateryna Broslavets.

> There were four loudspeakers [broadcasting the proceedings to] the people in the street. The judge announced that [the accused] confessed to their crimes [and described] how they robbed, killed, tortured, hanged,

> strangled children with their own hands, how they buried people alive in wells. It was impossible to listen; everyone cried. There were ten thousand people there. Two hundred people testified and proved [their guilt] in their face. Everyone screamed and called them murderers, cried for thirty minutes, and the court was unable to silence those who shouted, 'Kill the murderers,' rushed at them, but were rebuffed by the militia ... Never in my life have I seen such people. There was a meeting near the well where people were murdered. Everything was filmed for the cinema. The court sentenced them to be shot. For thirty minutes everyone clapped and shouted 'Right! Death for death.'[107]

Some who arrived in the region after the war and had never met real-life nationalists were horrified to identify neighbours among the accused, while others were angry at the initial leniency the regime showed the criminals. Many sent their relatives newspaper articles and photos of the exhumed bodies in the wells, and all expressed shock at the murder of children, the disposal of corpses in the wells, and the utter indifference of the perpetrators, who were laughing in court. One of them told the court that 'it was all the same to him. He just seized the kids by the throat, strangled [them] and threw them into the well.' 'Had the court not sentenced them to death, people would surely have shot these vile bandits on the spot,' wrote one villager to a relative. With thousands involved in the public legal process, as active spectators or aspiring executioners, the totalitarian dream (or nightmare) of entire communities policing themselves under the auspices of an all-powerful party-state was becoming a reality.

It was still a far cry from the vision articulated by Khrushchev three years later when he authorized the creation of the Party-State Control Commission: 'We have ten million party members, twenty million Komsomol members, sixty-six million members of the trade unions. If we could put all these forces into action, if we could use them in the interests of control, then not even a mosquito could pass unnoticed.'[108] Nevertheless, it was a step in the implementation of a Bolshevik vision of Communism in practice, drawing on both the national historical traditions of the Russian village and the full-blown vision of Communism offered by Lenin in his 1917 *The State and Revolution* ('universal, general, and popular control [over a variety of strayers]; there will be no getting away from it, there will be "nowhere to go"'). That vision was abandoned after the demise of war Communism, but it was not forgotten – at least not by the one person whose direct exposure to the wartime sacrifice and exploits of Soviet people reinforced his trust in the citizenry, and who viewed his mission as reviving 'true Leninism': Nikita Khrushchev.[109]

Closure

With the final dismantling of the special settlements on the horizon, the ministers of internal affairs of the Soviet republics met in January 1958 to discuss the release process. As expected, the Ukrainian MVD consented to releases from the special settlements as long as those released would have no right to return to the western provinces. Embittered by the brutal struggle of the post-war years and weary of the revival of nationalist activity in the wake of the events in Poland and Hungary, the Ukrainian ministry's objections were apparently supported by the all-Union ministry, which had persistently rejected such requests in the preceding months.[110] The Lithuanian and Latvian ministries opted for the removal of all restraints, arguing that restrictions would be impractical and would require mass repression to implement. The Estonian minister consented to a right to return to the republic, with the exception of the home districts of the deportees and several restricted cities.[111] There followed a series of amnesty decrees that by late 1963 finally released all deportees from the special settlements. The localities continued to complain about the unauthorized return of nationalists and the ongoing problem of restitution. But their own data showed that the stream of returnees was brought under control and practically curtailed.[112]

The stern warning issued approximately at that time by Lithuanian First Secretary Sniečkus applied to the entire region. To ensure that the returnees would know their place and that the images of the crushed Hungarian uprising would not fade away, Sniečkus reminded the delegates to the Tenth Congress of the Lithuanian Communist Party 'that anyone who would stir up antagonism toward the Russian nation, anyone who would tear the Lithuanian people away from the Russian people, would be digging a grave for the Lithuanian people.'[113] If the next decade was any indication, his warning was not lost on anyone. Behind the scenes, however, Sniečkus and fellow Baltic leaders advanced a more balanced interpretation of the causes of the 1956 eruption, pointing to the under-representation of the indigenous population in local power as a factor that played into the hands of nationalist elements and demoralized even Communists. Sniečkus did not hesitate to scold all-Union ministries that viewed any promotion of indigenous cadres as a sign of chauvinism. Tellingly, the Baltic leaders got their way, and the indigenization of local party organizations progressed steadily.[114] Throughout the region, the authorities continued to register anti-Russian and anti-Soviet incidents but with a significantly decreased frequency. Returnees continued to demand the return of their property, Estonian students continued to taunt the militia, and Lithuanian villagers in the Belorussian Republic continued to protest the liquidation of their schools and culture and requested the transfer to the Lithuanian republic of districts where they constituted a majority. However, the western frontier appeared to be settling down.[115]

The remaking of the frontier was accelerated when Moscow returned in full force to the policy of ethno-national homogenization of the borderlands. [116] Having identified the enduring appeal of external homelands to Gulag returnees as a key to the destabilization of the region in the wake of the Polish-Hungarian crisis, the Kremlin moved fast to reduce the number of the remaining former Polish citizens on the frontier. The Soviet-Polish agreement of 25 March 1957, on the repatriation of Polish citizens approved the departure of some 74,000 Poles and Jews by the end of the year – including 69,000 who came from the western republics – in addition to the 27,000 who had already left in the preceding three months. The mass repatriation may not have erased the scars of 1939–40, but it resulted in far fewer disgruntled individuals.[117] As the 1950s drew to a close, the once multi-ethnic and cultural mosaic that comprised the western frontier had few if any advocates. Eighteen years of class, ethnic, and racial engineering drives by practically every political movement in the region left little appetite for pluralism and the accommodation it required. By then, stability, the most desired political commodity, was equated with consolidation and even homogenization.

The closure of this episode on the western frontier witnessed the return of class as an operational category in Soviet politics. To be sure, class had been the raison d'être of the revolutionary enterprise from its inception to the very end, a concept written into the structure of each and every Soviet institution. However, the 'Great Transformation' and the ensuing declaration of 'socialism built' in the mid-1930s saw the downgrading of class structure as an explanatory paradigm and class struggle as a modus operandi in recruitment into the party, state bureaucracy, and higher education, and the struggle against the real and imagined enemies of the socialist enterprise, which were increasingly identified in the ethno-national domain.[118] With Khrushchev in power, class came back with a vengeance. For Stalin's successor, class was a guiding principle in restructuring the Soviet landscape and drawing 'all the people' into the process of 'moulding the New Man and building communism,' his two cherished goals. It was a key to the revitalization of stifled public life, the expansion of the pool of social activists, the intimidation and break-up of nepotistic, bureaucratic clans (*semeistvennost'*), and the restoration of the diminished proletarian traits of the polity.[119]

The western frontier was part of this shift, but given its unique history and location, in a more acute way than elsewhere. There, class was a tool for both breaking Communists' isolation among the population at large and simultaneously penetrating the ranks of amnestied nationalists. After years of party stagnation, workers and peasants were enrolled en masse in party cells. In 1958, workers and peasants accounted for 55.9 per cent of those admitted to candidacy to the Estonian party, increasing their share in the party to 52.3 per cent. The share of peasants and workers among those admitted to candidacy to the Lithuanian party rose from 43.4 per cent in 1953 to 59.1 per cent in 1964, bringing their overall share in the party to 52.8 per cent that year. The Latvian party increased the share of these groups from 44.5 per cent in 1953 to 50 per cent in 1964.[120] Notably, the pro-'toiling classes' orientation in recruitment to party organizations in the Baltic republics continued well after it slowed down in the union as a whole.

With the Gulag on its last legs, those deported as nationalists had to be reclassed. Perhaps unwittingly, Solzhenitsyn's bitter quip on the formation of shock workers' brigades (*udarnye brigady*) from among the nationalist rebels following the crushing of the uprising in the summer of 1954 pointed to more than just a return to camp routine.[121] Seemingly anachronistic in the late 1950s, the reclassing of this contingent was perfectly rational, particularly in light of its experience in the camps and the troubles with returning nationalists at home. Class categorization was the Soviet way to break, remould, control, and eventually reintegrate hitherto impenetrable groups. The decree of 12 October 1957 of the Presidium of the Supreme Soviet of the Estonian Republic that ordered the continued incarceration of the hard core of the nationalist movement also gave the rehabilitation committees the right to release former members of the nationalist underground and guerrilla organizations and their families if they had come from the ranks of 'the poor and middle peasants, workers, and white-collar workers who were drawn to nationalist activity unconsciously or due to a momentary lapse of will and redeemed themselves during their stay in the special settlements.'[122] So much and yet so little had changed. After all these years, class still mattered.

Conclusion

The 1956–7 events marked an ironic twist in the Soviet borderlands policy. Following decades of experiments with ethno-national minorities, ranging from their use as bridgeheads in approaching their diaspora brethren to deportations and eventual territorial and national consolidations, the Soviets found themselves fending off traditional irredentist pressures, only this time from the very satellites they had established in their own image. To make things worse, these pressures came at the delicate moment when they were set on a reformist course at home. To be sure, this was not a life-threatening crisis, but it brought back the centuries-old ghosts that haunted the Russian empire, saddled with endemically unstable and unassimilated borderlands that still had not been reintegrated after civil wars and suppressed rebellions.[123] This time around, the crisis was met by a regime confident in its ability to take risks, even when it dispensed with the primary tool of mass terror, and despite its awareness that many locals still harboured enmities and expectations for a chain reaction that would shake the foundations of the union.

Still, the events of the second half of the 1950s in the western borderlands left an indelible mark on Soviet policies at home and abroad. They revealed Soviet resolve, confidence, and impressive flexibility in moving from mass terror to communal policing, launched, of all places, in the bastions of anti-Soviet nationalist movements. Without shedding much blood, the regime conveyed unequivocally that resisting Soviet power by force was futile. Moreover, the regime continued to pursue the ethno-national consolidation of the borderlands without resorting to mass deportations and redrawing of the borders. Finally, surveillance reports revealed that the main consumers of foreign radio broadcasts were the political and cultural elites, a fact whose importance for the inner erosion of the system would become clear only decades later. Simply put, this world was much more complex than the one the Soviets had hitherto inhabited.

Relating the lessons of the era to its young apprentices some twenty years later, the KGB directors sounded almost nostalgic for an earlier, simpler age, when borders were controllable and the enemy recognizable and straightforward in its tactics and ideology. In an age of foreign radio broadcasts, expanding tourism, and cross-ethnic collaboration between nationalist activists employing legal means offered by the system itself, this was almost a plus. Paraphrasing, perhaps not unwittingly, Stalin's famous characterization of the elusive new enemy that confronted

Soviet power following the building of socialism, KGB historians quoted an unnamed Ukrainian nationalist leader who allegedly claimed that the era of armed struggle had ended and the era of subverting Soviet power from within had begun: 'This must be a joint struggle, otherwise nothing will be gained. We don't care who will be our accomplices – atheists, Communists, or Jews.'[124] If the post-1956 career of Danylo Shumuk was any indication, then the agency's historians were not far off the mark. Back in Mordovian Camp 1–6, Shumuk launched a long and torturous journey as one of the most prominent dissidents in the Soviet Union and as a living link between the generation of anti-Soviet guerrillas and the younger democratic Ukrainian dissidents. Using the Soviet courts and the international community, Shumuk shifted his struggle to the promotion of human rights and collaboration between political prisoners across national, religious, political, and ideological divides.[125]

Indeed, the events of 1956 and their aftermath marked the tenuous transition from an era of opposition seeking to depose Soviet power to an era of dissidence looking for ways to reform the system with the help of non-violent tools provided by the system itself. And these tensions would continue to mark Soviet policies in the region, fluctuating between the often-incompatible choices between viability and stability, between tightening the political reins and experimenting with economic liberalization, and between Russification and indigenization of culture and education.[126] Amidst the travails and upheavals, the Soviet quest for a safe passage from a Wild West to a window to the West was bound to continue.

NOTES

Reprinted with permission from the *Journal of Modern History* 78 (June 2006): 333–76.

1 Valentyn Malanchuk, *Torzhestvo Leninskoi natsional'noi polityky: Komunistychna partiia – orhanizator rozviazannia natsional'noho pytannia v zakhidnykh oblastiakh URSR* (L'viv, 1963), 564–5. Notable exceptions to the inattention to the Soviet domestic-external axis during the 1956 crisis have been Mark Kramer, Borys Lewytzkyj, Romuald Misiunas, and Rein Taagepera, whose works are referred to below. For a pioneering effort (that regrettably was not followed) to map the impact of the newly acquired empire on the Soviet core, see Roman Szporluk, ed. *The Influence of East Europe and the Soviet West on the USSR* (New York, 1975).

2 The Lithuanian KGB did not mince words in its condemnation of the release of anti-Soviet activists and guerrillas who 'in our view were erroneously and prematurely released from incarceration' and for whom, as well as for other hidden enemies of socialism, 'the recent events in Poland and Hungary provoked the hope for restoration of capitalist order in the Soviet Union ... [these were people] who had not renounced their hostile views of Soviet power, [who] exerted negative influence on unstable segments of the population ... [and who] resumed their efforts to form an anti-Soviet nationalist underground in the republic.' Lietuvos ypatingasis archyvas (LYA) 1771/190/11/24–5, 41.

3 *Khrushchev Remembers: The Last Testament*, trans. and ed. Strobe Talbott (Boston, 1974), 78–9. For insightful discussions of the dilemmas of de-Stalinization, especially the balancing acts required by the renunciation of mass terror and the cult of the late leader, while preserving the remaining pillars of the Soviet enterprise (a non-market economy and a single-party system), see John Armstrong, *The Politics of Totalitarianism: The Communist Party of the Soviet Union from 1934 to the Present* (New York, 1961), 281–93, 321–3; Martin Malia, *The Soviet Tragedy: A History of Socialism in Russia, 1917–1991* (New York, 1994), 315–50; Andrzej Walicki, *Marxism and the Leap to the Kingdom of Freedom: The Rise and Fall of Communist Utopia* (Stanford, CA, 1995), 495–521.

4 On the explosive fusion of the ethno-national problem and the attempt at institutional restructuring on the western borderlands in the immediate aftermath of Stalin's death, see Amir Weiner, 'Robust Revolution to Retiring Revolution: The Life Cycle of the Soviet Revolution, 1945–1968,' *Slavonic and East European Review* 86, no. 2 (April 2008): 214–22.

5 Between 1944 and 1952 some 203,662 people were deported from western Ukraine, of whom the majority (182,543) were categorized as nationalist guerrillas, members of the nationalist underground, and their supporters and family members. On 1 January 1953, deportees from the Baltic republics numbered 172,362 people in the camps and special settlements. Tentral'nyi derzhavnyi arkhiv hromads'kykh ob"iednan Ukraïny (TsDAHOU) 1/24/4531/76; Viktor Zemskov, 'Prinudatel'nye migratsii is pribaltiki v 1940–1950-kh godakh,' *Otechestvennye arkhivy* 1 (1993), 6. For a list of amnesty decrees issued between March 1953 and May 1956, see Gosudarstvennyi Arkhiv Rossiiskoi Federatsii (GARF) 9479/1/949/11–13.

6 Eesti riigiarhiivi filiaali (ERAF) 131/1/362/39–53; Mart Laar, *War in the Woods: Estonia's Struggle for Survival, 1944–1956*, trans. Tiina Ets (Washington, DC, 1992), 194; TsDAHOU 1/24/4297/4, 8–9; *Politychnyi terror i terorizm v Ukraïny, xix–xx st. Istorychni narysy* (Kiev, 2002), 769; *Istoriia Sovetskikh*

organov gosudarstvennoi bezopasnosti, ed. V.M. Chebrikov, G.F. Grigorenko, N.A. Dushin, and F.D. Bobkov (Moscow, 1977), 524 (this KGB internal textbook was prepared for the training of the agency's officers; it is still classified in Russia but is available at http://www.fas.harvard.edu/~hpcws); LYA 1771/190/11/27–8, 31–2, 37–8.

7 Natsyianal'ny arkhiu Respubliki Belarus' (NARB) 99/6/232/2–4.

8 NARB 4/62/427/255–9, 265–6.

9 *Litopys UPA. Nova seriia*, 7 vols. (Kyiv/Toronto, 2001–3), 7:536–44.

10 Nanci Adler, *The Gulag Survivor: Beyond the Soviet System* (New Brunswick, NJ, 2002), 166, 172–73; EKLA, no. 642, 46, 49; EKLA no. 529, 34; LYA 1771/190/11/126–30; TsDAHOU 1/24/4307/188–95.

11 See, e.g., the case of Tadii Terlets'kyi, who told a KGB informant in June 1956 that it was in the camps where he converted to Ukrainian nationalism – an ideology he was now hoping to implement at home. TsDAHOU 1/24/4377/125–6.

12 GARF 9479/1/612/73–7.

13 GARF 9401s/1s/4365/36; GARF 9479/1s/925/325–7.

14 *Reabilitatsiia: Kak eto bylo, Fevral' 1956-nachalo 80-x godov*, ed. A. Artizov, 3 vols. (Moscow, 2003), 2:19–20.

15 GARF 9401/1a/568/338–9; NARB 4/62/444/512; TsDAHOU 1/24/4297/12.

16 In February 1956, the Central Committee and the Presidium of the Supreme Soviet ordered the creation of sixty-five review committees with a mandate to issue immediate releases, rehabilitation, and reduced terms of sentences. The committees were ordered to take into consideration the activities of convicts prior to arrest, social position, party membership, role in the Great Patriotic War, partisan movement, attitude toward work in the camps, and the social danger posed by their past crimes. The committees were also asked to report to the corresponding party organs the names of those guilty of fabricating cases and violators of socialist legality inside the camps. Detailed instructions on the composition and mandate of the committees are in TsDAHOU 1/24/4306/211–19. For a firsthand account by a chair of one such committee, see Petro Shelest, '*Spravzhnii sud istorii shche poperedu*,' ed. Iuri Shapoval (Kiev, 2003), 111–13.

17 ERAF 1/5/54/1–6. Decisions by the Estonian state commission that reviewed applications for release and permission to return to native places of residence did not display clear patterns, and that in itself was a break from past practices. In some sessions the commission rejected en bloc appeals by former Omakaitse members, but in others it granted release and the right to return to all applicants. However, appeals by veterans of prewar organiza-

tions such as Kaitseliit were turned down in toto. ERAF 17-2/1/46/1–14, 34–42, 112–20, 179–98; ERAF 17-1/1/57/21–8.

18 TsDAHOU 1/24/4306/166–75.

19 Danylo Shumuk, *Life Sentence: Memoirs of a Ukrainian Political Prisoner* (Edmonton, AB, 1984), 279, 282–5.

20 GARF 9479/1/925/53–3b.

21 TsDAHOU 1/24/4306/42–3.

22 TsDAHOU 1/24/2774/70–1.

23 Robert Sullivant, *Soviet Politics and the Ukraine, 1917–1957* (New York, 1962), 288–91; Amir Weiner, *Making Sense of War: The Second World War and the Fate of the Bolshevik Revolution* (Princeton, 2000), 129–90.

24 Maria Savchyn Pyskir, *Thousands of Roads: A Memoir of a Young Woman's Life in the Ukrainian Underground during and after World War II* (Jefferson, NC, 2001), 191.

25 The KGB noted with evident satisfaction that Gulag returnees counted for more than 60 per cent of the agents recruited by its Ukrainian branch in 1956–7 for the struggle against Ukrainian nationalists. Chebrikov et al., *Istoriia,* 523.

26 *Khrushchev Remembers,* trans. and ed. Strobe Talbott (Boston, 1970), 457.

27 Ibid., 459.

28 TsDAHOU 1/24/4377/117–19.

29 Derzhavnyi arkhiv Ministerstva vnutrishnikh sprav Ukraïny (DAMVSU) Kiev 3/1/184/29, 12–13; TsDAHOU 1/24/4297/42–3; TsDAHOU 1/24/4307/188–94; TsDAHOU 1/24/4624/11–12.

30 *Litopys UPA: Nova seriia,* 7:542. Yanichars (Janissaries) were special infantry soldiers in the Ottoman army who had been taken away from their Christian parents and then raised and trained as zealot fighters for Islam. 'They look at us as if we were beasts,' and 'they say about the returnees that they would stray and murder people again,' complained other returnees in letters to friends. *Litopys UPA. Nova seriia,* 7:541, 543. For a similar account, see Shumuk, *Life Sentence,* 295–6.

31 Shumuk, *Life Sentence,* 300–1, 303–4.

32 Jaan Kross, 'The Day Eyes Were Opened,' in *The Conspiracy and Other Stories,* trans. Eric Dickens (London, 1995), 215–37.

33 TsDAHOU 1/24/4377/121–2.

34 TsDAHOU 1/24/4377/123–4.

35 For recanting former inmates, see Adler, *Gulag Survivor,* 81, 101; and Eugenia Ginzburg, *Journey into the Whirlwind,* trans. Paul Stevenson and Max Hayward (New York, 1967), 417.

36 GARF 9479/1/547/3, 71.

37 GARF 9479/1/547/6, 10b, 59.
38 GARF 9479/1/547/4, llb, 57, 58, 227.
39 GARF 9479/1/547/3, 4, 131, 11b.
40 Joseph Scholmer, *Vorkuta*, trans. Robert Kee (New York, 1954), 133. See also Aleksandr Solzhenitsyn, *Arkhipelag Gulag, 1918–1956: Opyt khudozhestvennogo issledovaniia*, 3 vols. (Moscow, 1989), 3:254–5.
41 Scholmer, *Vorkuta*, 138, 40. One Estonian returnee noted with pride that while many fellow Estonians had families and children born in exile, none of them had married a Russian. EKLA no. 620, 51a.
42 On the role of Ukrainian and Baltic nationalists in the strikes and uprisings, see 'Vosstanie v Steplage,' *Otechestvennye arkhivy* 4 (1994): 33–82, esp. 52–3, 63–77; Solzhenitsyn, *Arkhipelag Gulag*, 3:305–6, 329.
43 Scholmer, *Vorkuta*, 139–40.
44 LYA 1771/190/11/37, 40–1, 44–7. For Soviet concerns about the enduring influence of the church on social life in western Ukraine during the trying time of the 1956 crisis, especially in the countryside, see, *Kul'turne zhyttia v Ukraïni: Zakhidni zemli*, 2 vols. ed. Iurii Slyvka, Tamara Halaichak, and Oleksandr Luts'kyi (L'viv, 1996), 2:268–71.
45 *Radians'ka kultura*, 7 October 1956, cited in Borys Lewytzkyj, *Politics and Society in Soviet Ukraine*, 1953–80 (Edmonton, AB, 1984), 29.
46 TsDAHOU 1/24/4255/59–63.
47 ERAF 1/211/5/84–5, 35–6, 42. For other and similar reactions throughout the Soviet Union, see Mark Kramer, 'The Soviet Union and the 1956 Crisis in Hungary and Poland: Reassessments and New Findings,' *Journal of Contemporary History* 33 (1998): 195–6; Elena Zubkova, *Russia after the War: Hopes, Illusions, and Disappointments, 1945–1957*, trans. and ed. Hugh Ragsdale (New York, 1998), 186–90. For identical reactions in Poland, see Tony Kemp-Welsh, 'Khrushchev's "Secret Speech" and Polish Politics: The Spring of 1956,' *Europe-Asia Studies* 48, no. 2 (1996): 181–206. Khrushchev delivered a second de-Stalinization speech on 20 March 1956, on the occasion of the special session of the Polish United Workers' Party in the wake of Boleslaw Bierut's death. For an excerpt of the Warsaw speech, see 'Khrushchev's Second Secret Speech,' intro. and ed. L.W. Gluchowski, *Cold War International History Project Bulletin* 10 (March 1998): 44–9.
48 General Andrei Vlasov, one of the heroes of the Battle of Moscow, was later captured by the Germans and under their auspices formed the Russian Liberation Army. After the war, Vlasov and his close associates were convicted of treason and hanged. ERAF 1/211/5/45–6.
49 TsDAHOU 1/46/7055/245, 251.
50 In early 1953, the republic's Central Committee ordered intensification of

jamming, including a plea for help to the Baltic fleet, curtailment of the sale of long-range wireless radios, and an increase in supply of short-range receivers, along with improvement of the quality of the admittedly unattractive local radio programs. ERAF 1/5/52/1–3, 5.

51 TsDAHOU 1/24/4373/177.

52 ERAF 1/211/5/44, 47–9. For a detailed account of the mass disorder in Georgia following Khrushchev's speech, see Vladimir Kozlov, *Massovye besporiadki v SSSR pri Khrushcheve i Brezhneve* (Novosibirsk, 1999), 155–83.

53 TsDAHOU 1/24/4373/168.

54 ERAF 1/211/5/123, 125–7.

55 ERAF 1/211/5/35–6, 43.

56 TsDAHOU 1/24/4265/3–4; TsDAHOU 1/46/7070/65; *Kul'turne zhyttia v Ukraïni,* 2:213.

57 See, e.g., the reports by the Drohobych Regional Party Committee (*obkom*) in TsDAHOU 1/46/7070/33–4; Transcarpathian *obkom,* TsDAHOU 1/46/7070/40–1; and L'viv *obkom,* TsDAHOU 1/46/7070/66–7, 70.

58 By late November 1956, some one thousand copies of leading Polish newspapers circulated in L'viv alone, providing readers with information on the Yugoslav government's reaction to the abduction of Imre Nagy to Romania, Nehru's statement on the 'crisis of Communism,' critical essays on socialist realism and 'Zhdanovshchina' in literature, and reports on the Polish government's consent to American aid. *Kul'turne zhyttia v Ukraïni,* 2:220, 274.

59 The authorities in L'viv noted that the events in Hungary and Poland and information from foreign radio broadcasts and the socialist-bloc media reignited debates over the sensitive issues of nationality policy, collectivization, and the sources of the Soviet victory in the Second World War and soured relations between Ukrainian and Russian students. *Kul'turne zhyttia v Ukraïni,* 2:274–5.

60 TsDAHOU 1/24/4265/9.

61 TsDAHOU 1/24/4265/11–12.

62 *United Nations Report of the Special Committee on the Problem of Hungary,* General Assembly Official Records: 11th session, suppl. no. 18 (A/3592) (New York, 1957), 125; *Sovetskii Soiuz i Vengersnkii krizis 1956 goda: Dokumenty,* ed. István Vida and Tofik Islamov (Moscow, 1998), 652–5.

63 Bohdan Nahaylo and Victor Swoboda, *Soviet Disunion: A History of the Nationalities Problem in the USSR* (New York, 1989), 127; Shumuk, *Life Sentence,* 302.

64 TsDAHOU 1/24/4624/9–10.

65 GARF 9401s/1s/4444/27–7b, 28.

66 EKLA no. 519, 206.

67 TsDAHOU 1/24/4297/43–4.

68 'Sotsial'no-politicheskaia obstanovka v Pribaltike v 50-e gody,' *Voennye arkhivy Rossii* 1 (1993): 247–8. The KGB estimated that 140,000 Lithuanians corresponded with the outside world with some 720,000 letters reaching the republic between January 1956 and April 1957. According to the agency, the influx of anti-Soviet letters drastically increased during the Polish-Hungarian crisis. Many letters directed the correspondents to foreign radio broadcasts. LYA 1771/190/11/26–7.

69 Faculty members and students in the Ivan Franko University in L'viv figured prominently in the party's reports on trouble spots in the wake of the Hungarian crisis, but mainly as individuals and not as a group capable of collective action. *Kul'turne zhyttia v Ukraïni*, 2:238–40, 266–77.

70 Rossiiskii Gosudarstvennyi Arkhiv Sotsial'no-Politicheskoi Istorii (RGASPI) M-1/46/192/6–8, 10, 19–20, 179.

71 ERAF 1/211/5/108–11; RGASPI 1/46/192/147–9.

72 Romuald Misiunas and Rein Taagepera, *The Baltic States: Years of Dependence, 1940–1990* (Berkeley, 1993), 136; Thomas Remeikis, *Opposition to Soviet Rule in Lithuania, 1945–1980* (Chicago, 1980), 275–8; 'Sotsial'no-politicheskaia obstanovka v Pribaltike v 50-e gody,' 250–4; LYA K-1/3/510/331.

73 When locals applied Marxist mythology in their protests, they used the figure of Spartacus, the leader of the slave rebellion against the Roman Empire, as did a group of schoolchildren who circulated anti-Soviet leaflets and named themselves the 'Union of the Spartacists.' The teenager who initiated this activity claimed he was inspired by the broadcasts of the Voice of America on the events in Hungary. ERAF 1/211/5/110, 113–14.

74 'Sotsial'no-politicheskaia obstanovka v Pribaltike v 50-e gody,' 250.

75 ERAF 151/12/2/67, 71, 73–4.

76 LYA 1771/190/11/31–2, 42–4; Misiunas and Taagepera, *Baltic States*, 152–5. The confusion the demonstrations caused among members of the Lithuanian Komsomol was aptly conveyed in Vytautas Rimkevičius, *Studentai* (Vilnius, 1957), a candid novel whose very publication was a sign of the confusion. For excerpts and insightful comments by Thomas Remeikis and Rimvydas Šilbajoris, see *Lituanus* 7 (1960) 2:68–74.

77 ERAF 1/211/5/114, 118–20, 128–32.

78 ERAF 1/211/6/18–19; LYA 1771/190/11/42.

79 ERAF 1/211/5/48–50.

80 Jews everywhere were singled out for expressing pride in the successful Israeli-French-British joint campaign against Egypt that month. ERAF 1/211/6/17.

81 TsDAHOU 1/24/4265/1–5.

82 TsDAHOU 1/24/4297/12–22.

83 DAMVSU Kiev 3/1/184/15–18, 46.
84 TsDAHOU 1/24/4297/44, 46–8.
85 TsDAHOU 1/24/4297/32–41.
86 TsDAHOU 1/24/4087/377.
87 TsDAHOU 1/24/4531/76–7. Sixty released nationalist leaders were sent back to the camps. Chebrikov et al., *Istoriia*, 524.
88 ERAF 17–1/1/299/86–7; TsDAHOU 1/24/4297/199–200; Zemskov, 'Prinudatel'nye migratsii,' 12–13.
89 Rossiiskii Gosudarstvennyi Arkhiv Noveishei Istorii (RGANI) 89/6/2/1–12, esp. 8, 10–11. For the protocol of the Presidium meeting on 6 December that discussed the letter and included a reference to a party 'purge' and a remark by Khrushchev about the undeserved release of some inmates, see *Presidium TsK KPSS, 1954–1964: Chernovye protokol'nye zapisi zassedanii; Stenogrammy*, ed. Aleksandr Fursenko, 3 vols. (Moscow, 2003), 1:212–13.
90 The restless students were confronted, too, but with different measures. The party authorities in L'viv responded to the Presidium's letter with intensified propaganda among the students, including excursions to leading collective farms and industrial centres in eastern Ukraine. Iurii Slyvka et al., *Kul'turne zhyttia v Ukraïni*, 2:275.
91 Shumuk, *Life Sentence*, 302–5.
92 NARB 4/62/444/513–14.
93 ERAF 1/211/6/18, 21–2.
94 ERAF 1/211/5/50–1.
95 The authorities were similarly troubled by a number of religious people who either did not vote ('We already have one God, we won't elect another one') or successfully formed a bloc against certain party candidates. ERAF 1/211/5/52–8.
96 Valeriu Pasat, *Trudnye stranitsy istorii Moldovy, 1940–1950-e gg.* (Moscow, 1994), 721–3, 726–9, 736–8.
97 For updated figures of casualties in Hungary, see Kramer, 'The Soviet Union and the 1956 Crisis,' 210–12.
98 Notably, the Ukrainian Ministry of Justice vetoed one of the public trials on legal grounds. *Litopys UPA: Nova seriia*, 3:375–9; TsDAHOU 1/24/31/83–93, 437–9; TsDAHOU 1/24/42/27–38; TsDAHOU 1/24/98/308–9; TsDAHOU 1/24/874/358–62.
99 TsDAHOU 1/16/77/8.
100 During the campaign against postwar collectivization, the guerrillas allegedly displayed decapitated heads of three supporters of the Soviets on stakes in the village centre and chopped off the right arms of two other

peasants who voted for the establishment of collective farms. TsDAHOU 1/24/4297/195–201.

101 Ibid.

102 TsDAHOU 1/24/4738/1–4, 81–3. For useful discussions of the law, see Armstrong, *Politics of Totalitarianism*, 324–5; Rene Beerman, 'A Discussion on the Draft Law against Parasites, Tramps and Beggars,' *Soviet Studies* 9 (1957): 214–22.

103 Concerning the young, the alarmed authorities in Tallinn noted that one of the dance instructors who introduced youngsters to vulgar rock and roll was a former political prisoner. ERAF 1/191/46/9–10.

104 TsDAHOU 1/24/4532/16.

105 'Tse bilshe ne povtoryt'sia,' *Chervonyi prapor*, 13 March 1957.

106 The following account draws on the report sent by the Rivne *obkom* secretary to Mykola Pidhornyi, the secretary of the Ukrainian Central Committee, in TsDAHOU 1/24/4944/10–28. A report from 18 September 1959 to the Central Committee in Kiev stated that in recent years fourteen public trials were staged in L'viv, Rivne, Stanyslaviv, Ternopil, and Volhyn, in which some fifty-one former OUN terrorists were tried and twenty-four were sentenced to death. TsDAHOU 1/16/85/248–9.

107 TsDAHOU 1/24/4944/19–20.

108 Cited in Oleg Kharkhordin, *The Collective and the Individual in Russia: A Study of Practices* (Berkeley, 1999), 299.

109 On the profound impact of the war on Khrushchev, see William Taubman, *Khrushchev: The Man and His Era* (New York, 2003), 147–78.

110 GARF 9479/1/949/119; GARF 9479/1/946/173, 214; GARF 9479/1/948/77–8.

111 GARF 9479/1/949/119.

112 Summing up the past decade, the Ukrainian MVD and Procuracy noted that 90.5 per cent of the approximately sixty thousand political exiles who returned to western Ukraine did so with the consent of the local authorities. On 20 May 1970, the agencies offered the final removal of all restriction on former nationalists, including resettlement in western Ukraine. This, however, did not amount to rehabilitation, an act that entailed recovery of confiscated property, which the agencies kept tightly under their jurisdiction. By January 1971, barely 6,117 people had obtained full rehabilitation. TsDAHOU 1/25/637/35–41.

113 Misiunas and Taagepera, *Baltic States*, 137.

114 ERAF 1/4/2034/23–4; 'Sotsial'no-politicheskaia obstanovka v Pribaltike v 50-e gody,' 260–2. The share of Lithuanians in the republic's party organization grew from 44.1 per cent in 1955 to 63.7 per cent in 1965. *Kommu-*

nisticheskaia partiia Litvy v tsifrakh, 1918–1976, ed. Konstantinas Surblys (Vilnius, 1977), 125.

115 For the enduring problem of property in the western Ukrainian countryside in the late 1950s, see TsDAHOU 1/24/4944/35–6. On Estonian students, see GARF 9401/2/492/187, 224. While cultural concerns received a positive response, demands for territorial adjustments were rejected and eventually dropped, following an intimidation campaign by the Belorussian authorities. Remeikis, *Opposition to Soviet Rule in Lithuania,* 313–18.

116 In the course of the population exchange in the immediate post-war years, 786,546 out of 872,917 Poles who resided in western Ukraine had moved to Poland, while 296,459 Polish Ukrainians resettled in the region. Malanchuk, *Torzhestvo Lenins'koi natsional'noi polityky,* 492.

117 In the course of a preparatory meeting with the Soviet MVD in December 1957, Polish officials estimated that out of half a million Poles who had the right of repatriation, some three hundred thousand wished to exercise it, although it was not clear whether all of them wanted to leave for Poland. The Soviets countered that the actual number was significantly lower, but both agreed that the recent decline in the number of applications was due to the economic crisis in Poland. Both sides were confident that the process would be completed by the end of 1958. RGANI 89/67/2/1–2, 7–8; TsDAHOU 1/24/4749/31–2.

118 On the tenuous balance between social and ethnic origin and the shift toward the latter from the early 1930s on, see Terry Martin, *The Affirmative Action Empire* (New York, 2001); Weiner, *Making Sense of War,* 138–90.

119 See T.H. Rigby, *Communist Party Membership in the U.S.S.R, 1917–1967* (Princeton, NJ, 1968), 302, 304; Robert A. Feldmesser, 'Equality and Inequality under Khrushchev,' *Problems of Communism* 9:2 (1960): 31–39; George W. Breslauer, *Khrushchev and Brezhnev as Leaders: Building Authority in Soviet Politics* (Boston, 1982), 23–133; 'On Strengthening the Relationship of the School with Life and on the Further Development of the System of Public Education in the Country: Theses of the Central Committee of the Communist Party and the Council of Ministers of the USSR,' in George S. Counts, *Khrushchev and the Central Committee Speak on Education* (Pittsburgh, 1959), 38–40, 43–4, 55–6.

120 ERAF 1/4/2034/222; Rigby, *Communist Party Membership,* 305, n.18; ERAF 1/4/2286/1–2; *Kommunisticheskaia partiia Litvy v tsifrakh,* 86, 94, 105; *Kommunisticheskaia partiia Latvii v tsifrakh, 1904–1983 gg.* (Riga, 1984), 91, 151.

121 Solzhenitsyn, *Arkhipelag Gulag,* 3:331.

122 ERAF 17-1/1/299/80–81.

123 For an intriguing treatise of the Russian borderlands dilemma, see Alfred Rieber, 'Persistent Factors in Russian Foreign Policy,' in *Imperial Russian Foreign Policy*, ed. Hugh Ragsdale (Cambridge, MA, 1993), 315–59.

124 Chebrikov et al., *Istoriia*, 494–6, 511, 522–31, 544–5.

125 Shumuk, *Life Sentence*, epilogue.

126 Not surprisingly, these tensions reflected the Soviet trade-off between cohesion and viability in the eastern bloc after 1956. Kramer, 'The Soviet Union and the 1956 Crisis,' 213.

9 The Revival of Soviet Internationalism in the Mid to Late 1950s

ELEONORY GILBURD

Around the corner from Nikitskii Boulevard, on Vozdvizhenka, stands one of the strangest buildings in Moscow. An ornamented castle with heavy arched portals, laced balcony rails, shell-shaped stucco moulding, two round towers, twisted columns of sandstone, and an entrance in the shape of a horseshoe for luck, this building transports visitors to the Lisbon of Vasco da Gama and the Age of Discovery, to the Salamanca of Isabel and Ferdinand.

If the building's central ensemble and its decorative grapevines bear strange similarity to the Sintra Castle near Lisbon, while the shell-embossed facade is reminiscent of the Casa de las Conchas in Salamanca, then it is because the building also belongs to another context – the Moscow eclecticism of the Russian fin-de-siècle. These symbols, together with late gothic, Renaissance, and Mudejar architectural elements, were imported to Moscow in the 1890s, after a tour of Europe, by Arsenii Morozov, a scion of the Morozov dynasty of merchants and philanthropists. The building and its interior embodied a fusion of all things and times, serving as a meeting ground of East and West in the heart of Moscow, only a short distance from the Kremlin. After the Revolution, the building was home to an avant-garde theatre, and then to Proletkul't.[1] Following the eclipse of Proletkul't, the house lost its cultural liveliness and became solemn and unapproachable; for the next thirty years it would house diplomatic missions.

But there was another context to the life of this building and another incarnation of universalist yearnings within its walls – when Vozdvizhenka was the street's colloquial name, when only old-timers knew who had built this castle, when guidebooks to Moscow listed Kalinin Street, 16, the House of Friendship. In 1958, ownership of the castle was transferred to the recently founded Union of Soviet Friendship Societies (SSOD), and the building regained its associations with both culture and internationalism. It also became an unambiguously public structure for the first time. The reorganization of the interior highlighted the building's new status. Partitions, columns, and entire walls were demolished in an effort to enlarge the space of the foyer, cinema, coat rooms, and theatre, and to make room for the potential visitors, with which SSOD plans and reports were crammed.[2] In the best traditions of Moscow eclecticism, the building was now adorned with Soviet insignia.

The House of Friendship epitomized Soviet international efforts of the mid-1950s, which combined exuberant populism and information hierarchy, conspicuous new openness and gnawing suspicions. Within its walls, a distinctly Soviet conception of cultural universalism was superimposed upon Russian eclecticism. The house had long-standing associations with exclusivity, thus, its open doors symbolized the difference between the mid- to late-1950s and the xenophobia of the late 1940s, when the Soviet Union had seemed to have conclusively abandoned its early internationalism – a process that began in the second half of the 1930s, if not earlier.[3] However, as a political project, Soviet internationalism had an incredible staying power, despite the various degrees of public prominence and discursive investment.[4] And in this project, most consequential was the Thaw, marked by a democratization of privileged knowledge about foreign cultures as ever more and diverse information became available to ever greater numbers of people.[5] In the mid-1950s, the initiatives for citizen diplomacy and cultural exchange created a breach in the information hierarchy. During the 1957 Moscow International Youth Festival, the breach was filled with the names of iconic performers, sounds of music and foreign speech, token objects, and charming images. As emblems of the 1950s, as memorabilia, and as the context for the habituation of Western imports to come, these names, objects, sounds, and images would prove formative for late Soviet culture. The festival has been locked in the legacy of its own – and of the Cold War's – making. Indeed, the Komsomol chiefs intended it as propagandistic fanfare for the 'socialist way of life,' and that is how both its detractors and advocates understood the festival at the time.[6] But, above all, it was an intense aesthetic and intellectual experience, emblematic of the Thaw-era opening to the West writ large. Short-lived propagandistic projects brought the Soviet Union into the global circulation of sounds, images, and goods; and diplomatic contingencies brought a permanent presence of Western culture that would define

Soviet life for the next thirty years. However, neither Stalin's death nor even the new diplomatic course *had* to result in cultural exchanges; there was nothing 'natural' about the policy, which required a profound rethinking of the relationship between culture and social order.[7] Asking what visions guided the new exchange projects, this chapter seeks to return an element of surprise to the process. The story that follows is part diplomacy and part fancy.

The Origins of Cultural Exchange Agreements

The year 1955–6 was of far-reaching change in Soviet-Western cultural relations. After the Soviet delegation returned home with renewed confidence from the Geneva Summit in the summer of 1955, the Central Committee passed a series of nearly identical resolutions on the 'expansion of cultural ties' with various countries.[8] Earlier, only cultural relations with the socialist bloc had been subject to planning; now the practice was extended to capitalist countries – with important implications.[9] The new policy erased the formal distinction between approaches to socialist and capitalist cultures. Cultural exchanges in the socialist world were based on bilateral agreements, and mixed commissions oversaw the fulfilment of these treaties. Soviet propaganda claimed for this system a unique conceptual foundation: here was a novel type of foreign relations based on 'socialist internationalism,' juridical parity, and respect for all cultures.[10] This model, its structure and rationale, was now transferred to relations with capitalist countries. Placing exchange with the West on the books assured regularity: however carefully measured and censored, Western culture would be an accepted and recurrent presence in Soviet theatres, libraries, and museums.

Diplomatic conferences and summits not only produced official communiqués, they were also surrounded by first-time-ever cultural events – foreign exhibitions, film festivals, tourist delegations, radio concerts.[11]

In the summer of 1955, following the summit, the resolution on the expansion of Soviet-British cultural exchange framed the preparations for Nikita Khrushchev's trip to Britain.[12] Under the resolution's mandate, the Ministry of Culture directed a comprehensive effort to introduce English culture to Soviet audiences. 'Cultural measures' to be carried out efficiently, 'in operational order,' affected all media: in the spring of 1956, Soviet information space was inundated with things British. Items from Britain were now included in newsreels, and English films from the early 1940s – reminders of the wartime alliance – reappeared in Soviet movie theatres. In Moscow, sixty theatres, clubs, and houses of culture screened the films, and over a million people rushed to see them during the first week. The Lenin Library showcased English literature published in the Soviet Union, and the Ministry of Culture made sure to invite the British ambassador to the exhibit of English porcelain, glazed pottery, and precious stones from 'unique [Soviet] collections.' Everywhere in Moscow there were lectures, evenings, or programs – the All-Union conference 'Shakespeare on the Soviet Stage' and the festival of Shakespearian film adaptations, the evening on 'English Literature and Art' at the Central House for Artistic Workers, and yet another at the House of Cinema. These performances were limited to the capital, but the radio and newspapers reached the rest of the country with classical and contemporary music, readings of English fiction, literary reviews, and surveys of British culture commissioned by the Central Committee.[13] For its part, the British Council invited the Soviet minister of culture to London in the summer of 1955. Several limited agreements on exhibitions and performing troupes were settled during this visit, and reciprocal film festivals were decided the following spring.[14]

Also in 1955–6, the Pushkin Museum in Moscow opened two exhibitions of French art in quick succession. Drawn from Soviet collections, the first exhibition was enormous, extravagant, an embarrassment of riches: antique furniture, enamel, porcelain, tapestries, medals, ivory daggers, miniatures, drawings, prayer books of parchment and gold, popular prints from the French Revolution, sculptures, and hundreds of paintings in ornate frames.[15] In July 1955, the Central Committee and the Council of Ministers passed a resolution 'On the Expansion of Cultural Relations between the Soviet Union and France,' and the Ministry of Culture saw the art exhibition as a first step.[16] Diplomatic confirmation followed shortly thereafter. No sooner had this exhibition left Moscow for Leningrad than the French government sent to Moscow an exhibition of its own – an example of the new Soviet-French rapprochement after the 1954 Paris Agreements (which had solidified the division of Europe). In an effort to improve relations, the new Prime Minister Guy Mollet and the Minister of Foreign Affairs Christian Pinot visited the Soviet Union in May 1956.[17] The result of this first official visit in over a decade was the Declaration on Cultural Exchange, announced on 19 May.

That year France was celebrated in the Soviet Union unequivocally and passionately. In late summer 1955, hundreds of French tourists disembarked at the Leningrad port as crowds flocked to the Neva embankment, waving and chanting greetings. Meanwhile, Marseille and Odessa became sister cities; the first French film festival sparked the Soviet love affair with Gérard Philipe; and the first USSR-France football match drew 80,000 thrilled fans and ended diplomatically, in a draw. Yves Montand's songs aired in 1954–5, acquiring Russian lyrics and Russian admirers in the farthest reaches of the country, and his figure assumed cult-like proportions following landmark concerts at the end of 1956. The streets around the concert venues in Moscow, Leningrad, and Kiev were crowded with girls waiting in the brutal cold of late December and early January to catch a glimpse of their darling.[18] In the provinces, young men organized their own Montand concerts in a perfectly Soviet manner – or, rather, in a peculiar hybrid of foreign sounds and Soviet cultural practices: a local club, friendship slogans, lectures on French culture, and a gramophone pulsing 'C'est si bon.'[19] Another song, 'Les Grands Boulevards,' gained enormous popularity, thanks to the catchy melody and to the people who engaged with it. The handsome and sweet-voiced Gleb Romanov, whose fame peaked precisely in the mid-1950s, sang it in French. Leonid Utesov, a Soviet classic of the genre and probably the most influential entertainment artist, sang the Russian translation. And Mark Bernes, the voice of sincere feelings and stern male friendships, crooned about what happens 'when a faraway friend sings.' 'Huge distances shorten,' 'the smile of Paris' illuminates Moscow, and *les Grandes Boulevards* join the Garden Ring. Bernes's song was dedicated to Montand, the 'faraway friend' who effected such physical transformations.

In giving air time to French music in the spring of 1956, the Soviet Radio Administration and the Ministry of Culture intended the broadcasts to coincide with the visit of Mollet and Pinot, and thus convince French officials of Soviet interest in their culture. The month was May, the windows were open, the sounds of Paris filled Soviet apartments and courtyards and remained there after the politicians had left.[20] Of course, both the British and the French campaigns were orchestrated, but no less significant for that. Nor does campaigning necessarily imply disingenuousness: the government was eager to sign cultural exchange agreements, and throughout 1956, negotiations with Western powers proceeded in earnest, until the dual crises, Hungary and Suez, forestalled further talks.

These projects, however, were resumed as soon as the crises had subsided. Already in the summer of 1957, the French were willing to discuss cultural exchange, and by the fall, the diplomats were back at the negotiating table. Still, these meetings were not easy. The French refused to sign the Cultural Convention drawn up in Moscow, making any such agreement conditional on the lifting of Soviet travel restrictions and the distribution of foreign publications.[21] The convention, which would have assured the stability of exchange while keeping the door open to extemporized changes, had been the key negotiation priority for the Soviets. The document had symbolic value. It had originated in Moscow, and its acceptance would have signified recognition of the Soviet Union within the customary practices of Western cultural diplomacy.[22] Instead, the talks yielded only a short-term but still comprehensive program of exchanges for 1958, to be evaluated and renegotiated annually.[23]

The French-Soviet program of exchanges became the prototype for the initial conversations with the Americans that same fall, 1957.[24] The American negotiators, like the French before them and the British after, staked the whole project upon a single article – the exchange of uncensored information, including the press, radio, and television programs. Or else, President Eisenhower's special assistant on East-West Exchanges, William Lacy, seemed to imply, the State Department would not be able to convince businessmen and interest groups to uphold the American side of the bargain. The famous U.S.-Soviet agreement signed in January 1958, after three months of talks and almost three years of false starts, papered over this division and left Soviet officials to negotiate many clauses directly with the relevant agencies in the United States.[25]

In the summer of 1957, as the exchange of notes with the French and the Americans began, Chairman of the Council of Ministers Nikolai Bulganin also sent a letter to Prime Minister Harold Macmillan, inviting the British government to resume the 1956 projects.[26] In Britain, however, Hungary had left a more permanent trace than elsewhere in the West, and for another two years, the British Council refused to formalize cultural relations with the Soviet Union. The same story, with yet more mistrust and tension, was repeated. The Soviets wanted to put cultural exchange on 'a sound and permanent basis.' The British called for open travel and correspondence, uncensored distribution of foreign press, and a halt to radio jamming.[27] By the time the negotiations finally started in 1959, there was no mention of a permanent convention, and only a limited program for the next year was signed.[28]

At first, it seemed, the Italian story would be different. Regularized cultural exchange with the Soviet Union had a sympathetic ally in President Giovanni Gronchi, who had been carried to the Quirinale Palace by Communist and Socialist votes and who had worked to bring both parties into the government. In February 1960, Gronchi paid a visit to Moscow, and cultural programs – specifically, an exchange agreement between Italy and the USSR – were to frame the talks. But while the cultural diplomats negotiated a generous convention, the conversations between the heads of state did not go quite as well, according to eyewitnesses, on account of Khrushchev's impromptu jokes, toasts, threats, and invitations for Gronchi to join the Communist Party. At the last minute, the Italian delegates postponed the ratification of the convention until the spring of 1961, and in the meantime, the Soviets would have to be content with 'a temporary program of cultural exchange.'[29]

The French, American, British, and Italian negotiations illustrate how cultural exchange was defined by different patterns of diplomatic relations as well as pre-existing perceptions, domestic politics, and Cold War contingencies. The American approach was pragmatic, based on potential propagandistic dividends in the psychological war against the Soviet Union.[30] Even as relations soured after Hungary, in 1956 it was clear to both parties that the hiatus would be temporary. In Britain, moral outrage had the upper hand over propaganda interests and tainted all conversations. Nor was this attitude unique to the post-Hungarian moment: mutual suspicion had a long history in both countries.[31] The Italians brought to the Soviet Union domestic political divisions and compromises, but it was, above all, the personal disconnect between Gronchi and Khrushchev that poisoned whatever leftist common ground the two may have shared. The French delegation carried, in addition to its trampled international ambitions (from Germany to Algiers), a tradition of cultural cooperation with Russia. Despite the jolt of the 1956 crises, the fundamental document that the diplomats recalled and on which they relied to rescue the faltering conversation was the Declaration on Cultural Exchange of 19 May 1956 – when the windows were open and the sounds of Paris filled Moscow courtyards.[32] The cultural exchange agreements were shaped by the Western powers as much as by the Soviet Union.

With the terms of only a year or two, none of these agreements was permanent, and, as practice demonstrated, none was particularly binding. There were no juridical mechanisms for enforcing the agreements. Everything hinged on goodwill, interpersonal relations, and mutual propagandistic benefits. Yet, remarkably, this system of cultural exchange between the USSR and Western countries proved durable, lasting as long as the Soviet Union.

Conceptual Foundations

How did cultural exchange come to occupy so central a place in the Soviet conception of foreign relations between the Twentieth Party Congress in 1956, when it became a clearly articulated policy, and the Twenty-Second Party Congress in 1961, when it entered the party program?[33] It did not have to be so. Peaceful coexistence could have been limited to disarmament, neutrality treaties, trade, technical cooperation, and even travel; but it did not have to include paintings, books, films, musicians, and performing troupes. Indeed, in the early 1950s, cooperation had been limited to trade and negotiations over Korea and Germany.[34] To read what was appearing in the press during 1951–4 is to watch how, slowly and hesitantly, 'cultural relations' emerged as a distinct and legitimate concept, sometimes mentioned once, sometimes forming a subordinate clause; at first attached to a socialist or a decolonizing country – India, for example, or Iran – then to neighbours like Finland, until the expression finally shed socio-geographical qualifiers altogether.[35]

Soviet commentators did not take peaceful coexistence for granted: they tried to explain on what grounds and for what purposes socialist and capitalist cultures could, and would, interact. The question of the incompatibility between socialism and capitalism was so troubling as to require repeated answers for years to come. The people who invested much effort in explicating the principles of cultural exchange often had first-hand international experience and a professional stake in the issue. One such person was Gennadii Mozhaev, a young graduate of Moscow University who came to work for the Soviet Commission at UNESCO in 1956 and, in the late 1950s–early 1960s, provided some of the more comprehensive and consistent justifications for cultural coexistence. Mozhaev held dear the idea of a great humanistic culture shared by all. Socialist and capitalist cultures might be incompatible and incomparable, but some capitalist creations had enduring and universal value: 'In every socially antagonistic formation, we find cultural valuables common to all mankind [*obshchechelovecheskie*].'[36] Such findings derived from Lenin's theory of two cultures, corresponding to two classes.[37] Classes rise and fall; their culture is progressive at birth and degenerates at death; therefore, nascent capitalism had left a lasting cultural heritage. On these grounds, Soviet cultural theoreticians argued that 'spiritual culture' had certain classless 'components.'[38] Lenin's two cultures came to mean that 'the culture of any bourgeois nation is not monolithic or homogenous,' and that there was something called 'democratic culture' that capitalist countries could offer to Soviet audiences.

Foreign affairs journalists and academics did not make foreign policy, of course, but they did become its public voice. Their writings provided the new policy with philosophical foundations, made coexistence 'historically' necessary rather than circumstantial, and linked it to cultural exchange.[39] Coexistence, however, did not have to be peaceful. So long as capitalism existed, war seemed inevitable. War was central to the Soviet cosmos, to the Marxist-Leninist understanding of both international relations and history. War was expected, hoped for (at least theoretically) as a cataclysm that would destroy capitalism, and feared at the same time.[40] In justifying cultural exchange, the first step, then, was to prove the very possibility of peace.[41] Hence the proliferation of new legal treatises on international organizations and international law, whose potential to preserve peace had been dismissed or derided for decades.[42] Hence, too, the invocations of politically unconventional but intellectually authoritative figures: Russian translations of Thomas More and Tommaso Campanella, Erasmus and Hugo Grotius, Abbé Saint Pierre, Rousseau and Lessing, Voltaire, Mably, William Penn and Wilhelm Weitling, Fichte, Bentham, and the Saint-Simonians aided in the search for the legitimate origins of peaceful coexistence.

Reinterpretation accompanied translation and publication. For example, before the late 1950s, Soviet publications had faulted Grotius for confounding natural and divine law, using religious terminology, grounding his juridical system in morality, and for his services to the powers-that-be in Holland and France. But in 1958, on the heels of the Russian-language republication of his treatise *On the Law of War and Peace*, scholar of the Enlightenment A.I. Kazarin offered a defence of Grotius's oeuvre. No longer an offshoot of theologians, Grotius emerged from Kazarin's pen as a forerunner of the Enlightenment and the encyclopedists.[43] The new Soviet readings of such thinkers devoted much space to exploring how the idea of 'perpetual peace' evolved in its socio-economic context. The birth of the concept was linked to the transition from feudalism to capitalism, and peace was declared productive of other historic shifts, including that from capitalism to socialism.[44]

Perhaps most important in this intellectual effort was the reassessment of Immanuel Kant and his essay on *Perpetual Peace*.[45] Kant had been on the margins of official philosophical writings, but in the late 1950s three aspects of his thinking became useful. First, harbouring few illusions about the harmonious state of nature, Kant accepted the antagonism of states and admitted an obligation to go to war under certain circumstances. Second, nonetheless, peace was possible – but not by way of a supranational state, a merging of states, or a world government (the anathema of cosmopolitanism in Soviet discourse), for Kant resolutely defended sovereignty.[46] However, if states were to retain their sovereignty, then the only way of ensuring peace was with a 'union of nations.' As Kant envisioned it, this union would be held together by three linchpins – mutual commercial interests, increased communications, and a shared world culture. All three were also the main goals, practices, and slogans of 'peaceful coexistence.'[47] For Soviet philosophers, Kant's treatise 'not only had a historical value as evidence of its author's humanistic aspirations.' For all its 'utopianism and some mistaken propositions,' Kant's program was 'generally consonant with the one for which millions of simple people all over the world are struggling today.'[48] Like many authors writing in the West, Soviet thinkers saw in Kant's 'union of nations' a prophesy of the United Nations.[49] In the late 1940s and early 1950s, Soviet leaders had shown little interest in that organization, at once seeing it as contrived by imperialists and fearing that it might be demolished by those same imperialists. But from 1955 on, Soviet politicians commented favourably on the UN's work, began to cooperate with its specialized councils, and called its charter a manifestation of 'peaceful coexistence.'[50] Such pronouncements and the accompanying philosophical writings in justification of coexistence constituted a substantial alteration of Marxist political theory, for it was now suggested that social and economic transformations could happen peacefully.

Two assumptions about culture underpinned these intellectual endeavours: first, that culture was a transparent medium of communication, and second, that the reason for its transparency was its universality (when culture was not intelligible, it was not 'true' culture). Like science, culture spoke a shared language.[51] Universality became the key principle (*printsip universal'nosti*) of cultural exchange, an invitation to 'all nations, all peoples, and all the countries of the globe,' no matter how small, to 'make a contribution to the common treasury of world culture' on 'an equal footing.'[52] For the most part, the 'treasury' was a metaphor for the common stock of books, paintings, and music scores available to each according to his needs. But occasionally, universality shaded into universalism, into the all-human, despite the party's reminders that it was class that mattered, not humanity in the abstract.[53] There was good reason for such lapses into universalism, and that reason was communism.[54] The starting points were familiar – communism as the embodiment of the eternal quest for justice, as the ultimate enlightened 'society of reason.' But the conclusions were controversial: if communism was supposed to fulfil 'humankind's centuries-old historical dream,' then did this not suggest that the universal, the 'all-human' (*obshchechelovecheskoe*), rather than the exclusively proletarian, would ultimately prevail under communism? And if Soviet society was so close to communism, then did this not mean that 'there are elements of social life, which, in their development, take on universal character, become universal morality' already in the present?[55]

Nobody talked yet about humanity in the abstract, but as early as 1955, the Academy of Sciences resolved to participate in a multi-volume, internationally authored, UNESCO-sponsored *History of Mankind: Cultural and Scientific Development.* The Soviet archeologists and historians invited for the project as consultants imagined a *History* that would show how, over centuries, cross-cultural interactions had created a common 'world culture' and 'the unity of human society.' People had traded goods from time immemorial, and, travelling with goods, they had spread their primitive technologies and alphabets along the way. Isolated civilizations, whose development was doomed to repetition, à la Arnold J. Toynbee, were decidedly unpalatable for Soviet historians.[56] Even the proliferation of civilizations was strange, because in the Russian Soviet language, 'civilization' carried unifying rather than divisive implications. The term itself, *tsivilizatsiia,* had meta-historical and global connotations and was used rather sparingly, primarily in conjunction with antiquity, modernity, the East, the West, and the world. As Soviet historians envisioned it, the cultural process (progress, in their vocabulary) was the flow of goods, ideas, discoveries, and artistic movements from nations to 'the common world usage' and back to nations. It is this kind of reading that the Soviet Commission on the UNESCO project expected from the *History.*

They were disappointed. The substantive disagreements were mainly about the foreign scholars' elevation of race or religion into an explanatory factor at the expense of socio-economic relations.[57] The *History*'s treatment of Russia and 'the East' spurred another set of controversial issues. Soviet consultants wished to see more attention devoted to 'the countries of Eastern Europe and to non-European countries,' to Tokugawa thought, Iranian miniature, architecture in Central Asia and the Caucuses, murals in India, and non-Western confessions. As for Russia, everything about it seemed slighted: its church, state, and wars; its travellers and explorers, scientists and thinkers. Its definition on the map as a 'white civilization beyond Europe' was grating.[58] For five years, the Group for the Study of World Culture argued for its version of human development, but ultimately broke away from the UNESCO project and, in the early 1960s, proceeded to work on a Soviet counter-account. As its guiding principle, the Soviet version took 'the idea of the original and permanent unity of mankind' (*iznachal'noe i neprekhodiashchee edin-*

stvo chelovechestva).[59] This vision of common humanity was fundamental to both the Soviet scholars' involvement in the UNESCO project and their frustration with it. The academy's early decision to participate in UNESCO's *History* inspired more explicitly universalist thinking and brought to the fore a language long dormant.

Institutions: A Project and Its Time

Cultural policymakers insisted on setting the internationalism of the mid- to late-1950s apart from its predecessors. The Soviet government's political appeals to 'the people' of foreign countries were nothing new, but the cultural exchange policies of the mid-1950s were suffused with a new-fangled populism. Populism first emerged at home, when Khrushchev renewed the perennial attack on the bureaucracy as he tried to restructure state institutions, replace many of them with public (*obshchestvennye*) organizations, champion accountability, and inspire initiative from below.[60] Hundreds of ministerial departments and thousands of state offices were abolished, to be replaced by unions, committees, societies, and other public organizations.

Among the thousands was VOKS, the All-Union Society for Foreign Cultural Ties. Although nominally not part of the state bureaucracy then under attack, in fact, 'boasting a network of representatives in Soviet embassies abroad and complete integration into the branches of the bureaucracy,' VOKS 'most resembled a regular state agency.'[61] It had been established in 1925 to cultivate relations with foreign intellectuals and coordinate the activities of the 'friends of new Russia.' Its main function and field of expertise was information. Its main participants and beneficiaries were cultural elites at home and abroad, whose elite status would be conferred or confirmed by privileged access to information about each other.[62] Over the years, VOKS had acquired its own patrons, clients, and perks as well as an aura of secrecy. Historians and memoirists alike expose VOKS as a facade: a public organization providing cover for police networks and state control.[63] VOKS was abolished for these reasons – for its bureaucracy, secrecy, hypocrisy, and elitism.[64]

The Union of Soviet Societies for Foreign Cultural Relations (SSOD) that came to replace VOKS in 1958 was conceived as its opposite on all these counts. Decentralization was one of the main goals of the new union; indeed, it was a union of friendship societies in the plural, not a single society as VOKS had been.[65] Another major goal, a matter of self-definition and a rewarding sign of success in its early years, was mass participation.[66] Unlike VOKS, whose associates were prominent writers and scholars, friendship societies boasted 'broad' membership of ordinary people. There was a catch, however. In 1958, the new societies and the propaganda campaign that accompanied SSOD's founding conference attracted much enthusiasm and curiosity, but, as many letter writers petitioning for membership in the societies would discover, membership was collective, not individual. The 'wide circles of the Soviet public' entered the picture as entire factories, institutes, libraries, collective farms, and unions.[67] SSOD was created in the spirit of activism and participation, but its founders sought supervised participation and controlled activism.[68]

Why did the Central Committee go to the trouble of establishing friendship societies?

One of the more remarkable (though least remarked upon) aspects of the new diplomatic course was the belief in the effectiveness of public and personal diplomacy.[69] It was a literal reading of an old story: 'the masses' make history, including international history, not diplomats and governments.[70] What made for the novelty was the attempt to put this reading into practice. At the SSOD founding conference in 1958, hardly a speaker missed the most prominent theme of the campaign for public activism in international affairs – personal relations (*lichnye sviazi, lichnye kontakty*) with foreigners.[71] This idea was a departure from the usual propaganda methods that centred on demonstrating superiority and embodying it in photographic images of success. Photographs and success stories were still important, but now they were to be distributed by ordinary people rather than state-sponsored magazines. And they were to come with a personal touch, by word-of-mouth, first (good) impressions, and letters from Soviet citizens to pen pals abroad. International personal correspondence seemed especially promising because of a perception that foreigners took first impressions to heart. 'For people abroad, personal contact starts with mutual sympathy,' and 'it would be interesting,' argued the SSOD president, 'to have a comrade send a letter in which he would speak his mind extensively. We need documents that will awaken sympathies.'[72]

These ideas did not remain backstage for long; soon enough, the press was talking about personal contacts and foreign correspondence. It was unprecedented, and, like the friendship societies, elicited an upsurge of enthusiasm. At the same time, similar kinds of announcements were being disseminated through friendship societies abroad. The combined effect was a 'flood' of letters from Soviet and foreign citizens, requesting addresses and help in finding pen pals.[73] Officials were taken by surprise and had no idea what to do with these requests. The main problem was control. Until the requests started arriving, nobody had thought through regulatory mechanisms – how correspondence would be supervised and the right content assured. While officials scratched their heads and wrote reports, letters continued to pile up, and no bureaucracy wanted to take responsibility for them. In desperation, SSOD officials turned to their Presidium: 'The SOD departments want to know how to respond to such requests ... The main question has not been settled – is it allowed to give Soviet citizens' addresses to foreigners and foreigners' addresses to Soviet citizens? ... The question of correspondence has outgrown the institutional framework ... and become a political matter.'[74]

Several solutions were proposed. One was to establish a special SSOD department that would maintain a database of addresses, translate letters, and 'be responsible for international correspondence from the point of view of state secrets' (read: exercise censorial supervision). Another solution was to channel correspondence through local party and trade union cells, which would review individual candidates, issue permissions, and 'help with letter writing' (read: exercise censorial supervision).[75] Not much came of either. Despite all the talk about personal relations, the decision against individual membership in friendship societies and direct correspondence with foreigners had the upper hand. Perhaps this was to be expected, but the fact that the other option was considered seriously and debated, even defended, intensely, is equally important and indicative of the times.

Cosmopolitan Lessons

The culmination of the conceptual shift toward cultural universalism and coexistence was the Moscow International Youth Festival in the summer of 1957. A signature event, a landmark moment in the mythology of the Thaw, and a watershed in numerous biographies, the festival was unparalleled in scale, scope, investment, excitement, and impact on the subsequent lives of participants.

What made it, in part, a spectacular cultural event was the Hungarian revolution. By 1957, youth festivals had had only a decade-long history, but each one – from the Prague Festival of 1947, the year Czechoslovakia joined the Cominform, to the Bucharest Festival staged literally days after the ceasefire in Korea, to the Warsaw Festival of 1955, held less than two weeks after the Geneva summit – had taken place at turning points in the Cold War.[76] The Moscow Festival planners recalled the earlier festivals (as participants, observers, creators, or manipulators) and understood well that the crisis in Eastern Europe could tarnish their own. In October–December 1956, national preparatory committees everywhere in Europe faced the disintegration of the festival as activities on its behalf were suspended.[77] In an attempt to pick up its broken pieces, the Europeans in the International Festival Committee staked their propaganda efforts on the cultural program – because it was entertaining and innocent, and it held promise of universal appeal. That is how the festival became *conceivable* as an expressly cultural event, despite the Komsomol's insistence on its political goals, program, and ramifications.[78] And that, in part, is how the festival did become a cultural event, one of the most spectacular in Soviet history.

The festival's visual and ceremonial order set it distinctly apart from Soviet celebrations. Soviet holidays were centripetal, with a parade proceeding down the main street toward the seat of power, in Moscow – the Red Square. The festival opening procession was linear, circumventing the centre and connecting the opposite ends of the city, the northeast and the southwest. Attempts to impose Soviet celebratory rituals onto this international event were rather limited. Instead, the artists designing the festival decor sought universal symbols – dove, torch, fire, water, white and blue colours, the symbols of purity – that anybody could decipher on the spot.[79] The festival flag was a white silk field with an emblem invented specifically for this event – a daisy of five semi-circular colourful petals standing for the five continents. The closest visual and symbolic kin of its red, blue, green, yellow, and purple petals were the Olympic rings.[80] Whereas the standard holiday colours were solemn red and gold, here the whole rainbow brought a carnivalesque spirit to festival sequences. To turn Moscow into a celebratory city, the artists resolved to colour streetcars, buses, taxis, all public transport, as well as vans, cars, and pickup trucks carrying the foreigners. To paint trucks and vans – from olive green to orange, blue, yellow, lilac; to paint them twice over – with exotic flowers, birds and butterflies, with wavy azure stripes.[81] This was one of the most memorable spectacles; to this day, the mention of the festival triggers recollections in colour and of colour.[82] There was something wild about purple cars: aesthetic and emotional abandon replaced homogeneity and solemnity.

Dozens of sketches and pages of scripts fashioned Moscow into an international thoroughfare, a meeting point of the five continents. The drawings for Gogol' Boulevard disclose the story of 'literary heroes at the

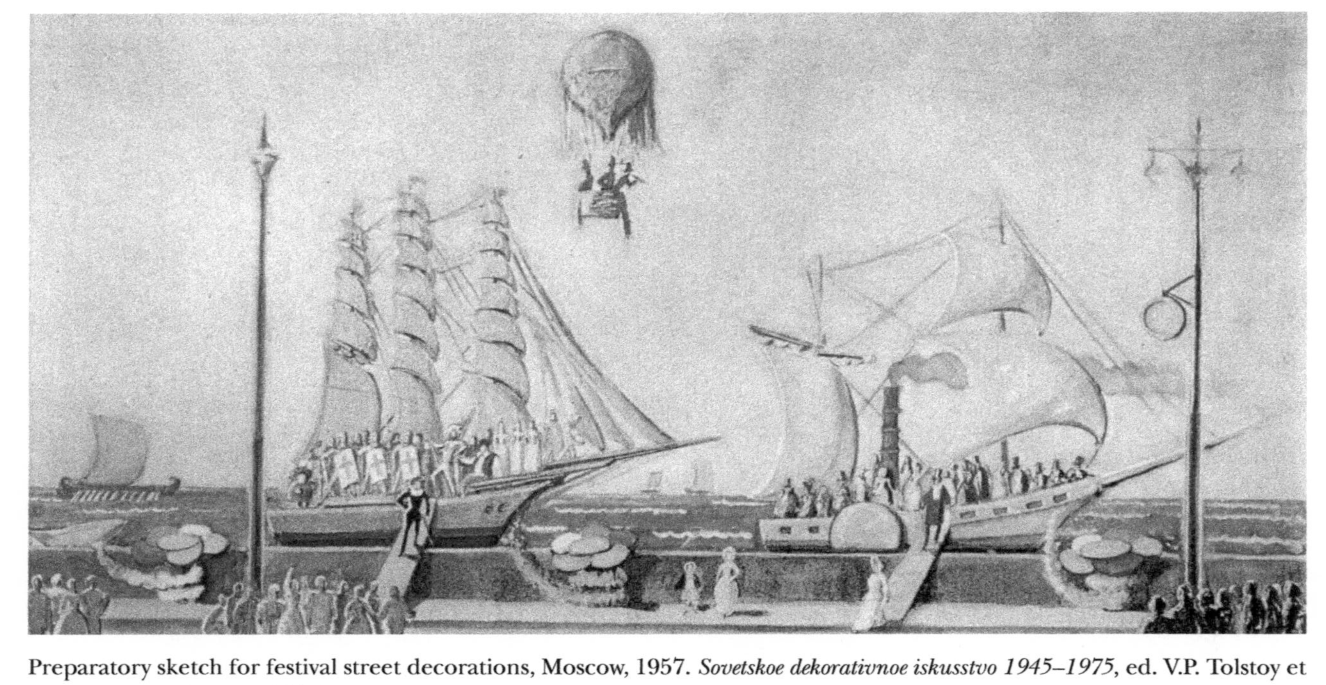

Preparatory sketch for festival street decorations, Moscow, 1957. *Sovetskoe dekorativnoe iskusstvo 1945–1975*, ed. V.P. Tolstoy et al. (Moscow: Iskusstvo, 1989).

Festival street decorations, Tverskoi Boulevard, Moscow, 1957. *Sovetskoe dekorativnoe iskusstvo 1945-1975*, ed. V.P. Tolstoy et al. (Moscow: Iskusstvo, 1989).

festival.' A multidimensional installation would turn Kropotkin Square into a wharf, with a street in the immediate foreground, followed by the sea, mooring ships, and disembarking travellers. The wind would blow the pink and yellow sails, and the festival daisy would hold the mooring lines. The blue band in the sketch may have been the real Moscow River; it certainly cast Moscow as the proverbial port of five seas. And the travellers, courtiers in puffed trousers and ruffed collars, gentlemen in long overcoats and tall cylindrical hats, from sixteenth-century Spain to Victorian Britain, would fulfil the wishful prophecy of Peter the Great (in Pushkin's rendition): 'Ay, ships of every flag shall come.' Ultimately, this particular composition did not take shape. But the main ideas – literary themes triggering universal recognition, the arrival of ships of every flag, the re-creation of foreign cityscapes in Moscow – did materialize. Tverskoi Boulevard was transformed into a veritable encyclopedia of fairy tales and legends. A 'magic village' mixed and matched different cityscapes. Here, a caliph's palace stood side by side with a Chinese pagoda, palm trees doubled as partitions between curling eaves and domes crowning octagonal arcades, and real tree-leaves embraced all this strangeness. Not only here, on Tverskoi Boulevard, but throughout Moscow, miniature foreign cities appeared.[83]

The idea of the 'ships of every flag' arriving in Moscow was most explicit in the water show, when all the world's ships did indeed arrive in Moscow. Every kind of ship imaginable, staffed with sailors and passengers in historical and national costumes, was here: galleys, frigates, clippers, corvettes, barges, schooners, sloops, launches, canoes, pirogues, feluccas, and even a raft. Chinese junks carried the sounds of dizi flutes, bells, cymbal drums, and lutes; gondolas, sentimental barcarolles. The hundreds of ships were accompanied by real and fantastic creatures: bands of mermaids with flower-wreaths, whales turned into fountains, crocodiles and dragonflies, swans and dolphins, monsters covered with seashells and seaweeds, floating islands with palm trees, and the lord of the show, Neptune. The vision of the 'ships of every flag' was the guiding concept for the creators of the water show: Pushkin's verse was on the very first page of their script. It is surprising to see just how closely the festival matched these sketches and scripts, which betray the meanings and imaginings invested in this event. The festival had been a literary enterprise, a spectacular invention on paper, before it became real.[84]

The preparations not only set the interpretive lens, shaping the expectations and thus, in part, the outcome, but also radically democratized the elite knowledge of foreign places, languages, and cultures. Reoriented toward the festival, the publishing industry exploded with information about exotic places: medieval castles, crooked side streets, palm trees, tropical forests, skyscrapers, piazzas and arcades, ice-lined expanses, and much more. The Distributing Centre for Research Libraries compiled a bibliographical reference about the 131 countries represented at the festival. Besides the reading lists, the guide contained 'concise physical and geographical information about the political structure, economy, population, and language.' With this guide at hand, librarians could readily recommend books and articles and could brief readers on basic facts about any country.[85] Such encyclopedic bibliographies – all countries from A to Z – registered a remarkable expansion of the geographical imagination.

The frequency with which maps were mentioned strikingly reflected the new disposition. Or, rather, it was the map in the singular – the map of the whole world, the material proof that encompassing everything on a single sheet of paper was possible. The map was a concept on the order of the festival itself, whose planners were trying to encompass the world in one city. The activists of the Torch club in the Moscow Kuibyshev district called their 'spoken journal' *At the Map of the World.* A similar 'spoken journal' in the Sokol'niki district took the audience *Around the World* in a series of lectures. Maps of the world covered the walls of neighbourhood libraries, where bookcases displayed artefacts, postcards, fact sheets, and novels from different countries. The initial sketches of decor for the Manezh Square included 'photo[graphic] landscapes of the most beautiful places: the mountains of Tibet and India, the canyons of America, Siberian taiga, Norwegian fiords, the lakes of Switzerland.'[86] Nooks of all kinds – library 'corners,' theatre foyers, billboard stands at park entrances – could unexpectedly reveal a foreign site in a collage of images or a montage of articles and salutations. 'The map' was a vocabulary as well. It functioned as an indicator of curiosity and knowledge and filled Soviet spaces with foreign appellations.

Clubs and houses of culture were eager to invite people who had travelled abroad and could give colour, voice, and substance to contours on the maps. In 1956, a group of writers and journalists toured Europe on the steamship *Pobeda* in a much publicized voyage. Afterward, they helped to produce a documentary about the trip and wrote moving travelogues. Among the earliest audiences for their manuscripts were the residents of the working-class Stalin district in Moscow who came one March evening to their local library no. 72. For hours that evening, they listened to the writers speak of summertime Europe.[87] Another local library invited a journalist who had recently visited Brazil to 'share his impressions about [that] country's culture and political life.' Besides his impressions, he brought to the lecture a music recording, and the evening ended with the assembly tapping to Brazilian songs.[88] Gossip and frenzy surrounded music albums purchased abroad. New recordings were the talk of fashionable Moscow, objects of much devotion, advantageous exchanges, and underground business, and to this day memoirists write about them with considerable emotion.[89] But in 1957, these desirable and inaccessible objects were spinning at local libraries and clubs throughout the city.

Flowing from dormitory windows, dancing grounds, clubs, parks, and courtyards, foreign sounds saturated Soviet auditory spaces.[90] The idea of an international festival legitimized foreign pieces in the amateurs' repertoires, so much so that practising for the festival and learning something foreign became interchangeable notions. Here were countless moments of creative appropriation: Russian lyrics invented for foreign melodies, popular Soviet theme songs rearranged with foreign inflections, dance steps learned from foreign movies and retraced from memory. A new band established at the Central House of the Art Workers in 1957 offered an irreverent remix of Isaak Dunaevskii's classic songs, which had been changed beyond recognition: 'A triple meter song in a Russian melodious style is given in *style moderne*, in the style of American jazz. From the aesthetic point of view, this is a perversion.' The person who rallied against this composition was Aleksandr Tsfasman, an old jazzman, one of the Soviet Union's most celebrated and versatile. Tsfasman was not against jazz as such; what, then, was the matter? The stylistic incongruity that jarred him was the contamination of the familiar-by-heart lyrical songs with the foreign. The foreign was not necessarily bad; it was simply somebody else's, while the Soviet melodies in question were the lyrical songs and spirited marches of 'the happy-go-lucky guys' from the beloved musicals of the 1930s.[91]

According to the politicians in the Preparatory Committee, the trouble was twofold: the foreign had overtaken Soviet spaces, and, in the process, the festival was being reinterpreted as a cultural event once again, and this time right at home. From the screen and the press, from radios and television sets, it looked as if there was nothing more to the preparations or to the festival itself than music and dance – than foreign music and dance. No 'interesting labour initiatives' and no politics. By the time the Preparatory Committee caught up with the action and began to issue one warning after another, it was already too late. Jazz quartets and girls doing the *Cachucha pas de basques* were everywhere.[92]

Conventional wisdom, based on memoirs, suggests that foreigners, bringing to the festival unthinkable sounds, dance steps, and images, set in train a stylistic revolution. They did bring unthinkable sounds, dance steps, and images. But the aesthetic mobilization had begun before their arrival and hinged on the anticipation of foreigners.

The Tower of Babel

For the majority of Soviet citizens, the festival was the most concentrated exposure to foreigners they had ever experienced. The novelty struck people even second hand; for one such memoirist, who was not in Moscow that summer, the festival still marked the beginning of 'a new life, *vita nova*' – the repetitive mix of Russian and Latin conveying the momentous significance of the event.[93] For another memoirist, who was in Moscow and saw the jostling crowds, the festival as a spectacle, as a popular fête (*prazdnik, gulian'e*) was almost comparable to the spontaneous celebrations in May 1945.[94] There was something of the same communal elation when, on the opening day of the festival, 28 July 1957, people poured out onto the streets to watch the motorcade with foreigners along Garden Ring Road. The Muscovites' place was on the sidewalks, waving hands in welcome. They would be separated from the procession by an invisible (to foreigners at least) human barrier, Komsomol patrols standing in the first row along the route. But when the painted trucks and buses with the delegates came in sight, the crowd nudged the first row and overflowed onto the road. In a split second, the human cordon gave way, cracked simultaneously everywhere, dissipated, disappeared.[95]

Leaping into trucks, Soviet citizens pulled the foreigners onto the ground to embrace them in dance. People stretched out hands not just to wave or salute, no – to partake in another world physically. This was the 'enchanting feeling' of belonging in the world, 'of being a tiny particle, a grain of sand in an immense celebration,' as one student in the Komsomol patrol experienced it. Mothers offered their toddlers to the foreigners to hold, thousands of hands picking up children, passing them to the trucks and back to the women. Giving of themselves (and there were instances of people offering precious objects to the delegates) was another way of joining the world. The motorcade stopped completely. Buses and trucks drowned in flowers. In turn, the impulse entranced the foreigners; they began to jump over truck rails, uniting with the crowd,

Festival opening procession, Moscow, 28 July 1957. TsAADM 0-6487.

or to lift people from the sidewalks onto the trucks and chair them in the air. The next day, translators reported, some delegates' voices turned hoarse from all the shouting and singing.[96]

The moment was marked by an incredible release of energy, which found an outlet in screams, dances, jumps, and tears. Shortly after the festival, with a touch of retrospectiveness but without losing immediacy, the documentary filmmaker Vasilii Katanian described what he had felt: 'I will probably never forget the first day. Until then, I had not seen anything of the kind.... Nobody had expected it, we were blown away.' In the trucks, in the crowd, people cried, and his camera caught their tears.[97] The outpouring in May 1945 is understandable, but how to interpret this 'flow and flood of joy,' as the festival has been remembered? It defied all reason, this inordinate emotionality. Later, trying to make sense of what had happened, some described their own state as intoxication; others referred to the hypnotism of the motorcade. Maybe the baking heat was responsible. Maybe this was madness, ecstasy, mass hysteria. Or maybe this was *communitas*, all the more astonishing because the people who united with such abandon were strangers worlds apart. And what was it that they celebrated without restraint? Perhaps just themselves – themselves in unison with the world, as all things, people, sounds mixed and melded in this Babel of biblical proportions.[98]

In dances, songs, and physical expressiveness, the opening procession epitomized a central quest of the festival: the search for a universal language with which to confirm and proclaim common humanity, for ways to speak not only beyond geopolitical and ideological borders but linguistic ones as well. Even before the festival began, journalists and documentary filmmakers had referred to a special 'festival language' that would allow people to communicate across linguistic barriers. The festival dreamers, who had choreographed the sequences and scripted the city, envisioned an event that would undo God's punishment and reverse our post-Babelian condition. Like sketches for the festive city, documentary footage does not so much depict what happened at the festival as reveal the visions and aspirations of its planners. An early screenplay of the documentary *Above Us Is One Sky* bound the festival to the story of the origin of languages, thereby imparting to this event world-historical, prophetic significance: 'Once upon a time, as legend has it, God confounded the tongues of nations that had dared to build the Tower of Babel reaching the skies; then people speaking different languages ceased to understand each another, and the Tower remained unfinished.' Would the festival participants, 'so different, so unalike,' 'build their own Tower

American festival participants dancing in a Moscow street, 1957. TsAADM 1-59333.

of Friendship and Peace?' The question was rhetorical; the rest of the film – and the entire festival – would answer in the affirmative.[99]

During the festival, the search for a universal tongue went beyond linguistic fluency. Even as dictionaries became bestsellers, there was a sustained discourse on the superfluity of grammatical forms and verbal coherence in general. Polyglottism was suspect unless the speakers were appointed translators.[100] Rather than celebrating linguistic fluency, the press at the time, as well as post-festival fiction and eyewitness accounts, relished the moments of misunderstanding and inarticulateness. Such accounts were filled with dialogues in multiple languages, grammatically misconstrued Russian sentences, transliterated foreign words and expressions inserted into Russian texts, and awkward, good-natured laughter. And the worse the mistakes, the more good-natured the laughter.[101]

Inarticulateness was ultimately compensated for by gestures, exchange of objects, songs, dance, art. Objects rescued and completed exchanges that failed on the most literal, verbal level:

> A Moscow boy, maybe a college freshman, ran up to a tall, curly-haired guy standing by the wall and asked in broken English:
>
> – *Forin* [foreigner]?
>
> The guy started searching his pockets with embarrassment and at long last held out a coin, the forint.
>
> The Moscow boy looked in bewilderment and then exclaimed happily: 'Are you Hungarian? Yes?' And so they made acquaintance.[102]

Hungary was a refrain throughout the festival. The hand-picked Hungarian delegates were some of the most paraded and photographed, and the camera typically captured them in close physical contact with Russians, holding hands, embracing, dancing. In this propagandistic snippet, until the coin appears, the boys speak past each other. Language proves an inadequate marker of identity and an equally ineffective way of communicating; it is the object that prompts recognition and cements the acquaintance.

Out in the streets, gifts nearly replaced speech. People bartered pins, pens, stamps, signatures, addresses, toys, and anything else that could serve as a keepsake. In lieu of a common language, pins told stories. Flags and other country symbols did the honour of introduction. Professional and political badges revealed life choices. Pins from previous festivals spoke of journeys. What they meant in the festival context is best illustrated by immaterial exchanges: addresses and signatures. Photographs show public, crowded, and indiscriminate interactions around the address book. Multiple hands hold out address books for signatures; people scribble their addresses in one pad after another; several signatories are writing at once, as if in an assembly line. Such exchanges were about accumulation; witnesses to foreignness, address books held meaning as collections. According to the festival lore, they had the power to compensate for absence, as one old woman discovered when she arrived in Moscow to 'get something from the fair' for her sick grandson. She shyly held out her notebook to a group of Chinese: 'Listen, my dear, write something in your way for me.' The crowd grew; the notebook began to make rounds, at first accompanied by somebody's translation, then without any words or questions, 'in silence.' While it travelled from the Chinese hands to those of an African, passing on to the Italians, then to the Britons, people affixed pins to the old woman's blouse. In the end, she departed with a collection of pins and signatures as valuable as anything that the festival participants could have assembled. Pins and autographs were thus seen as repositories of foreign presence.[103] The meaning of these gifts derived from the very situation of exchange or gift-giving. And that situation, as photographs attest, involved excited polyglot groups, people in widely different attire and headgear, sharing *this* moment, *this* literal incomprehension, *this* immediate sense of surrounding others, *this* experience – of which the gifts were now tokens.

The pride of place in non-verbal communication belonged to the arts. Soviet cultural policies, theoretical writings, and practices ranging from artwork exhibitions to prose translation were grounded in a fundamental assumption of cultural transparency. Now, at the festival, it seemed that cultural performances could say it all. Here, visual, kinetic, and auditory arts predominated. Songs were a greeting. The French would sing 'Katiusha' as a salutation to the Russians; in response, the Russians would hum 'C'est si bon.' Along with 'The Anthem of Democratic Youth,' festival songbooks also printed 'Les Grands Boulevards.'[104] Montand had only recently appeared on the screens and radio waves – and his songs were immediately recycled and reinterpreted at the festival. They became symbolic of how a melody can cross borders and become a shared transnational identifier. Contemporaries revelled in his songs and in the symbolism.[105] In a delightful circus act, a Russian clown ridiculed a pile of dictionaries when a foreigner attempted a phrase-book conversation. Words only caused confusion, so the clown traded dictionaries for an accordion and presented his guest with recognizable choices: *Krakowiak* –

no, *Csárdás* – no, *pas d'Espagne* – no. And thus the accordion played until the clown luckily stumbled upon Maurice Chevalier's waltz 'Sous les toits de Paris' and was immediately rewarded by rousing applause from the audience as well as a cheerful 'Oui, je suis parisien!' from the foreigner. Waltzing, hand in hand, the two departed, no longer strangers.[106]

Most readily, musical 'gifts' were exchanged in the streets, where professionals and amateur passersby alike would burst into dance and song with abandon that rarely happens in modern urban settings.[107] Even now, over fifty years later, as the journalist Nikolai Eremchenko describes a dance scene around the Moscow University, his voice gains momentum, then halts in laughter: 'You should have just seen what went on at the Lenin Hills! I went there only once, this was not my territory ... just went to see what was happening, and there was dancing and so on in every corner, in the squares, on the staircases, in the fountain and so on and so on [*laughs*]. How we romped! How Moscow frisked about. It was all awesome, from the heart. This really was fun and exciting.'[108]

Much of the dancing consisted of jumping in circles – a way to express the overwhelming emotionality that, participants often said, they could not convey in words. During a dance of Russian and Hungarian passers-by in the Alexander Gardens, 'we join[ed] hands, hop[ped] around in circle, and [sang] together: "Rich-rach, riblebum, riblebum, riblebum! / Rich-rach, riblebum, riblebum, bum!"' Here was a breakdown of language; the Russians had no idea what these sounds meant, if anything at all, and as far as they were concerned, it did not matter. The gibberish proved only that gestures were truer than words and surely more meaningful.[109] Dance was an escape from the verbal order. It disrupted dialogues: oftentimes, an invitation to dance immediately followed a reciprocal introduction, an exchange of names. Or so said the journalists, whose professional being depended on verbal communication but who repeatedly announced the lexicon's inability to do justice to the festival.[110] 'Rich-rach, riblebum,' romping in circles or lines, was emotionally bonding in a primitive and physical way, for to synchronize one's steps with the bodies and sounds of others was to become manifestly absorbed into a community.[111]

In keeping with a mission to depict cross-cultural communication amid linguistic heterogeneity, documentary films about the festival arrayed the shots from gala concerts, open-air performances, and untutored street dancing into a story of universal harmony and interchangeability. In the film *Above Us Is One Sky*, the story unfolds through a montage of sequences from a Japanese lion dance, a Mexican courtship dance, a fast-paced Russian character dance, a Scottish jig, and the *Cueca.* In each case, the camera – focusing on the dancing feet – seeks a common step to relate one dance to the next in a chain of associations. This composition actually begins a segment earlier, with a French pantomime in which an impoverished rope-walker stretches out his hat for some coins. Technically, this performance is of an order different from the dances that follow, yet it conveys the same communicative imperative – kinesics. The camera concentrates on the rope-walker's feet; the next shot begins with the plodding feet of the dancers hidden under the lion costume and ends as the camera zooms in on the same stomping feet, then glides up and away to reveal the Mexican dance. Such editing was a common festival motif. The associational linkage was even more pronounced in *The Art of Our Friends,* devoted entirely to the cultural program. The shots were edited for a flawless transition from one culture to another through the same movements. With a half-spin of the body or a turn of the head, a traditional Korean dance becomes a classic Indian dance becomes a Japanese flower dance becomes an Egyptian belly dance.[112] Through analogous gestures, steps, turns, and whirls, the editing techniques thus elaborated the notion of a common cultural lineage.

Conclusion

As the foreigners departed and the makeshift stages were torn down, the festival spirit crumbled. For the next several years, offences ranging from prostitution to 'Zionist propaganda,' from illegal trade in foreign goods to high treason would be traced to the festival. In principle, the new diplomatic policy – popular participation in transnational cooperation – was to be based on trust in the Soviet people. In practice, however, officials could not give up controlling and censoring the population. The project for citizen diplomacy was stillborn, while the cultural exchange conventions that Soviet diplomats tried so stubbornly to negotiate may seem to be little more than a cover for cultural export.

But whereas the idea of public diplomacy flared briefly and died down by the early 1960s, the impulse behind it – the notion of a shared world culture – remained, sustaining continued Soviet participation in international cultural traffic. From the mid-1950s to the early 1960s, a group of Soviet philosophers came to postulate a set of values they declared to be 'universal' – fundamental behavioural norms, scientific discoveries, a great 'world culture,' and the desire to avert war. Class understanding of social life, class analysis of culture, and class morality were by no means abandoned, but the language of common humanity helped to legitimize the new policy of cultural exchange with capitalist countries. 'Peaceful coexistence,' as the Soviet press never tired of saying, was a long-term policy that would last until it would no longer be necessary, that is, until capitalism would disintegrate under the weight of its internal contradictions; then peace would become natural and eternal. In fact, Soviet commentators on international relations spoke of permanent peace right then and there. The vocabulary of peaceful coexistence and cultural universalism would remain unchanged for the next thirty years. Before perestroika, there would be no *conceptual* innovations in foreign relations, and when the new concepts did appear in the mid-1980s, they were, in turn, directly inspired by the Thaw-era language.[113]

So even as the foreigners departed and the makeshift stages were torn down, the sounds, dance steps, and words, pins and autographs, memorabilia and memories, and, above all, enchantment have remained. The festival artists called their masterpiece 'a time of miracles,' when fairy tales came alive in the streets. The festival overturned familiar time, space, and routine. Its planners sought universality; what they discovered was an infinite variety of people, colours, sounds, costumes, and movements. In subtle ways (more subtle than the propaganda factor), however, the festival was a quintessentially Soviet project – a work of fiction, initially taking shape, and place, in hundreds of pages of scripts before turning into reality. Before the decorations were drawn and painted, they were narrated; before the documentaries were filmed, they were written. It was no accident that fairy tales, literary characters, poetic verses, fantastic creatures, and enchanted vistas made frequent appearances in the scripts and on the streets. The festival asked its creators and participants alike to suspend disbelief and become children. In return, it delivered magic that rarely, if ever, visits us and our daily routine. This was a long-standing Soviet trope: art into life, fairy tale into reality.

To be sure, there was a darker side to it: foreigners were correct in suspecting police presence in the hotels and on the buses, and there was surveillance, manipulation, and detailed training of the thousands of Soviet participants.[114] And yet, the people who worked as translators at the festival would be hard pressed to remember this training; it simply did not matter much. Perhaps that is because the preparatory lectures were unsurprising; the correct answers and invisible boundaries were unquestionable; the presence of Komsomol overseers was part of the normal order of things. It was easy not to notice. Even so discerning a memoirist as the jazzman Alexei Kozlov did not. In his memoirs, he contrasts the 'crowded, joyous' festival with the 1980 Olympics, 'devoid of people, all prearranged, cheerless.' Kozlov remembers how beggars, tramps, prostitutes, and ex-prisoners were expelled from Moscow for the duration of the Olympics, how the police made apartment rounds looking for people without Moscow registration, how cordons on approaches to the city blocked entrance. Of course, the same thing, and on a mass scale, had taken place in 1957, but it had not affected the festival or its domestic reception.[115] What was so out of the ordinary, so beyond the conceivable in 1957, was the opportunity to stand surrounded by foreigners on a street corner or to sit in their company on a park bench, to exchange whispers with them in dimly lit theatres, to invite them home for tea, walk them back to the hotels, and speak to them first-hand.[116] And this is what became singularly memorable.[117]

The festival marked a generational shift in the entertainment industry and, because of the state monopoly on communications, a sea change in the entire audio-visual environment. Many of the household names in the 1960s and 1970s, some of them still performing today as aged pop stars, famous theatre directors, and conservatory conductors, first came to prominence during the summer of 1957. Earlier, they had worked at local houses of culture and university amateur troupes, and without the festival they might have gone on to become engineers, architects, doctors. The twenty-nine-year-old composer who rearranged Dunaevskii's songs for the band of the Central House of Art Workers was Yuri Saul'skii. He would spearhead the jazz revival of the 1960s as the conductor of the Moscow music hall, the creator of the celebrated big band VIO-66, and a founder of Soviet jazz festivals in the 1970s. He also wrote music that would become ubiquitous – pop hits, musicals, pieces for the theatre and cinema.[118] The festival's impact on the senses, soundscapes, and fields of vision would remain unparalleled by any other cultural event in Soviet history.

The festival encounters set the interpretive context for the reception of future imports. New imports would interact with the older ones, one song, one film triggering recollections of the next, until the chain of foreign inflections in Soviet culture would become endless. This, then, was the most important result of the exchange agreements: these repetitive protocols assured a constant – controlled, censored, distorted in many ways, but nonetheless constant – presence of Western books, paintings, films, or songs in the Soviet Union. In the years to come, there would be rigorous selection, editorial excisions of book pages and metres of film, loud arguments against the contamination of the Russian language with foreign words and of Soviet ethics with bourgeois mores. But there would be no serious attempt to wipe out foreignness from the Soviet – or Russian – cultural scene, which, like never before, now partook of the Western audio-visual world. Although a singular event, in fact, the festival was central to the routinization of the exotic in the late Soviet decades. The festival presented Soviet citizens with sounds, colours, and gestures that would be infinitely multiplied in urban decor and in urban comportment, on the variety stage and on the radio, in the cinema, in the design of book and magazine covers, in millions of knick-knacks of both foreign and domestic origin. Finally, and importantly, the festival highlighted cross-cultural communication as an intellectual problem and a source of creative expression.

In the mid- to late 1950s, when cultural exchange was a novel project, there was one building in Moscow that symbolized foreignness: the House of Friendship. A meeting place of East and West, the House had been exotic even among the architecture of Moscow's fin-de-siècle eclecticism. It was certainly outlandish in the Soviet urban context, and what went on inside this strange house on Vozdvizhenka during the late 1950s was a good match for its exterior. As the SSOD headquarters, the House staged exhibits of foreign books and photographs, as well as welcoming foreign artists and intellectuals for lectures, conferences, and performances. But the House would soon lose its exclusive significance. By the 1960s, in the process of cross-cultural transfer that began in the mid-1950s, the foreign had become a constant, diffused, and intimate presence in Soviet cities. Western imports filled Soviet public places: movie theatres, museums, dancing grounds, university dormitories, and libraries. And they also filled Soviet homes – eventually so seamlessly and imperceptibly that, by the late Soviet decades, many people had forgotten about the House of Friendship.

NOTES

I thank the audiences at conferences 'The Thaw: Soviet Culture and Society in the 1950s and 1960s' (Berkeley, 2005), 'Universalities in History' (Harvard, 2006), and 'Remembering 1957: Fifty Years of Slavic Studies at Berkeley' (Berkeley 2007), where I presented portions of this article. For attentive readings and good advice, I am grateful to Margaret Lavinia Anderson, Julia Gilburd, Denis Kozlov, Elizabeth McGuire, Andrey Shlyakhter, and Yuri Slezkine.

1 An early Soviet organization of writers and artists striving to create a distinctly proletarian culture as well as to educate and encourage workers to become culture-makers themselves.
2 Gosudarstvennyi arkhiv Rossiiskoi Federatsii (GARF) 9576/1/8/204–34.
3 David Brandenberger, *National Bolshevism: Stalinist Mass Culture and the Formation of Modern Russian National Identity, 1931–1956* (Cambridge, MA, 2002), esp. 28, 58–9, 109, 123–9, 132, 141–3, 186–96. For a view of isolationism, grounded not in nationalism but in 'Sovietness,' see Malte Rolf, 'A Hall of Mirrors: Sovietizing Culture under Stalinism,' *Slavic Review* 68, no. 3 (Fall 2009): 601–30.
4 Katerina Clark, 'Germanophone Intellectuals in Stalin's Russia: Diaspora and Cultural Identity in the 1930s,' *Kritika* 2, no. 3 (Summer 2001): 529–51; Katerina Clark, *Moscow, the Fourth Rome: Stalinism, Cosmopolitanism, and the Evolution of Soviet Culture, 1931–1941* (Cambridge, MA, 2011); Michael David-Fox, 'The "Heroic Life" of a Friend of Stalinism: Romain Rolland and Soviet Culture,' *Slavonica* 11, no. 1 (April 2005): 3–29; David-Fox, *Showcasing the Great Experiment: Cultural Diplomacy and Western Visitors to the Soviet Union, 1921–1941* (Oxford, 2012); David-Fox, 'Stalinist Westernizer? Aleksandr Arosev's Literary and Political Depictions of Europe,' *Slavic Review* 62, no. 4 (Winter 2003): 733–59; David-Fox, 'Transnational History and the East-West Divide,' in *Imagining the West in Eastern Europe and the Soviet Union,* ed. György Péteri (Pittsburgh, 2010), 258–67; Ekaterina Sal'nikova, *Sovetskaia kul'tura v dvizhenii: ot serediny 1930-x k seredine 1980-x. Vizual'nye obrazy, geroi, siuzhety. Otechestvennaia kul'tura za predelami 'sovetskosti'* (Moscow, 2008); Alexei Yurchak, *Everything Was Forever, Until It Was No More: The Last Soviet Generation* (Princeton, 2006), chap. 5, esp. 162–70, 203–4. Indeed, as Clark, David-Fox, and Yurchak suggest, internationalism was a structural feature of Soviet ethos and polity.
5 On geographically and socially widespread experiences of Western cultures, see Anne E. Gorsuch, *All This Is Your World: Soviet Tourism at Home and Abroad after Stalin* (Oxford, 2011); Susan E. Reid, 'Who Will Beat Whom? Soviet Popular Reception of the American National Exhibition in Moscow, 1959,' in *Imagining the West,* 194–236; Kristin Roth-Ey, *Moscow Prime Time: How the Soviet Union Built the Media Empire That Lost the Cultural Cold War* (Ithaca, 2011), chaps. 2, 3; Sergei I. Zhuk, *Rock and Roll in the Rocket City: The West, Identity, and Ideology in Soviet Dniepropetrovsk, 1960–1985* (Baltimore, 2010).
6 Pia Koivunen, 'The 1957 Moscow Youth Festival: Propagating a New, Peaceful Image of the Soviet Union,' in *Soviet State and Society under Nikita Khrushchev,* ed. Melanie Ilič and Jeremy Smith (London, 2009), 46–65; Kristin Roth-Ey, '"Loose Girls" on the Loose? Sex, Propaganda and the 1957 Youth

Festival,' in *Women in the Khrushchev Era*, ed. Melanie Ilič, Susan E. Reid, and Lynne Attwood (Basingstoke, UK, 2004), 75–95.

7 But also see David-Fox, *Showcasing*, for an important argument that cultural diplomacy was a noteworthy aspect of the Stalinist 1930s and, moreover, that the Soviet Union was an innovator in this area.

8 Rossiiskii gosudarstvennyi arkhiv noveishei istorii (RGANI) 5/36/11/17; for taking Soviet confidence seriously, Nigel Gould-Davies, 'The Logic of Soviet Cultural Diplomacy,' *Diplomatic History* 27, no. 2 (April 2003): 193–214; on Khrushchev's emerging international confidence, Vladislav Zubok, 'Soviet Policy Aims at the Geneva Conference, 1955,' in *Cold War Respite: The Geneva Summit of 1955*, ed. Günter Bischof and Saki Dockrill (Baton Rouge, LA, 2000), 61–4, 72–3.

9 RGANI 5/36/4/40–78.

10 G.A. Mozhaev, 'Kul'turnoe sotrudnichestvo sotsialisticheskikh gosudarstv,' *Vestnik istorii mirovoi kul'tury* (hereafter *VIMK*) 7 (1957): 144–55.

11 See also Vladislav Zubok's observations in *A Failed Empire: The Soviet Union in the Cold War from Stalin to Gorbachev* (Chapel Hill, 2007), chap. 4, esp. 102–3.

12 RGANI 5/36/7/120–3; RGANI 5/36/11/17.

13 *Ezhegodnik kino 1956* (Moscow, 1957), 132–3; 'Kul'turnyi obmen mezhdu SSSR i Angliei,' *Literaturnaia gazeta*, 29 March 1956; Samuil Marshak, 'Dorogi druzhby,' *Pravda*, 1 April 1956; David Oistrakh, 'Desiat' dnei v Anglii,' *Literaturnaia gazeta*, 12 April 1956; RGANI 5/36/7/17–21, 86–7; Rossiiskii gosudarstvennyi arkhiv literatury i iskusstv (RGALI) 2329/8/239/39, 40, 44, 130–2, 134–5; RGALI 2329/8/235/123–5; Marietta Shaginian, 'Na vystavke angliiskogo iskusstva,' *Pravda*, 25 March 1956; Shaginian, 'Na vystavke angliiskoi knigi,' *Pravda*, 24 March 1956.

14 GARF 9518/1/168/46; RGALI 2329/8/235/123–6; RGALI 2329/8/239/39–47, 134–5; RGANI 5/30/161/113–16.

15 RGANI 5/28/367/83–86; *Vystavka frantsuzskogo iskusstva, XV–XX vv. Katalog* (Moscow, 1955).

16 RGANI 5/36/7/120–3.

17 Zhorzh Marten [Georges Marten], Vol'f Sedykh, *Moskva-Parizh: velenie serdtsa i razuma* (Moscow, 1998), 80–2.

18 RGALI 2732/1/1125/113–14.

19 RGALI 2732/1/1066/50–2ob, 60, 101–2ob, here esp. l. 102; RGALI 2732/1/1125/21, 36–8, 86–8.

20 RGALI 2329/8/364/128.

21 GARF 9518/1/276/4–6, 20, 44; RGANI 5/36/43/116–18. On French books, see also RGANI 5/30/235/103, 105; RGANI 5/30/274/34–5; RGANI 5/30/304/10.

22 GARF 9518/1/276/21–4, 58, 76–7; RGANI 5/36/43/116–18; RGANI

5/30/235/103, 129; RGANI 5/36/304/1–2, 6–7; on the advantages of general conventions, RGANI 5/30/370/77; on the usual terms of conventions, GARF 9518/1/166/124–6.

23 GARF 9518/1/276/46–55.

24 GARF 9518/1/346/83.

25 GARF 9518/1/346/54–9, 66, 70–1; separate contracts, GARF 9518/1/348/6–27, 145–6; RGANI 5/36/86/167–9; RGANI 5/36/82/61–4; RGANI 5/30/338/52.

26 RGANI 5/30/274/21; GARF 9518/1/166/1, 19, 230.

27 GARF 9518/1/166/5, 6, 10–11, 26, 96, 112–13, 230–1, 238.

28 RGANI 5/30/394/13; GARF 9518/1/168/29–36.

29 RGANI 5/30/338/ 15, 23–4, 25–31. On Gronchi's visit, Giulio Andreotti, 'O vstrechakh s Khrushchevym,' *Kentavr* (July–August, 1992): 65–6; 'In Dispraise of Macaroni,' *Time*, 22 February 1960.

30 On American psychological war aims in the Cold War, see Walter L. Hixson, *Parting the Curtain: Propaganda, Culture, and the Cold War, 1945–1961* (New York, 1997).

31 N.A. Erofeev, *Tumannyi Al'bion: Angliia i anglichane glazami russkikh, 1825–1853 gg.* (Moscow, 1982).

32 RGANI 5/30/235/103, 128; RGANI 5/30/274/34.

33 N.S. Khrushchev, *The Report of the Central Committee of the Communist Party of the Soviet Union to the 20th Party Congress* (Ottawa, 1956), 19–23, 29–46; *Programma Kommunisticheskoi partii Sovetskogo Soiuza. Priniata XXII s"ezdom KPSS* (Moscow, 1962), 120–31, esp. 131; 'Proekt: Programma kommunisticheskoi partii Sovetskogo Soiuza,' *Pravda*, 30 July 1961; G.I. Tunkin, 'XXII s"ezd KPSS i mezhdunarodnoe pravo,' *Sovetskii ezhegodnik mezhdunarodnogo prava* (1960) (hereafter *SEMP*).

34 Ia. Kotovskii, 'Ozdorovlenie mezhdunarodnoi torgovli ukrepit delo mira,' *Kommunist* 4 (1954): 81–95; F.I. Novik, *'Ottepel'' i inertsiia kholodnoi voiny (Germanskaia politika SSSR v 1953–55 gg)* (Moscow, 2001), 29–38; Aleksandr Pyzhikov, *Khrushchevskaia 'ottepel''* (Moscow, 2002), 16–17.

35 For a sample of articles, see A. Leont'ev, 'O mirnom sosushchestvovanii dvukh sistem,' *Kommunist* 13 (1954): 43–58; G. Malenkov, 'Rech' na piatoi sessii Verkhovnogo Soveta SSSR,' *Kommunist* 12 (1953): 12–34, here 26–31; A. Solodovnikov, 'Mezhdunarodnye kul'turnye sviazi,' *Mezhdunarodnaia zhizn'* 2 (1954); E. Voznesenskii, 'Vzaimnoe doverie i druzhba – osnova dobrososedskikh otnoshenii mezhdu SSSR i Finliandiei,' *Kommunist* 17 (1954): 85–97; 'Za mirnoe uregulirovanie mezhdunarodnykh voprosov,' *Kommunist* 13 (1953): 36–48. This change is reflected in diplomatic dictionaries: Vyshinskii's 1950 dictionary contains no entry on cultural cooperation, but a well-elaborated entry on 'trade agreements,' while Gromyko's 1960 diction-

ary contains rather lengthy entries on 'cultural cooperation' and 'scientific and technological cooperation.' *Diplomaticheskii slovar'* ed. A. Ia. Vyshinskii (Moscow, 1948, 1950), 1:846, 2:818–19; *Diplomaticheskii slovar'* ed. A.A. Gromyko et al. (Moscow, 1960, 1961, 1964), 2:154–6, 378–80.

36 E.A. Baller, 'Problema preemstvennosti v razvitii kul'tury,' *Vestnik istorii mirovoi kul'tury* (hereafter *VIMK*) 5 (1961): 18; G.A. Mozhaev, 'Kul'turnye sviazi sluzhat ukrepleniiu mira i druzhby mezhdu narodami,' *VIMK* 5 (1961): 78.

37 V.I. Lenin, *Sobranie sochinenii* (Moscow, 1948), 20:8, 16; 27:278, 376; 29:54–5; 31:259–65, 343.

38 GARF 9576/2/4/105–6, 109; Baller, 'Problema preemstvennosti,' 16.

39 M.Z. Selektor, 'Ob ob"ektivnykh osnovakh mirnoi politiki SSSR,' *Voprosy filosofii* (hereafter *VF*) 6 (1955): 31–44; editorial, *VF* 2 (1958): 3–8.

40 Margot Light, *The Soviet Theory of International Relations* (New York, 1988), 221–8.

41 Leont'ev, 'O mirnom,' 47–8; A. Nikonov, 'V sovremennuiu epokhu voiny mogut byt' predotvrashcheny,' *Kommunist* 6 (1956): 31–45; editorial, 'Leninskii kurs na mirnoe sosushchestvovanie – general'naia liniia vneshnei politiki Sovetskogo Soiuza,' *Kommunist* 11 (1957): 3–11.

42 V.N. Durdenevsky and S.B. Krylov, eds., *Organizatsiia Ob"edinennykh Natsii: sbornik dokumentov, otnosiashchikhsia k sozdaniiu i deiatel'nosti*, (Moscow, 1956); D.B. Levin, *Osnovnye problemy sovremennogo mezhdunarodnogo prava* (Moscow, 1958); E.G. Panfilov, 'Marksizm-Leninizm o demokraticheskom i spravedlivom mire,' *VF* 4 (1958): 15–27; G.I. Tunkin, 'Mirnoe sosushchestvovanie i mezhdunarodnoe pravo,' *Sovetskoe gosudarstvo i pravo* 7 (1956): 3–13; Tunkin, 'Sorok let sosushchestvovaniia i mezhdunarodnoe pravo,' *SEMP* (1958): 15–49; G.P. Zadorozhnyi, *OON i mirnoe sosushchestvovanie gosudarstv* (Moscow, 1958).

43 A.I. Kazarin, 'Gugo Grotsii kak politicheskii myslitel',' *VIMK* 6 (1958): 59–81. See also A.L. Sakketti, 'Gugo Grotsii kak uchenyi-gumanist, iurist i istorik,' *SEMP* (1959): 261–70; Sakketti, 'Gugo Grotsii o voine i mire,' *SEMP* (1964–5): 202–3.

44 Iu. Ia. Baskin, 'Ideia "vechnogo" mira v filosofskoi i politicheskoi literature novogo vremeni,' *SEMP* (1964–5): 190–201; Baskin, 'Ideia,' *SEMP* (1966–7): 166–81

45 Excepting *The Critique of Pure Reason.* For a very early attempt at rehabilitation of Kant as a rightful heritage and undeniable foundation of Marxist thought, see T. Oizerman, 'Nemetskaia klassicheskaia filosfiia – odin iz istochnikov marksizma,' *Kommunist* 2 (1955): 84–98. For a more inclusive and appreciative attitude, see Z.A. Kamenskii, 'I. Kant v russkoi filosofii nachala 19 veka,' *VIMK* 1 (1960): 49–64.

46 Immanuel Kant, *Perpetual Peace: A Philosophical Essay* (1795; London, 1903), 108–9, 113, 117–19, 128–36, 155; Allen W. Wood, 'Kant's Project for Perpetual Peace,' in *Cosmopolitics: Thinking and Feeling beyond the Nation*, ed. Pheng Cheah and Bruce Robbins (Minneapolis, 1998): 59–76; for the Soviet reception: A.V. Glebov, 'Vokrug traktata Kanta "O vechnom mire,"' *VF* 2 (1958): 173–5.

47 Glebov, 'Vokrug traktata'; Kant, *Perpetual*, 156–7; see also B.T. Grigorian, 'Filosofiia kul'tury Kanta,' *VIMK* 3 (1959): 24–38.

48 Glebov, 'Vokrug traktata'; Kant, *Perpetual*, 156–7.

49 For example, Carl Joachim Friedrich, *Inevitable Peace* (1948; New York, 1969).

50 Alexander Dallin, *The Soviet Union at the United Nations: An Inquiry into Soviet Motives and Objectives* (New York, 1962), 27–41, 45–50, 54–5, 61–6, 88–90, 95–7, 122–3; Tunkin, 'XXII s"ezd.'

51 Solodovnikov, 'Mezhdunarodnye,' 101.

52 GARF 9576/2/4/99, 105, 106; Mozhaev, 'Kul'turnye sviazi,' 78, 79, 82–3; for earlier Soviet uses of 'world culture,' which were picked up during the Thaw, see Katerina Clark, *Moscow, the Fourth Rome*, chap. 5.

53 Mozhaev, 'Kul'turnye sviazi,' 77. For a critical discussion of the connection between cosmopolitanism, universalism, and various related notions of common humanity, ethical and cultural, see Catherine Lu, 'The One and Many Faces of Cosmopolitanism,' *Journal of Political Philosophy* 8 no. 2 (2000): 244–67; Rossiiskii gosudarstvennyi arkhiv sotsial'no-politicheskoi istorii (RGASPI) 606/1/486/3, 15–20, 60–2, 67–72, 77–9; V.P. Tugarinov, *O tsennostiakh zhizni i kul'tury* (Leningrad, 1960).

54 The sentences that follow are indebted to Vail' and Genis's discussion of the party program as a literary text and an exercise in utopics, *60-e: mir sovetskogo cheloveka* (Moscow, 2001), 12–18. I also borrow from them the interpretation of the program as 'universal' and agree with their contention about the yearnings for universalism at this time.

55 RGASPI 606/1/486/15, 19, 43, 60, 66, 67, 71.

56 'Materialy k planu 5-go toma "Istorii nauchnogo i kul'turnogo razvitiia chelovechestva,"' *VIMK* 4 (1957): 146–78.

57 'Nekotorye problemy nauchnogo i kul'turnogo razvitiia chelovechestva v period s 1300 po 1775 gg.,' *VIMK* 3 (1959): 106–26; 'Nekotorye voprosy istorii obshchestva bronzovogo veka,' *VIMK* 6 (1958): 122–48; 'Po povodu materialov L. Vulli,' *VIMK* 1 (1957): 148–65; 'Zamechaniia po proektu prospekta IV toma, razrabotannogo professorom Luisom Gotshokom,' *VIMK* 3 (1957): 159–75, here 161–2.

58 'Nekotorye problemy nauchnogo,' 109–12, 124–5; 'Nekotorye voprosy

istorii,' 143–7; 'Zamechaniia po proektu prospekta III toma,' *VIMK* 2 (1957): 119–39; 'Zamechaniia po proektu prospekta IV toma,' 160–1, 166–7.

59 'Proekt istorii mirovoi kul'tury,' *VIMK* 25, no. 1 (1961): 98.

60 George W. Breslauer, 'Khrushchev Reconsidered,' *Problems of Communism* (September–October 1976): 18–33, esp. 23–5; Pyzhikov, *Khrushchevskaia 'ottepel',*' 33, 35, 90, 136–7.

61 Michael David-Fox, 'From Illusory "Society" to Intellectual "Public": VOKS, International Travel, and Party-Intelligentsia Relations in the Interwar Period,' *Contemporary European History* 11 (2002): 7–32, here 25.

62 Ibid.; V.I. Fokin, *Mezhdunarodnyi kul'turnyi obmen i SSSR v 20–30-e gody* (Saint Petersburg, 1999); N.V. Kiseleva, *Iz istorii bor'by sovetskoi obshchestvennosti za proryv kul'turnoi blokady SSSR: VOKS, seredina 20x-nachalo 30x godov* (Rostov-na-Donu, 1991).

63 For some recollections of former *voksovtsy*, see V.N. Kuteishchikova, *Moskva – Mekhiko – Moskva: Doroga dlinoiu v zhizn'* (Moscow, 2000), 7–22, 152–6, 182; Raisa Orlova, *Vospominaniia o neproshedshem vremeni. Moskva, 1961–1981 gg.* (Ann Arbor, 1983), 103–18.

64 RGANI 89/46/28/5–6.

65 For example, GARF 9576/2/89/13; GARF 9576/2/7/ll. 4–5.

66 GARF 9576/2/89/13; GARF 9576/2/7/ll. 4–5; GARF 9576/2/75/15, 440; GARF 9576/2/127/48; Solodovnikov, 'Mezhdunarodnye,' 101.

67 GARF 9576/2/7/57; GARF 9576/2/9/170–1 (second set of pagination).

68 GARF 9576/2/82/187.

69 See also Gorsuch, *All This,* chap. 4.

70 Solodovnikov, 'Mezhdunarodnye.'

71 GARF 9576/2/4.

72 GARF 9576/1/386/66.

73 GARF 9576/1/388/83, 141–3; GARF 9576/1/390/1 (second set of pagination); GARF 9576/2/75/1, 8.

74 GARF 9576/1/388/157–9; GARF 9576/2/120/76; GARF 9576/2/90/172; see also GARF 9576/2/9/62–3.

75 GARF 9576/1/388/34, 158–9. For a similar dynamic – a vision of popular diplomacy via tourism combined with inability to relinquish control – see Gorsuch, *All This,* 17, 20, 106–29.

76 RGASPI M-3/15/83/95; RGASPI M-3/15/19/4; for the chronology of the festivals, see *Vsemirnaia federatsiia demokraticheskoi molodezhi. Daty i sobytiia (1945–75)* (Moscow, 1975); on previous festivals, see Jöel Kotek, *Students and the Cold War* (New York, 1996), chap. 7; A. Kuranov, *Prazdnik molodosti* (Moscow, 1957), 5–13.

77 RGASPI M-3/15/19/22; RGASPI M-3/15/83/1, 102–3; RGASPI M-3/15/265/79, 80–1; RGASPI M-3/15/19/8; RGASPI M-3/15/406–7; Tsentral'nyi arkhiv obshchestvenno-politicheskoi istorii Moskvy (TsAOPIM) 4/113/23/30–32; RGANI 5/30/233/155.

78 RGASPI M-3/15/35/23; TsAOPIM 4/113/23/25–7.

79 RGASPI M-3/15/10/62, 149, 150, 153.

80 G. Senchakova, 'Emblema Vsemirnogo,' *Vecherniaia Moskva*, 6 July 1957.

81 Boris Knoblok, *Grani prizvaniia* (Moscow, 1986), 382–3; Rossiiskii gosudarstvennyi arkhiv kinofotodokumentov (RGAKFD) no. 1-19325; RGASPI M-3/15/10/118; L. Rozanova and Gal. Sheveleva, 'My vdvadtsaterom idem po Moskve,' in *Tri dnia otpuska* (Moscow, 1973), 394; *Sovetskoe dekorativnoe iskusstvo, 1945–1975. Ocherki* (Moscow, 1989), 191.

82 Armen Medvedev, *Territoriia kino* (Moscow, 2001), 91.

83 RGASPI M-3/15/10/123; *Sovetskoe*, 190–1.

84 This paragraph is based on Betti Glan, *Prazdnik vsegda s nami* (Moscow, 1988), 132–41; *Massovye prazdniki* (Moscow, 1961), 142–58; RGASPI M-3/15/19/19; TsAOPIM 147/1/524/44–53.

85 RGASPI M-3/15/83/141–3.

86 Mikhail Ladur, 'Puteshestvie po festival'noi Moskve,' in *Bloknot agitatora k festivaliu* (Moscow, 1957), 43–51, here 50–1; V. Panchenko, 'Avtozavodtsy – k prazdniku iunosti,' in *Bloknot agitatora k festivaliu*, 101; TsAOPIM 4/113/23/126.

87 *Festival'nyi sbornik no. 1* (Moscow, 1957), 5, 50; GARF A-501/1/1636/197; on the popularity of people who had written about foreign countries and the great demand for lectors who had been abroad, see RGASPI f. M-3/15/19/36; TsAOPIM 147/1/546/21.

88 TsAOPIM 147/1/528/22.

89 Artem Dotsenko, 'Chuvaki na khatakh: stiliagi kak obshchestvennyi ferment,' *Rodina* 7 (2005). Aleksei Kozlov, *'Kozel na sakse' – i tak vsiu zhizn'* (Moscow, 1998), 70–1, 80.

90 TsAGM 1609/2/428/15; TsAOPIM 4/113/42/133.

91 RGALI 2329/3/575/2, 4; TsAOPIM 4/113/23/151.

92 *Khudozhestvennaia samodeiatel'nost' Leningrada* (Leningrad, 1957), 236, 255; RGANI 5/36/46/55; RGASPI M-3/15/19/25; TsAOPIM 4/113/23/151.

93 Viacheslav Kabanov, *Odnazhdy prisnilos'. Zapiski diletanta* (Moscow, 2000), 150.

94 A.M. Biriukov, 'Sovsem nedavno, letom 57-go,' in *Proshchanie so Zmeem: rasskazy i povesti* (Magadan, 2003), 148, 159.

95 Ibid., 149.

96 RGASPI M-3/15/198/16.

97 Vasilii Katanian, *Loskutnoe odeialo* (Moscow, 2001), 143–4.

98 This and the previous paragraphs are based on Vasilii Ardamatskii, *Piat' lepestkov: reportazh o VI Vsemirnom festivale molodezhi i studentov v Moskve* (Moscow, 1958), 26, 25–8, 116–17; Biriukov, 'Sovsem nedavno,' 147–9 (quotation at 149); GARF 9415/3/315/26; N. Grand and V. Tkachenko, *Festival'nye vstrechi* (Kalinin, 1958), 15; Katanian, *Loskutnoe*, 143–4; Knoblok, *Grani*, 386–8; *Prazdnik mira*, 59–60; RGASPI M-3/15/199/30, 178; RGASPI M-3/15/198/16, 17, 29ob, 38; Rozanova, 'My,' 394.

99 RGALI 2487/1/446/78, 237–8.

100 GARF 9415/3/315/58, 99, 110; RGASPI M-3/15/189/71, 96; RGASPI M-3/15/197/97; RGASPI M-3/15/198/62.

101 'What is your name? Wie heist du? – Menia voobshche-to Kolia zovut,' Rozanova, 'My,' 396.

102 Ibid., 401.

103 Ibid., 396.

104 *Festival'nyi sbornik*, 15–16.

105 RGASPI M-3/15/124/28.

106 Maksimilian Nemchinskii, *Tsirk Rossii naperegonki so vremenem: Modeli tsirkovykh spektaklei 1920–1990 godov* (Moscow, 2004), 260–1.

107 For the discussion of dance and abandon, see Barbara Ehrenreich, *Dancing in the Streets: A History of Collective Joy* (New York, 2007).

108 Nikolai Vladimirovich Eremchenko interview recording, 13/03/03, tape 5, Tsentral'nyi arkhiv elektronnykh i audiovizual'nykh dokumentov Moskvy (TsAE ADM).

109 Rozanova, 'My,' 395.

110 For example: Rozanova, 'My,' 394–5; for a different interpretation of such encounters, see Roth-Ey, '"Loose Girls."'

111 Ehrenreich, *Dancing in the Streets*, 23–7.

112 RGAKFD no. 1-10633; RGAKFD no. 1-10702; RGALI 2487/1/341/3, 13–14, 35; RGALI 2487/1/446/14–17.

113 Robert D. English, *Russia and the Idea of the West: Gorbachev, Intellectuals and the End of the Cold* War (New York, 2000).

114 RGASPI M-3/15/10/74; RGASPI M-3/15/12/160–2, 178; RGASPI M-3/15/3/203–14; RGASPI M-3/15/4/18; RGASPI M-3/15/194; RGASPI M-3/15/221/30–1, 104.

115 Kozlov, *Kozel*, 354–5. There are many parallels between the two events, including the international context – Hungary and Afghanistan. Also, the festival could not have been more meticulously scripted or planned.

116 Interview with Alla Davydovna Shereshevskaia, Saint Petersburg, 24 July 2004.

117 Interviews with Marina Nikolaevna, Moscow, 15 June 2003, and Alla Davydovna Shereshevskaia, Saint Petersburg, 24 July 2004.

118 'Moi "chernyi kot" byl pervym sovetskim tvistom,' http://www.sem40.ru/famous2/m37.shtml; 'Mir muzyki proshchaetsia s kompozitorom Iuriem Saul'skim,' http://www.fashion-monitor.com/news.php/614; Aleksei Kozlov, 'Vospominaniia o Iurie Saul'skom,' http://alexeykozlov.com/?p=1977; Tat'iana Dvornikova, 'Tvorcheskii donor,' http://www.isurgut.ru/~company/NG/stat.asp?ida=20301.

10 Soviet Fashion in the 1950s–1960s: Regimentation, Western Influences, and Consumption Strategies

LARISSA ZAKHAROVA

The plan to create a society of abundance that would satisfy the material needs of Soviet citizens is well known as one of the most ambitious projects of the Khrushchev decade. Public statements by the leader, who aimed to catch up and overtake the United States in consumer goods production, helped to stigmatize the political meaning of this campaign as yet another aspect of the Cold War and competition between the two systems. The Novocherkassk events, following an increase (31 May 1962) in prices of staple foodstuffs, signalled the clear failure of national food supply reform. The aim of this chapter is to assess the results of reforms in the field of clothing consumption. What particular measures did the state undertake to supply clothes to the population? What kinds of clothing were Soviet people supposed to wear, and what did they actually wear? In what consumer behaviours did their reaction to production policy and the clothing distribution system manifest itself?

To answer these questions, we must reconstruct the entire system of Soviet fashion, encompassing the conception, production, distribution, and consumption of fashion products. Reconstructing the Soviet fashion system entails a multilevel analysis. The first level, that of theory and production, lies within the framework of political, economic, and cultural history, as well as the history of ideas. The second level pertains to the history of Soviet–Western economic contacts, revealing the official channels by which Western fashion penetrated Soviet society. The third level reveals everyday life – the realities of clothing consumption and fashion preferences of Soviet consumers.

The Theory of Soviet Fashion and Its Implementation

In the Soviet context, as a result of the well-known tendency of the party-state apparatus to regiment everyday life, one cannot speak of fashion without reference to policy. Numerous mechanisms were employed to effect this regimentation. One of them was rhetoric intended to manipulate and regulate material needs. Most often the rhetoric targeted women, on whom the state partly counted in reforming everyday culture.[1] An army of theoreticians and economists helped to buttress this rhetoric with the theory of socialist consumption. The main postulate of this theory was a respectful attitude toward products of socialist labour: goods were not to be discarded until completely worn out. As far as economists were concerned, thus fashion stood as a negative factor, foreign to socialist economics and hindering the planned production, distribution, and consumption of clothing.[2]

For their part, designers, when advocating in print the place of fashion in a socialist society, defined fashion's primary function as the education of consumer taste. In this they followed a course charted previously by Stalin, the struggle for 'culturedness' in Soviet society. 'Beautiful and comfortable clothing, which adorns a person and pleases him or her with its comfort, to a significant extent aids in the aesthetic education of the Soviet public.'[3] At the same time, designers conceptualized a socialist fashion that would typify Soviet conditions of life and reflect, in clothing, the style of socialist realism: 'In the course of the turbulent development of all aspects of social life in the USSR, fundamental changes have taken place in the content and forms of works of art; a new style of Soviet decorative art is being created in our country, as well as a new style of clothing, devoid of garishness, affectation, and formalism.'[4]

Socialist fashion was characterized not by sensationalism and extravagance, but rather by comfort, practicality, functionality, and hygiene. The emphasis on Soviet fashion's rationality was at times taken to the absurd: 'The length of the item is what is most appropriate: covering the knee, and for the full-figured and elderly, 5–8 cm longer.'[5] Designers themselves sought to demonstrate that their creative quests were in keeping with the general development of Soviet art: 'Our design trends follow the path taken by Soviet applied arts generally, and take up the challenge of satisfying, to the greatest extent possible, the lofty requirements of the people, from both the aesthetic and utilitarian points of view.'[6]

The nature of Soviet fashion was distinctively bound up with the idea of harmony as a sign of 'good taste.' The rules of good taste impressed upon consumers were based on a specific vision of aesthetics amounting to a 'correct' combination of colours, fabrics, and forms: 'When choosing a fabric for a new dress, keep in mind the colour of your shoes and purse. It is a plus, of course, if their colour matches everything. For example, white shoes and a white purse go well with any summer dress. For light sandals, red or beige is a good choice. You should get a green or blue purse or shoes only if you have several purses or several pairs of shoes.'[7]

Despite its concessions to modest budgets, this text is a model of conventional prescriptivism that abides no clashing colours and demands flawless harmony. These criteria of good taste remained frozen and unbending in Soviet fashion even as the late 1960s democratization of fashion in the West was overturning convention. But despite the stability of these criteria, designers nevertheless maintained that fashion was akin to art and hence subject to stylistic evolution, which was cited to justify seasonal pattern shifts: 'Fashion ... is the concrete form through which style is realized; when style cannot take shape, it is reflected in fashion.'[8]

The need to periodically update garment silhouettes had a similar basis: 'The very concept of "fashion," that is, people's preference over some period of time for particular clothing lines, fabric types and colours, trimmings, etc., is, in our view, a completely natural phenomenon. Changing from year to year, fashion reflects the successes of our textile, leather goods, and chemical industries as well as people's tastes and their natural aspiration to update their clothes. In the Soviet Union and the people's democracies, fashion follows a more logical progression than in capitalist countries, where the principle of competition reigns.'[9]

Implementing this conception of fashion was yet another way to regiment appearances. In the course of production, and as magazines published patterns, clothing was subject to strict classification according to socio-professional characteristics and activity types.[10] Good taste presupposed following these norms in everyday practice, arranging and using wardrobe in accordance with function – clothing for work, housework, a resort vacation, hiking, the theatre, dancing, etc. Ideally, a woman with taste would dress fashionably in any situation: 'It is wrong to wear out-of-style dresses at home until they fall apart.'[11]

Party and government regulations, edicts, and decrees on garment production were another form of regimentation. Thanks to its program of reforms aimed at improving the material well-being of Soviet citizens, the Khrushchev period saw a substantial number of such policy decisions. This populist program was at once a response to the Cold War (the desire to prove the superiority of socialism to the entire world) and a strategy for unfolding the policies of the Thaw, when the regime's popularity was to be maintained at all costs. In the context of the Thaw, there emerged a particular state paternalism, as the task of carrying out reforms was entrusted to experts and specialists. With regard to clothing, this meant professionals in the design, textile, and sewing industries, as well as in the retail network. In practice, involvement of this sort hindered the implementation of reforms. The specialists were to provide Soviet citizens with better-looking, more durable clothing, but it was left to the specialists themselves to figure out how to realize this goal, as the vague formulations of government edicts needed interpretation. As a result, several distinct professional cultures clashed with each other.

Designers of fashion houses (*Doma modelei*), who saw their primary function as educating consumer taste, sought to mass-produce patterns reflecting their cultural preferences. In this they envisioned fashion as artistically dynamic, presuming the periodic introduction of new lines and silhouettes. As the All-Union Fashion House senior designer L.K. Efremova put it, 'Our industry should be free of haphazard items that do not reflect our notions of contemporaneity and beauty; toward this end, fashion houses pay particular attention to elaborating a distinct fashion style.'[12]

Representatives of the textile and sewing industries who took part in sessions of the fashion houses' Great Artistic Council, which selected patterns for mass production, often refused to accept patterns of complicated new design. They preferred to keep producing goods with which the factory was well familiar, so as to avoid glitches in fulfilling the plan and be able to over-fulfil it: thus, they presumed, the people's growing demand could be more fully satisfied.[13] The problem remained a pressing one throughout the Khrushchev decade. The Leningrad Statistics Administration's sales statistics division noted that 'new clothing styles are being introduced into production very slowly. In the first quarter of 1962, 70% of clothing was made according to outmoded styles.'[14]

Measuring the population's needs, meanwhile, fell to the economists at Gosplan (State Planning Committee). Their task was highly complex: to draw up a clothing and footwear production plan, taking into account the tendency of material needs to grow constantly. They based their work on the results of research on Soviet household budgets conducted by the Central Statistics Administration, which sought to quantify actual clothing and footwear consumption by various categories of the population.[15] Using the methods of Western econometricians to process these data, Soviet economists (such as Nazarov, Shvyrkov, and Shnirlin) came to the conclusion that the increase in spending on clothing associated with rising incomes was not unlimited. Upon attaining a certain hypothetical level of income, clothing expenses cease to rise, remaining at a theoretical maximum plateau. Using this plateau, economists from nineteen research institutes calculated a 'rational norm' for clothing consumption, which characterized the reasonable needs of healthy, cultured, conscientious members of communist society.[16] All social and economic distinctions were meanwhile erased; according to this theory, Soviet citizens in the city and countryside alike were to use the same quantity of clothing and footwear, using these items until completely worn out – that is, uninfluenced by fashion. The Soviet system of clothing production was to arrive at this ideal quantity. Thus, the plan stressed quantity over quality, the latter being inextricably linked with fashion. Even custom tailoring shops were saddled with a plan to sell ready-to-wear, often out-of-date items refused by customers or produced without customer orders, as at a factory.[17] At a tailor shop in Cheliabinsk, custom tailoring made up only 10–30 per cent of the yearly plan, while the bulk of production capacity went to the mass making of clothes.[18] Because of this levelling approach to consumers' needs, an approach that ignored income differences and fashion preferences, the retail network was flooded with goods for which there was no demand.

Against this backdrop, there appeared an opposite trend in economic theory, represented by I.I. Korzhenevskii.[19] Here the goal was to find methods of ensuring the correct proportion of supply and demand. The initial postulate was that, under conditions of personal ownership of consumer goods, the purchase and sale of goods could not be regimented by any physiological or 'rational' norms. Consumer demand was defined as the sum total of the demands of millions of customers, who had their own individual needs and tastes. The idea was to draw up differential models of consumption based on household budget research data, and then, using these, to set current and long-range production plans, guided by consumption patterns typical of various economic groups.

For Soviet retailers, orientation toward consumer needs and tastes was paramount. They kept track of the movement of goods in stores and arranged buyers' conferences to inform designers of consumer demand.[20] However, in ordering items that had been in demand the previous season, representatives of the retail industry created a Soviet consumption culture at odds with the dynamic of fashion – one that did not take into account the effect fashion has on changes in consumer tastes. Designers understood that such an approach by the retail industry would render their efforts useless: 'Retail must become a true partner in the popularization of fashion; it is precisely retail that must be highly cognizant of the nature and essence of contemporary fashion, without an understanding of the developmental laws of which all production orders will be haphazard. A method that determines product releases based on last year's sales is subjective and useless.'[21]

The difference between professional cultures and approaches to the customer, the dilemma of balancing the desires to educate taste and satisfy demand in accordance with existing consumer tastes inexorably led to a conflict between designers and sellers. Soviet fashion had a hard time making it to store shelves.

Borrowing Western Techniques and Fashion Trends

This far-from-perfect system was neither self-sufficient nor autarkic. The second level of our analysis of the Soviet fashion system pertains to the history of Soviet–European economic ties and the history of cultural contacts. Such a perspective shift is required by the general historical context of the Thaw, when Soviet trade relations with capitalist countries intensified. Trade agreements were one of the official channels through which Western fashion penetrated the USSR. Imported goods helped to fill lacunae in the domestic market. Moreover, the aim was to correct officially acknowledged shortcomings in the Soviet system, including those in the area of clothing supply, by taking advantage of superior Western experience.[22] This aim was institutionalized through creating special committees at the Council of Ministers, as well as research institutes that explored Western developments, selecting those to be adopted. This facilitated the establishment of contacts between Soviet specialists and their Western colleagues. Despite the publicly declared differences between socialist and capitalist fashion, Soviet specialists preferred to draw on the achievements of Paris houses of haute couture, for example that of Christian Dior, citing its high degree of professionalism and reputation as an undisputed trendsetter.[23] Business trips abroad by Soviet garment engineers, technicians, and designers brought Western techniques and fashion trends to Soviet industry.

However, this was not a matter of blind imitation. Designers themselves described their approach to Western fashion as a creative one: they borrowed only such ideas as could be applied under Soviet conditions. The introduction of folkloric elements into the verbal or material expression of a fashion trend was supposed to convince public opinion once and for all that Soviet fashion was distinct from that of the West. Descriptions of new silhouettes often included references to elements of traditional Russian dress, which evinced a desire to underscore their belonging to

A female fashion-follower (Ministry of Textile Industry employee), dressed in a sarafan custom-tailored at an atelier. 1964. Private archive.

a national context: 'The bell-shaped silhouette of a coat already familiar to us as the "Russian sarafan" is back. But whereas this used to mean a rather bulky affair with tails in the back, now, while still offering freedom of movement, the bell-shape is a restrained one, flaring downward right from the shoulder-line. The tails are gone. This is perhaps the very latest silhouette, as yet not widely known, but sure to catch on and gain admirers.'[24] However, when we consider that this item appeared in the Soviet fashion press just a few months after Yves Saint Laurent introduced his 'Trapeze' line – which indeed vaguely recalled a truncated sarafan – the point of this scholastic formulation becomes clear.

Official channels for the arrival of Western fashion in the USSR, such as business trips abroad and foreign national and industry exhibitions (accompanied by fashion shows), were a prism that refracted the ideas of peaceful coexistence and competition between the two systems. The Soviet strategy of proving the superiority of socialism was ostensibly to democratize the symbols of luxury clothing through mass production. Women's magazines recommended completing one's ensemble with furs, which bore highly symbolic French or French-derived names like *pèlerine, manteau,* and *gorgette,*[25] or with capron gloves. This was considered a sign of good taste and conformity with the accepted norms of appearance.[26]

Clothing Consumption Strategies and Cultures

Given the inertia inherent in planned clothing production, is it possible to speak of fashion in Soviet society? The third level of our analysis, which relates to the history of everyday life and cultures of consumption, helps answer this question. The special nature of the Soviet clothing market forced individuals to seek clothing-consumption strategies befitting their own social, economic, and cultural motivations. These strategies can be divided into legal and illegal. Among the former were buying fabrics and ready-made clothing in stores, having garments made to order at a tailor shop, and independently making clothing or transforming it from unfashionable to fashionable. Illegal strategies included ordering clothes from private tailors moonlighting at home, as well as acquiring clothes from speculators and black marketeers.

The Socio-economic Factor and the Choice of Consumption Strategies

Despite the party's and government's constant efforts to coordinate ef-

French fashion exhibition, Moscow, 1958. TsAADM 0-23423.

Finnish fashion exhibition, Moscow, October 1966. Photograph by B. Trepetov. TsAADM 0-5846.

ficiently, via decree, the actions of the clothing production and distribution system, the selection of goods in Soviet stores never met consumer demands throughout the period under discussion. This was not even a matter of the 70 per cent of clothing patterns being out of style, as mentioned above. Rather, the problem was in the absence of many categories of essential goods. For instance, according to the findings of a survey of retail establishments in Rostov for the second half of 1953,

> Woollen fabrics in critically short supply include cheviot, Boston, tricot … covert, gabardine, thick woollen cloth, and others.… Silks in short supply include spun fabric, artificial crepe-satin, serge, and artificial silk.… As for apparel, there is a critical shortage of women's winter coats, men's suits, and men's wool pants.… These items are sold within several hours of their arrival in stores, and a significant percentage of them wind up in the hands of speculators. Also in short supply are men's overcoats, raincoats, dark-coloured women's suits, and other items. There is a critical shortage of fur

Austrian fashion exhibition, Moscow, May 1960. Photograph by V. Shustov. TsAADM 1-4292.

goods: fur coats, caps, sealskin collars, and other items. Out of season, the retail network retains some stock of these goods, whereas in winter they are in critically short supply. In the category of knitwear, there is a shortage of women's underwear, kerchiefs, mufflers and scarves, wool stockings and socks, as well as women's wool and semi-wool jackets and woven silk blouses and jerseys. Such items as calf boots, Central Asian–style slippers, leather-soled sneakers, girls' shoes and low-heeled and leather-soled dress shoes for school, patent-leather sandals, fur-lined boots, fur-trimmed, leather-soled boots – during the second half of 1953, these items never appeared in the retail network of the Rostov Department Store at all, even as the sale of these items, unhindered and in large quantities, was taking place at the Rostov manufactured goods market. Also in critically short supply are women's patent-leather shoes, which, despite the high demand, come in very meagre quantities (1.5–2% of the total for leather shoes) and are similarly repurchased by private individuals for sale at marked-up prices.[27]

Data for other cities and regions of the USSR provide a more or less similar list of goods in short supply, and this list remained almost constant for the duration of the period.[28] The stores in Moscow were no exception, as for instance Central Department Store (TsUM) customers attested:

- Stores in Moscow have almost no tall-size suits. There are only cheap ones, and even these are a rare find. A memo isn't enough to put the supply of size 6 and 7 suits in order; you actually have to *have* the item. I've been going from store to store since mid-December, and I still can't buy a suit.
- For such a big store to have no selection of pants in popular sizes and at a reasonable price is unacceptable. There are absolutely no inexpensive-but-decent suits for ninth- and tenth-graders, nor affordable size 41–42 shoes. Schoolchildren cannot wear dress shoes every day; not everyone is in a position to buy them.
- Why are there no good short coats, just frieze coats? After all, the demand for good short coats is huge.
- The whole family has been looking for a dressing gown for our mother for a week, but we can't find one anywhere.
- There are absolutely no vinyl women's raincoats for sale. They're really convenient in the summer; you can put them in your purse.
- It's impossible to find girls' sandals either in winter or summer; the same goes for men's sandals.
- The salespeople say that the store has boots once every three years; selling them every day would be a good idea.
- Your store has no ladies' underwear. You don't respect women.
- The spun fabric department is out of the 23.50 ruble per metre dark-blue *shtapel'*.[29] The salespeople tell me this is a rare guest to the store. Why?
- There is a lot of good cloth and suit material, but no dark- or light-toned 270–280 ruble per metre overcoat wool.[30]

In fulfilling the plan and keeping with the general atmosphere of economizing, it was not profitable for enterprises to produce garments in larger sizes: these required more fabric, yet sold for the same price as identical items in smaller sizes. Another nationwide problem was that

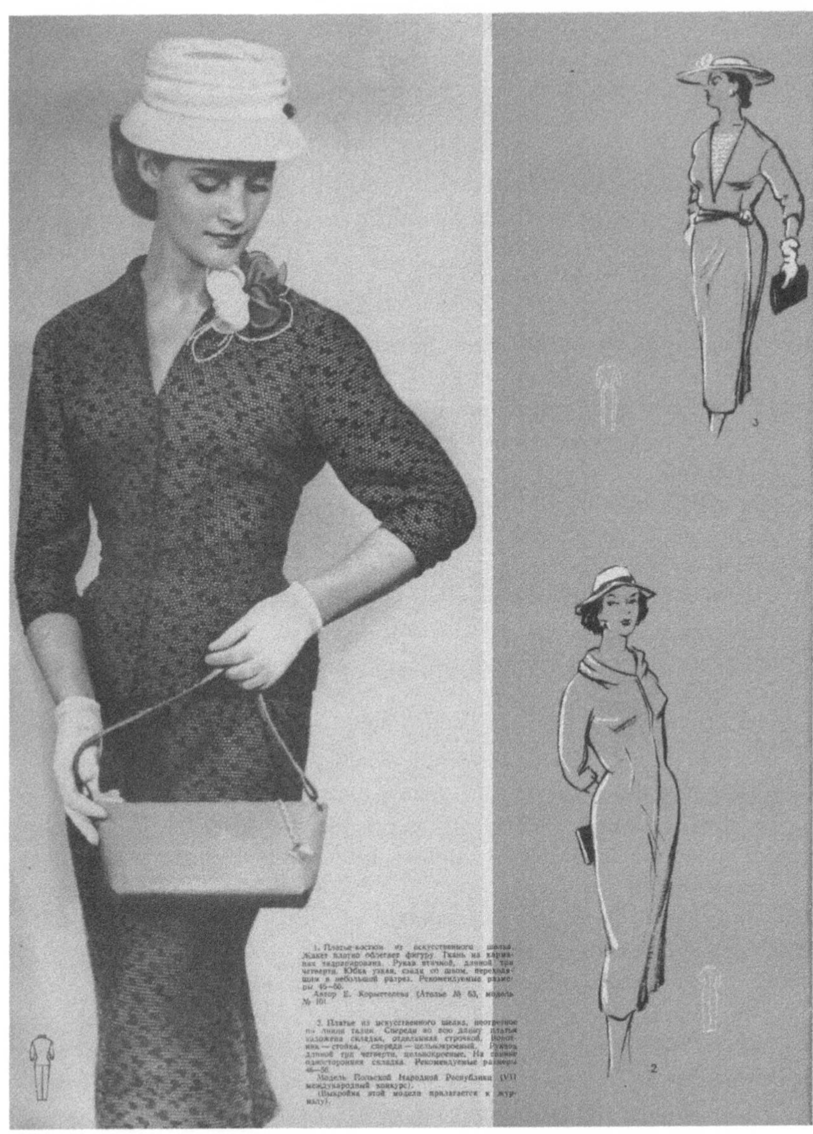

A 'dress-suit' made of artificial silk. *Zhurnal mod* 1 (1957), 29. Reproduced with permission.

retail establishments would get goods out of season, so that store shelves in winter featured summertime goods, and vice versa.

The economy of scarcity contributed to the rise of market mechanisms. If state stores were incapable of satisfying customer demand, then this function was successfully fulfilled by private, illegal middlemen – in Soviet parlance, speculators. One could always acquire scarce goods from them at a markup price. These enterprising individuals bought up goods in the state retail network and then resold them at markets originally intended for the sale of second-hand goods, or right in stores, or at the homes of 'friends.' The directors of many industrial enterprises enriched themselves on scarcity and fuelled it further, as they arranged fictitious 'thefts' of high-demand goods from their factories and received a percentage of the profit from speculators.[31] Retail personnel also cashed in on the shortages:

> In Kiev a form of speculation has become widespread by which speculators resell not goods themselves but merchandise receipts, and this makes it easier for them to hide from the police. The Kiev city inspector's office has uncovered a number of cases of shop workers abetting speculators. This year, for example, instances have been uncovered at the ORS NOD-1 store and stores no. 1011 and 1526 of the first Kievpromtorg of salespeople hiding scarce goods (thick woollen cloth, Boston, double satin, cashmere, men's 388- and 899-ruble suits, children's coats, leather mittens, etc.) for the purpose of selling them to speculators.[32]

When speculators resold goods produced by 'local industry,' there was little effect on the consumers' appearance: they paid more but were still dressed in 'provincial fashion.' But speculators also traded in clothing and shoes brought from other cities. Organized groups of speculators shipped goods from one population centre to another through the mail.[33] As a result, in Kiev cases were discovered when 'workers' families had purchased manufactured goods shipped from other cities by speculators: patent-leather dress shoes from Tbilisi, wool kerchiefs from Riga, etc.'[34] In Tashkent, 'at one of the markets, in a special place reserved for the sale of second-hand goods, thousands of people on Sundays are engaged in the person-to-person sale of new items: clothing, shoes, and hosiery from Moscow and Leningrad factories, and other goods.'[35] This allowed the inhabitants of one city to dress in the fashion of another.

Given the substantial scale of speculation as a phenomenon, law-enforcement agencies had difficulty defining the parameters of violations.

Article 107 of the 1926 RSFSR Criminal Code (with amendments as of 1957) defined speculation as the buying up or reselling of agricultural or mass consumer goods by private individuals for profit. Those found guilty of such acts were subject to imprisonment for a period of no less than five years and full or partial property confiscation, whereas 'the average citizen's occasional sale or exchange of goods acquired for personal use rather than resale' did not constitute a criminal act.[36] This amendment was due to the widespread practice of unplanned, hurried purchases made when a line suddenly formed for goods at a store would send customers the psychological signal that a quantity of otherwise scarce products was about to be dumped onto the store counter. In these cases, people bought indiscriminately, hoping that the item was something they would need; and if it was not, they would sell it. Such actions remained legal, so long as the item was resold at the same price as the state one. The arrest of a suspected speculator thus always required an appraisal of the value of items by store merchandise experts. These were often unable to indicate an exact value, and that complicated the investigation and determination of the suspect's guilt or innocence. Speculators, well-versed in the law, took advantage of this legal shortcoming, and the war on speculation was not very effective. The search for a solution to the problem boiled down to attempting to make the laws of certain republics stricter. In 1955, Kirgizia outlawed the person-to-person sale of new goods (regardless of price).[37] The executive committees of some councils of workers' deputies in Belorussia went even further, promulgating 'binding resolutions forbidding citizens to sell their belongings person-to-person at markets, regardless of whether the items are new or used.'[38]

Demand for used items can serve as an indirect indicator of the state of consumer life. Public prosecutors' accounts of cases in which persons were wrongfully convicted of speculation for having sold second-hand clothes include information on the defendants' grave material situation.[39] In some cases, women sold their clothes in order to clothe their children. In such situations, of course, the question of a desire to follow fashion does not come up. By taking away these people's right to sell used items, the state was denying them supplemental means of eking out a living. Taking clothes to consignment shops could not satisfy this group of the population, since consignment shops paid money only if the item was sold.

The anti-speculation decisions were formally adopted in the course of implementing the program to satisfy the people's needs and improve their material well-being. The USSR Prosecutor General's Office, however, determined the republican authorities' resolutions to be in violation

Table 10.1 Price differences (rubles) for factory- and craftsmen-made goods in Krasnodar in 1953

Item	Price when sold at a market	State retail price
Printed dressing gown	50	80
Cotton dress	80	95
Silk dress	150	198
Leather cap	80	135
Men's shoes	200	240
Leather shoes for children of preschool age	23	40

Source: RGAE 1562/26/219/41.

of the constitutional right of Soviet citizens to dispose of legally protected personal property as they saw fit. Nevertheless, according to the special rules that the USSR government adopted on the sale of personal items in Moscow, selling new items person-to-person at markets in the capital was forbidden.[40]

Competing with speculators were private craftsmen, who produced items lacking in state retail and offered them at a reduced price (see table 10.1). Craftsmen-made goods were not subject to regimentation, and to a certain extent their consumers wore and circulated an 'alternative' to official fashion. Such an underground economy roused the censure of power-structure representatives: 'The production of shoes by craftsmen from "their own" material is at bottom the worst sort of speculation. They make dress shoes from fine leather that is not sold in state or cooperative retail and thus can only be stolen from the state.'[41]

What options remained, meanwhile, for consumers dissatisfied with the quality and selection of ready-made clothes in state stores but at the same time unable to afford to overpay speculators for scarce items?

The most economical consumption strategy was to make one's own clothing. Because the prospect that the system of mass garment production in factories would function efficiently remained remote, the authorities went to great lengths to encourage do-it-yourself garment-making. This official orientation is directly reflected in a handbook of maxims for Soviet girls published in 1959:

> Any girl can learn to cut and sew well enough to make herself a summer dress, sarafan, blouse, dressing gown – in short, to make several simple things herself, without any outside help. The ability to sew teaches one to

"Ensembles." *Odezhda i byt* 1 (1961): 12–13.

> pay attention to detail and focus on one's work, and it gives a sense of satisfaction at the results achieved. After all, isn't it nice to put on a dress you've made with your own hands, or alter something for your little sister? Skills learned in youth last a lifetime, and every woman, regardless of her occupation, always wants to be well dressed and to dress her children tastefully. This isn't hard to achieve when you know how to do it all yourself.[42]

To regiment this self-service, Soviet designers produced patterns, which were promoted in supplements to women's magazines and cutting-and-sewing guides, as well as in separate kits.[43] The fact that patterns were offered for every single wardrobe item (including underwear) attests, on the one hand, to the low level of the sewing industry's development, or at least its meagre scale of production, and on the other hand, to the fact that a woman who knew how to sew could get by without factory-made clothing. All of this is clearly tinged with the gender trouble that characterized Soviet society in the 1950s and 1960s. If, in the 1920s, the state made every effort to free women from the burden of housework and traditional women's duties, establishing twenty-four-hour childcare centres and 'factory-kitchens,' in the 1950s and 1960s women were once again saddled with the duty of arranging house and home, which was now declared to be not burdensome but pleasant, thanks to the rationalization and modernization of household appliances.[44] As women also constituted 49 per cent of the Soviet labour force in 1964, home duties such as sewing consumed a vast proportion of their leisure time.[45] This gender orientation was also apparent in evaluative norms of appearance: for a woman to wear pants in an urban setting was considered the height of *mauvais ton* and poor taste, whereas luxurious skirts à la the Dior 'new look' gained a firm foothold in Soviet fashion, promoted as a choice for young women for more formal occasions.[46]

There is no single profile of the consumers engaged in do-it-yourself garment making. Of course, there were specific socio-occupational groups that made use of this strategy. If we look at the average consumption pattern of Leningrad sewing-industry workers from 1955 to 1964, for instance, we see that their purchases of fabrics exceeded their spending on ready-made clothing by a factor of almost three to one.[47] This group of the population employed their professional skills to provide themselves with clothing.

One obstacle to prioritizing do-it-yourself garment production was the absence not only of skills but also of the key technological means – a sewing machine. At the beginning of the Khrushchev period, it was a scarce item: 'Sewing machines come in to the Rostov department store in very limited quantities, and even despite the help of the police their sale still takes place amid literal fighting.'[48] Heightened demand for sewing machines is attested to by numerous instances of their being acquired from 'certain citizens' for sums marked up from the state price. In Stalingrad during the second half of 1953, for instance, 'Singer hand sewing machines with a high degree of wear and tear cost 800–850 rubles at the market, while new ones sold in state retail cost 600–640 rubles.'[49] The official turn toward encouraging do-it-yourself garment making was reflected in an attempt to control this situation and provide the necessary equipment to everyone who wished. A 22 August 1962 memo by the vice-chairman of the Leningrad Statistics Administration P. Voronov attested to this goal:

> With the exception of the electric sewing machines 'Tula' and 'Volga,' sewing machines, both imported and domestic, were in high demand as recently as 1960. Starting in 1961, demand for sewing machines has been

> completely satisfied; their supply has sharply increased, and at present the market for them has normalized. Demand for sewing machines produced by the Podolsk factory (the brands 'Tika' and 'Panoniia') has fallen sharply. The outer appearance and workmanship of the Podolsk sewing machines is very bad; they are of low quality.... To increase sales and reduce inventories, all sewing machine brands, imported and domestic, have to be sold on credit.[50]

This last proposal drew something of a positive response from the government, and by decree (18 August 1962) of the USSR Ministry of Trade, the '100' and 'Iskra' sewing machines could be sold on credit.[51]

However, by this time, it seems, the public demand for sewing machines was not as high as at the start of the Khrushchev decade. This can be explained by the 31 May 1962 increase in prices for milk, meat, and butter, as a result of which the spending patterns of all categories of the population shifted toward an increase in expenditures on food items and a substantial decrease in spending on fabric and clothing.[52]

Household budget data for workers in Leningrad (1961) shows that, as incomes rose, increases in spending on the acquisition of fabrics and ready-made clothing were not uniform. As seen in table 10.2, workers' families with a yearly income of more than 1200 rubles per person spent 13.5 times more on the purchase of fabrics and almost 11 times more on the purchase of ready-made clothing than families with an income of 420 rubles per person. Thus, as incomes rose, spending on fabrics increased at a higher rate than spending on ready-made clothing (the income percentage per family member spent on these items increased, respectively, 4.5 times for fabrics and 3.8 times for ready-made clothing). This pattern speaks to the tendency of better-off consumers to engage the services of tailor shops or private contractors for clothing made to order.

Having clothing made at a tailor shop involved certain difficulties, chief among them long lines (numerous sources attest to the practice of waiting in line overnight) and a lengthy wait – up to two months – for tailoring to be completed.[53] In Stalingrad, for instance, the shortcomings of custom tailoring could be summarized in this record:

> The city still does not have enough tailor shops; as a result, the shops cannot serve everyone who wants tailoring done. Shops receive tailoring customers once a week; some shops take orders once every two weeks. Nor is it clear beforehand on what particular day customers will be received: announcements are hung up two or three days in advance. Receiving hours are from 1 to 5 p.m. or 2 to 6 p.m., i.e., at times when most people are at

Table 10.2 Spending on fabrics and ready-made clothing, Leningrad, 1961

Income per family member (post-reform rubles)	Amount spent on fabrics (rubles)	Average % of income	Amount spent on ready-made clothing, underwear, and head-wear (rubles)	Average % of income
Up to 420	1.97	0.5	9.94	2.4
421–480	3.80	0.8	25.52	5.7
481–600	7.30	1.4	31.09	5.8
601–720	10.21	1.5	48.17	7.3
721–900	15.98	2.0	59.34	7.3
901–1200	21.75	2.1	68.40	6.5
1201 and up	26.76	2.2	108.70	9.1

Source: TsGA SPb 4965/6/1000/28.

work. Moreover, having women's dresses made is expensive: the same silk dress a private seamstress would make for 80 or 90 rubles costs 114 rubles at a tailor shop. Having a dress made from spun fabric at a tailor shop costs 90 rubles, i.e., more than the cost of the material itself, whereas privately such dresses cost 40 or 50 rubles. Tailor shops try not to take orders for children's coats or dresses, or for clothing made of cotton, on the grounds that these are 'not profitable.'[54]

Thus, because the services of a tailor shop were difficult to access, and because of their rather high prices, consumers lacking the skills or time necessary for sewing and dissatisfied with the selection of items in stores turned for their garment-making needs to private individuals. In the course of its budget surveys, the state closely watched the scale of the tailor shops' illegal competition. The RSFSR Criminal Code (article 99, on 'engagement in unlawful crafts') made private garment-making for commercial purposes punishable by up to two years' imprisonment.[55] Illegal activities were to be eradicated not only through criminal prosecution, but also by correcting deficiencies in the custom tailoring system. A reform of the tailor shops made them better adjusted to consumer demand: hours of operation were extended, while the introduction of semi-finished products in garment making made it possible for the shops to cut waiting periods for order fulfilment.[56] Over the course of the Khrushchev period, the number of tailor shops in cities increased: in Leningrad, for instance, by 6.8 per cent in 1959–63. As a result of these changes, the incidence of ordering from private tailors in Leningrad fell by 53.5–55.5 per cent during these years.[57]

The introduction of semi-finished products in garment production, together with struggles against private garment making, increased regimentation as it reduced the customers' freedom of choice and room to indulge their fancies, saddling them with semi-finished items. This fit the intended purpose of clothing designers: 'Pattern-makers and dress-cutters at tailor shops are not there merely to fulfil orders; they also serve as the public's educators of and conduits for good taste.... Often the client herself cannot decide which fabric or cut to choose; an experienced dress-cutter with good taste is there to help her.'[58]

Tailor shops also served as censors guarding against Western fashion trends then coming to the USSR. As a general rule, patterns were chosen from Soviet fashion magazines, less often from Central and East European publications – and in very rare cases (at 'deluxe,' high-end tailor shops), 'a dress-cutter, in using foreign fashion magazines, especially the leading French publications, should make a critical determination as to which patterns to recommend to this or that client, and which it is better to avoid.'[59]

However, socio-economic considerations were not the only factor in the choice of consumption strategies. Interviews with individuals who were consumers during the 1950s and 60s suggest that cultural factors, specifically attitudes toward fashion, played a crucial role in determining such choices.

The Cultural Factor and Consumption Strategy Choices

The analysis of sixteen interviews with former consumers allows us to posit three types of consumption cultures during those years: 'fashionable,' 'mixed,' and 'conservative.' The first group consisted of seven consumers who described themselves as having dressed fashionably and who indicated that toward this end they engaged the services of tailor/dressmaker shops and private tailors, as well as making their own clothes. The second group included five persons who followed fashion not consistently but on a case-by-case basis, and who used, besides the consumption strategies of the first group, Soviet factory-made ready-made clothing. The third consumption culture, represented by four interviewees, neglected fashion: here purchasing ready-made clothes in stores and at markets predominated, although other consumption strategies may also have been practised.

Each group was marked by a high degree of social heterogeneity, further confirming the secondary importance of socio-economic factors in the formation of consumer profiles. The first group included a radio engineer, an unskilled labourer, a librarian, a township council deputy, a Textile Industry Ministry staff person (who subsequently chaired the light industry section of the Moscow Party committee), a teachers college student, and a theatre institute student. The second group included two factory employees, a worker, a university lab technician, and a soldier. The third group consisted of a vocational school teacher, an unskilled labourer, a high school geography teacher, and a student at an agricultural college. It was not possible to establish a relationship between social origin and a particular consumption culture.

In terms of combined strategies, the first group was an exception, as its members seldom bought Soviet off-the-rack clothing in stores. Their purchases of ready-made clothes, usually at markets or consignment shops, were ad hoc and generally involved hard-to-find fashionable, especially foreign items.

Let us attempt to account for the remaining consumption strategies in the groups. A Leningrad native M.N.N. (radio engineer, born 1932), whose parents were an artist and an architect, explained her preference for homemade clothing in the 1950s and 1960s by a desire to follow fashion. The fact that her circle of acquaintances did not include retail workers meant that she had no special access to scarce items. She could not afford buying them at markets. Items sold in stores did not meet her needs on aesthetic grounds. She took dress-making courses, periodically went to see new collections shown at the Leningrad Fashion House, consulted all available fashion magazines, and independently reproduced fashion trends in her clothing.[60]

An interview with another Leningrader, Ch. M. Iu. (vocational school teacher, born 1923), revealed a contrasting motivation for do-it-yourself garment-making. This informant could not buy clothing in stores because of her body type, and numerous attempts to find suitable factory-made garments did not pay off. So she made her own clothes, occasionally also engaging the services of tailor shops and a private tailor, with whom she was acquainted. In choosing patterns, she paid little attention to the latest fashions. Her consumption culture was marked by a high degree of conservatism: unconcerned with 'obsolescence,' she would wear a garment till the end of its physical functionality and then remake the same pattern with new fabric. Nor did she see any shame in buying an outmoded dress left at a tailor shop because it had been rejected by the customer who originally ordered it.[61]

The issue of the non-standard body type as an obstacle to buying clothing off the rack came up in another interview, with Shch. Z.P., born in 1932 into a family of workers in Gor'kii *oblast'*. Having begun work at the *Russkie samotsvety* jewellery factory in 1949, she signed up for a dress-making course but did not complete it because she did not have a home sewing machine. Her predominant consumption strategy was to have clothing made at tailor shops and by a private tailor; this, in her opinion, allowed her to look fashionable. At tailor shops, she trusted the advice of dress-cutters based on the choice of patterns in Soviet fashion magazines; when ordering from a private tailor, she would explain her conception of a fashionable silhouette based on what she had seen at fashion house shows or on city streets.[62] This interviewee seemed to have formed a fashion culture based on whatever consumption strategies were available to her. Originally she refrained from factory-made Soviet items, not on aesthetic grounds but the result of a circumstance beyond her control: the absence of ready-made clothing in her size. It seems logical to assume that, had she been able to wear mass-produced Soviet clothing, her consumption culture might have been different.

The mixed consumption culture was marked by a lack of insistence on high standards in goods sold in the state retail system. Representatives of this group took fashion into consideration only when engaging the services of a tailor shop or private tailor. They had no complaint about the tasteless, ready-made goods available for sale. This last statement held also for the third group, whose members, by virtue of their disregard for fashion and the fact that they stuck with products of Soviet garment factories, did not stigmatize these products as unfashionable. As government-run stores were largely alien to fashion, the selection of Soviet mass-produced goods had little to do with consumers' search for fashionable clothing. The dissemination of fashion trends took place mostly via other kinds of clothing, particularly garments made abroad.

Mechanisms for Propagating Fashion Trends

Aside from the already mentioned mechanisms by which fashion trends spread through Soviet society (shows of new collections at fashion houses, fashion magazines, street fashion), Soviet and foreign cinema and theatre also played an important part in the shaping consumer fashion preferences. Women in movie theatres would draw heroines' outfits in order to reproduce them later at home, at a dressmaker's shop, or with a private tailor. Among the actresses and singers whom the interviewees named as fashion trendsetters were Tat'iana Piletskaia in her role in *Dif-*

ferent Fortunes (*Raznye sud'by*, 1956), where she appeared 'in a chic dress with a bow on the side'; Nikolai Cherkasov's wife, 'who loved Parisian outfits'; the Argentine singer Lolita Torres;[63] Liudmila Gurchenko, who popularized the Dior 'new look' in the Soviet Union thanks to El'dar Riazanov's film *Carnival Night* (*Karnaval'naia noch'*, 1956);[64] and actresses from Italian neo-realist films, such as *Roma, ore 11* and *Napoli milionaria.*[65] These stars were unwitting accomplices in cultural transfer, as they helped Western fashion and taste find ways into Soviet society. The fashion preferences of Soviet and Western actresses were very similar, oriented as they were toward Parisian trends. Soviet performers' entry into the culture of Western fashion took place in various ways. For instance, in 1959 a certain people's artist of the RSFSR 'Z' on tour in France 'ordered several dresses at a Paris dress shop, which were paid for by White émigrés; she compensated the Parisians with payments to their relatives living in Moscow.'[66] In June 1959, artists of the Bolshoi Theatre filled the auditorium of the Moscow club Kryl'ia sovetov, where over the course of five days fashion shows featured the collection of the House of Christian Dior.[67]

An important milestone in Soviet society's formation of fashion preferences was the Sixth World Festival of Youth and Students that took place in Moscow in 1957. This official event, along with the Western films purchased with the approval of the Central Committee culture section served as a powerful conduit for Western fashion in the Soviet Union. The USSR Ministry of Internal Affairs meticulously recorded instances of foreign festival guests selling 'personal effects on a person-to-person basis,' as well as the quantity and value of items they submitted at ad hoc resale locations and consignment stores. For the duration of the festival, Moscow was transformed into a big bazaar. In the courtyards, near consignment stores, and at spontaneous places of resale, students from Austria, Hungary, Denmark, Italy, Sweden, Finland, Czechoslovakia, Poland, and Bulgaria trafficked in shoes, capron and nylon stockings,[68] men's pants, women's camisoles, nylon blouses, suits, neckties, shirts, chemises, women's jacket-and-skirt sets, men's wool sweaters, knit caps, and 'PVC raincoats.'[69] The police responded by issuing warnings about the illegality of these activities, noting the locations of ad hoc resale centres and arresting not the sellers but the buyers, who faced 'measures of administrative pressure.' Those from out of town were compelled to sign notes promising to depart Moscow within twenty-four hours.[70] The fact that sellers were not punished increased the scale of the phenomenon: in the early days of the festival, 'foreigners asked to show their festival cards became uncomfortable and sought to leave, but now they readily show their documents and pay no heed to warnings.'[71] In most cases, the buyers were Soviet students, including Komsomol members; competing with them were Poles who sought to offer foreign guests a higher price for their 'goods.'[72] Some Soviet students received second-hand clothing from foreign festival delegates as gifts. According to the Ministry of Internal Affairs, there were instances of these wardrobe items being subsequently sold at markets.[73]

Another illegal channel for the penetration of Western fashion items into the USSR was smuggling. The sale of contraband goods was most prevalent in the nation's port cities, such as Odessa. Crewmembers of foreign vessels, as well as Soviet citizens returning from foreign business trips and tourist travel, were sources for new arrivals of contraband. Smuggled goods included the usual fashionable and hard-to-find nylons, shoes, women's and men's shirts, wool jackets, perfume, neckties, 'ladies' hosiery,' and other items. Uncovering organized groups of black marketeers allowed the police to trace their clients. The December 1955 exposure of a group of smugglers in Odessa who bought American goods from Bulgarian sailors and subsequently distributed those goods through major Soviet cities led to the discovery that some of the smuggled items had been sold to the composer Nikita Bogoslovskii and the Moscow performers Lidiia Atmanaki, Aleksandr Menaker, Mariia Mironova, Nikolai Rykunin, and Efim Berezin when they were in Odessa.[74]

The imitation of fashion trends from state-approved Western movies posed no major threat to official Soviet taste, as it was oriented toward the finest examples of French haute couture. But the consumption of illegally acquired Western clothes, as well as the borrowing of fashion ideas from banned foreign films, helped disseminate untested and unapproved fashions, whose influence was held to be corrosive.[75] Paradoxically, it was the mass-produced items put out by Western factories, rather than haute couture trends, that came in for official censure and criticism. And while high-profile cultural figures could be forgiven their passion for Western clothes, Soviet youth inevitably became a target for attack. Any Soviet youth dressed in non-Soviet clothing, particularly tight-fitting pants, could be accused of *stiliazhnichestvo* (hipsterism). However, the war on *stiliagi* ended in the authorities' defeat, although concealed by the gradual official adoption of the *stiliagi* fashion sense. During the Khrushchev decade, designers gradually narrowed men's pant-bottoms from twenty-eight to twenty-one or twenty-two centimetres, and, to the amazement of conservative consumers, inert industry commenced releasing once-popular slim-fit trousers:

- In every store, including the Central Department Store, the pants on sale have narrow bottoms (25 cm), but this style is not to everyone's liking. So, along with narrow pants, produce pants with bottoms 29–30 cm wide.
- It would be nice to have 28–30 cm wide pants, since the fashion for narrow pants does not go far beyond the capital.
- Stop making narrow pants. They make it impossible to buy a suit. Apparently, soon respectable people won't buy suits, but instead will have to have them custom-made.[76]

As the bitter struggle against the *stiliagi* ended peacefully with elements of their fashion penetrating mass factory production, this state of affairs had to be explained. Designers found a way out by appealing to their beloved theme of taste:

> Ignorance of the fundamental principles of fashion and its development often leads to serious mistakes. One of the crudest of these is overdoing a fashion. There are certain people who consider themselves the bearers of everything advanced and progressive in attire; but in reality these people have no elementary feel for this realm, not even the foggiest idea of what the essence of fashion is. Lacking internal culture and possessing bad taste, they grasp in fashion only the superficial and haphazard; they exaggerate these forms, seeking to show off their attire, and appear in loud, hideous, supposedly 'extra-trendy' outfits. The vulgar appearance of such young men and women is underscored by their free-and-easy behaviour and the slovenliness and garishness of their clothing. These are the *stiliagi*. Unfortunately, they are sometimes confused with fashionably dressed people, and instead of struggling against the inner bankruptcy and bravado of the *stiliagi*, many people take up arms against the narrow pants and short skirts of the modest but fashionably dressed.[77]

Conclusion

Analysing fashion and consumption allows us to establish connections among the politics, economics, and culture of Soviet society in the 1950s and 1960s and to trace the ways in which economic structures influenced everyday culture. Fashion reveals the contradictions of the Thaw. Formally, all the conditions were in place to work fashion harmoniously into the functioning of the Soviet system, with its planned economy and administrative-command logic of governance. Reforms aimed at satisfying the people's needs, while the project of building communism implied a material abundance that could justify the existence of fashion. However, the rational norms calculated by economists set boundaries for abundance, condemning fashion to vanish in the future egalitarian society. Revived contact with the outside world and competition with the capitalist bloc also created conditions favourable for updating the Soviet system through Western borrowings. Attempts to balance supply and demand implicitly relied upon market mechanisms. Yet the inflexibility and inertia of the planned economy suffering from resource shortages hindered the establishment of this balance.

The arrival of Western fashion in the USSR through informal channels in turn contributed to a certain dynamic in Soviet society. The Thaw in the arts led to a reconsideration of the stylistic principles of socialist realism: artists turned to the Russian and Soviet avant-garde of the 1920s and to contemporary Western modernism. Liberalization in art extended to the realm of fashion and clothing design. However, in the context of the Cold War, ideological control remained firmly in place. With each new wave of imitation of Western fashion, the standardization of appearance was imposed as an inviolable principle, and attempts to defy these norms met with stigmatization and social ostracism of the non-conformists. Fashion stands as a magnifying glass through which the rigidity of the Soviet system is plain to see. The reforms of the Thaw involved a quest for flexibility in the planned economy and tolerance for norms of representation, but the inflexibility of the regime's foundations thwarted attempts at transformation.

During the Khrushchev period, Soviet fashion remained the subject of debates that centred on its role and place in socialist society. Fashion was criticized as a locus of competition and social distinction incompatible with the idea of general equality and a nationalized economy. Fashion's fragile status obliged its defenders to resort to the argument that it was important for the inculcation of good taste. This led designers to draw up rigid norms in clothing that conflicted with fashion's need for constant renewal. Aspiring to keep up with developments in Western fashion, Soviet designers were caught in the trap of their own arguments. The result was a watered-down version of fashion that ossified everyday consumption practices: for some consumers, the rigid norms of good taste gradually replaced the need to renew silhouettes. Fashion magazines and sewing-and-cutting handbooks, while helping to get around the problem of scarcity, became timeless manuals of good taste for consumers, as the same issue of a magazine could be used to sew clothing for decades. This was a result of the designers' civilizing mission: despite the persistence of the administrative-command system, official fashion did have a certain influence on clothing practices, although in a sense contrary to the idea of fashion itself.

And yet, if leaders thus hoped to defend Soviet society from the influence of Western consumer values, their hopes were thwarted. Acquaintance with imported goods at international exhibitions and by many other means led to the rise of a heterogeneous consumer environment, in which Western styles and fashion trends were adopted through informal channels. The authorities' and society's reaction to this arrival of Western influences depended on the consumers' status and fashion's relative marginality.

The Thaw did not fundamentally alter the relationship between consumers and the state. The authorities' interference in society's everyday life, including their war on illegal strategies of clothing supply, continued as before. Nevertheless, the state proved unable to eradicate speculation and the unlawful private practice of made-to-order garment making. Shortages in the retail network reinforced the competitiveness of these forms of supply.

Despite the fact that the Soviet fashion system featured all the requisite elements – verbal, iconographic, and material – it was specifically in the system of clothing production that the breakdown occurred. Fashionable clothing was made in various ways: by consumers on their own, by professional seamstresses in tailor shops, and by semi-professional private tailors. Yet the industry, subject as it was to a plan, was unable to include fashion in its production cycle.

In terms of distinction between consumption cultures, the unfashionable nature of mass-produced Soviet clothing was definitive: such clothing could be worn only by people who paid little or no regard to fashion. Those who sought to follow fashion preferred homemade clothing, or items made to order at tailor shops and by private tailors. The differences in the costs of these strategies gave consumers with varying incomes a range of options in creating consumption cultures and finding their niche in the mechanisms of social distinction. High-income families interested in fashion preferred to have garments made to order at tailor shops. Middle-income consumers wishing to follow fashion could do so by engaging private tailors. People in low-income families, for whom fashion nonetheless mattered, made clothing themselves. Income disparities were therefore not an obstacle to dressing fashionably. Consumers of various income levels who did not follow fashion not only bought Soviet-made clothing off the rack but also made clothing themselves or had it made by tailors. It was thus not only income but also attitudes toward fashion that defined the nature of consumer culture.

The concept of 'Soviet fashion' encompassed not one but a great number of manners of dressing: some consciously disdained fashion, while others followed sanctioned or informal trends. Soviet fashion was a world featuring in concentrated form all the peculiarities of the system: methods of waging polemics, modelling and regimenting society, drawing on foreign experience, and both conforming to norms and getting around them. All of these practices underwent changes during the Thaw – despite the burdensome legacy of the Stalinist system. The transformation of the decision-making mechanism into a complex process of 'negotiation' led to the involvement in this process of experts with various professional cultures. This consensus-building particularly affected the level of freedom that was granted to experts – those given the task of rehabilitating the image of socialism. Clothing served as a material expression of this image. Claims to the superiority of the Soviet system and the desire to perfect it through borrowings from Western fashion industries were a pretext for renewing contacts with the outside world. But it was precisely this half-lifting of the Iron Curtain that undermined the communist project, as contact with capitalist countries led to the Westernization of Soviet everyday culture. Attempts to halt this underlying dynamic saddled the reform process with contradictions and incompleteness.

Translated by Avram Brown

NOTES

I would like to express my deep appreciation to Eleonory Gilburd and Denis Kozlov for the valuable comments and advice they provided at various stages of this essay. Part of this research was published in the Russian-language version of the journal *Fashion Theory*: see Larissa Zakharova, 'Sovetskaia moda 1950–60-kh godov: politika, ekonomika, povsednevnost',' *Teoriia mody: odezhda, telo, kul'tura* 3 (Spring 2007): 54–80.

1 Susan E. Reid, 'Cold War in the Kitchen: Gender and the De-Stalinization

of Consumer Taste in the Soviet Union under Khrushchev,' *Slavic Review* 61, no. 2 (Summer 2002): 220–1.

2 A. Braverman, 'Moda glazami ekonomista,' *Dekorativnoe iskusstvo SSSR* 10 (1963): 13; *Nekotorye voprosy razvitiia sovremennoi odezhdy. Novaia tekhnika i tekhnologiia shveinogo proizvodstva* (Kiev, 1964), 31–2.

3 I.A. Ter-Ovakimian, *Modelirovanie i konstruirovanie odezhdy v usloviiakh massovogo proizvodstva* (Moscow, 1963), 8.

4 *O trebovaniiakh k odezhde. Lektsiia dotsenta S.I. Rusakova* (Moscow, 1958), 12.

5 Ibid., 4.

6 *Mody odezhdy na 1962–63 god. Uchebnik dlia inzhenerov i rukovoditelei legkoi promyshlennosti* (Moscow, 1963), 2. See also N. Dmitrieva, 'Diskussiia o mode i stile,' *Dekorativnoe iskusstvo SSSR* 4 (1963): 32; E.V. Kireeva, *O kul'ture odezhdy (kostium, stil', moda)* (Leningrad, 1970), 4.

7 L. Efremova, 'S pervymi luchami solntsa ...,' *Modeli sezona* (Spring–Summer 1959), inside cover.

8 L. Pazhitnov, 'Diskussiia o mode i stile,' *Dekorativnoe iskusstvo SSSR* 1 (1963): 27.

9 V.A. Ivanova, 'O napravlenii mody v odezhde na 1963–1964,' in *Novaia tekhnika i tekhnologiia shveinogo proizvodstva*, issue 2 (Leningrad, 1963), 3–4.

10 See, for instance, L. Efremova, *O kul'ture odezhdy* (Moscow, 1960); L.M. Litvina, I.S. Leonidova, and L.F. Turchanovskaia, *Modelirovanie i khudozhestvennoe oformlenie zhenskoi i detskoi odezhdy* (Moscow, 1964); *Mody odezhdy na 1962–63 g.* (Moscow, 1963); *Novoe v konstruirovanii i modelirovanii odezhdy i napravlenie mody na 1963–64 gg.* (Simferopol', 1963); L.M. Shipova, 'Novoe v modelirovanii legkogo zhenskogo plat'ia,' in *Mody i modelirovanie* (Moscow, 1960), 3; A.M. Viaznikova, 'Novoe v modelirovanii legkogo zhenskogo plat'ia,' in *Mody i modelirovanie*, 2nd ed. (Moscow, 1962): 3–15; see also the journals *Modeli sezona*, *Odezhda i byt*, and *Zhurnal mod* for 1953–64.

11 Kireeva, 13.

12 Efremova, *O kul'ture odezhdy*, 57.

13 E.g., Tsentral'nyi Gosudarstvennyi Arkhiv Sankt-Peterburga (Central State Archive of Saint Petersburg – hereafter TsGA SPb) 9610/1/162/4, 5–8, 12, 30, 32, 39–40, 43, 66–7.

14 TsGA SPb 4965/6/858/24.

15 RGAE 1562, op. 26 (1951–62), op. 37 (1964); TsGA SPb 4965, op. 2–6. These data were not public in the period under discussion. Basing their theory of socialist consumption on these materials, Soviet economists presented them in a 'revised' form.

16 N. Ia. Bromlei, 'Uroven' zhizni v SSSR (1950–65),' *Voprosy istorii* 7 (1966):

3–17; A. Korneev, 'K voprosu o proizvodstve i potreblenii tekstil'nykh izdelii v SSSR,' *Voprosy ekonomiki* 7 (1956): 43–58; V.F. Medvedev, V.V. Shvyrkov, and L.P. Chernysh, *Modeli prognozirovaniia potrebitel'skogo sprosa dlia tselei planirovaniia* (Minsk, 1969); R.S. Nazarov, V.M. Siniutin, and Iu. L. Shnirlin, *Potreblenie v SSSR i metodika ego ischisleniia* (Moscow, 1959); I. Iu. Pisarev, ed., *Metodologicheskie voprosy izucheniia urovnia zhizni trudiashchikhsia,* (Moscow, 1959); Iu. L. Shnirlin, *Nauchno obosnovannye normy potrebleniia* (Moscow, 1961); *Voprosy modelirovaniia potrebitel'skogo sprosa. Chast' 1. Metodika prognoza sprosa i planovogo rascheta roznichnogo tovarooborota* (Minsk, 1969); V.V. Shvyrkov, *Metodologicheskie voprosy izucheniia struktury potrebitel'skogo biudzheta. Avtoreferat dissertatsii na soiskanie uchenoi stepeni kandidata ekonomicheskikh nauk* (Moscow, 1959); V.V. Shvyrkov, *Pokazatel' elastichnosti potrebleniia i ego prakticheskoe znachenie pri izuchenii urovnia zhizni trudiashchikhsia* (Moscow, 1959); V.V. Shvyrkov, *Zakonomernosti potrebleniia promyshlennykh i prodovol'stvennykh tovarov* (Moscow, 1965); V.S. Tiukov, *Planirovanie roznichnogo tovarooborota. V pomoshch' ekonomistu i planoviku* (1960); V.S. Tiukov and R.A. Lokshin, *Sovetskaia torgovlia v period perekhoda k kommunizmu* (Moscow, 1964).

17 E.g., TsGA SPb 9798/1/69/8.

18 RGAE 1562/26/219/57.

19 *Izuchenie sprosa i obosnovanie zakazov promyshlennosti na kozhanuiu obuv' (Metodicheskie ukazaniia)* (Kiev, 1970); I.I. Korzhenevskii, 'Opredelenie sprosa naseleniia na otdel'nye tovary,' *Sovetskaia torgovlia* 3 (1959): 19–23; Korzhenevskii, *Osnovnye zakonomernosti razvitiia sprosa v SSSR* (Moscow, 1965); *Metodicheskie rekomendatsii po sostavleniiu i obosnovaniiu zakazov promyshlennosti na shveinye izdeliia* (Kiev, 1971).

20 Tsentral'nyi Munitsipal'nyi Arkhiv Moskvy (Central Municipal Archive of Moscow – hereafter TsAGM) 1953/2/174; TsAGM 1953/2/238; TsAGM 474/1/37/38.

21 N.T. Savel'eva, *Moda i massovyi vkus* (Moscow, 1966), 53–4.

22 E.g., RGANI 5/43/69/83, 89.

23 RGAE 523/1/205/5.

24 *Zhurnal mod* 1 (1959): 7. See also *Odezhda i byt* 3 (1962): 22, 42.

25 French names for items of clothing in Russia have a tradition preceding the Revolution, as the upper strata of Russian society had long dressed according to Parisian fashion and spoken French.

26 On the official channels through which Western fashion and clothing-industry technologies arrived in the USSR, see also Larissa Zakharova, 'La mode soviétique et ses sources d'inspiration occidentales dans les années 1950–1960,' *Matériaux pour l'histoire de notre temps* 76 (October–December 2004): 34–40; Larissa Zakharova, *S'habiller à la soviétique. La mode et le Dégel en URSS* (Paris, CNRS Editions, 2011), 135–96.

27 RGAE 1562/26/219/24–7.
28 RGAE 1562/26, dd. 783, 784.
29 Viscose manufactured to resemble cotton.
30 TsAGM 1953/2/238/43, 44, 45, 46, 49, 59, 60, 75, 83.
31 E.g., GARF R-8131/28/3182.
32 RGAE 1562/26/433/76.
33 GARF R-8131/28/5117/3; D. Nazarov, 'O bor'be so spekuliatsiei,' *Sotsialisticheskaia zakonnost'* 11 (1957): 60.
34 RGAE 1562/26/433/76.
35 RGAE 1562/26/433/87.
36 *Ugolovnyi kodeks RSFSR. Ofitsial'nyi tekst s izmeneniiami i dopolneniiami na 1 marta 1957 goda i s prilozheniem postateino sistematizirovannykh materialov* (Moscow, 1957), 49, 189. Here we might note that punishments and prison terms varied from republic to republic, thus complicating the investigation of cases in which a citizen of one republic was accused of engaging in profiteering in another republic. In nine republics (Azerbaijan, Estonia, Kazakhstan, Kirgizia, RSFSR, Tadzhikistan, Turkmenistan, Ukraine, Uzbekistan), petty speculation as a first-time offence carried an administrative punishment of detention for three to fifteen days or a fine of up to 500 rubles. In Tadzhikistan, the detention period for petty speculation was set at five to twenty days, while in Azerbaijan the fine was 300 to 500 rubles. A repeat offence of petty speculation carried a criminal penalty of imprisonment for up to a year or correctional labour for the same period, or a fine of up to 2,000 rubles. In Azerbaijan, a repeat petty speculation offence carried a penalty of 1,500 to 2,000 rubles. In five republics (Armenia, Georgia, Moldova, Lithuania, Latvia), petty speculation was treated strictly as a criminal offence, although punishments varied. In Belorussia, no edict on petty speculation was published. GARF R-8131/28/5837/169–70.
37 GARF R-8131/28/6032.
38 GARF R-8131/28/6031.
39 E.g., GARF R-8131/28/5837.
40 GARF R-8131/28/6031/4.
41 RGAE 1562/26/43/70.
42 A. Stroev, ed., *Podruga* (Moscow, 1959), 352.
43 E.g., K.P. Mavrina, *Kroika i shit'e. Konstruirovanie, modelirovanie i tekhnologiia poshiva odezhdy* (Leningrad, 1960).
44 Susan E. Reid, 'Women in the Home,' in *Women in the Khrushchev Era*, ed. Melanie Ilič, Susan E. Reid, and Lynne Attwood, 149–76 (Houndmills, UK, 2004).
45 Melanie Ilič, 'Women in the Khrushchev Era: An Overview,' in Ilič, Reid, and Attwood, *Women in the Khrushchev Era*, 7.

46 E.g., N.B. Lebina and A.N. Chistikov, *Obyvatel' i reformy. Kartiny povsednevnoi zhizni gorozhan v gody NEPa i khrushchevskogo desiatiletiia* (Saint Petersburg, 2003); Reid, 'Cold War in the Kitchen'; *Zhurnal mod* 3 (1957): 22–3.

47 TsGA SPb 4965/2/5698/31.

48 RGAE 1562/26/219/27.

49 RGAE 1562/26/219/37.

50 TsGA SPb 4965/6/858/35.

51 TsGA SPb 4965/6/858/38.

52 TsGA SPb 4965/6/1000/11, 25; TsGA SPb 4965/6/1842/4, 5, 9, 10; TsGA SPb 7082/3/169/4.

53 RGAE 1562/26/219/2.

54 RGAE 1562/26/219/38.

55 *Ugolovnyi kodeks RSFSR*, 59, 184.

56 D. Ia. Zamkovskii, 'Novye formy obsluzhivaniia v atel'e,' in *Mody i modelirovanie*, 57–80.

57 TsGA SPb 4965/6/1842/11–12.

58 E.V. Semenova, 'Po stranitsam zarubezhnykh zhurnalov mod,' in *Mody i modelirovanie*, 102.

59 Ibid., 111.

60 Interview with M.N.N., Peterhof, 31 August 2004.

61 Interview with Ch. M. Iu., Saint Petersburg, 25 September 2004.

62 Interview with Shch. Z.P., Saint Petersburg, 26 August 2004.

63 Interview with M.L.V. (university lab technician, b. 1941), Saint Petersburg, 26 August 2004.

64 Interview with O.T.V. (teachers' college student, b. 1944), Novgorod, 14 August 2004.

65 Interviews with O.B.M. (garrison officer, b. 1925), Moscow, 27 September 2004; S.M.G. (Textile Industry Ministry staff person, b. 1924), Moscow, 19 October 2004; V.N.M. (Theatre Institute student), Moscow, 8 September 2004.

66 RGANI 5/14/19.

67 Centre des Archives Diplomatiques à Nantes. Fonds: Ambassade de France à Moscou. Série B, Carton 271.

68 In contemporary Russian there were two terms: *kapron* was a sort of nylon made in the Soviet Union or other countries of the socialist bloc. Thus when speaking about nylon, it was clear that one referred to goods of Western production. Indeed *kapron* was less prestigious than nylon because of where it was produced. A possible translation for *kapron* is *fosta nylon.*

69 GARF R-9401/2/491/257, 283, 284, 298, 299, 347, 376, 392.

70 GARF R-9401/2/491/347, 362.

71 GARF R-9401/2/491/375.

72 GARF R-9401/2/491/347, 361, 400, 407.

73 GARF R-9401/2/491/301, 348.

74 GARF R-9401/2/478/12, 20, 29, 170–2.

75 E.g., the 1957 Moscow case in which a group of students organized private showings of banned movies at Moscow colleges and institutes. GARF R-9401/2/490/357–61.

76 TsAGM 1953/2/238/47, 115, 117.

77 Efremova, *O kul'ture odezhdy*, 34.

11 Cine-Weathers: Soviet Thaw Cinema in the International Context

OKSANA BULGAKOWA

New developments in art during the Thaw are most often associated with the relaxation of censorship and the lifting of the Iron Curtain, with these two circumstances explaining the new agenda – that of speaking honestly about the present, returning the past from oblivion, and entering into a dialogue with contemporary Western culture. The discursive vocabulary of Thaw criticism was predicated upon the concepts of truth and sincerity (the categories of memory and dialogue were not predominant), but in various art forms – depending on the material – 'truth' and 'sincerity' take on several incarnations.

The cinema visualized these concepts.[1] In cinematic incarnations, 'memory' was transformed into mute dreams about the past by youthful characters bereft of 'historical memory.' 'Truth' in film was materialized in a documentary rhetoric that coincided with the 'redemption of physical reality' in world cinema. 'Dialogue' with Italian neo-realism,[2] the Polish school, the French New Wave, Bergman, Kurosawa, and Fellini became an important component of updating the national cinematic language. It was precisely at this time that the movie market, the development of which had been interrupted by the war,[3] became globalized, with radical technological changes influencing the course first of the motion picture industry, then of motion picture art, from Hollywood to Tokyo. But 'sincerity' – a category used in discussing literature, and countenanced there, and a category that helped establish the popularity of the lyrical-song genre – was highly problematic in the realm of non-verbal arts such as music, painting, sculpture, and film, because here it was connected with the *materialization* of the individual gaze. Such a focus on individual authorship did not fit the canonical notion of collective identity, which remained unaffected by the Thaw; this had merely exchanged a shiny, 'varnished' surface for a less vibrant, 'slushy,' 'sweaty' one, befitting a thaw.

The lifting of the Iron Curtain spelled not only a rendezvous with abstract expressionism, atonal music, and modern design; it also meant that previous standards would be challenged by new forms of pre-verbal physiognomic experience. This experience influenced even body motion – manners of walking and sitting – sharply severing the younger generation, raised not on Soviet films of the 1930s but rather on Western 'war trophy' films, from the world of their fathers.

> The Tarzan series alone, I daresay, did more for de-Stalinization than all Khrushchev's speeches at the Twentieth Party Congress and after. One should take into account our latitudes, our buttoned-up, rigid, inhibited, winter-minded standards of public and private conduct, in order to appreciate the impact of a long-haired naked loner pursuing a blonde through the thick of a tropical rain forest with his chimpanzee version of Sancho Panza and lianas as means of transportation. Add to that the view of New York (in the last bit of the series that was played in Russia), with Tarzan jumping off the Brooklyn Bridge – and almost an entire generation's opting out will become understandable.[4]

Here Joseph Brodsky explains the unfettering of thinking by way of the relaxation of joints, but this change in motility was only one aspect of a wide-ranging break with tradition. The non-verbal art forms of this period altered the paradigm of perception, both visual and auditory, and film became one of the most powerful conduits of new experience.[5] Examples of American abstract expressionism could be seen by visitors to the American exhibition in Sokol'niki Park, but these hardly constituted a majority of Muscovites; the sounds of the modernist music by Schoenberg, Volkonskii, and Schnittke belonged to similarly limited groups of House of Composers concert-goers. But several million saw François Reichenbach's *America as Seen by a Frenchman* (*L'Amérique insolite,* 1958) and heard Giovanni Fusco's soundtrack to Antonioni's *The Eclipse* (*L'Éclisse,* 1962). Accessible to all segments of the population, the cinema shapes manners of seeing, hearing, and moving; it is part of that universalization of perception and imagination noted by journalists, writers, sociologists, and anthropologists. In the late 1950s, French philosophers noted that visual information and communication can trigger social and psychological imbalance. The enthralment of the human imagination to visual information intensified with the introduction into everyday audio-visual experience of a telescreen alternating advertisements, serials, old movies, and news. When perceiving verbal information, a subject remains in his or her own world, whereas visual information, insinuating itself into the imagination, reconstitutes one's perception, becoming part of one's reality, or, more precisely, the subject sees himself or herself as part of this imagined world.[6] In the Soviet context, one of the first to draw attention to this phenomenon of psychological dissonance was Khrushchev, who remarked (in his 'Secret Speech') that Stalin judged reality from the images proffered by Soviet cinema and that he adopted behavioural models for governing his inner circle from American gangster movies.[7]

In keeping with the traditional historiography of Soviet cinema and film criticism, recent studies devoted to Thaw cinema have described mechanisms of censorship, narrative structures, and the type of the hero, the enemy, and the woman. Film has been analysed, naturally enough, as a literary, narrative, ideological, and discursive phenomenon.[8] Films of the Thaw updated the Bildungsroman narratives typical of Stalinist cinema with a new visual style and flipped the vertical axis of the plot to point not upward, to 'the father,' but down, to the son, at times a child. The criticism of this time, its plot synopses and even more so its film reviews, strikes us today as remarkably close to the rhetoric of the pre-Thaw period. But parallel to this verbal and narrative stability, all the physiognomic criteria of film – light, acoustic space, faces, the characters' somatic behaviour and affective makeup, their voices, their material surroundings – were changing.

The bright, sunny weather, shining light or deep shadows, and rich local colours of late Stalin-era films – the fiery reds, penetrating blues, and bright greens and yellows of Mikhail Chiaureli's *The Fall of Berlin* (*Padenie Berlina*) or Boris Barnet's *Bountiful Summer* (*Shchedroe leto*) – gave way to the greyscale of black-and-white films, the pastels of films in colour, and an abundant rainfall inundating the Soviet screen, and not only in the works of Tarkovskii. These torrents of water did not spring from any allegiance to the metaphor of 'thaw.' Rain was at this time also common in Italian, French, and German films, the makers of which attributed this climatic peculiarity to the fashion for Japanese cinema.[9] The rain in *The Rumiantsev Case* (*Delo Rumiantseva*, 1956) is dramatically motivated (because of the rain, the driver cannot brake in time and harms a girl; the criminal uses mud to obscure the car's licence plate), but at the same time, it changes visual parameters. Rain scatters light differently and softens colours. Slush and mud, wet, dark, body-moulding clothing, matted hair, and unshaven faces – these created a consciously perceived new style defined as 'documentary,' and a consciously unperceived atmospherics sharply altering the 'temperature of cinema.' In Stalin-era cinema, rain stood as an imposing menace – the harvest failure in *The Tractor Drivers* (*Traktoristy*), the enemies' conniving in *The Great Citizen* (*Velikii grazhdanin*), the intensity of emotions in *The Party Card* (*Partiinyi bilet*) – allowing dramatic tension to culminate and motivating dramatic light contrasts. In films of the Thaw – from *Spring on Zarechnaia Street* (*Vesna na Zarechnoi ulitse*) to *July Rain* (*Iul'skii dozhd'*) – rain turned into drizzling permanency, everyday ennui, which critics immediately decried: 'Our camera lenses have misted over in the fog and damp of a slushy thaw.'[10]

These atmospheric changes took place over the course of a decade in which films of the early 1960s differed sharply from films of the second half of the 1950s. However, radical changes took place in the late 1950s, and subsequent developments in cinema constitute a reaction to them. The timeline of the cinematic Thaw is therefore somewhat staggered. Making a movie takes time, especially given the lengthy preparatory and shooting period then entrenched in Russia.[11] A possible starting point in this context would be, therefore, not the death of Stalin or Khrushchev's speech, but reforms in movie production, the effects of which were seen in the films of 1956–8.[12] Similarly, the end of the Thaw is associated not so much with the removal of Khrushchev as with the mid-1960s wave of film bannings.[13] So long as the old narrative was reworked within the framework of new visual experience, discussion and criticism was engendered; but as soon as the new physiognomic experience was translated into narrative, a whole Pleiad of films was banned, which coincided with the end of the Thaw.

Within the framework of this modest article, I can address only a few features of Soviet cinematic globalization: the expansion of production and technological innovations and their application to Soviet cinema as compared with the experience of Hollywood; physiognomic and stylistic changes in films of the late 1950s alongside the preservation of old narratives; and the breakdown of collective identity, which cleared the way for the rise of auteur cinema. The emancipation of the national cinematic schools (the Ukrainian, Georgian, Armenian, and later those of the Central Asian republics) attendant upon the process of the Thaw and typologically reminiscent of post-colonial hybridization (the absorption of the achievements of neo-realism and Hollywood) in Indian, Japanese, Latin American, and later African cinema – this subject is of necessity beyond the scope of this article.[14] But it was precisely at this time, in 1958 –

a year before the revival of the Moscow International Film Festival – that Tashkent hosted the first Afro-Asian Film Festival, subsequently serving, for the Soviet cinema, as a platform for exchange with non-European cinematic cultures.

The Expansion of Film Production and Its Consequences

After the war, as the result of numerous complex reasons – of which the appearance of television was only one – Hollywood was forced to undergo a technological revolution.[15] The replacement of the expensive and technologically complicated Technicolor process with that of the simpler Eastman Color enabled a rapid increase in the number of films shot in colour.[16] At the same time, the studios introduced new screen (Cinemascope, Cinerama) and film (70 mm) formats, as well as 3-D cinema. This new quality of eye-catching shows on enormous screens was reinforced by the new quality of stereo sound recorded on magnetic tape and amplified by seven speakers in the movie theatre. The new formats' alternating systems of lenses enabled the attainment of a new level of sharpness and visual appeal, and the developing systems of recording and reproducing stereo sound furnished this spectacle with new sensations of presence. All of these technological metamorphoses transformed the visual and acoustic possibilities of the cinema, and with them, the traditional genres.

The reorganization of film production signalled a new beginning for Thaw-era Soviet cinema as well.[17] Film production increased by leaps and bounds: tenfold from 1951 to 1956 – from 9 to 104 films – and to 150 in 1969.[18] Such a growth spurt was made possible by changes in film-production financing policies (along with those pertaining to cultural production generally), allowing new studios to be built, old ones to be modernized, new technologies to be learned, and production strategies to be altered.[19] The number of movies in colour increased (in 1966 they made up only a third of the yearly total; in 1969, more than half – 82 of 150), as did the number of widescreen films (from 1 in 1956 to 67 in 1966 – more than a third of the yearly total of 151 movies – to 90, more than half of the 150 total, in 1969) and wide-format, 70 mm films (from 1 in 1960 to 9 in 1969).[20]

The number of movie theatres tripled,[21] and distribution policy changed markedly. In 1949, the Soviet moviegoer could, after a lengthy caesura, once again see foreign films: first 'war trophy' films brought from Germany, then movies bought for distribution, and new pictures screened at the Moscow International Film Festival – revived in 1959 after a twenty-four-year interlude – or during special 'foreign cinema weeks.'[22] In 1956, Moscow hosted a week of Italian cinema, in 1957, Chinese and Korean, and in 1958, French. In the 1940s, one American film was in Soviet release (John Ford's *Stagecoach*); in 1960, ten. Release strategy changed as well. In the 1930s, no more than four new movies were released per month; in 1956, these numbered twenty. A dancing Marika Rökk, who appeared on the Soviet screen clad only in a fur coat over suggestive undergarments, constituted the first erotically charged movie experience for post-war pubescents, and perhaps for their fathers as well.

The liberation of the cinema from the clutches of the general canon, the expansion of distribution, and the growth of the network of movie theatres resulted in the doubling of the movie-going audience over the course of a decade.[23] In 1955, the average Soviet citizen went to the movies 12.5 times; in 1966, 18.5 times, and in 1967, 19.1.[24]

This expansion of production required people. The All-Union State Institute of Cinematography (VGIK) was unable to supply a sufficient number of specialists, and so in October 1956 Mosfilm opened a two-year college for directors and screenwriters, graduates of which included Georgii Daneliia, Igor' Talankin, and later, when the college was transferred to the auspices of the Filmmakers' Union, Gleb Panfilov, Aleksandr Askol'dov, and many others. Now different generations of directors were making movies at the same time: classic directors of the 1920s and 1930s and veterans of the age of Stalin and the Cold War (Mikhail Romm, Ivan Pyr'ev, Mikhail Kalatozov) alongside war veterans such as Grigorii Chukhrai, Sergei Bondarchuk, and Iakov Segel' and debutants in their twenties and thirties, unacquainted with war and having only recently received their directorial diplomas (Andrei Tarkovskii, Andrei Mikhalkov-Konchalovskii, Elem Klimov, Larisa Shepit'ko). The coexistence of these generations was fraught with conflict, as the now-published minutes of film evaluations attest. These discussions were internal and closed, but it is significant that at this time filmmakers received the right to form their own union, which became a public vehicle for articulating these polemics.[25] Now Mikhail Romm, formerly one of the most Stalinist of film directors, became the personality cult's most popular spoken-word debunker (his speeches drew enormous audiences) – and teacher of the first generation of Soviet auteur cinema. Romm's method of oral commentary created a new genre in documentarism (*Ordinary Fascism* [*Obyknovennyi fashizm*], 1965) and historiography, laying the foundations for an oral history of Soviet cinema – a counterweight to the unchanged written canon.[26]

In 1991 the former paratrooper Grigorii Chukhrai recalled his beginnings in the movie industry and his 'non-standard' behaviour – arguing with his 'elders' – at artistic councils: 'How did I dare speak that way? Because I had been in the war. I saw a few things there that were scarier than bosses.'[27] Never in its history, replete as it was with dramatic shifts, had Soviet cinema undergone such rapid economic, structural, technological, generational, and artistic change.

The Soviet film industry followed developments in world cinema. As in Hollywood, the new capabilities for creating spectacle were used to revive historical epics and for special effects in the fantasy genre.[28] The latter half of the 1950s in Russia saw experimentation with the possibilities of eye-catching colour cinema. The bright colours reinforced the style of the Stalin-era 'varnished' opera. But while the rise of television led to the decline of the cheap 'B movie' in Hollywood, in the USSR expanded production had a different result. Under a more mobile method of organizing film production, by which studios and production units had more say in decision-making, the Stalin-era policy of making a small number of expensive movies gave way to the strategy of releasing a large number of low-budget ones. The expanding film industry relied on lowering the cost of a film by reducing its shooting period – on cheap black-and-white films in the 'documentary' style, for which there was no need for scenery (associated in cinematic discourse with 'window-dressing' and 'false art'), shot as they were in actual interiors and exteriors. We can see the association between cost and style in Minister of Culture Mikhailov's report to the Central Committee (13 April 1955) on 'filmmakers' break with party objectives': 'Movie budgets are generally overstated. Budgets for feature films this past year were cut by 15.5 million rubles, and still, 8 million rubles were saved by economizing during shooting.... Pageantry and ornamentality often lead to a retreat from life truth, to varnishing. Thus in the film *Land and People* ([*Zemlia i liudi*] dir. Rostotskii), a poor man's hut was to be furnished with lace curtains costing 2,000 rubles.'[29]

The studios' economic policy, oriented toward inexpensive films, encouraged the new style by which Russian cinema followed the *international* fashion for anonymous, uninterpreted reality. This agenda defined the aesthetics of the documentary, subversive auteur cinema of France and England – Free Cinema, cinéma vérité, nouvelle vague – and the New Wave in Poland and Czechoslovakia, which drew on the achievements of Italian neo-realism. The very concepts 'documentary,' 'objective,' and 'realistic' were changing.

In the 1930s, Soviet cinema had been turned into a medium for history and historical memory created anew. The idea of cinema as an objective chronicler ruled out all methods codifiable as signs of an individualized gaze or subjective perspective: the hand-held camera, lack of focus, exaggerated camera angles, unmotivated shifts in visual perspective. The camera was attached to a tripod, its height fixed at that of a table. Lowered and raised horizon lines were avoided, and travelling shots were virtually absent. Camera movement had typically been motivated by the movement of a character in the frame, but insofar as subjective perspective had vanished, so too had the unmotivated motion of the camera.

But in the mid-1950s, all of this neutralization of cinematic modes of expression came to be interpreted as 'window-dressing,' façade-like 'ornamentality,' 'untruth.' Under the new objectivity, artificial lighting was replaced by natural sunlight, constructed sets by street scenes and original interiors, plot by de-dramatization, colour by grainy black-and-white, actors by 'types.' The new objectivity privileged unkempt hair and faces without makeup, which had heretofore completely smoothed over the complexions of men and women alike, erasing signs of age, disease, insomnia, and social position. Masterfully 'crafted' art, including painstakingly composed shots, virtuoso lighting, harmonious, dramatically motivated plot development, well-turned dialogue acting, voice training – these were rejected in favour of the aesthetic of 'dilettantism.' The camera was taken down from the tripod and moved freely, observing silent protagonists indistinguishable from random passers-by, picking up incidentals in the flow of life and unarticulated moods. These methods, requiring no less filmmaking expertise than the rejected vestiges of 'window-dressing' of the previous period, were nevertheless coded as 'art without artifice.' Noise was valued more than dialogue, and characters' pointless ramblings around the city more than action calibrated for dramatic effect.[30] The appearance on screen of non-professional actors, incapable of learning long, complicated, artistically structured text, brought silence and change to dialogue; it was adapted to everyday speech. The camera observed and registered changes in the physiognomy of the city and of people, in their forms of communication, their manners of moving and intoning phrases; such observation was seen as more interesting than traditional movie plots.

This new style was understood in European auteur cinema as the agenda of the unconditional justification of 'reality,' beyond interpretation.

The theoretical platform of the style was worked out in books by André Bazin and Siegfried Kracauer, which were, albeit after a lengthy delay, translated into Russian.[31] Small life stories were not to be inscribed in a grand, meaning-conferring historical narrative; their flow not arranged according to ready-made, stereotypical narrative structures. Kracauer saw this onscreen 'redemption of physical reality' as a reaction against the ideological 'word machines' and cinematic propaganda of the 1930s and 1940s. Montage was seen in this regard as a trick that disrupts cinematic specificity, manipulating time, space, attention, vision, and therefore, the opinion of the viewer. Andrei Tarkovskii defined his project as the aesthetics of 'imprinted time'[32] and accused Eisenstein of misunderstanding the laws of cinematic specificity. The connection between private and shared history was breaking down. *Rome, Open City* (*Roma, città aperta*, 1945), a manifesto of Italian neo-realism, foregrounds not the story of a Resistance hero's martyr-like death, but the wedding, interrupted in the middle of the film, of a prosaic, pregnant, aging widow, who perishes 'randomly.'

Soviet directors considered themselves the heirs of neo-realism, while for their part the neo-realists declared themselves disciples of Mark Donskoi, famous for his screen adaptations of Maksim Gor'kii's autobiographical works *Childhood*, *My Apprenticeship*, and *My Universities* (1936–9). The French privileged the achievement of Dziga Vertov, and the very term *cinéma vérité* originated as a translation of Vertov's concept of *kino-pravda*. This 'cinema-truth' was realized in Soviet film first and foremost as a style, still functioning today, like other documentary styles (from the ethnographic cinema of Robert Flaherty to the 'Dogme' school), as a constructed artificiality, as one of the signifiers of reality.

It became fashionable in documentary filmmaking to make use of the hidden camera to follow shoppers, theatre patrons, and moviegoers. Whereas Stalin-era cinema privileged such interiors as the factory floor, the assembly hall, the office, and the large ('grandiose') apartment, late 1950s discussions of production problems shifted the scene to the small apartment or dormitory bedroom, which took precedence over public spaces. Viewers spied upon the intimate lives of others, in which they recognized details of their own. The everyday, the banal, the insignificant were to redeem the lies of grand art. Upon completing *Spring on Zarechnaia Street* (1956), Khutsiev and Mironer remarked, 'For a long time in art, we've been force-fed cardboard cut-outs of people, a dressed-up reality. The camera looked only "at the front door entrance." Now some films are turning off the avenues and into the back streets; filmmaker and camera are focused on back alleys, where not everything has been cleared away, where there's garbage, junk, and old rags. Into view come people without the fancy clothes (the *costumes*) they wear to the theatre.'[33] Moscow's Gor'kii Studio espoused this 'alleyway' realism. Iakov Segel', Lev Kulidzhanov, Sergei Rostotskii, and Marlen Khutsiev considered themselves the heirs of Mark Donskoi and Sergei Gerasimov, but followed the Verist line of Italian neo-realism. Continuing the project of Giuseppe De Santis (*Roma ore 11*, 1952), Segel' and Kulidzhanov observe the inhabitants of an apartment building on the outskirts of Moscow (*The House I Live In*, 1957). Family dramas, the birth of children, adultery, partings – these transform the 'grand narrative of history' in the banalities of private life and in concrete, object-oriented memory: in marble elephants, rubber plants, a Singer sewing machine. The favoured public space of film now became the school – the laboratory where modes of behaviour are formed. At Mosfilm, the Iunost' company created its own brand of inexpensive children's films. At Lenfilm, the new style was taken up by Iosif Kheifits. His modest film *The Rumiantsev Case* (1956, from the screenplay by Iurii German) tells the story of a kindly driver who gets entangled in a crime and tries to prove his innocence. Today it may be hard to understand what euphoric critics found so surprising in this unremarkable film, especially in the context of the return of the unjustly imprisoned from the camps.

The scene of the workplace film, in which is embedded the Bildungsroman, now shifted from the factory floor to nature: building a bridge, for instance, might force a high-ranking boss to abandon an apartment in the capital and move to a small cabin, or young people to settle in a barracks or tent. Examples of this oft-recycled storyline include *People on the Bridge* (*Liudi na mostu*, 1959), *The Girls* (*Devchata*, 1960), and *The Career of Dima Gorin* (*Kar'era Dimy Gorina*, 1964). The suggested scope of production is enormous, whereas production values are low. In these movies, five people and a tractor build a bridge (a railroad, a city), tame virgin lands, or lay power lines. Literally cut off from wider life, they are focused on small things. These films make use of a mass of sub-codes, which have little to do with the development of the plot (which remains within the framework of accepted narrative – the taming of nature and the socialization of the individual), but which give us an idea of what people have for breakfast (a cigarette, canned goods, or cream of wheat), what diet they're on, where and what kind of clothes they buy, what kind of perfume 'glamorous' women use, what kinds of gifts young women are getting (a wristwatch) and how much they cost, how much money a cook, savings bank director, taxi driver, and lumberjack make, what kinds of salads people are making for parties, what records they're dancing to, what movies they're going to, which hair-dos are fashionable, what kinds of sports people are engaging in (a secretary types up a copy of a yoga instruction book; an accountant works out to the radio in his office; a *stiliaga* goes to a boxing gym), where people are going on vacation (to Gagra or Lake Ladoga), what they're eating during lunch break (lumberjacks – cabbage soup and buckwheat porridge, but without meat; workers – kefir and a loaf of bread; junior researchers – just kefir; and a bank deputy director – fish sticks), what to do when the money runs out, how many years it takes to save up for a car, how much a long-distance call or a word in a telegram or an airplane ticket costs, what living space norm is typical in apartment allocation, and where it might be possible (though probably not) to finally sleep with one's beloved. (In *To Love* [*Liubit'*], Mikhail Kalik shows the lengths to which a man and woman will go to satisfy a spontaneous erotic urge, as they try to get a room in a hotel, to accommodate themselves on a park bench, the back seat of a taxi, the edge of an autumn forest, or in an entryway.)

Such details did not clutter the plots of movies in the 1930s to the 1950s. All the more surprising is the shift in characters' modes of *everyday* behaviour (leaving aside the plot) between *People on the Bridge* and *Into the Storm* (*Idu na grozu*, 1964). In the former, illicit relations must be legalized by marriage; characters are not shown having free time away from work (or a sense of humour); they have virtually no personal possessions, nor do they get sidetracked by 'the private.' In the latter, the heroine, whose profession we know nothing about, rides a motorcycle, takes yoga classes, buys home furnishings, imitates the hairstyles of actresses in movie magazines, and sunbathes on the embankment by the Peter and Paul Fortress. The characters are mobile, moving between Moscow, Leningrad, Novosibirsk, Marseilles, and the Caucasus. They kiss not only on deserted streets, but also on crowded buses; they make fools of police officers; and they are in no rush to get to the marriage bureau. In *Leap Year* (*Visokosnyi god*, 1961), the fact that the main character can desire to vacation in Gagra, dine in restaurants, and win the lottery and simultaneously be unwilling to marry his pregnant girlfriend is bewildering to his parents and criminalized by the storyline, whereas in *July Rain* (*Iul'skii dozhd'*, 1966), these are markers of the everyday life of the average Soviet scientist.

The emptiness and asceticism of the shot in Soviet cinema – whereby the corner of two white walls constituted a room interior; a table and chairs, apartment furnishings – now gave way to socially selected details. Objects in an interior became witnesses to the age, preservers of memory. In Muscovite topography, the very layout of an apartment of a boss, a member of the intelligentsia, or a worker reveals significant social nuances. Imitating a hidden camera, Khutsiev observes the manner in which people smoke, sit, listen to music, and exchange a-semantic gestures that establish contact. This is motivated by the fact that his protagonists are documentarian-like observers of the life around them. A young man on a trolley observes the young woman sitting across from him (*I Am Twenty* [*Mne dvadtsat' let*, 1961–4]), who, reading, does not notice the camera-observer that begins to follow her, watching her laugh, drink coffee in a street café, make a call in a telephone booth, look at posters, ride the subway, and walk down the street. Into the frame come parties, kitchens, transportation, dancing in a breezeway, singing by a bonfire, coffee drunk from paper cups, wine drunk right out of the bottle, macaroni eaten right from the saucepan, and a spontaneous little feast of canned goods eaten with a knife. This anthropological attention to the physical side of everyday life leads to a desire to go to the countryside and make films featuring peasants, just as Flaherty did with Eskimos and Polynesians – to observe workers and peasants, as do Kira and Aleksandr Muratov in *Our Honest Bread* (*Nash chestnyi khleb*, 1964) and Andrei Mikhalkov-Konchalovskii in *Asia Kliachina's Story* (*Istoriia Asi Kliachinoi*, 1966).

Film narratives still promoted the preservation of the communal (socialist) world. This world's hierarchy of values did not allow for realization of the individual personality, which greatly limited opportunities for updating dramatic structures. Only in screen adaptation policy do we observe a break. Now even the director of 1930s kolkhoz pastorals Ivan Pyr'ev adapted three Dostoevskii's novels in a row – *The Idiot* (1958), *White Nights* (1960), and *The Brothers Karamazov* (1968) – while Sergei Iutkevich took up *Othello* (1955), Grigorii Kozintsev *Don Quixote* (1956), and Iosif Kheifits *The Lady with a Lapdog* (1960). The change in course was noted immediately by young French critics. Regarding Samson Samsonov's adaptation of Chekhov's *The Grasshopper* (*Poprygunia*, 1955), François Truffaut remarked, 'Enfin un film russe avec adultère: on respire!' ('Finally, a Russian film with adultery – what a relief!') For the first time, he could draw parallels between films 'from there' (Russia) – which had hitherto left Truffaut with the impression of archaic 'fairy tales' – and something familiar, like the melodramas of Max Ophuls.[34]

Film storylines of this time (involving the unmasking of enemies, the reform of individualists, women's liberation, etc.) remained essentially unchanged; only the emphasis had shifted: now the enemy was not a foreign spy but a conservative, a bureaucrat, or an individualist. (In this sense *Into the Storm* [*Idu na grozu,* 1964] differs little from *Certificate of Maturity* [*Attestat zrelosti,* 1954].) The re-education plot is softened, to be sure, in the comedy genre (*Height* [*Vysota,* 1956], *Spring on Zarechnaia Street* [1956], *The Unamenables* [*Nepoddaiushchiesia,* 1959], *The Girls* [*Devchata,* 1960]); whereas the women's liberation plot shifts from the genre of comedy to drama (*The Lesson of Life* [*Urok zhizni,* 1955]). A working woman smokes and is vulgar (*Height*), a working man does not appreciate classical music and has poor grammar (*Spring on Zarechnaia Street*): here the classic couple from *The Fall of Berlin* – a steelworker ignorant of Pushkin and a schoolteacher, whose unequal union is blessed in the film by Stalin – is transplanted into a screwball-comedy battle of, and reconciliation of, the unequal sexes, the marriage of a refined young lady and a hooligan (with Blok and Rachmaninoff taking the place of Pushkin). These simple adjustments to the Soviet cinema's mythologizing of the proletariat as the hegemon of history were taken as signs of innovation and individualization.

The main criterion of art was now proclaimed to be 'truth,' which was analogous to the concept as understood in English and French cinema only on the level of the photographic 'surface.' The fact that actors' faces were unshaven, sweaty, and tired, and their clothes dirty and worn out, that home furnishings were meagre, and physiognomies now conveyed ethnic distinctions (suddenly joining the standard Ukrainian jokester and charming Georgian was the Jewish girl of marriageable age), and that streets were slushy and muddy – these were taken as signs of 'truth,' lending an everyday authenticity to the rather schematized action of *Spring on Zarechnaia Street,* which was little distinguished from previous re-education narratives. Storylines from contemporary life, history, and classic literature were processed in this rhetoric. Grigorii Kozintsev offered a 'neo-realist' Shakespeare (*Hamlet,* 1964, which, seen as striking a blow against the lies of 'the fathers,' was awarded the Lenin Prize); Mikhail Shveitser – a 'neo-realist' Leo Tolstoy (*Resurrection,* 1960–61).

None of these films was a box-office favourite. Moviegoers' preference was not for the prosaic dramas that became, for critics, the national trademark of Thaw cinema (whereas its *inter*national trademark was the tragic film, notable for its highly evocative rhetoric, about the broken individual vis-à-vis a collective destiny). Mosfilm head Ivan Pyr'ev discovered the young VGIK graduate El'dar Riazanov at a studio for documentary films (!) and offered him the chance to make a comedy in colour. The box-office champion of 1957 was not *The Cranes Are Flying* (*Letiat zhuravli*), which took the number ten spot with 28.3 million tickets sold, but Riazanov's comedy of errors *The Girl with No Address* (*Devushka bez adresa*), which sold 36.4 million.[35] In *Carnival Night* (*Karnaval'naia noch'*, 1956), Riazanov offered a musical – starring the Soviet Union's answer to Deanna Durbin, Liudmila Gurchenko, whose 18.5-inch waistline was much discussed and admired – half of which comprised a New Year's Eve revue. The film, which updated the storyline of the bureaucrat put in charge of amateur art, saw Igor Il'inskii end his twenty-year absence from the screen by repeating the caricature he had created in *Volga-Volga* (1938).

Moviegoers in 1962 preferred not *Clear Skies* (*Chistoe nebo*) and *Nine Days in One Year* (*Deviat' dnei odnogo goda*), which featured Thaw-redolent plots and protagonists (a rehabilitated pilot, a nuclear physicist) and won the main prizes at socialist film festivals in Moscow and Karlovy Vary, but rather *The Amphibian Man* (*Chelovek-Amfibiia*, 1961). The film set a record with 65.4 million tickets sold.[36]

The tender young man Ikhtiandr (Vladimir Korenev), half-human, half-fish, dwells like a creature of freedom at the bottom of the sea. His movements have an astonishingly unearthly grace; he acts like Robin Hood, coming to the aid of poor pearl-divers; he lives in a state of pure nature like the Rousseau ideal, innocent of social deformations, and targeted by greedy criminals. Sovremennik Theatre star Mikhail Kozakov, the handsome fascist from *Murder on Dante Street* (*Ubiistvo na ulitse Dante*, 1956), plays a charming cynic. Its exotic Mediterranean-city atmosphere, stylish, modern Western interiors, and dramatic underwater photography made *The Amphibian Man* the most successful film of the *entire* Thaw period.[37] Higher-ups found the film so disturbing that the director Vladimir Chebotarev was subsequently denied such storylines, while Korenev, who became an icon of the Soviet gay community, disappeared from the screen. Fumed *Literaturnaia gazeta*, 'Ikhtiandr? What Ikhtiandr!? Tarzan with gills!' – anticipating Joseph Brodsky's panegyric to Tarzan.[38]

The film is interesting not only in the context of Thaw-era fashion, or in view of the aesthetics of queer cinema, or the films of Pasolini (as Perestroika criticism saw it),[39] but also in the context of Hollywood in the 1950s. New media formats (3-D, widescreen, colour) were changing the Hollywood genre system, allowing science fiction and horror films to be produced on the level of big-budget features, the better to respond to what can be seen as the leading emotion of the time – fear.[40] (With good reason did W.H. Auden entitle his long post-war poem 'The Age of Anxiety'). This affect helped 3-D find its 'subject' (just as melodrama found powerful reinforcement in colour).[41]

This new, multisensory perception of fear went unnoticed by Soviet cinema. The first Soviet 3-D movie was the 1947 adaptation of the civilization saga *Robinson Crusoe*, while the second, 1949's *Happy Voyage* (*Schastlivyi reis*), visualized an exciting journey into space.[42] Prior to 1986, not a single Soviet movie was made about a potential nuclear war or 'day after,' à la 1959's *On the Beach*. While Hollywood used the new objects of terror born in the laboratories of Los Alamos to extrapolate nature and the body run amok (radioactive mutants, the awakening of prehistoric monsters, giant insects), Soviet cinema's faith in scientific and technological progress remained unshaken, its heroes unafraid in the face of modernization and the technological uncanny. This optimism, familiar from the experiments of Russian Futurists and Constructivists, was justified by the idea of historical progress, which coloured fantasies about aliens with the same euphoria. In the Soviet version, relations with extraterrestrials blossomed from friendship into love, as proposed already by Aleksei Tolstoy in *Aelita* (1923, adapted for the screen in 1925) or Aleksandr Bogdanov in *Red Star* (*Krasnaia zvezda*, 1925). Military conflicts erupt between American astronauts and the aggressive, cunning inhabitants of a *red* planet Mars, whereas in a 1961 film, the first voyage into space takes Soviet cosmonauts to Venus, the planet of love![43]

The amphibian man is in this vein, and as such can be compared to the 'creature from the Black Lagoon' of Jack Arnold's 3-D horror film of the same name – a prehistoric monster revived by a nuclear blast. The amphibian man, a creature from a *blue* lagoon, is the product of a consciously conducted scientific experiment, a noble, handsome Frankenstein creation who is loved by a pretty girl (unlike in the American version) and who upholds faith in scientific progress. Cinematic higher-ups were afraid of Ikhtiandr's popularity, but society was not afraid of anything, not even a new, uncontrollable social group – young people, who, along with rock music, motorcycles, and new fashions, were being criminalized in America (*The Wild One*, 1953; *The Blackboard Jungle*, 1955) and Europe (*Before the Deluge* [*Avant le déluge*, 1954] and *The Cheaters* [*Les tricheurs*, 1958] in France; *The Damned* [1963] in England; *Teenage Wolfpack* [*Die Halbstarken*, 1956] in West Germany; and *Berlin – Schönhauser Corner* [*Berlin – Ecke Schönhauser*, 1956] and *The Skinhead Gang* [*Glatzkopfbande*, 1960] in East Germany).

Even the combination of atomic peril and youth run amok – employed by Joseph Losey in *The Damned,* produced by Columbia Pictures and the British production company Hammer Films, which specialized in gothic horror films and had previously released colour remakes of *Dracula* and *Frankenstein* – found, in Russia, a happy ending, in the traditional form of self-sacrifice in the name of progress. While young people on the other side of the Iron Curtain were living in constant fear of nuclear apocalypse, as in André Cayatte's *Before the Deluge,* young Soviets were sacrificing their lives to advance the study of the atom. In *Nine Days in One Year,* Mikhail Romm portrays a young physicist who for the sake of science knowingly exposes himself to a high dose of radiation, after which he is furthermore ready to subject himself to a medical experiment – the first human bone marrow transplant. His fearlessness returns us to the idea of historical progress, faith in which was shaken only in films aimed at the past.

The Objective as Subjective: The Appropriation of History

External stylistic resemblances between films of the Thaw and those of Italian neo-realism or British Free Cinema cannot hide the fact that the deep foundation of Soviet cinema, like the socialist utopia itself, remained unaffected. That changes in the value system (and hence the narrative system) were minimal is most obvious when we consider a traditional genre in Soviet cinema, that of the 'revolution film.' Only Mikhail Chiaureli's Stalinist films *The Great Dawn* (*Velikoe zarevo*), *The Oath* (*Kliatva*), *The Fall of Berlin,* and *The Unforgettable Year 1919* (*Nezabyvaemyi 1919-i god*) were banned; from the remaining, no less cultic movies of the 1930s, the figure of Stalin was removed, sometimes via complicated technical operations (travelling mattes, rear projection, and frame-by-frame retouching).[44] Twenty years (!) after making *Lenin in 1918* (*Lenin v 1918 godu*), Romm reshot several scenes. However, amid such adjustments, the historical conception of such films remained unchanged: having undergone a process of 'technical de-Stalinization,' movies were re-released, shaping and conditioning collective memory. In the 1950s, 1960s, and 1980s, Sergei Iutkevich re-staged old cinematic rituals commemorating Lenin, grafting the new documentary style onto their fictional historical space. The figure of Stalin had vanished from the screen (paralleling the removal of his embalmed body from the mausoleum), but that of Lenin took on a mass of everyday detail. He rides a bicycle, wanders in the woods, maintains a meaningful silence, is occasionally indecisive, and goes to the movies – just like the protagonist of a 1960s film. In *Lenin in Poland* (*Lenin v Pol'she*, 1965), Sergei Iutkevich makes Lenin the hero of a modern French novel, complete with interior monologue, while in *The Sixth of July* (*Shestoe iiulia*, 1968), Mikhail Shatrov and Iulii Karasik situate this figure within the space of a Peter Weiss–style docudrama.

The October Revolution and the Second World War remained the central events of collective historical memory. Remarkably, however, it was films entering into a dialogue with this memory, thereby seeking to justify individualization, that constituted the international 'brand' of Thaw cinema. In the ecstatic mass events that were the trademark of 1920s Russian cinema, as in *The Battleship Potemkin* (*Bronenosets Potemkin*), the individual is dissolved. In Stalin-era cinema, the hero of a movie is the symbolic representative of the masses (the working class) who submits, as in *The Fall of Berlin*, to the common destiny. Films of the 1960s reveal the *drama* of this submission, and while the necessity of this submission remains beyond doubt, these films do often portray the breakdown of the personality. The hero of Andrei Tarkovskii's *Ivan's Childhood* (*Ivanovo detstvo*, 1961) is an insane child whom war has turned into a war machine. The blame is laid upon a merciless historical cataclysm in which the individual is denied free will and choice. Tarkovskii, who won the Golden Lion Award at the 1962 Venice Film Festival, was accused by Italian Communists of historical fatalism, of doubting the very idea of historical progress, but Jean-Paul Sartre defended Tarkovskii and his film.[45]

Grigorii Chukhrai debuted with *The Forty-First* (*Sorok pervyi*, 1956). Boris Lavrenev's story, repeating the conflict in classic melodrama between love and duty, had been adapted for the screen already in 1927. Prior to *The Forty-First*, it had been traditional in Soviet movies for passionate love to come to an abrupt halt the moment the woman discovers that her beloved is a class enemy or spy (*The Party Card*, 1936). In Chukhrai's film, a captured White lieutenant (Oleg Strizhenov) and a Red sniper (Izol'da Izvitskaia) are shipwrecked on a desert island. This situation takes them out of their historical-social reality, leaving them only a man and woman whose survival depends on mutual cooperation. Literally putting aside their uniform puttees, they – following the camera's lead – lay bare the sensual beauty of each other's (half-)naked bodies. Eroticism and nature, shot in the pastel tones of yellow sand and blue-green water, are affirmed by the film as something preserving life in a world defined by the violence and death associated with history (revolution, war, modernization). The end of the film brings the protagonists back to history, which has designated for them the role of enemies; hav-

Ivanovo detstvo (Andrei Tarkovskii, 1961)

ing learned of the approach of a White ship to the island, the Red sniper kills the lieutenant. What was new in this film was not the plot (which is old), but the fact that the director turned obeying an order into murder – and a personal drama. To contrast with the objective nature of narrative early in the film, cinematographer Sergei Urusevskii chose for the island scenes an almost monochromatic range of colour, while the director removed the verbal range – dialogue – replacing it with meditative music. Both these elements are suggestive of the subjectivized gaze of a woman whose biological and physiognomic perception does not conform to a rational framework (that of duty or ideology). Chukhrai compels the viewer, too, to be dismayed at the heroine's act, to discover the inhumanity of this just war, the necessity of which had previously never been subject to doubt.

When, ten years later, Askol'dov made another attempt, with *The Commissar* (*Komissar*), to oppose the historical to the biological and human, the film did not pass the censorship, nor did other films of the time that sought to represent a historical cataclysm as senseless violence (*The*

Ivanovo detstvo (Andrei Tarkovskii, 1961)

Angel [*Angel,* 1967]) or grotesque carnival (*The Intervention* [*Interventsiia,* 1967]). In 1956, *The Forty-First* had the support of *Party Card* director Pyr'ev, although Chukhrai did have to replace the close-up of the face of the heroine, in despair after the last shot is fired, with a more neutral wide angle.

Russian film scholars believe that Soviet cinema's interest in individual fate, in the exception to the common biography, constituted the main course correction of the decade. This adjustment coincides with a principal discovery of Western cinema: the personal appropriation of shared history, in which the objective is exchanged for the sharply subjective. The emphasis on objective black-and-white documentary qualities can at times blind the viewer to the heightened subjectivity and provocative individualization of the cinema of this period. Alain Resnais began his film career with documentaries about artists; his most famous was *Night and Fog* (*Nuit et brouillard,* 1955), on Auschwitz. He went to Hiroshima to make a documentary on the atomic bombing. The film that emerged from this, *Hiroshima My Love* (*Hiroshima mon amour*, 1959), which combines documentary footage of bombing victims with semi-documentary scenes of the Hiroshima Museum, asserts on the screen the personal drama of the heroine – her 'wrong' love for a German soldier, through whose loss she has suffered her own Hiroshima. Similar appropriations of history by 'wrong' characters took place in Soviet cinema, and these were resolved in the same stylistic key: the black-and-white photographic realism of observation is interrupted by unmotivated visual shifts – skewed proportions, close-ups so close they result in spatial disorientation, lack of focus – markers associated with the 'subjectivization' and 'intimization' of historical experience. Cinematographers of this period such as Urusevskii, Vadim Iusov, and Margarita Pilikhina became as famous as directors. This is a distinguishing characteristic of the most internationally famous Thaw-era film.

In 1958, a year before the release of *Hiroshima*, a Russian film – *The Cranes Are Flying* (*Letiat zhuravli*, 1957; dir. Mikhail Kalatozov, cin. Urusevskii), about an unfaithful fiancée – took the Golden Palm at Cannes for the first and only time. Eighteen-year-old Veronika cannot understand why her fiancé Boris volunteers to go to the front; in a moment of despair, she gives in to his step-brother Mark and marries him, then leaves him, hoping for Boris to return – but no such miracle comes to pass.[46]

Critics attempted to fit the movie into the usual storyline of mistake, guilt, 'fall,' repentance, and redemption. *Iskusstvo kino*, however, deemed the film's subject 'love and faithfulness to the people,' while the studio promised that the movie would 'reveal the true meaning of civic heroism.'[47] Maia Turovskaia, criticizing lapses in the film's dramatic motivations, believed that Veronika would find her way to 'great life,' a life of meaning and purpose.[48] But Veronika strays from the norm without any intention of returning to it, and Kalatozov, Urusevskii, and Tat'iana Samoilova tell neither the story of her censure nor that of her reform. The aura of ambivalence emanating from the heroine is not characteristic of the conventional types: the 'unfaithful fiancée,' the fallen – 'infernal,' as Turovskaia dubs her – woman, the Young Communist who falters in the face of adversity. The mysteriousness of her personality is furthered by the metaphysical connection established between the lovers through parallel montage and the film's dramatic structure: just as Veronika gives in to Mark, Boris is hit by a stray bullet; just as Veronika is about to throw herself under a train, fate leads her to save a lost child named Boris from the wheels of a truck; the expected and postponed wedding is visual-

Letiat zhuravli (Mikhail Kalatozov, 1957)

ized only as the hallucination of a dying man; and the dead man's letter reaches his bride many years too late.

This drama of metaphysical chance, resisting the usual motivations of acts and actions, constituted – much like Pasternak's *Doctor Zhivago*,

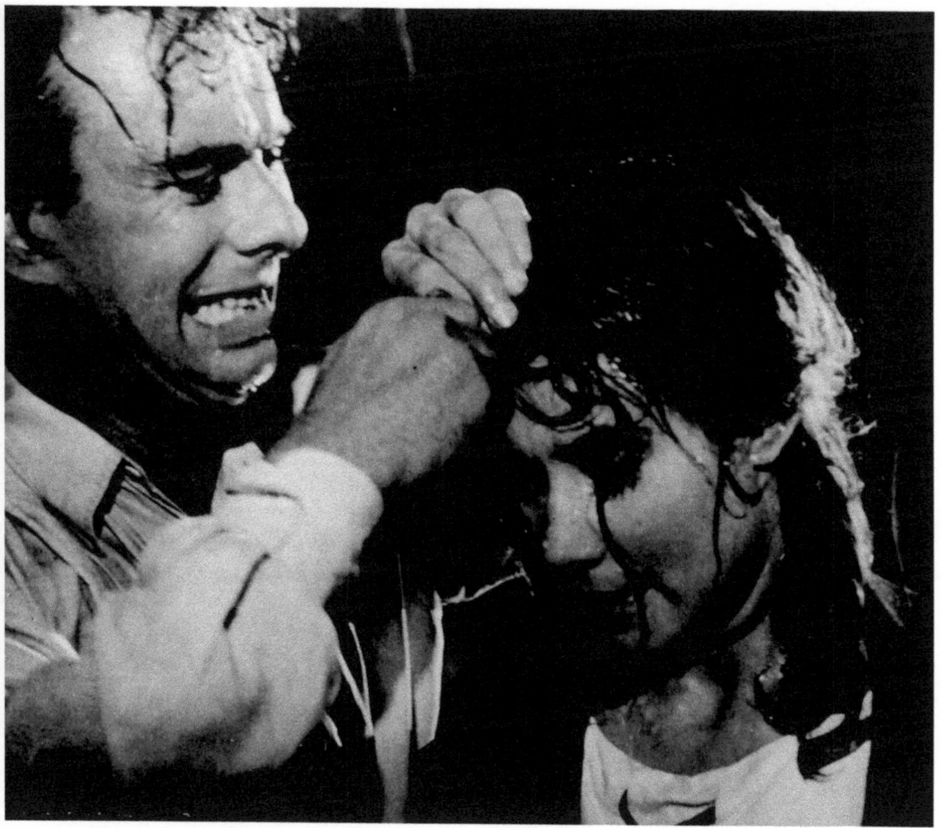

Letiat zhuravli (Mikhail Kalatozov, 1957)

published at the same time and discussed (unread) at Mosfilm on 31 January 1957 – a sharp break with the tradition of dramatic causality. Like Chukhrai and Alain Resnais, the makers of *Cranes* followed the traditional scheme of apportioning the individual vis-à-vis the general: the feminine, individually coded perspective of the heroine is at odds with the canon of the general and is situated within the framework of a private love story. Veronika's viewpoint is conveyed by way of subjectivized camerawork, off-centre compositions, sharp, exaggerated camera angles, and expressionistic, unmotivated lighting. Urusevskii's camera alternates between close-ups and wide shots, the former suggesting intimacy and the heroine's perspective, the latter, the view from the sky (the crane's-eye view?). Boris inscribes his story into the history of the entire

Letiat zhuravli (Mikhail Kalatozov, 1957)

kin, into the history of society; thus he is assigned neutral wide-angle shots. But at the moment of his death, and that of Veronika's suicide attempt, this balance is disrupted, and in the end the two perspectives merge. Lost in the kin's chaotic collective body, Veronika looks at her own story as if as it were from outer space.

Urusevskii used a hand-held camera; the virtuosity of its movements mesmerizes through long, continuous takes resulting in montage within the frame. The subjective viewpoint is reinforced by subjectivized sound: bits of dialogue, noises, and musical phrases placed one on top of another. The new short-focus lens revolutionized the way focus range was utilized, giving mass scenes a new dimension. Sharp, unmotivated alternations between a subjectivized perspective and the view from space, between close-ups of a face and the chaos of a crowd in which a small figure is lost; the nervous rhythm of the hand-held camera conveying the ragged breathing of a runner – these things lend the film an exaggerated emotionality bordering on kitsch; but the film's particular sublimation mechanism reinforces the unrealizability, the unreality

Letiat zhuravli (Mikhail Kalatozov, 1957)

of desire. A rhythmic montage of multiple-exposure space spinning or disintegrating into imperceptible segments interrupts Neo-realistic, everyday scenes with an avant-garde thrust, conveying a sense of mental shock, loss of consciousness, a shaken psyche. 'Documentalism' is suddenly revealed to be a mask for dreams, hallucinations, and visions that set 'correct' history straight; Andrei Tarkovskii made this displacement of cinematic reality in favour of hallucination and dream the foundation of his films.

The mysteriousness of the heroine played by Tat'iana Samoilova received as much critical attention as Urusevskii's camerawork and the film's alleged dramatic failings.[49] She remains a mystery even to herself, standing not as a victim of war, but a woman in love who, breaking free of the Thaw construct of 'reality,' believes in the metaphysical power of her love more than she believes in reality. Moviegoers – Soviet *and* Western – found this metaphysical faith hypnotic. This was a heroine seemingly distilled in the crucible of Russian literature.[50] After her, instead of komsomol girls, the Soviet screen was filled with Turgenevian young women and Chekhovian, self-conscious men. For Western critics, Samoilova was the screen resurrection of the mysterious Slavic soul, coinciding with *Zhivago*'s Lara. However, Kalatozov had reproduced in his film the physiognomy of the love triangle featured in the popular Italian melodrama *Bitter Rice* (*Riso amaro*, 1949; dir. De Santis). Here the heroine, played by Silvana Mangano, instead of marrying the fine young man played by Raf Vallone, falls under the spell of a criminal *homme fatal* (Vittorio Gassman), and perishes. The success of this rationally inexplicable attraction was quickly reinforced by a similar drama, *Anna* (1951; dir. Alberto Lattuada), starring the same actors. Like Mangano, Samoilova was hard to type: she was too 'light' for tragedy, too 'heavy' for comedy, and did not conform to the movie ideal of beauty, but her out-of-genre youthful authenticity was striking. Aleksei Batalov's Boris and Aleksandr Shvorin's Mark perfectly render the physiognomy of the kindly boy next door (a Russian engineer) and the erotically attractive 'infernal character' (a musician with a 'Jewish touch').

The film was an event, a completely unheralded phenomenon. Having begun his career as cinematographer for the visually arresting film *Salt for Svanetia* (*Sol' Svanetii*, 1930; screenplay by Sergei Tret'iakov), Kalatozov had directed movies in the typical Stalin-era genres: the bio-pic, the Cold War thriller, the 'varnished' film about the enthusiastic taming of the Virgin Lands (*Valerii Chkalov*, aka *Wings of Victory*, 1942; *Conspiracy of the Doomed* [*Zagovor obrechennykh*, 1950]; *The First Echelon* [*Pervyi eshelon*, 1955]). Urusevskii had previously filmed *Cossacks of the Kuban* (*Kubanskie kazaki*, 1949), following the style and colour palette of Palekh art and 'lacquered boxes.'[51] Neither the director, nor the cinematographer, nor the actress was subsequently able to recreate the expressive power of *Cranes*. Samoilova received many offers – from Italy, Hungary, and France – to replay the unique, mysterious Slavic woman, but she was unable to imbue any role with the suggestiveness of Veronika, not in the Hungarian *Alba Regia* (1961, dir. Mihâly Szemes), in which the mysteriousness is motivated by her character's slippery identity as a spy, nor in 1965's *Italiani brava gente* by Guiseppe De Santis, director of *Bitter Rice*. This emancipation of the personal from the general, of the individual from the mass, was felt especially by German critics (both East and West), who declared *Cranes* the most 'individual' of war movies.[52]

In his screen adaptation of Mikhail Sholokhov's story *The Fate of a Man* (1959), Sergei Bondarchuk further consolidated the theme of the uniqueness of individual fate by featuring the 'wrong' sort of hero, an 'exception' – an alcoholic and POW; here, too, the film's camerawork and soundtrack sharply subjectivize *personal* recollection. Cinematographer Vladimir Monakhov's graphic multidimensional compositions alternate with expressive close-ups, repeating the style by which objectivity is replaced with subjectivity. Tarkovskii would later repeat many of the visual motifs discovered by Bondarchuk and Monakhov: a wind that suddenly arises, causing grass to move expressively; the black silhouette of a destroyed, incinerated church against the background of the sky; black trees in a flooded, dead forest. Bondarchuk worked the tragic temperament in a very low-key manner and was able to convey the courage and long-suffering of a Russian hero whom the West recognized as the resurrection of a Tolstoyan hero – the Russian *muzhik*.[53] Just as Samoilova was supposed to reproduce her uniqueness, so too was Sergei Bondarchuk asked by Roberto Rossellini to recreate Andrei Sokolov in *Blackout in Rome* (*Era notte a Roma*, 1960). Rossellini insisted that Bondarchuk be filmed in the same costume as Sokolov and improvise the role of an escaped Russian POW who has joined the Italian Resistance.

In *The Fate of a Man*, this trend of 'wrong' heroes – the unfaithful fiancée, the Red partisan who falls in love with a White officer, the embittered child for whom war is reality and peace a dream – finds a courageous fulfilment. Bondarchuk's soldier can harden in his *personal* tragedy, excluding himself from the euphoria of the common victory, even against the backdrop of the conquered Reichstag. But historical cataclysm – war or revolution – is *the necessary* backdrop for the individual's breakout from the framework of collective fate and collective correctness. In this process, sensory and biological experience (fear, the survival instinct, erotic passion) ensure and justify the liberation of the personality (which is why most of these protagonists are women); but the cataclysm provides extenuating circumstances: the *individual* exception becomes a *general* one. A mass event such as a revolution or war, moreover, will always provide a chorus to comment upon this individual fate. In Grigorii Chukhrai's *Ballad of a Soldier* (*Ballada o soldate*, 1959), the main character's actions are corrected and guided by this chorus; in *The Forty-First*, the Red partisan woman in love has dreams about her fallen comrades; in *The Cranes Are Flying*, the lovers walk not only along a deserted embankment, but also past a symbol of Soviet collective identity, the Mausoleum – to which is immediately added, however, the silhouette of a church. They transform the Red Square into an intimate space, following the 1957 decree that not only parades and demonstrations be held there, but graduation dances as well.

The Physiognomy of the Protagonist

Western cinema of the time was marked by a sharp shift in gender roles. The usual plot structure was being subverted, on the one hand by excessively strong women who had gained their independence during the war, and on the other, by enfeebled, impotent, neurotic, androgynous men. The role of male romantic lead or femme fatale was played by teenagers such as James Dean and Brigitte Bardot. Incestuous libidinal energies were justified differently in Soviet cinema. As the 1950s gave way to the 1960s, here too a disproportionately large role was played by child protagonists – in adult, and not children's, cinema. This choice was justified both conceptually and in terms of production values. In the context of the new subjective appropriation of collective history, the most 'convenient' protagonist is a child, who is unburdened by oppressive historical memory. He is not associated with the guilt and mistakes of the world of the fathers, for which he can bear no responsibility. (For that matter, most of the children and teenagers appearing on screen were orphans.) Children appeared on screen as a palliative to the newly rising Gender Trouble, the Soviet variant of which was of necessity bereft of incestuous eroticism. Children's films were convenient also in terms of production values. They were cheap, hence not a great risk, and with this in mind, studio heads considered them proper for debuts of young, inexperienced directors. Andrei Tarkovskii's low-budget debut came in the form of reshooting a children's film whose director had been dismissed. To keep potential financial losses to a minimum, studios most often paired two debutant directors on one children's movie. Such compulsory tandem-work included Tengiz Abuladze and Rezo Chkheidze's debut *Magdana's Donkey* (*Lurdzha Magdany*, 1955), Georgii Daneliia and Igor' Talankin's *Seryozha* (1960, aka *A Summer to Remember*), and Aleksei Saltykov and Aleksandr Mitta's *My Friend, Kol'ka* (*Drug moi, Kol'ka*, 1961). Irina Poplavskaia and Larisa Shepit'ko were in preparations to shoot *Heat* (*Znoi*, 1963) in Kirghizia when Poplavskaia took ill, and Shepit'ko continued the work solo. Iulii Karasik debuted with *The Wild Dog Dingo* (*Dikaia sobaka Dingo*, 1962), Elem Klimov with *Welcome, or, No Trespassing* (*Dobro pozhalovat', ili postoronnim vkhod vospreshchen*, 1964), and in Tajikistan Vladimir Motyl' made *Children of the Pamir* (*Deti Pamira*, 1963), etc.

In English films, these unruly teenagers were socialized in the beds of grown women; their Soviet counterparts were socialized without erotica. The eccentric parabola of Klimov's film revives the pattern of Zamiatin's dystopian *We*, transposed by the director to a Young Pioneer summer camp and culminating in the children's revolt against a dictator in white pants, a 'father of all children' with the agricultural surname Dynin (melon) and a corncob in his hand. A combine harvester sweeps away an alley of alabaster hero-statues, and the children break through, instead of an iron curtain, the wooden fence that has kept them from elemental nature. The role of camp guard is taken up not by stern men but by fat, amorphous cleaning-matrons. The children parody adult conflicts with the power structure (dissidence, underground revolt). The grown-ups, either too fat or too thin, turn into comic-strip figures – figures the camera reduces to an enormous, gaping, siren-blaring mouth or a giant eavesdropping ear. Klimov included elements of silent-film slapstick in his comedy, and alternated camera speed, which underscored an alternative motility. The liberation of this spontaneous motor activity, and the appearance on screen of the graceful new 'wild' body, were part of the change taking place in the physiognomic structure of Soviet cinema. Klimov's 'little Tarzans,' whose nakedness was bereft of eroticism, hence acceptable, provided a tame alternative to 'Western' examples of the new body language from which Thaw-era young people were taking their cue.[54]

American and European teenagers copied James Dean's gestures and manner of dress, while Wajda made Zbigniew Cybulski Dean's Polish counterpart. Knees, hips, shoulders, arms, and the neck were liberated by the style of Elvis Presley and that of new Western dances. Young Soviet men took up the gait of American actors, thrusting their legs out from their hips like models on a catwalk. High heels changed how women walk everywhere. This provocative physicality was furthered by fashion: legs were emphasized by narrow pants and progressively shortening skirts, while male undershirts were undone, revealing the chest.[55] The Americanization of bodily techniques, communicative gestures, forms of greeting and farewell, manners of sitting and walking – this became a global process, significant not only for Russia but all of Europe, comprising an informal youth culture. Student unrest and the sexual revolution were still a long way off, but teenaged characters, played by sixteen- or seventeen-year-olds, were for the most part shown on screen embroiled in conflict with adults. Their alternative body language was further accentuated by the contrast between their thin, flexible, fragile bodies and the corpulent, athletic bodies of the older generation. In reality, there was nowhere to accommodate them (neither discos, clubs, nor cafes); hence their field of activity was the city. Their bodily techniques were adapted for the cityscape, but at the same time were presented as 'elemental' and 'natural.'

Brigitte Bardot introduced this new type into European cinema, where it was initially mitigated by the genre of comedy. The provocation was felt much more sharply in the melodrama *And God Created Woman* (*Et Dieu créa la femme*, dir. Roger Vadim, 1956). This child of nature, a problem child having grown up without parents or supervision among 'wild animal' friends, is possessed of a heightened sensualism and sense of her own body. All of her poses have an 'unaffected animalism.' She has the rhythmic, elastic gait of a fashion model or dancer, but walks barefoot on asphalt, sits on a table, lies on the floor during a decorous grown-up cocktail party, eats with her hands, licks her fingers, rolls in the sand. Her every movement and bodily habit is perceived as provocatively erotic: riding a bicycle, her manner of dancing, sitting, lying. The plasticity of James Dean, his cat-like gait, his dangerous stunts, were equally striking. He made jumping from a train at top speed look easy, but a similar trick cost the Dean-imitating Zbigniew Cybulski his life.

In Russia, too, young movie characters ceased following the code of 'cultured' and 'appropriate' behaviour established on screen in the 1930s. In *Height* (*Vysota*, 1957), the liberation of the body language of the young workers (Nikolai Rybnikov and Inna Makarova) is motivated in the plot by two circumstances: they grew up in orphanages (like Bardot's character in *And God Created Woman*) and lead a nomadic life beyond the norms of family structure. However, this 'homeless' freedom from 'norms' comes across as unaffectedly natural.

The main characters are high-riggers by trade, and so their working movements are marked by a swaggering ease, their bodies endowed with acrobatic adroitness. Into the workplace film is thus introduced the body of a character from a musical or circus act. During high installations, they perform dangerous stunts, clambering up sheer surfaces, tap-dancing on narrow planks, sliding down cables, descending from balconies by rope. Their everyday gestures, too, are in marked contrast to the reserved norm of cultured behaviour on display in the early 1950s. The workers eat lying down, sit in a lounging manner, open beer bottles with their teeth, and fight. But their crudeness and vulgarity are not presented as physiologically repulsive. Intimate conversation between the friends feature gestures different from those of tea-time orators of the 1950s, more mobile hands and palms.[56] A young woman takes on the mannerisms of a juvenile delinquent, smoking, greeting a young man with a broad, open-palm blow, riding piggyback on a friend, but this travesty of manners is now presented as flirty, provocative eroticism, of which the director is well aware and by which the male protagonist is aroused. She dances provocatively, bares her leg to take off a stocking, and walks barefoot through a city park, albeit for a different reason than that of Bardot's Juliette, whose 'natural' grace was hindered by constricting footwear – here the girl goes barefoot to save her shoes.

These emancipated mannerisms change toward the end of the movie as the main characters are re-educated, becoming more like the reserved members of the intelligentsia who are their teachers, a male engineer and a female doctor. The reining in of 'gestures' parallels the subduing of 'colour': in the end, Rybnikov's character is walking on crutches after an accident, and his girlfriend Katia (Inna Makarova) has exchanged her red-and-green clothes for a pastel palette and the white coat of a nurse; she stops smoking, learns to set a table, and starts drinking kefir from a glass rather than from the bottle.

Despite its traditional storyline of the disciplining of the anarchic body of a hooligan, the film made it clear that conceptions of poor manners and undue familiarity were changing; these were now evaluated not as vulgarity, but 'openness,' whereas formerly highly valued propriety and good manners (as signified by legs pressed together, arms folded or pressed against the body, the body tensed) now signified 'closedness,' constraint, a personality beset with complexes.

In *The Girls* appears a clumsy teenager, again the ill-mannered product of an orphanage, a tomboy with neither bust nor hips, her hair in rat-tails. The actress, Nadezhda Rumiantseva, took her cue from the clowning of Giulietta Masina, who in Fellini's *La Strada* (1956) had fired the imagination of Soviet filmmakers. In the film, Rumiantseva is bereft of 'old-fashioned' femininity – she does not know how to flirt or kiss, she engages in pillow fights, skips, and, like a clown, wears felt boots too big for her, stumbling and falling. The male contingent in the film is endowed with the chic of street toughs. These traditional cinematic masks – that of the clown and the street tough – are also encoded as 'authentic' and 'spontaneous.' Nikolai Rybnikov employed this bodily costume in every film; in *Spring on Zarechnaia Street*, his leather-coated steelworker character jumps from a moving car like James Dean from a train. Khutsiev pits against each other two kinds of bodies – the cultivated and the raw, which form the physiognomic basis of the re-education storyline. Workers do not wear jackets and ties; the proper dress code is reserved for the engineer. In the end, the street tough, his macho strut vanished, becomes an agile athlete with rhythmically moving arms.

Departure from the norms of plasticity is similarly motivated in *The Career of Dima Gorin,* in which high-riggers move along wires like tightrope-walkers. Aleksandr Dem'ianenko's character (also, incidentally, an orphan) plays an asexual 'overgrown adolescent' à la Jerry Lewis who, full of raging hormones, falls in love, like Lewis in *Artists and Models* (1955), with a girl from the 'comics.' He glues together his ideal of the beautiful woman with photos from *Sovetskii ekran,* creating her from Elizabeth Taylor (forehead and hair-do), Alla Larionova (mouth and chin), and the nose of Vsevolod Pudovkin as seen as the holy fool in *Ivan the Terrible.* The result is Tat'iana Koniukhova, whom Dem'ianenko discovers at a construction site in Siberia.

Protagonists of a new type were being introduced in the stories of Vasilii Aksenov and Anatolii Gladilin, the dramas of Viktor Rozov and Aleksei Arbuzov: 'star' children, 'little brothers,' runaway students, and teens who break their parents' polished furniture with Civil War–era sabres.[57] But the physiognomy and motility of these new protagonists was formed at the movies. A slew of films registered the new bodily techniques of young people, and the plot of many films amounted to roaming around Moscow; thus locomotion became the principal characteristic of the hero. Valentin Popov, Nikolai Gubenko, and Stanislav Liubshin create the characters of *I Am Twenty* (1961–4) with their gait. *The Cranes Are Flying* begins with a stroll through a completely empty downtown at dawn. In *I Walk around Moscow* (*Ia shagaiu po Moskve,* 1964), Nikita Mikhalkov introduced the walk of the sixteen-year-old flâneur: rolling, gawking, taking one's time. Teens were slouch-backed and long- and floppy-armed. Similarly relaxed was their 'open' style of sitting: slouched, knees apart, leaning on their elbows. Even soldiers walked with a rolling gait, their pace in no way distinct from that of civilians. In *I Am Twenty,* there is no marching, even at a 1 May demonstration, which proves utterly loose and undisciplined; everyone is running and laughing, unable and unwilling to keep in step and maintain ranks. Styles of walking were becoming 'thematized,' assimilated, differentiated. Marlen Khutsiev observes the gait of a professional fashion model (although in the plot of the film she is given village roots), while characters in his *July Rain* (1966) observe foreign diplomats getting out of cars and walking. All the signifiers of liberation – swinging arms, chewing while walking, leaning against a wall or doorframe, sitting on the arm of a chair dangling one's legs – these were imparted to young, flexible, slender, relaxed, undisciplined bodies. This conferred grace, unaffectedness, and lightness upon bodily techniques that might otherwise be perceived as 'uncultured' and vulgar.

With such changes came a simultaneous transformation in the expression of affects. Kira Muratova devoted lengthy observation to the automatic, erroneous, unconscious gestures of her characters and of documentary-style figures 'accidentally' wandering into frame, among whom were many amateurs and country people with behavioural styles differing from 'the norm' (*Brief Encounters* [*Korotkie vstrechi*], 1967). Attention to these symptomatic gestures, to the fingers, which drummed upon tables, crumpled biscuits, traced lines on plates – expressions of the instinctive unconscious – went hand-in-hand with attention to the crippled body: the legless, armless, blind, deformed, or clumsy move differently. The erotic was stifled. Violence and aggression were suppressed or erased in melancholy. Affects were not translated into body language.

For the first time, members of the intelligentsia appeared on the screen not as negative characters, and their confirmation in the lead role completely eclipsed the body language of the common man. On the screen, the gestural reticence of the typical *intelligent* became characteristic of all social strata at all times: Hamlet, a Russian prince, a provincial teacher, a peasant, a soldier, and a physicist living in the capital all had one and the same body language – that of Innokentii Smoktunovskii. The voice and manner of speaking were subject to a similar physiognomic change. Voices of movie characters in the 1930s and 1940s had been formed according to the requirements of articulate theatrical pronunciation. Their melodic way of speaking (almost singing the dialogue) was supported by the 'voice of Soviet history,' a 'disembodied voice' of Iurii Levitan, whose low baritone was likened to a military trumpet.

The voice, which has its own physiognomy, models not only character, but also the socio-historical body, defining, moreover, the 'temperature' of a culture. From descriptions of the effect of Aleksandr Blok's emotionless, 'blank,' monotone voice, we can understand what a break with the past his 'non-tenor' declamatory style signified.[58] Such a break was felt even more sharply in the late 1950s, when after two decades of 'shouters' with well-trained, sonorous, distinct voices marked by clarity of diction, an abundance of uniform, rhythmic accents, dramatic rising and falling of intonation, vibrato, and rich modulation – there appeared the weak (bordering on professionally unsuitable), muffled, cracking, androgynous, à-la-Marlon-Brando voice of Innokentii Smoktunovskii, with its unstable intonations, gaps, and arrhythmic pauses.[59] His 'ordinary' hero took the right to speak in a way of a former leader and its screen double with low, intimate, quiet voice.

Zastava Il'icha (Marlen Khutsiev, 1962, 1964)

The Thaw's first cases of censorship concerned two films about young people starting out in life: Mikhail Shveitser's *The Tight Knot* (*Tugoi uzel*, 1956) and Khutsiev's *Il'ich's Gate* (*Zastava Il'icha*), which drew Khrushchev's ire:

> Our remarkable young people are not represented in the movie, not even by its most positive characters – the three young workers, who are shown such that they don't know how to live or what to strive for.... No, society cannot rely on such people – they're not fighters; they're not world-changers. These are morally feeble, prematurely aged young people without lofty goals or callings in life.... The filmmakers were unable to carry out their intention of condemning idlers and spongers. They should have branded and pilloried these degenerates and renegades, but lacked the necessary civic courage and rage.[60]

After this, Khutsiev spent two years making changes to the film and in 1964 released an abridged version of it entitled *I Am Twenty*, which was shown at Venice. Western critics could not understand what was subversive or provocative about the film – a question that remained even after Khutsiev in 1987–8 restored the original version of the film and presented it at the Locarno Film Festival. Situations understood by the director as confrontations with 'Stalinists' – a young engineer's conflict with his boss, the young protagonist's discussions with his girlfriend's father – were so nebulous as to be accessible only to insiders. In European movies, teenagers and young men stole cars, fired weapons at policemen, and smuggled drugs. In the Moscow version, they went to work, courageous young men who just happened to be suffused with a longing, which even they themselves could not articulate, for something incomprehensible. But a protagonist's unverbalized physiognomic break, and the appearance of metaphysical longing in a film about everyday life – these were new, despite not being translated into narrative or action. It was precisely these 'physiognomic' aberrations, markers of an elusive 'something else,' that drew sharp reactions from two directors of the older generation, Sergei Gerasimov and Mark Donskoi, in discussions of the film:

> The trouble here, as I see it, is not, as some here have been saying, that the main character is unappealing; the trouble, rather, is a matter of *vocabulary*, *phonetics*, and *behavioural plasticity*.... The ones doing all this walking around are still just losers.... They even smoke like losers.... You took the *emaciated* Tarkovskii – he looks like he'd fall down if you spit on him – and you specially picked Voznesenskii. You didn't even pick angry young men.... You have to say: 'Listen, you boys who pity me – get away from me, I myself know what to do!... Along with my comrades, teachers, and the company and party organization chairmen, I understand what's what!'[61]

Despite the fact that the film's main character is close in appearance to the traditional physiognomy of the 'fine young man' – and to increase this impression, the actor's hair was dyed blond, as was done with Aleksandr Beliavskii in *Into the Storm*, visually 'whitening' him as a counterweight to the 'infernal' brunette Lanovoi – his actions are not such as had previously defined the status of hero, nor is he able to mark out a new, independent personality, which Thaw cinema had relegated to the old, collective acts of initiation – revolution and war. The strong, independent personality was introduced into the films of this time only in amended form. Its extraordinariness is an exception, and so the character displaying this personality was either made a criminal or relegated to the category of minor mental pathology (Vasilii Shukshin's 'odd-ball' heroes in his series of films beginning with *There Is Such a Lad* (*Zhivet takoi paren'*, 1964) or a pathology explained by the plot (*Ivan's Childhood*). Perhaps only two directors – Andrei Tarkovskii and Sergei Paradzhanov – rejected these palliatives and mitigating factors in the course of affirming individuality on the Russian screen, mounting a radical defence of art as an autonomous sphere of *authorship*. This position is not traditional in the peculiar construct that is Soviet cinema; it is rather close to that of Western Europe, and that is perhaps why, of all Russian directors, these two became the best known outside the USSR.

Auteur Cinema and National Tradition

Both Paradzhanov and Tarkovskii made names for themselves with films that sought to establish a place for the individual within national or mythologized-national tradition. It is at this time that, perhaps for the first time in the history of the Soviet national school, true auteur cinema was born.

By his very behavioural model, Paradzhanov created a new image of the independent eccentric: the homosexual, the blasphemer, the aesthete, the labour camp prisoner. Beginning with *Shadows of Forgotten Ancestors* (*Teni zabytykh predkov*, Ukraine, 1964), and continuing with *The Colour of Pomegranates* (*Tsvet granata*; Armenia, 1969) and *The Legend of the Suram Fortress* (*Legenda Suramskoi kreposti*; Georgia, 1984), Paradzhanov established a peculiarly archaic style that developed autonomously as *his own*, Paradzhanov's. His camera is emphatically immobile; space in the frame is flat, composition frontal and perspectiveless; the actors' gestures are ritualized; the stringently selected range of colours relies on solid red, blue, yellow, and black. Paradzhanov would seem to have gotten by without montage: every shot is constructed and displayed like a picture, requiring close examination, as if, against all the laws of the cinema, the viewer is not to associate one shot with another, but rather, as with painting, to plunge into the depths of a flat space.[62] Everything in his shots is laden with meaning: the symbolism of colour, of costume, of the poetic texts his films are based upon, the mysterious, exotic rituality of the actors' movements. All these details, which seem symbolic, are to be decoded and yet *cannot be*, because their meaning has been freely invented by the director himself, and he changed it just as freely from film to film. In Paradzhanov's compositions, aestheticized beauty would seem to be paramount, and yet his non-narrative, stylizedly naive film-making style is able to convey the tragic and philosophical themes of death and sacrifice, loss of faith and exile, loss of love and memory. All of Paradzhanov's films end on the threshold of death and are suffused with a tragic world view standing in marked contrast to the decorative, sensuously perceived, and very fragile beauty of his 'textile' film-world.

The emphatically asserted conception of art as the form and even the plot of Paradzhanov's first auteur film, *Shadows of Forgotten Ancestors* (1964), marked a programmatic break with Soviet tradition. A *hutsul* loses his beloved and, after her death, all connection with life. Paradzhanov examines that point of departure so crucial for 1960s cinema – the relationship between the individual and the general – on a new level: the individual breaks all ties with his own kind, and it is at this moment that Paradzhanov the artist discovers his individual language. Russian film scholar Irina Izvolova interprets this transition from the ritual and canon of others to a form of one's own as the transition from mythological to Christian (hence individual) thinking.[63] But it can also be understood as the discovery of one's own language and *gaze* by means of a peculiarly tactile sense of vision, constituted in Paradzhanov's films by colour and a particular sense of space.

Andrei Tarkovskii managed to assert his conception of the auteur film within the traditional storyline of an individual facing a choice – the cause of torment for the main characters of all of his movies, from *Andrei Rublev* (1966–71) to *Nostalgia* (1983) and *The Sacrifice* (*Offret*, 1986) (the latter two filmed after his emigration). His artist-characters, Rublev and Boriska, are entirely in keeping with all the physiognomic adjustments undergone by contemporary protagonists, including the absence of verbalization: Rublev falls silent for seven years, Boriska stutters. Silence is the condition of their non-verbal articulation within the plot. Tarkovskii's basic conflict, not only with Goskino authorities, but also with the tradition of 'Soviet cinema' itself, stemmed from his assertion of the right to an individual viewpoint unsupported by any authority, as well as the right to autonomy in his art, which constituted a value in itself. Describing this conflict in terms of ideological or aesthetic deviation would not do it justice. It is significant that Sergei Gerasimov, one of the leading directors of the 1930s, characterized this 'generational' conflict as ethical rather than aesthetic: 'This is an overestimation of one's own personality, a sense of exceptionalism regarding oneself, i.e., "I am a phenomenon, and as such it is within my power to form judgments unchecked even by the conscience of the people, by the people's reason; I am above the people." ... This is a desire to look down from hastily conquered heights, to take on the mantle of genius, to prophesy like the Pythian oracle. It is a position completely at odds with our communist morality.'[64]

In his later book *Sculpting in Time*, Tarkovskii contemplates not cinema, art, and aesthetics so much as the relationship between individuality and generality, freedom and conscience, the material and the eternal. He sees the twentieth century as an epoch – drawing to a close – of Grand Inquisitors haunted by the idea of making human society ever more fair, offering ever newer means of saving the world. This idea of common salvation must (in the view of these Grand Inquisitors) take precedence over the thoughts and actions of the loner, who gradually loses his or her ability to think and feel; world development is a collective effort. Against this view, in all his films, Tarkovskii posits the concept of the *individual* effort, upon which depend history, the progress or regress of civilization, and even, in a mystical way, the fate of the world itself, as in *The Sacrifice*. However, in this film, in order to save the world from global catastrophe, the main character must sacrifice his *individual* hypostases – his voice, his reason, his home.

Tarkovskii's conception of art is that it is to give form to transient individual experience, dreams, memories, and sensations; hence his most programmatic film, perhaps, is *The Mirror* (*Zerkalo*). It is Soviet cinema's *first* (1974) autobiographical film, the idea of which struck even Tarkovskii's perennial cinematographer Vadim Iusov as beneath the generally accepted standard of art and fit only for 8 mm home movies.

Tarkovskii's subjectivity closely aligned him to Western auteur cinema. On the other hand, he fit the stereotype of the mysterious, metaphysical, arcane Russian soul – not because of brief montage phrases, like in his time Eisenstein, who with this method solidified outside Russia the stereotype of the 'divided Slavic soul,' but rather because of his long, tedious sequence shots, in which orientation between right and left is lost, actors spin around the camera and the camera around actors, and contrasts are created, not via the splicing of shots, but by depth and proximity, alterations in scale and in warm versus cold lighting, slow-motion sustained by a barely perceptible time lag, and elliptical leaps between historical layers of culture.

We find this same aggressive defence of subjective experience in the films of Kira Muratova, who in the genre of the 'provincial melodrama' (*Brief Encounters* [*Korotkie vstrechi*, 1967] and *A Long Goodbye* [*Dolgie provody*, 1971] put forward the provocatively and manneristically aestheticized 'banal' as the antipode of the universal. She discovered a form of cinematographic individualism in the reconstruction of erased historical memory – memory, that is, of history *intimately* perceived, 'generally' forgotten and restored in private memory only in details, without an integrating historical 'grand meaning.'

Directors meanwhile perceived themselves in the tradition of the Russian artist as teacher unto the nation, as messiah. This lent their art, and a given film, a completely different axiological weight. The framework of autonomous art, within which Paradzhanov happily ensconced himself, was too narrow for this role.

The Thaw began with a remarkable expansion of filmmaking, and its end was signalled by the banning of numerous films already made. But the Thaw resulted in the splintering of the concept of Soviet cinema, which now included very disparate phenomena: large-scale directorial projects, socially engaged films, Bildungsromans, auteur cinema, and a substantial number of average, little-known Soviet melodramas, which, however, unlike the works of Tarkovskii or Bondarchuk, remain wildly popular in Russia.[65]

Thaw cinema began by rejecting the allegories of Stalinist filmmaking, which depicted visions of the future, asserting instead a sweaty prose of the everyday, and hallucinations and dreams of a lost past. From the viewpoint of perestroika, which initially defined itself as the logical continuation of the Thaw, the efforts and achievements of this art were evaluated in different ways. Vail' and Genis see in this period the rise of the romantic utopian, full of false hopes that sacrificed art in the name of social utility. Russian film historians, the authors of a two-volume study of Thaw cinema, see this as a time of departure from traditional norms of behaviour, and of the birth of a new, sober, post-socialist man. Although in my view the Thaw was not marked by any breakdown of Soviet cinema's meta-narrative per se, Evgenii Margolit notes de-ritualization,[66] while Igor Smirnov emphasizes the discovery of the semiotic nature of cinematic representation as a departure from naive conceptions about its 'reality.'[67] From today's standpoint, this cinema strikes me as an updated version of the engaged art of socialist realism, realized with a documentary faith in reality, as well as a few eruptions of metaphysical subjectivity. But, within these old narratives, the wealth of unverbalized detail physiognomically captured by these films served to adjust social roles and equip protagonists with techniques of 'private practice,' allowing them to turn off the main thoroughfares onto side streets.

Translated by Avram Brown

NOTES

1 It is significant that cinema does not play a central role in Petr Vail' and Aleksandr Genis's book *60-e: mir sovetskogo cheloveka* (1988; 1996), serving rather as part of the general 'atmosphere.' The choice of films mentioned, however, is telling: four Stalin-era comedies (*Cossacks of the Kuban, Hectic Days* [*Goriachie denechki*], *The Rich Bride* [*Bogataia nevesta*], *Seekers of Happiness* [*Iskateli schast'ia*]) are weighed against four Thaw films (*Ballad of a Solder, Ivan's Childhood, I Walk around Moscow, Nine Days in One Year*), as well as two box office record-setters (*The Hussar's Ballad* [*Gusarskaia ballada*], and *Operation ЫI*) and a film by Ingmar Bergman, *Wild Strawberries* – a work constructed around the inner monologue of an aging intellectual who, having lost his connection to the present, seeks a return to the past.

2 A discussion of neo-realism took place in *Iskusstvo kino* 1 (1957) and continued in subsequent issues. In 1961, Inna Solov'eva's *Italian Neo-Realism 1945–1960* came out in Moscow, while characters in Anatolii Efros's *Leap Year* (1961) watch *The Bicycle Thief.* In an interview with Viktor Bozhovich (*Kinematograf ottepeli: Dokumenty i svidetel'stva*, ed. Valerii Fomin [Moscow, 1998], 5), Marlen Khutsiev likened this film's effect on him to the 'peal of a bell.' However, the system of oppositions used to describe neo-realism was also used to describe Thaw-era cinema: 'varnishing' vs 'life without embellishment,' 'artificiality' vs 'documentalism,' 'window-dressing' vs 'real life,' the 'false values of ideology' (fascism) vs the 'simple values of life.' See Vladimir Semerchuk, 'Slova velikie i prostye. Kinematograf ottepeli v zerkale kinokritiki,' in *Kinematograf ottepeli. Kniga vtoraia*, ed. Vitalii Troianovskii (Moscow, 2002), 71.

3 In Europe and America, visual and acoustic experience was drastically altered by the circulation of new films, pictures, sounds, and bodies. See Jean Améry, *Geburt der Gegenwart. Gestalten und Gestaltungen der westlichen Zivilisation seit Kriegsende* (Open und Freiburg im Breisgau, 1961); Jean-Pierre Bertin-Maghit, *Les cinémas européens des années cinquante* (Paris, 2000); Pierre Sorlin, *European Cinemas, European Societies: 1939–1990* (London, 1991).

4 Joseph Brodsky, 'Spoils of War,' in his *On Grief and Reason* (New York, 1995), 8–9.

5 See Brodsky: 'I suppose my generation was the most attentive audience for all that pre- and postwar dream factories' production. Some of us became, for a while, avid cineastes, but perhaps for a different set of reasons than our counterparts in the West. For us, films were the only opportunity to see the West. Quite oblivious of the action itself, in every frame we tried to discern the contents of the street or of an apartment, the dashboard of the

hero's car, the types of clothes worn by heroines, the sense of space, the layout of the place they were operating in.' *On Grief and Reason*, 12.

6 Gilbert Cohen-Séat, *Problèmes actuels du cinéma et de l'information visuelle* (Paris, 1959).

7 *Khrushchev Remembers*, ed. and trans. Strobe Talbott (Boston, 1970), 298.

8 The history of the bannings of notable films of this period can be traced through key documents (discussions, internal reviews, and denunciations) published by Valerii Fomin. See Fomin, *Polka. Dokumenty. Svidetel'stva. Kommentarii* (Moscow, 1992); Fomin, *Zapreshchennye fil'my. Dokumenty. Svidetel'stva. Kommentarii*, vol. 2 (Moscow, 1993); and Vitalii Troianovskii, ed., *Kinematograf ottepeli: Dokumenty i svidetel'stva.* Troianovskii, ed., *Kinematograf ottepeli. Kniga pervaia* (Moscow, 1996); and Troianovskii, ed., *Kinematograf ottepeli. Kniga vtoraia (Moscow, 2002)* provide detailed analysis of new narratives and characters and their reception in contemporary criticism. This is also the focus of Josephine Woll, *Real Images: Soviet Cinema and the Thaw* (London, 2000). The publication of documents from the archive of the Central Committee (E.S. Afanas'eva and V. Iu. Afiani, eds., *Apparat TsK i kul'tura: 1953–1957. Dokumenty* [Moscow, 2001]) has also proved quite valuable. Taken together, these works trace the secret, private, and open history of the cinematic Thaw. Only a few articles have dealt with non-verbal criteria; see, for instance, Irina Izvolova's analysis of spatial distortion in Thaw-era films, 'Drugoe prostranstvo,' in Troianovskii, *Kinematograf ottepeli. Kniga pervaia, 77–98.*

9 This is discussed by Claude Sautet in a final, fifteen-hour interview conducted by N.T. Binh and Dominique Raburdin for their film *Claude Sautet ou La magie invisible* (France, 2002). Japanese cinema in its turn associated rain in the 1950s not only with actual climate conditions, but also with a new semantic richness – it suggested the washing away of radioactive dust after the bombings of Hiroshima and Nagasaki. German radio plays, for instance, were replete with this motif; see Justus Fetscher, 'Radioaktivität. Atomgefahr und Sendebewußtsein im Rundfunk der 1950er Jahre,' in *Navigation. Zeitschrift für Medien und Kulturwissenschaften Medieninnovationen und Medienkonzepte. 1950–2000* (Siegen, 2006), 143–57.

10 G. Aleksandrov, 'Nasha pravda iasna,' *Literaturnaia gazeta*, 14 March 1963.

11 An average feature film took a year to make. *The Dragonfly* (*Strekoza*, 1955) took as many as 566 days. Troianovskii, *Kinematograf ottepeli. Materialy*, 68.

12 In the case of Mosfilm, these innovations coincided with Ivan Pyr'ev's appointment (15 October 1954) to head the studio, where Pyr'ev proved an energetic reformer. Key in this regard was the reorganization of Mosfilm in March 1959 into three associations, each of which was granted wide latitude

in commissioning and accepting screenplays, hiring directors, and starting up film production. Troianovskii, *Kinematograf ottepeli. Kniga vtoraia*, 384–448.

13 In the opinion of Vladimir Baskakov, who at the time occupied a rather lofty position in the cinematic hierarchy (deputy chairman of the USSR Council of Ministers Committee on Cinematography), Khrushchev's removal had no effect on Soviet cinema or filmmakers. Baskakov, '"Serebrianyi vek" sovetskogo kino,' in Troianovskii, *Kinematograf ottepeli. Kniga vtoraia*, 176–8. From 1966 to 1969, a great variety of films fell victim to censorship, films offering alternative views of the revolution (*Commissar*, 1968; *Intervention* [*Interventsiia*], 1968), Russian history (*Andrei Rublev*, 1966–9), the Russian countryside (*The Story of Asia Kliachina* [*Istoriia Asi Kliachinoi*], 1966), young people (*To Love* [*Liubit'*], 1969), and classic Russian literature (*An Ugly Story* [*Skvernyi anekdot*], 1966).

14 Just as many Indian and African directors received their cinematic education in Paris or London, directors from these Soviet republics came to Moscow to study the narratives and visual language of Russian and European cinema, going on to make films in a peculiar mix of national and 'global' tradition. See Oksana Bulgakowa, 'Der Film der Tauwetterperiode (1954–1968),' in *Geschichte des sowjetischen und russischen Films*, ed. Christine Engel (Stuttgart, 1999), 109–81.

15 Post-war demographic, social, and cultural change (the return of the forty-two-hour work week and two-week vacation, the shift to the suburbs, rising income) led to changes in popular attitudes toward free time. Expensive, active hobbies cut into the cheaper and more passive pastime of moviegoing, and the number of moviegoers fell sharply. Having lost their monopoly on distribution rights and theatre ownership, studios were forced to change strategy. See Douglas Gomery, *The Hollywood Studio System: A History* (London, 2006); Gomery, *Shared Pleasures* (Madison, 1992).

16 In 1945, about 8 per cent of Hollywood films were shot in colour; by 1955, this figure had risen to 50 per cent. Geoffrey Nowell-Smith, ed., *An Oxford History of World Cinema* (Oxford, 1996), 266.

17 The structure and governance of the film industry once again underwent new institution-building. In 1948, the Main Cinematography Administration became a ministry; in March 1953, it lost its autonomous status and became a section of the Ministry of Culture; in 1963, it was separated to form the autonomous agency Goskino, under the immediate supervision of the Central Committee.

18 *Sovetskie khudozhestvennye fil'my: Annotirovannyi katalog*, 5 vols. (Moscow, 1961), vol. 3.

19 Cultural investment increased, from 54 million rubles in 1950 to 501 million in 1968. *Narodnoe khoziastvo SSSR. Statisticheskii ezhegodnik* (Moscow, 1971), 733. (Subsequent references indicate years of publication only.) On cuts in movie budgets, see Troianovskii, *Kinematograf ottepeli. Materialy,* 64. In 1959, the Soviet Union had twenty studios and forty-one film lots built in the 1920s and 1930s. A decision was adopted in July 1959 to modernize these studios and build new ones. By 1967, the number of film lots had increased to sixty-four, and Kirghizia and Moldavia, formerly lacking feature film facilities, saw the making of their first movies. *Istoriia sovetskogo kino,* in 4 vols. (Moscow: Iskusstvo, 1978) 4:19.

20 *Ekran* (Moscow, 1970), 73.

21 In 1956, there were 63,300 movie theatres in the USSR; in 1966, 149,700 (including 127,100 in rural areas); by 1968, the number had increased to 155,000. In 1966, 21,000 theatres were equipped for anamorphic (widescreen) projection; in 1970, 52,000. *Narodnoe khoziastvo SSSR* (1956), 165, 264; *Narodnoe khoziastvo SSSR* (1971), 733.

22 Roughly 5,200 movies from the *Reichsfilmarchiv* – not only German ones, but also Italian, French, and American (Disney productions and Hollywood musicals) – were brought to Russia as war trophies, and some of these went into Soviet release. Soviet movie theatres were showing nineteen foreign films in 1949; by 1956, their number – including movies from Austria, Belgium, East Germany, Greece, India, Italy, Japan, Mexico, and West Germany – had increased to seventy-nine. *Ezhegodnik kino* (Moscow, 1957), 73–128. From 1969 on, there were regularly ninety-nine foreign films in release, half of them from Eastern Europe.

23 In 1956, 2.812 billion tickets were sold; in 1966, 4.192, and in 1968, 4.717. *Narodnoe khoziastvo SSSR* (1971), 677. The increase in moviegoing led to greater revenue, more than making up for low ticket prices. *Narodnoe khoziastvo SSSR* (1986), 529.

24 *Ekran,* 73; *Ezhegodnik kino* (1957), 73; Troianovskii, *Kinematograf ottepeli. Materialy,* 90.

25 The first plenum of the Organizing Committee took place in 1957; the Union was established in 1965.

26 Mikhail Romm, *Ustnye rasskazy* (Moscow, 1991). The atmosphere surrounding Thaw-era speeches is well conveyed in 'Iz istorii odnogo vystupleniia. Vystuplenie v VTO osen'iu 1962,' *Iskusstvo kino* 9 (1995): 87–101; on reaction to this speech, see Troianovskii, *Kinematograf ottepeli. Materialy, 314–335.*

27 Troianovskii, *Kinematograf ottepeli. Kniga pervaia,* 175.

28 1956 saw the release of the first Soviet widescreen film (with its own anamorphic technology patent), *Il'ia Muromets,* in which the legendary hero

came to life amid impressive special effects and mass battle scenes; in 1957, Roman Karmen made the first Soviet Cinerama feature, *Broad Is My Native Land* [*Shiroka strana moia …*]; in 1960, Iuliia Solntseva completed the first 70-mm Soviet film with stereo sound, the war epic *Chronicle of Flaming Years*).

29 Troianovskii, *Kinematograf ottepeli. Materialy*, 64.

30 Viktor Demin, *Fil'm bez intrigi* (Moscow, 1966).

31 André Bazin's *Qu'est ce que le cinema?* (1958), which proposed a new aesthetics of cinematic realism, was published in Moscow by Iskusstvo in 1972; Siegfried Kracauer's *Theory of Film: The Redemption of Physical Reality* (1960) was published in Moscow in 1974.

32 Tarkovskii's essay of this title appeared in *Voprosy kinoiskusstva* 4 (1967): 69–79; the director later gave this title to a book first published by Ullstein (Berlin, 1984) and subsequently in English as Andrey Tarkovsky, *Sculpting in Time: Reflections on the Cinema*, trans. Kitty Hunter-Blair (London, 1989).

33 Marlen Khutsiev and Feliks Mironer, 'Oblik geroia,' *Iskusstvo kino* 1 (1957): 128.

34 François Truffaut, 'Faiblesses et qualités des films soviétiques,' *Arts*, 14 December 1955.

35 These figures were published in *Iskusstvo kino* and *Sovetskii ekran*; Soviet box office statistics in *Entsiklopediia kino Kirilla i Mefodiia* (CD ROM, 2003).

36 No Soviet movie had ever sold so many tickets; in the preceding five years, 32–35 million had been considered the upper limit. *Iskusstvo kino* 4 (1957): 151.

37 Only in 1966 was this record broken by *Operation Ы and Other Adventures of Shurik* (69.6 million tickets sold).

38 *Literaturnaia gazeta*, 20 January 1962.

39 Dunia Smirnova, 'Chelovek-amfibiia,' *Seans* 8 (1993); cited from http://www.russiancinema.ru/template.php?dept_id=15&e_dept_id=2&text_element_id=7197.

40 On horror and sci-fi movies in the new formats, see ed. Peter Lev, ed., *History of the American Cinema*. Vol. 7, *The Fifties: Transforming the Screen, 1950–1959* (New York, 2000), 170–85.

41 Oksana Bulgakowa, 'Wer hat Angst vor wem – Phobien in den Filmen der fünfziger Jahre,' in *Politics of Fear in the Cold War*, ed. Bernd Greiner, 347–74 (Hamburg, 2009).

42 The most popular 70-mm 3-D movie, however, with 37.6 million tickets sold, was *The Mysterious Monk* (*Tainstvennyi monakh*, 1968), a traditional thriller about Reds and Whites disguised as monks in a gothic monastery.

43 Pavel Klushantsev made *Storm Planet* [*Planeta bur'*] at the popular science film studio Lennauchfil'm. On Soviet science-fiction cinema, see Evgenii

Kharitonov and Andrei Shcherbak-Zhukov, *Na ekrane – chudo. Otechestvennaia kinofantastika i kinoskazka 1909–2002* (Moscow, 2003); Mathias Schwartz, *'Erfindung des Kosmos. Zur sowjetischen Zukunftsromane und populärwissenschaftlichen Publizistik vom Sputnikflug bis zum Ende der Tauwetterzeit* (Berlin 2003).

44 We demonstrate some of these techniques in our documentary *Stalin – eine Mosfilmproduktion* (WDR, 1993; dir. Enno Patalas, Oksana Bulgakowa, and Frieda Grafe). Some of the figures eradicated from memory appeared once again in movies: Grigorii Zinov'ev in Lev Kulidzhanov and Emmanuil Kazakevich's *The Blue Notebook* (*Siniaia tetrad',* 1964), Iakov Bliumkin and Mariia Spiridonova in *The Sixth of July* (*Shestoe iiulia,* 1968). But neither Trotskii nor Bukharin could be shown.

45 *L'Unita,* 9 October 1963. For Sartre's response, see Anetta Sandler, ed., *Mir i fil'my Andreia Tarkovskogo. Razmyshleniia. Issledovaniia. Vospominaniia. Pis'ma* (Moscow, 1991), 11–16, 17.

46 Aleksandr Stolper's *Wait for Me* (1944), featuring a similar plot but with a happy ending, forms part of the background of Soviet critics' reception of Kalatozov's film.

47 'Kinostudiia v 1957 g.,' *Iskusstvo kino* 2 (1957): 10; V. Surin, 'Problemy kinoiskusstva nashikh dnei,' *Iskusstvo kino* 2 (1957): 61.

48 Maia Turovskaia, 'Da i net,' *Iskusstvo kino* 12 (1957): 18.

49 Almost all Soviet critics saw these dramatic oddities as lapses and mistakes; a great deal was similarly written about Urusevskii's camerawork. 'Letiat zhuravli,' *Iskusstvo kino* 12 (1957): 5–26.

50 Even in an 'old' movie like *Certificate of Maturity,* Young Communists were already modelling themselves after Lermontov's Demon, Turgenev's Bazarov, and Pushkin's Tat'iana.

51 Such was Eisenstein's rather precise definition of the style of his pupil Pyr'ev's black-and-white films. Sergei Eisenstein, 'Ob Ivane Pyr'eve,' in Eisenstein, *Izbrannye proizvedeniia v shesti tomakh* (Moscow, 1963), 5:455.

52 Oksana Bulgakowa and Dietmar Hochmuth, eds., *Der Krieg gegen die Sowjetunion* (Berlin, 1992), 61–71.

53 However, the folkloric nature of the hero's absurd tribulation (demonstrating fortitude in drinking), and at the same time his Russian identity, were perhaps accessible only to Russian viewers.

54 The phenomena of *shtatniki* and *stiliagi* ('Americans' and 'hipsters'), who turned Gor'kii Street into 'Broadway,' are well known. Brodsky describes how for years he sought to imitate the jutting chin and independently arching left eyebrow of Errol Flynn, whose photo he had bought upon leaving a movie theatre. Brodsky, 'Spoils of War,' 10.

55 *Krokodil* ran caricatures of drug addicts dancing to boogie-woogie and rock-

and-roll; and too-tight pants were torn during *druzhina* (volunteer militia) raids upon hipsters; but the new fashion could not be stopped.

56 In *The Cranes Are Flying*, two Young Communists representing the factory committee come to bid farewell to the hero departing for the front; reciting the farewell, they accompany their words with the rhythmic gestures of an orator. The father, an old surgeon, stops them, mimicking their oratorical gesticulations, and suggests they shift to a different form of social intercourse – a meal – and raise their hands in a toast.

57 These stories and plays were adapted for the screen: Aleksandr Zarkhi turned Aksenov's *A Ticket to the Stars* (*Zvezdnyi bilet*) into *My Younger Brother* (*Moi mladshii brat*, 1962), while Aleksei Sakharov filmed his *Colleagues* (*Kollegi*, 1962); Anatolii Efros and Georgii Natanson adapted Viktor Rozov's play *A Noisy Day* (*Shumnyi den'*, 1961). It was not, however, these adaptations that became the most striking expressions of youth culture, but rather the films based on original screenplays by Gennadii Shpalikov, Evgenii Grigor'ev, and Anatolii Grebnev: *I Am Twenty* (1961/4), *I Walk around Moscow* (1964), and *Three Days in the Life of Viktor Chernyshev* (*Tri dnia Viktora Chernysheva*, 1968).

58 Sergei Bernshtein, 'Esteticheskie predposylki teorii deklamatsii,' *Poetika* 3 (Leningrad, 1927), 24–44; Bernshtein, 'Golos Bloka,' *Blokovskii sbornik* 2 (Tartu, 1972): 454–525; Boris Eikhenbaum, 'O kamernoi deklamatsii' (1923), in his *O poezii*, 512–41 (Leningrad, 1969).

59 Oksana Bulgakowa, 'Tonbremsspuren. Film-Stimmen der 1950er Jahre. Marlon Brando und Innokentij Smoktunovskij,' in *Resonanz-Räume*, ed. Oksana Bulgakowa (Berlin, in press).

60 Khrushchev's speech, 8 March 1963. Troianovskii, *Kinematograf ottepeli. Materialy*, 163.

61 Mark Donskoi at the meeting of the Gor'kii Studio's Party Bureau and the Commission to Assist Agencies of Party-State Control, 13 May 1963. Artem Demenok, '"Zastava Il'icha" – urok istorii,' *Iskusstvo kino* 6 (1988): 114. This particular physiognomic note was struck also by Andrei Voznesenskii, who entitled a 1987 article (*Ogonek* 9 (1987), 11) 'My byli *toshchie* i uzhe togda nichego ne boialis'.'

62 Iurii Lotman points out this aspect of Paradzhanov's language in his discussion of the director's last film, *The Legend of the Suram Fortress*, but this poetics had already taken shape in *Shadows of Forgotten Ancestors*. Lotman, 'Novizna legendy,' *Iskusstvo kino* 5 (1987): 65.

63 Izvolova, 'Drugoe prostranstvo,' 97.

64 Demenok, '"Zastava Il'icha,"' 101–2. These formulations were reproduced almost verbatim in the verdict on *Andrei Rublev* drawn up for the Central Committee. Troianovskii, *Kinematograf ottepeli. Materialy*, 146–7.

65 In its first year of release, the average film *Officers* (*Ofitsery*, dir. Viktor Rogovoi, 1971) sold 53.4 million tickets without any particular advertising campaign, and in this sense could compete with one of the most popular genre films in the history of Soviet cinema, *Moscow Does Not Believe in Tears* (dir. Vladimir Men'shov, 1979; Academy Award, 1980), which sold 84.4 million tickets.

66 Evgenij Margolit, 'Kinematograf "ottepeli." K portretu fenomena,' *Kinovedcheskie zapiski* 61 (2002): 195–212.

67 Igor Smirnov, 'Mertvyi rai proshlogo: semioticheskoe kinoiskusstvo 1960-kh gg.', in Smirnov, *Videoriad. Istoricheskaia semantika kino*, 260–88 (Saint Petersburg, 2009).

12 Afterword: The Thaw in Retrospect

SHEILA FITZPATRICK

The contributors to this volume have presented the Thaw in many different aspects and specific contexts. In this afterword, I want to return to some of the themes of the editors' introduction, reflecting in particular on the Thaw as an event and the Thaw as myth.

Events in History

What constitutes an 'event' in history? The word is used very differently in various disciplines, and its equivalents in other languages carry a variety of divergent connotations. For physicists and anglophone philosophers, an event is a data point, a fact, a physical change not in itself carrying the purposive significance of an action. For the French, *évènements* are the multitude of things that happen in the world – lucky, calamitous, perhaps sensational. Chateaubriand saw the pages of history as a palimpsest, with new events inscribed on top of the old ones.[1] This understanding of events is central to Braudel's famous disdain for *histoire évènementielle* – the flashy, visible, but ultimately superficial history of political, military, and diplomatic happenings that he opposed (to their detriment) to the history of deep structures. 'Events are the ephemera of history: they pass across its stage like fireflies, hardly glimpsed before they settle back into darkness and as often as not into oblivion.'[2]

Russians, too, seem to have a sense of events as accidental rather than predictable (*zakonomernye*) happenings. A *sluchai* is not only ephemeral but distinguished by its *sluchainost'*;[3] a *proissshestvie* is defined as 'something that violates the normal order of things.'[4] *Sobytie* is the weightiest Russian word for event, used in connection with international affairs (*mezhdunarodnye sobytiia*), but even it leaves open the question of significance.[5]

To find people who take events seriously, you have to go to the Germans. *Ereignis* – a favourite word of Goethe as well as Nietzsche – goes naturally with adjectives like *world-historical* or *remarkable*.[6] Ranke often writes of *Hauptereignissen* and *Großen Weltereignissen*; his events – seldom exactly datable – are often historical turning points, opening and closing epochs. For Nietzsche, an event is something that is experienced and thought as significant rather than something that just happens.[7] Marx used it in a similar sense, often functionally as a synonym for revolution: the June insurrection of 1848 in Paris, for example, was 'the most colossal event [*Ereignis*] in the history of European civil war' (whereas subsequent political victories were so cheaply bought, in Marx's view, that he explicitly denied them the status of *Ereignisse*).[8]

The Thaw as Historical Event

If the Thaw is an event, evidently it's a Germanic rather than Gallic or Anglo-Saxon one: something experienced, perceived, or remembered as significant. But what, then, is the nature of this particular event? It is not readily datable (though, according to Ranke, that's not a problem), nor is it self-evident what smaller events are its constituent parts. As so often in Russian history, the phenomenon was first identified and named in a literary work: Ehrenburg's *Ottepel'* (1954).[9] Thaw, the beginning of spring, symbolizes the (still tentative) triumph of love and honesty over denial of feelings and hypocrisy. The book ends on a note of cautious optimism: things can change, miracles like nature's annual rebirth can happen.

There is no real-life event in Ehrenburg that solves the would-be lovers' problems and helps them choose love and authenticity; these things just happen, albeit miraculously, like spring. But spring happens every year, part of a regular seasonal cycle, so in some respects it's an odd metaphor for an *Ereignis*. Still, as a result of good timing or happenstance it captured the Soviet imagination, so it's worth reflecting on the various things the word *ottepel'* conveys.[10] First, thaw is a matter of what was rigid (frozen) becoming fluid (the frozen emotions of Ehrenburg's protagonists coming back to life). Second (not in Ehrenburg, but highly relevant to the subsequent attachment of the metaphor to an event), thaw is revelatory, removing layers of winter snow and ice to expose what lies beneath – new growth, but also rubbish, things that have to be cleaned up. Third (implicit in Ehrenburg), winter and spring, frozen and fluid states, are cyclical: in due course, the earth will freeze again.

Ehrenburg's novel was not a description or summation of a process; its title was simply appropriated in the second half of the 1950s to describe phenomena that some contemporaries regarded as significant and mutually linked. Since we are in the realm of myth, it's hard to decide whose articulation of the myth to rely on: there are near-contemporary versions, foreign versions, dissident versions, perestroika versions, and so on. I'll try to outline the main characteristics, noting divergences in version where appropriate. It is important to note that 'the Thaw' (*ottepel'*) is one of those terms that are usually used affirmatively, pointing to a phenomenon or process that the speaker approves (is anyone in favour of freezing?). If you are against the phenomenon or sceptical about it, you use another term – in effect, like Marx, denying it the status of an *Ereignis.*

There is a consensus in literature and memoirs that the Thaw was a time of hope, excited expectation of change, rebirth, enthusiasm. It was 'our time of awakening,' 'a magical era,' 'a heroic period,' as contemporaries later remembered it.[11] The remembered emotion is vividly conveyed in recollections of the first day of Moscow Youth Festival 1957 – shouting, singing, dancing, joining hands, an 'enchanted feeling,' a 'flow and flood of joy'[12] – whose euphoric quality is reminiscent of the way contemporaries described the February (1917) Revolution.[13] Something remarkable was happening, and Evtushenko was there to mythologize it, later portraying himself and his poet-tribune contemporaries as commandos (*desantniki*) from the twenty-first century.[14]

Desantniki aside, the Thaw is associated in all versions of the myth with relaxation of tension – a move away from rigidity and repression, exemplified by the deconstruction of the Gulag and relaxation of controls on speech and publication. In some versions this relaxation is relatively neutrally described, as in the Russian Vikipediia entry, which characterizes the Thaw as 'a softening [*smiagchenie*] of state policies and more freedom in culture and art.'[15] But some interpretations carry a strong political connotation. Wikipedia's English-language entry,[16] for example, has a distinctly Cold-War flavour: the Thaw was 'a chain of unprecedented steps to free people from fear and dictatorship' which 'helped liberate minds of millions.' It was common for contemporary Western reports to describe what was going on in the Soviet Union as 'liberalization' – a term of approval but dubious accuracy, given the absence of pluralism or relativism on the Soviet reform side as well as the conservative one; and of course within the Soviet context highly damaging for the 'liberals' lauded by the West.[17] In dissident memoirs, 'the thaw was the time to search for an alternative system of belief' that would be truly 'ours,' not imposed from above.[18] For those rediscovering the Thaw during perestroika, 'openness' (*glasnost*) took the place of the Western 'liberalization,' emphasizing the relationship between the Thaw and the Gorbachev era.

De-Stalinization figures prominently in virtually all versions of the Thaw myth. It was both policy and process, including the collective release of political prisoners from the Gulag and the bureaucratic process of individual rehabilitation. De-Stalinization opened arenas of contestation about what exactly was the 'Stalinist' thing that had to be repudiated: in history, for example, was it collectivization or just its excesses? Stalin's rule in general or just the 'cult of personality'? De-Stalinization provided (and often imposed) a framework for intellectual debate in which the two sides were defined (by Thaw supporters) as pro- and anti-Stalinist. Evtushenko's poem 'Heirs of Stalin' is a key text here.

The other key element in all versions is the opening to the outside world, notably 'the West,' that is, the United States and Europe. The general relaxation of controls included those controls that had kept Soviet borders tightly closed against foreign cultural influences as well as restricting passage of people and goods. The 1957 Moscow Youth Festival was the symbolic moment of reconnection, and the cosmopolitan Ilya Ehrenburg a central figure, particularly through his memoirs. Evtushenko later claimed that his cohort of young poets in the Thaw had 'broken through the bars to make a window to Europe and America.'[19] This image suggests resistance by the regime, but, as Eleonory Gilburd reminds us,[20] there were significant 'from above' initiatives involved in opening the Soviet Union to the West as well as initiatives from Westernizing youth and intelligentsia.

In most accounts, Khrushchev's 'Secret Speech' at the Twentieth Party Congress in 1956 is the initiating moment and symbol of the Thaw, though in literature the first manifestations can be traced back to 1954. In their introductory article to this volume, Kozlov and Gilburd offer a mix of political and literary events as key aspects of the Thaw: the Twentieth and Twenty-Second Party Congresses, the 1956 Picasso exhibition, the 1957 Moscow Youth Festival, the launching of sputnik, Gagarin's 1961 space flight, publication of Solzhenitsyn's *One Day in the Life of Ivan Denisovich*, Ehrenburg's memoirs, and Dudintsev's *Not by Bread Alone.* These last three works were all published initially in *Novyi mir*, the 'thick' journal which, under Tvardovsky's editorship in the 1960s, exemplified the new spirit of openness.

Whose Thaw?

If the Thaw was one of those Events created in the minds of beholders, moreover sympathetic ones, the next question to ask is, who were the beholder-creators? For whom was the Thaw an Event? Who mythologized it as such? There clearly were many people who avoided the term, disliked its implicit claims, or were simply unaware that an Event had occurred. Khrushchev knew about the Event and no doubt regarded it as his own, but didn't like the term *Thaw*: the image suggested 'instability, uncertainty, incompleteness,' was completely inappropriate for a generation whose members looked optimistically to the future, knowing they would live under communism.[21] And the reform-minded element in the party – a substantial and influential group at this period – followed this lead. In the meagre sources available on lower-class Soviet opinion, one looks in vain not only for references to the Thaw but also for recognition that any such significant socio-political phenomenon existed.[22] Thus the Thaw, it appears, was peculiarly (exclusively?) the property of the intelligentsia and urban, educated youth. Young intelligentsia figures made the myth in the first place and then (under perestroika, by which time the erstwhile 'youth' had become middle-aged) perpetuated it.

The *Thaw generation* was a term coined outside the Soviet Union during the perestroika period.[23] But in the Soviet Union, too, the Thaw was often conflated with a particular generational cohort, and this tendency increased with the passing of time. The term *shestidesiatniki* – echoing and implicitly claiming spiritual connect to the radical Russian intellectuals of the 1860s – was first used in a 1960 essay by Stanislav Rassadin on an emerging literary type of New Man.[24] As Gilburd and Kozlov tell us, it came to suggest a character (young, urban, male) 'at once lyric and ironic, altruistic and critical,' who combined scientific scepticism with lofty ideals.[25] Later, a corresponding concept of 'the Sixties' (*shestidesiatye*) emerged. This referred not only to the decade that produced the *shestidesiatniki* but also to the spirit that they embodied, making 'the Sixties' and 'the Thaw' almost synonymous in retrospect, despite the fact that the key events of the Thaw took place in the second half of the 1950s.

In the late 1980s, perestroika gave a fresh impulse to mythologization of the Thaw and the Sixties. Within the Soviet Union, leading literary figures of the Sixties such as Evtushenko and Dudintsev were quick to point out the kinship of the two periods of glasnost.[26] Vail and Genis made a similar claim in their evocative study, *The 60s*, published in the United States in 1988.[27] By 2009, the cohort had become a subject of sociology as well as myth: according to one account, the *shestidesiatniki* constituted a 'Soviet intelligentsia subculture,' whose members, born mainly between 1925 and 1935 in intelligentsia or party families, inherited a Communist idealism, despite the fact that many of their fathers perished during the Great Purges.[28] *Novyi mir* – 'the main sounding-board of the *shestidesiat-*

niki' – is prominent in this account,[29] along with the bards and the poets of the Sixties, the *liriki-fiziki* debates, and even the new subculture of hiking (*turisty-pokhodniki*) in remote areas of the Soviet Union that emerged in the physicists' milieu.

The relationship of the Sixties cohort to the dissidents of the 'Seventies and Eighties is a key question for Russian interpreters. The question of whether reform was best promoted from within the system or by direct challenge to it caused a well-documented rupture in the latter part of the 1960s between *Novyi mir* (in favour of in-system activity) and Solzhenitsyn;[30] at stake here was also the question of socialism, to which *Novyi mir* remained loyal and Solzhenitsyn did not. As time passed, Solzhenitsyn's position gained more adherents within the intelligentsia, and many commentators on the Thaw now see dissidence as a direct and natural consequence of the Thaw, once the hopes of the *shestidesiatniki* were dashed. For Vail and Genis, dissidence (*inakomyslie*) was simply a logical outcome of the licence for independent thinking offered by the Thaw.[31]

In the post-Soviet period, it became fashionable to criticize the *shestidesiatniki* for naivety,[32] representing them as guitar-playing, backpacking romantics who were all talk but (in contrast to the dissidents) no action. Journals like *Novyi mir*, once represented as heroic truth-tellers, have been sharply criticized for failing to go the whole hog and embrace dissidence.[33]

Another recent development is the emergence of a competitor to the *shestidesiatniki* as an object of generational nostalgia. This is the so-called last Soviet generation, the one that came to maturity in the Brezhnev period. For Alexei Yurchak, who both coined the term and belongs to the group, this cohort was characterized by outward conformism and a surprising degree of inner freedom and flexibility, its members having mastered the *performance* of Sovietness, while being neither unduly constrained by it nor fully rejecting its values. In Yurchak's formulation, both the *shestidesiatniki* and the 'last Soviet generation' of the 1970s and 1980s belong to a period of Soviet history called 'late socialism,' which encompasses both the Khrushchev and Brezhnev periods.[34] This periodization scheme implicitly denies the Thaw the status of world-historic *Ereignis* claimed by the *shestidesiatniki* and their admirers.

'Say, I never knew you guys had a sixties over there'[35]

The more I wrote about 'the Sixties' and *shestidesiatniki*, thoughts of another mythic Sixties intruded – the one launched in America (circa

1958, according to Arthur Marwick) and associated with hippies, flower children, the anti-war movement, civil rights, drugs, and counter-culture. These Sixties, as Marwick emphasizes, were an international event, even if not all Americans realized the fact. But it was an internationalism apparently restricted to 'the west, particularly United States, Britain, France, Canada, Brazil, Australia, Spain, Italy, and West Germany,' though also finding an echo in 'such nations as Japan, Mexico, and others.'[36] Nowhere in Marwick or other authoritative texts is there any reference to the Soviet Union. Evidently there are two separate *Ereignisse* called the Sixties, one occurring in the Soviet Union and the other in the West, and consequently two discrete and non-connecting 'Sixties' myths.

There is one region of the world where this discrete separation seems to break down: Eastern Europe. Historians of Communism consider Khrushchev's Thaw to have been an event for Eastern Europe as well as the Soviet Union,[37] implying that the Soviet 'Sixties' had some sort of presence in Eastern Europe as well. Yet Eastern Europe also has a walk-on part in accounts of the international (Western) phenomenon of 'the Sixties.' In fact, the events that demonstrate 'Sixties" influence from the West seem very similar to the ones that demonstrated it from the East, namely student protests against restrictions on free speech in Poland and Yugoslavia and the 'Prague Spring' and 'socialism with a human face' in Czechoslovakia.[38]

The convergence of Sixties myths may even have reached post-Soviet Russia. When I typed '*Shestidesiatye gody*' into Russian Google, I arrived at a site for Russian women ('AskWoman') offering advice on fashion, lifestyle, and horoscopes. 'The 1960s are now the past century,' it pronounced. 'A remarkable time for all creative, unusual, vivid personalities. It was a breath of fresh air, the first steps towards freedom, the first scents and sensations of a new life.'[39] Wonderful, I thought; evidently the Thaw is not totally dismissed in post-Soviet times, even by women interested in horoscopes. Then I looked more closely and noticed the illustration – a blissed-out American hippie in dark glasses (à la Yoko Ono, or perhaps Ono herself).

So it was the wrong Sixties, the American one. Or could it be that 'AskWoman' was unaware of the distinction? If Montana and Kazakhstan are essentially the same thing, as Kate Brown memorably suggested in her article 'Gridded Lives,'[40] why not the Thaw and the counter-cultural Sixties in the West? In boring historical fact, Evtushenko may never have declaimed his poetry at Woodstock or Okudzhava have sung his guitar songs outside the Chicago Convention. Perhaps when Soviet *fiziki* went on the road, they were not actually travelling with Kerouac. But an *Er-*

eignis is not a boring fact or superficial happening; rather, it is something experienced and assigned significance *in thought*. If Russian 'AskWoman' is already thinking the two mythical Sixties as one, who are we to contradict her?

NOTES

1 Paul Robert, *Dictionnaire alphabétique et analogique de la langue française* (Paris, 1980), 10:712.
2 Fernand Braudel, *The Mediterranean and the Mediterranean World in the Age of Philip II*, trans. Siân Reynolds (London, 1973), 2:901. See Fernand Braudel, *Écrits sur l'Histoire* (Paris, 1969), 45.
3 For the definitions of *sluchai*, *proisshestvie*, and *sobytie* on which these comments are based, see *Tolkovyi slovar' russkogo iazyka v 4 tomakh.*, comp. V.V. Vinogradov et al., ed. D.N. Ushakov (Moscow, 1994).
4 As in the *chrezvychainye proisshestviia* – suicides and the like – on which the Army and other Soviet institutions kept records in the 1930s.
5 *Sobytiia v Kitae* was the standard heading for Soviet reports on the Chinese Cultural Revolution in the late 1960s, conveying the sense that something strange, rather than something of real historical significance, was happening there.
6 *Duden: Das grosse Wörterbuch der deutschen Sprache in acht Bänden* (Mannheim, 1993), 2:948.
7 Arno Borst, in *Geschichte – Ereignis und Erzählung*, Hsg. Reinhart Koselleck and Wolf-Dieter Stempel (Munich, 1973), 537–8.
8 Karl Marx, *Der achtzehnte Brumaire des Louis Bonaparte* (1852), from Karl Marx / Friedrich Engels, *Werke* (Berlin, 1972), 8:115–23.
9 Il'ia Erenburg, *Ottepel': povest'* (Moscow, 1954).
10 Here I am drawing on Katerina Clark's essay in this volume.
11 Epithets quoted in Stephen V. Bittner, *The Many Lives of Khrushchev's Thaw: Experience and Memory in Moscow's Arbat* (Ithaca, 2008), 7–9, from Ludmila Alexeyeva and Paul Goldberg, *The Thaw Generation: Coming of Age in the Post-Stalin Era* (Pittsburgh, 1993), 4–5; Masha Gessen, *Dead Again: The Russian Intelligentsia after Communism* (London, 1997), 12; Vladimir Shlapentokh, *Soviet Intellectuals and Political Power: The Post-Stalin Era* (Princeton, 1990), 148.
12 Eleonor Gilburd, 'The Revival of Soviet Internationalism in the Mid- to Late 1950s,' in this volume.
13 See Sheila Fitzpatrick, 'Lives and Times,' in *In the Shadow of Revolution: Life Stories of Russian Women from 1917 to the Second World War*, ed. Fitzpatrick and Yuri Slezkine (Princeton, 2000), 7.

14 Evgenii Evtushenko, 'Shestidesiatniki' (1993) in his *Pervoe sobranie sochinenii v vos'mi tomakh* (Moscow, 2003), 6:444.
15 Russian Vikipediia: entry for 'Khrushevskaia ottepel',' http://ru.wikipedia.org/wiki/%D0%A5%D1%80%D1%83%D1%89%D1%91%D0%B2%D1%81%D0%BA%D0%B0%D1%8F_%D0%BE%D1%82%D1%82%D0%B5%D0%BF%D0%B5%D0%BB%D1%8C), accessed 4 February 2009.
16 Wikipedia: entry for 'The Khrushchev Thaw,' http://en.wikipedia.org.wiki/Khrushchev_Thaw, accessed 4 February 2009.
17 The reform-minded journal *Novyi mir*, for example, cringed at such descriptions, not only because they put its editors' Soviet loyalty in doubt but because they actually were Communists, hostile to liberalism.
18 Alexeyeva and Goldberg, *Thaw Generation*, 4–5.
19 Evtushenko, 'Shestidesiatniki.'
20 Gilburd, 'Revival of Soviet Internationalism.'
21 N.S. Khrushchev, speech of 8 March 1963, published *Pravda* 10 March, reprinted in *Khrushchev and the Arts: The Politics of Soviet Culture, 1961–1964*, ed. Priscilla Johnson (Cambridge, MA, 1965), 180–81.
22 See, for example, the absence of references in the statements of persons accused of article 58 violations in *Kramola. Inakomyslie v SSSR pri Khrushcheve i Brezhneve 1953–1982 gg. Rasskrechenny dokumenty Verkhovnogo suda i Prokuratury SSSR*, ed. Vladimir A. Kozlov and Sergei V. Mironenko (Moscow, 2005); in English translation, *Sedition: Everyday Resistance in the Soviet Union under Khrushchev and Brezhnev*, ed. Vladimir A. Kozlov, Sheila Fitzpatrick, and Sergei V. Mironenko (New Haven, 2011).
23 See Alexeyeva and Goldberg, *Thaw Generation.* The book was not translated into Russian and published there until 2002.
24 Stanislav Rassadin, 'Shestidesiatniki: Knigi o molodom sovremennike,' *Iunost'* 12 (December 1960), 58–62, cited in Denis Kozlov and Eleonor Gilburd, 'The Thaw as an Event in Russian History,' in this volume.
25 Kozlov and Gilburd, 'The Thaw as an Event in Russian History,' in this volume.
26 See, for example, interviews with Bella Akhmadulina, Evgenii Evtushenko, Bulat Okudzhava, Robert Rozhdestvenskii, and Andrei Voznesenskii, in '"I byli nashi pomysli chisty" … Ob odnoi vstreche spustia tridtsadt' let,' *Ogonek* 9 (February 1987); Vladimir Dudintsev's interview with Aleksei Adzhubei, *Moscow News*, 15–22 March 1987; and Evtushenko's interview in Stephen F. Cohen and Katrina vanden Heuvel, *Voices of Glasnost: Interviews with Gorbachev's Reformers* (London, 1989), 261–79.
27 Petr Vail' and Aleksandr Genis, *60-e: Mir sovetskogo cheloveka* (Ann Arbor, 1988), 5.
28 Russian Google/Vikipediia: 'Shestidesiatniki': http://ru.wikipedia.org/

wiki/%D0%A8%D0%B5%D1%81%D1%82%D0%B8%D0%B4%D0%B5%D1%81%D1%8F%D1%82%D0%BD%D0%B8%D0%BA%D0%B8, accessed 24 January 2009.

29 See the article by Polly Jones in this volume.

30 For contrasting accounts, see Aleksandr Solzhenitsyn, *Bodalsia telenok s dubom. Ocherki literaturnoi zhizni* (Paris, 1975); and Vladimir Lakshin, *Solzhenitsyn, Tvardovsky and Novy Mir*, trans. Michael Glenny (Cambridge, MA, 1980).

31 Vail' and Genis, *60-e*, 176–86.

32 See, for example, Linor Goralik, 'Mir sovetskogo cheloveka: 60-e,' http://old.russ.ru/krug/razbor/19991022.html. Goralik was born in 1975. After reading Vail' and Genis, as she relates, she came to see the decade more in terms of seeking than naivety.

33 See, for example, the 1999 article by the influential publicist Valeriia Novodvorskaia, 'Shestidesiatniki i pustota,' *Novaia Iunost'* 1 (1999), http://magazines.russ.ru/znamia/1999/8/annot3.html.

34 He writes that 'because of the performative shift of authoritative discourse and the subsequent normalization of that discourse, the post-Stalinist period between the mid-1950s and mid-1980s may be thought of as a particular period with shared characteristics, which is here called late socialism.' Aleksei Yurchak, *Everything Was Forever, Until It Was No More: The Last Soviet Generation* (Princeton, 2006), 31.

35 Arthur Marwick, *The Sixties. Cultural Revolution in Britain, France, Italy, and the United States, c. 1958–1974* (Oxford, 1998), vi (comment of an unnamed American to Marwick, who was British).

36 Wikipedia: '1960s,' http://en.wikipedia.org/wiki/1960s, accessed 4 February 2009.

37 The entry for *Khrushchevskaia ottepel'* (see note 15) defines it as 'the period in the history of the USSR and countries of the "socialist camp" except Cuba, North Korea, Albania and China, beginning after the death of Joseph Stalin and characterized by a softening of state policies and more freedom in culture and the arts.' The English-language version of Wikipedia ('The Khrushchev Thaw,' see note 16) gives Eastern Europe a more marginal place, but even it recognizes the Polish and Hungarian revolts of 1956 and the political and social climate that gave rise to them as Thaw-related phenomena.

38 http://en.wikipedia.org/wiki/1960s, accessed 4 February 2009.

39 http://www.askwoman.ru/issues/?id=740. 'AskWoman,' accessed via Russian Google 24 January 2009.

40 Kate Brown, 'Gridded Lives: Why Kazakhstan and Montana Are Nearly the Same Place,' *American Historical Review* 106, no. 1 (2001): 17–48.

List of Contributors

Alan Barenberg is assistant professor of history at Texas Tech University. His publications include 'Prisoners without Borders: *Zazonniki* and the Transformation of Vorkuta after Stalin,' *Jahrbücher für Geschichte Osteuropas* 57, no. 4 (2008): 513–34; and 'Discovering Vorkuta: Science and Colonization in the Early Gulag,' *Gulag Studies* 4 (2011): 21–40. His monograph on the history of Vorkuta as a prison camp complex and company town is forthcoming from Yale University Press.

Oksana Bulgakowa is professor of film studies at the Johannes Gutenberg University in Mainz. She has published several books on Russian and German cinema: *The Adventures of Doctor Mabuse in the Country of Bolsheviks* (1995); *Sergei Eisenstein: Three Utopias; Architectural Drafts for a Film Theory* (1996); *FEKS: The Factory of Eccentric Actors* (1997); *The White Rectangle: Kazimir Malevitch on Film* (1997, English ed. 2002); *Sergej Eisenstein: A Biography* (German ed. 1998; English ed. 2003); *Factory of Gestures* (Moscow, 2005); and *Soviet Hearing Eye: Film and Its Senses* (Moscow 2010). She has also directed a number of films, curated exhibitions, and developed multimedia projects. She has taught at the Humboldt University and Free University in Berlin, as well as at Stanford, UC Berkeley, and the International Film School in Cologne.

Katerina Clark is professor of comparative literature and of Slavic languages and literatures at Yale University. She is the author of *The Soviet Novel: History as Ritual*, *Mikhail Bakhtin* (with Michael Holquist), *Petersburg, Crucible of Cultural Revolution*, and *Moscow, the Fourth Rome: Stalinism, Cosmopolitanism and the Evolution of Soviet Culture, 1931–1941.*

Marc Elie is a researcher with the Centre d'études des mondes russe, caucasien, et centre-européen (CNRS-EHESS). He holds a doctorate in history from École des hautes études en sciences sociales in France, with a thesis on the liberation, return, and rehabilitation of Gulag prisoners after Stalin's death. He co-edited, with Jan Plamper and Schamma Schahadat, *Rossiiskaia imperiia chuvstv: podkhody k kul'turnoy istorii emotsii* (2010). In his current research he focuses on disasters in the Soviet Union.

Sheila Fitzpatrick is Honorary Professor at the University of Sydney and Emerita Professor at the University of Chicago. She is working on a book on Stalin and his team, as well as a memoir of Moscow in the 1960s.

Eleonory Gilburd is assistant professor of history and Russian studies at New York University. She is revising for publication her UC Berkeley dissertation, '"To See Paris and Die": Western Culture in the Soviet Union, 1950s and 1960s.'

Polly Jones is the Schrecker-Barbour Fellow and University Lecturer in Russian at University College, University of Oxford. She was previously lecturer in Russian culture at University College London School of Slavonic and East European Studies. She has published widely on the cultural history of the post-Stalinist Soviet Union; publications include *The Dilemmas of De-Stalinization: Negotiating Cultural and Social Change in the Khrushchev Era* (Routledge, 2006; second paperback edition, 2009), *The Leader Cult in Communist Dictatorships: Stalin and the Eastern Bloc* (Palgrave, 2004), and a monograph, *Myth, Memory, Trauma: The Stalinist Past in Soviet Culture, 1953–68* (in press, Yale University Press).

Denis Kozlov is assistant professor of history at Dalhousie University. He has published articles and chapters in *Kritika: Explorations in Russian and Eurasian History, The Oxford History of Historical Writing, Russian Studies in History, Canadian Slavonic Papers,* and *Dilemmas of De-Stalinization,* as well as co-edited *The War against the Peasantry, 1927–1930.* He is completing a book about reading audiences, historical consciousness, and mechanisms of intellectual change in the Soviet Union during the 1950s and 1960s.

Michaela Pohl is associate professor of history at Vassar College. Her research focuses on the Soviet Union after Stalin, the history of socialism in Kazakhstan, and the Chechens and Germans in exile. She is completing a manuscript on Khrushchev's reforms in Kazakhstan and working on a memoir about growing up German after the Holocaust.

Amir Weiner is associate professor of history at Stanford University. He is the author of *Making Sense of War* (2001); *Landscaping the Human Garden* (2003); and the forthcoming *Getting to Know You: Surveillance in the USSR.*

Larissa Zakharova, doctor in history and civilizations, is *maître de conférences* at the École des hautes études en sciences sociales in Paris. She is the author of a book, *S'habiller à la soviétique: La mode et le Dégel en URSS* (Paris, CNRS Editions, 2011), and numerous articles on Soviet fashion and consumption in the USSR, as well as a co-editor of a special issue of *Cahiers du monde russe* on the Thaw (no. 47, 2006) and a book *Cacophonie d'empire: Le gouvernement des langues dans l'empire russe, en URSS et dans les États post-soviétiques* (2010).

Index